Cognition

SIXTH EDITION

MARGARET W. MATLIN
SUNY Geneseo

WILEY

John Wiley & Sons, Inc.

Executive Editor   Ryan Flahive
Associate Editor   Lili DeGrasse
Senior Production Editor   Norine M. Pigliucci
Marketing Manager   Kate Stewart
Media Editor   Tom Kulesa
Senior Designer   Dawn Stanley
Editorial Assistant   Deepa Chungi
Production Management Services   Elm Street Publishing Services, Inc.
Cover Photo   © George B. Diebold/CORBIS

This book was set in Janson by Pine Tree Composition and printed and bound by
R.R. Donnelley, Crawfordsville. The cover was printed by Lehigh Press.

This book is printed on acid free paper. ∞

Library of Congress Cataloging-in-Publication Data
Matlin, Margaret W.
    Cognition/Margaret W. Matlin.—6th ed.
        p. cm.
    Includes bibliographical references and index.
    ISBN 0-471-45007-3
    1. Cognition–Textbooks.

BF311.M426 2005
153–dc22   2004043472

ISBN: 0-471-45007-3.
WIE ISBN: 0-471-65834-0

Printed in the United States of America

10   9   8   7   6   5   4   3

Part A

RED	BLUE	GREEN	YELLOW	GREEN
RED	BLUE	YELLOW	BLUE	RED
YELLOW	GREEN	YELLOW	GREEN	BLUE
RED	RED	GREEN	YELLOW	BLUE

Part B

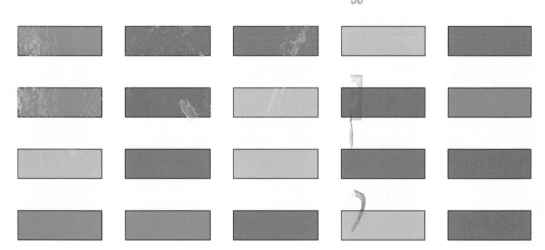

This book is dedicated to

Helen and Donald White

and

Clare and Harry Matlin

Preface

The day before I began to write this preface, I met with my new class in cognitive psychology. As I looked at them, I instantly recalled an event that had occurred when I was just a year or two older than most of my students. The year was 1967, and I was walking along a hallway in the Human Performance Center at the University of Michigan. A young man suddenly rushed past me, shouting, "Hey, everybody, I just got a copy of Neisser's *Cognitive Psychology*!" As my flashbulb memory suggests, the emerging cognitive perspective was welcomed enthusiastically, at least in certain circles. Many psychologists were intrigued that the mind could be viewed as an information-processing system, rather than the mechanical switchboard endorsed by the behaviorists (Treisman, 2003). I had the good fortune to watch the discipline of cognitive psychology develop during its infancy, with interesting early research on such topics as iconic memory, short-term memory, and language comprehension.

Almost 25 years ago, I began writing the first edition of my textbook, *Cognition*. That first edition, which was published in 1983, included 382 pages of text. It featured only one chapter on memory and one on language—and a mere 23 pages of references.

Now, in the year 2004, cognitive psychology has passed through childhood, and even adolescence. Our relatively mature discipline now features dozens of journals, hundreds of professional books, and numerous handbooks. In fact, I found it challenging to limit this sixth edition of *Cognition* to 493 pages of text and 69 pages of references.

As I write this preface for the current edition of *Cognition*, I'm reminded of the impressive advances in our discipline since that first edition was published. Cognitive psychologists have explored topics that were not even mentioned in the first edition—topics such as inattentional blindness, metamemory, bilingualism, and childhood amnesia. Researchers have also developed new theoretical approaches. For example, the fixed-capacity view of short-term memory has now been replaced by Baddeley's sophisticated working-memory model. Furthermore, the parallel distributed processing approach was not discussed in the first edition, and it was described in just one paragraph of the second edition. However, it now plays a major role in the discussion of semantic memory in Chapter 8.

Innovative research techniques have also opened new pathways. For example, neuroscience research allows us to investigate the biological basis of cognitive processes such as attention, memory, mental imagery, and language. Many of the new research methods are extremely creative, so it's exciting to contemplate how the field of cognition will expand during future decades!

This research continues to emphasize the impressive competence of our cognitive processes. For instance, college students can typically recall the names of their teachers from elementary school, details of a birthday party that happened a decade ago, and the meaning of foreign language vocabulary they haven't thought about since high school. Even infants are cognitively competent. For instance, 4-month-olds can discriminate between the language spoken by their parents and an unfamiliar language. Cognitive skills increase rapidly during childhood. In fact, 6-year-olds know about 12,000 words, which they use to construct grammatically accurate sentences that no human has previously uttered.

Still, many cognitive psychology textbooks are written in such a dry, academic style that they fail to capture these inherently interesting capabilities. Over the years, I've received letters and comments from hundreds of students and professors, telling me how much they enjoyed reading this textbook. Using their feedback, I have tried to write this sixth edition so that these positive characteristics are emphasized even more than in previous editions.

FEATURES OF THIS TEXTBOOK

I have now taught the cognitive psychology course at SUNY Geneseo approximately 35 times. Each time I revise *Cognition*, I try to think about students like those in my classes. This vigilance keeps me honest, because I must continually ask myself, "Would my own students really understand this, or would they simply give me a blank stare?"

Here are some of the ways in which I consider this textbook to be student-oriented:

1. The writing style is clear and interesting, with numerous examples.

2. The text demonstrates how our cognitive processes are relevant to our everyday, real-world experiences.

3. The book frequently examines how cognition can be applied to other disciplines, such as clinical psychology, social psychology, consumer psychology, education, communication, business, medicine, and law.

4. The first chapter introduces five major themes that I emphasize throughout the book. Because the research in cognitive psychology is now so extensive, students need a sense of continuity that helps them appreciate connections among many diverse topics.

5. An outline, a preview, and a brief anecdote introduce each chapter, providing an appropriate framework for new material.

6. Each new term is presented in **boldface print.** Every term is also accompanied by a concise definition that appears in the same sentence. In addition, I include pronunciation guides for new terms with potentially ambiguous pronunciation. Students who are hesitant about the pronunciation of terms such as *schema* and *saccadic* will be reluctant to use these words or ask questions about them.

7. Many easy-to-perform demonstrations illustrate important experiments in cognition and clarify central concepts in the discipline. I designed these demonstrations so that they would require equipment that undergraduate students would be likely to have on hand. (Yes, I'll admit that students may need to exercise their creativity in locating some items, such as a child under the age of 8 for Demonstration 13.2 in Chapter 13!)

8. Each major section within a chapter concludes with a summary. This feature enables students to review and consolidate material before moving to the next section, rather than wait until the chapter's end for a single, lengthy summary.

9. Each chapter includes comprehensive review questions and a list of new terms.

10. Each chapter concludes with a list of recommended readings, along with a brief description of each resource.

11. A glossary at the end of the book provides a definition of every new term. I tried to include additional contextual information wherever it might be useful, in order to clarify the terms as much as possible.

THE TEXTBOOK'S ORGANIZATION

A textbook must be interesting and helpful. It must also reflect current developments in the discipline, and it must allow instructors to adapt its structure to their own teaching plans. The following features should therefore be useful for professors:

1. *Cognition* offers a comprehensive overview of the field, including chapters on perceptual processes, memory, imagery, general knowledge, language, problem solving and creativity, reasoning and decision making, and cognitive development.

2. Each chapter is a self-contained unit. For example, terms such as *heuristics* or *top-down processing* are defined in every chapter in which they are used. This feature allows professors considerable flexibility in the sequence of chapter coverage. Some professors may wish to discuss the topic of imagery (Chapter 7) prior to the three chapters on memory. Others might want to assign the chapter on general knowledge (Chapter 8) during an earlier part of the academic term.

3. Each section within a chapter can stand as a discrete unit, especially because every section concludes with a section summary. Professors may choose to cover individual sections in a different order. For example, one professor may decide to cover the section on schemas prior to the chapter on long-term memory. Another professor might prefer to subdivide Chapter 13, on cognitive development, so that the first section of this chapter (on memory) follows Chapter 5, the second section (on metacognition) follows Chapter 6, and the third section (on language) follows Chapter 10.

4. Chapters 2 through 13 each include an "In Depth" feature, which focuses on recent research about selected topics in cognitive psychology and provides details on research methods. Seven of these features are new to this sixth edition, and the remaining five have been substantially updated and revised.

5. In all, the bibliography contains 1,829 references. More than 700 of them are new to the sixth edition, and 1,402 (77%) have been published within the last 10 years. As a result, the textbook provides a very current overview of the discipline.

HIGHLIGHTS OF THE SIXTH EDITION

The field of cognitive psychology has made impressive advances since the fifth edition of this textbook was published in 2002. Research in the areas of perception, memory, and language has been especially ambitious. In addition, theoretical approaches to the field have been greatly expanded. Neuroscience techniques have been used to provide information about cognitive topics as diverse as face recognition, mental imagery, and memory development during childhood.

I have made some structural changes in writing the sixth edition of *Cognition*. The most important change is that perceptual processes are now discussed in two separate chapters. Chapter 2 now explores visual and auditory recognition. It begins with some background on visual object recognition and top-down processing, and it includes research on face perception and speech perception. Chapter 3 examines three kinds of attention processes, explanations for attention, and consciousness.

In preparing this sixth edition, I also carefully reviewed each of the remaining chapters. In fact, every page of this textbook has been updated and rewritten. Some of the more substantial changes include the following:

- Chapter 1 examines some new examples of current issues in cognitive psychology, and the order of topics in this section has been rearranged.

- Chapter 2 now includes an introductory discussion of the figure-ground relationship and perceptual organization. In addition, the section on top-down processing has been reorganized and clarified. This chapter also features new applied research on face recognition. Because the topic of speech perception has been moved to this chapter, the text points out similarities between visual and auditory perceptual processes.

- Chapter 3 begins by emphasizing the connections between the perceptual processes discussed in Chapters 2 and 3. The discussion of divided attention includes new applied research about driving while using a hands-free cell phone, and the In Depth feature on selective attention discusses new research on individual differences in hearing one's own name in a noisy setting. Furthermore, a new section on explanations for attention includes both neuroscience research and theoretical approaches.

- Chapter 4, on working memory, has been reorganized, with reduced coverage of the early research on short-term memory. The major portion of this chapter closely examines Baddeley's working-memory approach, including the recently proposed episodic buffer. The chapter also includes updated research on individual differences in working memory.

- Chapter 5, on long-term memory, features a new In Depth section on emotions, mood, and memory, which includes applications to clinical psychology. New material has been added on flashbulb memories, source monitoring, and the relationship between memory confidence and memory accuracy. The discussion of the recovered memory/false memory controversy has been updated and reorganized.

- Chapter 6 now includes recent research on memory strategies, as well as updated information about prospective memory. The chapter has been reorganized in order to feature three components of metamemory. In addition, a new In Depth section focuses on metamemory and the regulation of study strategies.

- Chapter 7 now includes three sections, with cognitive neuroscience as a separate section. This chapter also features new research on topics such as video-game performance, motor-movement imagery, and individuals with brain lesions who cannot form visual images.

- Chapter 8, on general knowledge, begins with a discussion about why we need semantic memory and concepts. The discussion of theoretical approaches to semantic memory has been updated and slightly shortened. A new In Depth feature on schemas and inferences includes new research about inferences based on gender stereotypes, as revealed in implicit memory.

- Chapter 9 is now slightly shorter because the material on speech perception has been moved to Chapter 2. New topics in Chapter 9 include the English-centered nature of psycholinguistics research, an In Depth feature on neurolinguistics, and the constructionist view of inferences in discourse.

- In Chapter 10, new material has been added on the speed of sentence production, speech errors, and writing in real-world settings. The In Depth feature on bilingualism and age of acquisition includes new theoretical perspectives on the critical period hypothesis.

- Chapter 11, on problem solving and creativity, includes new research on the analogy approach, expertise, and the relationship between task motivation and creativity. A new In Depth feature examines stereotype threat and problem solving on mathematics tests.

- Chapter 12 includes new examples of deductive reasoning problems, as well as new material on the application of the confirmation bias to international politics. The section on decision making includes new research on illusory correlations, the anchoring and adjustment heuristic in courtroom settings, and overconfidence in decision making.

- Chapter 13 is now called "Cognitive Development Throughout the Lifespan," a title that reflects greater emphasis on cognitive aging. New research has been added to the topics of infant memory, children's working memory, and children's long-term memory. A new In Depth feature on long-term memory in elderly people clarifies which memory skills are most affected (and least affected) during the aging process. Other new material includes research on memory self-efficacy, how depressed mothers communicate with their infants, and children's first words.

In preparing this new edition, I made every possible effort to emphasize current research. I examined all relevant articles in eight cognitive psychology journals and five general psychology journals. This investigation was supplemented by numerous specific *PsycInfo* searches. Furthermore, I pursued every relevant book reviewed in *Contemporary Psychology*. I also wrote to more than 200 prominent researchers, requesting reprints and preprints. The research on cognition is expanding at an ever-increasing rate, and this textbook captures the excitement of the current research.

TEST BANK

As a classroom teacher, I know the importance of a high-quality Test Bank. The questions must be clear and unambiguous, and they must not focus on relatively trivial details. Also, the questions should be carefully reviewed and updated with each new edition of the textbook. Furthermore, each chapter of the Test Bank should contain enough questions that professors can select a different sample every time they create an examination.

I have extensively revised the Test Bank for the sixth edition of *Cognition*. It contains approximately 150 questions that are new to this edition. Furthermore, approximately half of the questions that had appeared in the fifth edition have been revised for this new edition. The questions continue to emphasize conceptual knowledge, as well as applications to real-world situations. Furthermore, each question is rated as "easy," "moderate," and "difficult." These difficulty ratings allow professors to create a test that is appropriate for the students in their classes. To learn more information, professors should contact their Wiley sales representative about the Test Bank for the sixth edition of *Cognition*. They can also visit the Wiley website for this book, www.wiley.com/college/matlin.

ACKNOWLEDGMENTS

I want to thank many individuals at John Wiley & Sons for their substantial contributions to the development and the production of the sixth edition of *Cognition*. Lili DeGrasse, Associate Editor at Wiley, was especially skilled in seeking out excellent reviewers who provided feedback about the chapters in the sixth edition. I would also like to acknowledge Anne Smith (Vice-President and Publisher, Higher Education) and Ryan Flahive (Executive Editor) for their editorial guidance throughout the planning and writing phases of this textbook.

The Production Department at Wiley is also wonderful! Norine M. Pigliucci is a top-notch Senior Production Editor, and she managed all aspects of production with intelligence and efficiency. Dawn Stanley, Senior Designer, created an elegant and user-friendly design for this sixth edition.

During the production phase of the sixth edition, I was extremely pleased with everyone who worked on this book! Amber Allen, my Project Editor at Elm Street Publishing Services, Inc., was masterful in answering questions about production, as well as managing the complex flow of edited material between Hinsdale, Illinois, and my home in Linwood, New York! Pine Tree Composition also deserves congratulations for their skill in making intelligent decisions about the layout of the sixth edition. After working with both Elm Street and Pine Tree, I developed a new heuristic: Whenever possible, choose companies whose names include a tree! In addition, I was very pleased with the art designed by Hadel Studio—special thanks to Fred Haynes and Al DeLuca!

The sixth edition of *Cognition* is the 20th book I have written. I have consistently found that the copyeditor for a book is the individual most responsible for my satisfaction with the production process. I was extremely fortunate to work with Elizabeth Jahaske, an intelligent and wonderfully conscientious copyeditor. Elizabeth has an astonishing ability to catch inconsistencies in the text, even when the inconsistencies are separated by dozens of text pages! She also has impressive skill in transforming awkward phrases and detecting unclear descriptions. Her editing skills clearly enhanced the entire textbook!

Once more, Linda Webster compiled both the subject index and the author index, and she also prepared the glossary. Linda has worked on all my recent textbooks, and I continue to be impressed with her intelligent and careful work on these important components of the textbook.

In addition, I would like to thank Kate Stewart, the marketing manager at Wiley, for her creativity, positive feedback, and excellent organizational skills. Thanks are also due to the Wiley sales representatives for their excellent work and enthusiastic support!

During my undergraduate and graduate training, many professors encouraged my enthusiasm for the growing field of cognition. I would like to thank Gordon Bower, Albert Hastorf, Leonard Horowitz, and Eleanor Maccoby of Stanford University, and Edwin Martin, Arthur Melton, Richard Pew, and Robert Zajonc of the University of Michigan.

Many others have contributed in important ways to this book. Allison Katter, Alexandra Feor, Kara Fitzgerald, and Jessica Majkowycz are exemplary student assistants who helped locate references and prepare the bibliography. Also, Carolyn Emmert and Connie Ellis kept other aspects of my life running smoothly, allowing me more time to work on this writing project.

Additional colleagues have helped in a variety of ways. Several members of Milne Library, SUNY Geneseo, deserve special thanks: Paula Henry ordered numerous books for me and kept me updated on interesting, relevant references. Judith Bushnell helped track down wayward references and elusive supplemental information. Harriet Sleggs and her staff efficiently ordered several hundred books and articles through interlibrary loan.

In addition, a number of students contributed to the book and provided useful suggestions after reading various editions of *Cognition*: Jennifer Balus, Mary Jane Brennan, A. Eleanor Chand, Miriam Dowd, Elizabeth Einemann, Michelle Fischer, Sarah Gonnella, Laurie Guarino, Benjamin Griffin, Jessica Hosey, Don Hudson, Jay Kleinman, Jessica Krager, Mary Kroll, Eun Jung Lim, Pamela Mead, Pamela Mino, Kaveh Moghbeli, Jacquilyn Moran, Michelle Morante, Jennifer Niemczyk, Danielle Palermo, Judith Rickey, Mary Riley, Margery Schemmel, Richard Slocum, John Tanchak, Brenna Terry, Dan Vance, Heather Wallach, and Rachelle Yablin. Several students at Stanford University's Casa Zapata provided insights about bilingualism: Laura Aizpuru, Sven Halstenburg, Rodrigo Liong, Jean Lu, Edwardo Martinez, Sally Matlin, Dorin Parasca, and Laura Uribarri.

Other students provided information about useful cognitive psychology articles: Ned Abbott, Angela Capria, Stacey Canavan, Elizabeth Carey, Melissa Conway, Patricia Kramer, Leslie Lauer, Sally Matlin, Christopher Piersante, Brooke Schurr, Laura Segovia, and Nancy Tomassino. Thanks also to colleagues Drew Appleby, Ada Azodo, K. Anders Ericsson, Hugh Foley, Mark Graber, Douglas Herrmann, Ken Kallio, Colin M. MacLeod, Lisbet Nielsen, Paul Norris, Bennett L. Schwartz, Douglas Vipond, Lori Van Wallendael, and Alan Welsh for making suggestions about references and improved wording for passages in the text.

Special thanks are also due to Lucinda DeWitt, who assisted in preparing the previous edition of the Test Item File for *Cognition* and also helped with the format of the current edition. Lucinda was also an exceptionally helpful reviewer who examined two earlier editions of this book for continuity, clarity, and accuracy. Her contributions continued to influence this sixth edition! In addition, thanks to Tracy Napper, now the Managing Editor for *Annals of Emergency Medicine*, for her fine work in pursuing elusive information and in examining the manuscript for passages that might mystify undergraduate students.

I would also like to express my continuing appreciation to the textbook's reviewers. The reviewers who helped on the first edition included: Mark Ashcraft, Cleveland State University; Randolph Easton, Boston College; Barbara Goldman, University of Michigan, Dearborn; Harold Hawkins, University of Oregon; Joseph Hellige, University of Southern California; Richard High, Lehigh University; James Juola, University of Kansas; Richard Kasschau, University of Houston; and R. A. Kinchla, Princeton University.

The reviewers who provided assistance on the second edition were: Harriett Amster, University of Texas, Arlington; Francis T. Durso, University of Oklahoma; Susan E. Dutch, Westfield State College; Sallie Gordon, University of Utah; Richard Gottwald, University of Indiana, South Bend; Kenneth R. Graham, Muhlenberg College; Morton A. Heller, Winston-Salem State University; Michael W. O'Boyle, Iowa State University; David G. Payne, SUNY Binghamton; Louisa M. Slowiaczek, Loyola University, Chicago; Donald A. Smith, Northern Illinois University; Patricia Snyder, Albright College; and Richard K. Wagner, Florida State University.

The third-edition reviewers included: Ira Fischler, University of Florida; John Flowers, University of Nebraska; Nancy Franklin, SUNY Stony Brook; Joanne Gallivan, University College of Cape Breton; Margaret Intons-Peterson, Indiana University; Christine Lofgren, University of California, Irvine; Bill McKeachie, University of Michigan; William Oliver, Florida State University; Andrea Richards, University of California, Los Angeles; Jonathan Schooler, University of Pittsburgh; and Jyotsna Vaid, Texas A & M University.

The reviewers of the fourth edition included: Lucinda DeWitt, Concordia College; Susan Dutch, Westfield State College; Kathleen Flannery, Saint Anselm College; Linda Gerard, Michigan State University; Catherine Hale, University of Puget Sound; Timothy Jay, North Adams State College; W. Daniel Phillips, Trenton State College; Dana Plude, University of Maryland; Jonathan Schooler, University of Pittsburgh; Matthew Sharps, California State University, Fresno; Greg Simpson,

University of Kansas; Margaret Thompson, University of Central Florida; and Paul Zelhart, East Texas State University.

The reviewers for the fifth edition included: Lise Abrams, University of Florida; Tom Alley, Clemson University; Kurt Baker, Emporia State University; Richard Block, Montana State University; Kyle Cave, University of Southampton (United Kingdom); Lucinda DeWitt, University of Minnesota; Susan Dutch, Westfield State College; James Enns, University of British Columbia; Philip Higham, University of Northern British Columbia; Mark Hoyert, Indiana University Northwest; Anita Meehan, Kutztown University of Pennsylvania; Joan Piroch, Coastal Carolina University; David Pittenger, Marietta College; and Matthew Sharps, California State University, Fresno. The excellent advice from the reviewers of these five earlier editions continued to guide me as I prepared this most recent version of the book.

Last—but certainly not least—I want to praise the reviewers of this sixth edition of *Cognition*. These individuals provided advice about how to restructure the chapters in this textbook, and they also suggested sections that could be shortened—advice that reviewers are typically reluctant to supply! I also appreciate their ability to review my manuscript from their own perspectives—as well-informed professors—and also from the perspective of fairly naïve psychology students. Enthusiastic thanks go to: Lise Abrams, University of Florida; Thomas R. Alley, Clemson University; Tim Curran, University of Colorado; Susan E. Dutch, Westfield State College; Ira Fischler, University of Florida; Kathy E. Johnson, Indiana University-Purdue University Indianapolis; Gretchen Kambe, University of Nevada, Las Vegas; James P. Van Overschelde, Univeristy of Maryland; Thomas B. Ward, University of Alabama.

The final words of thanks belong to my family members. My husband, Arnie Matlin, encouraged me to write the first edition of this book during the early 1980s. His continuing enthusiasm, superb sense of humor, and loving support always bring joy to my writing—and to my life! Our daughters and their spouses now live in other parts of the United States. I'd like to thank Beth Matlin-Heiger and Neil Matlin-Heiger, who live in the Boston area, and Sally Matlin and Octavio Gonzalez, who live in the San Francisco Bay area. Their continuing pride in my accomplishments makes it even more rewarding to be an author! Last, I would like to express my gratitude to four other important people who have shaped my life, my parents by birth and my parents by marriage: Helen and Donald White, and Clare and Harry Matlin.

Margaret W. Matlin
Geneseo, New York

⟳ Table of Contents

CHAPTER 3   Perceptual Processes II: Attention
         and Consciousness   **67**

CHAPTER 6   Memory Strategies and Metacognition   **171**

CHAPTER 1
An Introduction to Cognitive Psychology

PREVIEW

This chapter introduces you to cognition, an area within psychology that describes how we acquire, store, transform, and use knowledge. Human thought processes have intrigued theorists for more than 2,000 years. However, the contemporary study of cognition can be traced to Wundt's 1879 development of the introspection technique, the early research in memory, and William James's theories about cognitive processes. In the early twentieth century, the behaviorists emphasized observable behavior, rather than mental processes. New research in areas such as memory and language produced a disenchantment with behaviorism, and the cognitive approach started growing in popularity during the 1960s.

Cognitive psychology is influenced by research in cognitive neuroscience and artificial intelligence, as well as a theoretical framework called the parallel distributed processing approach. Cognitive psychology is also part of an active interdisciplinary area known as cognitive science.

This introductory chapter also gives you a preview of the chapters in this book and an overview of five themes in cognitive psychology. The chapter concludes with some tips on how to make the best use of your textbook's special features.

INTRODUCTION

At this exact moment, you are actively performing several cognitive tasks. In order to reach this second sentence of the first paragraph, you used pattern recognition to create letters and words from an assortment of squiggles and lines that form the letters and words on this page. You also consulted your memory and your knowledge about language to search for word meanings and to link together the ideas in this paragraph. Right now, as you think about those cognitive accomplishments, you are engaging in another cognitive task called *metacognition*, or thinking about your thought processes. In addition, you may have used decision making—yet another cognitive process—if you were debating whether to begin reading this textbook or to send an e-mail to a friend.

Cognition, or mental activity, describes the acquisition, storage, transformation, and use of knowledge. As you might imagine, cognition must include a wide range of mental processes, given that it operates every time you acquire some information, place it in storage, transform that information, and use it. This textbook will explore mental processes such as perception, memory, imagery, language, problem solving, reasoning, and decision making.

A related term, **cognitive psychology,** has two meanings: (1) Sometimes it is a synonym for the word *cognition*, and so it refers to the variety of mental activities we just listed. (2) Sometimes it refers to a particular theoretical approach to psychology.

Specifically, the **cognitive approach** is a theoretical orientation that emphasizes people's knowledge and their mental processes. For example, a cognitive psychology explanation of ethnic stereotypes would emphasize topics such as the influence of these stereotypes on the judgments we make about people from different ethnic groups (Wyer, 1998).

The cognitive approach is often contrasted with several other current psychological approaches. For example, the behaviorist approach emphasizes our observable behaviors, and the psychodynamic approach focuses on our unconscious emotions. To explain ethnic stereotypes, these two approaches would describe our behaviors or our emotions—rather than our cognitive processes.

Why should you and other students learn about cognition? One reason is that cognition occupies a major portion of the domain of human psychology. Think about this: Almost everything you have done in the past hour required you to perceive, remember, use language, or think. As you'll soon see, psychologists have discovered some impressive information about every topic in cognitive psychology.

A second reason to study cognition is that the cognitive approach has widespread influence on other areas of psychology. For instance, the cognitive approach has influenced educational psychology (e.g., Halpern & Hakel, 2002; Rayner et al., 2001), social psychology (e.g., Kunda, 1999), clinical psychology (e.g., Corrigan & Penn, 2001), and health psychology (e.g., Brannon & Feist, 2000). Cognitive psychology has also influenced interdisciplinary areas. For example, a journal called *Political Psychology* emphasizes how cognitive factors can influence political situations. In summary, your understanding of cognitive psychology will help you appreciate many other areas of psychology, as well as disciplines outside psychology.

The final reason for studying cognition is more personal. Your mind is an impressively sophisticated piece of equipment, and you use this equipment every minute of the day. If you purchase a computer, you typically receive a manual that describes its functions. However, no one issued an owner's manual for your mind when you were born. In a sense, this book resembles an owner's manual, describing what is known about how your mind works. This book—like a computer manual—also includes hints on how to improve performance.

This introductory chapter focuses on three topics. First, we'll briefly consider the history of cognitive psychology, and then we'll outline some important current issues. The final part of the chapter describes this textbook, including its content and major themes; it also provides suggestions for using the book effectively.

A BRIEF HISTORY OF COGNITIVE PSYCHOLOGY

The cognitive approach to psychology traces its origins to the classical Greek philosophers and to developments in nineteenth- and twentieth-century psychology. As we will also see in this section, however, the contemporary version of cognitive psychology emerged within the last 50 years.

The Origins of Cognitive Psychology

Human thought processes have intrigued philosophers and other theorists for at least 2,000 years. For example, the Greek philosopher Aristotle proposed laws for learning and memory, and he discussed the importance of mental imagery. Aristotle also emphasized that humans acquire knowledge through experience and observation (Sternberg, 1999a). Aristotle's views provided the original basis for cognitive psychologists' emphasis on **empirical evidence,** or scientific evidence obtained by careful observation and experimentation. Aristotle set the stage for centuries of philosophical debate about the acquisition of knowledge. However, psychology as a discipline did not emerge until the late 1800s.

Wilhelm Wundt. Theorists in the history of psychology often celebrate 1879 as the birth of scientific psychology. It was then that Wilhelm Wundt (pronounced "Voont") opened his laboratory in a small lecture room in Leipzig, Germany. This event marked the beginning of psychology as a new discipline that was separate from philosophy and physiology. Within several years, students journeyed from around the world to study with Wundt, who taught about 28,000 students during the course of his lifetime (Bechtel et al., 1998).

Wundt proposed that psychology should study mental processes, using a technique called introspection. **Introspection,** in this case, meant that carefully trained observers would systematically analyze their own sensations and report them as objectively as possible (Bechtel et al., 1998). For example, observers might be asked to objectively report their reactions to a specific musical chord, without attempting to provide any interpretation of this stimulus. Wundt also emphasized the importance of replications (Viney & King, 2003). **Replications** are experiments in which a phenomenon is tested under a variety of different conditions (e.g., different participants, different stimuli, or different testing situations). Most of the research described in this textbook has been replicated several times.

Wundt's introspection technique sounds subjective to most current cognitive psychologists (Sternberg, 1999a). As you'll see throughout this textbook, our introspections sometimes fail to correspond with our actual cognitive processes. For example, you may introspect that your eyes are moving smoothly across this page, but cognitive psychologists have determined that your eyes actually move in small jumps—as you'll learn in Chapter 3.

Early Memory Researchers. Not all of Wundt's contemporaries adopted the introspective technique, however. Another German psychologist named Hermann Ebbinghaus (1885/1913), for example, devised his own methods for studying human memory. He constructed more than 2,000 nonsense syllables (for instance, DAK) and tested his own ability to learn these stimuli. Ebbinghaus examined a variety of factors that might influence performance, such as the amount of time between list presentations. He specifically chose nonsense syllables—rather than meaningful material—so that the stimuli could not have previous associations with past experiences.

Meanwhile, in the United States, similar research was being conducted by psychologists such as Mary Whiton Calkins (1894), who was the first woman to be president of the American Psychological Association. For example, Calkins reported a memory phenomenon called the recency effect (Madigan & O'Hara, 1992). The **recency effect** refers to the observation that our recall is especially accurate for the final items in a series of stimuli.

Ebbinghaus, Calkins, and other pioneers inspired hundreds of researchers to examine how selected variables influenced memory. These early researchers typically used nonsense stimuli. As a result, they did not investigate the very different approach that people adopt when they try to recall meaningful material.

William James. Another crucial figure in the history of cognitive psychology is William James, an American whose theories became especially prominent at the end of the nineteenth century. James was not impressed with Wundt's introspection technique or Ebbinghaus's research with nonsense syllables. Instead, James preferred to theorize about our everyday psychological experiences. He is best known for his textbook *Principles of Psychology*, published in 1890. (Incidentally, try Demonstration 1.1 before you read further.)

Principles of Psychology provides detailed descriptions about humans' everyday experience and emphasizes that the human mind is active and inquiring. The book foreshadows numerous topics that currently fascinate cognitive psychologists, such as perception, attention, memory, reasoning, and the tip-of-the-tongue phenomenon. Consider, for example, James's vivid description of the tip-of-the-tongue experience:

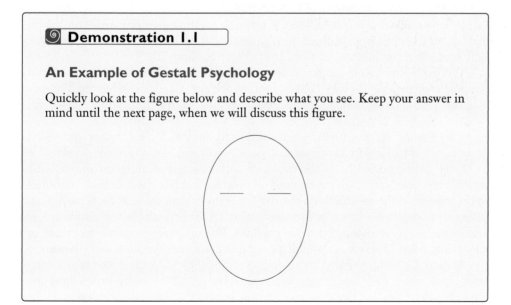

⑨ Demonstration 1.1

An Example of Gestalt Psychology

Quickly look at the figure below and describe what you see. Keep your answer in mind until the next page, when we will discuss this figure.

Suppose we try to recall a forgotten name. The state of our consciousness is peculiar. There is a gap therein but no mere gap. It is a gap that is intensely active. A sort of wraith of the name is in it, beckoning us in a given direction, making us at moments tingle with the sense of our closeness and then letting us sink back without the longed-for term. (1890, p. 251)

Behaviorism. Behaviorism was the most prominent theoretical perspective in the United States during the first half of the twentieth century. According to the **behaviorist approach,** psychology must focus only on objective, observable reactions; behaviorism therefore emphasizes the environmental stimuli that determine behavior (Pear, 2001). Strict behaviorists (often called *radical behaviorists*) rejected speculations about internal thoughts (Sternberg, 1999a). The most prominent early behaviorist was the American psychologist John B. Watson (1913).

The behaviorists' emphasis on observable behavior led them to completely reject Wundt's introspection approach (Bargh & Ferguson, 2000). They also avoided terms that referred to mental events, such as *image, idea,* or *thought.* Many behaviorists classified thinking as simply subvocal speech. Presumably, appropriate equipment could detect the tiny movements made by the tongue (observable behaviors) during thinking. For example, if you are thinking while reading this sentence, some early behaviorists would have said that you are really just talking to yourself, but so quietly that your vocalizations cannot be heard.

Behaviorists did not contribute to the study of mental activity. However, they did contribute significantly to the methods of current cognitive psychology. Behaviorists emphasized the importance of the **operational definition,** a precise definition that specifies exactly how a concept is to be measured. Current cognitive psychologists also emphasize operational definitions. For example, a cognitive researcher must specify exactly how memory is to be measured in an experiment. Behaviorists also valued experimental control. As a result, research psychologists primarily studied animals other than humans, because these animals can be reared under far more carefully controlled conditions (Staddon, 2001; Viney & King, 2003).

We must also acknowledge the important contribution of behaviorists to contemporary applied psychology. Their learning principles are extensively used in therapy, business, and education (Rachlin, 2002; Staddon, 2001).

The Gestalt Approach. Behaviorism thrived in the United States for several decades, but it had less influence on European psychology. An important development in Europe at the beginning of the twentieth century was Gestalt (pronounced "Geh-*shtahlt*") psychology. **Gestalt psychology** emphasizes that humans have basic tendencies to organize what they see and that the whole is greater than the sum of its parts. Consider, for example, the figure in Demonstration 1.1. You probably saw a human face, rather than simply an oval and two straight lines. This figure seems to have unity and organization. It is a **Gestalt,** or overall quality that transcends the individual elements.

Because Gestalt psychologists valued the unity of psychological phenomena, they strongly objected to Wundt's introspective technique of analyzing experiences into separate components. They also criticized the behaviorists' emphasis on breaking behavior into individual stimulus-response units (Sternberg, 1999a) and ignoring the context of behavior (Sharps & Wertheimer, 2000). Gestalt psychologists constructed a number of laws that explain why certain components of a pattern seem to belong together. We'll consider some of these laws in Chapter 2.

Gestalt psychologists also emphasized the importance of insight in problem solving (Sharps & Wertheimer, 2000; Viney & King, 2003). When you are trying to solve a problem, the parts of the problem initially seem unrelated to each other. However, with a sudden flash of insight, the parts fit together into a solution. Gestalt psychologists conducted most of the early research in problem solving. We will examine their concept of insight—as well as more recent developments—in Chapter 11 of this textbook.

Frederick C. Bartlett. In the early 1900s, the behaviorists were dominant in the United States, and the Gestalt psychologists were influential in Continental Europe. Meanwhile in England, a British psychologist named Frederick C. Bartlett conducted his research on human memory. His important book *Remembering: An Experimental and Social Study* (Bartlett, 1932) rejected the carefully controlled research of Ebbinghaus. Instead, Bartlett used meaningful materials, such as lengthy stories. He discovered that people made systematic errors when trying to recall these stories. Bartlett proposed that human memory is a constructive process in which we interpret and transform the original material, often making this material more consistent with our own personal experiences.

Bartlett's work was largely ignored in the United States during the 1930s, because American psychologists were committed to the experimental methods of behaviorism. However, about half a century later, American cognitive psychologists discovered his work and appreciated his use of naturalistic material, in contrast to Ebbinghaus's artificial nonsense syllables. Bartlett's emphasis on a schema-based approach to memory foreshadowed some of the research we will explore in Chapters 5 and 8 (Bechtel et al., 1998).

The Emergence of Modern Cognitive Psychology

We have briefly traced the historical roots of cognitive psychology, but when was this new approach actually "born"? Cognitive psychologists generally agree that the birth of cognitive psychology should be listed as 1956 (Eysenck, 1990; Viney & King, 2003). During this prolific year, many researchers published influential books and articles on attention, memory, language, concept formation, and problem solving.

Some psychologists even specify a single day on which cognitive psychology was born. On September 11, 1956, many important researchers attended a symposium at the Massachusetts Institute of Technology. As George Miller (1979) recalled the event:

> I went away from the Symposium with a strong conviction, more intuitive than rational, that human experimental psychology, theoretical linguistics, and computer simulation of cognitive processes were all pieces of a larger whole, and that the future would see progressive elaboration and coordination of their shared concerns. (p. 9)

Enthusiasm for the cognitive approach grew rapidly, so that by about 1960, the methodology, approach, and attitudes had changed substantially (Mandler, 1985). Another important turning point was the publication of Ulric Neisser's (1967) book *Cognitive Psychology* (Palmer, 1999).

In fact, the increasing enthusiasm for the cognitive approach has sometimes been called the "cognitive revolution" (Bruner, 1997). Let's examine some of the factors that contributed to the dramatic rise in popularity of cognitive psychology. Then we'll consider the information-processing approach, one of the most influential forces in the early development of cognitive psychology.

Factors Contributing to the Rise of Cognitive Psychology. The emerging popularity of the cognitive approach can be traced to psychologists' disenchantment with behaviorism, as well to new developments in linguistics, memory, and developmental psychology.

By the late 1960s, psychologists were becoming increasingly disappointed with the behaviorist outlook that had dominated American psychology. Complex human behavior could not readily be explained using only the concepts from traditional behaviorist theory, such as observable stimuli, responses, and reinforcement. This approach tells us nothing about psychologically interesting processes, such as the thoughts and strategies people use when they try to solve a problem (Bechtel et al., 1998).

New developments in linguistics also increased psychologists' dissatisfaction with behaviorism (Bargh & Ferguson, 2000). The most important contributions came from the linguist Noam Chomsky (1957), who rejected the behaviorist approach to language acquisition. Instead, Chomsky emphasized the mental processes we need in order to understand and produce language. Linguists such as Chomsky convinced many psychologists that the structure of language was too complex to be explained in behaviorist terms (Barsalou, 1992a). Many linguists argued that humans have an inborn ability to master language; this perspective clearly contradicted the behaviorist principle that language acquisition can be entirely explained by learning principles.

Research in human memory began to blossom at the end of the 1950s, further increasing the disenchantment with behaviorism. Psychologists examined the organization of memory, and they proposed memory models. They frequently found that material was altered during memory, for example, by people's previous knowledge. Behaviorist principles such as "reinforcement" could not explain these alterations (Bargh & Ferguson, 2000).

Another influential force came from research on children's thought processes. Jean Piaget (pronounced "Pea-ah-*zhay*") was a Swiss theorist who emphasized children's developing appreciation of concepts. For example, infants develop **object permanence,** the knowledge that an object exists, even when it is temporarily out of sight. Piaget's books began to attract the attention of American psychologists and educators toward the end of the 1950s.

Robins and his colleagues (1999) documented the emerging popularity of the cognitive approach—and the simultaneous decline of the behaviorist approach. Using a computerized database of psychology journals, these psychologists examined the articles that had been published in four prestigious, general-interest psychology journals. In particular, they counted the number of journal articles that used keywords such as *cognitive* and *cognition* (an indication of the popularity of the cognitive approach). They also counted the number of articles using keywords such as *reinforcement* and *conditioning* (an indication of the popularity of the behaviorist approach).

Figure 1.1 shows the number of articles with either cognitive or behaviorist keywords. As you can see, the number of cognitive articles has risen fairly steadily since 1950. The number of behaviorist articles increased to a maximum in the 1960s and has decreased fairly steadily since then.

We have seen that the growth of the cognitive approach was encouraged by research in linguistics, memory, and developmental psychology. Let's now consider an

FIGURE 1.1

The Percentage of Articles Published in Four Prominent Psychology Journals That Contain Keywords Relevant to the Cognitive and Behaviorist Approaches. Note: The four journals included in this study are *American Psychologist, Annual Review of Psychology, Psychological Bulletin,* and *Psychological Review.*

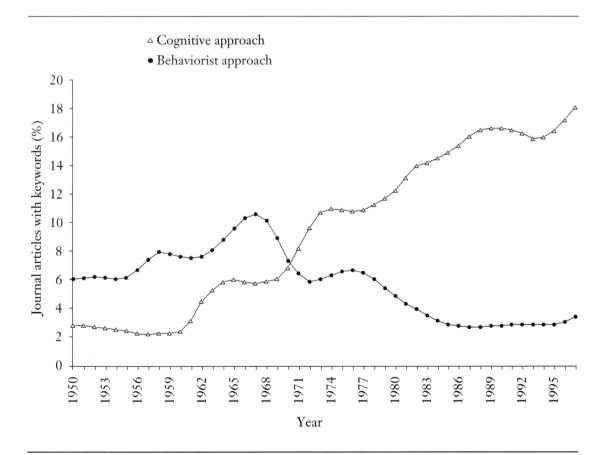

Source: Based on Robins et al., 1999.

additional factor contributing to that growth, which was the enthusiasm about the information-processing approach. For many years, the information-processing approach was the most popular theory within the cognitive approach.

The Information-Processing Approach. During the 1950s, communication science and computer science began to develop and gain popularity. Researchers then began speculating that human thought processes could be analyzed from a similar perspective (Palmer, 1999; E. Reed, 1997). Two important components of the **information-processing approach** are that (a) a mental process can best be understood by comparing it with the operations of a computer, and (b) a mental process can be interpreted as information progressing through the system in a series of stages, one step at a time (Groome, 1999; Massaro & Cowan, 1993).

Researchers proposed a number of information-processing models to explain human memory. For example, Richard Atkinson and Richard Shiffrin (1968) developed a multistore model that is often discussed. This model soon became tremendously popular within the emerging field of cognitive psychology (Squire et al., 1993). Because the Atkinson-Shiffrin theory quickly became the standard approach, it is often called the "modal model." The **Atkinson-Shiffrin model** proposed that memory can be understood as a sequence of discrete steps, in which information is transferred from one storage area to another. Let's look more closely at this model because it was so influential in persuading research psychologists to adopt the cognitive psychology perspective.

Figure 1.2 shows the Atkinson-Shiffrin model, with arrows to indicate the transfer of information. External stimuli from the environment first enter sensory memory. **Sensory memory** is a large-capacity storage system that records information from each of the senses with reasonable accuracy. During the 1960s and 1970s, psychologists frequently studied either iconic memory (visual sensory memory) or echoic memory (auditory sensory memory) (e.g., Darwin et al., 1972; Sperling, 1960). The model proposed that information is stored in sensory memory for 2 seconds or less, and then most of it is forgotten. For example, your echoic memory briefly stores the last words of a sentence spoken by your professor, but the "echo" of those words disappears within 2 seconds.

Atkinson and Shiffrin's model proposed that some material from sensory memory then passes on to short-term memory. **Short-term memory** (now called **working memory**) contains only the small amount of information that we are actively using. Memories in short-term memory are fragile—though not as fragile as those in sensory memory; these memories can be lost within about 30 seconds unless they are somehow repeated.

According to the model, material that has been rehearsed passes from short-term memory to long-term memory. **Long-term memory** has an enormous capacity because it contains memories that are decades old, in addition to memories that arrived several minutes ago. Atkinson and Shiffrin proposed that information stored in long-term memory is relatively permanent, and not likely to be lost.

Let's see how the Atkinson-Shiffrin model could account for the task you are working on right now. For instance, the sentences in the previous paragraph served as "external input," and they entered into your iconic memory. Only a fraction of that material passed into your short-term memory, and then only a fraction passed from

FIGURE 1.2

Atkinson and Shiffrin's Model of Memory.

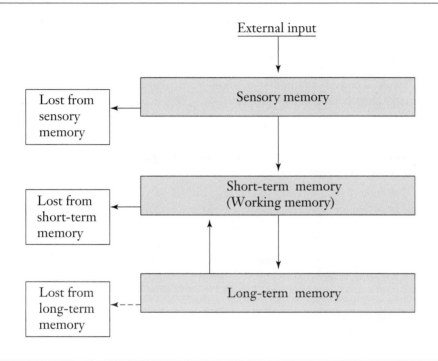

Source: Based on Atkinson & Shiffrin, 1968.

short-term memory to long-term memory. In fact, without glancing back, can you recall the exact words of any sentence in that previous paragraph?

Atkinson and Shiffrin's (1968) information-processing model dominated memory research for many years. However, its influence is now diminished. For instance, most cognitive psychologists now consider sensory memory to be the very brief storage process that is part of perception (Baddeley, 1995b).

Researchers also question Atkinson and Shiffrin's (1968) clear-cut distinction between short-term memory and long-term memory (Baddeley, 1995b; Healy & McNamara, 1996). Still, cognitive psychologists typically divide the huge topic of memory into two parts, more for the sake of convenience than a conviction that we have two entirely different kinds of memory. In this textbook, for instance, Chapter 4 examines short-term memory, although I use the current, more descriptive term "Working Memory" as the chapter title. Chapters 5, 6, 7, and 8 examine various components of long-term memory.

We have been discussing the Atkinson-Shiffrin (1968) model of memory because it is the best-known example of the information-processing approach. In general, enthusiasm for these information-processing models has declined; cognitive psychologists now acknowledge that we need more complex models to account for human thinking.

Instead, some emphasize either a neuroscience approach or the parallel distributed processing approach; we'll explore both of these in the next section. Still others no longer support the information-processing approach, and they do not have a strong theoretical framework within cognitive psychology. As many noted researchers in the field have remarked, the discipline has been experiencing an identity crisis for at least the last decade. Cognitive psychology lacks a unified theoretical direction for the future (Bechtel et al., 1998; Neisser, 1994). Throughout this book, however, we will consider a number of small-scale theoretical viewpoints as we examine the research in cognitive psychology.

⑨ Section Summary: *A Brief History of Cognitive Psychology*

1. The term *cognition* refers to the acquisition, storage, transformation, and use of knowledge; *cognitive psychology* is sometimes used as a synonym for cognition and sometimes as a term referring to a theoretical approach to psychology.

2. Scientific psychology is often traced to Wilhelm Wundt, who developed the introspection technique.

3. Hermann Ebbinghaus and Mary Whiton Calkins conducted early research on human memory.

4. William James examined everyday psychological processes, and he emphasized the active nature of the human mind.

5. Beginning in the early twentieth century, behaviorists such as John B. Watson rejected the study of mental processes; the behaviorists helped to develop the research methods used by current cognitive psychologists.

6. Gestalt psychology emphasized organization in pattern perception and insight in problem solving.

7. Frederick C. Bartlett conducted memory research using long stories and other meaningful material.

8. Cognitive psychology began to emerge in the mid-1950s; this new approach was stimulated by a disenchantment with behaviorism and also by a growth of interest in linguistics, human memory, developmental psychology, and the information-processing approach.

9. According to the information-processing approach, mental processes can best be understood by comparison with a computer; a particular cognitive process can be represented by information flowing through a series of stages.

10. The best-known example of the information-processing approach is the Atkinson-Shiffrin (1968) model, which proposes three different memory-storage systems. Enthusiasm has declined for both this model and for the general information-processing approach.

CURRENT ISSUES IN COGNITIVE PSYCHOLOGY

Cognitive psychology has had an enormous influence on the discipline of psychology. For example, almost all psychologists recognize the importance of mental representations, a term that behaviorists would have rejected in the 1950s. In fact, examples of "pure behaviorism" are now difficult to locate. For instance, the 2003 convention of the Association for Advancement of Behavior Therapy featured many presentations with cognitive terms in the title. Two representative titles were "Social, Cognitive, and Situational Predictors of Sexual Victimization and Perpetration" and "Cognitive Vulnerability to Depression: Data from Studies Using Mood Induction."

The cognitive approach has also permeated most areas of psychology that had not previously emphasized thought processes. Demonstration 1.2 illustrates this point. The discipline of cognitive psychology has its critics, however. One common complaint concerns the issue of ecological validity. Studies have **ecological validity** if the conditions in which the research is conducted are similar to the natural setting to which the results will be applied. Consider an experiment in which participants must memorize pairs of unrelated words, presented at 10-second intervals on a white screen in a barren laboratory room. The results of this experiment might tell us something about the way memory operates. However, this task may have limited ecological validity, because it cannot be applied to the way people learn in the real world (Sharps & Wertheimer, 2000). How often do you try to memorize isolated words in this fashion, when studying for an upcoming psychology exam?

Most cognitive psychologists prior to the 1980s did indeed conduct research in artificial laboratory environments, often using tasks that differed from daily cognitive activities. However, current researchers are much more likely to study everyday issues in natural settings (Bechtel et al., 1998; Woll, 2002). Psychologists interested in memory, for example, are currently studying real-life issues, such as remembering to take your medicine, comparing the prices of two brands of cheese, soap opera plots, and the lyrics to songs (Mazzoni et al., 1997; Reeve & Aggleton, 1998; Woll, 2002). In general, though, most cognitive psychologists acknowledge that the discipline

---

ⓢ Demonstration 1.2

The Widespread Influence of Cognitive Psychology

Locate a psychology textbook used in some other class. An introductory textbook is ideal, but textbooks in developmental psychology, social psychology, abnormal psychology, etc., are all suitable. Glance through the subject index for words related to *cognition* or *cognitive*, and locate the relevant pages. Depending on the nature of the textbook, you may also find entries under terms such as *memory*, *language*, and *perception*.

must advance by conducting both ecologically valid and laboratory-based research (Tulving, 1991; Winograd, 1993).

Several topics are important to our overview of current cognitive psychology. First, we will look at two areas within cognitive science that have contributed most to cognitive psychology: neuroscience and artificial intelligence. Our next topic is the new approach to cognitive psychology called parallel distributed processing. Finally, we will consider cognitive science, an interdisciplinary approach that includes all of these topics and contributions from other research-based disciplines.

Cognitive Neuroscience

Cognitive neuroscience combines the research techniques of cognitive psychology with various methods for assessing the structure and function of the brain (Raichle, 2001). In recent years, researchers have increased their efforts to discover what structures in the brain are activated when people perform a variety of cognitive tasks.

However, neurological explanations for complex higher mental processes are often elusive. For example, a complex task—such as remembering a word—is seldom accomplished by just one specific structure in the brain (Wheeler, 1998). Incidentally, be cautious when you read summaries of cognitive neuroscience research in the popular media. For example, I discovered a newspaper article that claimed "Scientists Find Humor Spot in the Brain." In reality, numerous parts of the brain work together to master the complicated task of appreciating humor.

Let's examine several neuroscience techniques that have provided particularly useful information for cognitive psychologists. We will begin with a method that examines individuals who have experienced brain damage. We'll next consider three methods used with normal humans: positron emission tomography, functional magnetic resonance imaging, and event-related potential. Finally, we will discuss the single-cell recording technique, which is used only with animals.

Brain Lesions. The term **brain lesions** refers to the destruction of tissue, most often by strokes, tumors, or accidents. The formal research on lesions began in the 1860s, but major advances came after World War II, when researchers examined the relationship between damaged regions of the brain and cognitive deficits (Feinberg & Farah, 2000; Gardner, 1985). The study of brain lesions has greatly increased our understanding of the organization of the brain. However, the results are often difficult to interpret. For example, people with brain lesions seldom have the damage limited to a specific area. As a result, researchers cannot associate a cognitive deficit with a specific brain structure (Gazzaniga et al., 2002). In this textbook, we will occasionally discuss research on people with lesions. However, the following neuroscience techniques provide better-controlled information (Hernandez-García et al., 2002). Let's first examine two brain-imaging techniques.

Positron Emission Tomography. When you perform a cognitive task, your brain needs oxygen to support the neural activity. The brain does not store oxygen. Instead, the blood flow increases in the activated part of the brain in order to carry oxygen to that site. Brain-imaging techniques measure brain activity indirectly. These techniques are based on the following logic: By measuring certain properties of the blood in different regions of the brain—while people perform a cognitive task—we can determine which brain regions are responsible for that cognitive task (Buckner & Logan, 2001; Raichle, 1999). Let's first examine a brain-imaging technique called positron emission tomography (PET) scans; we'll discuss functional magnetic resonance imaging (fMRI) in the following section. Both of these methods can detect activity in a region of the brain that is no larger than the period at the end of this sentence (Posner & DiGirolamo, 2000b).

In a **positron emission tomography (PET scan),** researchers measure blood flow by injecting the participant with a radioactive chemical just before this person performs a task. The chemical travels through the bloodstream to the parts of the brain that are activated during the task. A special camera makes an image of the accumulated radioactive chemical throughout the brain. By examining this image, researchers can determine which parts of the brain are activated when the participant works on the task (Buckner & Logan, 2001; Raichle, 2001). PET scans can be used to study such cognitive processes as attention, memory, and language (Binder & Price, 2001; Buckner & Logan, 2001; Nyberg & McIntosh, 2001). Color Figure 4 (inside the back cover) shows a series of PET scans, which we'll discuss in Chapter 9.

PET scans require at least 30 seconds to produce data, so this method is not very precise. If a brain area increases and then decreases its activity within this 30-second period, the PET scan will record an average of this activity level (Hernandez-García et al., 2002).

Functional Magnetic Resonance Imaging. We have just seen that PET scans measure the blood flow to various brain areas. In contrast, fMRIs measure the amount of oxygen in the blood in various brain areas. More specifically, **functional magnetic resonance imaging (fMRI)** is based on the principle that oxygen-rich blood is an index of brain activity (Raichle, 2000). The research participant reclines with his or her head surrounded by a large, donut-shaped magnet. This magnetic field produces changes in the oxygen atoms. A scanning device takes a "photo" of these oxygen atoms while the participant performs a cognitive task (Phelps, 1999). For example, researchers have used the fMRI method to examine regions of the brain that process visual information. They found that specific locations respond more to letters than to numbers (Polk et al., 2002).

The fMRI technique was developed during the 1990s, based on the magnetic resonance imaging (MRI) used in medical settings. In general, an fMRI is preferable to a PET scan because it is less invasive, with no injections and no radioactive material. In addition, an fMRI can measure brain activity that occurs fairly quickly—in about half a second (Buckner & Logan, 2001). As you can imagine, the fMRI technique is relatively precise in identifying the exact time sequence of cognitive tasks, compared to the 30-second time period required by the PET scan.

However, even the fMRI technique is not precise enough to study the sequence of events in the cognitive tasks that we perform very quickly (D'Esposito et al., 1999). For example, you can read the average word in this sentence out loud in about half a second. If someone used the fMRI technique while you were reading that word, the image would show simultaneous neural activity in both the visual and the motor parts of your brain (Buckner & Petersen, 1998). That is, the fMRI cannot identify that you actually looked at the word (a visual task) before you pronounced the word (a motor task).

In addition, neither PET scans nor fMRIs can provide precise information about a person's thoughts. For instance, some commentators have suggested using brain scans to identify terrorists. However, the current technology for this precise kind of identification is clearly inadequate (Farah, 2002).

Event-Related Potential. As we've seen, PET scans and the fMRI technique are too slow to provide precise information about the timing of brain activity. In contrast, the **event-related potential (ERP) technique** records the tiny fluctuations (lasting just a fraction of a second) in the brain's electrical activity, in response to a stimulus.

To use the event-related potential technique, researchers place electrodes on a person's scalp. These electrodes record the electrical activity generated by neurons located beneath the skull (Gazzaniga et al., 2002). The ERP technique cannot identify the response of a single neuron. However, it can identify electrical changes over very brief periods. The research participant is instructed to perform a particular task. For example, in a study of selective attention, the participant may be told to listen for tones of a particular pitch in the right ear, but ignore all tones in the left ear. The researchers repeat the task many times—usually more than 20 times. They average the signal across all these trials, to eliminate random activity in the brain waves (Phelps, 1999).

The ERP technique provides a reasonably precise picture about changes in the brain's electrical potential during a cognitive task. Research on selective attention, for example, showed a decrease in electrical potential about 100 milliseconds (1/10 of a second) after a tone was presented. However, this decrease was twice as large for the attended tones, in comparison to the tones that were to be ignored (Phelps, 1999). In other words, a fine-grained analysis shows that the brain adjusts its activity when a stimulus must be noticed, rather than ignored. We'll examine this research in more detail in the discussion of attention in Chapter 3.

Single-Cell Recording Technique. So far, we have examined four techniques that neuroscientists can use to study humans. In contrast, the single-cell recording technique cannot safely be used on humans. Specifically, in the **single-cell recording technique,** researchers study characteristics of an animal's brain and nervous system by inserting a thin electrode next to a single neuron (Gazzaniga et al., 2002). (A **neuron** is the basic cell in the nervous system.) Researchers then measure the electric activity generated by that cell.

The major goal of the single-cell recording technique is to identify which variations in a stimulus produce a consistent change in a single cell's electrical activity. For example, Hubel and Wiesel (1965, 1979) inserted an electrode next to a neuron in the visual cortex, at the back of a cat's brain. They found that some kinds of cells in the visual cortex responded vigorously only when a line was presented in a particular orientation. These same cells responded at a much lower level when the line was rotated only a few degrees. More details on this technique can be found elsewhere (e.g., Coren et al., 2004; Farah, 2000a; Hubel, 1982). Clearly, this research has important implications for visual pattern recognition: The cells provide a mechanism for recognizing specific patterns, such as letters of the alphabet. We will examine this research further in Chapter 2.

A detailed investigation of cognitive neuroscience techniques is beyond the scope of this book. However, these techniques will be mentioned further in the chapters on perception, memory, and language. You can also obtain more information from other resources (e.g., Gazzaniga et al., 2002; Kalat, 2001; Phelps, 1999).

Artificial Intelligence

Artificial intelligence (AI), a branch of computer science, seeks to explore human cognitive processes by creating computer models that exhibit "intelligent" behavior (Wagman, 1999). Researchers in artificial intelligence have tackled such cognitive tasks as medical problem solving, legal reasoning, spatial-map learning, and speech recognition (Sobel, 2001; Thrun et al., 1998; Wagman, 1999). In this textbook, you'll read about research on artificial intelligence in Chapter 7 (mental maps) and in Chapter 9 (language comprehension).

The Computer Metaphor. Throughout the history of cognitive psychology, the computer has been a popular metaphor for the human mind. According to the **computer metaphor,** our cognitive processes work like a computer, that is, a complex, multipurpose machine that processes information quickly and accurately. Of course, researchers acknowledge obvious differences in physical structure between the computer and the human brain that manages our cognitive processes. However, both may operate according to similar general principles. For example, both computers and humans can compare symbols and can make choices according to the results of the comparison. Furthermore, computers have a central-processing mechanism with a limited capacity. Humans also have a limited attention capacity. As we'll discuss in Chapter 3, we cannot pay attention to everything at once.

Researchers who favor the computer approach try to design the appropriate "software." With the right computer program and sufficient mathematical detail, researchers hope to mimic the flexibility and the efficiency of human cognitive processes (Guenther, 1995).

AI researchers favor the analogy between the human mind and the computer because computer programs must be detailed, precise, unambiguous, and logical. Researchers can represent the functions of a computer with a flowchart that shows the sequence of stages in processing information. Suppose that the computer and the human show equivalent performance on a particular task. Then the researchers can speculate that the computer program represents an appropriate theory for describing the human's cognitive processes (Carpenter & Just, 1999).

Every metaphor has its limitations, and the computer cannot precisely duplicate human cognitive processes. For example, humans have more complex and fluid goals.

If you play a game of chess, you may be concerned about how long the game lasts, whether you are planning to meet a friend for dinner, and how you will interact socially with your opponent. In contrast, the computer's goals are simple and rigid; the computer deals only with the outcome of the chess game.

Pure AI. We need to draw a distinction between "pure AI" and computer simulation. **Pure AI** is an approach that seeks to accomplish a task as efficiently as possible. For example, the most successful computer programs for chess will evaluate as many potential moves as possible in as little time as possible. Chess enthusiasts were fascinated by the 1996 and 1997 tournaments between Garry Kasparov, the world chess champion, and Deep Blue, the artificial intelligence program developed by IBM. Deep Blue was designed to evaluate 200 million chess moves per second, a capacity that completely dwarfs even the most expert human chess player (Carpenter & Just, 1999). After all, the goal of pure AI is to be efficient, not to be human. Not surprisingly, Deep Blue won most of the matches.

Franklin (1995) lists some of the tasks that can be accomplished by pure AI systems, such as playing chess, speaking English, and diagnosing an illness. However, as he points out,

> AI systems typically confine themselves to a narrow domain; for example, chess-playing programs don't usually speak English. They tend to be brittle, and thus break easily near the edges of their domain, and to be utterly ignorant outside it. I wouldn't want a chess-playing program speculating as to the cause of my chest pain. (p. 11)

Computer Simulation. As we have seen, pure AI tries to achieve the best possible performance. In contrast, **computer simulation** attempts to take human limitations into account. As the name implies, the goal of computer simulation is to design a system that resembles the way humans would perform a specific cognitive task (Carpenter & Just, 1999).

Computer-simulation research has been most active in such areas as basic visual processing, language processing, and problem solving. For example, Carpenter and Just (1999) created a computer-simulation model for reading sentences. The model was based on the assumption that humans have a limited capacity to process information. As a result, humans would read a difficult section of a sentence more slowly. Consider the following sentence:

> The reporter that the senator attacked admitted the error.

Carpenter and Just (1999) designed the computer similation so that it took into account the relevant linguistic information. The model predicted that processing speed should be fast for the words at the beginning and the end of the sentence. However, the processing should be slow for the two verbs, *attacked* and *admitted*. In fact, the human data matched the computer simulation quite accurately.

Interestingly, some tasks that humans accomplish quite easily seem to defy computer simulation. For example, a 10-year-old girl can search a messy bedroom for her watch, find it in her sweatshirt pocket, read the pattern on the face of the watch, and then announce the time. However, a computer cannot yet simulate this task. Computers also cannot match humans' sophistication in learning language, identifying objects in everyday scenes, or solving problems creatively (Jackendoff, 1997; Sobel, 2001).

So far, our discussion of current issues in cognitive psychology has examined (1) the techniques used in cognitive neuroscience and (2) the perspective of artificial intelligence. Let's now consider another development that has been applied to a wide variety of cognitive tasks, called the parallel distributed processing approach.

The Parallel Distributed Processing Approach

In 1986, James McClelland, David Rumelhart, and their colleagues at the University of California, San Diego, published an extremely influential two-volume book called *Parallel Distributed Processing* (McClelland & Rumelhart, 1986; Rumelhart et al., 1986). This approach contrasted sharply with the traditional information-processing approach. As we discussed on page 10, the information-processing approach argues that a mental process can be represented as information progressing through the system in a series of stages, one step at a time.

In contrast, the **parallel distributed processing** (or **PDP**) approach argues that cognitive processes can be understood in terms of networks that link together neuron-like units; in addition, many operations can proceed simultaneously—rather than one step at a time (O'Reilly & Munakata, 2000). Two other names that are often used interchangeably with the PDP approach are **connectionism** and **neural networks.**

An undergraduate textbook in cognition cannot examine this elaborate theory or its applications in detail. However, in this section we can outline its origins, its basic principles, and the reactions to the PDP approach. The PDP approach will also be covered in some detail as a model of general knowledge (Chapter 8), and it will be mentioned in several additional chapters.

The Development of the PDP Approach. The PDP approach grew out of developments in both neuroscience and artificial intelligence—the two topics we have just discussed. Neuroscientists developed research techniques during the 1970s that allowed them to explore the structure of the **cerebral cortex,** the outer layer of the brain that is responsible for cognitive processes. One important discovery was the numerous connections among neurons (e.g., Mountcastle, 1979). In fact, this pattern of interconnections resembled many elaborate networks.

This network pattern suggests that an item stored in your brain probably could not be localized in a specific pinpoint-sized region of your cortex (Woll, 2002). Instead, the neural activity for that item seems to be *distributed* throughout a section of the brain. For example, we cannot pinpoint one small portion of your brain in which the name of your cognitive psychology professor is stored. Instead, that information is probably distributed throughout thousands of neurons in a region of your cerebral cortex. The researchers who developed the PDP approach proposed a model that simulates many important features of the brain (Levine, 2002). Naturally, the model captures only a fraction of the brain's complexity. However—like the brain—the model includes simplified neuron-like units, numerous interconnections, and neural activity distributed throughout the system.

At the same time that theorists were learning about features of the human brain, they were becoming discouraged about the limits of the classical artificial intelligence approach favored by information-processing psychologists (Dawson, 1998). As we've discussed, classical AI models viewed processing as a series of separate operations. In other words, classical AI models emphasized **serial processing,** in which only one item is handled at a given time, and one step must be completed before the system can proceed to the next step in the flowchart.

This one-step-at-a-time approach may capture the leisurely series of operations you conduct when solving a long-division problem. However, it is difficult to use classical AI models to explain the kinds of cognitive tasks that humans do very quickly and accurately (Dawson, 1998). For example, these AI models cannot explain how you can instantly perceive a visual scene (Churchland & Churchland, 1990; Martindale, 1991). Glance up from your book, and then immediately return to this paragraph. When you looked at this visual scene, your retina presented about one million signals to your cortex—all at the same time. If your visual system had used serial processing in order to interpret these one million signals, you would still be processing that visual scene, rather than reading this sentence! Many cognitive activities seem to use **parallel processing,** with many signals handled at the same time, rather than serial processing. On these tasks, processing seems to be both parallel and distributed, explaining the name *parallel distributed processing approach.*

Basic Characteristics of the PDP Approach. The parallel distributed processing approach is characterized by several important principles. Let's begin with the two principles we have just discussed, and then add other major points.

1. Many cognitive processes are based on parallel operations, not serial operations.

2. The neural activity underlying a particular cognitive procedure (for example, remembering a word) is typically distributed across a relatively broad area of the cerebral cortex, rather than being limited to a single, pinpoint-sized location. Each location of neural activity is called a **node,** and the nodes are interconnected in a complex fashion with many other nodes.

3. When a node reaches a critical level of activation, it can affect another node to which it is connected, either by exciting it or inhibiting it.

4. When two nodes are activated at the same time, the connection between the nodes is strengthened. Thus, learning is defined as a strengthening of connections (Martindale, 1991).

5. If information is incomplete or faulty, you can still carry out most cognitive processes. For example, you can still recognize a friend's face, even if a scarf is covering her hair and forehead. Our pattern recognition, memory, and other

cognitive processes are extremely flexible. A simple machine will not work if one component is defective. In contrast, the human brain is designed to complete a task, even when the input is less than perfect (Dawson, 1998; Luger, 1994).

Keep in mind that the PDP approach uses the human brain—rather than the serial computer—as the basic model (Woll, 2002). This more sophisticated design allows the PDP approach to achieve greater complexity, flexibility, and accuracy as it attempts to account for human cognitive processes.

Reactions to the PDP Approach. Because the parallel distributed processing approach is still relatively new, we cannot assess its long-term impact. Many psychologists have welcomed the PDP approach as a groundbreaking new framework (e.g., Carpenter & Just, 1999; Levine, 2002; Ramsey, 1999). They have developed models in areas as unrelated to one another as reading (Carpenter & Just, 1999; Cohen et al., 1998), decision making (Levine, 2002), motivation (Lord et al., 2003), and social cognition (Levine, 2002; Read & Urada, 2003). With additional investigations, researchers should be able to determine whether the PDP approach can adequately account for the broad range of skills represented by our cognitive processes.

Cognitive Science

Cognitive psychology is part of a broader field known as cognitive science. **Cognitive science** is a contemporary field that tries to answer questions about the mind. As a result, cognitive science includes all the disciplines we've discussed so far—cognitive psychology, neuroscience, and computer science. It also includes philosophy, linguistics, anthropology, sociology, and economics (Bechtel & Graham, 1998b; Sobel, 2001).

According to cognitive scientists, thinking involves the manipulation of internal representations of the external world. Cognitive scientists focus on these internal representations. In contrast, you'll recall, the behaviorists focused only on observable stimuli and responses in the external world.

Cognitive scientists value interdisciplinary studies. As Carolyn Sobel (2001) describes cognitive science, "The proliferation of ideas, of experiments, of knowledge is so great that no one person can possibly become familiar with or absorb all of it. Yet if all these disparate fields remain separate, important insights may be missed and relevant connections will not be made" (p. xx). Consequently, cognitive science tries to coordinate information gathered by researchers throughout the relevant disciplines.

ⓢ Section Summary: *Current Issues in Cognitive Psychology*

1. Cognitive psychology has gained widespread support throughout the broader field of psychology. Still, the discipline has been criticized on such issues as ecological validity.

2. Cognitive neuroscientists search for brain-based explanations for cognitive processes, using brain-lesion studies, positron emission tomography (PET) scans, functional magnetic resonance imaging (fMRI), event-related potentials (ERPs), and single-cell recording.

3. Theorists interested in artificial intelligence (AI) approaches to cognition may design computer programs that accomplish cognitive tasks as efficiently as possible (pure AI) or programs that accomplish these tasks in a human-like fashion (computer simulation).

4. In contrast to the serial processing approach of classical AI, the parallel distributed processing (PDP) approach argues that the ideal model is provided by the human brain. According to the PDP approach, (a) cognitive processes operate in a parallel fashion, (b) neural activity is distributed throughout a relatively broad region of the cortex, (c) an activated node can excite or inhibit other nodes with which it is connected, (d) learning is associated with a strengthening of connections between nodes, and (e) cognitive processes can be completed even when the supplied information is incomplete or faulty.

5. Cognitive science tries to answer questions about the mind; it includes disciplines such as psychology, neuroscience, computer science, philosophy, linguistics, anthropology, and economics.

AN OVERVIEW OF YOUR TEXTBOOK

This textbook examines many different kinds of mental processes. We'll begin with perception and memory—two processes that contribute to virtually every other aspect of cognition. We'll then consider language, which is probably the most challenging cognitive task that humans need to master. Later chapters discuss "higher-order" processes. As the name suggests, these higher-order cognitive processes depend upon the more basic processes introduced at the beginning of the book. The final chapter examines cognition across the life span. Let's preview Chapters 2 through 13. Then we'll explore five themes that can help you appreciate some general characteristics of cognitive processes. Our final section provides hints on how to use your book more effectively.

Preview of the Chapters

Visual and auditory recognition **(Chapter 2)** are perceptual processes that use our previous knowledge to interpret the stimuli that are registered by our senses. For example, visual recognition allows you to recognize each letter on this page, whereas auditory recognition allows you to recognize the words you are hearing on the radio.

Another perceptual process is attention **(Chapter 3).** If you have ever tried to follow two conversations at the same time, you have probably noticed the limits of your attention. This chapter also examines a related topic, **consciousness,** or your awareness of the external world, as well as your thoughts and emotions about your internal world.

Memory—the process of maintaining information over time—is such an important part of cognition that it requires several chapters. **Chapter 4** describes working memory (short-term memory). You're certainly aware of the limits of working memory when you forget someone's name that you heard just 30 seconds ago!

Chapter 5, the second of the memory chapters, focuses on long-term memory. We'll examine several factors, such as mood and expertise, that are related to people's ability to remember material for a long period of time. We'll also explore memory for everyday life events. For example, do people really have highly accurate "flashbulb memories" for details of important events that occurred years ago?

Chapter 6, the last of the general memory chapters, provides suggestions for memory improvement. This chapter also considers **metacognition,** which is your knowledge about your own cognitive processes. For instance, do you know whether you could remember the definition for *metacognition* if you were to be tested tomorrow morning?

Chapter 7 examines **imagery,** which is the mental representation of things that are not physically present. An important controversy in the research on imagery is whether mental images truly resemble perceptual images. For example, does your mental image of a clock resemble the visual image formed when you actually look at a clock? Another important topic concerns the mental images we have for physical settings, such as the cognitive map you developed for your college campus.

Chapter 8 concerns general knowledge. One area of general knowledge is **semantic memory,** which includes factual knowledge about the world as well as knowledge about word meanings. General knowledge also includes **schemas,** which are generalized kinds of information about situations. For example, you have a schema for what happens during a child's birthday party in North America.

Chapter 9 is the first of two chapters on language, and it examines language comprehension. One component of language comprehension is perceiving spoken

---

⑨ Demonstration 1.3

Looking at Unusual Paragraphs

How fast can you spot what is unusual about this paragraph? It looks so ordinary that you might think nothing is wrong with it at all, and, in fact, nothing is. But it is atypical. Why? Study its various parts, think about its curious wording, and you may hit upon a solution. But you must do it without aid; my plan is not to allow any scandalous misconduct in this psychological study. No doubt, if you work hard on this possibly frustrating task, its abnormality will soon dawn upon you. You cannot know until you try. But it is commonly a hard nut to crack. So, good luck!

I trust a solution is conspicuous now. Was it dramatic and fair, although odd? *Author's hint:* I cannot add my autograph to this communication and maintain its basic harmony.

language. A friend can mumble a sentence, yet you can easily perceive the speech sounds. A second component of language comprehension is reading; you easily recognize familiar words and can figure out the meaning of unfamiliar words. You can also understand **discourse,** or long passages of spoken and written language.

Chapter 10, the second language chapter, investigates language production. One component of speaking is its social context. For example, we make certain that the person with whom we are speaking has the appropriate background knowledge. Psychologists are just beginning to examine writing as a form of language production, but writing clearly requires processes different from speaking. The final language topic is bilingualism; even though learning a single language is challenging, many people can speak two or more languages fluently.

Chapter 11 considers problem solving. Suppose you want to solve a problem, such as how to cook some soup when the electricity has gone out. You'll need to represent the problem, perhaps in terms of a mental image or symbols. You can then solve the problem by several strategies, such as dividing the problem into several smaller problems. Chapter 11 will also explore creativity. We'll see, for example, that people are often less creative if they have been told that they will be rewarded for their creative efforts.

Chapter 12 addresses deductive reasoning and decision making. Reasoning tasks require you to draw conclusions from several known facts. In many cases, our background knowledge interferes with drawing accurate conclusions on these problems. When we make decisions, we supply judgments about uncertain events. For example, people may cancel a trip to Europe after reading about a recent terrorist attack, even though statistics might show that chances of danger are small.

Chapter 13 examines cognitive processes in infants, children, and elderly adults. People in these three age groups are more competent than you might guess. For example, 6-month-old infants can recall an event that occurred 2 weeks earlier. Young children are also very accurate in remembering events from a medical procedure in a doctor's office. Finally, elderly people are very competent on many memory tasks, such as recalling sentences composed of English words shortly after they have been presented. Chapter 13 also encourages you to review your knowledge about three important topics in cognitive psychology: memory, metacognition (or your thoughts about your cognitive processes), and language.

Themes in the Book

This book will emphasize certain themes and consistencies in cognitive processes. The themes can guide you and can offer a framework for understanding many of the complexities of our mental abilities. These themes are also listed in abbreviated form inside the front cover; you can consult the list as you read later chapters. The themes are as follows:

Theme 1: *The cognitive processes are active, rather than passive.* The behaviorists viewed humans as passive organisms; humans wait until a stimulus arrives from the environment, and then they respond. In contrast, the cognitive approach proposes that people seek out information. In addition, memory is a lively process requiring active synthesis and transformation of information; memory is not just a passive storage system. When you read, you actively draw inferences that were never directly stated. In summary, your mind is not a sponge that passively absorbs information leaking out from the environment. Instead, you continually search and synthesize.

Theme 2: *The cognitive processes are remarkably efficient and accurate.* For example, the amount of material in your memory is awe-inspiring. Language development is similarly impressive because children must master thousands of new words and complex language structure. Naturally, humans make mistakes. However, these mistakes can often be traced to the use of a rational strategy. For instance, people frequently base their decisions on the ease with which examples spring to mind. This strategy often leads to a correct decision, but it can occasionally produce an error. Furthermore, many of the limitations in human information processing may actually be helpful. You may sometimes regret that you often forget information after just a few seconds. However, if you retained all information forever, your memory would be hopelessly cluttered with facts that are no longer useful. Before you read further, try Demonstration 1.3 on page 23, which is based on a demonstration by Hearst (1991).

Theme 3: *The cognitive processes handle positive information better than negative information.* We understand sentences better if they are worded in the affirmative—for example, "Mary is honest," rather than the negative wording, "Mary is not dishonest." Reasoning tasks are also easier with positive rather than with negative information. In addition, we have trouble noticing when something is missing, as illustrated in Demonstration 1.3 (Hearst, 1991). (If you are still puzzled, check the end of this chapter for the answer to this demonstration.) We also tend to perform better on a variety of different tasks if the information is emotionally positive (that is, pleasant), rather than emotionally negative (unpleasant). In short, our cognitive processes are designed to handle what is, rather than what is not (Hearst, 1991; Matlin, 2004a).

Theme 4: *The cognitive processes are interrelated with one another; they do not operate in isolation.* This textbook discusses each cognitive process in one or more separate chapters. However, this organizational plan does not imply that each process can function by itself, without input from other processes. For example, decision making requires perception, memory, general knowledge, and language. In fact, all higher mental processes require careful integration of the more basic cognitive processes. Consequently, such tasks as problem solving, logical reasoning, and decision making are impressively complex.

Theme 5: *Many cognitive processes rely on both bottom-up and top-down processing.* **Bottom-up processing** emphasizes the importance of information from the stimuli registered on your sensory receptors. This bottom-up processing involves a low-level sensory analysis of the stimulus. In contrast, **top-down processing**

emphasizes the influence of concepts, expectations, and memory upon the cognitive processes. This top-down processing requires higher-level cognition—the kind we will emphasize in Chapters 5 and 8 of this textbook. Both of these mechanisms work simultaneously to ensure that our cognitive processes are typically fast and accurate.

Consider pattern recognition. You recognize the professor for your cognitive psychology course partly because of the specific information from the stimulus—information about this person's face, height, shape, and so forth; bottom-up processing is important. At the same time, top-down processing operates because you have come to expect that the person standing in front of your classroom is that professor.

How to Use Your Book

Your textbook includes several features that are specifically designed to help you understand and remember the material. I would like to describe how you can use each of these features most effectively. In addition, Chapter 6 focuses on memory-improvement techniques. Table 6.1 on page 188 provides a summary of these techniques, which are explored in more detail throughout that chapter.

Chapter Outline. Notice that each chapter begins with an outline. When you start to read a new chapter, first examine the outline so that you can appreciate the general structure of a topic. For example, you can see that Chapter 2 has four major sections labeled (1) Background on Visual Object Recognition, (2) Top-Down Processing and Visual Object Recognition, (3) Face Perception, and (4) Speech Perception.

Chapter Preview. Another feature is the chapter preview, which is a short description of the material to be covered. This preview builds upon the framework provided in the outline and also defines some important new terms.

Opening Paragraph. Each chapter begins with a paragraph that encourages you to think how your own cognitive experiences are related to the material in the chapter. By combining the material from the outline, the preview, and the opening paragraph, you'll be well prepared for the specific information about the research and theories in each chapter.

Applications. As you read the actual chapters, notice the numerous applications of cognitive psychology. The recent emphasis on ecological validity has produced many studies that describe our everyday cognitive activity. In addition, research in cognition has important applications in such areas as education, medicine, business, and clinical psychology. These examples provide concrete illustrations of psychological principles.

These examples should also facilitate your understanding because research on memory has demonstrated that people recall information better if it is concrete, rather than abstract, and if they try to determine whether the information applies to themselves (Paivio, 1971, 1995; Rogers et al., 1977; Symons & Johnson, 1997). Finally, a third kind of application in this book is found in the demonstrations. The informal experiments in these demonstrations require little or no equipment, and you can perform most of them by yourself. Students have told me that these demonstrations help make the material more memorable.

New Terms. Notice also that each new term appears in boldface type (for example, **cognition**) when it is first discussed. I have included the definition in the same sentence as the term, so you do not need to search an entire paragraph to discover the term's meaning. A phonetic pronunciation is provided for words that are often mispronounced. Students tell me that they feel more comfortable using a word in class discussion if they are confident that their pronunciation is correct. (Pronunciation guides are also included for the names of some theorists and researchers, such as Wundt and Piaget.)

Also, some important terms appear in several different chapters. These terms will be defined the first time they occur in each chapter, so that the chapters can be read in any order.

"In Depth" Features. Chapters 2 through 13 each contain an "In Depth" feature, which examines research on a selected topic relevant to the chapter. These features focus on the research methodology and the outcome of the studies.

Section Summaries. A special component of this textbook is a summary at the end of each major section in a chapter, rather than at the end of the entire chapter. For example, Chapter 2 includes four section summaries. These summaries allow you to review the material more frequently and to master small, manageable chunks before you move on to new material. When you reach the end of a section, test yourself to see whether you can remember the important points. Then read the section summary and notice which items you omitted or remembered incorrectly. Finally, test yourself again and recheck your accuracy. You may also find that you learn the material more efficiently if you read only one section at a time, rather than an entire chapter.

End-of-Chapter Review. You will find a set of review questions and a list of new terms at the end of each chapter. Many review questions ask you to apply your knowledge to an everyday problem. Other review questions encourage you to integrate information from several parts of the chapter. Notice that the new terms are listed in order of their appearance in the chapter. Check each item to see whether you can supply a definition and an example. You can consult the chapter for a discussion of the term; the glossary also has a brief definition.

Recommended Readings. Each chapter also includes a list of recommended readings. This list can supply you with resources if you want to write a paper on a particular topic or if an area is personally interesting. In general, I tried to locate books, chapters, and articles that provide more than an overview of the subject but are not overly technical.

Glossary. Your textbook includes a glossary at the end of the book. The glossary will be helpful when you need a precise definition for a technical term. It will also be useful when you want to check your accuracy while reviewing the list of new terms in each chapter.

One unusual aspect of cognition is that you are actually using cognition to learn about cognition! These suggestions—combined with the material on memory improvement in Chapter 6—may help you use your cognitive processes even more efficiently.

CHAPTER REVIEW QUESTIONS

1. Define the terms *cognition* and *cognitive psychology*. Now think about a career that you are considering; suggest several ways in which the information from cognitive psychology may be relevant to your career.

2. Compare the following approaches to psychology, with respect to their emphasis on thinking: (a) William James's approach, (b) behaviorism, (c) Gestalt psychology, (d) Frederick Bartlett's approach, and (e) the cognitive approach.

3. This chapter addressed the trade-off between ecological validity and experimental control. Explain each of these concepts. Then compare the following approaches in terms of their emphasis on each concept: (a) Ebbinghaus's approach to memory, (b) James's approach to psychological processes, (c) Bartlett's approach to memory, (d) the cognitive psychology from several decades ago, and (e) current cognitive psychology research.

4. List several reasons for the increased interest in cognitive psychology and the decline of the behaviorist approach. In addition, describe the field of cognitive science, noting the disciplines that are included in this field.

5. The section on cognitive neuroscience described five different research techniques. Answer the following questions for each technique: (a) Can it be used with humans? (b) How precise is the information it yields? (c) What kind of research questions can it answer?

6. What is artificial intelligence, and how is the information-processing approach relevant to this topic? Think of a human cognitive process that might interest researchers in artificial intelligence, and give examples of how pure AI and the computer-simulation investigations of this cognitive process might differ in their focus.

7. How does parallel distributed processing differ from the classical artificial intelligence approach? How is this new approach based on discoveries in cognitive neuroscience? What are the basic characteristics of the PDP approach?

8. Theme 4 argues that your cognitive processes are interrelated. Think about a problem you have solved recently, and point out how the solution to this problem depended upon perceptual processes, memory, and other cognitive

activities. Use the description of chapter topics (see pp. 22–24) to help you answer this question.

9. As you'll see in Chapter 6, your long-term memory is more accurate if you carefully think about the material you are reading; it is especially accurate if you try to relate the material to your own life. Review the section called "How to Use Your Book" (pp. 26–28), and point out how you can use each feature to increase your memory for the material in the remaining chapters of this book.

10. Review each of the five themes of this book. Which of them seem consistent with your own experiences, and which seem surprising? From your own life, think of an example of each theme.

NEW TERMS

cognition
cognitive psychology
cognitive approach
empirical evidence
introspection
replications
recency effect
behaviorist approach
operational definition
Gestalt psychology
Gestalt
object permanence
information-processing approach
Atkinson-Shiffrin model
sensory memory
short-term memory
working memory
long-term memory
ecological validity

cognitive neuroscience
brain lesions
positron emission tomography (PET scan)
functional magnetic resonance imaging (fMRI)
event-related potential (ERP) technique
single-cell recording technique
neuron
artificial intelligence (AI)
computer metaphor
pure AI
computer simulation
parallel distributed processing (PDP)
connectionism
neural networks
cerebral cortex

serial processing
parallel processing
node
cognitive science
consciousness
memory
metacognition
imagery
semantic memory
schemas
discourse
Theme 1
Theme 2
Theme 3
Theme 4
Theme 5
bottom-up processing
top-down processing

RECOMMENDED READINGS

Bechtel, W., & Graham, G. (Eds.). (1998a). *A companion to cognitive science*. Malden, MA: Blackwell. This superb handbook contains 60 chapters on cognitive science, with 25 of these specifically addressing topics in cognitive psychology. The chapters on the history of cognitive science, neuroscience, and artificial intelligence are especially relevant to Chapter 1 in your textbook.

Gazzaniga, M. S., Ivry, R. B., & Mangun, G. R. (2002). *Cognitive neuroscience: The biology of the mind* (2nd ed.). New York: Norton. If you are intrigued by the developing field of cognitive neuroscience, this textbook will provide more information on research techniques, as well as research findings on topics such as perception, memory, language, and cognitive development; numerous full-color illustrations help to make the book more accessible than most competitors' books.

Izawa, C. (Ed.). (1999). *On human memory: Evolution progress, and reflections on the 30th anniversary of the Atkinson-Shiffrin model.* Mahwah, NJ: Erlbaum. Chizuko Izawa has assembled 11 chapters by memory researchers, tracing the history and current status of the "modal model," which had such a major influence on the development of cognitive psychology.

Pashler, H., & Wixted, J. (Eds.). (2002). *Stevens' handbook of experimental psychology* (3rd ed., Vol. 4). New York: Wiley. Here's an advanced-level volume that provides a sophisticated discussion of topics such as neuroscience methods and connectionism.

Sternberg, R. J. (Ed.). (1999). *The nature of cognition.* Cambridge, MA: MIT Press. Some especially useful chapters in this book are the initial chapters on the history of cognitive psychology, the chapter on computational modeling, and the chapter on neuroscience methods.

ANSWER TO DEMONSTRATION 1.3

The letter *e* is missing from this entire passage. The letter *e* is the most frequent letter in the English language. Therefore, a passage this long—without any use of the letter *e*—is highly unusual. The exercise demonstrates the difficulty of searching for something that is not there (Theme 3).

CHAPTER 2

Perceptual Processes I: Visual and Auditory Recognition

PREVIEW

When you perceive, you use your previous knowledge to gather and interpret the stimuli that your senses register. Chapter 2 explores recognition, a perceptual task that is especially relevant for cognitive psychology. (Chapter 3 will examine another equally relevant perceptual process, paying attention.)

When you recognize a visual object, you identify a complex arrangement of sensory stimuli, such as a letter of the alphabet, a human face, or a complex scene. We will briefly discuss the visual system, and then explore how this system organizes our visual world. Then we will consider three theories that try to explain how we recognize objects.

The concept of top-down processing emphasizes that our concepts, expectations, and memory influence perceptual processing. We will explore how top-down processing aids reading, and then we will see that overactive top-down processing can lead to errors in reading and in visual object recognition.

Face perception is vitally important in our social interactions, and we seem to process human faces differently from other visual stimuli. Neuroscience research helps to clarify the biological processes that are involved in face perception. This section also includes an "In Depth" section on the difficulty of recognizing faces from identification cards and from security surveillance systems.

Speech perception is more complicated than it appears, especially because people vary in the way they pronounce the basic speech sounds. However, we use context to fill in missing sounds and to create boundaries between sounds; we also use visual cues to help us interpret ambiguous sounds. Two theories have been created to account for speech perception.

INTRODUCTION

Take a minute to appreciate your perceptual abilities. For instance, hold a pen in your hand. You clearly perceive a solid object that includes distinctive characteristics. You can easily identify its size, shape, and color. You also notice that the pen appears to be a unified object, clearly separate from your hand. As you shift your gaze back to this textbook, you perceive a series of squiggles on this page. It doesn't seem remarkable that you can identify each squiggle as a letter of the alphabet. If a friend walks by, you can instantly recognize this person's face. Your auditory abilities are equally impressive; you can recognize speech sounds, music, squeaking chairs, and footsteps.

Most of us take perception for granted; *of course* we can see and hear. Chapters 2 and 3 should persuade you that perception is actually a remarkably complex human ability. Perception may seem to be far easier than other cognitive skills, such as playing chess. However, you could buy a chess machine that will beat a chess master, but you cannot buy a vision machine that will beat the visual skills of a 2-year-old child (Hoffman, 1998; Tarr, 1999). Perceptual processes provide clear evidence for Theme 2 of this textbook, because our visual and auditory achievements are remarkably efficient and accurate (Lappin & Craft, 2000).

In Chapters 2 and 3, we'll explore perception. **Perception** uses previous knowledge to gather and interpret the stimuli registered by the senses. For example, you use perception to interpret each of the letters on this page. Consider how you managed to perceive the letter *n* at the end of the word *perception*. You combined (1) information registered by your eyes, (2) your previous knowledge about the shape of the letters of the alphabet, and (3) your previous knowledge about what to expect when your visual system has already processed the fragment *perceptio-*. Notice that perception combines aspects of both the outside world (the visual stimuli) and your own inner world (your previous knowledge). You'll notice that this process of pattern recognition is a good example of Theme 5 of this book, because it combines bottom-up and top-down processing.

Most colleges offer an entire course on perceptual processes, so we cannot do justice to this discipline in just two chapters. Other resources can provide information about basic sensory processes, such as the nature of the receptors in the eye and the ear (Goldstein, 2001; Soderquist, 2002). You can find more details about perception in other books (e.g., Coren et al., 2004; Goldstein, 2001; Matlin & Foley, 1997; Palmer, 1999; Yantis, 2002). These books examine how we perceive important characteristics of visual objects, such as shape, size, color, texture, and depth. These resources also examine other perceptual systems—audition, touch, taste, and smell.

Our current chapter will explore several aspects of perceptual processing. We will begin with some background information on visual object recognition. Then we'll examine two important topics in vision: top-down processing and face perception. Finally, we will shift to the perceptual world of audition as we consider speech perception. These perceptual processes are vitally important because they prepare the "raw" sensory information so that it can be used in the more complex mental processes, which are discussed in later chapters of this book. For example, Chapter 9 explores how we recognize both spoken and written words, and how we understand more elaborate language passages.

BACKGROUND ON VISUAL OBJECT RECOGNITION

During **object recognition** or **pattern recognition** you identify a complex arrangement of sensory stimuli. When you recognize an object, your sensory processes transform and organize the raw information provided by your sensory receptors. You also compare the sensory stimuli with information in other memory storage. Let's briefly consider the visual system, how organization operates in visual perception, and three theories about object recognition.

The Visual System

Psychologists have developed two terms to refer to perceptual stimuli. The **distal stimulus** is the actual object that is "out there" in the environment—for example, the telephone sitting over there on your desk. The **proximal stimulus** is the information registered on your sensory receptors—for example, the image on your retina created by the telephone. When we recognize an object, we manage to figure out the identity of the distal stimulus, even when the information available in the proximal stimulus is far from perfect (Vecera & O'Reilly, 1998). For example, you can recognize your telephone, even when you view it from an unusual angle and even when it is partly hidden by your book bag. Try Demonstration 2.1 to illustrate your skill in identifying the distal stimulus.

Demonstration 2.1 noted that you can recognize objects in a new scene that has been presented for about 1/10 of a second (Biederman, 1995). Does this mean that your visual system manages to take the proximal stimulus, representing perhaps a dozen objects, and recognize all of these objects within 1/10 of a second? Fortunately, your visual system has some assistance from one of its other components. As you may recall from Chapter 1 (p. 10), your **sensory memory** is a large-capacity storage system that records information from each of the senses with reasonable accuracy. To be specific, **iconic memory,** or visual sensory memory, allows an image of a visual stimulus to persist for about 200 to 400 milliseconds—less than half a second—after the stimulus has disappeared (Cowan, 1995; Neisser, 1967; Sperling, 1960).

Visual information that is registered on the retina (the proximal stimulus) must make its way through the visual pathway, a set of neurons between the retina and the

---

◎ Demonstration 2.1

The Immediate Recognition of Objects

Turn on a television set and adjust the sound to "mute." Now change the channels with your eyes closed. Open your eyes and then immediately shut them. Repeat this exercise several times. Notice how you can instantly identify and interpret the image on the TV screen, even though you did not expect that image and have never previously seen it in that exact form. In less than a second—and without major effort—you can identify colors, textures, contours, objects, and people.

This demonstration was originally suggested by Irving Biederman (1995), who noted that people can usually interpret the meaning of a new scene in 1/10 of a second. Incidentally, you can also recognize the rapidly presented images on MTV even though they may be shown at a rate of five per second. Consistent with Theme 2, humans are impressively efficient in recognizing patterns.

primary visual cortex. The **primary visual cortex** is located in the occipital lobe of the brain; it is the portion of your cerebral cortex that is concerned with basic processing of visual stimuli. (See Figure 2.1.) If you place your hand at the back of your head, just above your neck, the primary visual cortex lies just beneath your skull at that location. As the name suggests, however, the primary visual cortex is only the first stop within the cortex. For instance, researchers have identified at least 30 additional areas of the cortex that play a role in visual perception (Frishman, 2001; Kosslyn, 1999). These regions beyond the primary visual cortex are activated when we recognize complex objects. However, researchers have not yet discovered a consistent relationship that identifies which brain region is connected with which component of object recognition (Farah, 2000a). Our examination of face recognition, later in this chapter, will focus on these more "sophisticated" regions of the cortex.

FIGURE 2.1

A Schematic Drawing of the Cerebral Cortex, as Seen from the Left Side, Showing the Four Lobes of the Brain. Notice the primary visual cortex (discussed in this section). The inferotemporal cortex (discussed on p. 54) plays an important role in recognizing complex objects such as faces.

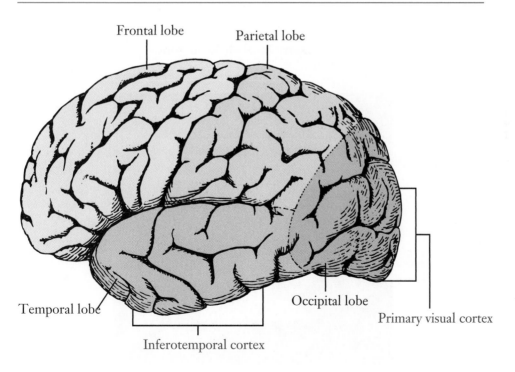

Organization in Visual Perception

At the beginning of this chapter, we emphasized that object recognition is a remarkable human achievement. As it happens, our visual system is designed to impose organization on the richly complicated visual world (Geisler & Super, 2000).

In Chapter 1, we introduced a historical approach to psychology called Gestalt psychology. One important principle in **Gestalt psychology** is that humans have basic tendencies to organize what they see; we see patterns, rather than random arrangements. For example, when two areas share a common boundary, the **figure** has a distinct shape with clearly defined edges. In contrast, the **ground** is the region that is left over, forming the background. As Gestalt psychologists pointed out, the figure has a definite shape, whereas the ground simply continues behind the figure. The figure also seems closer to us and more dominant than the ground (Kelly & Grossberg, 2000; Palmer, 1999; Rubin, 1915/1958). Even young infants demonstrate some of the Gestalt principles of organization (Quinn et al., 2002).

In an **ambiguous figure-ground relationship,** the figure and the ground reverse from time to time, so that the figure becomes the ground and then becomes the figure again. Figure 2.2 illustrates the well-known vase-faces effect. At first, you see a white vase against a blue background, but a moment later, you see two faces against

FIGURE 2.2

The Vase-Faces Effect: An Example of an Ambiguous Figure-Ground Relationship.

a white background. Even in this ambiguous situation, our perceptual system imposes organization on a stimulus, so that a portion stands out and the remainder recedes into the background.

Surprisingly, we can even perceive a figure-ground relationship when a scene has no clear-cut boundary between the figure and the ground. One category of visual illusions is known as illusory contours. In **illusory contours** (also called **subjective contours**), we see edges even though they are not physically present in the stimulus. In the illusory contour in Figure 2.3, for example, people report that a white triangle seems to loom in front of an inverted triangle and three small blue circles. Furthermore, the triangle appears to be brighter than any other part of the stimulus (Grossberg, 2000a; Palmer, 2002).

Two factors help to explain how we perceive these illusory contours: (1) Some cells in the visual system respond to these contours (Grossberg, 2003); and (2) the visual system tries to make sense of this disorderly jumble, and an efficient explanation is that a white triangle is covering the other figures. Illusory contours can therefore help us organize our visual perception (Gillam & Chan, 2002; Palmer & Nelson, 2000). In our everyday life, we typically perceive scenes more accurately if we "fill in the blanks." In the case of illusory contours, this rational strategy leads to a perceptual error (Mendola, 2003).

FIGURE 2.3

An Example of Illusory Contours.

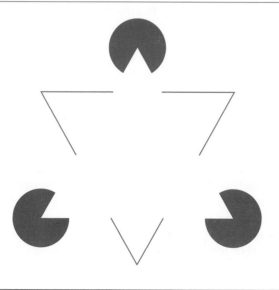

Theories of Visual Object Recognition

Researchers have proposed many different theories of object recognition, and we will consider three of them. The first theory, template matching, was designed to explain how we recognize 2-dimensional patterns such as numbers or letters. The template approach is now generally acknowledged to be inadequate. Nevertheless, our discussion begins with template matching because it was the first modern explanation for object recognition. The two other theories—feature analysis and recognition-by-components—are more sophisticated than the template approach. As you read about these two current theories, keep in mind that we don't need to decide that one theory is correct and the other is wrong. Humans are flexible creatures, and we may use different approaches for different object-recognition tasks (Riddoch & Humphreys, 2001).

Template-Matching Theory. You look at a letter *T* and you immediately recognize it. According to the **template-matching theory,** you compare a stimulus with a set of **templates,** or specific patterns that you have stored in memory. After comparing the stimulus to a number of templates, you note the template that matches the stimulus. You've probably had the experience of trying to find a piece of a jigsaw puzzle that will complete part of the puzzle. The piece must fit precisely, or else it won't work. Similarly, the stimulus must fit the template precisely. Thus, the letter *Q* will not fit the template for the letter *O* because of the extra line on the bottom.

Some machine recognition systems are based on templates. For example, if you have a checking account, look at one of your checks. Notice the numbers at the bottom of the check. These numbers are specially designed to be recognized by check-sorting computers. Each number has a constant, standardized shape. Each number is also distinctly different from the others. Humans sometimes write a number *4* that looks like a *9*. The *4* on your check, however, looks very different from the *9*, so the computer will not make errors in recognition when comparing the number with the templates.

A template system may work well for computers that process a standardized set of numbers. But notice why templates are totally inadequate for explaining the complex process of object recognition in humans. One problem with the template-matching theory is that it is extremely inflexible. If a letter differs from the appropriate template even slightly, the pattern cannot be recognized. However, every day we succeed in recognizing letters that differ substantially from the classic version of a letter. Notice in Figure 2.4 how all the *T*'s in *theory* differ from one another. Both the print types and the sizes vary. Some *T*'s are more slanted or more curved than others. Still, you can recognize each of those letters. When you recognize patterns and objects, your perceptual processes must therefore employ a more flexible system than matching a pattern against a specific template (Biederman, 1995).

Even if we could devise a modified template theory, we would still have difficulty when we view an object from a different perspective. Rotate Figure 2.4, and then view it from a slant. The shape of the image on your retina (the proximal stimulus) changes drastically for each *T*. Nevertheless, you still recognize the letters (Vecera,

FIGURE 2.4

An Example of Variability in the Shape of Letters. Notice specifically the difference in the shape of the letter *t* in *theory*.

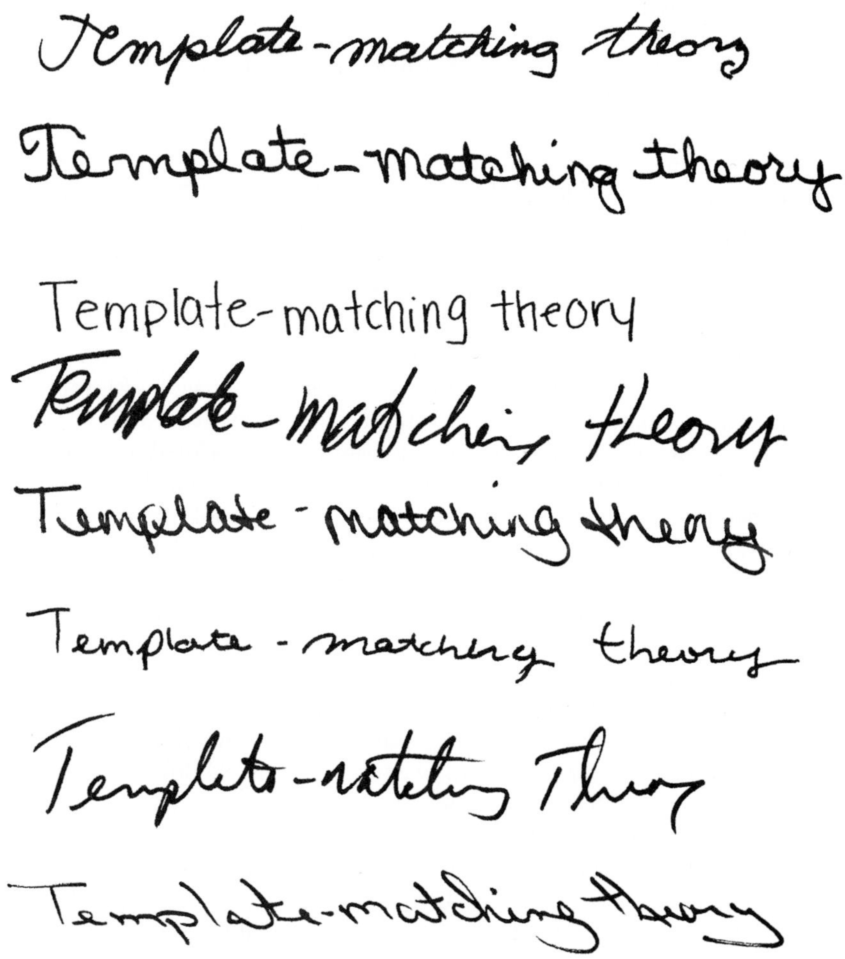

1998). A template-matching theory would require a different template for each rotation or slant of a figure, a clearly unwieldy proposal for a task we accomplish so quickly. In fact, using a template model to identify patterns would be like storing the answers to every possible arithmetic problem (Groome, 1999).

Finally, template models work only for isolated letters, numbers, and other simple objects presented in their complete form (Palmer, 1999). Look up from your textbook right now and notice the complex array of fragmented objects registered on your retina. Perhaps these include a lower edge of a lamp, a corner of a desk, and a portion of a book. Nonetheless, you can sort out this jumble and recognize the shapes. Your visual system could not possibly include templates for the lower edges of lamps and other fragments. Clearly, the template-matching theory cannot account for the complexity of human visual processing.

Feature-Analysis Theory. Several **feature-analysis theories** propose that a visual stimulus is composed of a small number of characteristics or components. Each characteristic is called a **distinctive feature.** Consider, for example, how feature-analysis theorists might explain the way we recognize letters of the alphabet. They argue that we store a list of distinctive features for each letter. For example, the distinctive features for the letter R include a curved component, a vertical line, and a diagonal line. When you look at a new letter, your visual system notes the presence or absence of the various features. It then compares this list with the features stored in memory for each letter of the alphabet. People's handwriting may differ, but each of their printed R's will include these three features.

Try Demonstration 2.2, which is based on a chart developed by Eleanor Gibson (1969). The feature-analysis theories propose that the distinctive features of alphabet letters remain constant, whether the letter is handwritten, printed, or typed. These models can explain how we perceive a wide variety of 2-dimensional patterns, such as figures in a painting, designs on fabric, and illustrations in books. However, most research on this topic focuses on our ability to recognize letters and numbers.

Feature-analysis theories are consistent with both psychological and neuroscience research. For example, the psychological research by Eleanor Gibson (1969) demonstrated that people require a relatively long time to decide whether one letter is different from a second letter when those two letters share a large number of critical features. According to the table in Demonstration 2.2, the letters P and R share many critical features; Gibson's research participants made slow decisions about whether these two letters were different. In contrast, G and M differ from each other on many of these critical features; in the research, people decided relatively quickly whether letter pairs like these were different from each other.

Other psychological research has focused on handwritten numbers found on envelopes that had been processed by the U.S. Postal Service. For example, Larsen and Bundesen (1996) designed a model based on feature analysis that correctly recognized an impressive 95% of these numbers.

The feature-analysis theories are also compatible with evidence from neuroscience (Palmer, 2002). As described in Chapter 1, the research team of Hubel and Wiesel used the single-cell recording technique to insert small wires into the visual cortex of anesthetized animals (Hubel, 1982; Hubel & Wiesel, 1965, 1979). Next they presented a simple visual stimulus—such as a vertical bar of light—directly in front of each animal's eyes. Hubel and Wiesel then recorded how a particular neuron responded to that visual stimulus. In this fashion, they tested a variety of visual stimuli and a variety of neurons in the primary visual cortex.

Hubel and Wiesel's results showed that each neuron responded especially vigorously when a bar was presented to a specific retinal region, and when the bar had a

---

⑨ Demonstration 2.2

A Feature-Analysis Approach

Eleanor Gibson proposed that letters differ from each other with respect to their distinctive features. She proposed the table that is reproduced below. Notice the top three kinds of features—straight, curve, and intersection. Notice the P and R share many features. However, Z and O have none of these kinds of features in common. Compare the following pairs of letters to determine the number of distinctive features they share: E and F; K and M; Z and B; N and M.

Features	A	E	F	H	I	L	T	K	M	N	V	W	X	Y	Z	B	C	D	G	J	O	P	R	Q	S	U
Straight																										
horizontal	+	+	+	+		+	+								+				+							
vertical		+	+	+	+	+	+	+	+	+						+		+				+	+			+
diagonal /	+							+	+		+	+	+	+	+											
diagonal \	+							+	+	+	+	+	+	+	+	+							+			
Curve																										
closed																+		+			+	+	+	+		
open V																				+						+
open H																	+		+	+					+	
Intersection	+	+	+	+			+	+					+			+						+	+	+		
Redundancy																										
cyclic change	+								+			+			+										+	
symmetry	+	+		+	+	+	+	+	+	+	+	+	+	+	+						+					+
Discontinuity																										
vertical	+			+	+	+	+	+	+	+					+							+	+			
horizontal		+	+			+	+								+											

Source: Gibson, 1969.

---

particular orientation. For example, suppose that a bar of light is presented to a particular location on the animal's retina. One neuron might respond strongly when that bar has a vertical orientation. Another neuron, just a hairbreadth away within the visual cortex, might respond most vigorously to a bar rotated about 10 degrees from the vertical. One small patch of the primary visual cortex could contain a variety of neurons, some especially responsive to vertical lines, some to horizontal lines, and some to specific diagonal lines. In summary, the visual system contains feature detectors that are "wired in." These detectors help us recognize certain features of letters and simple patterns.

However, we need to consider some problems with the feature-analysis approach. First, a theory of object recognition should not simply list the features contained in a stimulus; it must also describe the physical relationship among those features (Groome, 1999). For example, in the letter T, the vertical line *supports* the horizontal line. In contrast, the letter L consists of a vertical line resting at the side of the horizontal line.

Furthermore, bear in mind that the feature-analysis theories were constructed to explain the relatively simple recognition of letters. However, the shapes that occur in nature are much more complex. How can you recognize a horse? Do you analyze the stimulus into features such as its mane, its head, and its hooves? Wouldn't any important perceptual features be distorted as soon as the horse moved? Horses and other objects in our environment contain far too many lines and curved segments, and the task is far more complicated than letter recognition (Palmer, 1999; Vecera, 1998). The final approach to object recognition, which we discuss next, specifically addresses how people recognize these more complex kinds of stimuli found in everyday life.

The Recognition-by-Components Theory. Researchers such as Irving Biederman (1990, 1995) have developed an approach that attempts to explain how humans manage to recognize 3-dimensional shapes. The basic assumption of the **recognition-by-components theory** (also called the **structural theory**) is that a given view of an object can be represented as an arrangement of simple 3-D shapes called **geons.** Just as the letters of the alphabet can be combined into words, geons can be combined to form meaningful objects.

Five of the proposed geons are shown in Part A of Figure 2.5, together with several objects that can be constructed from the geons, shown in Part B. As you know, letters of the alphabet can be combined to form different meanings, depending upon the specific arrangements of the letters; for example, *no* has a different meaning from *on.* Similarly, geons 3 and 5 from Figure 2.5 can be combined to form different meaningful objects. A cup is different from a pail, and the recognition-by-components theory emphasizes the specific way in which these two geons are combined. Biederman (1995) has also described other ways in which a geon can vary, such as its orientation with respect to other geons in the figure, and also the ratio between the geon's length and width.

In general, an arrangement of three geons gives people enough information to classify any object. Notice, then, that Biederman's recognition-by-components theory is essentially a feature-analysis theory for the recognition of 3-D objects.

Research on the recognition-by-components theory has tested both normal humans and people with specific visual deficits. This research has demonstrated general support for the model (Biederman & Bar, 1999; Biederman & Kalocsai, 1997).

FIGURE 2.5

Five of the Basic Geons (A) and Representative Objects That Can Be Constructed from the Geons (B).

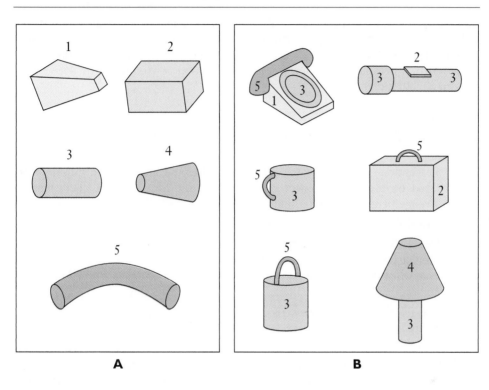

A   B

Source: Biederman, 1990.

However, the recognition-by-components theory requires an important modification because people recognize objects less quickly when those objects are seen from an unusual viewpoint, rather than the standard one (O'Reilly & Munakata, 2000; Tarr, 1995; Tarr & Bülthoff, 1998; Tarr et al., 1997). Notice, for instance, how your telephone is somewhat difficult to recognize if you look at it from an unusual perspective.

One modification of the recognition-by-components theory is called the **viewer-centered approach;** this approach proposes that we store a small number of views of 3-dimensional objects, rather than just one view. Suppose that we see an object from an unusual angle, and this object does not match any object shape we have stored in memory. We must then mentally rotate the image of that object until it matches one of the views that *is* stored in memory (Dickinson, 1999; Tarr & Vuong, 2002; Vecera, 1998). This mental rotation requires some time, and we can make errors in recognizing the object. (Chapter 7 discusses mental rotation in more detail.)

At present, both the feature-analysis theory and the recognition-by-components theory (modified to include the viewer-centered approach) can explain some portion of our remarkable skill in recognizing objects. In addition, researchers must explore whether these theories can account for our ability to recognize objects that are more complicated than isolated cups and pails. For example, how were you able to immediately identify numerous complex objects in the scene you viewed on your television screen in Demonstration 2.1? The topic of scene perception will undoubtedly inspire many research projects in the next decade (Henderson & Hollingworth, 1999; Tarr & Vuong, 2002).

⦿ Section Summary: *Background on Visual Object Recognition*

1. Perception uses previous knowledge to gather and interpret the stimuli registered by the senses; object recognition is the identification of a complex arrangement of sensory stimuli.

2. Visual information from the retina is transmitted to the primary visual cortex; other regions of the cortex are also involved when we recognize complex objects.

3. Gestalt psychology emphasizes that people tend to organize their perceptions, even when they encounter ambiguous figure-ground stimuli and even in illusory-contour stimuli, when no boundary actually separates figure from ground.

4. Several theories of object recognition have been proposed. Of these, the template-matching theory can be rejected because it cannot account for the complexity and flexibility of object recognition.

5. Feature-analysis theory is supported by research showing that people require more time to make decisions about letters of the alphabet when those letters share many critical features; the theory is also supported by neuroscience research using the single-cell recording technique.

6. The recognition-by-components theory argues that objects are stored in memory in terms of an arrangement of simple 3-D shapes called geons; according to the viewer-centered approach, we also store several alternate views of these 3-D shapes, as viewed from different angles.

TOP-DOWN PROCESSING AND VISUAL OBJECT RECOGNITION

Our discussion so far has emphasized how people recognize isolated objects. With the exception of illusory contours, we have not mentioned how knowledge and expectations can aid recognition. In real life, when you try to decipher a hastily written letter of the alphabet, the surrounding letters of the word might be helpful. When you try to identify an object that consists of a narrow, curved geon—attached to the side of a wider, cylindrical geon—the context of a coffee shop is probably useful.

Theme 5 emphasizes the difference between two kinds of processing. Let's first review that distinction. Then we'll see how these two processes work together in a complementary fashion to help us recognize words during the reading process. Finally, we'll see how we can sometimes make recognition errors if our top-down processing is overly active.

The Distinction Between Bottom-Up Processing and Top-Down Processing

So far, this chapter has focused on bottom-up processing (also called *data-driven processing*). **Bottom-up processing** emphasizes the importance of the stimulus in object recognition. Specifically, the physical stimuli from the environment are registered on the sensory receptors.

For example, at this moment, the sensory receptors in the retina of my left eye are registering information about an object. This information includes characteristics such as the object's shape (four straight lines), its color (red on the bottom, fading to white at the top), and the nature of its surface (shiny). The arrival of this information sets the object-recognition process into motion. This information starts from the most basic (or *bottom*) level, and it works its way *up* until it reaches the more sophisticated cognitive processes beyond the primary visual cortex. The combination of simple, bottom-level features allows us to recognize more complex, whole objects.

The very first part of visual processing may be bottom-up (Palmer, 2002). However, an instant later, the second process begins. This second process in object recognition is top-down processing (also called *conceptually driven processing*). **Top-down processing** emphasizes how a person's concepts and higher-level mental processes influence object recognition. Specifically, our concepts, expectations, and memory help in identifying objects. We expect certain shapes to be found in certain locations, and we expect to encounter these shapes because of past experiences. These expectations help us recognize objects very rapidly. In other words, our expectations at the higher (or *top*) level of visual processing will work their way *down* and guide our early processing of the visual stimulus. Top-down processing is especially strong when stimuli are incomplete, ambiguous, or presented for just a fraction of a second (Groome, 1999).

Here is a likely top-down account for the perceptual experience that I just described. For the last 3 hours, I have been surrounded by psychology books and journals. These journals have included several issues of a journal called *Psychological Science*, which has a shiny, red and white cover. My concepts, expectations, and memory help me recognize this journal very easily.

Cognitive psychologists propose that both bottom-up and top-down processing are necessary to explain the complexities of object recognition (Riddoch & Humphreys, 2001). We cannot ask whether perceivers interpret just the whole or just the parts, because both processes are necessary. For example, you recognize a coffee cup because of two almost simultaneous processes: (1) bottom-up processing forces you to register the component features, such as the curve of the cup's handle; and (2)

🌀 **Demonstration 2.3**

Context and Pattern Recognition

Can you read the following sentence?

THE MAN RAN.

---

the context of a coffee shop encourages you to recognize the handle on the cup more quickly, because of top-down processing. Let's now consider how this top-down processing facilitates reading.

Top-Down Processing and Reading

Researchers have demonstrated that top-down processing can influence our ability to recognize a variety of objects (e.g., Bar & Ullman, 1996; Becker, 1999; Riddoch & Humphreys, 2001; Tanaka & Curran, 2001). Let's explore one specific facet of this research, which demonstrates how top-down processing influences your ability to recognize letters during reading.

Before you read further, try Demonstration 2.3. As you can see, the same shape—an ambiguous letter—is sometimes perceived as an *H* and sometimes as an *A*. In this demonstration, you began to identify the whole word *THE*, and your tentative knowledge of that word helped to identify the second letter as an *H*. Similarly, your knowledge of the words *MAN* and *RAN* helped you identify that same ambiguous letter as an *A* in this different context.

Most of the research on this topic examines how context helps us recognize letters of the alphabet. Psychologists who study reading have realized for decades that a theory of recognition would be inadequate if it were based only on the information in the stimulus. When we read, suppose that we do identify each letter by analyzing its features. In addition, suppose that each letter contains four distinctive features, a conservative guess. Taking into account the number of letters in an average word—and the average reading rate—this would mean that a typical reader would need to analyze about 5,000 features every minute. This estimate is ridiculously high; our perceptual processes couldn't handle that kind of work load!

In addition, do you have the impression that you really see and identify each letter in every sentence? You probably could read most sentences fairly well, even if only half the letters were present. F-r -x—pl-, -t's e-s- t- r—d t—s s—t-n—.

One of the most widely demonstrated phenomena in the research on recognition is the **word superiority effect**. According to the **word superiority effect,** we can identify a single letter more accurately and more rapidly when it appears in a meaningful word than when it appears alone by itself or else in a meaningless string of unrelated letters (Palmer, 2002). For example, Reicher (1969) demonstrated that recognition accuracy was significantly higher when a letter appeared in a word such as *work*, rather than in a nonword such as *orwk*. Since then, dozens of studies have confirmed the importance of top-down processing in letter recognition (e.g., Jordan & Bevan, 1994; Krueger, 1992; Palmer, 1999). For example, the letter *s* is quickly recognized in the word *island*, even though the *s* is not pronounced in this word (Krueger, 1992).

Several theoretical explanations have been proposed to explain how top-down and bottom-up processing interact in a systematic fashion in order to produce the word superiority effect. One approach, which was introduced in Chapter 1, is called parallel distributed processing (McClelland & Rumelhart, 1981; Palmer, 1999; Rumelhart & McClelland, 1982). Specifically, **parallel distributed processing (PDP)** or **connectionism** argues that cognitive processes can be understood in terms of networks that link together related units. According to the PDP model, when a person sees features in a word, these features activate letter units. These letter units then activate a word unit in the person's mental dictionary for that combination of letters. Once that word unit is activated, excitatory neural feedback helps in identifying individual letters. As a result, people can identify a letter relatively quickly. When an isolated letter appears—without the context of a word—no excitatory feedback is provided. As a result, people identify an isolated letter relatively slowly.

So far, we've seen that letters can be more readily recognized in the context of a word, illustrating the importance of top-down processing. Researchers have also shown that the context of a sentence can facilitate the recognition of a word in a sentence. For example, people easily recognize the word *juice* in the sentence, "Mary drank her orange juice" (Forster, 1981; Stanovich & West, 1981, 1983).

Let's discuss a classic study that explored this word-in-a-sentence effect. Rueckl and Oden (1986) demonstrated that both the features of the stimulus and the nature of the context influence word recognition. That is, both bottom-up and top-down processing occur in a coordinated fashion. These researchers used stimuli that were letters and letter-like characters. For example, one set of stimuli consisted of a perfectly formed letter *r*, a perfectly formed letter *n*, and three symbols that were intermediate between those two letters. Notice these stimuli arranged along the bottom of Figure 2.6. In each case, the letter pattern was embedded in the letter sequence "bea-s." As a result, the study included five stimuli that ranged between "beans" and "bears." (In other words, this manipulated variable tests the effects of bottom-up processing.)

The nature of the context was also varied by using the sentence frame, "The _____ raised (bears/beans) to supplement his income." The researchers constructed four sentences by filling the blank with a carefully selected term: "lion tamer," "zookeeper," "botanist," and "dairy farmer." You'll notice that a lion tamer and a zookeeper are more likely to raise bears, whereas the botanist and the dairy farmer are more likely to raise beans. Other similar ambiguous letters and sentence frames were also constructed, each using four different nouns or noun phrases. (In other words, this manipulated variable tested the effects of top-down processing.)

FIGURE 2.6

The Influence of Stimulus Features and Sentence Context on Word Identification.

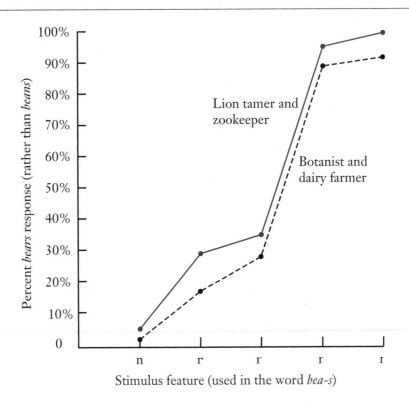

Stimulus feature (used in the word *bea-s*)

Source: Based on Rueckl & Oden, 1986.

Figure 2.6 shows the results. As you can see, people were definitely more likely to choose the "bears" response when the line segment on the right side of the letter was short, rather than long: The features of the stimulus are extremely important because word recognition operates in a bottom-up fashion. However, you'll also notice that people were slightly—but consistently—more likely to choose the "bears" response in the lion tamer and zookeeper sentences than in the botanist and dairy farmer sentences: The context is important because word recognition also operates in a top-down fashion. Specifically, our knowledge about the world leads us to expect that lion tamers and zookeepers would be more likely to raise bears than beans.

Think about how these context effects can influence the speed of reading. The previous letters in a word help you identify the remaining letters more quickly. Furthermore, the other words in a sentence help you identify the individual words more quickly. Without context to help you read faster, you might still be reading the introduction to this chapter!

Overactive Top-Down Processing and Occasional Errors in Word Recognition

Theme 2 of this book states that the cognitive processes are remarkably efficient and accurate. However, our discussion of Theme 2 in Chapter 1 pointed out that human mistakes can often be traced to the use of a rational strategy. Our perceptual processes use a rational strategy—namely, top-down processing—but they sometimes *overuse* it. As a result, people may ignore the information that is present in the stimulus, by means of bottom-up processing.

Mary Potter and her colleagues (1993) illustrated this tendency to "overuse a good strategy" in a study on reading. Specifically, participants were instructed to read a list of stimuli. Half of the stimuli on the list were actual words. The other half of the stimuli were nonwords, created by substituting a new vowel in a real word (for example, *dream* became *droam*, and *motor* became *mitor*). The list was presented very quickly, at the rate of only 1/10 of a second per word. This presentation rate was so fast that people read only 57% of the actual words correctly. However, they made even more errors on the nonwords; in fact, they were correct only 10% of the time. The most interesting finding, though, was that people converted the nonword into a real word on 42% of the trials. Their top-down processing was overactive, and they read *dream*, rather than the true stimulus, *droam*.

Overactive Top-Down Processing and Occasional Errors in Object Recognition

Suppose that you are walking along a sidewalk near your college campus, and a stranger asks you for directions to a particular building. Right in the middle of this interaction, two workers—who are carrying a wooden door—walk between you and the stranger. When they have passed by, the original stranger has been replaced by a different stranger. Would you notice that you are no longer talking with the same individual? You may be tempted to reply, "Of course!"

The research on a relatively new topic called change blindness certainly defies our commonsense ideas about object recognition. **Change blindness** refers to the inability to detect changes in an object or a scene (Simons & Levin, 1997a). Simons and Levin (1997b, 1998) tried the stranger-and-the-door study we just described. A stranger asks a bystander for directions (see Frame A of Figure 2.7). Then, as shown in Frame B of the figure, two individuals—carrying a door—perform a trick that could have come from an old Marx Brothers movie. The original stranger departs behind the door, leaving the substitute stranger talking to the bystander. The bystander is then asked if he or she noticed the change. Amazingly, only half of the bystanders reported that one stranger had been replaced by a different stranger—even when they were explicitly asked, "Did you notice that I'm not the same person who approached you to ask for directions?" (Simons & Levin, 1998, p. 646). Try Demonstration 2.4 to see how quickly you can detect the difference between two similar scenes.

FIGURE 2.7

A Study on Change Blindness. These photos are four frames from a video of a study on change blindness. Frames A through C show the sequence of the shift, and Frame D shows the original stranger and the "substitute stranger," standing side by side.

Source: Simons & Levin, 1998.

Laboratory research provides other examples of change blindness. For instance, Rensink and his colleagues (1997) asked participants to look at a photo, which was briefly presented twice. Then a slightly different version of the photo was briefly presented twice. This sequence of alternations was repeated until the participant detected the change. This research demonstrated that people quickly identified the change when the change was important. For example, when a view of a pilot flying a plane showed a helicopter either nearby or far away, participants required only 4.0 alternations to report the change. In contrast, they required 16.2 alternations to report a change that was unimportant, such as the height of a railing behind two people seated at a table. Additional studies confirm that people are surprisingly blind to fairly obvious changes in the objects that they are perceiving (e.g., Archambault et al., 1999; Intraub, 1999; Rensink, 2002; Simons et al., 2002).

Other researchers have reported a related phenomenon. When you are paying attention to some events in a scene and an unexpected but completely visible object suddenly appears, you sometimes fail to notice this new object; this phenomenon is called

◎ Demonstration 2.4

Detecting the Difference Between Two Pictures

Look back and forth between these two scenes, until you have detected which feature is different. The answer is at the end of the chapter, on p. 66.

inattentional blindness. In general, psychologists use the term *change blindness* when people fail to notice a change in some part of the stimulus. In contrast, they use the term *inattentional blindness* when people fail to notice that a new object has appeared. In both cases, however, people are using top-down processing as they concentrate on some objects in a scene. As a result, when an object appears that is not consistent with their concepts, expectations, and memory, people often fail to recognize this changed object (change blindness) or this new object (inattentional blindness).

Let's now consider a dramatic study about inattentional blindness. Simons and Chabris (1999) asked participants to watch a videotape of people playing basketball. They were instructed to mentally tally the number of times that members of a specified group made either a bounce pass or an aerial pass. Shortly after the video began, a person dressed in a gorilla suit wandered into the scene and remained there for 5 seconds. Amazingly, 46% of the participants failed to notice the gorilla! Other research confirms that people often fail to notice a new object, if they are paying close attention to something else (Intraub, 1999; Most et al., 2001). Incidentally, Daniel Simons's Web site contains some interesting demonstrations of his research: http://viscog.beckman.uiuc.edu/djs_lab/demos.html

Theme 2 of this textbook states that our cognitive processes are remarkably efficient and accurate. How can we reconcile the data on change blindness with this theme? As Simons and Levin (1997a) explain, we actually function very well in our visual environment. If you are walking along a busy city street, a variety of perceptual representations will rapidly change from one glance to the next. People move their legs, shift a bag to another arm, and move behind traffic signs. If you precisely tracked each detail, your visual system would rapidly be overwhelmed by the trivial changes. Instead, your visual system is accurate in integrating the gist or general interpretation of a scene. You focus only on the information that appears to be important, such as the distance of an approaching bus as you cross the street, and you ignore unimportant details. Change blindness and inattentional blindness illustrate a point we made in connection with Theme 2: Our cognitive errors can often be traced to the use of a rational strategy.

We have been discussing research that illustrates how we make errors in object recognition if we are not paying close attention to the object. In Chapter 3 (Perceptual Processes II: Attention and Consciousness), we will examine attention in more detail.

So far, we have discussed the visual system, perceptual organization, and theories of object recognition. We have also emphasized the importance of top-down processing in perception. Now let's consider another topic in some detail. One of the most active areas of research on object recognition is the challenging topic of face perception.

Ⓢ Section Summary: *Top-Down Processing and Visual Object Recognition*

1. Bottom-up processing emphasizes the importance of the stimulus in object recognition; top-down processing emphasizes how a person's concepts, expectations, and memory influence object recognition. Both processes must work together to allow us to recognize objects.

2. Context can facilitate recognition; for example, the word superiority effect shows that we can identify a single letter more accurately and more rapidly when it appears in a meaningful word than when it appears by itself or in a meaningless string of letters.

3. Overactive top-down processing can encourage us to make errors in recognizing letters of the alphabet, so that we convert nonwords into real words.

4. Overactive top-down processing can also encourage us to make errors in recognizing that an object has changed (change blindness) or that a new object has appeared (inattentional blindness).

FACE PERCEPTION

So far, our exploration of visual recognition has emphasized how we perceive letters of the alphabet and geometric objects. Now let's consider the most socially significant kind of recognition: How do we perceive human faces?

If you're like most people, you haven't given much thought to a problem that has intrigued cognitive psychologists for decades: How do humans manage to recognize someone they know by simply looking at this individual's face? The task *should* be challenging because all faces have generally the same shape. A further complication is that you can recognize the face of your friend Monica even when you see her face from a different angle, in an unusual setting, and wearing an unexpected facial expression. Impressively, you manage to overcome all these sources of variation (Moses et al., 1996). Almost instantly, you perceive that this is indeed Monica's face.

We'll consider three areas of research in this section of the chapter. First, we'll examine some laboratory-based research showing that our perceptual system processes human faces differently from the way it processes other visual stimuli. Then, we'll consider the neuroscience research on face perception. Finally, in the In Depth section, we'll explore some applied research on face perception; this research suggests that some kinds of face-perception tasks are surprisingly challenging.

Recognizing Faces Versus Recognizing Other Objects

Some psychologists argue that we perceive faces in a different fashion from other stimuli; in other words, face perception is somehow "special." For example, young infants track the movement of a photographed human face more than other similar stimuli (Farah, 2000a; Johnson & Bolhuis, 2000).

Similarly, Tanaka and Farah (1993) found that people were significantly more accurate in recognizing facial features when they appeared within the context of a whole face, rather than in isolation. That is, they could recognize a whole face much more accurately than, say, an isolated nose. In contrast, when they judged houses, they were just as accurate in recognizing isolated house features (e.g., a window) as in recognizing house features within the context of a complete house. We recognize most objects—such as houses—by identifying the individualized features that combine together to create these objects.

In contrast to other objects, faces apparently have a special, privileged status in our perceptual system. We recognize faces on a **holistic** basis—that is, in terms of their overall shape and structure. In other words, we perceive a face in terms of its **Gestalt,** or overall quality, that transcends its individual elements (Farah, 2000a; Farah et al., 1998).

Neuroscience Research on Face Recognition

Much of the research on face recognition comes from people with brain lesions. The term **brain lesions** refers to the destruction of tissue, most often by strokes, tumors, or accidents. For example, McNeil and Warrington (1993) studied a professional man who lost his ability to recognize human faces after he had experienced several strokes. He then decided on a dramatic career change, and he began to raise sheep. Amazingly, he could recognize many of his sheep's faces, even though he still could not recognize human faces! In contrast, most people—even those who routinely work with sheep— are much more accurate in recognizing people's faces. This man has **prosopagnosia** (pronounced "pro-soap-ag-*know*-zhia"). Prosopagnosia is a condition in which people cannot recognize human faces visually, though they perceive other objects relatively normally (Farah et al., 2000). For example, a woman with prosopagnosia might be able to elaborately describe the facial features of the person standing in front of her, yet she fails to recognize that this person is her own daughter (Palmer, 1999).

Earlier, we mentioned that the occipital lobe, at the back of your brain, is the location in the cortex that is responsible for the initial, most basic visual processing. Information then travels from that location to numerous other locations throughout the brain. The location most responsible for face recognition is the temporal cortex, at the side of your brain (Bentin et al., 2002; Farah, 2000a). The specific location is known as the *inferotemporal cortex*, in the lower portion of the temporal cortex. (See Figure 2.1 on p. 35.)

In a representative study on the inferotemporal cortex, Rolls and Tovee (1995) tested monkeys, using the single-cell recording technique, a neuroscience technique described in Chapter 1. They presented a variety of different photos, one at a time. Certain cells in the inferotemporal cortex responded especially vigorously to the full-face photos of monkey faces. The cells' response rate was somewhat lower when a side-view picture of a monkey was presented, and lowest of all when photos of other objects—perhaps a human hand—were shown. Similar results were obtained in a replication study (Wang et al., 1996).

Chapter 1 also mentioned the fMRI technique, one of the most sophisticated techniques for obtaining images of the brain's activity in humans. A representative study used the fMRI technique to determine that the brain responds more quickly to faces presented in the normal, upright position, in comparison to faces presented upside-down (D'Esposito et al., 1999).

The neuroscience research suggests that specific cells in the inferotemporal cortex are responsible for perceiving faces (Farah, 2000a; Kanwisher et al., 2001). The research is far from complete. However, these cells may help to explain why face perception seems to follow different rules, emphasizing holistic processing rather than isolated components.

| **IN DEPTH** |

Applied Research on Face Recognition

Chapter 1 noted that many cognitive psychologists now emphasize the importance of **ecological validity;** they believe that the conditions in which research is conducted should be similar to the natural setting to which the results will be applied. Richard Kemp and his coauthors (1997) conducted an applied study on face recognition that is high in ecological validity. Their research suggests that humans are not especially skilled at some face-recognition tasks. Specifically, people have difficulty matching the ID photo of a stranger with the real-life face of that stranger. Kemp and his colleagues (1997) noted that several credit card companies were issuing credit cards that included the photo of the credit card holder. The photo is in full color, and approximately 1″-by-1″ in size. These credit card companies believe that the photo will decrease the rate of fraud.

Kemp and his coauthors (1997) worked together with a credit card company to create four different credit cards for each of 46 undergraduates:

1. A card with an actual photo of the student (unchanged-appearance condition);
2. A card with a photo of the student with some attribute changed, such as the removal of eyeglasses (changed-appearance condition);
3. A card with a photo of some other individual who looked fairly similar in appearance (matched-foil condition); and
4. A card with a photo of some other individual of the same gender and ethnicity, but otherwise very different in appearance (unmatched-foil condition).

Each student went to a supermarket, selected some items, and presented his or her card to the cashier. (The cashiers were all trained employees, and they had been informed about the nature of the study.) The **dependent variable** in this study (i.e., the behavior that the researchers measured) was the cashier's decision either to accept or to reject the credit card.

The results showed that the cashiers were quite accurate in recognizing the photos in the unchanged-appearance condition; 93% of the time, they correctly decided to accept the credit card. They were slightly less accurate in recognizing the photos in the changed-appearance condition; 86% of the time, they correctly decided to accept the card. However, the results were less encouraging for students carrying the photo ID of another person. Specifically, the cashiers correctly decided to *reject* the credit card in the matched-foil condition only 36% of the time. (In other words, they let someone with the photo ID of a different but similar-looking person slip past them 64% of the time!) And amazingly, the cashiers correctly decided to reject the card in the unmatched-foil condition only 66% of the time. (In other words, when the student presented a photo ID of a very different-looking person, the cashiers still accepted it 34% of the time.)

In the United States, airplane personnel are required to inspect a passenger's photo ID before allowing this person to board the plane. The results from this study by Kemp and his coauthors (1997) are not optimistic about the usefulness of this precaution; people can often escape detection when using someone else's ID.

Another application of the research on face recognition focuses on security surveillance systems. Many banks, businesses, and institutions use a video security system, typically recording people who walk through a door. A. Mike Burton and his coauthors (1999) asked people to look at video clips of psychology professors walking through the entrance of the department of psychology at the University of Glasgow in Scotland. The video system had already been in use in the department, a factor that increased the ecological validity of the study. The participants in the study saw a series of video clips of 10 professors, followed by a series of high-quality photos of 20 professors; 10 of these professors had appeared in a video, and 10 had not. The participants were instructed to rate each photo, using a scale from 1 (indicating certainty that the person in the photo had not appeared in a video) to 7 (indicating certainty that the person in the photo had appeared in a video).

Burton and his colleagues (1999) also tested three categories of participants. Twenty of the participants were psychology students who had been taught by all 20 professors in the video clips. Twenty were other students from the same university who had never been taught by any of these professors. Twenty were experienced police officers enrolled in a course at a police training school. (We would hope that these officers would be especially accurate in matching the photographs with the faces that had appeared in the video clips.)

Figure 2.8 shows the ratings provided by the three categories of participants. As you can see, the students who were familiar with the professors had highly accurate recognition. These students were very confident in identifying the 10 professors who had actually appeared in the videos, and they were equally confident that the other 10 professors had not appeared in the videos. Notice the responses of the students who were unfamiliar with the professors. They were only slightly more confident about the professors they had seen, compared to the professors they had not seen. Even more alarming, the experienced police officers were no more accurate than the second group of students.

Notice why these results are distressing: Suppose that police officers are trying to track down a robber, after a theft at a jewelry store. The videotape from the surveillance system probably won't allow accurate identification of the robber's face. Yes, we may be quite accurate in identifying the faces of familiar people, but these people are probably unlikely to commit robbery. Additional studies conducted by this same research group have confirmed that people are accurate in identifying familiar faces and inaccurate in identifying unfamiliar faces, under a variety of viewing conditions (Bruce et al., 2001; Bruce et al., 1999; Henderson et al., 2001).

FIGURE 2.8

Participants' Confidence About Having Seen a Target Person in an Earlier Video, as a Function of Kind of Observers and Whether the Target Had Been Seen or Not Seen.

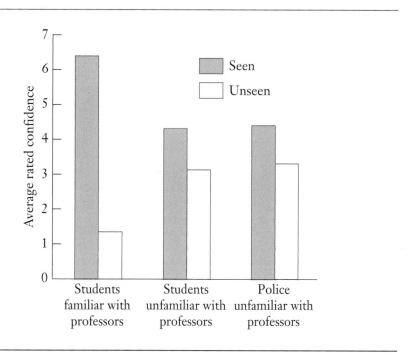

Section Summary: *Face Perception*

1. People can quickly recognize the faces of people they know; we seem to process faces in terms of their overall shape and structure.

2. A variety of neuroscience techniques—including research with people who have prosopagnosia, the single-cell recording technique, and the fMRI technique—have demonstrated that cells in the inferotemporal cortex are responsible for perceiving faces.

3. The In Depth section explored some applied research, suggesting that people are not very accurate in judging whether a small photo on a credit card matches the face of the cardholder. Furthermore, people are not very accurate in judging whether a photo of an unfamiliar person matches a person in an earlier video.

SPEECH PERCEPTION

When we hear spoken language, we must first analyze the sounds of speech. During **speech perception,** our auditory system translates sound vibrations into a sequence of sounds that we perceive to be speech. Speech perception seems perfectly easy and straightforward . . . until you begin to think about some of the components of this process. For example, adult speakers produce about 15 sounds each second (Kuhl, 1994a). Therefore, a listener must somehow perceive 900 sounds each minute! In order to perceive a word, you must distinguish the sound pattern of one word from the tens of thousands of irrelevant words that are stored in your memory. And—as if these tasks are not challenging enough—you must separate the voice of the speaker from a noisy background that typically includes other, simultaneous conversations as well as a wide variety of nonspeech sounds. In fact, it's astonishing that we ever manage to perceive spoken language!

Speech perception is extremely complex, and more details on the process may be pursued in other books (Coren et al., 2004; Goldstein, 2002; Jusczyk & Luce, 2002; Matlin & Foley, 1997). We'll consider two aspects of speech perception in this section: (1) characteristics of speech perception and (2) theories of speech perception.

Characteristics of Speech Perception

The next time you listen to a radio announcer, pay attention to the sounds you are hearing, rather than the meaning of the words. When discussing these speech sounds, psychologists and linguists use the term *phoneme* (pronounced "*foe*-neem"). A **phoneme** is the basic unit of spoken language, such as the sounds *a*, *k*, and *th*. Phonemes include both vowels and consonants. You hear vowels for which the vocal tract remains open (for example, the sounds *a* and *e*), stop consonants for which the vocal tract closes completely and then quickly opens up (for example, the sounds *p* and *k*), and other sounds (such as *f* and *r*) in which the vocal tract performs other contortions. You may hear brief quiet periods throughout this string of sounds. However, most of the words are simply run together in a continuous series.

Let's consider several important characteristics of speech perception:

1. Phoneme pronunciation varies tremendously.
2. Context allows listeners to fill in missing sounds.
3. Listeners can impose boundaries between sounds, even when these sounds are not separated by silence.
4. Visual cues from the speaker's mouth help us interpret ambiguous sounds.

All these characteristics provide further evidence for the Theme 2 of this book. Despite a less-than-perfect speech stimulus, we perceive speech with remarkable accuracy and efficiency.

Variability in Phoneme Pronunciation. Perceiving phonemes does not initially seem like a challenging task. After all, don't we simply hear a phoneme and instantly perceive it? Actually, phoneme perception is not that easy. For example, speakers vary tremendously in the pitch and tone of their voices, as well as their rate of producing phonemes. Fortunately, we listeners seem to retain information about each speaker's phoneme production in our memory. We use this information to help us perceive a particular speaker's stream of phonemes (Green et al., 1997; Jusczyk & Luce, 2002; Miller & Eimas, 1995b).

A second source of variability is that speakers often fail to produce phonemes in a precise fashion. Try Demonstration 2.5 to appreciate the problem of sloppy pronunciation that listeners must decode.

⊙ Demonstration 2.5

Variability in Phoneme Pronunciation

Turn on the radio and locate a station on which you hear someone talking. After hearing one or two sentences, turn the radio off and try to determine whether the speaker produced each phoneme in a precise fashion. For instance, did the speaker omit some portion of a word (e.g., *sposed* instead of *supposed)?* Did he or she pronounce consonants such as *k* or *p* precisely? Now try pronouncing the words in each sentence very carefully, so that every phoneme can be clearly identified.

A third source of variability is called **coarticulation;** when you are pronouncing a particular phoneme, your mouth remains somewhat the same shape as it was in pronouncing the *previous* phoneme; furthermore, your mouth is also preparing to pronounce the *next* phoneme—all at the same time. As a result, the phoneme you produce varies slightly from time to time, depending upon the surrounding phonemes (Jusczyk & Luce, 2002; Massaro, 1999a; J. L. Miller, 1999). For example, notice that the *d* in *idle* sounds slightly different from the *d* in *don't.*

Despite this remarkable variability in phoneme pronunciation, we still manage to understand the speaker's intended phoneme. Factors such as context, word boundaries, and visual cues help us achieve this goal.

Context and Speech Perception. People are active listeners, consistent with Theme 1. Instead of passively receiving speech sounds, they can use context as a cue to help them figure out a sound or a word (Cleary & Pisoni, 2001; Massaro, 1999a). We saw earlier in this chapter that context and other top-down factors influence visual perception. Top-down factors also influence speech perception (Theme 5).

For example, when you are listening to your professors' lectures, extraneous noises will sometimes mask a phoneme. People knock books off desks, cough, turn pages, and whisper. Still, without much effort, you can usually reconstruct the missing sound. People tend to show **phonemic restoration:** They can fill in a missing phoneme, using context as a cue.

In a classic study, Warren and Warren (1970) showed that people are skilled at using the meaning of a sentence to select the correct word from several options. They played tape recordings of four sentences for their subjects:

It was found that the *eel was on the axle.

It was found that the *eel was on the shoe.

It was found that the *eel was on the orange.

It was found that the *eal was on the table.

A coughing sound was inserted in the location indicated by the asterisk. The four sentences sounded identical with one exception: A different word was spliced onto the end of each sentence. The results showed that the "word" *eel/eal was heard as *wheel* in the first sentence, *heel* in the second sentence, *peel* in the third, and *meal* in the fourth. In this study, then, people could not use surrounding sounds to reconstruct the word, yet they were able to reconstruct the word on the basis of a context cue that occurred four words later!

Notice that phonemic restoration is a kind of illusion. People think they hear a phoneme, even though the correct sound vibrations never reach their ears. Phonemic restoration is a well-documented phenomenon, and it has been demonstrated in numerous studies (Carroll, 2004; Samuel, 1987; Samuel & Ressler, 1986). Our ability to perceive a word on the basis of context also allows us to handle sloppy pronunciations, the problem we mentioned earlier.

Because we are so tolerant of mispronunciations in sentences, we often fail to notice startling mispronunciations that children make. Think back about a song that you sang when you were a child in which you included totally inappropriate words. One of my students recalled singing a Christmas carol in which the shepherds "washed their socks by night," rather than "watched their flocks by night." Many songs that children learn are never explained, and so they make up versions that make sense to them. As an experienced listener, your top-down processing is well developed, so the context encourages you to ignore children's mispronunciations.

One likely explanation for the influence of context on perception is top-down processing, although other explanations have also been offered (Carroll, 2004; Grossberg, 1999; Grossberg & Myers, 2000; Miller & Eimas, 1995b). The top-down processing approach argues that we use our knowledge and expectations to facilitate recognition, whether we are looking at objects or listening to speech. Understanding language is not merely a passive process in which words flow into our ears, providing data for bottom-up processing. Instead, we actively use the information we know to create expectations about what we might hear. Consistent with Theme 5 of this textbook, top-down processing influences our cognitive activities.

Word Boundaries. Have you ever heard a conversation in an unfamiliar language? The words seem to run together in a continuous stream, with no boundaries of silence to separate them. You may think that the boundaries between words seem much more distinct in English—almost as clear-cut as the white spaces that identify the boundaries of written English. In most cases, however, the actual acoustical stimulus of spoken language shows no clear-cut pauses to mark the boundaries (Davis et al., 2002; Miller & Eimas, 1995b). An actual physical event—such as a pause—marks a word boundary less than 40% of the time (Cole & Jakimik, 1980; Flores d'Arcais, 1988).

Impressively, we are rarely conscious of the difficulty of resolving ambiguities concerning word boundaries. Researchers have discovered that our speech recognition system initially considers several different hypotheses about how to segment a phrase. This system immediately and effortlessly uses our knowledge about language in order to place the boundaries in appropriate locations (Vroomen & de Gelder, 1997). Most of the time, this knowledge leads us to the correct conclusions.

Visual Cues as an Aid to Speech Perception. Try Demonstration 2.6 when you have the opportunity. This simple exercise illustrates how visual cues contribute to speech perception (Smyth et al., 1987). Information from the speaker's lips and face helps resolve ambiguities from the speech signal, much as phoneme contextual cues help us choose between *wheel* and *peel* (Dodd & Campbell, 1986). Similarly, you can hear conversation more accurately when you closely watch a speaker's lips, instead of listening to a conversation over the telephone (Massaro & Stork, 1998). Even with a superb telephone connection, we miss the lip cues that would inform us whether the speaker was discussing *Harry* or *Mary*.

---

⑨ Demonstration 2.6

Visual Cues and Speech Perception

The next time you are in a room with both a television and a radio, try this exercise. Switch the TV set to the news or some other program where someone is talking straight to the camera; keep the volume low. Now turn on your radio and tune it between two stations, so that it produces a hissing noise. Turn the radio's volume up until you have difficulty understanding what the person on television is saying; the radio's "white noise" should nearly mask the speaker's voice. Face the TV screen and close your eyes; try to understand the spoken words. Then open your eyes. Do you find that speech perception is now much easier?

Source: Based on Smyth et al., 1987.

Adults with normal hearing seldom notice or take full advantage of these visual cues. In fact, we are likely to appreciate visual cues only in unusual circumstances. For example, you may notice a poorly dubbed movie, perhaps one that was filmed in French with American actors' voices substituted afterward. The actors' lips often move independently of the sounds presumably coming from those lips. However, researchers have demonstrated that we do integrate visual cues with auditory cues during speech perception—even if we don't recognize the usefulness of these visual cues (Massaro, 1999b). These results have been replicated for speakers of English, Spanish, Japanese, and Dutch (Massaro, 1998; Massaro et al., 1995). Furthermore, a black-and-white talking face can provide the appropriate visual cues; we don't even need full-color visual information (Jordan et al., 2000).

Research by McGurk and McDonald (1976) provides a classic illustration of the contribution of visual cues to speech perception. These researchers showed participants a video of a woman whose lips were producing simple sounds, such as "gag." Meanwhile, the researchers presented different auditory information (coming from the same machine), such as "bab." When the observers were asked to report what they perceived, their responses usually reflected a compromise between these two discrepant sources of information. Typically, they reported hearing the word "dad." The **McGurk effect** refers to the influence of visual information on speech perception, when individuals must integrate both visual and auditory information (Massaro, 1999b). Usually, however, a speaker's lips move in a manner that is consistent with the speaker's auditory message, therefore improving the listener's accuracy.

In summary, then, we manage to perceive speech by overcoming the problems of a less-than-ideal speech stimulus. We do so by using context to resolve ambiguous phonemes and to carve out boundaries between words. If we can watch the speaker who is producing the stream of speech, the visual information from the speaker's lips provides additional helpful clues.

Theories of Speech Perception

The theoretical approaches to speech perception generally fall into two categories. Some theorists believe that there must be a special mechanism that explains our impressive skill in speech perception. Others admire humans' skill in speech perception, but they argue that the same general mechanism that handles other cognitive processes also handles speech perception.

The Special Mechanism Approach. According to the **special mechanism approach** (also called the **speech-is-special approach**), humans are born with a specialized device that allows us to decode speech stimuli. As a result, we process speech sounds more quickly and accurately than other auditory stimuli, such as instrumental music. Supporters of this approach argue that humans possess a **phonetic module,** a special-purpose neural mechanism that specifically facilitates speech perception, rather than other kinds of auditory perception. This phonetic module would presumably enable listeners to perceive ambiguous phonemes accurately. It would also help them segment the blurred stream of auditory information that reaches their ears, so that they can perceive distinct phonemes and words (Liberman, 1996; Liberman & Mattingly, 1989).

Notice that the special mechanism approach to speech perception suggests that the brain is organized in a special way. Specifically, the module that handles speech perception does *not* rely on the general cognitive functions discussed throughout this book—functions such as recognizing objects, remembering events, and solving problems (Trout, 2001). Incidentally, this modular approach is not consistent with Theme 4 of this textbook, which argues that the cognitive processes are interrelated and dependent upon one another.

One argument in favor of the phonetic module was thought to be categorical perception. Computers can generate a range of sounds that form a gradual continuum between two speech sounds—for example, a gradual continuum between the phonemes *b* and *p*. However, in the early research, people who heard this series of sounds typically showed **categorical perception;** they heard either a clear-cut *b* or a clear-cut *p*. Intriguingly, people did not report hearing a sound partway between a *b* and a *p* (Liberman & Mattingly, 1989).

When the special mechanism approach was originally proposed, supporters argued that people processed speech sounds very differently from nonspeech sounds. Specifically, they believed that people show categorical perception for speech sounds, but nonspeech sounds are heard as a smooth continuum. However, more recent research has shown that humans also exhibit categorical perception for some complex nonspeech sounds (Pastore et al., 1990). Also, when different research methods are used to present speech sounds, people report that they hear a smooth continuum (Cleary & Pisoni, 2001).

The General Mechanism Approaches. Although some still favor the special mechanism approach (Trout, 2001), most theorists now favor one of the general mechanism approaches (e.g., Cleary & Pisoni, 2001; Massaro & Cole, 2000). The **general mechanism approaches** argue that we can explain speech perception without proposing any special phonetic module. People who favor these approaches believe that humans use the same neural mechanisms to process both speech sounds and nonspeech sounds. Speech perception is therefore a learned ability—indeed, a very impressive learned ability—but it is not really "special."

Current research seems to favor the general mechanism approach. As we already noted, humans exhibit categorical perception for complex nonspeech sounds (Pastore et al., 1990). Other research supporting the general mechanism viewpoint uses event-related potentials (ERPs), which we discussed in Chapter 1. This research demonstrates that adults show the same sequence of shifts in the brain's electrical potential, whether they are listening to speech or to music (Patel et al., 1998).

Other evidence against the phonetic module is that people's judgments about phonemes are influenced by visual cues, as we saw in the discussion of the McGurk effect. For example, suppose that people hear the auditory stimulus *ba* and see lip movements appropriate to a sound somewhere between *ba* and *da*. They rarely report hearing the clear-cut sound *ba*—even though that is the sound reaching their ears (Cleary & Pisoni, 2001; Massaro, 1998). Thus, speech perception is more flexible than the special mechanism approach suggests, because phoneme perception can be influenced by nonspeech, visual information.

Several different general mechanism theories of speech perception have been developed (e.g., Cleary & Pisoni, 2001; Jusczyk & Luce, 2002; Massaro, 1998). These theories tend to argue that speech perception proceeds in stages and that it depends upon familiar cognitive processes such as feature recognition, learning, and decision making.

In summary, our ability to perceive speech sounds is impressive. However, this ability can probably be explained by our general perceptual skill, combined with our other cognitive abilities—rather than any special, inborn speech mechanism. We learn to distinguish speech sounds, the same way we learn other cognitive skills.

⑨ Section Summary: *Speech Perception*

1. Speech perception is an extremely complex process that demonstrates humans' impressive cognitive skills.

2. The pronunciation of a specific phoneme varies greatly, depending upon vocal characteristics of the speaker, imprecise pronunciation, and variability caused by coarticulation.

3. When a sound is missing from speech, listeners demonstrate phonemic restoration, using context to help them perceive the missing sound.

4. Even when the acoustical stimulus contains no clear-cut pauses, people are able to determine the boundaries between words with impressive accuracy.

5. People also use visual cues to facilitate speech perception, as illustrated by the McGurk effect.

6. According to the special mechanism approach to speech perception, humans have a special brain device (or module) that allows us to perceive phonemes.

7. At present, the evidence supports a general mechanism approach to speech perception; research suggests that humans perceive speech sounds in the same way we perceive nonspeech sounds, and phoneme perception can be influenced by other cognitive processes.

CHAPTER REVIEW QUESTIONS

1. How would you describe perception to a friend who has never had a course in cognitive psychology? Point out five different perceptual tasks that you have accomplished in the past 5 minutes, including examples of both visual and auditory perception.

2. Imagine that you are trying to read a sloppily written number that appears in a friend's class notes. You conclude that it is an *8*, rather than a *6* or a *3*. Explain how you recognized that number, using the template-matching and feature-analysis theories.

3. What is the goal of Biederman's recognition-by-components theory? Look up from your book and identify two nearby objects; how would this theory describe how you recognize these objects?

4. Distinguish between bottom-up and top-down processing. Explain how top-down processing can help you recognize the letters of the alphabet in this paragraph; also cite relevant studies.

5. This chapter emphasized visual and auditory object recognition; provide examples of how top-down processing could help you recognize tastes, odors, and touch sensations.

6. According to the material in this chapter, face recognition seems to be "special," and it probably uses different processes from the processes used in other recognition tasks. Discuss this statement, mentioning research on the comparison between faces and other visual stimuli. Be sure to include material from neuroscience research on this topic.

7. What evidence do we have that speech stimuli are less than ideal? Describe several sources of variability, and discuss why each factor presents a problem when psychologists try to explain speech perception.

8. Consulting your answer to Question 7, explain how our auditory processes manage to overcome the difficulties in recognizing speech stimuli.

9. What kinds of arguments support the general mechanism approach to speech perception? Contrast this approach with the special mechanism approach, and describe why the general mechanism approach is more consistent with the view that cognitive processes are interrelated.

10. Throughout this book, we will emphasize that the research from cognitive psychology can be applied to numerous everyday situations. For example, the In Depth section described several practical applications of the research on face perception. Skim through this chapter and describe at least five other practical applications of the research on visual and auditory recognition.

NEW TERMS

perception
object recognition
pattern recognition
distal stimulus
proximal stimulus
sensory memory
iconic memory
primary visual cortex
Gestalt psychology
figure
ground
ambiguous figure-
    ground relationship

illusory contours
subjective contours
template-matching
    theory
templates
feature-analysis theories
distinctive feature
recognition-by-
    components theory
structural theory
geons
viewer-centered
    approach

bottom-up processing
top-down processing
word superiority effect
parallel distributed
    processing (PDP)
connectionism
change blindness
inattentional blindness
holistic (recognition)
Gestalt
brain lesions
prosopagnosia
ecological validity

NEW TERMS (continued)

dependent variable
speech perception
phoneme
coarticulation
phonemic restoration

McGurk effect
special mechanism
  approach
speech-is-special
  approach

phonetic module
categorical perception
general mechanism
  approaches

RECOMMENDED READINGS

Coren, S., Ward, L. M., & Enns, J. T. (2004). *Sensation and perception* (6th ed.). Hoboken, NJ: Wiley. Coren and his colleagues' mid-level textbook emphasizes vision and hearing; however, other chapters provide information on taste, smell, the skin senses, and the perception of time.

Goldstein, E. B. (Ed.). (2001). *Blackwell handbook of perception*. Malden, MA: Blackwell. In this advanced-level book, the chapters on vision and audition are especially relevant to the chapter you have been reading, but the book also includes the other sensory systems as well as chapters on perceptual development and the synthesis of perceptual information.

Palmer, S. E. (1999). *Vision science: Photons to phenomenology*. Cambridge, MA: MIT Press. This advanced-level book is a comprehensive overview of visual perception; it explores topics such as object perception, attention, depth perception, color perception, and motion perception.

Pashler, H. (Ed.). (2002). *Stevens' handbook of experimental psychology* (3rd ed.). New York: Wiley. I strongly recommend this four-volume series of books on cognitive psychology and other related research areas. Volume 1, on sensation and perception, is especially relevant to the chapter you have been reading.

ANSWER TO DEMONSTRATION 2.4:

Look at the right-hand edge of each photo. About halfway down this edge, you can see that the lower photo has a solid dark patch, which is missing in the upper photo.

CHAPTER 3

Perceptual Processes II: Attention and Consciousness

PREVIEW

If you've ever tried to study while a friend is talking, you know that attention can be limited. Research confirms that performance usually suffers on *divided-attention tasks*, where you must perform two or more tasks simultaneously. Research also reveals limits on three kinds of *selective-attention tasks*: (1) You usually cannot follow two simultaneous conversations; (2) on a task where ink of one color—such as blue—is used for printing the name of a different color—such as *red*—people have trouble producing the name of the ink's color; (3) people have trouble searching quickly for visual stimuli when the task is difficult. Finally, our *saccadic eye movements* regulate our visual attention during reading.

This chapter also discusses neuroscience and theoretical explanations of attention. For instance, neuroscience research suggests that one part of the brain is responsible for visual search, whereas a different part is responsible for processing word meaning and for inhibiting automatic responses. In addition, neuroscience research using the event-related potential technique examines systematic changes in the brain when we perform an attention task. Theoretical explanations of attention include the idea that the brain resembles a bottleneck in the way it limits our attention. According to a second theoretical explanation, we can use either automatic or controlled processing on an attention task. The third theoretical explanation proposes that we can register some visual features automatically via distributed attention, but more challenging tasks require focused attention and serial processing.

One issue related to consciousness is how often people are unaware of the way their cognitive processes operate. In addition, they may have difficulty eliminating some thoughts from consciousness. Finally, in a rare condition called "blindsight," people with a damaged visual cortex can detect an object, even though they believe that they cannot see it.

INTRODUCTION

Take a few minutes to pay attention to your attention processes. First, look around you and try to take in as many visual objects as possible. If you are reading this book in a room, for instance, try to notice all the objects that surround you. Be sure to notice their shape, size, location, and color. If your room is typical, you'll have the sensation that your visual attention is overworked, far beyond its limits, even after a single minute.

Now try the same exercise, but also try to notice every sound in your environment, such as the hum of your computer, the noise of a clock ticking, and a distant automobile. Next, try to maintain all these visual and auditory stimuli, but also notice your skin senses. Can you feel the pressure that your chair creates on your back and your watch creates on your wrist, and can you sense a slight itch or a subtle pain? If you somehow manage to pay simultaneous attention to your vision, hearing, and skin senses, try expanding your attention to include smell and taste. You'll easily discover that you cannot attend to everything at once. Interestingly, though, we seldom give much thought to our attention. Instead, attention just "happens," and it seems as natural to us as breathing (LaBerge, 1995).

Attention is a concentration of mental activity. Attention allows your cognitive processes to take in selected aspects of your sensory world in an efficient and accurate manner (Fernandez-Duque & Johnson, 2002; Palmer, 1999). Notice, therefore, that the *unattended* aspects of your sensory world lose out, and they are not processed in detail. Even William James (1890) speculated about the number of ideas that could be attended to at one time—a speculation that still intrigues psychologists more than a century later.

You'll notice that many of the concepts in this chapter are related to concepts in the previous chapter on perceptual recognition, consistent with Theme 4. As you will see, attention tasks use both top-down and bottom-up processing (Chun & Marois, 2002; Downing & Treisman, 1997; Egeth & Yantis, 1997). Specifically, we sometimes concentrate our mental activity because an interesting stimulus in the environment has captured our attention (bottom-up processing). For example, an object in your peripheral vision might suddenly move. Other times we concentrate our mental activity because we want to pay attention to some specific stimulus (top-down processing). For example, you might be searching for the face of a particular friend in a crowded cafeteria.

Chapter 2 also discussed several visual phenomena that illustrate how shape perception and attention work cooperatively. Consider, for example, ambiguous figure-ground relationships (see Figure 2.2 on p. 36). When you pay attention to the central white form, you see a vase; when you shift your attention to the two outer blue forms, you see two faces. Other relevant concepts from Chapter 2 include change blindness (when you fail to notice a change in an object) and inattentional blindness (when you fail to notice that a new object has entered a scene).

Attention also has implications for many of the chapters in the remaining part of this book. For example, attention plays a major role in regulating how many items we can process in working memory (Chapter 4). Attention is also intertwined with both long-term memory (Chapter 5) and concepts (Chapter 8; Logan, 2002a). Furthermore, as Chapter 11 describes, when people read a description of a problem, they need to pay attention to certain information, while ignoring trivial details. Also, Chapter 12 explains how people make incorrect decisions when they pay too much attention to relatively unimportant information.

We will begin our discussion by considering three interrelated cognitive tasks—divided attention, selective attention, and saccadic eye movements. Our second section examines both biological and theoretical explanations for attention. Our final topic, consciousness, focuses on our awareness about the external world, as well as our cognitive processes.

THREE KINDS OF ATTENTION PROCESSES

As you read this section, you are probably engaged in the three kinds of attention processes that we will discuss. For example, you may momentarily try to use divided attention, concentrating on a nearby conversation, as well as the words in your cognition textbook. You'll easily discover, though, that you cannot accurately attend to both categories of stimuli. As a result, you will try to use selective attention, focusing on just one category of stimuli; let's be optimistic and presume that your selective attention is directed toward your textbook. Selective attention will not allow you to take in much information about the unattended conversation. Finally, as you read your textbook, your visual system will produce saccadic movements; your eyes will move systematically to the right to take in an appropriate amount of new information.

Divided Attention

In a **divided-attention task,** you try to pay attention to two or more simultaneous messages, responding to each as needed. The consequences of divided attention can be disastrous. For example, in the former country of Yugoslavia in 1976, two airplanes collided and all 176 passengers and crew members were killed. The air-traffic controller had been working without an assistant, and he was monitoring 11 aircraft simultaneously! In the preceding minutes, he had transmitted 8 messages and received 11 (Barber, 1988). Humans are extremely competent, yet they cannot pay attention to everything at the same time.

Research on Divided Attention. In the laboratory, divided attention is typically studied by instructing participants to perform two tasks at the same time. For example, Duncan (1993) asked participants to make judgments about a single object. They were able to make two simultaneous judgments about this object—what it was, as well as where it was located—without any loss in accuracy. However, they made many errors when asked to make two simultaneous judgments about two different objects—for example, where both objects were located. In other words, our perceptual system can handle some divided-attention tasks, but we fail when the tasks become too demanding.

The research on divided attention has important implications for people who use cell phones while driving, especially because U.S. residents owned about 156,000,000 cell phones as of February, 2004 (Cellular Telecommunications & Internet Association, 2004), and 12,000,000 Canadian households owned at least one cell phone by 2002 (Statistics Canada, 2004). I live in New York, and our state passed a law prohibiting the use of handheld phones during driving. Still, I wonder whether some people might carry on distracting conversations by using their hands-free cell phones.

David Strayer and his colleagues (2003) tested the effects of hands-free cell phones by instructing undergraduate students to use a driving simulator. This simulator provided a realistic experience of driving behind another car on a highway. From time to time, this other car would brake unexpectedly, and the researchers measured the amount of time before the participant reacted and depressed the brake in his or her car. The participants in the control group simply drove the simulated car. In contrast, the participants in the experimental group conversed on a hands-free cell phone with a research assistant; they spoke about a variety of topics that the participant had previously rated as being personally interesting.

The results during low-traffic conditions showed that people in the cell-phone group took slightly longer to apply the brake than those in the control group. However, the results during high-traffic conditions showed that people in the cell-phone group took significantly longer than those in the control group. With further testing, the researchers discovered that the participants who used cell phones showed a form of inattentional blindness (see pp. 50–52 of Chapter 2). For example, their attention had been reduced for information that appeared in the center of their visual field. Apparently, ongoing cell-phone conversations can be genuinely dangerous because they draw drivers' attention away from the roadway information they require in order to drive safely.

Divided Attention and Practice. "Practice makes perfect," according to the familiar saying. The research on practice and divided attention confirms the wisdom of that phrase. For example, in two classic studies, college students were trained to read stories silently at the same time that they copied down irrelevant words dictated by the experimenter (Hirst et al., 1980; Spelke et al., 1976). At first, the students had trouble combining the two tasks; their reading speed decreased substantially, and their handwriting was illegible. However, after 6 weeks of training, they could read as quickly while taking dictation as when they were only reading. Their handwriting also improved.

Still, even at this well-practiced stage, the students were not really attending to the dictated words. In fact, they were able to recall only 35 of the several thousand words they had written down. However, with more extensive training, they became so accomplished at this divided-attention task that they could even categorize the dictated word (for example, by writing "fruit" when they heard the word *apple*) without any decline in their reading rate.

Consider some applied research—again about driving—that compared experienced drivers with novice (inexperienced) drivers. Wikman and her colleagues (1998) instructed all the participants to drive as they normally would, while performing several routine, secondary tasks: changing an audiocassette, dialing a cell phone, and tuning the radio. The novices divided their attention ineffectively. Specifically, they frequently glanced away from the highway for longer than 3 seconds. More worrisome still, their cars often swung to the side as they glanced away. The experienced drivers managed to complete each task quickly and efficiently, glancing away from the road for less than 3 seconds for each task. (Still, can't you imagine roadside conditions that could create an accident in less than 3 seconds?)

The topic of divided attention has also been applied to sport psychology. For example, researchers have discovered that well-practiced volleyball players are able to shift their visual attention to some important action in the periphery of their visual field—without actually moving their eyes in that direction (Castiello & Umilta, 1992; Moran, 1996).

IN DEPTH

Selective Attention

Selective attention is closely related to divided attention. In divided-attention tasks, people try to pay equal attention to two or more sources of information. In a **selective-attention task,** people are instructed to respond selectively to certain kinds of information, while ignoring other information (Milliken et al., 1998). Selective-attention studies often show that people notice little about the irrelevant tasks (McAdams & Drake, 2002). Perhaps you've noticed that you can usually follow closely only one conversation at a noisy party; in contrast, you typically cannot process the content of the other conversations.

At times, you might wish that attention were not so selective. Wouldn't it be wonderful to participate in one conversation, but still notice the details of all the other conversations going on around you? On the other hand, think how confusing this would be. Perhaps you would be in the midst of talking with a friend about a new job prospect, and then you might suddenly start talking about baseball—the topic of a neighboring conversation. Furthermore, imagine the chaos you would experience if you simultaneously paid attention to all the information your senses register. As we discussed at the beginning of this chapter, you would notice hundreds of sights, sounds, smells, tastes, and touch sensations. It would be extremely difficult to focus your mental activity enough to respond appropriately to just a few of these sensations. Fortunately, then, selective attention simplifies our lives. As Theme 2 suggests, our cognitive apparatus is impressively well designed. Features such as selective attention—which may initially seem to be drawbacks—may actually be beneficial.

The research on selective attention is extensive, making it an ideal topic for an In Depth discussion. In general, the research that has been conducted on selective attention can be divided into three basic categories: (1) an auditory task called dichotic listening; (2) a visual task called the Stroop effect; and (3) other visual selective-attention tasks. Several additional selective-attention tasks are discussed in other resources (e.g., McAdams & Drake, 2002; Milliken et al., 1998).

Dichotic Listening. Have you ever held a phone to one ear, while your other ear registers a message from a nearby radio? If so, you have created a situation known as dichotic listening (pronounced "die-*kot*-ick"). In the laboratory, **dichotic listening** is studied by asking people to wear earphones; each ear is presented with a different message. Typically, the research participants are asked to **shadow** the message in one ear; that is, they listen to the message and repeat it after the speaker.

In the classic research, people noticed very little about the unattended, second message (Cherry, 1953). For example, people didn't even notice that the second message was sometimes switched from English words to German words. People did notice, however, when the voice of the unattended message was switched from male to female.

When performing a dichotic listening task, people sometimes notice when their name is inserted in the unattended message (Moray,1959; Wood & Cowan, 1995). The so-called "cocktail party effect" refers to a phenomenon that occurs at a cocktail party or other gathering when you are surrounded by many simultaneous conversations. According to the **cocktail party effect,** when you are paying close attention to one conversation, you can often notice if your name is mentioned in a nearby conversation. Wood and Cowan (1995), for example, found that 35% of the participants recalled hearing their name in the message that they were supposed to ignore. Surprisingly, then, we ignore even our own name about two-thirds of the time. One possible explanation for why people did not report hearing their names more frequently is that the Wood and Cowan study was conducted in a laboratory, so this research may not have high ecological validity (Baker, 1999). Most social gatherings are much less structured, and our attention may easily wander to other intriguing conversations.

In more recent research, Conway, Cowan, and Bunting (2001) examined whether the capacity of a person's working memory could help explain why some people hear their name, but others do not. As we'll see in Chapter 4, **working memory** is the brief, immediate memory for material we are currently processing. These researchers found that students who had a high working-memory capacity noticed their name only 20% of the time. In contrast, students with a low working-memory capacity noticed their name 65% of the time in a dichotic-listening task. Apparently, people with a relatively low capacity have difficulty blocking out the irrelevant information about their name, and so they are easily distracted from the task they are supposed to be completing.

In some cases, however, people notice the meaning of the unattended message in a dichotic listening situation . For example, if both messages are presented slowly, people can sometimes process the meaning of the message they are supposed to ignore (e.g., Cowan & Wood, 1997; Duncan, 1999; Treisman, 1960).

In summary, when people's auditory attention is divided, they can notice some characteristics of the unattended message—such as the gender of the speaker, whether their own name is mentioned, and occasionally the meaning of the message. On the other hand, under more challenging conditions, they may not even notice whether the unattended message is in English or in a foreign language.

The Stroop Effect. So far, we have examined selective attention on auditory tasks. In these tasks, people are instructed to shadow the message presented to one ear and ignore the message presented to the other ear. However, researchers have conducted a greater number of studies on selective visual attention. Try Demonstration 3.1, which illustrates the famous Stroop effect. After reading these instructions, turn back to Color Figure 2 and notice the word in the upper-left corner of Part A. Here, the word RED is printed in yellow ink. You'll probably find that it's much more difficult to name the color of the ink (YELLOW) than to name the color of the ink in any of the yellow rectangles in Part B. According to the **Stroop effect,** people have trouble naming the ink color when that color is used in printing an incongruent word; in contrast, they can easily name that same ink color when it appears as a solid patch of color. Notice why the Stroop effect demonstrates selective attention. People take longer to name a color when they are distracted by another feature of the stimulus, namely, the meaning of the words themselves.

🌀 Demonstration 3.1

The Stroop Effect

For this demonstration, you will need a watch with a second hand. Turn to Color Figure 2 inside the front cover. First, measure how long it takes to name the colors in Part A. Your task is to say out loud the names of the ink colors, ignoring the meaning of the words. Measure the amount of time it takes to go through this list *five* times. (Keep a tally of the number of repetitions.) Record that time.

   Now you will try a second color-naming task. Measure how long it takes to name the colors in the rectangular patches in Part B. Measure the amount of time it takes to go through this list five times. (Again, keep a tally of the number of repetitions.) Record the time.

   Does the Stroop effect operate for you? Are your response times similar to those obtained in Stroop's original study?

In the discussion of dichotic listening, we noted that people's auditory attention can sometimes be distracted by the meaning of an irrelevant message. In the current discussion on the Stroop effect, we'll see that people's visual attention can also be distracted by the meaning of an irrelevant characteristic.

   The effect was first demonstrated by James R. Stroop (1935), who found that people required an average of 110 seconds to name the ink color of 100 words that were incongruent color names (for example, blue ink used in printing the word *red*). In contrast, people required an average of only 63 seconds to name the ink color of 100 solid-color squares.

   Since the original experiment, hundreds of additional studies have examined variations of the Stroop effect. For example, some research has compared the ways that older and younger adults perform this task. In Chapter 13, we will emphasize that older adults perform as well as younger adults on many cognitive tasks. However, older adults experience even greater difficulty on the Stroop task than do younger adults (Hartley, 1993).

   Clinical psychologists have studied individuals with psychological disorders, using the Stroop task. For example, **schizophrenia** is a psychological disorder characterized by severely disordered thoughts. People with schizophrenia have particular difficulty controlling their attention (Grossberg, 2000b; Leonhard & Corrigan, 2000). Carmi Schooler and her colleagues (1997) studied participants with schizophrenia and found that they experienced even greater difficulty on the Stroop task than did individuals in the normal control group. Suppose that clinical psychologists want to test the effectiveness of a treatment for schizophrenia. They can examine whether people perform better on the Stroop test after they have received treatment, in comparison with people in a control group.

Other clinical psychologists have created a technique called the emotional Stroop task, in order to test people who have a phobic disorder. (A **phobic disorder** is an excessive fear of a specific object.) On the emotional Stroop task, people are instructed to name the ink color of words that are related to the objects they fear. For example, someone with a fear of spiders is instructed to name the ink colors of printed words such as *hairy* and *crawl*. People with phobias are significantly slower on these anxiety-related words than on control words. In contrast, people without phobias show no difference between the two kinds of words (Williams et al., 1996). These results suggest that people who have a phobic disorder are hyper-alert to words related to their phobia, and they show attentional bias to the meaning of these stimuli. As a result, they pay relatively little attention to the ink color of the words.

Researchers have examined a variety of explanations for the Stroop effect. Some have suggested that it can be explained by the parallel distributed processing (PDP) approach (e.g., Cohen et al., 1997; MacLeod, 1991). According to this explanation, the Stroop task activates two pathways at the same time. One pathway is activated by the task of naming the ink color, and the other pathway is activated by the task of reading the word. Interference occurs when two competing pathways are active at the same time. As a result, task performance suffers.

Another potential explanation focuses on the fact that we have had much more practice in reading words than in naming colors (T.L. Brown et al., 2002; Luck & Vecera, 2002; MacLeod, 1997). The more automatic process (reading the word) interferes with the less automatic process (naming the color of the ink). As a result, we automatically—and involuntarily—read the words that are printed in Part A of Color Figure 2.1. In fact, it's difficult to prevent ourselves from reading those words—even if we want to! MacLeod (1997) suggests a simple demonstration to illustrate the automatic nature of reading: The next time you are driving, try *not* to read the signs along the road!

In the earlier discussion of divided attention, we saw that practice improved people's ability to perform two simultaneous tasks, such as reading while copying a separate set of words. Emily Elliot and Nelson Cowan (2001) examined whether practice could also improve people's selective attention, as measured by the Stroop task. These researchers employed a cross-modal task. A **cross-modal task** uses two different perceptual systems, in this case, vision and hearing. Specifically, these researchers presented a series of colored squares. At the same time, participants heard an auditory stimulus, either a spoken color name, which did not match the color of the square, or a tone. The participants were instructed to name the color of each square. By the end of the training session, the people in the color-name group could now identify the squares much more quickly, though still not as quickly as those in the tone group. In summary, spoken color names can interfere with performance on a color-identification task, but performance can improve (somewhat) with practice.

Other Visual Selective-Attention Effects. So far, our exploration of selective attention has emphasized that people have trouble paying attention when two or more sets of stimuli are presented simultaneously. We have seen that they have difficulty processing two auditory messages at the same time (dichotic listening). In addition, they have difficulty processing both the color of a stimulus and a word referring to a different color (the Stroop effect).

Researchers have also explored how visual selective attention operates when too much visual information is presented at one time (e.g., Shih & Sperling, 2002) or when visual information is presented too rapidly (e.g., Palmer, 1999; Visser et al., 1999).

In Chapter 2, you learned that people sometimes fail to notice shapes. As we discussed, **change blindness** refers to our inability to detect changes in an object or a scene. We also discussed a related phenomenon, **inattentional blindness,** which occurs when you are paying attention to some events in a scene and you fail to notice an unexpected but completely visible object that suddenly appears. Troy Visser and his colleagues (1999) reviewed the research on a third phenomenon, called the attentional blink. In an **attentional blink,** a series of stimuli is presented rapidly, and the system becomes overloaded; viewers can accurately identify the first stimulus, but they miss the second. For example, suppose you are seeing a series of letters at a rate of five letters per second. You might be able to report the first letter, but you would still be processing it when the second letter arrives. The name "attentional blink" is appropriate, because you fail to perceive that second letter, just as you would miss it if your eyes blinked shut when that second letter was presented.

However, we know even more about another kind of visual selective-attention task, called visual search. You've probably conducted several visual searches within the last hour. For example, you may have searched for your yellow marking pen, or you may have scanned through Chapter 2 to find the term *change blindness.* You've probably found that some visual searches are genuinely easy—in fact, almost automatic. In contrast, other visual searches are time consuming and frustrating.

◉ Demonstration 3.2

The Isolated-Feature/Combined-Feature Effect

After reading this paragraph, turn to Color Figure 3 inside the back cover. First, look at the two figures marked Part A. In each case, search for a blue *X*. Notice whether you take about the same amount of time on these two tasks. After trying Part A, return to this page and read the additional instructions.

Additional instructions: For the second part of this demonstration, return to Part B inside the back cover. Look for the blue *X* in each of the two figures in Part B. Notice whether you take the same amount of time on these two tasks or whether one takes slightly longer.

Researchers have identified an impressive number of variables that influence visual searches. We'll limit our attention to just two variables: (1) whether we are searching for a single, isolated feature or a combined set of features; and (2) whether we are searching for a target for which the feature is present or a target for which the feature is absent. As you'll see, two researchers—Anne Treisman and Jeremy Wolfe—have been especially active in studying visual search. Before you read further, however, try Demonstration 3.2.

1. *The isolated-feature/combined-feature effect.* Demonstration 3.2 is based on classic research by Treisman and Gelade (1980). According to their research, if the target differed from the irrelevant items in the display with respect to a simple feature such as color, observers could detect the target just as fast when it was presented in an array of 25 items as when it was presented in an array of only 3 items (Treisman, 1986; Treisman & Gelade, 1980). If you tried Part A of Demonstration 3.2, you probably found that the blue *X* seemed to "pop out," whether the display contains 2 or 23 irrelevant items.

In contrast, Part B of Demonstration 3.2 required you to search for a target that is a combination (or conjunction) of two properties. When you searched for a blue *X* among red *X*'s, red *O*'s, and blue *O*'s, you probably found that you had to pay attention to one item at a time, using serial processing. This task is more complex, and the time taken to find the target increases dramatically as the number of distractors increases (Wolfe, 2000, 2001). Thus, Figure B2 required a more time-consuming search than Figure B1 did. Now try Demonstration 3.3 before you read further.

Ⓢ Demonstration 3.3

Searching for Features That Are Present or Absent

In Part A, search for the circle with the line. Then, in Part B, search for the circle *without* the line.

A

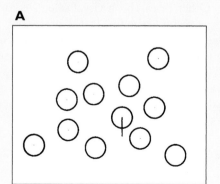

B

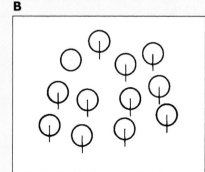

Source: Based on Treisman & Souther, 1985.

2. *The feature-present/feature-absent effect.* Theme 3 of this book states that our cognitive processes handle positive information better than negative information. Turn back to Demonstration 1.3 on page 23 to remind yourself about this theme. The research of Treisman and Souther (1985) provides additional support for that theme, as you can see from Demonstration 3.3.

Notice, in Part A of this demonstration, that the circle with the line seems to "pop out" from the display. The search is rapid when we are looking for a particular feature that is *present*. Treisman and Souther (1985) found that people performed rapid searches for a feature that was present (as in Part A), whether the display contained 0 or 11 irrelevant items. When people are searching for a feature that is *present*, the target item in the display usually captures their attention automatically (Johnston & Schwarting, 1997; Wolfe, 2000, 2001).

In contrast, notice what happens when you are searching for a feature that is *absent* (as in Part B). Treisman and Souther (1985) found that the search time increased dramatically as the number of irrelevant items increased. People who are searching for a feature that is *absent* must use focused attention. This task is substantially more challenging, as Wolfe (1998, 2000, 2001) has also found in his extensive research on the feature-present/feature-absent effect.

Another example of the feature-present/feature-absent effect was discovered by Royden and her coauthors (2001). According to their research, people can quickly locate one moving target when it appears in a group of stationary distractors. In contrast, they take much longer to locate one stationary target when it appears in a group of moving distractors. In other words, it's easier to spot a movement-present object than a movement-absent object.

Let's review what we have discussed in this section on selective attention. According to the research on dichotic listening, people usually have trouble picking up much information about the auditory message that they were instructed to ignore. The research on the Stroop effect shows that people have trouble naming the color of a stimulus when the letters of the stimulus are used to spell the name of a different color; because we read words quite automatically, it's difficult to pay attention to the less automatic part of the message. Other research on visual selective attention shows us that we may fail to perceive a second stimulus if it is presented too soon after a first stimulus. Furthermore, we search more quickly for an isolated feature (as opposed to a combination of two features) and for a feature that is present (as opposed to a feature that is absent).

Now let's consider a third kind of attention task that you are performing right now: You are moving your eyes forward so that you can read the next words in this sentence.

Saccadic Eye Movements

One of the most obvious ways we can regulate our visual attention is by moving our eyes. Let's examine how these eye movements operate in reading, although researchers have also studied how our eyes move when we are looking at a scene (e.g.,

Findlay & Gilchrist, 2001; Irwin & Zelinsky, 2002; Underwood, 1998) and when we are driving (Recarte & Nunes, 2000; Underwood, 1998).

Two perceptual processes are central to reading. In Chapter 2, on object recognition (pp. 40–42), we considered how people recognize letters of the alphabet. In that section, we also discussed how context facilitates the recognition of both letters and words.

Eye movement is the second perceptual process that is central to reading. For a moment, pay attention to the way your eyes are moving as you read this paragraph. Your eyes actually make a series of little jumps as they move across the page. This very rapid movement of the eyes from one spot to the next is known as saccadic (pronounced "suh-*cod*-dik") eye movement. The purpose of a **saccadic eye movement** is to bring the center of the retina into position over the words you want to read. The center of the retina, known as the **fovea,** has better acuity than other retinal regions. Therefore, saccadic movement is essential in order to move the eye so that new words can be registered on the fovea. Saccadic eye movement is another example of Theme 1 (active cognitive processes); we actively search for new information, including the material we will be reading (Findlay & Gilchrist, 2001; Findlay & Walker, 1999).

When you read, each saccade moves your eye forward by about 7 to 9 letters. Researchers have estimated that people make between 150,000 and 200,000 saccadic movements every day (Abrams, 1992; Cooper & Hochberg, 1994). **Fixations** occur during the period between these saccadic movements; during each fixation, the visual system acquires the information that is useful for reading.

The term **perceptual span** refers to the number of letters and spaces that you perceive during a fixation (Rayner, 1998). This perceptual span normally includes letters lying about 4 positions to the left of the letter you are directly looking at, and the letters about 15 positions to the right of that central letter. Notice that the perceptual span is definitely lopsided. After all, when we read English, we are looking for reading cues in the text that lies to the right, and these cues provide some general information (Findlay & Gilchrist, 2001; Findlay & Walker, 1999; Inhoff et al., 2000). For instance, the material in the extreme right side of the perceptual span is useful for spotting the white spaces between words, which provide information about word length. However, we usually cannot identify a word that lies more than 8 spaces to the right of the fixation point (Rayner, 1998).

Other research has demonstrated that saccadic eye movements show several predictable patterns. For example, when the eye jumps forward in a saccadic movement, it rarely moves to a blank space between sentences or between words. The eye usually jumps past short words, function words such as *the,* and words that are highly predictable in a sentence (Rayner, 1998; Reichle et al., 1998). In contrast, the size of the saccadic movement is small if the next word in a sentence is misspelled or if it is unusual (Kennedy, 2000; Reichle et al., 1998). All these strategies make sense, because a large saccadic movement would be unwise if the material is puzzling or challenging.

Good readers differ from poor readers with respect to their saccadic eye movements. Figure 3.1 shows how two such readers might differ. The good reader makes larger jumps and is also less likely to make **regressions,** by moving backward to earlier

FIGURE 3.1

Eye Movement Patterns and Fixations for a Good Reader (top numbers) and a Poor Reader (bottom numbers).

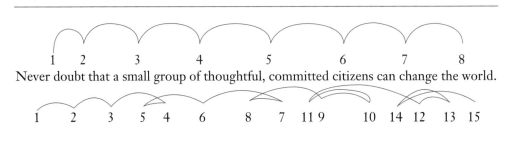

material in the sentence. Furthermore—although this cannot be seen in Figure 3.1—the good reader pauses for a shorter time before making the next saccadic movement. A typical good reader might pause for 1/5 second each time, whereas a poor reader might pause for 1/2 second (Liversedge & Findlay, 2000; Rayner, 1998). Thus, good and poor readers differ with respect to the size of the saccadic movement, the number of regressions, and the duration of the fixation pause.

Our saccadic movements are also sensitive to thematic aspects of the material we are reading (Deubel et al., 2000; Liversedge & Findlay, 2000). We'll be discussing these more sophisticated aspects of language in more detail in Chapter 9. However, if we read a paragraph with a surprise ending, we make a larger number of regression movements as we reread the puzzling passage (Underwood & Batt, 1996). In summary, the research shows that a wide variety of cognitive factors have an important influence on the pattern and speed of our saccadic eye movements (Reichle et al., 1998). Saccadic eye movements clearly help us become more active, flexible readers (Findlay & Gilchrist, 2001).

⑨ Section Summary: *Three Kinds of Attention Processes*

1. Attention is a concentration of mental activity, and it allows our cognitive processes to take in selected aspects of our environment.

2. The first kind of attention process discussed in this chapter is divided attention. Research on divided attention shows that performance often suffers when people must attend to several stimuli simultaneously. For example, we cannot talk on a hands-free cell phone and drive carefully at the same time. However, with extensive practice, performance on some divided-attention tasks can improve.

3. The second kind of attention process is selective attention, and the chapter provides an in-depth inspection of three different selective-attention examples:

a. The first example is the dichotic listening technique, which shows that people may notice little about an irrelevant message. Occasionally, however, they may notice the gender of the speaker, their own name, or some semantic aspects of the irrelevant message.

b. A second example of a selective-attention task is the Stroop effect; the task is especially difficult for older adults and for individuals with schizophrenia; a variant called the "emotional Stroop task" demonstrates that people with a phobic disorder have difficulty identifying the ink color of words related to feared objects.

c. A third example of selected-attention findings includes other visual effects, such as the attentional blink, and phenomena related to visual search (e.g., the isolated-feature/combined-feature effect and the feature-present/feature-absent effect).

4. The final kind of attention process is saccadic eye movements, which the visual system makes during reading; saccadic movement patterns are influenced by such factors as the predictability of the text, individual differences among readers (e.g., the number of regressions during reading), and the more general meaning of the text.

EXPLANATIONS FOR ATTENTION

So far, we have examined three attention processes that help humans regulate how much information they take in from their visual and auditory environment. Specifically, we have difficulty paying attention to two or more messages at one time (divided attention). In addition, when we are paying attention to one message, we have difficulty noticing information about irrelevant messages (selective attention). Furthermore, our saccadic eye movements regulate the way our eyes move in order to acquire information. Researchers have tried to account for these components of attention by conducting neuroscience studies and by devising theories to explain the characteristics of attention.

Neuroscience Research on Attention

During recent decades, researchers have developed a variety of sophisticated techniques for examining the biological basis of behavior; we introduced these approaches in Chapter 1. Research using these techniques has identified a network of areas throughout the brain that accomplish various attention tasks (Farah, 2000a; Parasuraman, 1998; Posner & Fernandez-Duque, 1999).

Several regions of the brain are responsible for attention, including some structures that are below the surface of the cerebral cortex (Just et al., 2001; Umilta, 2001; Webster & Ungerleider, 1998). For example, several brain structures below your cortex are now coordinating their actions in order for your eye to

FIGURE 3.2

A Schematic Drawing of the Cerebral Cortex, as Seen from the Left Side, Showing the Four Lobes of the Brain and the Two Regions That Are Most Important on Attention Tasks.

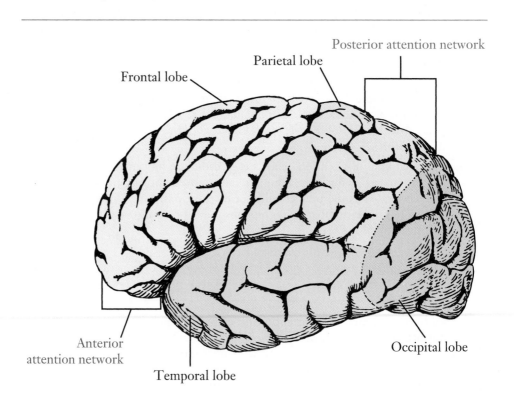

jump forward in saccadic movements until you reach the end of this sentence (Findlay & Walker, 1999). In this discussion, however, we'll focus on structures in the cerebral cortex, as shown in Figure 3.2. Take a moment to compare Figure 3.2 with Figure 2.1 (p. 35), which showed the regions of the cortex that are most relevant in object recognition.

Most of the research suggests that attention is managed by two regions of the cortex: (1) the posterior attention network in the parietal lobe and (2) the anterior attention network in the frontal lobe. (Incidentally, *posterior* means "toward the back" and *anterior* means "toward the front.") Let's consider these two areas, and then we'll discuss how the event-related potential technique provides additional information about the biological underpinnings of attention.

The Posterior Attention Network. Imagine that you are searching the area around a bathroom sink for a lost contact lens. When you are attending to a location in space, the posterior attention network is activated. The **posterior attention network** is responsible for the kind of attention required for visual search, in which you must shift your attention around to various spatial locations (Chun & Wolfe, 2001; Luck & Vecera, 2002). Notice that the posterior attention network is located in the parietal lobe of the cortex.

How was the parietal cortex identified as the region of the brain used in attention tasks related to visual searches? Much of the research uses **positron emission tomography (PET scan),** in which researchers measure blood flow in the brain by injecting the participant with a radioactive chemical just before he or she performs a cognitive task. As discussed in Chapter 1, this chemical travels through the blood to the parts of the brain that are active during the cognitive task; a special camera makes an image of the accumulated chemical. According to PET-scan research, the parietal cortex shows increased blood flow when people perform visual searches and pay attention to spatial locations (e.g., Palmer, 1999; Posner & Raichle, 1994).

Another important method used to determine the biological basis of attention focuses on people with **brain lesions,** which are specific brain damage caused by strokes, accidents, or other traumas. People who have brain damage in the parietal region of the right hemisphere of the brain have trouble noticing a visual stimulus that appears on the left side of their visual field. Those with damage in the left parietal region have trouble noticing a visual stimulus on the right side (Luck & Vecera, 2002; Posner & DiGirolamo, 2000a).

The lesions produce remarkable deficits. For instance, a woman with a lesion in the left parietal region may have trouble noticing the food on the right side of her plate. She may eat only the food on the left side of her plate, and she might even complain that she didn't receive enough food (Farah, 2000a; Humphreys & Riddoch, 2001). Amazingly, however, she may not seem to be aware of her deficit.

Part A of Figure 3.3 shows a simple figure—a clock—that was presented to a man with a lesion in the right parietal lobe. He was asked to copy this sketch, and Part B shows the figure he drew. Notice that the left part of the drawing is almost completely missing. The drawing demonstrates that this man is experiencing **unilateral neglect,** defined as a spatial deficit for one half of the visual field.

The Anterior Attention Network. The illustration of the brain in Figure 3.2 also shows an area in the frontal lobe of the cortex responsible for attention tasks that focus on word meaning. The **anterior attention network** is active when people try the Stroop task, in which word meaning interferes with color identification (Fan et al., 2002; Posner & Fernandez-Duque, 1999). This part of the brain is responsible for inhibiting your automatic responses to stimuli (Stuss et al., 2002). This function makes sense: On the Stroop task, you need to inhibit your automatic response of reading a word, in order to name the color of the ink.

The anterior attention network is also active for top-down control of attention (Farah, 2000a). Finally, this network operates when people are asked to listen to a list

FIGURE 3.3

The Original Figure (A) Presented to a Man with a Lesion in the Right Parietal Lobe, and the Figure He Drew (B).

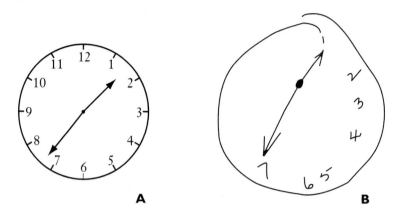

A   **B**

Source: Bloom & Lazerson, 1988.

of nouns and to state the use of each word, such as listening to the word *needle* and responding "sew" (Posner & DiGirolamo, 2000a).

In summary, PET scans and other neuroscience techniques have identified one brain region that is active when we are searching for objects (the posterior attention network). These techniques also show that a different brain region is active when we must inhibit an automatic response and produce a less obvious response (the anterior attention network).

Using the Event-Related Potential Technique to Explore Attention. Chapter 1 described the event-related potential technique, in which electrodes are placed on the scalp, and researchers record electrical signals generated by a large number of neurons located underneath each electrode (Chun & Wolfe, 2001). The **event-related potential (ERP) technique** records the tiny fluctuations in the electrical activity of the brain in response to a stimulus such as a tone. The ERP technique provides information about the sequence of events in a cognitive task.

For example, researchers in Finland measured ERPs after they had instructed participants to listen to a series of tones. Most were tones of a particular pitch, but sometimes a higher-pitched tone was included (e.g., Näätänen, 1985; Sams et al., 1985; Tiitinen et al., 1993). In one condition, the participants were instructed to press a response key whenever they heard this unexpected higher-pitched tone. In this condition, the ERP showed a burst of electrical activity when the tone was presented. However, when participants had been instructed to *ignore* the higher-pitched tone, this particular electrical activity was absent. This series of studies therefore identifies a clear-cut neurological correlate of attention.

Similar research on visual attention has identified systematic changes in ERPs when people are searching for visual targets (e.g., Luck & Girelli, 1998). According to this ERP research on the visual system, one early component of the electrical activity shows inhibition of the unattended stimulus; a slightly later component shows facilitation of the attended stimulus. However, as Näätänen and his colleagues (2002) conclude, different kinds of attention tasks produce a variety of responses throughout different regions of the brain.

In summary, neuroscience research on attention has employed PET scans as well as case studies of people with lesions. This research has identified the regions of the brain—such as the parietal cortex and the frontal cortex—that are responsible for attention. In addition, the event-related potential technique has documented neuronal activity that corresponds to components of attention. Future researchers will continue to combine the results of various neuroscience techniques to help us understand the biological explanations of attention.

Theories of Attention

Let us first consider some theories of attention that were proposed several decades ago, when cognitive psychology was in its infancy. Then we will discuss Schneider and Shiffrin's theory of automatic versus controlled processing. The final portion of this discussion examines Treisman's feature-integration theory.

Early Theories of Attention. The first theories of attention emphasized that people are extremely limited in the amount of information that they can process at any given time. A common metaphor in these theories was the concept of a bottleneck. This metaphor was especially appealing because it matches our introspections about attention. The neck of a bottle restricts the flow into or out of the bottle. **Bottleneck theories** proposed a similar narrow passageway in human information processing. In other words, this bottleneck limits the quantity of information to which we can pay attention. Thus, when one message is currently flowing through a bottleneck, the other messages must be left behind. Many variations of this bottleneck theory were proposed (e.g., Broadbent, 1958; Treisman, 1964). Updated discussion of these theories can be found in other resources (Luck & Vecera, 2002; Pashler & Johnston, 1998).

You may recall from the discussion of the theories of object recognition (Chapter 2) that the template theory was rejected because it was not flexible enough. Similarly, the bottleneck theories must be rejected because they underestimate the flexibility of human attention (Cowan & Wood, 1997; Meyer & Kieras, 1997). As Chapter 1 pointed out, no metaphor based on a simple machine or a simple structure can successfully account for the sophistication of human cognitive processes. A bottleneck is far too simple. For example, current neuroscience research demonstrates that information is not lost at just one phase of the attention process, as the bottleneck theories suggest. Instead, information is lost throughout many phases of attention, from early processing through later processing (Kanwisher et al., 2001; Posner & DiGirolamo, 2000a). As Luck and Vecera (2002) conclude,

The term *attention* applies to many separable processes, each of which operates within a different cognitive subsystem and in a manner that reflects the . . . structure and processing demands of that cognitive subsystem. (p. 261)

Let's now consider two theories that emphasize the flexibility of human attention. Specifically, they illustrate that the way people use attention is influenced by the nature of the task, the amount of practice, and the stage in processing.

Automatic Versus Controlled Processing. During the 1970s, theoretical research shifted to another aspect of attention. Specifically, we can classify attention tasks in terms of the kind of processing they require. According to Walter Schneider and Richard Shiffrin, humans have two levels of processing that are relevant to attention (Schneider & Shiffrin, 1977; Shiffrin & Schneider, 1977):

1. We can use **automatic processing** on tasks that are easy and on tasks that use highly familiar items. (For example, imagine scanning a list of students' names to see if your own name is included.) Furthermore, automatic processing is **parallel;** that is, we can handle two or more items at the same time.

2. We need to use **controlled processing** on tasks that are difficult and on tasks that use unfamiliar items. (For example, imagine scanning that same list of names, except that you must search to see whether the list includes any of the following three unfamiliar names: Samantha Augusta Williams, Arturo Octavio Gomez, and Elizabeth Louise Blaisdell.) Furthermore, controlled processing is **serial;** we can handle only one item at a time.

Let's relate automatic processing to the research on selective attention and divided attention, which we discussed in the first part of this chapter. We mentioned that people can use automatic processing on easy tasks with familiar items. Therefore, on a simple selective-attention task where you are using *automatic* processing, it should be relatively easy for you to pick up features of the unattended message. Similarly, on a divided-attention task where both tasks use automatic processing, it should also be relatively easy for you to perform two tasks simultaneously. In addition, the definition of automatic processing specified that it is used for familiar items. As a result, you will typically use automatic processing if you have practiced a task extensively.

Now let's relate *controlled* processing to the research on selective and divided attention. On a difficult selective-attention task where you use controlled processing, you will notice very few features of the unattended message. Similarly, on a difficult divided-attention task, you will have trouble performing two tasks simultaneously. You'll also use controlled processing on both selective-attention and divided-attention tasks that are unfamiliar. To help you distinguish between these two terms, try thinking of examples of tasks you've accomplished today that require either automatic or controlled processing.

Let's consider part of the classic research by Schneider and Shiffrin, which examined the difference between automatic and controlled processing (Schneider & Shiffrin, 1977; Shiffrin & Schneider, 1977). Participants in these studies saw a rapid series of 20 pictures, or frames, on each trial. Each of four locations in a particular frame could be occupied by a number or a letter. On some tasks, people conducted an easy search, for instance, by searching for one or more letters when all the irrelevant items were numbers. On this easy task, people were equally accurate, whether they were searching for one letter or for four letters. In other words, people used automatic processing on this easy task; they apparently conducted a *parallel* search when they searched for the four letters simultaneously.

On other tasks, people conducted a difficult search. On one trial they might have been instructed to search for the letter *E*, when the irrelevant letters in the frame were *A*, *C*, *N*, and *S*. On the next trial, they might have been instructed to switch, so that they would now search for the letter A, when the irrelevant letters were now *C*, *N*, *S*, and *E*. This instructional condition basically resembled a card game in which the rules keep changing! On this difficult search task, people were fairly accurate when searching for a single target; however, they made numerous errors when searching for several targets at the same time. People in this condition apparently conducted a *serial* search, looking for each target—one at a time—through all items in a frame. As some researchers emphasize, however, it's often difficult to demonstrate whether the search process is parallel or serial, based simply on participants' response patterns in a single study (Logan, 2002b).

Feature-Integration Theory. Let's now consider a related approach, which has been studied extensively. Anne Treisman has developed an elaborate theory of attention and perceptual processing. Her original theory, proposed in 1980, was elegantly simple (Treisman & Gelade, 1980). As you might expect, the current version is more complex. Let's consider (1) the basic elements of feature-integration theory, (2) research on the theory, and (3) the current status of the theory.

1. *The Basic Elements:* According to Treisman's **feature-integration theory,** we sometimes look at a scene using distributed attention,* with all parts of the scene processed at the same time; on other occasions, we use focused attention, with each item in the scene processed one at a time. Furthermore, distributed attention and focused attention form a continuum, so that you frequently use a kind of attention that is somewhere between those two extremes.

Let's examine these two kinds of processing in more detail before considering other components of Treisman's theory (Treisman & Gelade, 1980; Treisman, 1993). The first stage of the theory uses distributed attention. **Distributed attention** allows you to register features automatically, using parallel processing across the field. Distributed attention, the relatively low-level kind of processing, is similar to Schneider and Shiffrin's (1977) automatic processing. This kind of processing is so effortless that you are not even aware that you're using it.

---

*In some of her research, Treisman uses the phrase "divided attention," rather than "distributed attention." However, I will use "distributed attention" in this textbook, in order to avoid confusing the concept with the research on divided attention discussed on pages 70–71.

The second stage of Treisman's theory, **focused attention,** requires serial processing, and you identify one object at a time. This more demanding kind of processing is necessary when the objects are more complex. Thus, focused attention is roughly equivalent to Schneider and Shiffrin's (1977) controlled search. Focused attention identifies which features belong together—for example, which shape goes with which color.

2. *Research on the theory:* Treisman and Gelade (1980) examined distributed attention and focused attention by studying two different stimulus situations. One situation used isolated features (and therefore it used distributed attention). In contrast, the other situation used combinations of features (and therefore it used focused attention). Let's first consider the details of the research on distributed attention. Treisman and Gelade proposed that, if you processed isolated features in distributed attention, then you should be able to rapidly locate a target among its neighboring, irrelevant items. That target should seem to "pop out" of the display automatically, no matter how many items are in the display.

To test their hypothesis about distributed attention, Treisman and Gelade conducted a series of studies. You already tried Demonstration 3.2 (p. 76), which illustrated part of their study. Remember the results: If the target differed from all the irrelevant items in the display with respect to a simple feature such as color, you could quickly detect this target. In fact, you could detect it just as fast when it appeared in an array of 23 items as when it appeared in an array of only 3 items (Treisman, 1986; Treisman & Gelade, 1980). Distributed attention can be accomplished in a parallel fashion and relatively automatically; the target seemed to "pop out" in Demonstration 3.2A.

In contrast, consider the details of the research on focused attention. Demonstration 3.2B required you to search for a target that was an object—that is, a conjunction (or combination) of properties. When you searched for a blue *X* buried among red *X*'s, red *O*'s, and blue *O*'s, you needed to use focused attention. In other words, you were forced to focus your attention on one item at a time, using serial processing. You searched at the object level, rather than at the feature level. This task was more complex, and you required more time to find the target when there were a large number of distractors.

We already discussed another important component of feature-integration theory, in connection with Demonstration 3.3. As you learned, the feature-present/feature-absent effect tells us that people search much more rapidly for a feature that is present—as in Part A—compared to searching for a feature that is absent—as in Part B (Treisman & Souther, 1985).

So far, we have reviewed the isolated-feature/combined-feature effect and the feature-present/feature-absent effect. A third effect related to feature-integration theory is called an *illusory conjunction*. Specifically, when we are overwhelmed with too many simultaneous tasks, we may form an illusory conjunction (Treisman & Schmidt, 1982; Treisman & Souther, 1986). An **illusory conjunction** is an inappropriate combination of features, perhaps combining one object's shape with a nearby object's color. Many studies by other researchers have demonstrated, for example, that a blue *N* and a green *T* can produce an illusory conjunction in which the viewer actually perceives a blue *T* (e.g., Ashby et al., 1996; Hazeltine et al., 1997).

This research on illusory conjunctions confirms a conclusion demonstrated in other perception research. Contrary to our commonsense intuitions, the visual system actually processes an object's features independently. For example, when you look at a red apple, your visual system actually analyzes its red color separately from its round shape (Goldstein, 2002; Hazeltine et al., 1997). In other words, the human visual system sometimes has a **binding problem** because the important features of an object are not represented as a unified whole by your visual system (Wolfe & Cave, 1999).

When you use focused attention to look at the apple, you will accurately perceive an integrated figure—a red, round object. Attention allows the binding process to operate. However, suppose that a researcher presents two arbitrary figures, for example, a blue *N* and a green *T*. Suppose also that your attention is overloaded or distracted, so that you must use distributed attention. In this situation, the blue color from one figure may combine with the *T* shape from the other figure. As a result, you may perceive the illusory conjunction of a blue *T*.

Other research shows that our visual system can create an illusory conjunction from verbal material (Treisman, 1990; Wolfe, 2000). For example, an observer whose attention is distracted might be presented with two nonsense words, *dax* and *kay*. This observer may report seeing the English word *day*. When nonsense words do not receive focused attention, we form illusory conjunctions that are consistent with our expectations. Top-down processing—which we emphasized in Chapter 2—helps us screen out inappropriate combinations (Treisman, 1990).

3. *Current status of the theory:* The basic elements of feature-integration theory were proposed more than 20 years ago. Since that time, dozens of additional studies have been conducted, and the original, straightforward theory has been modified. For example, Treisman and her colleagues (1992) found that people can search very quickly for conjunction targets (like a blue *X*), if they have had extensive practice.

As we will see throughout this textbook, researchers often propose a theory that initially draws a clear-cut distinction between two or more psychological processes. With extensive research, however, theorists frequently conclude that reality is much more complex. Rather than two clear-cut categories, we find that—in some conditions—distributed attention can occasionally resemble focused attention. As Palmer (1999) concludes in his evaluation of this theory of attention, feature-integration theory will probably be modified after additional research has been conducted, but it still provides an important framework for understanding visual attention.

◎ Section Summary: *Explanations for Attention*

1. Neuroscience research on attention has used the PET scan to establish that the posterior attention network—located in the parietal cortex—is active during visual search. In addition, when people have a lesion in the parietal cortex, they cannot notice visual objects in the opposite visual field.

2. Neuroscience research has also used the PET scan to establish that the anterior attention network—located in the frontal lobe—is active during the Stroop task and other tasks focusing on word meaning.

3. In addition, the event-related potential (ERP) technique has documented systematic neuronal activity during attention.

4. Early theories of attention emphasized a "bottleneck" that limits attention at a particular part of processing, but this perspective is too simplistic.

5. Somewhat later, Schneider and Shiffrin suggested that automatic processing is parallel, and it can be used on easy tasks with highly familiar items. In contrast, controlled processing is serial, and it must be used with difficult or unfamiliar tasks.

6. Treisman proposed a feature-integration theory that contains two components: (a) distributed attention, which can be used to register single features automatically, and (b) focused attention, which is used to search for combinations of features and for a feature that is missing. Illusory conjunctions may arise when attention is overloaded. With some modifications, feature-integration theory accounts for many important aspects of visual attention.

CONSCIOUSNESS

Our final topic—consciousness—is a controversial subject. One reason for the controversy is the variety of different definitions for the term (Groome, 1999; Schacter, 2000). I prefer a broad definition: **Consciousness** means the awareness people have of the outside world and of their perceptions, images, thoughts, memories, and feelings (Davies, 1999; Hobson, 1997). The contents of consciousness can therefore include your perceptions of the world around you, your visual images, the comments you make silently to yourself, the memory of events in your life, your beliefs about the world, your plans for activities later today, and your attitudes toward other people (Baars, 1997).

Consciousness is closely related to attention, but the processes are not identical. After all, we are not aware or conscious of the tasks we are performing with the automatic-processing kind of attention. For example, when you are driving, you may use automatic processing to put your foot on the brake in response to a red light. However, you may not be at all *conscious* that you performed this motor action. In general, consciousness is associated with the kind of controlled, focused attention that is not automatic (Cohen & Schooler, 1997a; Dehaene & Naccache, 2001).

As Chapter 1 noted, the behaviorists considered topics such as consciousness to be inappropriate for scientific study. However, consciousness edged back into favor as psychologists began to adopt cognitive approaches (Cohen & Schooler, 1997a; Dehaene & Naccache, 2001; Jacoby et al., 1997) Since the mid-1980s, consciousness has become a popular topic for numerous books (e.g., Baars & Newman, 2002; Cohen & Schooler, 1997b; Dehaene, 2001; Hameroff et al., 1998; Wegner, 2002).

🌀 **Demonstration 3.4**

Thought Suppression

This demonstration requires you to take a break from your reading and just relax for 5 minutes. Take a sheet of paper and a pen or pencil to record your thoughts as you simply let your mind wander. Your thoughts can include cognitive psychology, but they do not need to. Just jot down a brief note about each topic you think about as your mind wanders. One final instruction:

  During this exercise, do not think about a white bear!

In recent years, cognitive psychologists have been especially interested in three interrelated issues concerned with consciousness: (1) our ability to bring thoughts into consciousness; (2) our inability to let thoughts escape from consciousness; and (3) blindsight, which reveals that people can perform quite accurately on a cognitive task, even when they are not conscious of their accuracy. Before you read further, however, try Demonstration 3.4.

Consciousness About Our Higher Mental Processes

To what extent do we have access to our higher mental processes? For example, answer the following question: "What is your mother's maiden name?" Now answer this second question: "How did you arrive at the answer to the first question?" If you are like most people, the answer to the first question appeared swiftly in your consciousness, but you probably cannot explain your thought process (Miller, 1962). The name simply seemed to "pop" into your memory.

Richard Nisbett and Timothy Wilson (1977) challenged cognitive psychologists' assumptions by arguing that we often have little direct access to our thought processes. As they argued, you may be fully conscious of the *products* of your thought processes (such as your mother's maiden name), but you are usually not conscious of the *processes* that created these products (such as the memory mechanisms that produced her maiden name). Similarly, people may solve a problem correctly; however, when asked to explain how they reached the solution, they may reply, "It just dawned on me" (Maier, 1931; Nisbett & Wilson, 1977). We'll discuss this topic further in Chapter 11 on problem solving.

Psychologists currently believe that our verbal reports are somewhat accurate reflections of our cognitive processes (Nelson, 1996; Wilson, 1997). As we'll see in Chapter 6, we do have relatively complete access to some thought processes (e.g., judgments about how well you will perform on a simple memory task). However, we have only limited access to other thought processes (e.g., how well you understand the information in an essay).

We need to raise this topic of consciousness about thought processes, because it points out that cognitive psychologists should not rely on people's introspections (Nisbett & Wilson, 1977; Wegner, 2002). For example, when several people are talking to me at once, it genuinely *feels* like I am experiencing an "attention bottleneck." However, as we saw earlier in this section, humans actually have fairly flexible attention patterns; we really do not experience a rigid bottleneck. Throughout this book, we'll see that the research findings sometimes do not match our commonsense introspections. This discrepancy points out the importance of conducting objective research.

Thought Suppression

I have a friend who decided to quit smoking. So he tried valiantly to get rid of every idea associated with cigarettes. As soon as he thought of anything remotely associated with smoking, he immediately tried to push that thought out of his consciousness. Ironically, however, this strategy backfired, and he was haunted by numerous ideas related to cigarettes. Basically, he was unsuccessful in suppressing these undesirable thoughts. How successful were you in suppressing your thoughts in Demonstration 3.4? Did you have any difficulty carrying out the instructions?

The original source for the white bear study is literary, rather than scientific. Apparently, when the Russian novelist Tolstoy was young, his older brother tormented him by instructing him to stand in a corner and *not* think about a white bear (Wegner, 1996; Wegner et al., 1987). Similarly, if you have ever tried to avoid thinking about food when on a diet, you know the difficulty of trying to chase these undesired thoughts out of consciousness. The topic of thought suppression is also relevant for clinical psychologists (Shoham & Rohrbaugh, 1997; Wegner, 1997a). For example, suppose that a client is experiencing depression, and the therapist encourages the client to stop thinking about depressing topics. Ironically, this advice may produce an even greater number of depressing thoughts!

Wegner (1997b, 2002) uses the phrase **ironic effects of mental control** to describe how our efforts can backfire when we attempt to control the contents of our consciousness. Suppose that you try valiantly to banish a particular thought. Ironically, that same thought is *especially* likely to continue to creep back into consciousness.

Wegner and his coauthors (1987) decided to test Tolstoy's "white bear" task scientifically. They instructed one group of students *not* to think about a white bear during a 5 minute period, and then they were allowed to think about a white bear during a second 5 minute period. The participants in this group were very likely to think about a white bear during the second period, even more so than students in a control group who were instructed to think freely about a white bear—without any previous thought-suppression session. In other words, initial suppression of specific thoughts can produce a rebound effect.

Wegner (1992) relates the components of thought suppression to the concepts of controlled and automatic processing, which we introduced earlier in this chapter. According to Wegner, when you try to suppress a thought, you engage in a controlled search for thoughts that are *not* the unwanted thought. For example, when you are on a diet, you consciously, systematically search for items other than food to think about—a friend, a movie, exercise. At the same time, however, you also engage in an automatic search for any signs of the unwanted thought; this process demands little attention and it occurs automatically. On a diet, this automatic search effortlessly produces thoughts about rich pastries and other caloric treats. When you stop trying to suppress a thought, you discard the controlled search for irrelevant items. Unfortunately, however, the automatic search continues. Consequently, you experience a rebound effect, with thoughts about the previously forbidden topic now over-populating your consciousness!

Many studies have replicated the rebound effect following thought suppression (e.g., Clark et al., 1993; Wegner, 1997a; Wegner, 2002). Furthermore, this rebound effect is not limited to suppressing thoughts about white bears and other relatively trivial ideas. For example, when people are instructed not to notice a painful stimulus, they are likely to become even more aware of the pain. Similar ironic effects—which occur when we try to suppress our thoughts—have been documented when people try to concentrate, relax, and avoid movement (Wegner, 1994).

Blindsight

The first topic in this discussion on consciousness illustrated that we often have difficulty bringing some information about our cognitive processes into consciousness. The discussion of thought suppression suggested another concern: We often have difficulty *eliminating* some information from consciousness. The research on a visual condition called blindsight reveals a third point about consciousness: In some cases, people can perform a cognitive task quite accurately, with no conscious awareness that their performance is accurate. **Blindsight** refers to an unusual kind of vision without awareness. In more detail, blindsight is a condition in which an individual with a damaged visual cortex (e.g., from a stroke) claims not to be able to see an object. Nevertheless, he or she can accurately report some characteristics of that object (Farah, 2000a, 2001; Güzeldere et al., 2000; Merikle et al., 2001; Weiskrantz, 1997).

Individuals with blindsight believe that they are truly blind in part or all of their visual field. In other words, their consciousness contains the thought, "I cannot see." In a typical study, the researchers present a stimulus in a region of the visual field that had previously been represented by the damaged cortex. For example, a spot of light might be flashed at a location 10° to the right of center. People with blindsight are then asked to point to the light. Typically, these individuals report that they did not even see the light, so they could only make a guess about its location. Surprisingly, however, researchers have discovered that the participants' performance is significantly better than chance—and often nearly perfect (Weiskrantz, 1997).

Additional research has eliminated several obvious explanations. Furthermore, the individuals do have genuine, complete damage to the primary visual cortex (Farah, 2001; Weiskrantz, 1997). The most likely current explanation focuses on the fact that a portion of the information from the retina travels fairly directly to other locations on the cerebral cortex, even though most information travels first to the primary visual cortex (Goldstein, 1999). A person with blindsight can therefore identify some characteristics of the visual stimulus—even with a damaged primary visual cortex—based on information registered in those other cortical locations.

The research on blindsight is especially relevant to the topic of consciousness. In particular, it suggests that visual information must pass through the primary visual cortex in order to be registered in consciousness. If that information takes a detour and bypasses the primary visual cortex, the individual will not be conscious of the visual experience (Baars et al., 1998; Farah, 2001). In Chapter 5, we will consider a related phenomenon in our discussion of implicit memory; people can often remember some information, even when they are not aware of this memory.

In summary, this discussion has demonstrated that consciousness is a challenging topic. Our consciousness is not a perfect mirror of our cognitive processes; that is, we often cannot explain how these processes operate. It is also not a blackboard; we cannot simply erase unwanted thoughts from our consciousness. Consciousness is not even an accurate reporter, as the research on blindsight demonstrates. As Wegner (2002) concludes, we usually assume that "How things seem is how they are" (p. 243). However, this convergence between our consciousness and reality is often an illusion.

⊚ Section Summary: *Consciousness*

1. Consciousness, or awareness, is now a popular topic. Research suggests that we are often unaware of our higher mental processes; for instance, you may solve a problem but not be conscious of how you actually reached the solution.

2. Research on thought suppression illustrates the difficulty of eliminating some thoughts from consciousness; ironically, if you try to suppress your thoughts, you may experience a rebound effect.

3. Studies of individuals with blindsight suggest that they can identify characteristics of objects, even when they are not consciously aware of these objects.

CHAPTER REVIEW QUESTIONS

1. What is divided attention? Give several examples of divided-attention tasks you have performed within the past 24 hours. What does the research show about the effects of practice on divided attention? Can you think of some examples of your own experience with practice and divided-attention performance?

2. What is selective attention? Give several examples of selective-attention tasks—both auditory and visual—that you have performed within the past 24 hours. Based on the discussion of practice and *divided attention*, what would you predict about how practice on a selective-attention task would affect your ability to notice information about the irrelevant task?

3. The In Depth discussion on selective attention examines three topics: dichotic listening, the Stroop effect, and other visual effects (primarily search). Describe how the information in this discussion could be applied to your academic activities. (Note: The Stroop effect may be difficult to apply.)

4. Imagine that you are trying to carry on a conversation with a friend at the same time you are reading an interesting article in a magazine. Describe how the bottleneck theories and automatic versus controlled processing would explain your performance. Then describe Treisman's feature-integration theory and think of an example of this theory, based on your previous experiences.

5. Chapter 2 discussed change blindness and inattentional blindness; the current chapter defines these terms again and then introduces a third term, attentional blink. Define each term and then discuss how each of them emphasizes the connection between visual object recognition (Chapter 2) and attention (Chapter 3).

6. Imagine that you are searching the previous pages of this chapter for the term "dichotic listening." What part of your brain is activated during this task? Now suppose that you are trying to pay attention to the meaning of the phrase *dichotic listening*. What part of your brain is activated during this task? Describe how research has clarified the biological basis of attention.

7. Summarize the three theoretical approaches to attention that were discussed in this chapter: the bottleneck approach, the automatic-processing/serial-processing distinction, and Treisman's feature-integration theory. Then for each of these approaches think of a situation you have recently experienced and apply the approach to this situation.

8. Define the word *consciousness*. Based on the information in this chapter, do people have complete control over the information stored in consciousness? Does this information provide an accurate account of your cognitive processes? How is consciousness different from attention?

9. Cognitive psychology has many practical applications. Based on what you have read in this chapter, what applications can you suggest for driving and highway safety? Name the two points mentioned directly in this chapter, and then list three or four additional issues.

10. Cognitive psychology can also be applied to clinical psychology. Discuss some applications of the Stroop effect and thought suppression to the area of psychological problems and their treatment.

NEW TERMS

attention
divided-attention task
selective-attention task
dichotic listening
shadow

cocktail party effect
working memory
Stroop effect
schizophrenia
phobic disorder

cross-modal task
change blindness
inattentional blindness
attentional blink
saccadic eye movement

NEW TERMS   (continued)

fovea

fixations

perceptual span

regressions

posterior attention
   network

positron emission
   tomography (PET
   scan)

brain lesions

unilateral neglect

anterior attention
   network

event-related potential
   (ERP) technique

bottleneck theories

automatic processing

parallel (processing)

controlled processing

serial (processing)

feature-integration
   theory

distributed attention

focused attention

illusory conjunction

binding problem

consciousness

ironic effects of mental
   control

blindsight

RECOMMENDED READINGS

Goldstein, E. B. (Ed.). (2001). *Blackwell handbook of perception*. Malden, MA: Blackwell. Two chapters in this handbook are most relevant to attention and consciousness, one on visual object and space perception, and the other on visual attention.

Pashler, H. (Ed.). (2002). *Stevens' handbook of experimental psychology* (3rd ed., Vol. 1). New York: Wiley. Sensation and perception are the focus of this first volume of a four-volume series on cognitive psychology and other related research areas. The most relevant chapters of this volume are on attention and on auditory perceptual processes.

Rapp, B. (Ed.). (2001). *The handbook of cognitive neuropsychology*. Philadelphia: Psychology Press. This advanced-level handbook includes chapters on atten-

tion and consciousness that are especially relevant for the current chapter of your textbook.

Wegner, D. M. (2002). *The illusion of conscious will*. Cambridge, MA: MIT Press. Daniel Wegner conducted the initial research on thought suppression, and that is one of many topics examined in this book. However, the scope is much broader because Wegner also examines topics such as voluntary action and illusions about our cognitive processes; this book is interesting and even humorous!

Wolfe, J. M. (2000). Visual attention. In K. K. De Valois (Ed.), *Seeing* (2nd ed., pp. 335–386). San Diego: Academic Press. Wolfe's chapter is probably the most readable comprehensive summary of the research and theory on visual attention.

CHAPTER 4
Working Memory

Introduction

The Classic Research on Working Memory (Short-Term Memory)

The Working-Memory Approach

PREVIEW

Our topic in this chapter is working memory. At this moment, you are using your working memory to remember the beginning of this sentence until you reach the final word in this sentence. On other occasions, your working memory helps you remember visual and spatial information. In addition, working memory coordinates your cognitive activities, and it plans strategies.

We'll begin this chapter by inspecting some influential milestones in the history of working-memory research. The first section starts with George Miller's classic view that our immediate memory can hold approximately seven items. We'll also explore other early research and theories. In addition, we'll examine two factors that influence how much information we can store in working memory. For example, pronunciation time is important; you can remember roughly the number of words that you can pronounce in 1.5 seconds. Another important factor is semantic similarity; sometimes words that are similar in meaning can interfere with one another and produce forgetting.

The second part of this chapter explores the working-memory approach originally proposed by Alan Baddeley. His research showed that people can perform a verbal task and a spatial task at the same time, with little loss of speed or accuracy. This research led Baddeley to propose that working memory has two separate components—the phonological loop and the visuospatial sketchpad—which have independent capacities. We'll examine these two components as well as the central executive, the component that coordinates our ongoing cognitive activities. We'll also consider the episodic buffer, a temporary storehouse where information from the phonological loop and the visuospatial sketchpad is combined with information from long-term memory. The chapter ends with an In Depth feature that discusses some individual differences in working memory.

INTRODUCTION

You can probably recall a recent experience like this: You are talking on the phone to a friend, who tells you the number where you can reach him tonight. You repeat the number silently, hang up, and look for a pen and paper to write it down. Amazingly, you cannot remember the number. The first digits were 586, and a 4 appeared somewhere, but you have no idea what the other three numbers could be! Perhaps only 15 seconds pass while you hang up the phone and search for the pen and paper, but some memories are so fragile that they evaporate before you can begin to use them. As you'll soon see, research confirms that your short-term memory is limited when you must recall an arbitrary sequence of numbers or letters, even after a delay of less than 1 minute.

When you try to remember material for a short period of time, you're probably also aware that your memory cannot store many items. Suppose that you will be shopping for groceries, and a friend is giving you a list of items to purchase for her. You've already mentally stored five items. Doesn't it seem that, if one more item is added, one of the original items will need to be shoved out? You also become aware of these limits when you try mental arithmetic, read complicated sentences, or solve complex problems (Just & Carpenter, 1992; Kareev, 2000; Waltz et al., 2000). Demonstration 4.1 illustrates the limits of our immediate memory for two of these tasks; try each task before reading further.

In Demonstration 4.1, you probably had no difficulty with the first mathematics task and the first reading task. The second math and reading tasks may have seemed more challenging, but you could still manage. The third tasks probably seemed beyond the limits of your immediate memory.

In the preceding chapter, we saw that attention is limited. Specifically, you have difficulty dividing your attention between two simultaneous tasks. Furthermore, if you are paying selective attention to one task, you notice very little about the unattended task. Therefore, these attention processes limit the amount of information that can be passed on to your working memory.

The current chapter also emphasizes the limited capacity of cognitive processes, though it focuses on limited memory instead of limited attention. Specifically, this chapter examines working memory. **Working memory** is the brief, immediate memory for material that you are currently processing; a portion of working memory also coordinates your ongoing mental activities. In other words, working memory lets you

---

⑨ Demonstration 4.1

The Limits of Short-Term Memory

A. Try each of the following mental multiplication tasks. Be sure not to write down any of your calculations. Do them entirely "in your head."

1. $7 \times 9 =$
2. $74 \times 9 =$
3. $74 \times 96 =$

B. Now read each of the following sentences, and construct a mental image of the action that is being described. (*Note: Sentence 3 is technically correct, though it is confusing.*)

1. The repairman departed.
2. The deliveryperson that the secretary met departed.
3. The salesperson that the doctor that the nurse despised met departed.

keep information active and accessible, so that you can use it in a wide variety of cognitive tasks (Cowan, 2001; Engle, 2001; E.E. Smith, 2000). (The term *working memory* is currently more popular than a similar but older term, **short-term memory.**) In contrast, Chapters 5, 6, 7, and 8 will explore long-term memory. **Long-term memory** has a large capacity and contains our memory for experiences and information that have accumulated over a lifetime.

In discussing working memory, we need to repeat a point we made in connection with the Atkinson-Shiffrin model of memory in Chapter 1. According to some psychologists, the research evidence supports the proposal that working memory and long-term memory are basically the same (e.g., Crowder, 1993; Nairne, 2002). Another important point is that those who *do* believe in two different systems may not all share the same theoretical explanations (e.g., Atkinson & Shiffrin, 1968; Baddeley, 2001a; Engle & Kane, 2005; Izawa, 1999; Miyake & Shah,1999a).

In this discussion, we also need to repeat a different point we made in Chapter 1: Our performance on everyday tasks is often different from our performance on tasks in the psychology laboratory. In everyday life, for instance, your memory is often much more impressive, especially because you are working on a variety of complex tasks within a short period of time (Miyake & Shah, 1999b). Your working memory must decide what kind of information is useful to you right now, and it selects this material out of an enormous wealth of information you possess (Goldberg, 2001).

At this moment, for example, your working-memory system is rapidly inspecting your vast knowledge of words, grammar, and concepts, with the goal of interpreting the meaning of this sentence. However, you may soon shift toward several other memory tasks. Within a 2-minute time period, you may consider the following: (1) the contents of your refrigerator, with the goal of making lunch; (2) the time your next class starts, with the goal of eating lunch before you walk to class; and (3) the psychology terms you'll use later today in a computer search, with the goal of beginning your cognitive psychology paper.

So let's begin by inspecting some of the classic research on working memory. As you'll notice, the concept of limited memory capacity has been an important feature of this research for many decades. Then we'll explore the multicomponent model—originally proposed by Alan Baddeley—which is currently the most widely accepted theoretical explanation of working memory. As you'll see, this theory is more flexible than earlier explanations. However, it still emphasizes that each of the major components of working memory has a limited capacity.

THE CLASSIC RESEARCH ON WORKING MEMORY (SHORT-TERM MEMORY)

We'll start by discussing George Miller's perspective on the limitations of memory, as well as some early studies that attempted to measure these limitations. Our next topic in this section is the Atkinson-Shiffrin model, and we'll end by considering two factors that affect the capacity of working memory.

George Miller's "Magical Number Seven"

More than a century ago, early psychologists speculated that humans could retain only a limited number of items at a time in active memory (Baldwin, 1894; Engle, 1996). However, this observation was not extensively examined until much later. In 1956, George Miller wrote his famous article titled "The Magical Number Seven, Plus or Minus Two: Some Limits on Our Capacity for Processing Information." Miller proposed that we can hold only a limited number of items in short-term memory (as this brief memory was called at the time). Specifically, he suggested that people can remember about seven items (give or take two), that is, between five and nine items.

Miller uses the term *chunk* to describe the basic unit in short-term memory. According to the current definition, a **chunk** is a memory unit that consists of several components that are strongly associated with one another (Bellezza, 1994; Cowan, 2001). Miller suggests, therefore, that short-term memory holds approximately seven chunks.

A chunk can be a single numeral or a single letter, because people can remember a random sequence of about seven numerals or letters. However, you can organize several numbers or letters so that they form a single chunk. For example, suppose that your area code is 617, and all the phone numbers at your college begin with the same digits, 346. If 617 forms one chunk and 346 forms another chunk, then the phone number 617-346-3421 really contains only six chunks (that is, 1 + 1 + 4). The entire number may be within your memory span. Miller's (1956) article received major attention, and the magical number 7 ± 2 became a prominent concept known to almost all psychology students.*

Miller's article was unusual because it was written at a time when behaviorism was very popular. Nonetheless, the article proposed that people engage in internal *mental* processes in order to convert stimuli into a manageable number of chunks. The article emphasized the active nature of our cognitive processes—consistent with Theme 1—rather than focusing only on the visible stimuli and the visible responses (Baddeley, 1994). Miller's work also helped to inspire some of the classic research on short-term memory.

Other Early Research on Short-Term-Memory Capacity

Between the late 1950s and the 1970s, two methods were frequently used to assess how much information our short-term memory could hold. Two especially popular measures were the Brown/Peterson & Peterson Technique and a measure derived from the serial position effect. (Incidentally, here we will use "short-term memory"—the term used during that era—rather than the more current "working memory.")

---

*In more recent research, Nelson Cowan (2001) argues that the magical number is really 4 ± 1, when we consider the "pure capacity" of short-term memory—without the possibility of chunking.

The Brown/Peterson & Peterson Technique. Demonstration 4.2 shows a modified version of the Brown/Peterson & Peterson Technique, a method that provided much of our original information about short-term memory. John Brown (1958)—a British psychologist—and Lloyd Peterson and Margaret Peterson (1959)—two American psychologists—independently demonstrated that material held in memory for less than a minute is frequently forgotten. The technique therefore bears the names of both sets of researchers.

Peterson and Peterson (1959), for example, asked people to study three letters. The participants then counted backward by threes for a short period, an activity that prevented them from rehearsing the stimuli during the delay. (**Rehearsal** means repeating the items silently.) Finally, the participants tried to recall the letters they had originally seen. On the first few trials, people recalled most of the letters. However, after several trials, the previous letters produced interference, and recall was poor.

---

⑨ Demonstration 4.2

A Modified Version of the Brown/Peterson & Peterson Technique

Take out six index cards. On one side of each card, write one of the following groups of three words, one underneath another. On the back of the card, write the three-digit number. Set the cards aside for a few minutes and practice counting backward by threes from the number 792. Then show yourself the first card, with the side containing the words toward you, for about 2 seconds. Then immediately turn over the card and count backward by threes from the three-digit number shown. Go as fast as possible for 20 seconds. (Use a watch with a second hand to keep track of the time.) Then write down as many of the three words as you can remember. Continue this process with the remaining five cards.

1. appeal			4. flower	
simple	687		classic	573
burden			predict	
2. sober			5. silken	
persuade	254		idle	433
content			approve	
3. descend			6. begin	
neglect	869		pillow	376
elsewhere			carton	

After a mere 5-second delay—as you can see from Figure 4.1—people forgot approximately half of what they had seen. This early research therefore yielded important information about the fragility of memory for material stored for just a few seconds. This technique also inspired hundreds of studies on short-term memory, and it played an important role in increasing the support for the cognitive approach (Bower, 2000; Kintsch et al., 1999).

The Recency Effect. Another technique that has often been used to examine short-term memory makes use of the serial position effect. The term **serial position effect** refers to the U-shaped relationship between a word's position in a list and its probability of recall. Figure 4.2 shows a classic illustration of the serial position effect in research (Rundus, 1971). The U-shaped curve is very common, and it continues to be found in more recent research (e.g., Page & Norris, 1998; Roediger et al., 2002; Tremblay & Jones, 1998).

As you can see, the curve shows a strong **recency effect,** with better recall for items at the end of the list. Many researchers have argued that this relatively accurate memory for the final words in a list means that these items were still in short-term memory at the time of recall. Thus, one way of measuring the size of short-term memory is to count the number of accurately recalled items at the end of the list (Cowan, 1994; Cowan, 2001; Murdock, 2001). Typically, the size of short-term memory is estimated to be two to seven items when the serial-position curve method is used. (Notice that the serial-position curve also shows a strong **primacy effect,**

FIGURE 4.1

Typical Results for Percentage Recalled with the Brown/Peterson & Peterson Technique.

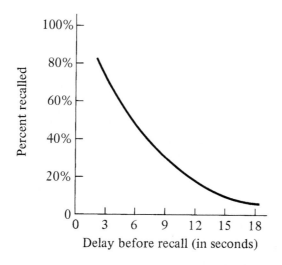

FIGURE 4.2

The Relationship Between an Item's Serial Position and the Probability That It Will Be Recalled.

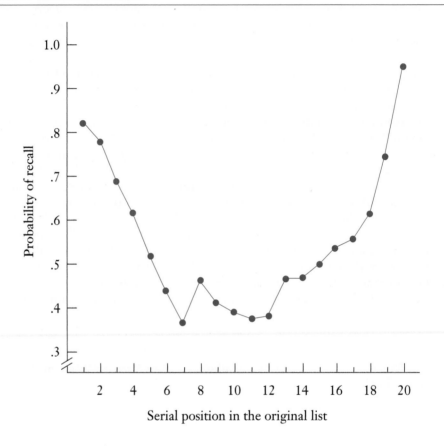

Source: Based on Rundus, 1971.

with better recall for items at the beginning of the list, presumably because early items are rehearsed more frequently.) The information gathered from these two re-search methods was useful in the construction of an extremely influential approach to human memory, developed by Atkinson and Shiffrin.

Atkinson and Shiffrin's Model

Richard Atkinson and Richard Shiffrin (1968) proposed the classic information-processing model that we presented in Chapter 1. Turn back to this model, presented in Figure 1.2 on page 11. As you can see, short-term memory (as it was then called) is distinctly separate from long-term memory in this diagram. Atkinson and Shiffrin argued that memories in short-term memory are fragile, and they could be lost within about 30 seconds unless they are repeated. In addition, Atkinson and Shiffrin proposed **control processes,** or strategies—such as rehearsal—that people use to improve their memory (Raaijmakers & Shiffrin, 2002; Shiffrin, 1999). The original form of this model focused on the role of short-term memory in learning and memory. The model did not explore how short-term memory is central when we perform other cognitive tasks (Roediger et al., 2002).

The Atkinson-Shiffrin model played a central role in the growing appeal of the cognitive approach to psychology. As Chapter 1 noted, researchers conducted numerous studies to determine whether short-term memory really is distinctly different from long-term memory—a question that still does not have a clear-cut answer. Research on this question declined during the mid-1970s, partly because Baddeley's new approach did not emphasize this distinction. Before we consider Baddeley's approach, however, let's examine two factors that have an important effect on working memory.

Other Factors Affecting Working Memory's Capacity

We have already considered one important factor that influences the capacity of working memory. As Miller's (1956) work demonstrated, we can increase the number of items in memory by using the chunking strategy. Let's focus on two additional influential variables: (1) pronunciation time, and (2) the semantic similarity of the items.

Pronunciation Time. The research shows that pronunciation time strongly influences the number of items that can be stored in working memory (Cowan, 1994, 1995; Hulme et al., 1999; Page & Norris, 1998). For example, Schweickert and Boruff (1986) tested memory span for a variety of stimuli, such as consonants, numbers, nouns, shape names, color names, and nonsense words. With impressive consistency, people tended to recall the number of items that they could pronounce in about 1.5 seconds. Apparently, then, the capacity of working memory is determined by the limited time for which the verbal trace of the items endures. In the case of nonsense syllables, a person might be able to pronounce only four items in 1.5 seconds; therefore, only four items will be recalled. In the case of numbers in the English language, a person can typically pronounce six items in 1.5 seconds, and so the number of recalled items is somewhat greater.

Researchers also tested the pronunciation-time hypothesis for other kinds of items. Try Demonstration 4.3, which is a modification of a study by Baddeley and his colleagues (1975). These researchers found that people could accurately recall an average of 4.2 words from the list of countries with short names, but only 2.8 words from the list of countries with long names.

One of the most systematic studies about pronunciation time was conducted on the recall of numbers in a variety of languages. Naveh-Benjamin and Ayres (1986) tested memory spans for people who spoke English, Spanish, Hebrew, or Arabic. The names for English numbers between 1 and 10 can be spoken rapidly; almost all numbers are one-syllable words. Spanish and Hebrew names for these numbers have

---

◉ Demonstration 4.3

Pronunciation Time and Memory Span

Read the following words. When you have finished, look away from the page and try to recall them.

Burma, Greece, Tibet, Iceland, Malta, Laos

Now try the task again with a different list of words. Again, read the words, look away, and recall them.

Switzerland, Nicaragua, Botswana,
Venezuela, Philippines, Madagascar

---

a somewhat greater average number of syllables, and Arabic numbers have even more syllables.

As Figure 4.3 shows, the memory span for numbers is greater for people speaking English than for people speaking the other three languages. Furthermore, the dotted line shows the pronunciation rate for each of the four languages. As you can see, greater memory spans are associated with languages whose numbers can be spoken rapidly. Clearly, pronunciation rate—as well as number of chunks—needs to be considered when discussing the capacity of short-term memory.

Semantic Similarity of the Items in Working Memory. The research on pronunciation time emphasized the importance of the acoustic properties of stimuli— that is, the *sound* of words. Now let's emphasize the semantic properties of stimuli: The *meaning* of words can also have an important effect on the number of items that can be stored in working memory.

For example, consider a study by Wickens and his colleagues (1976). Their technique is based on a classic concept from memory research called proactive interference. **Proactive interference (PI)** means that people have trouble learning new material because previously learned material keeps interfering with new learning. Suppose you had previously learned three items—XCJ, HBR, and TSV—in a Brown/Peterson & Peterson test of memory. You will then have trouble remembering a fourth item, KRN, because the three previous items keep interfering. However, if the experimenter shifts the category of the fourth item from letters to, say, numbers, your memory will improve. You will experience a **release from proactive interference;** performance on a new, different item (say, 529) will be almost as high as it had been on the first item, XCJ.

Many experiments have demonstrated release from PI when the category of items is shifted, as from letters to numbers. However, Wickens and his coauthors

FIGURE 4.3

Memory Span and Pronunciation Rate for Numbers in Four Different Languages.

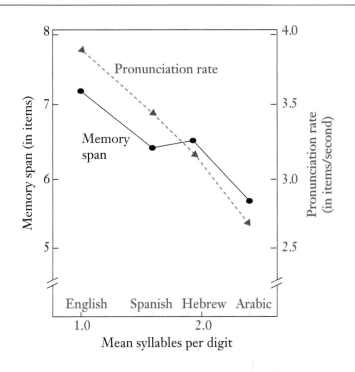

Source: Naveh-Benjamin & Ayres, 1986.

(1976) demonstrated that release from PI could also be obtained when they shifted the *semantic category* of the items. Their study employed five semantic categories, which you can see in Figure 4.4. Wickens and his colleagues initially gave people three trials on the Brown/Peterson & Peterson test. In other words, on each trial they saw a list of three words, followed by a three-digit number. After counting backward from this number for 18 seconds, they tried to recall the three words.

On each trial in this study, participants saw three related words. For example, those in the Occupations condition might begin with "lawyer, firefighter, teacher" on the first trial. On Trials 2 and 3, the people in this condition saw lists of additional occupations. Then on Trial 4, they saw a list of three fruits—such as "orange, cherry, pineapple"—as did the people in the other four conditions.

Look through the five conditions shown at the right side of Figure 4.4. Wouldn't you expect the buildup of proactive interference on Trial 4 to be the greatest for those in the fruits (control) condition? After all, people's memories should be filled

FIGURE 4.4

Release from Proactive Interference, as a Function of Semantic Similarity. On Trials 1, 2, and 3, each group saw words belonging to the specified category (e.g., occupations). On Trial 4, everyone saw the same list of three fruits.

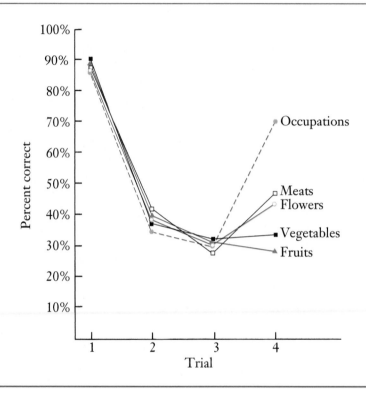

Source: Based on Wickens et al., 1976.

with the names of other fruits that would be interfering with the three new fruits. But how should the people in the other four conditions perform? If meaning is important in working memory, recall in these conditions should depend upon the semantic similarity between these items and fruit. For example, people who had seen vegetables on Trials 1 through 3 should do rather poorly, because fruits and vegetables are similar—they are both edible and grow in the ground. People who had seen either flowers or meats should do somewhat better, because flowers and meats each share only one attribute with fruits. However, people who had seen occupations should do the best of all, because occupations are not edible and do not grow in the ground.

Figure 4.4 is an example of the kind of results every researcher hopes to find. Note that the results match the predictions perfectly. In summary, semantic factors influence the number of items that we can store in working memory; words that have been previously stored can interfere with the recall of new words that are similar in meaning. Furthermore, the degree of semantic similarity is related to the amount of interference.

The importance of semantic factors in working memory has also been confirmed by other researchers (Humphreys & Tehan, 1999; Potter, 1999; Walker & Hulme, 1999). We know, then, that the number of items stored in working memory depends on chunking strategies, word length, and word meaning. Let's summarize the information in this section and then examine Baddeley's approach to working memory.

Section Summary: *The Classic Research on Working Memory (Short-Term Memory)*

1. Working memory is the very brief, immediate memory for material that we are currently processing.

2. In 1956, George Miller proposed that we can hold about seven chunks of information in memory.

3. Research using the Brown/Peterson & Peterson Technique has demonstrated that, when rehearsal is prevented, people forget material after a brief delay. The recency effect in a serial-position curve has also been interpreted as a measure of the capacity of short-term memory.

4. The Atkinson-Shiffrin model proposed that short-term memories can be lost from memory within about 30 seconds unless they are repeated.

5. Pronunciation time has an important effect on the number of items that can be stored in working memory; in general, people can recall the number of items they are able to pronounce in 1.5 seconds. This effect has been confirmed with a variety of stimuli, such as consonants, color names, nonsense words, names of countries, and names of numbers.

6. Word meaning can also influence the recall of items that are stored in working memory; when the semantic category changes between adjacent trials, recall increases.

THE WORKING-MEMORY APPROACH

For many years, researchers eagerly explored the characteristics of short-term memory. However, no one developed a comprehensive theory for this brief kind of memory. Now that you are familiar with several factors that influence working-memory capacity, we can explore the working-memory model in some detail. This model was originally proposed by Alan Baddeley and his colleagues. In recent decades, other researchers have also contributed to its development.

During the early 1970s, Alan Baddeley and Graham Hitch were examining the wealth of research on short-term memory. They soon realized that researchers had ignored one very important question: What does short-term memory accomplish for our cognitive processes? Eventually, they agreed that its major function is to hold several interrelated bits of information in our mind, all at the same time, so that this information can be worked with and then used (Baddeley & Hitch, 1974).

For example, if you are trying to comprehend the sentence you are reading right now, you need to keep the beginning words in mind until you know how the sentence is going to end. (Think about it: Did you in fact keep those initial words in your memory until you reached the word *end*?) Baddeley and Hitch also realized that this kind of working memory would be necessary for a wide range of cognitive tasks, such as language comprehension, mental arithmetic, reasoning, and problem solving.

According to the **working-memory approach** proposed by Baddeley, our immediate memory is a multipart system that temporarily holds and manipulates information as we perform cognitive tasks. Figure 4.5 illustrates the current design of the model, featuring the phonological loop, the visuospatial sketchpad, the central executive, and the episodic buffer—which was added more recently (Baddeley, 2000a, 2000b, 2000c, 2001a, 2001b).

Baddeley's approach emphasizes that working memory is not simply a passive storehouse, with a number of shelves to hold partially processed information until it moves on to another location, presumably long-term memory. Instead, the emphasis on the manipulation of information means that working memory is more like a workbench where material is constantly being handled, combined, and transformed. Furthermore, this workbench holds both new material and old material that you have

FIGURE 4.5

A simplified version of Alan Baddeley's (2000b) Model of Working Memory, Showing the Phonological Loop, the Visuospatial Sketchpad, the Central Executive, and the Rehearsal Buffer—as Well as Their Interactions with Long-Term Memory.

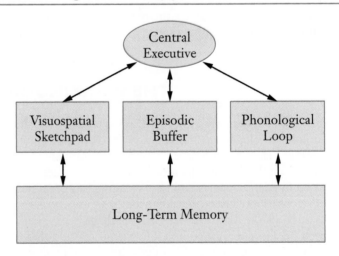

Source: Based on Baddeley (2000b).

retrieved from storage (long-term memory). Notice that, as Figure 4.5 illustrates, working memory has access to several kinds of long-term memory (represented by the large rectangle at the bottom of the figure).

Let's begin our analysis of the research by first considering why Baddeley felt compelled to conclude that working memory is not unitary. Next we'll consider each of the four components—the phonological loop, the visuospatial sketchpad, the central executive, and the episodic buffer. Then our In Depth feature will consider several important skills that are associated with individual differences in working memory.

Evidence for Components with Independent Capacities

An important study by Baddeley and Hitch (1974) provided convincing evidence that working memory is not unitary. These researchers presented a string of random numbers to participants, who were instructed to rehearse them in order. The string of numbers varied in length from zero to eight items. In other words, the longer list approached the upper limit of short-term memory, according to Miller's (1956) 7 ± 2 proposal. At the same time, the participants also performed a spatial reasoning task. The reasoning task required them to judge whether certain statements about letter order were correct or incorrect. For example, when the two letters *BA* appeared, participants should respond to the statement "*A* follows *B*" by pressing a "yes" button. If *BA* was accompanied by the statement "*B* follows *A*," participants should press the "no" button.

Imagine yourself performing this task. Wouldn't you think you would take longer and make more errors on the reasoning task if you had to keep rehearsing eight numerals, instead of only one? To the surprise of everyone—including the participants in the study—people performed remarkably quickly and accurately on these two simultaneous tasks. For example, Baddeley and Hitch (1974) discovered that these participants required less than a second longer on the reasoning task when instructed to rehearse eight numerals, in contrast to a task that required no rehearsal. Even more impressive, the error rate remained at about 5%, no matter how many numerals the participants rehearsed!

The data from Baddeley and Hitch's (1974) study clearly contradicted the view that temporary storage has only about seven slots, as Miller (1956) had proposed. Instead, short-term memory or working memory seems to have several components, which can operate partially independently of each other. Specifically, this study suggested that people can indeed perform two tasks simultaneously—for instance, one task that requires verbal rehearsal and another task that requires spatial judgments. Memory theorists now agree that working memory cannot be unitary (Miyake & Shah, 1999b).

As we've already described, Baddeley and his colleagues proposed four components for working memory: a phonological loop, a visuospatial sketchpad, a central executive, and—more recently—an integrative component that Baddeley calls an "episodic buffer" (Baddeley, 1999, 2000a, 2000b, 2000c, 2001a, 2001b; Gathercole & Baddeley, 1993; Logie, 1995). Let's examine each of these components.

Phonological Loop

According to the working-memory model, the **phonological loop** stores a limited number of sounds for a short period of time. Susan Gathercole and Alan Baddeley (1993) argue that the pronunciation-time research you learned about in Demonstration 4.3 (p. 106) can be explained by the limited storage space in the phonological loop (Baddeley, 2000c; Gathercole, 1997; Gathercole & Baddeley, 1993). You can pronounce country names such as *Burma* and *Greece* fairly quickly, so you can rehearse a large number of them quickly. In contrast, you can pronounce only a limited number of longer names, such as *Switzerland* and *Nicaragua*. When you have a large number of these long names to rehearse, some will inevitably be lost from the phonological loop.

Other Research on the Phonological Loop. Some additional studies on the phonological loop have examined acoustic confusions. We noted that the phonological loop stores information in terms of sounds. Therefore, we would expect to find acoustic confusions in people's memory errors; people would be likely to confuse similar-sounding stimuli.

Consider, for example, the setup in Demonstration 4.4. At some point in the near future, find someone who can help you try this demonstration. It is based on a classic study by Wickelgren (1965), who presented a tape recording of an eight-item list to participants. Each list consisted of four letters and four digits in random order, like the lists in the demonstration. As soon as the tape recording was finished, people tried to recall the list in order. The participants were tested in this fashion with a series of eight-item lists.

Wickelgren was particularly interested in the kinds of substitutions people made. For example, if they did not correctly recall the *P* at the end of the first list of items in Demonstration 4.4, what did they recall in its place? Wickelgren found that people tended to substitute an item that was acoustically similar. For example, instead of that last *P*, they might substitute a *B*, *C*, *D*, *E*, *G*, *T*, or *V*—all letters with the "ee" sound. Furthermore, if they substituted a number for *P*, it would most likely be the similar-sounding number *3*. When you try Demonstration 4.4, notice whether your friend shows a similar pattern of substituting acoustically similar stimuli. Does he or she also confuse an *M* with an *N*? Is this person fairly accurate in recalling the *W* on the second trial? After all, no letter or number is acoustically similar to a *W*.

Wickelgren's research confirmed that people confuse similar-sounding letters and numbers. In other classic research, Kintsch and Buschke (1969) demonstrated that people confuse similar-sounding words. Let's now consider some of the ways in which we use the phonological loop, and then we'll note some of the neuroscience research about this process.

Other Uses for the Phonological Loop. The phonological loop plays an important role in our daily lives, beyond its obvious role in working memory (Baddeley, 1999). Try counting the number of words in the previous sentence, for example. Can you hear your "inner voice" saying the numbers silently? Now try counting the number of

⑨ Demonstration 4.4

Acoustic Confusions in the Phonological Loop

Find a friend who can help by trying this brief study. Read the following instructions to your friend:

> I am going to read you several lists of items. Each list will include both letters and numbers. After I read one list, I want you to write down as many items as you can recall from this list, in the correct order. After you have finished recalling the list, we'll go on to the next list. OK? Let's begin.

(Use a ruler or sheet of paper to help you read each row more accurately.)

```
4 N F 9 G 2 7 P
B 3 Q 6 7 W 1 L
5 A 7 Z 3 M 4 T
6 8 C H 5 R 3 A
Y 2 D 9 J V 1 6
3 K N S 8 X 4 7
9 Q 7 M 2 Y 3 Z
T 8 R 3 A L 2 5
```

If you cannot find a friend to try this study, you can test yourself by uncovering one line of items, then covering it up again and trying to recall the items in order. This variation of the demonstration may be somewhat less effective, however, because the items would not be presented acoustically. You'll probably encode most of them in your phonological loop anyway, but you might confuse some items with visually similar items, rather than acoustically similar items.

words in that same sentence, but rapidly say the word *the* while you are counting. When your phonological loop is preoccupied with saying *the*, you cannot perform even a simple counting task! Notice how these uses for the phonological loop illustrate Theme 4 of this textbook: The cognitive processes are interrelated with one another; they do not operate in isolation. For example, some problem-solving tasks (see Chapter 11) require the phonological loop from working memory in order to keep track of numbers and other information. The phonological loop also plays an important role in reading, as we'll see in Chapter 9. (Be honest: The first time you see a long word, such as *phonological*, can you read that word without silently pronouncing it?) In addition, the phonological loop is crucial when we acquire new vocabulary words (Burgess & Hitch, 1999; Knott & Marslen-Wilson, 2001; Schacter, 2001).

Neuroscience Research on the Phonological Loop. Recent studies have also been conducted with brain-imaging techniques. In general, these studies have shown that phonological tasks activate parts of the frontal lobe and the temporal lobe in the left hemisphere of the brain (Baddeley, 2000c; Gazzaniga et al., 2002; Schacter, 2001). This finding makes sense, as you may recall from other psychology courses. Compared to the right hemisphere of the brain, the left hemisphere is more likely to process information related to language. More fine-grained brain-imaging research suggests that the phonological loop stores auditory information in the parietal lobe of the cortex. (See Figure 2.1, p. 35.) Furthermore, the regions of your frontal lobe that handle speech are activated when you rehearse verbal material (Newman et al., 2002; Smith & Jonides, 1998, 1999).

Visuospatial Sketchpad

A second component of Baddeley's model of working memory is the **visuospatial sketchpad,** which stores visual and spatial information. This sketchpad also stores visual information that has been encoded from verbal stimuli (Baddeley, 1999; Logie, 1995). For example, when a friend tells a story, you may find yourself visualizing the scene. Incidentally, the visuospatial sketchpad has been known by a variety of different names, such as *visuo-spatial scratchpad* and *visuo-spatial working memory;* you may encounter these alternate terms in other discussions of working memory.

As you begin reading about the visuospatial sketchpad, keep in mind the research by Baddeley and Hitch (1974) that we discussed earlier. People can work simultaneously on one verbal task (rehearsing a number) and one spatial task (making judgments about the relative position of the letters *A* and *B*)—without much alteration in their performance.

However, like the phonological loop, the capacity of the visuospatial sketchpad is limited (Baddeley, 1999; Frick, 1988, 1990). I remember tutoring a high school student in geometry. When working on her own, she often tried to solve her geometry problems on a small scrap of paper. As you might imagine, the restricted space caused her to make many errors. Similarly, when too many items enter into your visuospatial working memory, you cannot represent them accurately enough to recover them successfully.

Alan Baddeley (1999) describes a personal experience that made him appreciate how one visuospatial task can interfere with another. As a British citizen, he became very intrigued with American football while spending a year in the United States. On one occasion, he decided to listen to a football game while driving along a California freeway. In order to understand the game, he found it necessary to form clear, detailed images of the scene and the action. While creating these images, however, he discovered that his car began drifting out of its lane!

Apparently, Baddeley found it impossible to perform one task requiring a mental image—with both visual and spatial components—at the same time that he performed a spatial task requiring him to keep his car within specified boundaries. In fact, Baddeley found that he had to switch the radio to music in order to drive safely.

Baddeley's dual-task experience inspired him to conduct some laboratory studies. This research confirmed the difficulty of performing two visuospatial tasks simultaneously (Baddeley, 1999; Baddeley et al., 1973).

In general, less research has been conducted on the visuospatial sketchpad than on the phonological loop (Engle & Oransky, 1999). However, we will examine related topics in Chapter 7. In particular, that chapter explores the mental manipulations we perform on visuospatial information. In this present discussion, let's consider a study on visual coding, as well as some other applications of the visuospatial sketchpad. We'll also briefly consider some relevant brain-imaging research.

Visual Coding in Working Memory. Students in disciplines such as engineering, art, and architecture frequently use visual coding and the visuospatial sketchpad in their academic studies. It's probably safe to say that students in psychology and other social sciences are more likely to use verbal/acoustic encoding and the phonological loop.

In our everyday, nonacademic activities, we often use acoustic coding when we maintain information in working memory. However, when we cannot use acoustic coding, we often code items in terms of their visual characteristics. Let's consider the research conducted by Maria Brandimonte and her colleagues (1992), which shows that people use visual coding when acoustic coding has been suppressed.

In particular, let's compare the performance of two groups of participants in one of Brandimonte's studies. In one condition, which we'll call the control group, people saw a series showing six pictures of objects, such as the ones labeled "Original picture" in Figure 4.6. During Task 1, the series was repeated until the participants knew the pictures in order.

On Task 2, the control-group participants were asked to create a mental image of each picture in the series, and to subtract a specified part from each image. They were then told to name the resulting image. For example, suppose they had created a mental image of the piece of candy at the top of Figure 4.6, and then they subtracted the specified part. Notice that they should end up describing the resulting image as a fish. Similarly, the pipe minus the specified part should be described as a bowl. The participants in this control condition succeeded in naming an average of only 2.7 items correctly, out of a maximum of 6.0 items. During Task 1, these participants had probably used acoustic encoding to learn the names of the stimuli; that is, they silently rehearsed the names "candy," "pipe," and so on. They typically did not create a visual code for the stimuli. As a result, they usually had no available visual image from which they could subtract a specified part on Task 2. Without a visual image, Task 2 was so challenging that they answered less than half of the items correctly.

The participants in the experimental group performed most of the same tasks as the control group did. There was one exception, however: While they were learning the original list of pictures in Task 1, they were instructed to repeat an irrelevant sound ("la-la-la . . . "). Notice that this repetition would block the acoustic representation of each picture, creating verbal suppression. After all, you can't say "candy" or "pipe" to yourself if you are chanting "la-la-la" out loud!

FIGURE 4.6

Two of the Stimuli Used in the Study by Brandimonte and Her Colleagues.

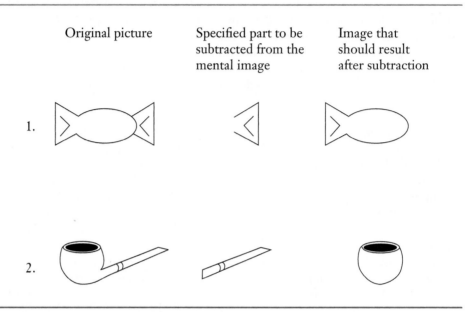

Original picture   Specified part to be   Image that
                          subtracted from the   should result
                          mental image   after subtraction

1.

2.

Source: Based on Brandimonte et al., 1992.

How well did the participants in the verbal-suppression group do on Task 2, identifying the image that was created by subtracting the specified part? As it turned out, they performed significantly better than people in the control condition. In fact, they named an average of 3.8 items correctly. Because acoustic coding had been difficult, they were probably more likely to use visual coding. As a result, on the picture-subtraction task, they had little difficulty subtracting a part from a visual image.

This study is particularly intriguing because participants in the experimental group were actually given extra work: They had to recite the sound "la-la-la." However, despite this extra assignment, they actually performed *better* on the visual task!

Other Uses for the Visuospatial Sketchpad. The study by Brandimonte and her coauthors (1992) emphasizes visual images, specifically the shape of certain stimuli. Other research emphasizes spatial tasks, specifically the location of certain stimuli. For example, Toms and her colleagues (1994) found that people have trouble working on a task requiring spatial imagery if they are required to simultaneously view a shifting design on a television screen. As Baddeley (2001a) suggests, most relevant tasks have both spatial and visual components.

Neuroscience Research on the Visuospatial Sketchpad. In general, the brain-imaging research suggests that visual and spatial tasks are especially likely to activate the right hemisphere of the cortex, rather than the left hemisphere (Awh & Jonides, 1999; Gazzaniga et al., 2002; Smith & Jonides, 1997). Again, these studies are consistent with information you probably learned in other courses; the right hemisphere is generally responsible for processing visual and spatial tasks.

Visual and spatial tasks often activate a variety of regions of the cortex. For example, working-memory tasks with a strong visual component typically activate the occipital region, a part of the brain that is responsible for visual perception (Baddeley, 2001a; Smith & Jonides, 1997). (Refer again to Figure 2.1, p. 35.) In addition, various regions of the frontal cortex are active when people work on visual and spatial tasks (Courtney et al., 1998; E.E. Smith, 2000; Smith & Jonides, 1998). Research on spatial working memory also suggests that people mentally rehearse this material by shifting their selective attention from one location to another in their mental image (Awh et al., 1998). As a result, this mental rehearsal activates areas in the frontal and parietal lobes (Diwadkar et al., 2000). These are the same areas of the cortex that are associated with attention, as we discussed in Chapter 3.

Central Executive

According to the working-memory model, the **central executive** integrates information from the phonological loop, the visuospatial sketchpad, and the episodic buffer. The central executive also plays a major role in attention, planning strategies, and coordinating behavior (Baddeley, 2001a; Gathercole & Baddeley, 1993; Healy & Mc-Namara, 1996). In addition, the central executive is responsible for suppressing *irrelevant* information (Engle & Conway, 1998). In your everyday activities, your central executive helps you decide what to do next. It also helps you decide what *not* to do, so that you do not become sidetracked from your primary goal.

Characteristics of the Central Executive. Most researchers emphasize that the central executive plans and coordinates, but it does not store information (Baddeley, 2000b; Richardson, 1996a, 1996b). As you know, the phonological loop and the visuospatial sketchpad both have specialized storage systems.

Compared to the two systems we've discussed, the central executive is more difficult to study using controlled research techniques. However, the central executive plays a critical role in the overall functions of working memory. As Baddeley (1986) points out, if we concentrate on, say, the phonological loop, the situation would resemble a critical analysis of Shakespeare's play *Hamlet* that focuses on Polonius—a minor character—and completely ignores the prince of Denmark!

Baddeley (1986, 1999) proposes that the central executive works like an executive supervisor in an organization. According to this metaphor, the executive decides which issues deserve attention and which should be ignored. The executive also selects strategies, figuring out how to tackle a problem. (We will examine this issue of strategy selection more completely in Chapter 6, in connection with metacognition.)

Furthermore, a good executive also knows not to keep repeating a strategy that doesn't work (Baddeley, 2001a). Also, like any executive in an organization, the central executive has a limited ability to perform simultaneous tasks. Our cognitive executive cannot make numerous decisions at the same time, and it cannot work effectively on two simultaneous projects.

The Central Executive and Daydreaming. Let's look at a representative study about the central executive. At this very moment, you may be engaging in the slightly embarrassing activity we typically call "daydreaming." For example, right now you may be thinking about a TV show you saw last night or what you will be doing next weekend—rather than the words that are being registered by your sensory receptors.

Interestingly, daydreaming requires the active participation of your central executive. Consider part of a study by Teasdale and his colleagues (1995), which is illustrated in Demonstration 4.5. These researchers examined a task that should compete for your central executive's limited resources. This task, called the *random-number generation task*, requires people to supply one digit every second, in a random sequence described in this demonstration. As Demonstration 4.5 illustrates, the task is challenging. Approximately every 2 minutes, the researcher interrupted the task and asked the participants to write down any thoughts.

The researchers then inspected the trials on which the participants reported that they had been thinking about the numbers. On those trials, the results showed that the participants had been able to successfully generate a random sequence of numbers. In contrast, when the participants reported daydreaming, their number sequences were far from random. Apparently, their daydreaming occupied enough of the resources of the central executive that they could not create a truly random sequence of numbers.

⊚ Demonstration 4.5

A Task That Requires Central-Executive Resources

Your assignment for this demonstration is to generate a sequence of random numbers. In particular, make sure that your list contains a roughly equal proportion of the numbers 1 through 10. Also, be sure that your list does not show any systematic repetition in the sequence. For example, the number 4 should be followed equally often by each of the numbers 1 through 10.

As quickly as you can, write a series of digits on a piece of paper (at the rate of approximately one digit per second). Keep performing this task for about 5 minutes. If you find yourself daydreaming, check back at the numbers you have generated. During these periods, you'll probably find that your numbers do not form a truly random sequence.

Neuroscience Research on the Central Executive. In general, researchers know less about the biological underpinnings of the central executive than they know about the phonological loop or the visuospatial sketchpad. However, the brain-imaging research clearly shows that the frontal lobe of the cortex is the most active portion of the brain when people work on a variety of central-executive tasks (Smith & Jonides, 1997). Furthermore, the executive processes do not seem to be confined to any particular locations within the frontal lobe (Beardsley, 1997; Carpenter et al., 2000).

To some extent, this uncertainty about frontal-lobe activity is due to the fact that the central executive actually handles a large number of distinctive tasks (Baddeley, 2000a; Smith & Jonides, 1999). For example, suppose you are writing a paper for your cognitive psychology course. While you are working on the paper, your central executive may inhibit you from paying attention to some research that is irrelevant to your topic. It may also help you plan the order of topics in your outline. In addition, it guides you as you make decisions about your time frame for writing the paper. Each of these central-executive tasks seems qualitatively different, though all are clearly challenging. Perhaps we'll have more definitive answers about the biological correlates of the central executive once we have more clear-cut classifications of the kinds of tasks that the central executive performs.

Episodic Buffer

Approximately 25 years after Alan Baddeley proposed his original model of working memory, he proposed a fourth component of working memory called the *episodic buffer* (Baddeley, 2000a, 2000b, 2001a, 2001b). You can locate this component in Figure 4.5 on page 110. The **episodic buffer** serves as a temporary storehouse where we can gather and combine information from the phonological loop, the visuospatial sketchpad, and long-term memory. (As Chapter 5 will explain, the term "episodic" refers to your memories of events that happened to you; these memories describe episodes in your life.)

This episodic buffer actively manipulates information so that you can interpret an earlier experience, solve new problems, and plan future activities. For instance, suppose that you are thinking about an unfortunate experience that occurred yesterday, when you unintentionally said something rude to a friend. You might review this event and try to figure out whether your friend seemed offended; naturally you'll need to access some information from your long-term memory about your friend's customary behavior. You'll also need to decide whether you do have a problem, and—if so—how you can plan to resolve the problem.

Because the episodic buffer is new, we do not have details about how it works and how it differs from the central executive. However, Baddeley proposes that it has a limited capacity—just as the capacities of the phonological loop and the visuospatial sketchpad are limited. Also, this episodic buffer is just a temporary memory system, unlike the relatively permanent long-term memory system. Some of the material in the episodic buffer is verbal (e.g., the specific words you used) and some is visuospatial (e.g., your friend's facial expression and how far apart you were standing). Finally, just as you are consciously aware of the information you retrieve from long-term memory, you are also consciously aware of the information you are integrating in the episodic buffer.

We have examined four components of the working-memory model, as proposed by Alan Baddeley. Although this model is widely supported, other psychologists have devised somewhat different theories about working memory (e.g., Izawa, 1999; Miyake & Shah, 1999a). However, the theories consistently argue that working memory is complex, flexible, and strategic. The current perspective is certainly different from the view held during the 1950s and 1960s that short-term memory was relatively rigid and had a fixed capacity.

Meanwhile, other psychologists have begun to examine individual differences in working memory. This area of research has become especially productive during the last decade, so let's examine this topic in depth.

IN DEPTH

Individual Differences in Working Memory

Cognitive psychologists usually conduct research that focuses on typical human skills. For example, researchers who are interested in perception might acknowledge that people may differ from one another in their ability to recognize faces or their accuracy in performing a divided-attention task. However, their research and theories typically emphasize general rules that can be applied to the human perceptual system.

One notable exception is the research on working memory, in which psychologists have conducted many studies on individual differences (e.g., Engle, 2002; Engle & Kane, 2005; Kane et al., 2001; Miyake, 2001a). Let's consider three different questions about these individual differences:

1. How is working-memory capacity related to verbal fluency?
2. How is working-memory capacity related to other cognitive skills?
3. How can the theory of working memory explain the extraordinary memory abilities of individuals with expertise in certain areas?

Working Memory and Verbal Fluency. Virginia Rosen and Randall Engle (1997) speculated that working-memory capacity is related to one particular form of language skills—specifically, people's general level of verbal fluency. Think about some people you know who are extremely fluent. These people speak without hesitation, and they seem to be able to retrieve a large variety of words with little difficulty. In contrast, others speak more hesitantly, and their vocabulary is more limited.

Rosen and Engle devised a test of working memory that focuses especially on the central executive. This test is illustrated in Task 1 of Demonstration 4.6.

🌀 Demonstration 4.6

The Relationship Between Working Memory and Verbal Fluency

Task 1: Your first task is a measure of working memory that focuses on the central executive. You will need to perform a series of arithmetic problems while keeping some material in memory. Suppose that you see the following item:

IS $(3 \times 4) - 2 = 10$?   TREE.

First, answer "yes" or "no" to the arithmetic problem (in this case, "yes"). Then look at the word that follows the question mark, and remember this word.

Now take a blank piece of paper and cut out a window so that it exposes only one item at a time. Move through the following list quickly, but try to be accurate. When you are done, close the book and recall the six words in order. Your accuracy on this memory task is the measure of working memory that Rosen and Engle (1997) used.

IS $(5 \times 3) + 4 = 17$?   BOOK
IS $(6 \times 2) - 3 = 9$?   FLOWER
IS $(9 \times 3) - 4 = 21$?   CHAIR
IS $(4 \times 4) + 6 = 22$?   FROG
IS $(3 \times 8) - 8 = 16$?   PAPER
IS $(7 \times 5) - 2 = 32$?   SHIRT

Now recall the words in the correct order.

Task 2: Now take out a watch. During the next 2 minutes, write down as many names of animals as you can. Try not to repeat any. This is the measure of verbal fluency used in Rosen and Engle's study.

Notice that this test assesses more than just the number of stimuli you can memorize (Engle, 2002). Instead, the test assesses how you can control and coordinate your working memory. Specifically, you must coordinate your problem-solving ability (the arithmetic task) with your phonological loop (remembering the words).

Rosen and Engle (1997) tested a large group of college students, and they presented many test items in order to obtain a reliable measure of working memory. Then the students in the highest 25% of the group (high working-memory score) and the lowest 25% of the group (low working-memory score) were invited to participate in the second part of the study. This second part resembled Task 2 in Demonstration 4.6, except that the participants generated names of animals for a total of 15 minutes, rather than just 2 minutes. The total number of different animal names was used as the measure of verbal fluency.

Figure 4.7 compares the average verbal fluency of the students with high scores to that of the students with low scores. As you can see, the two groups differ even during the first minute of the verbal-fluency test. By the end of the 15-minute period, the students with the high working-memory scores had listed about 50% more animal names than the students with the low scores. Keep in mind, too, that Rosen and Engle tested only college students. A sample of participants that included a more general population would undoubtedly show an even greater difference in verbal fluency between those with high and low scores on the working-memory test.

In summary, Rosen and Engle's (1997) study illustrates that the concept of working memory is indeed related to language skills. Specifically, people who can remember a list of words in order—while performing mental arithmetic—are able to demonstrate verbal fluency by searching their memory for a large number of relevant words.

FIGURE 4.7

The Average Number of Animal Names Supplied by Individuals Who Have High Working Memory and Low Working Memory. This figure shows cumulative recall.

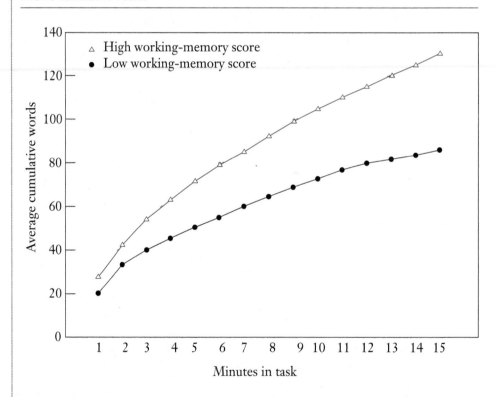

Source: Rosen & Engle, 1997.

Working Memory and Other Cognitive Skills. Other measures of working memory, similar to Rosen and Engle's test, are correlated with people's ability to take notes, follow directions, and perform reasoning tasks (Engle, 2002). Furthermore, research shows that working-memory performance is related to the ability to learn vocabulary in a foreign language (Atkins & Baddeley, 1998).

Working memory is also related to measures of reading ability. For example, people with large working-memory spans are especially skilled in guessing the meaning of unusual words on the basis of sentence context (Daneman & Green, 1986). Apparently, their large memory span allows them to read efficiently, so that they have more attention "left over" to remember the important contextual cues. Furthermore, students with high working-memory ability also earn higher scores on the reading comprehension part of the Scholastic Assessment Test (SAT; Daneman & Hannon, 2001).

According to the research we've discussed so far, individual differences in working-memory skills are correlated with a variety of cognitive skills. Another approach to individual differences is to study people who have outstanding cognitive talents—for example, people who could be called "memory experts."

Working Memory and Memory Experts. K. Anders Ericsson has been studying memory experts for about 25 years. Consider a classic study of two individuals who were able to expand their memory span dramatically (Chase & Ericsson, 1981). As you know, most of us are able to recall about seven numbers in a row. Nevertheless, one man named S.F. was able to attain the extraordinary memory span of about 80 numbers. S.F. received no coaching or instruction in memory improvement. However, he was a good long-distance runner and soon began to encode the numbers into running times for various races. For example, he recalled the sequence 3492 as "3 minutes and 49.2 seconds, near world-record time for running a mile." He constructed similar codes for additional numbers in the series.

More recently, Ericsson and his coauthor Peter Delaney (1998, 1999) developed a theory to account for the exceptional memory performance of individuals such as S.F. As we've discussed, working memory has limited storage capacities. Therefore, Baddeley's standard four-component model of working memory cannot explain how someone like S.F. can remember a list of numbers that is far longer than his storage capacity.

To address this storage problem, Ericsson and Delaney propose that highly skilled individuals can overcome the limited capacity of working memory by using abilities that allow them to store relevant material in their long-term memory. Furthermore, these memory experts keep—in their working memory—the specific retrieval cues connected with this particular material. The retrieval cues allow experts to retrieve this material quickly and accurately. According to Ericsson and Delaney, the term **long-term working memory** is defined as a set of acquired strategies that allow memory experts to expand their memory performance for specific types of material within their domain of expertise.

S.F.'s expertise in running speeds, together with the strategies he acquired for segmenting the sequence of numbers, allowed him to develop a long-term working memory. Other memory experts develop their own unique forms of long-term working memory in specific areas. These experts include a waiter who could memorize up to 20 complete dinner orders, chess players who can play several games of chess simultaneously (while wearing a blindfold!), and medical experts who can quickly evaluate alternative diagnoses for a disease (Ericsson, 1985; Ericsson & Delaney, 1999). The topic of expertise is now a lively issue in cognitive psychology that we'll continue to examine throughout this textbook. For example, Chapter 5 explores other aspects of memory expertise, and Chapter 11 discusses expert problem solvers.

◎ Section Summary: *The Working-Memory Approach*

1. Alan Baddeley and his coauthors proposed a working-memory approach in which immediate memory is not a passive storehouse; instead, it resembles a workbench where material is continuously being combined and transformed.

2. In a classic study, Baddeley and Hitch (1974) demonstrated that people could perform a verbal task and a spatial task simultaneously, with minimal reduction in speed and accuracy.

3. In the working-memory approach, the phonological loop stores a limited number of sounds, as demonstrated by the pronunciation-time research; additional research shows that items stored in the loop can be confused with other similar-sounding items.

4. Neuroscience research reveals that phonological tasks typically activate the left hemisphere, especially the parietal lobe and the frontal lobe.

5. A second component of the working-memory approach is the visuospatial sketchpad, which stores visual and spatial information. The capacity of this feature is also limited; two visuospatial tasks will interfere with each other if they are performed simultaneously.

6. According to Brandimonte's research, when people are prohibited from using acoustic coding, they are more likely to use visual coding, and they can perform better on a task that requires the manipulation of visual information.

7. Activation of the visuospatial sketchpad is typically associated with the right hemisphere, especially the occipital region (for visual tasks), the frontal region, and the parietal region.

8. The central executive integrates information from the phonological loop, the visuospatial sketchpad, and the episodic buffer—as well as from long-term memory. The central executive is important in attention and selecting strategies.

9. The central executive cannot perform two challenging tasks simultaneously; for example, daydreaming interferes with generating a random-number sequence.

10. The central executive primarily activates various regions within the frontal lobe.

11. Baddeley recently proposed a new component to the working-memory approach called the "episodic buffer"; this component temporarily stores material from the phonological loop, the visuospatial sketchpad, and long-term memory.

12. Psychologists are now investigating individual differences in working memory; this research focuses on the relationship between working memory and verbal fluency, the relationship between working memory and other cognitive skills, and the impressive memory spans of memory experts.

CHAPTER REVIEW QUESTIONS

1. Describe Miller's classic notion about the magical number 7 ± 2. Why are chunks relevant to this notion? How did the Atkinson-Shiffrin model incorporate the idea of limited memory?

2. What is the serial position effect? Why is this effect related to short-term memory? Also discuss another classic method of measuring short-term memory.

3. What does the research on pronunciation time tell us about the limits of working memory? What specific aspect of Baddeley's model is most likely to be related to pronunciation time?

4. Suppose that you have just been introduced to five students from another college. Using the information on pronunciation time and semantic similarity, why would you find it difficult to remember their names immediately after they have been introduced? How could you increase the likelihood of your remembering their names?

5. According to the discussion of Baddeley's approach, working memory is not just a passive storehouse; instead, it is like a workbench where material is continually being handled, combined, and transformed. Explain why the workbench metaphor is more accurate for Baddeley's model than for the Atkinson-Shiffrin model.

6. Why does Baddeley and Hitch's (1974) research on remembering numbers and performing a spatial reasoning task suggest that a model of working memory must have at least two separate stores?

7. Name some tasks that you have performed today that required the use of your phonological loop, the visuospatial sketchpad, the central executive, and the episodic buffer. Can you think of a task that uses all four of these working-memory components, as well as long-term memory?

8. In the research by Brandimonte and her colleagues (1992), people in one group were prevented from using verbal methods to encode the various shapes. Usually, we think it's helpful to describe something in words. Why does this study suggest that verbal encoding can actually decrease memory accuracy on some tasks that require spatial information?

9. What does the central executive do? Why is the metaphor of a business executive an accurate one in discussing its role in working memory?

10. Our discussion of individual differences in working memory examined three areas in which individual differences might be prominent. Describe each of those areas. Based on your knowledge of working memory, what other areas would be useful to examine for the presence of individual differences? What kinds of professions would be appropriate for individuals who have outstanding abilities in each of these areas?

NEW TERMS

working memory
short-term memory
long-term memory
chunk
rehearsal
serial position effect

recency effect
primacy effect
control processes
proactive interference (PI)
release from proactive
    interference

working-memory approach
phonological loop
visuospatial sketchpad
central executive
episodic buffer
long-term working memory

RECOMMENDED READINGS

Baddeley, A. D. (2001a). Is working memory still working? *American Psychologist, 56,* 849–864. After Alan Baddeley received the American Psychological Association's Award for Distinguished Scientific Contributions, he was asked to deliver a scholarly presentation about his research; this article provides a succinct summary of his work, including information about the episodic buffer.

Logie, R. H., & Gilhooly, K. J. (Eds.). (1998). *Working memory and thinking.* Hove, England: Psychology Press. This book contains eight chapters that relate working memory to tasks such as comprehension, problem solving, and reasoning.

Miyake, A. (Ed.). (2001b). Individual differences in working memory [Special issue]. *Journal of Experimental Psychology: General, 130,* 163–168. The June 2001 issue of this journal presents six articles about individual differences in working memory, which is the subject of the current chapter's In Depth feature. The topics include children's working-memory capacity, working memory and math anxiety, and working memory and the Scholastic Assessment Test.

Miyake, A., & Shah, P. (Eds.). (1999a). *Models of working memory: Mechanisms of active maintenance and executive control.* New York: Cambridge University Press. Here is an excellent resource featuring a variety of theoretical approaches to working memory, including several that are beyond the scope of the present chapter. This book is especially strong because the final chapters compare the proposed models of working memory.

Long-Term Memory

PREVIEW

Chapter 5 focuses on long-term memory, or memory for information you've gathered throughout your lifetime. This chapter first examines factors that are relevant when we acquire new information. For example, we know from research on depth of processing that memory is more accurate if we process information in terms of its meaning, rather than more superficial characteristics. Memory is especially accurate if we try to relate that information to our own lives. If you have ever returned to a once-familiar location and experienced a flood of long-lost memories, you know the importance of another factor, called encoding specificity. In addition, emotional factors influence your memory in several ways. For example, if you have been watching a violent show on television, your memory will be relatively poor for the advertisements appearing during that show.

The next section of the chapter, on the retrieval of memories, demonstrates that memory accuracy can also be influenced by the way memory retrieval is measured. For instance, individuals with amnesia earn low scores on traditional recall tests, but they perform quite well on some nontraditional memory tests. This section also looks at the memory abilities of individuals with expertise in a particular subject area.

Autobiographical memory, the topic of the last section in this chapter, refers to our memory for the everyday events in our lives. This discussion points out that so-called flashbulb memories are typically not especially accurate. Our memory is influenced by our general knowledge about objects and events; this general knowledge is usually helpful but may create memory errors. This section also examines source monitoring, a process we use when we try to determine whether we really performed an action or merely imagined it. Finally, the chapter looks at eyewitness testimony, which shows that misleading information can sometimes alter our memory.

INTRODUCTION

Take a minute to think about the contents of your own long-term memory. For example, can you remember some of the details about the first day that you attended classes at your current college or university? Now try to recall several of your close friends during high school. Can you remember some of the characteristics of your teachers from fourth or fifth grade?

Chapter 4 emphasized the fragility of working memory. As that chapter illustrated, information that we want to retain can disappear from memory after less than a minute. In contrast, Chapter 5 will demonstrate that material retained in long-term memory can be amazingly resistant to forgetting.

Before we examine long-term memory, let's review some familiar terminology and introduce some important new distinctions. As we noted in earlier chapters, psychologists often divide memory into two basic categories called **working memory** (the brief, immediate memory for material we are currently processing) and long-term memory. **Long-term memory** has a large capacity and contains our memory for experiences and information that have accumulated over a lifetime. Like many psychologists, I'm not firmly convinced that working memory and long-term memory are two distinctly different forms of memory. However, I *do* believe that the division is a convenient way to partition the enormous amount of research about our memory processes.

Psychologists often subdivide long-term memory into more specific categories. Once again, this subdivision reflects convenience, rather than a conviction that the subdivisions are distinctly different forms of memory. One popular system subdivides long-term memory into episodic memory, semantic memory, and procedural memory, (Hoerl, 2001; Tulving, 1999a, 1999b, 2002).

Episodic memory focuses on your memories for events that happened to you; it allows you to travel backward in subjective time to re-experience earlier *episodes* in your life. Episodic memory includes your memory for an event that occurred 10 years ago, as well as a conversation you had 10 minutes ago. Episodic memory is the major focus of this chapter.

In contrast, **semantic memory** describes your organized knowledge about the world, including your knowledge about words and other factual information. For example, you know that the word *semantic* is related to the word *meaning*, and you know that an oak tree has acorns. Chapter 8 of this textbook focuses on semantic memory and our general knowledge about the world.

Finally, **procedural memory** refers to your knowledge about how to do something. For instance, you know how to ride a bicycle, and you know how to send an e-mail message to a friend. We will mention some aspects of procedural memory in this chapter, in connection with implicit memory (pp. 145–147), and also in Chapter 6, in connection with prospective memory (pp. 185–189).

In the current chapter, we'll look at three aspects of long-term memory. We'll begin with **encoding,** which refers to your initial acquisition of information; during encoding, information enters your memory (Buckner, 2000). Then we'll explore **retrieval,** which refers to locating information in storage and accessing that information. Our final section examines **autobiographical memory,*** or memory for events and topics related to your own, everyday life. Incidentally, we'll continue to examine long-term memory in Chapter 6 of this textbook; it emphasizes memory-improvement strategies.

---

*Many psychologists consider episodic memory and autobiographical memory to be highly similar. However, others argue that episodic memory emphasizes accuracy, whereas autobiographical memory emphasizes the qualitative "match" between the event and the memory for the event (Koriat et al., 2000).

ENCODING IN LONG-TERM MEMORY

In this section, we'll look at three important questions about encoding in long-term memory:

1. Are we more likely to remember items that we processed in a deep, meaningful fashion, rather than items processed in a shallow, superficial fashion?

2. Are we more likely to remember items if the context at the time of encoding matches the context at the time of retrieval?

◎ Demonstration 5.1

Levels of Processing

Read each of the following questions and answer "yes" or "no" with respect to the word that follows.

1.	Is the word in capital letters?	BOOK
2.	Would the word fit this sentence: "I saw a _____ in a pond"?	duck
3.	Does the word rhyme with BLUE?	safe
4.	Would the word fit this sentence: "The girl walked down the _____"?	house
5.	Does the word rhyme with FREIGHT?	WEIGHT
6.	Is the word in small letters?	snow
7.	Would the word fit this sentence: "The _____ was reading a book"?	STUDENT
8.	Does the word rhyme with TYPE?	color
9.	Is the word in capital letters?	flower
10.	Would the word fit this sentence: "Last spring we saw a _____"?	robin
11.	Does the word rhyme with SMALL?	HALL
12.	Is the word in small letters?	TREE
13.	Would the word fit this sentence: "My _____ is 6 feet tall"?	TEXTBOOK
14.	Does the word rhyme with SAY?	day
15.	Is the word in capital letters?	FOX

Now, without looking back over the words, try to remember as many of them as you can. Count the number correct for each of the three kinds of tasks: physical appearance, rhyming, and meaning.

3. How do emotional factors influence memory accuracy? This third question is one we will examine in an In Depth discussion.

Before you read further, though, be sure to try Demonstration 5.1.

Levels of Processing

In 1972, Craik and Lockhart wrote an article about the depth-of-processing approach, and this article became one of the most influential publications in the history of research on memory (Roediger, Gallo, & Geraci, 2002). The **levels-of-processing approach** argues that deep, meaningful kinds of information processing lead to more permanent retention than shallow, sensory kinds of processing. (This theory is also called the **depth-of-processing approach.**) The levels-of-processing approach predicts that you will recall many words when you use a deep level of processing. In Demonstration 5.1, for instance, you used deep processing when you considered a word's meaning (e.g., whether it would fit in a sentence). In contrast, the levels-of-processing approach predicts that your recall will be poor when you use a shallow level of processing. For example, you will be less likely to recall a word when you considered its physical appearance (e.g., whether it is typed in capital letters) or its sound (for example, whether it rhymes with another word).

In general, then, people achieve a deeper level of processing when they extract more meaning from a stimulus. When you analyze for meaning, you may think of other associations, images, and past experiences related to the stimulus. Stimuli analyzed at a very deep level will probably be remembered (Roediger, Gallo, & Geraci, 2002). As we'll see in Chapter 6, most memory-improvement strategies emphasize deep, meaningful processing.

Let's examine some of the research on the levels-of-processing approach. We'll first consider general verbal material, and then we'll consider an especially deep level of processing called *self-reference*. Finally, we'll shift to visual material, specifically, memory for faces.

Levels of Processing and Memory for Verbal Material. The major hypothesis emerging from Craik and Lockhart's (1972) paper was that deeper levels of processing should produce better recall. This hypothesis has been widely tested. For example, in an experiment similar to Demonstration 5.1, Craik and Tulving (1975) found that people were about three times as likely to recall a word if they had originally answered questions about its meaning rather than if they had originally answered questions about the word's physical appearance. Numerous reviews of the research conclude that deep processing of verbal material generally produces better recall than shallow processing (Craik, 1999; Lockhart, 2001; Roediger & Gallo, 2001; Zimmer & Engelkamp, 1999).

Deep levels of processing encourage recall because of two factors: distinctiveness and elaboration. **Distinctiveness** means that a stimulus is different from all other memory traces. If you've met someone whose name you want to remember, you'll need to use deep processing to figure out something unusual about that name that makes it different from others you've recently learned.

The second factor that operates with deep levels of processing is **elaboration,** which requires rich processing in terms of meaning and interconnected concepts (Craik, 1999). For example, if you want to understand the term *levels of processing,* you'll need to appreciate how this concept is related to both distinctiveness and elaboration. Think about the way you processed the word *duck* in Demonstration 5.1, for example. Perhaps you thought about the fact that you had indeed seen ducks on ponds and that some people like to eat roast duck with an orange sauce. The semantic encoding encouraged rich processing. In contrast, if the instructions for that item had asked whether the word *duck* was printed in capital letters, you would simply have answered "yes" or "no"; extensive elaboration would have been unlikely.

Let's consider research on the importance of elaboration. Craik and Tulving (1975) asked participants to read sentences and decide whether the words that followed were appropriate to the sentences. Some of the sentence frames were simple, such as "She cooked the _____." Other sentence frames were elaborate, such as "The great bird swooped down and carried off the struggling _____." The word that followed these sentences was either appropriate (for example, *rabbit*) or inappropriate (for example, *book*). You'll notice that both kinds of sentences required deep or semantic processing. However, the more elaborate sentence frame produced far more accurate recall.

Levels of Processing and the Self-Reference Effect. According to the **self-reference effect,** you will remember more information if you try to relate that information to yourself. Self-reference tasks tend to encourage especially deep processing. Let's look at some representative research on the self-reference effect and then consider a problem with participants who do not follow instructions. Then we'll discuss several potential explanations for the self-reference effect, as well as its biological correlates.

1. *Representative research.* In the classic demonstration of the self-reference effect, Rogers, Kuiper, and Kirker (1977) asked participants to process lists of words according to three kinds of instructions usually studied in levels-of-processing research. These three instructions included: (1) the words' visual characteristics, (2) their acoustic (sound) characteristics, or (3) their semantic (meaning) characteristics. Still other words were to be processed in terms of self-reference: (4) people were asked to decide whether a particular word could be applied to themselves.

The results showed that recall was poor for the two tasks that used shallow processing—that is, processing in terms of visual characteristics or acoustic characteristics. Recall was much better when people had processed in terms of semantic characteristics. However, the self-reference task produced by far the best recall. Apparently, when we think about a word in connection with ourselves, we develop a particularly memorable coding for that word. For example, suppose that you are trying to decide whether the word *generous* applies to yourself. You might remember how you loaned your notes to a friend who had missed class, and you shared a box of candy with your friends—yes, *generous* does apply. The mental processes and elaboration required in the self-reference task seem to increase the probability that we will recall an item.

The research on the self-reference effect also demonstrates one of the themes of this book. As Theme 3 proposes, our cognitive system handles positive instances more effectively than negative instances. In the self-reference studies, people are more likely to recall a word that does apply to themselves rather than a word that does not apply (Bellezza, 1992; Ganellen & Carver, 1985; Roediger & Gallo, 2001). For example, the participants in Bellezza's (1992) study recalled 46% of the adjectives that applied to themselves, compared with 34% of the adjectives that did not apply.

The self-reference effect has been demonstrated repeatedly with participants from different age groups and with a variety of instructions and stimuli (e.g., Thompson et al., 1996). Furthermore, Symons and Johnson (1997) gathered the results of 129 different studies that had been conducted on the self-reference effect, and they performed a meta-analysis. The **meta-analysis technique** provides a statistical method for synthesizing numerous studies on a single topic. A meta-analysis computes a statistical index that tells us whether a variable has a statistically significant effect. Symons and Johnson's meta-analysis confirmed the pattern we have described: People recall significantly more items when they use the self-reference technique, rather than semantic processing or any other processing method.

2. Participants' failure to follow instructions. The self-reference effect is definitely robust. However, Mary Ann Foley and her coauthors (1999) have shown that the research may actually *underestimate* the power of self-reference. Specifically, they speculated that research participants may sometimes "cheat" when they have been instructed to use relatively shallow processing for stimuli, and they may use the self-reference technique instead.

In one of their studies, Foley and her coauthors (1999) instructed students to listen to a list of familiar, concrete nouns. However, before hearing each word, they were told about the kind of mental image they should form. Let's consider two of the conditions, in which the students were instructed (1) to "visualize the object," or (2) to "imagine yourself using the object." For the first analysis of the data, the results were classified according to the instructions supplied by the experimenter, prior to each word. Notice in Table 5.1 that the two conditions produced identical recall. That is, students recalled 42% of the words, whether they had been instructed to use relatively shallow processing or deep, self-reference processing.

TABLE 5.1

Percentage of Items Recalled, as a Function of Imagery Condition and Analysis Condition.

	Visualize the Object	Imagine Yourself Using the Object
First analysis of data	42%	42%
Second analysis of data	23%	75%

Source: Based on Foley et al., 1999.

Fortunately, however, Foley and her colleagues had also asked the students to describe their visual image for each word during the learning task. As the researchers had suspected, people in the "visualize the object" condition often inserted themselves into the mental image, so that they had actually used self-reference processing. In the second analysis, the researchers sorted the words according to the processing methods that the students had actually used, rather than the instructions they had been given. As you can see, the second analysis revealed that the recall was more than three times as high for the self-reference condition as for the visualized-object condition.

The research by Foley and her colleagues (1999) has important implications beyond this particular study. The research shows that our cognitive processes are active (Theme 1). People do not assume that people will just passively follow instructions and do what they are told. Researchers need to keep in mind that participants are likely to transform the instructions, and this transformation may have an important impact on the results of the study.

3. *Explanations for the self-reference effect.* Let's now turn our attention to another issue: Why should we recall information especially well when we apply it to ourselves? One explanation is that the self is treated as an especially rich set of cues. You can easily link these cues with new information that you are trying to learn. These cues are also very different from one another. For example, your trait of honesty seems quite different from your trait of intelligence (Bellezza, 1984; Bellezza & Hoyt, 1992).

A second explanation suggests that self-reference instructions encourage people to consider how their personal traits are related to one another. As a result, retrieval will be easier and more effective (Klein & Kihlstrom, 1986; Thompson et al., 1996).

A third possible explanation is that we probably rehearse material more frequently if it is associated with ourselves. We're also more likely to use rich, complex rehearsal when we associate material with ourselves (Thompson et al., 1996). These rehearsal strategies facilitate later recall.

4. *Biological correlates of the self-reference effect.* Neuroscience research has made tremendous progress in recent years in identifying brain activity during memory processes. The research on memory encoding has focused on the frontal lobe of the cortex. (See Figure 2.1, p. 35.) More specifically, the research has recorded brain activity in the **prefrontal cortex,** which is the region in the front portion of the frontal lobe.

Research by Craik and his colleagues (1999) examined how both level of processing and self-reference are related to brain activity. These researchers conducted PET scans (see p. 15) while participants judged adjectives. In one condition, participants performed a shallow processing task; they judged the number of syllables in each word. In two other conditions, they were instructed to use much deeper levels of semantic processing, judging either the social desirability of the word or its relevance to a prominent government official. In the fourth condition, they were told to use self-reference processing, judging whether the word applied to themselves.

The results showed that the level of processing was related to brain activity. Specifically, the three deeper levels of processing were associated with activation of the left prefrontal cortex, a result that is consistent with other research (Brewer et al., 1998; Wagner et al., 1998). This finding makes sense because all three of these deep-level tasks were verbal. However, the shallow-processing task had not activated this region. Furthermore, the self-reference condition also activated another region of the brain, the *right* prefrontal cortex; none of the other three tasks had activated this specific region. This finding about the right prefrontal region also matched the conclusions from other research, which suggests that the self-concept may be represented in the right prefrontal cortex. This unique pattern of brain activity for self-reference processing—with both the left and the right prefrontal regions showing activation—must somehow be related to the high probability of recall.

Levels of Processing and Memory for Faces. We have emphasized that deep levels of processing can improve your memory for verbal material. The same conclusions also apply to face recognition. You can probably recall an embarrassing incident where you failed to recognize someone you know reasonably well. For example, you may have had several conversations with a woman who sits near you in class. However, you fail to recognize her with her new haircut; apparently, you had never used deep processing to notice her facial features.

Research has confirmed that shallow processing of faces—like shallow processing of words—leads to poor recall. For instance, research participants recognize a large number of photos of faces if they had made earlier judgments about whether each person is honest. In contrast, recognition is poor if they had used shallow processing—for example, making judgments about the width of each person's nose (Sporer, 1991).

How can we explain why deep processing facilitates memory for faces? Let's consider two answers. For example, we saw that distinctiveness helps to explain the levels-of-processing effect for verbal stimuli, and it may also operate for facial memory. Mäntylä (1997) found that participants were more likely to remember photos of faces if they had been instructed to pay attention to the *distinctions* between the faces.

Bloom and Mudd (1991) provided a second explanation. Their research demonstrated that people who had been instructed to judge whether a person was honest looked at the faces for a long time and made many eye movements. These measures were substantially reduced for people who had been instructed to judge whether a person was male or female. Deeper processing apparently leads to encoding a greater number of features, and therefore to superior recall. Notice that this explanation resembles the elaboration explanation proposed for verbal material (Craik & Lockhart, 1986).

In general, then, a deep level of processing is an effective way of enhancing recall for both verbal and visual material. In the next section, however, we'll note an important exception to this principle.

The Effects of Context: Encoding Specificity

Does this scenario sound familiar? You are in the bedroom and realize that you need something from the kitchen. Once you arrive in the kitchen, however, you have no idea why you made the trip. Without the context in which you encoded the item you wanted, you cannot retrieve this memory. You return to the bedroom, which is rich with contextual cues, and you immediately remember what you wanted. Similarly, an isolated question on an exam may look completely unfamiliar, although you would have remembered the answer in the appropriate context.

These examples illustrate the **encoding specificity principle,** which states that recall is better if the retrieval context is similar to the encoding context (Brown & Craik, 2000; Tulving, 1983). In contrast, forgetting often occurs when the two contexts do not match. Two other, similar terms for the encoding specificity principle are **context-dependent memory** and **transfer-appropriate processing** (Roediger & Guynn, 1996). Let's now consider this topic of encoding specificity in more detail. We'll begin with some representative research, and then we'll see how the research forces us to modify our earlier conclusions about levels of processing.

Research on Encoding Specificity. In a representative study, Geiselman and Glenny (1977) presented words visually to the participants in their experiment. The participants were asked to imagine each of the words as being spoken by a familiar person; some were instructed to imagine a female voice, and others were instructed to imagine a male voice. Later, the researchers tested recognition by having either a male or a female speaker say each word; the participants indicated whether each word was old or new. For some people, the gender of the speaker matched the gender of the imagined voice; others had a mismatch between the encoding context and the retrieval context. As Figure 5.1 illustrates, recognition was substantially more likely when the contexts matched. This study also illustrates that "context" is not limited to physical locations; context can include other cues present during encoding and recall, such as a speaker's voice.

Everyone reading this book can readily recall real-life examples of the encoding specificity principle. Psychologists have also explained why context effects help us to function competently in our daily lives. Basically, we often forget material associated with contexts other than our present context. After all, we don't need to remember numerous details that might have been important in a previous setting but are no longer relevant at the present time (Bjork & Bjork, 1988). For instance, you don't want your memory to be cluttered with details about your third-grade classroom or the senior trip you took in high school.

Context effects are easy to demonstrate in real life, but they are sometimes difficult to demonstrate in the laboratory (e.g., Roediger & Guynn, 1996). For example, why should context effects be important in one experiment (e.g., Smith et al., 1978), and yet have absolutely no influence in a highly similar replication experiment (e.g., Bjork & Richardson-Klavehn, 1987)? Let's consider two potential explanations.

1. *Different kinds of memory tasks.* One explanation for the discrepancy between real life and the laboratory is that the two situations typically test different kinds of memory (Roediger & Guynn, 1996). To explore this point, we need to introduce two important terms: *recall* and *recognition*. When memory researchers test **recall,** the participants must reproduce the items they learned earlier. (For example, can you recall the definition for *elaboration*?) In contrast, when memory researchers test **recognition,** the participants must identify which items had been presented at an earlier time. (For example, did the word *morphology* appear earlier in this chapter?)

FIGURE 5.1

FIGURE 5.1

Percentage of Participants Who Correctly Recognized a Word, as a Function of Encoding Condition and Retrieval Condition.

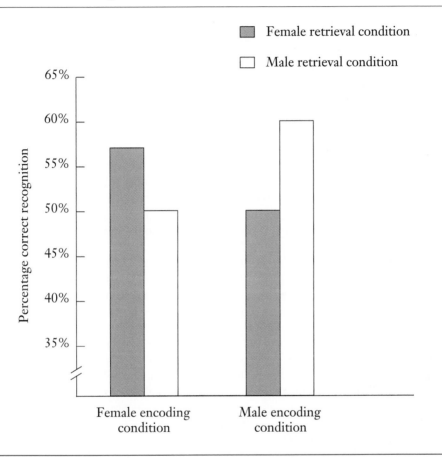

Source: Based on Geiselman & Glenny, 1977.

Let's return to encoding specificity. Our real-life examples typically describe a situation in which we *recall* an earlier experience, and that experience occurred many years earlier (Roediger & Guynn, 1996). Encoding specificity is typically strong in these real-life, long-delay situations. For example, when I smell a particular flower called verbena, I am instantly transported back to a childhood scene in my grandmother's garden. I specifically recall walking through the garden with my cousins, an experience that happened decades ago. In contrast, the laboratory research focuses on *recognition*—"Did this word appear on the list you saw earlier?" Furthermore, that list was typically presented less than an hour earlier. Encoding specificity is typically weak in these laboratory, short-delay situations.

In summary, then, the encoding-specificity effect is most likely to occur in memory tasks that (a) test recall; (b) use real-life incidents; and (c) examine events that happened long ago.

2. *Physical versus mental context.* In their studies on encoding specificity, researchers often manipulate the *physical* context in which material is encoded and retrieved. However, physical context may not be as important as *mental* context. It is possible that physical details—such as the characteristics of the room—are relatively trivial in determining whether the encoding context matches the retrieval context. Instead, as Eich (1995a) points out, "How well information transfers from one environment to another depends on how similar the environments feel, rather than on how similar they look" (p. 293).

Eich's comment should remind you of the study by Foley and her colleagues (1999), in which participants' mental activities often did not match the researchers' instructions. (See pp. 133 to 134, earlier in this chapter.) Researchers need to look beyond the variables that they think they are manipulating, and pay attention to the processes going on inside the participant's head. This importance of mental activities is also crucial to the next topic, which brings us back to the level-of-processing issue.

Levels of Processing and Encoding Specificity. Craik and Lockhart's (1972) original description of the levels-of-processing approach emphasized encoding, or how items are placed into memory. It did not mention details about retrieval, or how items are recovered from memory. In a later paper, Craik and another colleague proposed that people recall more material if the retrieval conditions match the encoding conditions (Moscovitch & Craik, 1976). Thus, encoding specificity can override level of processing. In fact, shallow processing can be more effective than deep processing when the retrieval task emphasizes superficial information. Notice that this point is *not* consistent with the original formulation of the levels-of-processing approach.

Let's consider a study that emphasizes the importance of the similarity between encoding and retrieval conditions (Bransford et al., 1979). Suppose that you performed the various encoding tasks in Demonstration 5.1 on page 130. Imagine, however, that you were then tested in terms of rhyming patterns, rather than in terms of recalling the words on that list. For example, you might be asked, "Was there a word on the list that rhymed with *toy*?" People usually perform better on this rhyming test if they had originally performed the shallow-encoding task (rhyming), rather than the deep-encoding task (meaning).

This area of research demonstrates that deep semantic processing may not be ideal unless the retrieval conditions also emphasize these deeper, more meaningful features (Roediger & Guynn, 1996). This research also emphasizes that memory often requires problem solving: To determine how to store some information, you'll need to figure out the characteristics of the retrieval task (Phillips, 1995). For example, how would you study the material in this chapter if you knew you would be tested on your *recall* (e.g., by answering essay questions like those at the end of each chapter)? Would your study techniques be different if you were tested on your *recognition* (e.g., by having to answer multiple-choice questions)?

In summary, then, memory is sometimes enhanced when the retrieval context resembles the encoding context. However, the benefits of encoding specificity are more likely when items are tested by recall (rather than recognition) and when the items have been in memory for a long time. In addition, encoding specificity depends on mental context more than physical context. Furthermore, we saw that encoding specificity can modify the level-of-processing effect; in some cases, the match between encoding and retrieval is even more important than deep processing. As you'll see next, context is also relevant when we examine how emotions and mood can influence memory.

IN DEPTH

Emotions, Mood, and Memory

In everyday speech, we often use the terms *emotion* and *mood* interchangeably, and the terms are somewhat similar. However, psychologists define **emotion** as a reaction to a specific stimulus. In contrast, **mood** refers to a more general, long-lasting experience (Bower & Forgas, 2000). For example, you may have a negative emotional reaction to the stale slice of pizza you just consumed, whereas you may be in a relatively positive mood today. Before you read further, try Demonstration 5.2.

Demonstration 5.2

Lists of Items

Take out a piece of paper and make three columns of numbers from 1 to 10. For the first set of numbers, list 10 colors in any order you wish. For the next set, list 10 names of vegetables. Finally, list 10 students from your college whom you know reasonably well.

Now arrange each of the three lists in alphabetical order on a separate piece of paper, and set the original lists aside. Rank each item in the alphabetized list, with respect to the other members of the list. For example, give your favorite color a rank of 1 and your least favorite color a rank of 10. Finally, transfer each of those ranks back to the original list. At this point, each of the 10 items on all three original lists should now have a rank next to it. Save your results; we will discuss them later in this section.

Cognitive psychologists acknowledge that emotion and mood can influence our cognitive processes. In this In Depth discussion, we'll consider three ways in which emotion and mood can affect our memory: (1) We typically remember pleasant stimuli more accurately than other stimuli; (2) we typically recall material more accurately if our mood matches the emotional nature of the material, an effect called *mood congruence*; and (3) we often recall material more accurately if our mood during encoding matches our mood during retrieval, an effect called *mood-dependent memory*.

Memory for Items Differing in Emotion. In 1978, my coauthor and I proposed that the selective recall of pleasant items is part of a more general *Pollyanna Principle* (Matlin & Stang, 1978). The **Pollyanna Principle** states that pleasant items are usually processed more efficiently and more accurately than less pleasant items. The principle holds true for a wide variety of phenomena in perception, language, and decision making (Matlin, 2004a). However, our focus in this chapter is on long-term memory. Let's consider several ways in which the emotional nature of the stimuli can influence memory.

1. *More accurate recall for pleasant stimuli.* For nearly a century, psychologists have been interested in the way that emotional tone can influence memory (e.g., Hollingworth, 1910; Rychlak, 1994; Thompson et al., 1996). In a typical study, people learn lists of words that are pleasant, neutral, or unpleasant. Then their recall is tested after a delay of several minutes to several months. In a review of the literature, we found that pleasant items are often recalled better than negative items, particularly if the delay is long (Matlin & Stang, 1978). For example, in 39 of the 52 studies that we located on long-term memory, pleasant items were recalled significantly more accurately than unpleasant items. Incidentally, neutral items are usually recalled *least* accurately of all, suggesting that the intensity of an item's emotional tone is also important.

In more recent research, Walker and his colleagues (1997) reported similar findings; people generally recalled the pleasant events from their lives more accurately than the unpleasant events. One potential explanation is that visual imagery is more vivid for pleasant events than for unpleasant events (D'Argembeau et al., 2003). A related finding is that drivers quickly forget their near-accidents; in fact, they remember only 20% of these accidents just 2 weeks later (Chapman & Underwood, 2000).

2. *More accurate recall for neutral stimuli associated with pleasant stimuli.* Media violence is an important issue in North American culture. Surveys suggest that about 60% of television programs depict violence. Furthermore, numerous studies have concluded that media violence has an impact on children's aggression (Bushman & Huesman, 2001; Matlin, 1999; National Television Violence Study, 1997). However, Brad Bushman (1998) examined a different component of media violence: Would people remember commercials less accurately if they were associated with violent material? To answer this question, he recorded 15-minute segments of two films. One film, *Karate Kid III*, showed violent fighting and destruction of property. The other film, *Gorillas in the Mist*, was judged equally exciting by undergraduate students, but it contained no violence. Bushman selected two 30-second advertisements for neutral items, one for laundry detergent and one for glue. These ads were inserted 5 minutes and 10 minutes into each of the two video film clips.

Undergraduate students were randomly assigned to one of the two conditions. Immediately after watching the film clip, the students were asked to recall the two brand names that had been featured in the commercials and to list everything they could recall about the commercials. The results showed significantly better recall—

on both measures—for commercials that had appeared in the nonviolent film. Additional research demonstrates that anger typically reduces memory accuracy (Bushman,1998; Levine & Burgess, 1997).

Individuals who are concerned about societal violence should be interested in Bushman's research because they should use this research in persuading advertisers to place their ads during nonviolent programs. Advertisers obviously want viewers to remember their product's name, as well as information about the product. In light of this research, they should be hesitant to sponsor violent programs.

3. *Faster recall for pleasant stimuli.* Demonstration 5.2 illustrates another aspect of the Pollyanna Principle: When constructing a list of items, we remember pleasant items *prior* to remembering less pleasant items (Matlin, 2004a). Inspect your responses for Demonstration 5.2. Did you list the colors you like (those with ranks of 1, 2, and 3) before you listed the colors you detest (those with ranks of 8, 9, and 10)? Are your favorite vegetables first on the list? My colleagues and I found that when people made lists of fruits, vegetables, and professors, the pleasant items "tumbled out" of memory prior to neutral or unpleasant items (Matlin et al., 1979). For example, the correlation* between an item's pleasantness and its order in the list was +.87 for colors, +.83 for animals, and +.86 for friends. All of these correlations are highly significant.

Matlin and Stang (1978) proposed that pleasant items seem to be stored more accessibly in memory. As a result, they can be recalled quickly and accurately. The Pollyanna Principle is consistent with Theme 3 of this book: Positive information is processed more efficiently than negative information.

4. *Over time, unpleasant memories fade faster.* Richard Walker and his coauthors (1997) asked undergraduate students to record one personal event each day for about 14 weeks and to rate both the pleasantness and the intensity of the event. Three months later, the participants returned, one at a time, for a second session. A researcher read off each event from the previous list, and the student was instructed to rate the current pleasantness of that event. In the analysis of the results, the rating did not change for those events that were originally considered to be neutral. However, the events originally considered to be pleasant were now considered to be slightly less pleasant. In contrast, the events originally considered to be unpleasant were now considered to be much more pleasant. Consistent with the Pollyanna Principle, the change in pleasantness ratings was significantly larger for the unpleasant items than for the pleasant items.

We should note, however, that aspects of the Pollyanna Principle don't apply for people with tendencies toward depression. Walker and his colleagues (2003) conducted the same study with two new groups of students. All the students completed an inventory that assessed tendencies toward depression. Those who did not have depressive tendencies showed the usual trend: Unpleasant events faded more dramatically than pleasant events. However, some students had scores on this inven-

---

*A correlation is a statistical measure of the relationship between two variables, in which .00 represents no relationship and +1.00 represents a strong positive relationship.

tory that indicated they were **dysphoric** (toward the depressed end of the scale). The dysphoric students showed equal fading for unpleasant and pleasant events. In other words, when people at risk for depression look back on their lives, the unpleasant events still remain unpleasant! As you can imagine, this research has important implications for clinical psychologists. Therapists must address a depressed client's interpretation of past events, as well as the current situation.

So far, we have considered how the pleasantness of the stimuli influences memory. As we've seen, pleasant stimuli usually fare better than less pleasant ones: (1) We remember them more accurately; (2) we remember neutral information better when it is associated with the pleasant stimuli; (3) we remember pleasant items sooner than other items; and (4) over time, pleasant memories fade less than unpleasant memories. Let's now see how memory is influenced by the match between your mood and the emotional tone of the stimuli.

Mood Congruence. A second major category of studies about mood and memory is called *mood congruence*. **Mood congruence** means that memory is better when the material to be remembered is congruent with a person's current mood (Ellis & Moore, 1999; Fiedler, 2001; Parrott & Spackman, 2000; Schwarz, 2001). Thus, a person who is in a pleasant mood should remember pleasant material better than unpleasant material, whereas a person in an unpleasant mood should remember unpleasant material better.

One way to examine mood congruence is to compare nondepressed individuals and individuals with tendencies toward depression. Consider, for example, a study by Laura Murray and her colleagues (1999). These researchers located undergraduate students whose scores on two scales of depression allowed them to be categorized as either nondepressed or dysphoric. The participants were instructed to look at a series of 20 positive- and 20 negative-trait words and to press a key to indicate whether or not each word applied to themselves. Later, the participants were asked to recall all the words from the original list. Consistent with previous research, the nondepressed individuals recalled a greater overall percentage of the words than did the dysphoric individuals. As you can see from Table 5.2, the nondepressed students also recalled a significantly greater percentage of positive words than negative words. The dysphoric students recalled a slightly greater percentage of negative words than positive words.

TABLE 5.2

Percentage of Items Recalled, as a Function of Mood and the Nature of the Stimulus.

Mood category	Type of stimulus	
	Positive	Negative
Nondepressed	49%	38%
Dysphoric	35%	39%

Source: Murray et al., 1999.

In these studies about mood congruence, nondepressed people typically recall more positive than negative material. In contrast, depressed people tend to recall more negative material (Ellis & Moore, 1999; Fiedler, 2001; Parrott & Spackman, 2000; Schwarz, 2001). Like the results of the research by Walker and his colleagues (in press), these findings are important for clinical psychologists. If depressed people tend to forget the positive experiences they have had, their depression could increase still further (Schacter, 1999b).

Mood-Dependent Memory. According to the principle of **mood-dependent memory,** you are more likely to remember material if your mood at the time of retrieval matches the mood you were in when you originally learned the material. Unlike all the other research we've discussed about emotion and memory, this research does not focus on the emotional nature of the *stimulus.* Instead, the important variable is whether the mood during encoding *matches* the mood during recall. Notice, then, that mood-dependent memory is one example of the encoding specificity principle, a concept we discussed earlier in this chapter. (See pp. 135 to 138.)

The research on mood-dependent memory is inconsistent (e.g., Balch et al., 1999; Bower & Forgas, 2000; Ellis & Moore, 1999; Forgas, 2001; Parrott & Spackman, 2000). In fact, mood-dependent memory is a much weaker phenomenon than the mood-congruence effect. However, mood-dependent memory is more likely to operate if the stimulus material involves real-life events, rather than material such as sentences constructed by the researchers (Ucros, 1989). Also, mood-dependent memory is more likely to occur when the mood of the participant is intense—for example, strongly negative during both encoding and retrieval (Ryan & Eich, 2000). In contrast, mood-dependent memory is unlikely to operate when the participant's mood is either weakly positive or weakly negative. However, these inconsistent results for mood-dependent memory shouldn't surprise us, because we saw a similar inconsistency with the encoding-specificity effect that it resembles.

⊚ Section Summary: *Encoding in Long-Term Memory*

1. Long-term memory can be subdivided into three categories: episodic memory, semantic memory, and procedural memory; episodic memory is most relevant for the current chapter.

2. The research on levels of processing shows that stimuli are remembered better with deep, meaningful processing, rather than with shallow, sensory processing.

3. With verbal material, deep processing encourages recall because of distinctiveness and elaboration.

4. Research on the self-reference effect demonstrates that memory is greatly improved by relating stimuli to your own personal experience; to obtain a valid assessment of the self-reference effect, the stimuli must be classified in terms

of the participant's actual mental activities, rather than in terms of the experimenter's instructions.

5. The self-reference effect works because the self is a rich source of memory ideas and because self-reference increases elaborative rehearsal. In addition, deep levels of processing and self-reference processing are associated with patterns of activation within the prefrontal cortex.

6. For remembering faces, deep processing encourages distinctiveness, elaboration, and holistic encoding strategies.

7. The encoding-specificity effect is most likely to operate when memory is tested by recall, when real-life events are studied, when the original event happened long ago, and when mental context is emphasized. In addition, encoding specificity can modify the depth-of-processing effect.

8. Research on the influence of emotions and mood on memory shows that (a) people generally recall pleasant stimuli more accurately than unpleasant stimuli; (b) recall is decreased for information presented during a violent television program; (c) pleasant stimuli are recalled faster than unpleasant stimuli; and (d) unpleasant memories fade faster than pleasant memories

9. Memory is more accurate when the material to be learned is congruent with a person's current mood (mood congruence). Also, in many cases, memory is more accurate when the mood during retrieval matches the mood during encoding (mood-dependent memory).

RETRIEVAL IN LONG-TERM MEMORY

So far in this chapter, we have emphasized encoding processes. We examined how your long-term memory could be influenced by the level of processing that you used in encoding the material, by the context at the time of encoding, and by emotional and mood-related factors during encoding. Naturally, we cannot discuss encoding without also mentioning retrieval; to examine how effectively you encoded some information, psychologists need to test how accurately you can retrieve the information. However, retrieval was relatively unimportant in the preceding section of this chapter. Now we'll move retrieval to the center stage. Let's first consider two categories of retrieval tasks, called explicit and implicit memory tasks. Then we'll focus on the two extremes of memory ability by exploring the topics of amnesia and memory expertise.

Throughout this section, keep Theme 1 in mind; our cognitive processes are active, rather than passive. Yes, sometimes we retrieve material from memory in an effortless fashion; you see a friend, and her name seems to spontaneously appear in your memory. Other times, retrieval requires hard work! For example, you might try to recover someone's name by strategically re-creating the context in which you met this person (Koriat, 2000; Roediger, 2000). Who else was present, how long ago was it, and where did this event take place?

Explicit Versus Implicit Memory Tasks

Imagine this scene: A young woman is walking aimlessly down the street, and she is eventually picked up by the police. She seems to be suffering from an extreme form of amnesia, because she has lost all memory of who she is. Unfortunately, she is carrying no identification. Then the police have a breakthrough idea—they ask her to begin dialing phone numbers. As it turns out, she dials her mother's number—though she is not aware whose number she is dialing.

Daniel Schacter tells this story to illustrate the difference between explicit and implicit measures of memory (as cited in Adler, 1991). This difference can be demonstrated for people with normal memory as well as for those who have amnesia. Let us clarify the basic concepts of this distinction and then look at some research.

⊚ Demonstration 5.3

Explicit and Implicit Memory Tasks

Take out a piece of paper. Then read the following list of words:

> picture   commerce   motion   village   vessel
> window   number   horse   custom   amount
> fellow   advice   dozen   flower   kitchen   bookstore

Now cover up that list for the remainder of the demonstration. Take a break for a few minutes and then try the following tasks:

A. *Explicit Memory Tasks*

1. *Recall:* On the piece of paper, write down as many of those words as you can recall.
2. *Recognition:* From the list below, circle the words that appeared on the original list:

> woodpile   fellow   leaflet   fitness   number   butter
> motion   table   people   dozen   napkin
> picture   kitchen   bookstore   horse   advice

B. *Implicit Memory Tasks*

1. *Word completion:* From the word fragments below, provide an appropriate, complete word. You may choose any word you wish.

(continued)

---

⑨ Demonstration 5.3

Explicit and Implicit Memory Tasks   *(continued)*

v_s_e_ l_t_e_ v_l_a_e p_a_t_c m_t_o_ m_n_a_
n_t_b_o_ c_m_e_c_ a_v_c_ t_b_e_ f_o_e_ c_r_o_
h_m_w_r_ b_o_s_o_e

2. *Repetition priming:* Perform the following tasks:

- Name three rooms in a typical house.
- Name three different kinds of animals.
- Name three different kinds of stores.

Definitions and Examples. Demonstration 5.3 provides two examples of explicit memory tasks and two examples of implicit memory tasks. Try these examples before you read further.

On an **explicit memory task,** the researcher instructs participants to remember information; the participants are conscious that their memory is being tested, and the test requires intentional retrieval of previously learned information. Almost all the research we have discussed in Chapters 4 and 5 has used explicit memory tests. The most common explicit memory test is *recall*; as we discussed in the preceding section, a recall test requires the participant to reproduce items that were learned earlier. Another explicit memory test is *recognition*, in which the participant must identify which items on a list had been presented at an earlier time.

In contrast, on an **implicit memory task,** people see the material (usually a series of words or pictures); later, during the test phase, people are instructed to complete a cognitive task that does not directly ask for recall or recognition (Lockhart, 2000; Roediger, Marsh, & Lee, 2002). For example, in part B1 of Demonstration 5.3, you filled in the blanks in several words. Previous experience with the material—in this case, the words at the beginning of the demonstration—facilitated your performance on the task (Schacter & Buckner, 1998).

An implicit memory task typically seems unrelated to any previous material that participants had learned. In fact, words such as *remember* or *recall* are not even mentioned in the instructions. For example, in Schacter's anecdote about the woman with amnesia, dialing a phone number was a test of implicit memory. Implicit memory shows the effects of previous experience that creep out in our ongoing behavior, when we are not making a conscious effort to recall the past (Kihlstrom, 1999; Roediger, Marsh, & Lee, 2002).

Researchers have devised numerous measures of implicit memory (Toth, 2000). You tried two of these in Demonstration 5.3. For example, in Task B1, if the words in the original list were stored in your memory, you would be able to complete those words (for example, *commerce* and *village*) faster than words in Task B1 that had not been on the list (for example, *letter* and *plastic*). Furthermore, you would be likely to supply those words on a repetition priming task. In a **repetition priming task,** recent exposure to a word increases the likelihood that this word will later come to mind, when you are given a cue that could evoke many different words. For example, on Task B2, you were likely to supply the words *kitchen, horse,* and *bookstore*—words you had seen at the beginning of the demonstration. In contrast, you were less likely to supply words you had not seen, such as *dining room, cow,* and *drugstore.*

During the last 20 years, implicit memory has become a popular topic in research on memory (Roediger, 2000; Schacter, 1999a). Psychologists are intrigued by paradoxes, and paradoxes are common when we compare performance on explicit and implicit memory tasks. For example, in some studies, amnesic patients perform very poorly on explicit memory tasks that require either recall or recognition. However, they score well on implicit memory tasks that simply require them to complete a word or carry out some task (Schacter, 1998). Later in this section, we'll examine some of the research on implicit memory in amnesic patients. For now, let's look at the research with normal individuals.

Research with Normal Adults. A variety of studies demonstrate that normal adults often cannot remember stimuli when they are tested on an explicit memory task, but they do remember the stimuli when tested on an implicit memory task. For example, DeSchepper and Treisman (1996) showed undergraduates a series of meaningless shapes that resembled pieces in a jigsaw puzzle. As you can imagine, an explicit memory test showed that they quickly forgot these shapes. However, an implicit memory test showed that they had some memory for the shapes, even a month after they had originally seen them—and even when 200 other shapes had been presented during the interval between encoding and retrieval.

Another intriguing finding focuses on patients who have been anesthetized during surgery. These patients show no evidence of memory for information transmitted under anesthesia (for example, a conversation between the surgeon and the anesthesiologist) when memory is assessed with explicit memory tests. However, they do remember a substantial amount of information when memory is assessed with implicit memory tests (Kihlstrom et al., 1990; Sebel et al., 1993).

Some of the studies on explicit and implicit memory illustrate a pattern that researchers call a dissociation. A **dissociation** occurs when a variable has large effects on Test A, but little or no effects on Test B; a dissociation also occurs when a variable has one kind of effect if measured by Test A, and exactly the opposite effect if measured by Test B (Neath, 1998). The term *dissociation* is similar to the concept of a statistical interaction, a term that might sound familiar if you've taken a course in statistics.

Let's consider an illustration of a dissociation based on the research on the level-of-processing effect. As you know, the typical pattern is that people recall more words if they have used deep levels of processing to encode them. For example, scores are higher on an explicit memory test if participants had used semantic encoding rather than perceptual encoding. On an *implicit* memory test, however, semantic and perceptual encoding may produce similar memory scores, or people may even score lower if they had used semantic encoding (e.g., Jones, 1999; Richardson-Klavehn & Gardiner, 1998). Notice that these results fit the definition of a dissociation because depth of processing has a large effect on memory scores on Test A (an explicit memory task), but depth of processing has no effect on Test B (an implicit memory task).

We need to emphasize, however, that some variables have the same effect on both explicit and implicit memory. For example, in Chapter 4 we discussed proactive interference. **Proactive interference** means that people have trouble learning new material because previously learned material keeps interfering with new learning. Researchers have demonstrated that proactive interference operates on both explicit and implicit memory tasks (Lustig & Hasher, 2001a, 2001b). In both cases, memory for new material is less accurate because the earlier material keeps interfering.

The research on implicit memory illustrates that people often know more than they can reveal in actual recall. As a result, this research has potential implications for applied areas such as education, clinical psychology, and advertising (Jones, 1999).

Individuals with Amnesia

In this section and the next, we'll consider individuals whose memory abilities are unusual. We'll first discuss people with amnesia; then we'll examine the impressive performance of memory experts.

One form of amnesia is **retrograde amnesia,** or loss of memory for events that occurred *prior* to brain damage (Kalat, 2001). For example, a woman known by the initials L.T. cannot recall events in her life that happened prior to an accident that injured her brain. However, her memory is normal for events after the injury (Conway & Fthenaki, 2000; Riccio et al., 2003).

The other form of amnesia is **anterograde amnesia,** or loss of memory for events that have occurred *after* brain damage (Kalat, 2001). For several decades, researchers have studied a man with amnesia who is known only by his initials, H.M. (James & MacKay, 2001; Milner, 1966). H.M. had such serious epilepsy that neurosurgeons operated on his brain. Specifically, in an operation in 1953, they removed a portion of his temporal lobe region and his hippocampus (a structure that is important in many learning and memory tasks).

The operation successfully cured H.M.'s epilepsy, but it left him with a severe kind of memory loss. H.M. can accurately recall events that occurred before his surgery. However, he cannot learn or retain new information. For example, in 1980, he moved to a nursing home. Four years later, he still could not describe where he lived. For many years after the operation, he persisted in reporting that the year was 1953 (Corkin, 1984).

The research demonstrates that people with anterograde amnesia often recall almost nothing on tests of explicit memory such as recall or recognition. That is, they do poorly when asked to *consciously* remember an event that happened after they developed amnesia. Interestingly, however, they usually perform quite accurately on tests of implicit memory (Schacter & Badgaiyan, 2001; Weiskrantz, 2000).

Let's consider the pioneering work conducted by Elizabeth Warrington and Lawrence Weiskrantz (1970). These researchers presented some English words to amnesic individuals and then gave them several recall and recognition tasks. Compared to normal control-group participants, the amnesics performed much poorer on both of these explicit memory tasks. So far, then, the results are not surprising.

Warrington and Weiskrantz (1970) also administered two implicit memory tasks. The tasks were presented as word-guessing games, though they actually assessed memory for the words shown earlier. In one task, the previously presented English words were shown in a mutilated form that was difficult to read. Participants were told to guess which word was represented. Amazingly, the implicit memory scores of the amnesics and the control-group participants were virtually identical. Both groups correctly supplied the words from the previous list for about 45% of the mutilated stimuli.

In the second implicit memory task, people saw the first few letters of a word, and they were instructed to produce the first word that came to mind. On this task, both groups correctly supplied the words from the previous list for about 65% of the word stems. These results have been replicated many times since the original research, with both visual and auditory tasks (e.g., Bower, 1998; Roediger et al., 1994; Schacter et al., 1994).

Notice that the research by Warrington and Weiskrantz (1970) is another good example of a dissociation. As we noted, a dissociation occurs when a variable has a large effect on one kind of test, but little or no effect on another kind of test. In this case, the dissociation was evident because the variable of memory status (amnesic versus control) had a major effect when measured by explicit memory tests, but this same variable had no effect when measured by implicit memory tests.

The research on individuals with amnesia reminds us that memory is an extremely complex cognitive process. Specifically, people who apparently remember nothing when their memory is tested on a recall task can actually perform quite well when memory is measured in a different fashion.

Expertise

In contrast to research about amnesia, researchers who study expertise concentrate on people with impressively strong memory abilities. **Expertise** is defined as consistently superior performance on a set of tasks relevant for a specific skill or topic, which is achieved by deliberate practice over a period of at least 10 years (Ericsson & Lehmann, 1996). You may recall that we introduced the topic of expertise in Chapter 4. In connection with working memory, we noted that memory experts seem to develop a special long-term working memory related to their area of expertise. By storing a stable retrieval strategy in working memory, they can easily access that long-term working memory (Ericsson & Delaney, 1998, 1999).

Our first topic in this discussion illustrates that people's expertise is context-specific. Next we'll examine some of the ways in which memory experts and novices differ. We'll then consider the memory skills displayed by professional actors as they learn their parts for a play. Our final topic—indirectly related to expertise—explores how people can identify individuals from their own ethnic background more accurately than individuals from another ethnic group.

The Context-Specific Nature of Expertise. Researchers have studied memory experts in numerous areas, such as chess, sports, ballet, maps, and musical notation. In general, researchers have found a strong positive correlation between knowledge about an area and memory performance in that area (Vicente & Wang, 1998).

Interestingly, however, people who are expert in one area seldom display outstanding *general* memory skills (Ericsson & Pennington, 1993; Kimball & Holyoak,

2000; Wilding & Valentine, 1997). For instance, chess masters are outstanding in their memory for chess positions, but they do not differ from nonexperts in their basic cognitive and perceptual abilities (Cranberg & Albert, 1988). Furthermore, memory experts typically do not receive exceptional scores on tests of intelligence (Wilding & Valentine, 1997). For example, men who are experts in remembering information at the horse races do not score especially high on standard IQ tests. In fact, one horse race expert had an eighth-grade education and an IQ of 92 (Ceci & Liker, 1986). Incidentally, in Chapter 11, we'll see that memory expertise for specific areas of knowledge helps people solve problems in these areas.

How Do Experts and Novices Differ? From the information we've discussed, as well as from other resources, we know that memory experts have several advantages over nonexperts (Ericsson & Kintsch, 1995; Ericsson & Lehmann, 1996; Ericsson & Pennington, 1993; Kimball & Holyoak, 2000; Noice, 1992; Roediger, Marsh, & Lee, 2002; Simon & Gobet, 2000; Wilding & Valentine, 1997). Let's consider these advantages:

1. As we noted, experts possess a well-organized, carefully learned knowledge structure. This structure may be stored in long-term working memory so that it can be easily accessed from working memory. For instance, chess players store a number of common patterns that they can quickly access.
2. Experts typically have more vivid visual images for the items they must recall.
3. Experts are more likely to reorganize the new material they must recall, forming meaningful chunks that group related material together.
4. Experts rehearse in a different fashion. For example, an actor may rehearse his or her lines by focusing on words that are likely to trigger recall.
5. Experts are better at reconstructing missing portions of information from material that is partially remembered.

Throughout this book, we have emphasized that our cognitive processes are active, efficient, and accurate (Themes 1 and 2). These cognitive processes also employ top-down as well as bottom-up strategies (Theme 5). As we can see in the foregoing list, these characteristics are especially well developed for someone with memory expertise in a given area. Let's now consider how the topic of expertise is relevant in the strategies of professional actors, as well as how own-race bias is relevant to the topic of expertise.

Professional Actors. Have you ever watched an actor in a play, delivering an entire monologue flawlessly . . . and felt embarrassed that you can't even remember the first verse of "The Star-Spangled Banner" or "O Canada"? Professional actors specifically avoid rote memorization when learning a new script (Noice, 1992). Instead, they read the script numerous times, trying to determine the motivation for each line. As one actor commented about memorization strategies, "What was the impulse that created the thought that created the words?" (Noice, 1992, p. 421).

In addition, professional actors report that they use effortful, deep levels of processing (Noice & Noice, 1997a). Furthermore, when memorizing a section of dialogue, they try to visualize the person with whom they are talking. They also emphasize other principles we've discussed in this chapter, such as mood congruence, encoding specificity, and the self-reference effect (Noice & Noice, 1997b). As a result, these actors' recall is highly accurate, even several years after they performed the role (Noice & Noice, 2002). In summary, these actors gained their expertise by using many of the same memory-improvement devices that psychologists have identified in their research.

Own-Race Bias. The information on expertise has a practical application for eyewitness testimony, a topic we will examine more thoroughly later in the chapter. Specifically, people are generally more accurate in identifying members of their own ethnic group than members of another ethnic group, a phenomenon called **own-race bias** (Ng & Lindsay, 1994; O'Toole et al., 1994). This effect is also known as the *other-race effect* or the *cross-race effect*. Basically, people develop expertise for the facial features of the ethnic group with whom they typically interact. For example, Van Wallendael and Kuhn (1997) found that Black students rate Black faces as more distinctive than European American faces; European American students rate European American faces as more distinctive than Black faces.

Reviews of the literature show that both Black and European American individuals are substantially more accurate in recognizing faces of people of their own ethnic group (Anthony et al., 1992; MacLin & Malpass, 2001; Wright et al., 2003). Similar findings are reported for face recognition in European American and Asian individuals (Ng & Lindsay, 1994).

We would expect to find that own-race bias decreases somewhat when people have greater contact with members of other ethnic groups. Some studies do report greater accuracy when people have had this kind of extensive contact (Brigham & Malpass, 1985; Chance & Goldstein, 1996). In other studies, the findings are unclear (Ng & Lindsay, 1994; Wright et al., 2003). Under ideal circumstances, though, we might expect that European American college students with many Black friends will develop expertise in recognizing the facial features of Black individuals.

Researchers are beginning to explore expertise in social categories other than ethnicity. For example, Anastasi and Rhodes (2003) studied younger-adult and older-adult participants. They found that participants from these two age groups are most accurate in identifying people in their own group. In the next section, we will explore several additional factors that influence accuracy in identifying faces.

🌀 **Section Summary:** *Retrieval in Long-Term Memory*

1. Explicit memory tasks instruct participants to recall or recognize information, whereas implicit memory tasks ask participants to perform a cognitive task, such as completing a word that has missing letters.

2. Research shows that adults may remember meaningless shapes a month after viewing them if memory is measured by an implicit memory task, even when an explicit memory task shows that the shapes have been forgotten. Research also indicates that depth of processing has no impact on an implicit memory task, even though it has a major effect on an explicit memory task.

3. Individuals with anterograde amnesia often recall almost nothing on tests of explicit memory; however, on tests of implicit memory, they can perform as accurately as people without brain damage.

4. Expertise has an important effect on long-term memory, although expertise is context-specific. Research on memory expertise shows that experts are superior to novices with respect to their well-organized knowledge structure, vivid visual images, reorganizing material during learning, rehearsal strategies, and reconstruction. Professional actors acquire their memory expertise by using effortful, deep levels of processing. The own-race bias is related to the research on expertise.

AUTOBIOGRAPHICAL MEMORY

As we noted at the beginning of the chapter, autobiographical memory is memory for events and issues related to yourself. Autobiographical memory usually includes a verbal narrative; it may also include imagery about the events, emotional reactions, and procedural information (Roediger, Marsh, & Lee, 2002; Rubin, 1996). In general, the research in this area examines recall for naturally occurring events that happen outside the laboratory. Your autobiographical memory is a vital part of your identity, shaping your personal history and your self-concept (Bluck & Habermas, 2001; Pasupathi, 2001).

The previous two sections in this chapter focused on encoding and retrieval in long-term memory, and they primarily examined laboratory research. In general, the dependent variable in these studies is the number of items correctly recalled—a *quantity*-oriented approach to memory (Koriat et al., 2000). In contrast, in autobiographical memory, the dependent variable is memory *accuracy*; does your recall match the actual events that happened, or does it distort the events? Therefore, autobiographical memory usually focuses on the correspondence between the actual event and an individual's memory for that event. We need to mention, incidentally, that autobiographic memory does not refer to a category of memory, such as episodic or semantic memory. Instead, it represents a particular approach to studying memory (Roediger, Marsh, & Lee, 2002).

The studies of autobiographical memory are typically high in ecological validity (Eichenbaum, 1997; Koriat & Goldsmith, 1996; Neisser & Libby, 2000). As we noted in Chapter 1, a study has **ecological validity** if the conditions in which the research is conducted are similar to the natural setting to which the results will be applied.

Interest in autobiographical memory has grown rapidly during the last 25 years. A glance through some of the recent studies in this area suggests the wide variety of topics within autobiographical memory: estimating the dates of personal events and academic lectures (Burt et al., 1998; Thompson et al., 1996); immigrant Latinas/os recalling their life stories in both English and Spanish (Schrauf & Rubin, 2001); older adults describing themes in their life stories (Bluck & Habermas, 2001; Pasupathi, 2001); college graduates remembering grades from college courses (Bahrick et al., 1993); people recalling the most momentous events of their lives (Pillemer, 1998); memory for the events of a Thanksgiving dinner (Friedman & deWinstanley, 1998); and brain-imaging studies of autobiographical memory (Conway, 2001; Conway & Pleydell-Pearce, 2000; Conway et al., 2000).

This section on autobiographical memory first examines especially vivid memories, and then it shows how our personal memories can be shaped to become more consistent with our current viewpoints. We'll also see what kinds of errors occur when we try to remember where and when we learned certain information. The final topics focus on eyewitness testimony, a topic with obvious applications in the courtroom.

Several important themes are interwoven throughout this material on autobiographical memory:

1. Although we sometimes make errors, memory is typically accurate across many different situations (Theme 2). In a representative study on memory accuracy, Howes and Katz (1992) found that middle-aged adults showed accurate recall for public events 98% of the time.

2. When people do make mistakes, they generally concern peripheral details and specific information about commonplace events, rather than central information about important events (Sutherland & Hayne, 2001). In fact, it's usually helpful *not* to remember numerous small details (Schacter, 2001).

3. Our memories often blend together information; we actively construct a memory at the time of retrieval (Kelley & Jacoby, 2000; Koriat, 2000). Notice that this constructive process is consistent with Theme 1: Our cognitive processes are typically active, rather than passive.

Flashbulb Memories

At some point in the near future, try Demonstration 5.4. This demonstration illustrates the so-called flashbulb-memory effect. **Flashbulb memory** is your memory for the situation in which you first learned of a very surprising and emotionally arousing event (Brown & Kulik, 1977).

One of my clearest flashbulb memories, like many of my generation, is of learning that President John Kennedy had been shot. I was a sophomore at Stanford University, just ready for a midday class in German. As I recall, I had entered the classroom from the right, and I was just about to sit down at a long table on the right-hand side of the room. The sun was streaming in from the left. Only one other person was seated in the classroom, a blond fellow named Dewey. He turned around and

---

⑤ Demonstration 5.4

Flashbulb Memory

Ask several acquaintances whether they can identify any memories of a very surprising event. Tell them, for example, that many people believe that they can recall—in vivid detail—the circumstances in which they learned about the death of President Kennedy, the 1999 shootings at Columbine High School, or the September 11, 2001, terrorist attacks.

Also tell them that other vivid memories focus on more personal important events. Ask them to tell you about one or more memories, particularly noting any small details that they recall.

---

said, "Did you hear that President Kennedy has been shot?" I also recall my reaction and the reactions of others as they entered the room.

President Kennedy was shot more than 40 years ago, yet trivial details of that news still seem stunningly clear to many people (Neisser & Libby, 2000). You can probably think of personal events in your own life that triggered flashbulb memories, such as the death of a relative, a piece of important good news, or an amazing surprise. Most of us believe that our memory for these events is highly accurate. We'll see, however, that these memories are often less accurate than we believe them to be.

The Classic Research. In the first description of this controversial topic, Roger Brown and James Kulik (1977) pointed out that flashbulb memories are definitely not as accurate as a photograph in which a true flashbulb has been fired. For example, I don't remember what books I was carrying or what Dewey was wearing. Nonetheless, flashbulb memories sometimes include details that are missing from the memory of a neutral event from the same period.

To examine flashbulb memories, Brown and Kulik questioned people to see whether various national events triggered these memories. Six kinds of information were most likely to be listed in these flashbulb memories: the place, the ongoing event that was interrupted by the news, the person who gave them the news, their own feelings, the emotions in others, and the aftermath. (Check the responses to Demonstration 5.4 to see if these items were included in the recall.)

Brown and Kulik concluded that the two main determinants of flashbulb memory are a high level of surprise and a high level of emotional arousal. These authors also proposed that these surprising, arousing events were very likely to be rehearsed, either silently or in conversation. Consequently, the memory of these events is more elaborate than memories of more ordinary, daily experiences.

These vivid memories may capture highly positive as well as tragic events. For example, an Indian friend of mine recalls in detail the circumstances in which Mohandas Gandhi, the nonviolent political leader, spoke to a crowd of people in Gauhati, India.

My friend was only 5 years old at the time, yet he vividly recalls Gandhi who was wearing a white outfit and was accompanied by two women. He can recall that his aunt, who was with him, was wearing a white sari with a gold and red border. He can also distinctly remember how the heat of the day had made him very thirsty.

The Recent Research. Most of the research conducted in recent years has focused on whether flashbulb memories are somehow special. Alternately, do they simply represent the more impressive end of normal memory? For example, Conway showed that British students had very clear, persistent memories for the unexpected resignation of British prime minister Margaret Thatcher (Conway et al., 1994). Conway is one of the strongest supporters of the "pro–flashbulb memory" viewpoint. He argues that true flashbulb memories are most likely to be formed when an event is surprising, important, and emotional, and when that event has important consequences for the individual (Conway, 1995).

However, Conway seems to be in the minority. For example, Neisser and Harsch (1992) found that people made numerous errors in recalling details about the *Challenger* space shuttle disaster; memories for national events like this do not seem to be unusually strong. Indeed, people do claim that their memories for these events are very vivid. They are also confident that these memories are accurate, but in fact their accuracy is far from perfect (Roediger, Marsh, & Lee, 2002; Schooler & Eich, 2000; Shum, 1998).

Some skeptics concede, however, that our memory for an event of national importance may be quite vivid if we directly experienced this event. For example, Ulric Neisser and his colleagues (1996) asked students at two California universities and one Georgia university to describe—several days after the event—their memory for the 1989 Loma Prieta earthquake in California. Their recall was tested again 1½ years later. The California students had almost perfect recall for details such as the activity they were doing at the time of the event. Neisser and his coauthors speculate that these students frequently rehearsed the events by retelling their stories to friends and family members. In contrast, the Georgia students made many errors in reconstructing how they had heard about the earthquake. For instance, one student originally reported that her father had told her about the quake on the telephone. In her recall 1½ years later, she was confident that she had heard the news on the radio.

Talarico and Rubin (2003) studied recall of a national event that is especially vivid for most U.S. students—the terrorist attacks of September 11, 2001. On September 12, the day after the attacks, these researchers asked students at a North Carolina university to report specific details about how they had learned about the attacks. The students also provided similar information for an ordinary event that had occurred at about the same time; this ordinary event served as a control condition for the "flashbulb memory" of the attack. The students were then randomly assigned to one of three recall-testing sessions; some returned to be tested 1 week later, others returned 6 weeks later, and still others returned 32 weeks later. At these recall-testing sessions, Talarico and Rubin asked the students a variety of questions, including the details of their memory for the attack and for the everyday event. These details were checked against the details that had been supplied on September 12, and the researchers counted the number of consistent and inconsistent details.

Figure 5.2 shows the results. The number of details provided on September 12 provides the baseline for the number of consistent details. As you can see, the consistency drops over time for each of the three testing sessions. However, the drop was similar for the terrorist-attack memory and for the everyday memory. The number of inconsistent details could not be assessed until the 1-week recall-testing session. As the figure shows, the number of inconsistent details increases slightly over time for both kinds of memories. Interestingly, however, the students in all conditions reported that they were highly confident that their recall of the terrorist attacks had been accurate.

So, what can we conclude from all this information about flashbulb memories? It's likely that we do not need to invent any special mechanism to explain them. Yes, these memories can sometimes be more accurate than our memories for ordinary events (for example, as they were for the California students in the 1996 study by Neisser and his colleagues). However, these enhanced memories can be explained by standard mechanisms such as rehearsal frequency, distinctiveness, and elaboration (Koriat et al., 2000; Neisser & Libby, 2000; Schmolck et al., 2000; Schooler & Eich, 2000).

FIGURE 5.2

Average Number of Consistent and Inconsistent Details Reported for a Flashbulb Event (September 11, 2001, Attacks) and an Ordinary Event, as a Function of the Passage of Time.

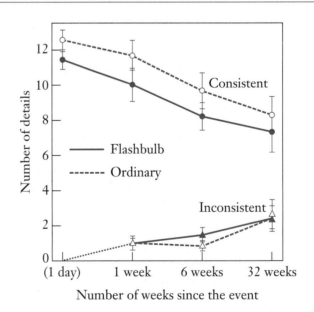

Source: Talarico & Rubin, 2003.

Schemas and Autobiographical Memory

The discussion of flashbulb memories emphasizes memory for unusually important events. In contrast, our discussion of schemas emphasizes memory for common, ordinary events. A **schema** consists of our general knowledge or expectation, which is distilled from our past experiences with an event, an object, or a person (Koriat et al., 2000; Roediger, 1997). Schemas are abstracted from a large number of specific examples of events in our lives, and these schemas summarize the important characteristics contained in the events. For example, you have probably developed a schema for "eating lunch." You tend to sit in a particular area with the same group of people. Your conversation topics may also be reasonably standardized. You also have developed a schema for buying a concert ticket, for the events that occur during the first day of a class, and for purchasing items in a grocery store. You have even developed a schema for yourself.

We use schemas to guide our recall, and Chapter 8 explores in more detail how schemas influence a variety of cognitive processes. However, in the present chapter we'll examine a topic that is especially relevant to autobiographical memory, called the consistency bias.

During recall, we often reveal a **consistency bias;** that is, we tend to exaggerate the consistency between our past and present feelings and beliefs (Levine, 1997; Robinson, 1996; Schacter, 1999b, 2001). As a consequence, our memory of the past may be distorted. For example, suppose that a researcher asks you today to recall how you felt about feminism when you were a high school student. You would tend to construct your previous emotions so that they would be consistent with your current emotions. We generally see ourselves as being consistent and stable (Greenwald et al., 2002). As a result, we underestimate how we have changed throughout our lives. For example, we recall our previous political views and activities as being similar to our current perspective. As Schacter (2001) summarizes the consistency bias, "The way we were depends on the way we are" (p. 139).

The consistency bias suggests that we tell our life stories so that they are consistent with our current schemas about ourselves (Ceballo, 1999). For example, Honig (1997), a historian, interviewed Chicana garment workers who had participated in a strike at a garment manufacturing company in El Paso, Texas. Shortly after the strike, these women viewed the strike as a life-transforming experience that had changed them from timid factory workers into fearless, self-confident strikers.

When Honig returned to interview the women several years later, they recalled that they had *always* been assertive and nonconforming—even prior to the strike. Possibly, they selectively recalled assertive episodes from their pre-strike lives—episodes consistent with their current self-schemas. As Honig argues, these Chicana garment workers are "not inventing nonexistent past experiences, but they are retelling them with the language, perceptions, and mandates of their present" (1997, p. 154). Notice the interdisciplinary nature of research on the consistency bias: It explores the interface of cognitive psychology, personality/social psychology, and history.

In this discussion, we have seen how schemas can influence our memories of the past, so that they seem more similar to our present feelings, beliefs, and actions. Now let's move away from schemas to consider another component of autobiographical memory, called source monitoring.

Source Monitoring

Something like this has certainly happened to you: You borrowed a book from a friend, and you distinctly remember returning it. However, the next day, you find that the book is still on your desk. Apparently, you simply *imagined* returning the book. Or perhaps you are trying to recall where you learned some background information about a movie you saw. Did a friend tell you this information, or did you learn it from a review of the movie? This process of trying to identify the origin of memories and beliefs is called **source monitoring** (Johnson, 1997, 2002). According to Marcia Johnson and Carol Raye (2000), we often try to sort out the source of information in our memory. The clues we use include our schemas and expectations, as well as the nature of the details. Unfortunately, our source monitoring sometimes produces mistakes.

Source monitoring has become a popular topic for research. Consider a study by Marsh and his colleagues (1997), for example. These researchers studied groups of about 20 college students who had been instructed to discuss an open-ended question on a topic such as the ways in which their university could be improved. One week later, the participants returned for a second session. Half of the participants took a recognition test. Specifically, each person saw a list of items and was asked to identify whether each item on the list had been his or her own idea, the idea of someone else in the group, or an idea that had not been generated during the first session. Participants in this condition seldom made source-monitoring mistakes; that is, they seldom claimed that an idea generated by another person had really been their own idea.

The other half of the participants were tested in a different fashion when they returned for the second session. Instead of taking a recognition test, they were given the original open-ended topic, and they were then asked to write down new answers to the question—answers that no one had supplied before. Interestingly, this group of individuals frequently committed source-monitoring errors. That is, they frequently wrote down answers that another person had supplied one week earlier. Apparently, a recognition test forces us to adopt stricter criteria with respect to source monitoring. In contrast, our criteria are more relaxed when we generate ideas.

Other research by Henkel and her colleagues (2000) demonstrated that people falsely remembered seeing events that they didn't actually see (such as a basketball bouncing) when they had both heard the event and visually imagined seeing it. These source-monitoring errors were more common than when people had (1) just heard the event, (2) just visually imagined it, or (3) just imagined it both visually and auditorily. Notice, then, that we seem to accumulate "evidence" for an event from both vision and hearing—and from both perception and imagery. An ideal combination of memories can persuade us that we saw something we never actually saw. Thinking about an imagined event can sometimes increase its vividness until we think it actually happened (Koriat et al., 2000).

For many years, Marcia Johnson (1996, 1998, 2002) has emphasized that source-monitoring errors occur at a societal level, and not just at the individual level. Our government, the media, and corporations must engage in vigorous source monitoring in order to determine which events really happened and which are fictional. Sadly, individuals are seldom aware of source monitoring until they make a source-monitoring error. Similarly, society is seldom aware of source monitoring until we discover that this monitoring has failed.

Ironically, I was writing this paragraph on July 17, 2003, when my copy of *Newsweek* arrived. One item on the front cover caught my eye, "Bush vs. the CIA: The intel mess." The corresponding news article discussed one important reason that had been provided by the United States in order to justify invading Iraq. Specifically, in his State of the Union address earlier in 2003, President Bush had announced that Iraq was attempting to buy uranium from Africa. Six months later, it seems that this claim was based on clearly falsified documents from Niger, a country in west-central Africa. Also, the Central Intelligence Agency claims that their agents had tried to warn the President that the information from Niger was false. Furthermore, the President maintains that his State of the Union address had been cleared by the CIA (Isikoff & Lipper, 2003). Unfortunately, several errors in source monitoring on "the uranium question" probably helped to push the United States into an expensive, destructive war.

Johnson emphasizes that government agencies, the media, and corporation executives need to be meticulous about checking the accuracy of their information. Their goal should be to limit both the frequency and the size of source-monitoring errors.

So far, our discussion of autobiographical memory has explored flashbulb memories, memory schemas, and source monitoring. Now let's consider eyewitness testimony, the most extensively researched topic within the domain of autobiographical memory. As you'll see, some of the errors in eyewitness testimony can be traced to faulty source monitoring: People believe they really witnessed something that had actually been suggested to them in a different situation (Mitchell & Johnson, 2000).

Eyewitness Testimony

In 1981 in Houston, Texas, a man named Gary Graham was a suspect in the murder of Bobby Lambert. In truth, there was no convincing evidence for Graham's guilt—nothing like DNA or fingerprint evidence. When Graham came to trial, jury members were informed that Graham had a pistol *similar* to one that had shot Lambert. They were not told that the Houston police had concluded that it was not the *same* pistol. Eight eyewitnesses had seen the killer near the store, but seven of them were unable to identify Graham as the killer. His fate—the death penalty—was sealed by one woman's eyewitness testimony, even though she testified that she had seen his face at night for about 3 seconds, from a distance of about 30 feet. In addition, the court never heard the testimony of two eyewitnesses whose information contradicted the testimony of that one woman. Graham's case was never reviewed. Was Gary Graham genuinely guilty? We'll never know, because he was executed on June 22, 2000 (Alter, 2000).

Reports like this one have led psychologists to question the reliability of eyewitness testimony. In many criminal cases, the only evidence available for identifying the culprit is the eyewitness testimony provided by people who were present at the crime scene. For example, researchers have conducted analyses of legal cases in which people were mistakenly convicted by juries. These analyses show that mistakes in eyewitness testimony account for more than half of all cases of mistaken conviction (Wells & Bradfield, 1999).

Furthermore, DNA testing became more common during the late 1990s, and it can now be performed on some individuals who had been convicted before the tests were available. Wells and Olson (2003) report on a sample of about 100 imprisoned people whose DNA did not match the biological sample from the scene of the crime; more than 75% had been pronounced guilty because of erroneous eyewitness testimony.

Throughout our discussion of memory, we have emphasized that human memory is reasonably accurate, but it is not flawless. Eyewitness testimonies, like other memories, are generally accurate. However, the reports can contain errors (Wells & Olson, 2003; Wells et al., 2000). When eyewitness testimony is inaccurate, the wrong person may go to jail or—in the worst cases—be put to death.

In our discussion of eyewitness testimony, let's first consider how inaccuracies can arise when people are given misleading information after the event that they had witnessed. Then we'll summarize several factors that can influence the accuracy of eyewitness testimony. Our final topic in this discussion is the recovered memory/false memory debate.

The Misinformation Effect. Errors in eyewitness testimony can often be traced to the misinformation effect. In the **misinformation effect,** people first view an event, and then afterward they are given misleading information about the event; later on, they mistakenly recall the misleading information, rather than the event they actually saw (Zaragoza et al., 1997).

Earlier in the chapter, on page 148, we discussed proactive interference, which means that people have trouble recalling new material because previously learned, old material keeps interfering with new memories. The misinformation effect resembles another kind of interference called retroactive interference. In **retroactive interference,** people have trouble recalling old material because recently learned, new material keeps interfering with old memories. For example, suppose that an eyewitness saw a crime, and then a lawyer supplied some misinformation while asking a question. Later on, the eyewitness may have trouble remembering the events that actually occurred at the scene of the crime, because the new misinformation is interfering.

In the classic experiment on the misinformation effect, Elizabeth Loftus and her coauthors (1978) showed participants a series of slides. In this sequence, a sports car stopped at an intersection, and then it turned and hit a pedestrian. Half the participants saw a slide with a yield sign at the intersection; the other half saw a stop sign.

Twenty minutes to a week after the slides had been shown, the participants answered a questionnaire about the details of the accident. A critical question contained information that was either consistent with a detail in the original slide series, inconsistent with that detail, or neutral (i.e., did not mention the detail). For example, some people who had seen the yield sign were asked, "Did another car pass the red Datsun while it was stopped at the yield sign?" (consistent). Other people were asked, "Did another car pass the red Datsun while it was stopped at the stop sign?" (inconsistent). For still other people, the sign was not mentioned at all (neutral). To answer this question, all participants were shown two slides, one with a stop sign and one with a yield sign. They were asked to select which slide they had previously seen.

As Figure 5.3 shows, people who saw the inconsistent information were much less accurate than people in the other two conditions. Their selections were based on the information in the questionnaire, rather than the original slide. Many studies have replicated the detrimental effects of misleading post-event information (e.g., Cutler & Penrod, 1995; Roediger & McDermott, 2000; Schacter, 2001; Weingardt et al., 1995; Zaragoza et al., 1997). As Belli and Loftus's (1996) review points out, the misinformation effect has convinced people that they have seen nonexistent objects such as hammers, eggs, mustaches, broken glass, and even barns.

FIGURE 5.3

The Effect of Type of Information and Delay on Proportion of Correct Answers.

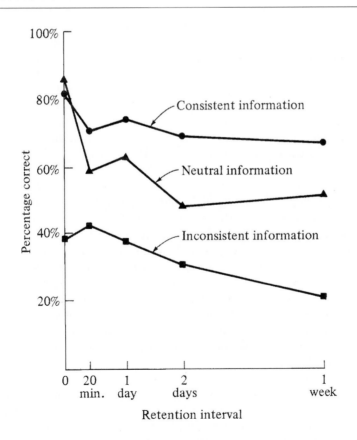

Source: Loftus et al., 1978.

The misinformation effect can be at least partly traced to faulty source monitoring (Schacter et al., 1998). For example, in the study by Loftus and her colleagues (1978), the post-event information in the inconsistent-information condition encouraged people to create a mental image of a stop sign. During testing, they had trouble deciding which of the two images—the stop sign or the yield sign—they had actually seen in the original slide series.

In some studies, participants are asked to judge how confident they are about the accuracy of their eyewitness testimony. Interestingly, in many situations, participants are almost as confident about their misinformation-based memories as they are about their genuinely correct memories (Koriat et al., 2000; Lindsay et al., 1998; Penrod & Cutler, 1999; Wells & Olson, 2003). In other words, people's confidence about their eyewitness testimony is not strongly correlated with the accuracy of their testimony. In fact, the correlations are typically between +.30 and +.50. This research has a practical application for the legal system. Jury members are much more likely to believe a confident eyewitness than an uncertain one (Koriat et al., 2000; Penrod & Cutler, 1999). Unfortunately, however, the research shows that a *confident* eyewitness is not necessarily an *accurate* eyewitness.

The research on the misinformation effect emphasizes the active, constructive nature of memory. As Theme 1 points out, cognitive processes are active, rather than passive. The **constructivist approach** to memory argues that "recollections change as people revise the past to satisfy their present concerns and reflect their current knowledge" (Ross & Buehler, 1994, p. 207). Notice, then, that the consistency bias—discussed on page 157—is one component of the constructivist approach. In short, memory does not consist of a list of facts, all stored in intact form and ready to be replayed like a videotape. Instead, we construct a memory by blending information from a variety of sources (Goldsmith & Koriat, 1998; Hyman & Kleinknecht, 1999).

Factors Affecting the Accuracy of Eyewitness Testimony. As you can imagine, a variety of factors influence whether eyewitness testimony is accurate. We have already mentioned two potential problems in eyewitness testimony: (1) People may create memories that are consistent with their schemas; and (2) people may make errors in source monitoring. Here are several other important variables:

1. *Errors are more likely if the witness's attention has been distracted by something arousing at the time of the event* (Brown, 2003). For example, if a robber is holding a gun, eyewitnesses are likely to focus on the gun rather than the details of the robber's face, a phenomenon called **weapon focus** (Baddeley, 1999; Stanny & Johnson, 2000; Wells & Olson, 2003).

2. *Errors are more likely if the misinformation is plausible.* For instance, in the classic study by Loftus and her colleagues (1978), a stop sign is just as plausible as a yield sign, so participants in that study often made errors. People are also likely to say that an event occurred in their own life (when it really did not) if the event seems consistent with other similar experiences (Hyman & Kleinknecht, 1999; Hyman & Loftus, 2002; Koriat et al., 2000; Pezdek et al., 1997).

3. Errors are more likely if there is social pressure (Roebers & Schneider, 2000; Roediger & McDermott, 2000). People make many errors in eyewitness testimony if they have been pressured to provide a specific answer (for example, "Exactly when did you first see the suspect?"). In contrast, the testimony is more accurate when people are allowed to report in their own words, when they are given sufficient time, and when they are allowed to say, "I don't know" (Koriat et al., 2000; Loftus, 1997; Wells et al., 2000).

4. Errors are more likely if eyewitnesses have been given positive feedback. Wells and Bradfield (1998) cite the case of an eyewitness inspecting a lineup of possible suspects. This eyewitness spent 30 minutes trying to identify the perpetrator, and then

---

⊚ Demonstration 5.5

Remembering Lists of Words

For this demonstration, you must learn and recall two lists of words. Before beginning, take out two pieces of paper. Next, read List 1, then close the book and try to write down as many of the words as possible. Then do the same for List 2. After you have recalled both sets of words, check your accuracy. How many items did you correctly recall?

List 1	List 2
bed	water
rest	stream
awake	lake
tired	Mississippi
dream	boat
wake	tide
snooze	swim
blanket	flow
doze	run
slumber	barge
snore	creek
nap	brook
peace	fish
yawn	bridge
drowsy	winding

hesitantly said, "Number 2?" The police officer administering the lineup then said, "Okay." Months later, she was asked at the trial whether she was certain about the suspect, and she replied, "There was no maybe about it. . . . I was absolutely positive" (p. 360). Of course, factors other than positive feedback may have encouraged her to change her level of confidence. However, Wells and Bradfield (1998, 1999) found that people were much more certain about the accuracy of their decision if they had previously been given positive feedback—even a simple "Okay." Unfortunately, in real-life lineups, the eyewitnesses often hear this kind of encouragement (Wells & Olson, 2003).

The Recovered Memory/False Memory Controversy. If you scan popular magazines such as *Newsweek* or *People,* you seldom come across articles on working memory, the encoding-specificity principle, or source monitoring. However, one topic from cognitive psychology has attracted media attention for many years: the controversy about recovered memory versus false memory. Numerous books on the subject have also been written by cognitive psychologists, therapists, and professionals concerned with legal issues (e.g., Brown et al., 1998; Conway, 1997; Eisen et al., 2002; Freyd & DePrince, 2001; Lynn & McConkey, 1998; Read & Lindsay, 1997; Stein et al., 1997; Williams & Banyard, 1999). A complete discussion of this controversy is beyond the scope of a cognitive psychology textbook, but we will summarize five important components of this issue. Before you read further, however, be sure that you have tried Demonstration 5.5.

1. *The two contrasting positions in the controversy.* Most of the discussion about false memory focuses on childhood sexual abuse. One group of researchers argues that memories can be forgotten and then recovered. According to this **recovered-memory perspective,** some individuals who experienced sexual abuse during childhood managed to forget that memory for many years; at a later time, often prompted by a specific event or by encouragement from a therapist, this presumably forgotten memory comes flooding back into consciousness (Briere, 1997; Brown et al., 1998; Conte, 1999; Dorado, 1999; Schacter, 2001).

A second group of researchers interprets phenomena like this in a different light. We must emphasize that this second group agrees that childhood sexual abuse is a genuine problem that needs to be addressed. However, these people deny the accuracy of many reports about the sudden recovery of early memories. Specifically, the **false-memory perspective** proposes that many of these recovered memories are actually incorrect memories; that is, they are constructed stories about events that never occurred (Hyman & Kleinknecht, 1999; Hyman & Loftus, 2002; Loftus, 2000; Loftus & Guyer, 2002a, 2002b; Pressley & Grossman, 1994; Tavris, 2002).

2. *The potential for memory errors.* Our discussion throughout this section on autobiographical memory should convince you that memory is less than perfect. For example, people are often guided by schemas, rather than their actual recall of an event. In addition, people cannot recall with absolute accuracy whether they performed an action or merely imagined performing it. We also saw that eyewitness testimony can be flawed, especially when misinformation has been provided (Hyman & Loftus, 2002).

Similar problems arise in recalling memories from childhood. For instance, some psychotherapists provide suggestions that could easily be blended with reality to create a false memory (Kihlstrom, 1998). One therapist often approached clients with the following comment: "You know, in my experience, a lot of people who are struggling with many of the same problems you are, have often had some kind of really painful things happen to them as kids—maybe they were beaten or molested. And I wonder if anything like this ever happened to you?" (Forward & Buck, 1988, p. 161). As you can imagine, this statement invites the client to invent a false memory, especially because we noted earlier that people make more errors when they have experienced social pressure (Smith et al., 2003). Hypnosis also encourages false memories (Loftus, 2000; Lynn et al., 1997; McConkey et al., 1998).

We cannot easily determine whether or not a memory of childhood abuse is correct. After all, the situation is far from controlled, and other, independent witnesses can rarely be found (Berliner & Briere, 1999; Koriat et al., 2000; Schooler, 1994). Furthermore, PET scans and other techniques cannot reliably distinguish between correct and incorrect recall of abuse (McNally, 2003; Schacter, 2001). However, psychologists have conducted research and created theories that are designed to address the recovered memory/false memory issue. Let's first consider laboratory research that demonstrates false memory. Then we'll discuss why the situation of sexual abuse during childhood may require a different kind of explanation, rather than one that can explain false memory for emotionally neutral material.

3. *Laboratory evidence of false memory.* Research in the psychology laboratory has clearly demonstrated that people can create a false memory for a word they have not actually seen. In contrast to the real-life recall of sexual abuse, the laboratory research is very straightforward. People are simply asked to remember a list of words they had seen earlier, and their accuracy can be objectively measured. For example, Demonstration 5.5 asked you to memorize and recall two lists of words, and then you checked your accuracy. Take a moment now to check something else. On List 1, did you write down the word *sleep?* Did you write *river* on List 2?

If you check the original lists on page 163, you'll discover that neither *sleep* nor *river* was listed. In research with lists of words like these, Roediger and McDermott (1995) found a false-recall rate of 55%; people created false memories of words that did not appear on the lists. Intrusions are common on this task because each word that *does* appear on a list is commonly associated with a missing word, in this case *sleep* or *river.* This experiment has been replicated many times, using different stimuli and different testing conditions (Brainerd & Reyna, 1998; Dobbins et al., 1998; Roediger & McDermott, 2000; Roediger et al., 2001; Wixted & Stretch, 2000). False-recall rates remain high—and sometimes even increase—if there is a long delay before people are asked to recall the words (Koriat et al., 2000; Toglia et al., 1999). These researchers argue that similar intrusions could occur with respect to childhood memories. People may "recall" events that are related to their actual experiences, but these events never really occurred.

Other studies have demonstrated that laboratory-research participants can construct false memories for events in their own lives that never actually happened (e.g., Hyman et al., 1995; Hyman & Kleinknecht, 1999; Leichtman & Ceci, 1995; Pezdek et al., 1997). For example, Hyman and his colleagues (1995) sent a questionnaire to the parents of college students who would be participating in a study. The questionnaire asked the parents to supply information about several events, such as going on a family vacation, attending a wedding, and going to the hospital. The researchers then interviewed each student individually about several events that really did occur. However, in the course of the interview, they also planted several false memories. For example, a researcher said that the student's parent had described a wedding reception at which the student, then 6 years old, had accidentally bumped into a table and turned the punch bowl over on a parent of the bride. During this first session, students reported that they had no recall of this event.

Interestingly, however, some students gradually began to create a false memory. When asked again about the event during the second session, 18% now "recalled" that this event had actually occurred. During the third session, 25% recalled this false memory—an entire event that did not actually occur (Hyman & Loftus, 2002). Notice, however, that 75% of the students refused to "remember" the specific event.

4. *Arguments for recovered memory.* One problem is that these laboratory studies have little ecological validity with respect to memory for childhood sexual abuse (Freyd & Quina, 2000). Consider the studies on recalling word lists. There's not much similarity between a false memory for a word that never appeared on a list and a false memory of childhood sexual abuse. In addition, the event of spilling a punch bowl is somewhat embarrassing, but it has no sexual content and it could be discussed in public. Students cannot be convinced to create false memories for more embarrassing events, such as having had an enema as a child (Pezdek et al., 1997).

Many people who have been sexually abused as children have continually remembered the incidents, even decades later. However, some people may genuinely not recall the abuse. For example, researchers have studied individuals who had been treated in hospital emergency rooms for childhood sexual abuse, or individuals whose sexual abuse had been documented by the legal system. Still, some of them fail to recall the episode when interviewed as adults (Goodman et al., 2003; Pezdek & Taylor, 2002; Schacter et al., 1999; Schooler, 2001). Indeed, some people can forget about the incident for many years, but they suddenly recall it decades later.

Freyd (1996, 1998) proposes an explanation for these cases of recovered memory. She emphasizes that childhood sexual abuse is genuinely different from relatively innocent episodes such as spilled wedding punch. In particular, Freyd proposes the term **betrayal trauma** to describe how a child may respond adaptively when a trusted parent or caretaker betrays him or her by sexual abuse; the child depends on this adult and must somehow forget about the abuse, to maintain an attachment to the adult. The child must make an active effort to inhibit these painful memories (Anderson, 2001).

5. *Both perspectives are partially correct.* In reality, we must conclude that both the recovered-memory perspective and the false-memory perspective are at least partially correct (Schacter, 1996; Schooler et al., 1997). Indeed, some people have truly experienced childhood sexual abuse, and they may forget about the abuse for many decades until a critical event triggers their recall. In addition, other people may never

have experienced childhood sexual abuse, but a suggestion about abuse creates a false memory of childhood experiences that never really occurred. In still other cases, children can provide accurate testimony about how they have been abused, and they resist "remembering" false information, even years later (Bidrose & Goodman, 2000; Goodman et al., 2001).

We have seen throughout this chapter that human memory is both flexible and complex. This memory process can account for temporarily forgetting events, it can account for the construction of events that never actually happened, and it can also account for accurate memory—even when the events are horrifying.

⑨ Section Summary: *Autobiographical Memory*

1. Research on autobiographical memory typically has high ecological validity; this research shows that our memories are usually accurate, though we may make errors on some details and we may blend together information from different events.

2. Flashbulb memories are rich with information, and we are confident that they are accurate; however, they are typically no more accurate than memories for other important events.

3. Memory schemas encourage us to make errors in recalling events; in addition, we may reveal a consistency bias by exaggerating the similarity between our current self-schema and our previous characteristics.

4. The research on source monitoring shows that we may have difficulty deciding whether something really happened, instead of imagining it, and we may have difficulty deciding where we learned some information.

5. The misinformation effect can occur when misleading information is introduced after a witness has seen an event even though the witness is confident that the memory is accurate.

6. Errors in memory are more likely if the witness's attention had been distracted, if the misinformation is plausible, if social pressure was applied, or if positive feedback was supplied.

7. Both sides of the recovered memory/false memory controversy are at least partially correct; some people may indeed forget about a painful childhood memory, recalling it years later, and some people apparently construct a memory of abuse that never really occurred.

CHAPTER REVIEW QUESTIONS

1. Suppose that you are in charge of creating a public service announcement for television. Choose an issue that is important to you, and point out at least five tips from this chapter that would help you make an especially memorable advertisement. Be sure to include depth of processing as one of the tips.

2. What is encoding specificity? How is encoding specificity related to the topic of mood-dependent memory, and how strong is the evidence for mood-dependent memory?

3. Give several examples of explicit and implicit memory tasks you have performed in the past few days. What is dissociation, and how is it relevant in the research that has been conducted with both normal adults and patients with amnesia?

4. According to one saying, "The more you know, the easier it is to learn." What evidence do we have for this statement, based on the material discussed in this chapter? Be sure to include information on expertise and schemas as part of your answer.

5. Define autobiographical memory and mention several topics that have been studied in this area. How does research in this area differ from more traditional laboratory research? List the advantages and disadvantages of each approach. Point out how Roediger and McDermott's (1995) study on false memory for English words highlights both the advantages and disadvantages of the laboratory approach.

6. Describe how schemas could lead to a distortion in the recall of a flashbulb memory. How might misleading post-event information also influence this recall? In answering the two parts of this question, use the terms *proactive inhibition* and *retroactive inhibition*.

7. The constructivist approach to memory emphasizes that we actively revise our memories in the light of new concerns and new information. How would this approach be relevant if a woman were to develop a false memory about her childhood, and she also shows a strong consistency bias? How would this approach be relevant for other topics in the section on autobiographical memory?

8. Chapter 6 emphasizes methods for improving your memory. However, the present chapter also contains some relevant information and hints about memory improvement. Review Chapter 5, and make a list of suggestions about memory improvement that you could use to help study for your next examination in cognitive psychology.

9. Although this textbook focuses on cognitive psychology, several topics discussed in this chapter are relevant to other areas, such as social psychology, personality psychology, and abnormal psychology. Summarize this research, discussing topics such as the self-reference effect, emotions and memory, and the consistency bias.

10. Researcher Daniel Schacter (2001) wrote a book describing several kinds of memory errors. He argues, however, that these errors are actually by-products of a memory system that usually functions quite well. What textbook theme is related to his argument? Review this chapter and list some of the memory errors people may commit. Explain why each error is a by-product of a memory system that works well in most everyday experiences.

NEW TERMS

working memory
long-term memory
episodic memory
semantic memory
procedural memory
encoding
retrieval
autobiographical memory
levels-of-processing
  approach
depth-of-processing
  approach
distinctiveness
elaboration
self-reference effect
meta-analysis technique
prefrontal cortex

encoding specificity principle
context-dependent memory
transfer-appropriate processing
recall
recognition
emotion
mood
Pollyanna Principle
dysphoric (person)
mood congruence
mood-dependent memory
explicit memory task
implicit memory task
repetition priming task
dissociation
proactive interference
retrograde amnesia

anterograde amnesia
expertise
own-race bias
ecological validity
flashbulb memory
schema
consistency bias
source monitoring
misinformation effect
retroactive interference
constructivist approach
weapon focus
recovered-memory perspective
false-memory perspective
betrayal trauma

RECOMMENDED READINGS

Martin, L. L., & Clore, G. L. (Eds.). (2001). *Theories of mood and cognition.* Mahwah, NJ: Erlbaum. Here's an excellent overview of the relationship among emotion, mood, and memory. It includes eight chapters that emphasize theoretical issues, but they also describe the relevant research.

Schacter, D. L. (2001). *The seven sins of memory.* Boston: Houghton Mifflin. Daniel Schacter discusses seven areas in which memory initially appears to be faulty (e.g., misattribution, suggestibility, and bias), but he also argues that each of these apparent flaws makes sense in terms of general human functioning.

Tulving, E., & Craik, F. I. M. (Eds.). (2000). *The Oxford handbook of memory.* New York: Oxford University Press. I strongly recommend this handbook, which contains 40 chapters on both autobiographical and laboratory-based components of memory. For a book written mostly by active researchers, it's remarkably jargon-free.

Wells, G. L., & Olson, E. A. (2003). Eyewitness testimony. *Annual Review of Psychology, 54,* 277–295. This brief chapter provides a clear overview of eyewitness testimony, and it includes topics beyond the scope of your textbook, such as the nature of the lineup, characteristics of the eyewitness, and how to improve the system.

Memory Strategies and Metacognition

PREVIEW

Chapter 4 focused on working memory, the brief, immediate memory for material you are currently processing. Chapter 5 explored long-term memory, or memory for events that occurred minutes, days, or even years earlier. Both of those chapters emphasized the research and theory about memory. In contrast, Chapter 6 explores more practical issues concerned with memory strategies and metacognition (knowledge about your cognitive processes). The information in this chapter should help you develop more effective memory strategies; it should also help you learn how to monitor both your memory and your reading techniques.

The section on memory strategies begins by reviewing some memory suggestions derived from Chapters 3, 4, and 5. Next we'll consider several ways in which different forms of practice can enhance your memory. We'll then look at memory techniques that emphasize imagery and organization. However, we'll see that a truly conscientious effort to improve memory requires a comprehensive approach that includes factors such as mental and physical health. Our final topic in this section explores ways to improve prospective memory, or remembering to do something in the future.

The second section examines metacognition. The research on metamemory suggests that college students can accurately predict which items they will remember on a memory test, but they are often overconfident and unaware of the effectiveness of memory strategies. They may also spend too long studying material they already know. The research on the tip-of-the-tongue phenomenon points out that people are fairly knowledgeable about characteristics of the target word, such as the first letter of this word. Unfortunately, however, the research suggests that students are often overconfident in judging whether they have understood a passage they have recently read. Throughout the discussion of metacognition, we'll point out techniques to help you learn course material more effectively.

INTRODUCTION

How many thousands of hours did you spend during high school listening to lectures, engaging in class discussions, taking notes, reading textbooks, and then studying for examinations? The goal of these examinations was to assess your memory for the information you had learned. Now think about the amount of time your high school teachers spent in teaching you how to improve your memory. Perhaps a history teacher urged the class to begin studying early for an upcoming exam, rather than trying to master everything the night before the exam. Maybe a math teacher taught you how to remember the abbreviations for the trigonometry formulas. Possibly a foreign language teacher mentioned that you could learn vocabulary terms by using mental imagery. What was the total amount of time your teachers spent helping you learn how to improve your memory?

When the students in my cognitive psychology class arrive at the chapter on memory strategies and metacognition, we try the exercise I've just described. In contrast to the thousands of hours my students have spent presumably learning and remembering, most of them estimate that their high school teachers spent a grand total of about 1 hour discussing memory improvement. Furthermore, some students report that their teachers recommended some study strategies that contradict the information they have learned about human memory. For instance, one student told our class about her history teacher's recommendations: Repeat a sentence out loud three times, and then write it three times, and you'll have it memorized! Even if you read no further in this current chapter, you should be able to explain why students should avoid this particular recommendation.

We'll start this chapter by reviewing some strategic tips that you learned about memory improvement, based on the chapters you've already read. Then we'll look at several other memory strategies that psychology researchers have discovered. As it happens, your choice of memory strategies will be guided by your metacognition, the second major topic in this chapter. **Metacognition** is your knowledge about your cognitive processes. As you'll see later in the chapter, the research on metacognition provides some suggestions that will help you (1) monitor and regulate your study strategies; (2) understand the tip-of-the-tongue phenomenon as you struggle to recall an important term; and (3) read material in your textbooks more effectively.

MEMORY STRATEGIES

When you use a **memory strategy**, you perform mental activities that are designed to improve your encoding and retrieval (Bransford et al., 2000; Herrmann et al., 2002). Most memory strategies help you remember something that occurred in the past, whether it is information relevant to a college course, the name of a new acquaintance, or something that is personally important. We'll first explore strategies for remembering the past. Our last topic in this section is quite different, however, because it focuses on improving your memory for tasks you must remember to do in the future.

Suggestions from Previous Chapters: A Review

The advice about memory from previous chapters emphasizes some concepts you learned in Chapter 5: levels of processing, the encoding specificity principle, and the overconfidence problem. We'll also address divided attention, an important concept from Chapter 3.

Levels of Processing. The most useful guiding principle for memory improvement comes from the discussion about levels of processing in Chapter 5. Specifically, the research on **levels of processing** shows that you will recall information more accurately if you process it at a deep level, rather than a shallow level. Therefore, when you need to learn some information, be sure to concentrate on its meaning and try to develop rich, elaborate encodings (Chi, 2000; deWinstanley & Bjork, 2002; Herrmann et al., 2002). In contrast, simple **rehearsal,** or repeating the information you want to learn, is "an extraordinarily poor technique for memorization" (Payne et al., 1999, p. 91).

Deep processing clearly helps students remember more information in their psychology courses. For instance, students scored higher on introductory psychology tests if they had paused from time to time to summarize the material they just learned (Davis & Hult, 1997). Furthermore, students learned more in a developmental psychology course if they tried to analyze newspaper advice columns from a developmental perspective (Cabe et al., 1999). Also, students earned higher scores in a psychology course on personality theories if they had maintained a journal in which they applied various theories to personal friends, political figures, and characters from television programs (Connor-Greene, 2000). In all these cases, students elaborated on the material and analyzed it in a complex, meaningful fashion, rather than simply reheared the material.

One especially deep level of processing takes advantage of the **self-reference effect,** in which you enhance long-term memory by relating the material to your own experiences. For example, one of the reasons that I include demonstrations in your textbook is to provide you with personal experiences with some of the important principles of cognitive psychology. If you read your textbook in a reflective fashion, you'll try to think how to apply major concepts to your life. I'm hopeful, for instance, that this chapter will encourage you to see how memory strategies and metacognitive principles can be applied to the way you learn in your other college courses.

Encoding Specificity. Chapter 5 also discussed the **encoding specificity principle,** which states that recall is often better if the context at the time of encoding matches the context at the time when your retrieval will be tested. A specific suggestion, then, is that you should consider how you will be tested on your next examination when you are trying to devise your study strategies (Bjork, 1999; Koriat, 2000; Payne et al., 1999). For example, suppose that your exam will contain essays, a format that requires you to *recall* information—not simply to *recognize* it. As you are learning the material, make an effort to quiz yourself periodically by closing your notebook and trying to remember the material on the pages you've just read. During studying, you can also try to create some essay questions and then answer them, a strategy that would also increase your deep processing of the material.

Overconfidence. Our examination of autobiographical memory in Chapter 5 provides a general caution, rather than a specific memory strategy. In that section, we saw that people often believe that their memories about their life experiences are highly accurate. However, even their so-called flashbulb memories may contain some errors. This area of research suggests that we may sometimes be overconfident about our memory skills. If we can make mistakes in remembering important life events, then we can certainly make mistakes in remembering material from a course! The issue of overconfidence is also an important topic in the second half of the chapter.

Divided Attention. We've reviewed three suggestions from Chapter 5. That chapter is especially relevant because the examinations in your courses assess your long-term memory. However, the material in Chapter 3 provides another general caution. As you'll recall, people cannot pay full attention to two tasks in a divided-attention situation. Suppose that you aren't paying attention to your course material when you are studying (or weren't, for that matter, when you were taking notes in class). This material will be unlikely to make its way into your long-term memory. Research confirms that memory performance is substantially reduced if attention had been divided during the encoding phase (deWinstanley & Bjork, 2002; Naveh-Benjamin et al., 1998; Payne et al., 1999).

Also, let's consider some related research on the topic of divided attention and memory. My students often ask whether their memory will be helped or hindered by listening to background music while they study. The answer—like many answers in psychology—is, "It depends." On the one hand, outgoing people who are extraverts may not be distracted by background music played at a quiet volume during memory encoding, though the music probably will not improve their memory encoding. In contrast, people who are introverts—that is, shy and withdrawn—are likely to find that their memory will suffer if they listen to background music during encoding (Furnham & Bradley, 1997). During divided-attention tasks like this, introverted individuals are apparently more distracted by the music, and they cannot focus their attention sufficiently on the memory task.

Practice

So far, we've considered several memory-improvement suggestions based on concepts discussed in earlier chapters. Let us now turn to some new suggestions about memory strategies. The first of these memory-improvement strategies sounds almost too obvious to mention: The more you practice, the more you remember. However, even college students forget this rule. Every semester, students will come to my office to discuss how they can improve their performance on examinations. One of my first questions is, "How long did you spend studying for the last test?" An amazing number will say something like, "Well, I read every chapter, and I looked over my notes."

Most of us cannot master material with only one exposure to a textbook and a cursory inspection of lecture notes. Instead, the task requires reading the material two or three times; each time, you should also practice retrieving the information. (For example, what are the memory-improvement techniques we have discussed so far in this chapter?) This retrieval practice also makes use of the encoding specificity principle, and the research shows that retrieval practice improves test performance (Bjork, 1999; deWinstanley & Bjork, 2002; Herrmann et al., 2002).

Total Time Hypothesis. According to the **total time hypothesis,** the amount you learn depends on the total time you devote to learning (Baddeley, 1997). Keep in mind, however, that 1 hour spent actively learning the material—using deep levels of processing—will usually be more helpful than 2 hours in which your eyes simply drift across the pages.

Incidentally, let's clarify an important point about practice: Practice improves your memory for the material you are currently studying. However, practice does not strengthen your general memory ability. Many well-meaning educators have misinterpreted the research on practice. They mistakenly believe that memory exercises "strengthen" your brain, much like weight lifting strengthens your muscles. If you spend several hours each week memorizing Spanish vocabulary, you're sure to expand your Spanish skills. Unfortunately, however, you won't improve your general ability to memorize material more effectively (Glisky, 1995). Now, before you read further, be sure to try Demonstration 6.1.

⊚ Demonstration 6.1

Instructions and Memory

Learn the following list of pairs by repeating the members of each pair several times. For example, if the pair were CAT–WINDOW, you would say over and over to yourself, "CAT–WINDOW, CAT–WINDOW, CAT–WINDOW." Just repeat the words, and do not use any other study method. Allow yourself 1 minute to learn this list.

CUSTARD–LUMBER	IVY–MOTHER
JAIL–CLOWN	LIZARD–PAPER
ENVELOPE–SLIPPER	SCISSORS–BEAR
SHEEPSKIN–CANDLE	CANDY–MOUNTAIN
FRECKLES–APPLE	BOOK–PAINT
HAMMER–STAR	TREE–OCEAN

Now, cover up the pairs above. Try to recall as many responses as possible:

ENVELOPE	_____	JAIL	_____
FRECKLES	_____	IVY	_____
TREE	_____	SHEEPSKIN	_____
CANDY	_____	BOOK	_____
SCISSORS	_____	LIZARD	_____
CUSTARD	_____	HAMMER	_____

Next, learn the following list of pairs by visualizing a mental picture in which the two objects in each pair are in some kind of vivid interaction. For example, if the pair were CAT–WINDOW, you might make up a picture of a cat jumping through a closed window, with the glass shattering all around. Just make up a mental image and do not use any other study method. Allow yourself 1 minute to learn this list.

(continued)

SOAP–MERMAID   MIRROR–RABBIT
FOOTBALL–LAKE   HOUSE–DIAMOND
PENCIL–LETTUCE   LAMB–MOON
CAR–HONEY   BREAD–GLASS
CANDLE–DANCER   LIPS–MONKEY
DANDELION–FLEA   DOLLAR–ELEPHANT

Now, cover up the pairs above. Try to recall as many responses as possible:

CANDLE	_____	DOLLAR	_____
DANDELION	_____	CAR	_____
BREAD	_____	LIPS	_____
MIRROR	_____	PENCIL	_____
LAMB	_____	SOAP	_____
FOOTBALL	_____	HOUSE	_____

Now, count the number of correct responses on each list. Did you recall a greater number of words with the imagery instructions? Incidentally, you may have found it very difficult to avoid using imagery on the first list, because you are reading a section about memory improvement. In that case, your recall scores were probably similar for the two lists. You may wish to test a friend, instead.

Distribution of Practice Effect. The research shows that some practice schedules are more effective than others. Specifically, the **distribution of practice effect** (also called the **spacing effect**) points out that you learn more if you spread your learning trials over time, rather than learning the material all at once. The studies generally support the effect for both recall tasks and recognition tasks (Dempster, 1996; Donovan & Radosevich, 1999; Russo et al., 1998). Research also confirms the spacing effect with real-life material, such as high school math and Spanish vocabulary (Bahrick & Hall, 1991; Bahrick et al., 1993; Payne & Wenger, 1992).

According to Robert Bjork (1999), distributed practice is helpful because it introduces "desirable difficulties." Suppose that you need to learn some key concepts for a biology class. If you test yourself on one concept several times in a row, the concept will seem easy by your third or fourth repetition. However, if you allow several minutes to pass before the second repetition, you'll pay more attention to the concept. In addition, the task will be slightly more difficult because you will have begun to forget the concept (Bjork, 1999; deWinstanley & Bjork, 2002). As a result, you'll make some mistakes, and you won't be overconfident that you have mastered the concept. Incidentally, I have tried to apply the distribution of practice effect to some extent in this textbook. For instance, this chapter began with a review of some concepts you learned in Chapter 5. Furthermore, you'll have another opportunity to review many memory concepts in Chapter 13, when we examine memory processes in children and elderly adults.

Mnemonics Using Imagery

The preceding discussion demonstrated the usefulness of strategies related to practice. This section, as well as the next one on organization, emphasizes the use of mnemonics (pronounced "ni-*mon*-icks," with a silent initial *m*). **Mnemonics** is the use of a strategy to help memory. When we use mnemonics that emphasize **imagery,** we mentally represent objects or actions that are not physically present. Chapter 7 examines the nature of these mental images; in the present chapter, however, we'll focus on how imagery can enhance memory.

Now check your results for Demonstration 6.1. Which set of instructions produced the highest recall—the repetition or the imagery instructions? This demonstration is a simplified version of a study by Bower and Winzenz (1970). They used concrete nouns in their study and tested participants in several different conditions. In the repetition condition, for example, people repeated the pairs silently to themselves. In contrast, in the imagery condition, people tried to construct a mental picture of the two words in vivid interaction with each other. After learning several lists of words, the participants saw the first word of each pair and were asked to supply the second word. The results showed that people in the imagery condition recalled more than twice as many items as did the people in the repetition condition.

Visual imagery is a powerful strategy for enhancing memory (Bellezza,1996; deWinstanley & Bjork, 2002; Neath, 1998). The research consistently shows that imagery is especially effective when the items that must be recalled are shown interacting with each other (McKelvie et al., 1994; West, 1995). For example, if you want to remember the pair *elephant–apple*, try to visualize an elephant holding the apple in its trunk, rather than these two items separated from each other. Participants in memory studies report that imagery mnemonics are more motivating and enjoyable than a simple repetition strategy, and this factor probably helps to explain the success of this technique (Herrmann et al., 2002; Higbee, 1999). Let's now consider two specific mnemonic devices that employ mental imagery: the keyword method and the method of loci.

The Keyword Method. If you need to remember unfamiliar vocabulary items, the keyword method is especially helpful. In the **keyword method,** you identify an English word (the keyword) that sounds similar to the new word you want to learn, and then you create an image that links the keyword with the meaning of the new word (Bellezza, 1996; Iannuzzi et al., 1998). For example, imagine that you are learning Spanish, and you want to remember that the unfamiliar Spanish word *rodilla* means *knee* in English. From the word *rodilla* (pronounced "roe-*dee*-ya"), you could derive a similar-sounding English word, *rodeo*. Then imagine a cowboy at a rodeo with his knees conspicuously protruding, as in Figure 6.1.

The research on the keyword method shows that it seems to help students who are trying to learn new English vocabulary words, foreign language vocabulary, or people's names (Groninger, 2000; Gruneberg, 1998; Herrmann et al., 2002; Kasper & Glass, 1988; Searleman & Herrmann, 1994). The keyword method has also been used to help individuals with Alzheimer's disease learn people's names (Hill et al., 1987). This research matches my own personal experience with learning Spanish vocabulary over a period of several years. Some researchers, however, are more pessimistic

FIGURE 6.1

The Keyword Representation for the Pair of Words *Rodilla–Knee.*

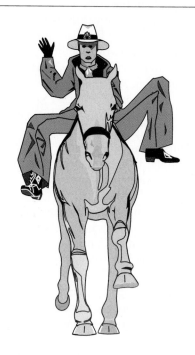

🌀 **Demonstration 6.2**

Remembering Lists of Letters

Read this list of letters and then cover up the list. Try to recall them as accurately as possible.

    YMC AJF KFB INB CLS DTV

Now read this list of letters and then cover them up. Try to recall them as accurately as possible.

    AMA PHD TWA VCR CIA CBS

Finally, read this list of letters and then cover them up. Try to recall them as accurately as possible.

  N Z K L E Q B N P I J W U Y H R T M

about its effectiveness (Thomas & Wang, 1996; Wang & Thomas, 1999). (Try Demonstration 6.2 before you read further.)

Let's look at a recent example of the effectiveness of mental imagery. Carney and Levin (2001) used a slight modification of the keyword method, because the material in their study consisted of sketches of unfamiliar animals, each paired with the animal's name. (Strictly speaking, the keyword method pairs together two words.) For example, in one study, college undergraduates were randomly assigned to one of two conditions. In the control condition, students were instructed to use their own most effective method for learning the animals' names. (Notice, therefore, that these students would probably perform better than if they had been instructed to use simple repetition—the instructions provided to people in the control condition in most memory studies.) The students in the experimental condition were taught how to use a visual mnemonic. For example, the instructions said that they should imagine an animal called a *capybara* with a *cap* pulled down over its eyes. A similar phrase was provided for the other pairs in the list.

After a brief delay, students in both conditions saw a brief video clip of each animal, and they were asked to provide the animal's name. (Notice that the video clip enhances the ecological validity of this study; in real life, you would see a moving 3-dimensional animal, not a simple sketch.) Finally, the students saw each sketch and were again instructed to provide the animal's name. As Figure 6.2 shows, students' memory was much more accurate when they used the imagery mnemonic. Carney and Levin (2001) point out that this memory strategy can be applied in numerous educational settings in which the stimulus is visual, including courses in geography, anatomy, and botany.

The Method of Loci. If you want to use the **method of loci**, you must associate the items to be learned with a series of physical locations. The method of loci (pronounced "*low*-sigh") is especially useful when you want to learn a list of items in a specific order (Bellezza, 1996; Herrmann et al., 2002; Neath, 1998).

In more detail, the rules for using the method of loci require you to (1) visualize a series of places that you know well, arranged in a specific sequence; (2) make up an image to represent each item you want to remember; and (3) associate the items, one by one, with the corresponding location in memory. A clear strength of the method of loci is that it takes advantage of the encoding specificity principle that we've discussed earlier. Notice that the new material is encoded together with memory cues that are so familiar that you can easily remember them when you need to recall the items.

For example, you might use the method of loci for a familiar sequence of loci associated with a home, such as the driveway, the garage, the front door, the coat closet, and the kitchen sink (Bower, 1970). If you need to remember a grocery shopping list (for example, hot dogs, cat food, tomatoes, bananas, and orange juice), you could make up a vivid image for each item. Then imagine each item in its appropriate place. You could imagine giant *hot dogs* rolling down the *driveway*, a monstrous *cat eating food* in the *garage*, ripe *tomatoes* splattering all over the *front door*, a bunch of *bananas* swinging in the *coat closet*, and a quart of *orange juice* gurgling down the *kitchen sink*. When you enter the supermarket, you can mentally walk the route from the driveway to the kitchen sink, recalling the items in order.

FIGURE 6.2

Percentage of Animal Names Remembered Correctly, as a Function of Instructions ("Free Choice" vs. Imagery Mnemonic) and Format of the Stimuli (Video Clip vs. Sketch).

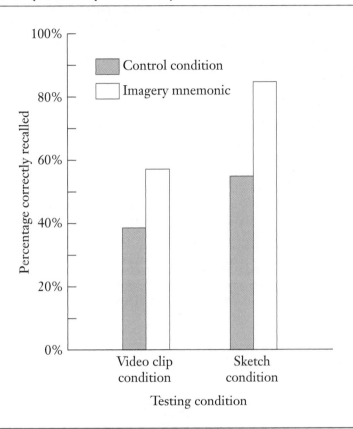

Source: Based on Carney & Levin, 2001.

The method sounds unlikely to work, but it is helpful. In a classic experiment, participants in the method of loci condition recalled about twice as many words as participants in the control condition, when recall was measured 5 weeks after the original learning session (Groninger, 1971).

Mnemonics Using Organization

Organization is the attempt to bring systematic order to the material we learn. This category of mnemonics makes sense, because retrieval is easier when you have constructed a well-organized framework (Bellezza, 1996; West, 1995). Let's consider four mnemonics that emphasize organization.

Chunking. Chapter 4 discussed an organizational strategy called **chunking**, in which we combine several small units into larger units. For instance, Demonstration 6.2 on page 179 is a modification of a study by Bower and Springston (1970). These researchers found that people recalled much more material when a string of letters was grouped according to meaningful, familiar units, rather than in arbitrary groups of three. In Demonstration 6.2, you may have recalled a large number of items on the second list, which was organized according to familiar chunks. You probably recalled far fewer items from the list where the letters were grouped in arbitrary units and from the ungrouped list.

Hierarchy Technique. A second effective way to organize material is to construct a hierarchy. A **hierarchy** is a system in which items are arranged in a series of classes, from the most general classes to the most specific. For example, Figure 6.3 presents part of a hierarchy for animals.

Gordon Bower and his colleagues (1969) asked people to learn words that belonged to four hierarchies similar to the one in Figure 6.3. Some people learned the words in an organized fashion, in the format of the upside-down trees you see in Figure 6.3. Other people saw the same words, but the words were randomly scattered throughout the different positions in each tree. The group who had learned the organized structure performed much better. For instance, on the first trial, the group who learned the organized hierarchy structure recalled an average of 73 words, in comparison to only 21 for the group who learned the random structure. Structure and organization clearly enhance recall (Baddeley, 1999; Herrmann et al., 2002).

FIGURE 6.3

An Example of a Hierarchy.

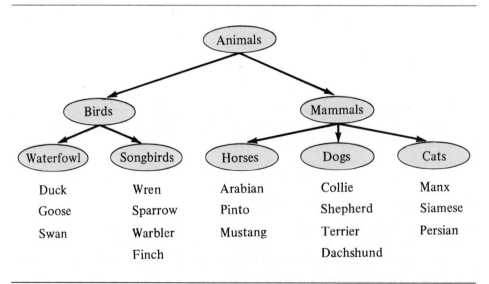

An outline is a form of a hierarchy, because an outline is divided into general categories, and each general category is further subdivided. An outline is valuable because it provides organization and structure for concepts that you learn in a particular discipline. Naturally, the material is usually not as simple as a list of individual words, but the ideas can still be arranged into a series of classes. For example, this chapter is divided into two general categories: memory strategies and metacognition. When you have finished reading this chapter, see if you can construct—from memory—a hierarchy similar to Figure 6.3. Begin with the two general categories, and then subdivide these categories into more specific topics. Then check the chapter outline on page 171 to see whether you omitted anything. If you study the outline of each chapter, you will have an organized structure that can enhance your recall on an examination.

Unfortunately, students in introductory psychology classes report that they seldom use chapter outlines when studying for exams (Gurung, 2003). However, it's possible that students in more advanced courses (such as cognitive psychology!) are aware that they can learn more effectively if they know how a topic is organized.

First-Letter Technique. Another popular mnemonic that makes use of organization is the **first-letter technique;** you take the first letter of each word you want to remember and compose a word or a sentence from those letters (West, 1995). Maybe you learned the order of the colors of the rainbow by using the letters ROY G. BIV to recall Red, Orange, Yellow, Green, Blue, Indigo, and Violet. As you may have learned in a statistics class, the nominal, ordinal, interval, and ratio scales conveniently spell *noir*, the French word for "black."

Students frequently use first-letter mnemonics. Unfortunately, however, the effectiveness of this technique has not been consistently demonstrated in laboratory research (Gruneberg & Herrmann, 1997; Herrmann et al., 2002; West, 1995). In cases where it *does* work, its effectiveness can probably be traced to the fact that these first letters frequently enhance retrieval. For instance, suppose that you are experiencing a memory block for a certain term, and someone supplies you with the first letter of that term. About half of the time, that clue will allow you to retrieve the item (Herrmann et al., 2002).

Narrative Technique. So far, we have looked at three mnemonic strategies that focus on organization: chunking, hierarchies, and the first-letter technique. A fourth organizational method, called the **narrative technique,** instructs people to make up stories that link a series of words together.

In one study focusing on the narrative technique, Bower and Clark (1969) told a group of people to make up narrative stories that incorporated a set of English words. In contrast, people in the control group spent the same amount of time learning these words, but they were simply told to study and learn each list. In all, each group learned 12 lists of words. The results showed that the people in the narrative-technique group recalled about six times as many words as those in the control group.

The narrative technique is clearly an effective strategy for enhancing memory, and it has also been used successfully with memory-impaired individuals (Wilson, 1995).

However, we should emphasize that techniques such as this are effective only if you can generate the narrative easily and reliably during both learning and recall. A narrative will not be helpful if it hangs together so loosely that you cannot remember the story!

A Comprehensive Approach to Memory Improvement

In recent years, psychologists have become increasingly critical of the mnemonics approach to memory improvement. These researchers complain that the traditional approach to memory improvement has been too simplistic (e.g., Baddeley et al., 1995; Herrmann, 1996; Herrmann et al., 2002; Searleman & Herrmann, 1994). That approach implies that we can find a single solution to help all people with their memory difficulties, and it also suggests that people can cure their memory problems with just a few days' effort.

Researchers now emphasize that we need a more comprehensive approach to solving memory problems. For example, Douglas Herrmann's **multimodal approach** emphasizes that people who seriously want to enhance their memory must adopt a comprehensive approach to memory improvement; this approach focuses on many different *modes* or factors (Herrmann, 1991; Herrmann et al., 1999; Herrmann et al., 2002). Specifically, this comprehensive approach requires attention to physical condition (for example, by getting sufficient sleep, maintaining an optimal level of daily activity, and attending to health problems). Psychological well-being is also important. For instance, depressed individuals are more likely than other individuals to experience memory problems on tests of both explicit and implicit memory (Gilbert, 2002; Jenkins & McDowall, 2001; Kizilbash et al., 2002).

People who want to improve their memories should develop a repertoire of several memory techniques. According to the research, students who earn high grades in a college course typically report using a large number of different memory strategies, compared to students who earn average grades (Herrmann et al., 2002). The flexible use of memory strategies can also be useful outside the classroom. Suppose, for example, that you want to improve your memory for people's names. Here are some steps to follow (Herrmann, 1991):

1. Say the person's name aloud.
2. Ask the person a question, using his or her name.
3. Say the name at least once in conversation.
4. End the conversation by thinking of a rhyme for the name, deciding whom the person looks like, or—if possible—jotting down the name unobtrusively.

Ellen Langer (2000) has developed a perspective called mindfulness that provides another dimension to comprehensive memory improvement. According to Langer, **mindfulness** requires a flexible approach to the world, with a particular sensitivity to new things and an appreciation for new ways of approaching a problem. In contrast, we demonstrate mindlessness when we approach everything in the same, routine fashion we've used in the past.

I recall a student in my introductory psychology course several years ago who provided an unfortunate example of mindlessness. Dave had earned a low D grade on the first exam in the course, and I wrote a note asking him to come to my office to discuss study strategies. Together we discussed several of the concepts mentioned in this chapter, including a heavy emphasis on metacognition (the topic we'll address in the second half of this chapter). Eagerly, I inspected Dave's second exam. Another low D. When Dave came to my office for the second time, I asked him whether he had tried any of the ideas we had discussed. Dave replied, "No, they would have been too much work, so I studied the way I always study."

The current research suggests that Dave's mindless perspective is fairly common; in many cases, failure comes from not trying (Claxton, 1999). Students often resist using resources that could help them. For instance, students enrolled in a Web-based introductory psychology course seldom used any of the online study material until just two days before their exam (Maki & Maki, 2000). Furthermore, students enrolled in a traditional introductory psychology course made use of the boldface terms in their textbook, but they seldom used other helpful features, such as outlines (as we noted earlier), chapter summaries, or practice-test questions (Gurung, 2003).

Let's take a moment to review the strategies we've examined for improving your memory for information you've acquired in the past. In previous chapters, we emphasized the value of deep processing, for example by using the self-reference approach and elaborate encodings. These previous chapters also provided advice about the usefulness of encoding specificity, the importance of not being overconfident, and the problems of divided attention.

The current chapter pointed out the helpfulness of two components of practice (the total time hypothesis, and the distribution of practice effect). This chapter also explored mnemonics using imagery (visualizing the objects in vivid interaction, the keyword method, and the method of loci) and mnemonics using organization (chunking, the hierarchy technique, the first-letter technique, and the narrative technique). Finally, we emphasized the value of a comprehensive orientation to memory, which includes Herrmann's multimodal approach and Langer's concept of mindfulness.

Improving Prospective Memory

Let's move away from memory for information acquired in the past. Instead, we'll focus on **prospective memory,** or remembering to do things in the future. A prospective-memory task has two components. First, you must establish that you intend to accomplish a particular task at some future time. Second, at that future time, you must fulfill your intention (Marsh et al., 1998; McDaniel & Einstein, 2000).

Some typical prospective-memory tasks might include remembering to pick up a friend at work, to mail a letter, to let the dog out before you leave the house, and to keep your office-hour appointment with a professor. In many cases, the primary challenge is simply to remember to perform an action in the future. However, sometimes the primary challenge is to remember the *content* of that action (Schaefer & Laing, 2000). You've probably experienced the feeling that you know you are supposed to do something, but you cannot remember what it is. You may also find—as I do—that you need to leave written messages and other physical reminders in conspicuous places, in order to remind yourself of all the things you need to do tomorrow.

Before we can examine the methods for improving prospective memory, we need to understand how this aspect of memory operates. Let's first compare prospective memory with more standard memory tasks, and then we'll consider some of the research on prospective memory. Next we'll explore the related topic of absentmindedness. With this background in mind, we'll consider several specific suggestions about the improvement of prospective memory.

Comparing Prospective and Retrospective Memory. This textbook's discussions of memory have focused on **retrospective memory,** or recalling information that you have previously learned. Prospective memory is studied much less often than retrospective memory. However, most people rank prospective memory errors among the most common memory lapses and also among the most embarrassing (Baddeley, 1995a; Sellen, 1994).

In contrast to retrospective memory, prospective memory requires plans about the future. In this respect, prospective memory resembles problem solving, a topic we'll explore in Chapter 11, and it also focuses on action (Einstein & McDaniel, 1996). Retrospective memory is more likely to focus on remembering information and ideas.

Despite their differences, prospective memory and retrospective memory are governed by some of the same variables. For example, both kinds of memory are facilitated by distinctive encoding and by effective retrieval cues. Furthermore, both kinds of memory are less accurate when you have a long delay, filled with irrelevant activities, prior to retrieval (Roediger, 1996). Finally, prospective memory relies on regions of the frontal lobe that also play a role in retrospective memory (Burgess & Shallice, 1997; McDaniel et al., 1999; West et al., 2000).

Naturalistic Research on Prospective Memory. Most of the research on prospective memory is naturalistic and reasonably high in ecological validity. For example, Marsh and his colleagues (1998) asked students to complete some "planning activity sheets," in which they were instructed to list the activities they had planned for the next 7 days. One week later, these activity sheets were returned to them, and the students were asked to specify whether they had actually performed each task. Students reported that they had forgotten to perform only 13% of the activities. Surprisingly, students who habitually used a daily planner were no more accurate in their prospective memory than those who did not maintain a formal list of commitments. As you might imagine, though, lapses in prospective memory are more likely when you are preoccupied with many other tasks that you must perform before you complete the prospective-memory task (Marsh & Hicks, 1998).

Absentmindedness. One intriguing component of prospective memory is absentmindedness (e.g., Reason, 1984; Reason & Mycielska, 1982; Sellen, 1994). Most people do not publicly reveal their absentminded slips. You may therefore think that you are the only person who forgets to pick up a quart of milk on your way home from school, who dials Chris's phone number when you want to speak to Alex, who forgets why you walked from one room in your house to another, or who fails to include an important attachment when sending an e-mail.

One problem is that the typical prospective-memory task represents a divided-attention situation; you must focus on your ongoing activity, as well as on the task you need to remember in the future (D'Ydewalle et al., 1999; Marsh et al., 2000; Mc-Daniel & Einstein, 2000). Absentminded behavior is especially likely when the intended action requires disrupting the customary schema surrounding an action (Morris, 1992). That is, you have a customary schema or habit that you usually perform, which is Action A (for example, driving from school to your home). You also have a prospective-memory task that you must perform on this occasion, which is Action B (for example, stopping at the grocery store). In cases like this, your long-standing habit dominates the more fragile prospective memory, and you fall victim to absentminded behavior (Hay & Jacoby, 1996).

These errors are more likely in highly familiar surroundings when you are performing tasks automatically (Schacter, 2001). Errors are also more likely if you are preoccupied, distracted, or feeling time pressure. In most cases, absentmindedness is simply irritating. However, sometimes these slips can produce airplane collisions, industrial accidents, and other disasters that influence the lives of hundreds of individuals.

Suggestions for Improving Prospective Memory. Earlier in the chapter, we discussed numerous suggestions that you could use to aid your retrospective memory. Some of these internal strategies could presumably be used to aid your prospective memory as well. For example, a vivid, interactive mental image of a quart of milk might help you avoid driving past the grocery store in an absentminded fashion.

However, the reminders that you choose must be specific if you want to perform a prospective-memory task (Engelkamp, 1998; Guynn et al., 1998). For example, suppose you want to remember to give Tonya a message tomorrow. It won't be helpful just to rehearse her name or just to remind yourself that you have to convey a message. Instead, you must form a strong connection between these two components, linking both Tonya's name and the fact that you must give her a message. A distinctive, unusual reminder is also useful (McDaniel & Einstein, 2000).

External memory aids are likely to be especially helpful on prospective-memory tasks. An **external memory aid** is defined as any device, external to yourself, that facilitates your memory in some way (Herrmann et al., 2002). Some examples of external memory aids include a shopping list, a rubber band around your wrist, asking someone else to remind you to do something, and the ring of an alarm clock, to remind you to make an important phone call.

The placement of your external memory aid is especially important. For example, my nephew sometimes drives to his mother's home for dinner, and she typically tells him about some items in the refrigerator that he must remember to take home when he leaves. After several prospective-memory lapses, he thought of an ideal external memory aid: When he arrives for dinner, he places his car keys in the refrigerator (White, 2003). Notice his mindfulness in designing the placement of this memory aid; he is highly unlikely to drive home without the refrigerated items.

My students report that they often use informal external mnemonics to aid their prospective memory. When they want to remember to bring a book to class, they place it in a location where they will have to confront the book on the way to class. They also place letters to be mailed in a conspicuous position on the dashboard of their car. Other students describe the sea of yellow Post-its that decorate their dormitory rooms.

Many commercial memory aids are also available to assist your prospective memory (Herrmann et al., 1999; Herrmann et al., 2002). For example, many people now carry "palm pilots," which can be programmed to provide reminders about prospective-memory tasks. External memory aids are designed to ease the burden of remembering too much information. However, these aids are helpful only if they can be easily used and if they successfully remind us of what we are supposed to remember. If you switch your ring to another finger to remind you to turn off your stove before leaving the apartment, you may find yourself pondering, "Now what was this reminder supposed to remind me to do?"

Now that you are familiar with the challenges of prospective memory, try Demonstration 6.3. Also, review the memory-improvement techniques listed in Table 6.1.

⟲ Demonstration 6.3

Prospective Memory

Make a list of five prospective-memory tasks that you need to accomplish within the next week. These must be tasks that you can remember to complete on your own, without anyone else providing a reminder.

For each item, first describe the method you would customarily use to remember to do the task. Also note whether this method is typically successful. Then, for each task where you typically make a prospective-memory error, try to figure out a more effective reminder. Note whether this reminder is an internal mnemonic or an external memory aid.

TABLE 6.1

Memory-Improvement Techniques

---

1. Suggestions from previous chapters

   a. Process information in terms of its meaning, rather than at a shallow level.

   b. Relate information to your own experiences.

   c. Try to learn material in the same context as the one in which you will be tested.

   d. Don't be overconfident about the accuracy of your memory for life events.

   e. Do not divide your attention between several simultaneous tasks.

2. Techniques related to practice

  a. The amount you learn depends on the total time you spend practicing.

  b. You'll learn more if you spread your learning trials over time (the spacing effect).

3. Mnemonics using imagery

  a. Use imagery, especially imagery that shows an interaction between the items that need to be recalled.

  b. Use the keyword method; for example, if you are learning vocabulary in a foreign language, identify an English word that sounds like the foreign word, and link the English word with the meaning of the foreign word.

  c. Use the method of loci when learning a series of items by associating each item with a physical location.

4. Mnemonics using organization

  a. Use chunking by combining isolated items into meaningful units.

  b. Construct a hierarchy by arranging items in a series of classes (e.g., Figure 6.3 on p. 182).

  c. Take the first letter of each item you want to remember, and compose a word or sentence from these letters (first-letter technique).

  d. Create a narrative, or a story that links a series of words together.

5. The multimodal approach

  Memory improvement must be comprehensive, with attention to physical and mental health, and the flexible use of memory strategies.

6. Improving prospective memory

  a. Create a vivid, interactive mental image to prompt future recall.

  b. Create a specific reminder or an external memory aid.

◎ Section Summary: *Memory Strategies*

1. Previous chapters presented several strategies for memory improvement: deep processing (including elaborate encodings and the self-reference effect) and encoding specificity, as well as the dangers of overconfidence and divided attention.

2. Two general memory-improvement strategies focus on components of practice: the total time hypothesis and the distribution of practice effect.

3. Some useful mnemonics focus on imagery; these include visualizing the items in vivid interaction, the keyword method, and the method of loci.

4. Other useful mnemonics focus on organization; these include chunking, the hierarchy technique, the first-letter technique, and the narrative technique.

ach to memory improvement proposes that memory
factor solutions that focus on physical, mental, and
s training in the flexible use of a variety of memory
hensive approach also emphasizes a mindful approach

esearch focuses on retrospective memory, the area of
amines how people remember to do something in the
wo kinds of memory have somewhat different focuses,
tant similarities.

pective memory suggests that college students are rea-
their everyday prospective-memory tasks. However,
nay create a divided-attention situation, which can lead

memory aids are useful in improving the accuracy of

METACOGNITION

The first half of this chapter focused on memory strategies, or methods of improving our memory. This second half focuses on the related topic of metacognition. We noted earlier that *metacognition* is your knowledge about your cognitive processes. In more detail, metacognition is your knowledge, awareness, and control of your cognitive processes.

Think about the variety of metacognitive knowledge you possess. For example, you know what kind of factors influence your own memory—factors such as the time of day, your motivation, the type of material, and social circumstances. In addition, you know how to regulate your study strategies; if something looks difficult to remember, you'll spend more time trying to commit it to memory. You also have metacognitive knowledge about whether information is currently on the "tip of your tongue." Try to recall, for instance, the name of the psychologist who is primarily responsible for developing the theory of working memory, which we discussed in Chapter 4. Is his name on the tip of your tongue? Still another kind of metacognitive knowledge focuses on your understanding of material that you've read. For example, do you understand the definition of *metacognition*? All these examples apply to your knowledge and awareness of your cognitive processes.

In addition, your metacognitive processes allow you to *control* your cognitive activities (Moses & Baird, 1999; Nelson, 1999). For example, your assessment that you are not yet prepared to take a test on memory strategies may encourage you to spend extra time studying that section.

Metacognition is an intriguing topic because we use our cognitive processes to contemplate our cognitive processes. Metacognition is important because our knowledge about our cognitive processes can guide us in arranging circumstances and selecting strategies to improve our future cognitive performance. Surprisingly, some memory-improvement books do not highlight metacognition (e.g., Claxton, 1999; Collins & Kneale, 2001; Iannuzzi et al., 1998), although metacognition is important if you want to approach memory improvement in a mindful fashion.

In previous chapters of this book, we discussed topics related to metacognition. For instance, in Chapter 3, we saw that people often have limited consciousness about their higher mental processes. As a result, they may not be able to identify which factors helped them solve a problem. In that chapter, we also saw that people often have difficulty controlling the contents of consciousness. As a result, they may not be able to stop thinking about a particular topic.

In addition, Chapter 4 explored Alan Baddeley's (2001a) theory of working memory. That theory proposes that the central executive plays an important role in planning and controlling our behavior; metacognition uses these processes, for example, when you decide which topics you'll spend the most time studying, in preparation for an exam. In Chapter 5, we discussed how people may have difficulty on source-monitoring tasks; for instance, you may not be able to recall whether you actually gave a book to a friend—or whether you merely imagined you had done so. We also noted that people are sometimes unaware of the errors they have made with respect to remembering life events.

In this section of the current chapter, we will examine three important kinds of metacognition. Our first topic is **metamemory,** a topic that refers to people's knowledge, awareness, and control of their memory. Metamemory plays a major part in memory improvement, and so we'll explore several components of metamemory. In addition, we'll examine two other kinds of metacognition, the tip-of-the-tongue phenomenon, and metacomprehension.

We'll also discuss related components of metacognition in later chapters. For example, in Chapter 11 we will discuss whether people can accurately judge how close they are to solving a cognitive problem. Also, Chapter 13 addresses the development of metacognition across the lifespan. Let's begin by focusing on three different aspects of metamemory: (1) People's accuracy in predicting memory performance; (2) people's knowledge about memory strategies; and (3) people's knowledge about how to regulate their study strategies. This third topic will be the focus of this chapter's In Depth feature.

Metamemory and the Prediction of Memory Performance

Have you ever been in this situation? You thought that you knew the material for a midterm, and—in fact—you expected to receive a fairly high grade. However, when the midterms were handed back, you received a C. If this sounds familiar, you realize that your metamemory isn't always accurate in predicting memory performance.

In what circumstances does metamemory accurately predict memory performance? In other words, if you are confident about your performance on some memory task, is your memory indeed accurate? The answer to this question depends on which aspect of metamemory we are examining:

1. When people have a number of items to remember, they can accurately predict which individual items they'll remember and which ones they'll forget.

2. When people estimate their *total score* on a memory test, they are generally overconfident, rather than accurate.

Metamemory on an Item-by-Item Basis. Let's look at a study that investigates this first aspect of metamemory. In other words, this study demonstrates how people's metamemory can be highly accurate when we consider their predictions about which individual items they'll remember and which ones they'll forget. In a classic study, Eugene Lovelace (1984) presented pairs of unrelated English words, such as *disease–railroad.* The participants were told that they would be tested for paired-associate learning; that is, they would later see the first word in each pair and be asked to supply the second word.

The participants learned the pairs under four different exposure conditions: S1 people saw each pair for 8 seconds on a single study trial; S2 people saw each pair for 4 seconds on each of two successive study trials; S4 people saw each pair for 2 seconds on each of four successive study trials; and T2 people saw each pair for 4 seconds on each of two successive study trials with a test trial in between. After the final exposure of each pair, the participants in all four conditions rated each pair for the likelihood of their answering the item correctly on a later test. Finally, they saw the first word of each pair, and they were told to supply the appropriate second word.

Figure 6.4 shows the results, which were similar for all four conditions. The most striking finding is that people *can* accurately predict which items they will recall. When they give an item a rating of 5, they do in fact recall it about 90% of the time when they are tested later. In contrast, when they give a rating of 1, they recall the item less than 50% of the time. You can apply these findings to your classroom performance. If you know that you'll be tested on a specific list of items—such as Spanish vocabulary or definitions for specific psychology terms—you are likely to be reasonably accurate in estimating which items you'll recall and which you'll forget.

In general, the research shows that college students are fairly accurate in predicting which items they'll remember when they are learning straightforward material like pairs of words (Hall & Bahrick, 1998; Izaute et al., 2002; Koriat & Goldsmith, 1998; Koriat et al., 2000). Metamemory is less accurate when the task is not so clearcut. In most college courses, you seldom know exactly what material will be on the test. Furthermore, you need to master concepts, not pairs of words. Metamemory judgment about conceptual material seems to be more difficult (Nelson, 1999).

We have noted that the kind of material influences the accuracy of your metamemory. Remember that, in this case, we are no longer discussing *memory accuracy*, the central topic in Chapters 4 and 5. Instead, we are discussing *metamemory accuracy*. For example, the participants in Lovelace's (1984) study had high metamemory accuracy. In other words, the participants were much more likely to remember those items they predicted they would remember, in contrast to those items they predicted they would not remember.

Other research shows that metamemory can be highly accurate—on an item-by-item basis—when people delay their judgments, rather than making them im-

FIGURE 6.4

Probability of Recalling an Item, as a Function of Experimental Condition and Rated Likelihood of Answering the Question.

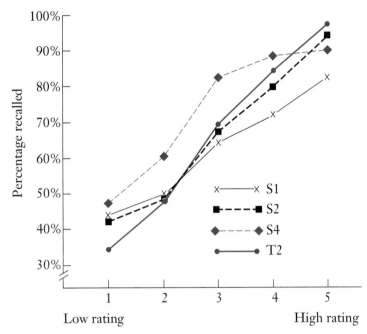

Source: Lovelace, 1984.

mediately after learning (Dunlosky & Nelson, 1994; Dunlosky et al., 2002; Kelemen & Weaver, 1997; Nelson, 1996; Son & Schwartz, 2002). These delayed judgments are especially likely to provide accurate assessments of your memory performance because they assess long-term memory—and the actual memory task requires long-term memory.* In contrast, immediate judgments assess working memory, which is less relevant to the memory task.

These particular findings suggest an important practical application. Suppose that you are studying your notes for an exam, and you are trying to determine which topics need more work. Be sure to wait a few minutes before assessing your memory (Dunlosky & Nelson, 1994). Your metamemory is more likely to be accurate if you wait than if you make an immediate judgment.

---

*In fact, it could be argued that this measure is actually a long-term memory test, rather than a true test of metamemory (Lovelace, 1996).

Metamemory on a Total-Score Basis. So far, we've looked at metamemory accuracy on an *item-by-item basis*, and we've seen that you can generally predict which items you'll remember and which you'll forget. However, as we noted on page 192, when people estimate their *total score* on a memory test, they are generally overconfident, rather than accurate.

Let's consider a recent study that demonstrates this overconfidence about total scores on a test. Dunning and his coauthors (2003) asked students in a sophomore-level psychology course to estimate the score they thought they had earned on an examination they had just completed. Then these researchers graded the test and divided the students into four groups, based on their actual test score. Figure 6.5 shows the performance for these four groups, the bottom quartile, second quartile, third quartile, and top quartile. Notice that the students in the top quartile estimated their total actual scores very accurately, and that students in the third quartile were almost as accurate. However, the less competent students clearly overestimated their performance. For instance, the students in the bottom quarter of the class overestimated their performance by about 30%. Ironically, this group of students is unaware of their limitations; they do not know that they do not know the material!

FIGURE 6.5

Estimated Score vs. Actual Score, as a Function of Actual Test Performance.

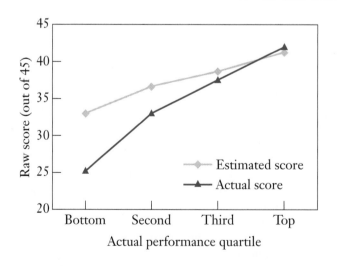

Source: Dunning et al., 2003.

Similar findings about overconfidence have been reported in other research. For example, college students are typically overconfident (Koriat, 2002; Koriat et al., 2002; Metcalfe, 1998a, 2000; Renner & Renner, 2001). This overconfidence is even more pronounced for people with frontal-lobe damage. These individuals are likely to be especially inaccurate on metacognitive tasks (Moses & Baird, 1999; Nelson, 1999; Shimamura, 1996). Ironically, these people are not aware that they have any cognitive deficits, and so they may believe that they are functioning very well. Notice the problem: People with frontal-lobe difficulties do not think they need to make any special efforts to remember information. As a result, they do not compensate appropriately for their memory deficits.

In Chapter 4, on working memory, we noted that the frontal lobe is the location for central-executive processing. This information makes sense, because planning, regulating, and other metacognitive tasks are the major responsibilities of the central executive.

Let's summarize the information about people's ability to predict their performance on a memory test. When we look at metamemory on an item-by-item basis, college students are fairly accurate in judging which individual items they'll remember and which ones they'll forget. In contrast, when we look at metamemory in terms of estimating total score on a memory test, the strongest college students are accurate, but the weaker students are overconfident.

Metamemory About Factors Affecting Memory

According to cognitive psychologists, many college students are not sufficiently aware of the importance of strategic factors that may affect their memory performance (Cornoldi, 1998). In fact, students who earn low scores on exams are likely to use no specific memory strategies in learning material for an exam (McDougall & Gruneberg, 2002).

Furthermore, metamemory should also help students identify which memory strategies work best for them and which ones are inefficient. However, Suzuki-Slakter (1988) found that students weren't aware that "all memory strategies are not created equal." For example, she instructed one group of students to memorize material by simply repeating it—a strategy that you know is relatively ineffective. These students seriously overestimated their performance. Another group was told to make up stories and images about the items—a strategy you know to be effective. These students actually *underestimated* their performance.

Other studies have found that people are not aware that the keyword method (illustrated in Figure 6.1, p. 179) is more effective than mere repetition (Pressley et al., 1984, 1988). However, when people practiced both methods and saw their superior performance with the keyword method, they were much more likely to use this method in the future. This research highlights an important point: Try using various study strategies, and then on your next test, see how you do. Identify which method or methods were most effective. You'll be much more likely to revise your strategies if you can demonstrate that they improve your own performance.

IN DEPTH

Metamemory and the Regulation of Study Strategies

You may have developed your metamemory to the point that you know exactly which study strategies work best in which circumstances. However, your exam performance may still be poor unless you effectively regulate your study strategies. For example, you need to control your time allotment, so that you spend much more time on the items you have not yet mastered than on those that you know you'll remember. The research on the regulation of study strategies emphasizes that memory tasks require a substantial amount of *decision making* as you plan how to master the material (Metcalfe, 2000). Consistent with Theme 4, many everyday cognitive activities require the coordination of two or more cognitive processes—in this case, memory and decision making.

This In Depth feature examines the way students make decisions about how they will allocate their study time, in preparing for a memory test. As you'll see, in some circumstances, students will spend more time on the difficult items than on the easy items. When the material is more challenging and the time is more limited, students will spend the most time learning the items that are just within their grasp.

Allocating Time When the Task is Easy. In a classic study, Thomas Nelson and R. Jacob Leonesio (1988) examined how students distribute their study time when they are allowed to study at their own pace. In this study, students were allowed a reasonable amount of time to study the material. Nelson and Leonesio found that students allocated more study time for the items that they believed would be difficult to master. The correlations here averaged about +.30 (where .00 would indicate no relationship and +1.00 would be a perfect correlation between each item's judged difficulty and its study time). In other words, the students did not passively review all the material equally. The research on metamemory reveals that people take an active, strategic approach to this cognitive task, a finding that is consistent with Theme 1 about active processing.

One of my professors in graduate school suggested an interesting perspective on research data (Martin, 1967). As he pointed out, whenever you see a number, you should ask yourself, "Why is it so high, and why is it so low?" In this case, the correlation is as *high* as +.30 because students do realize that they should study the difficult items more diligently. This general relationship has been replicated in later research (Cull & Zechmeister, 1994; Koriat, 1997; Nelson et al., 1994; Son & Schwartz, 2002; *see also* Son & Metcalfe, 2002). But why is this crucial correlation as *low* as +.30? Unfortunately, students are less than ideal in regulating their study strategies. They spend longer than necessary studying items they already know, and not enough time studying the items they have not yet mastered.

Let's translate these findings so that they apply to the way you might study this current chapter for an examination tomorrow. Let's assume that you are a typical student and that—fortunately—you have a fairly generous amount of time to devote to studying the chapter. You may decide that you know the material on the imagery mnemonics fairly well, but you are not confident about the section called "Metamemory and the Prediction of Memory Performance."

You might indeed spend somewhat longer studying the material on predicting memory performance. However, you would be likely to distribute your study time too evenly across the chapter, reviewing the comfortably familiar topics you already know. Can't you see yourself pausing to review the imagery mnemonics, but breezing too quickly over the distinctions between the two kinds of prediction tasks?

Here's another point. Students might *enjoy* thinking about a familiar topic, even if they have already mastered it. We can hardly condemn students for pausing to think about something that they find interesting, even if it is an easy concept. (Phillips, 1995). After all, efficient studying is not the only goal in a student's education!

Lisa Son and Janet Metcalfe (2000) reviewed the research on students' allocation of study time. They discovered that 35 out of the 46 published studies demonstrated that students spend more time on the difficult items. However, they found that all these studies examined relatively easy material, such as learning pairs of words. In addition, the students typically had enough time to study all of the items. Son and Metcalfe speculated that students might choose a different strategy in other circumstances.

Allocating Time When the Task is Difficult. Think about the exams you've taken so far this term. In psychology courses, for instance, your exams require you to remember conceptual information about psychology, rather than a list of paired words. In addition, you probably have only a limited time to study for your exams. Son and Metcalfe (2000) decided to design a situation that more closely resembles the more challenging learning situation that college students often face.

Let's consider the details of one of Son and Metcalfe's (2000) three studies. The test material was a series of eight encyclopedia-style biographies; a good reader would need about 60 minutes to read them all completely. The researchers increased the time pressure for this task by allowing the students only 30 minutes to read all the material. The students began by reading a single paragraph from each biography; they ranked the biographies in terms of their perceived difficulty. Then the researchers informed them that they had 30 minutes to read the material, and they could choose how to spend their time. In this study, students spent the majority of their study time on the biographies they considered easy, rather than those they considered difficult. Notice that this strategy was wise, because they could master more material within the limited time frame.

In further studies, Metcalfe (2002) demonstrated that, when students are facing time pressure, they choose to study material that they are especially likely to master. This material is typically either easy or moderately difficult, rather than very difficult. As you might expect, however, when Metcalfe tested students with expertise in a given area, they chose to concentrate their time on more challenging material than did the novices.

Conclusions About the Regulation of Study Strategies. As you can see from this In Depth feature, students can regulate their study strategies in a sophisticated fashion. When they have time to master a relatively easy task, they allocate the most time to the difficult items. On a more challenging task, with time pressure, they realistically adjust their study strategies so that they focus on the items they are likely to master in the limited time frame. In other words, students regulate their study strategies. Furthermore, they also regulate the *regulation* of their study strategies! That is, they choose one style for easy tasks, and a different style for difficult tasks. As Metcalfe (2000) concludes, "Rather than simply being passive repositories for knowledge and memories, humans can use their knowledge of what they know to exert control over what they know [and] what they will know" (p. 207).

Let's review the information about metamemory. We have explored how attention to your metamemory can improve your performance. Naturally, you need to know memory strategies, such as those described in the first part of this chapter. You also need to have the time and motivation to devise an appropriate plan for mastering the material (Langer, 2000; Winne & Hadwin, 1998). Finally, you need to know how to use memory strategies effectively by selecting those strategies that work well for you and by distributing your study time appropriately.

The Tip-of-the-Tongue Phenomenon

Try Demonstration 6.4 to see whether any of the definitions encourages a tip-of-the-tongue experience. The **tip-of-the-tongue phenomenon** refers to the subjective feeling you have when you are confident that you know the target word for which you are searching, yet you cannot recall it (Schwartz, 2002). In our discussion of this topic, let's first consider the classic study by Brown and McNeill (1966). Then we'll examine some of the later research, including the related topic of the feeling of knowing.

Brown and McNeill's Classic Research. Roger Brown and David McNeill (1966) conducted the first formal investigation in this area. Their description of a man "seized" by a tip-of-the-tongue state may capture the torment you sometimes feel when you fail to snatch a word from the tip of your tongue:

> The signs of it were unmistakable; he would appear to be in mild torment, something like the brink of a sneeze, and if he found the word his relief was considerable. (p. 326)

The similarity between "the brink of a sneeze" and the irritating tip-of-the-tongue experience is amazing! Don't you wish you had a substance similar to pepper that could coax the missing word out of memory?

In their research, Brown and McNeill produced the tip-of-the-tongue state by giving people the definition for an uncommon English word—such as *cloaca, ambergris,* or *nepotism*—and asking them to identify the word. Sometimes people supplied the appropriate word immediately, and other times they were confident that they did

---

🌀 Demonstration 6.4

The Tip-of-the-Tongue Phenomenon

Look at each of the definitions below. For each definition, supply the appropriate word if you know it. Indicate "don't know" for those that you are certain you don't know. Mark "TOT" next to those for which you are reasonably certain you know the word, though you can't recall it now. For these TOT words, supply at least one word that sounds similar to the target word. The answers appear at the end of the chapter. Check to see whether your similar-sounding words actually do resemble the target words.

1. An absolute ruler, a tyrant.
2. A stone having a cavity lined with crystals.
3. A great circle of the earth passing through the geographic poles and any given point on the earth's surface.
4. Worthy of respect or reverence by reason of age and dignity.
5. Shedding leaves each year, as opposed to evergreen.
6. A person appointed to act as a substitute for another.
7. Five offspring born at a single birth.
8. A special quality of leadership that captures the popular imagination and inspires unswerving allegiance.
9. The red coloring matter of the red blood corpuscles.
10. A flying reptile that was extinct at the end of the Mesozoic Era.
11. A spring from which hot water, steam, or mud gushes out at intervals, found in Yellowstone National Park.
12. The second stomach of a bird, which has thick, muscular walls.

---

not know the word. However, in some cases, the definition produced a tip-of-the-tongue state. In these cases, the researchers asked people to provide words that resembled the target word in terms of sound, but not meaning. For example, when the target word was *sampan*, people provided these similar-sounding words: *Saipan, Siam, Cheyenne, sarong, sanching,* and *symphoon.*

When Brown and McNeill analyzed the results, they found that the similar-sounding words were indeed very similar to the target words. Specifically, the similar-sounding words matched the target's first letter 49% of the time, and they matched the target's number of syllables 48% of the time.

Think about why the tip-of-the-tongue phenomenon is one kind of metacognition. People know enough about their memory for the target word to be able to say, "This word is on the tip of my tongue." Their knowledge is indeed fairly accurate, because they are likely to be able to identify the first letter and the number of sylla-bles in the target word. They are also likely to provide similar-sounding words that really do resemble the target word. In addition to metacognition, the tip-of-the-tongue phenomenon is related to several other topics in cognitive psychology, in-cluding consciousness (discussed in Chapter 3), semantic memory (discussed in Chapter 8), and language production (discussed in Chapter 10). As we have seen re-peatedly, cognitive processes are interrelated.

Later Research on the Tip-of-the-Tongue Phenomenon. Reviewing dozens of studies, researchers have concluded that people report having approximately one tip-of-the-tongue experience each week in their daily lives, although elderly people re-port it somewhat more often than younger adults (James & Burke, 2000; Schwartz, 2002). People successfully retrieve the word they are seeking about half the time, often within the first 2 minutes of the tip-of-the-tongue feeling. As you might expect, words that produce a strong tip-of-the-tongue sensation are especially likely to be correctly recognized at a later time (Schwartz, 2002; Schwartz et al., 2000).

In general, the research also shows that people correctly guess the first letter of the target word between 50% and 70% of the time. They are also highly accurate in identifying the appropriate number of syllables, with accuracy rates between 47% and 83% (Brown, 1991; Schwartz, 2002).

Furthermore, researchers have documented the tip-of-the-tongue phenomenon in non-English languages such as Polish, Japanese, and Italian (Schwartz, 1999, 2002). Research in these other languages demonstrates that people can retrieve other charac-teristics of the target word, in addition to its first letter and number of syllables. For example, Italian speakers can often retrieve the grammatical gender of the target word that they are seeking (Caramazza & Miozzo, 1997; Miozzo & Caramazza, 1997). In-terestingly, most languages have a descriptive phrase for the tip-of-the-tongue phe-nomenon that specifically contains the *tongue* metaphor (Schwartz, 2002).

Feeling of Knowing. Another topic related to the tip-of-the-tongue phenome-non is called the **feeling of knowing,** or the prediction about whether you could cor-rectly recognize the correct answer to a question (Schwartz & Perfect, 2002). The tip-of-the-tongue phenomenon is generally an involuntary effect. In contrast, the feeling of knowing is more conscious; we thoughtfully assess whether we could rec-ognize the answer if we were given several options.

We are likely to have a strong feeling of knowing if we can retrieve a large amount of partial information (Koriat et al., 2000; Schwartz et al., 1997; Schwartz & Smith, 1997). For example, as I was preparing to write this section, a friend men-tioned that she was going to a wedding in India, and she had been reading fiction about India. I recalled several books with which she was familiar, and then I recom-mended a book called *The Death of Vishnu.* I could recall reading it 2 years earlier and that the author is a math professor. A strong feeling of knowing enveloped me; what was the author's name? The available mental clues were that both his first and last names were short and fairly easy to pronounce. In this case, however, the name wasn't really on the tip of my tongue, and I wasn't able to recall the answer. However, I knew I could select the correct answer from a set of options. A quick check of some resources revealed his name: Manil Suri. Presumably this feeling of knowing would have been weaker if fewer mental clues had been available.

Metacomprehension

Did you understand the material on the tip-of-the-tongue phenomenon? How much longer can you read today before you feel that you can't absorb any more? Are you aware that you've started reading a new subtopic, in this current section on metacognition? As you think about these issues, you are engaging in metacomprehension. **Metacomprehension** refers to our thoughts about comprehension. Most research on metacomprehension focuses on reading comprehension, rather than on the comprehension of spoken speech (Maki & McGuire, 2002). The general term, *metacognition*, includes both metamemory (pp. 191 to 198) and metacomprehension (pp. 201 to 203).

Let's consider two topics in connection with metacomprehension. First, how accurate is the typical college student's metacomprehension? Second, how can you improve your metacomprehension skills?

Metacomprehension Accuracy. In general, college students are not very accurate in their metacomprehension skills. For example, they may fail to detect inconsistencies in a written passage; instead, they think they understand it (Maki, 1998; Metcalfe, 1998a). They also think that they have understood something they have read because they are familiar with its general topic (Chi, 2000). However, they often fail to retain specific information, and they overestimate how they will perform when they are tested on the material (Maki, 1998; Maki et al., 1994; Maki & McGuire, 2002).

Let's consider a representative study on metacomprehension. Pressley and Ghatala (1988) tested introductory psychology students to assess their metacomprehension as well as their performance on two other metacognitive tasks. Metacomprehension was tested using the reading comprehension tests from the Scholastic Aptitude Test, an earlier form of the Scholastic Assessment Test (SAT). If you took the SAT, you'll recall that the items on this portion of the test typically contain between one and three paragraphs, in essay form, accompanied by several multiple-choice questions.

The students in Pressley and Ghatala's study answered the multiple-choice questions, and then they rated how certain they were that they had answered each question correctly. If they were absolutely certain that their answer had been correct, they were told to answer 100%. If they were just guessing, they were told to report 20%. (Because the test items each had five possible answers, a person who simply guessed on an answer would be correct 20% of the time.) This certainty rating served as the measure of metacomprehension. (Notice, incidentally, that this task would have assessed metamemory—rather than metacomprehension—if there had been a delay between the reading task and the presentation of the multiple-choice questions.)

Let's consider the results. When a student had answered a reading comprehension question *correctly*, he or she supplied an average certainty rating of 73%. In other words, the students were fairly confident about these items, which is appropriate. However, when a student answered a question *incorrectly*, he or she supplied an average certainty rating of about 64%. Unfortunately, this is about the same level of confidence they showed for the items they answered correctly! Furthermore, these data suggest that students are highly overconfident in many cases. They believe that they understand what they have just finished reading, even when they answered the questions incorrectly.

These same students also completed two other tasks on the SAT. Interestingly, the students were much more accurate in assessing their comprehension of vocabulary terms and their comprehension of relationships between vocabulary terms, compared with their poor metacomprehension on the essays.

People with excellent metacomprehension sometimes receive higher scores on tests of reading comprehension (Maki & Berry, 1984; Maki et al., 1994; Maki & McGuire, 2002; Schraw, 1994). For example, Maki and her coauthors (1994) reported that readers who were good at assessing which sections of a text they had understood were also likely to receive higher scores on a reading comprehension test. In fact, metacomprehension accuracy and reading comprehension scores were significantly correlated ($r = +.43$).

Students also become somewhat more accurate in assessing their performance as they gain experience in reading the text and as they receive feedback (Maki & Berry, 1984; Maki & Serra, 1992). However, the improvement is not dramatic. College students clearly need some hints on how to increase their metacomprehension abilities and how to take advantage of their reading experiences.

Improving Metacomprehension. Ideally, students should be accurate in assessing whether they understand what they have read; in other words, their subjective assessments should match their performance on an objective test. One effective way to improve metacomprehension is to take a pretest, which can supply feedback about comprehension, before taking the actual examination (Glenberg et al., 1987; Maki, 1998).

Another effective method for improving metacomprehension is to wait a few minutes after reading a passage and then try to think of some words or phrases that summarize the passage. This procedure not only improves your judgment about how well you know the passage, but it should also increase your score on a test about this material (Thiede et al., 2003).

Several studies show that students' predictions are more accurate when they have used deep, elaborative processing while reading a passage (Maki, 1998). This deep processing may encourage them to assess how well they know the material. Throughout Chapter 5 and the beginning of this chapter, we've emphasized that deep processing directly increases your retention. Deep processing also offers a second advantage: It forces you to decide whether you really understand the material you are currently reading.

As we have seen, one component of metacomprehension requires you to accurately assess whether or not you understand a written passage. However, metacomprehension also requires you to *regulate* your reading, so that you know how to read more effectively. For example, good and poor readers differ in their awareness that certain reading strategies are useful. Good readers are more likely to report that they try to make connections among the ideas they have read. They also try to create visual images, based on descriptions in the text (Kaufman et al., 1985; Pressley, 1996). In addition, good readers outline and summarize material when they are reading textbooks (McDaniel et al., 1996).

Psychologists have also discovered that good readers can categorize different kinds of reading situations. They know that their approach to reading a chemistry chapter in preparation for an exam must be different from their approach to reading a Shakespeare play before writing an essay (Lorch et al., 1995; McDaniel et al., 1996; Pressley & Afflerbach, 1995). As we have seen in this chapter, good students regulate their use of memory strategies; they regulate the way they allocate their study time; and they regulate their approach to reading, according to the nature of the material.

Demonstration 6.5 will help you consider your own metacomprehension skills and think about some strategies for self-management.

---

⑨ Demonstration 6.5

Assessing Your Metacomprehension Skills

Answer each of the following questions about your own metacomprehension. If you answer "no" to any question, devise a plan for improving metacomprehension that you can apply as you read the next assigned chapter in this textbook.

1. Before beginning to read an assignment, do you try to assess how carefully you should read the material?

2. In general, are you accurate in predicting your performance on exam questions related to reading?

3. After reading a chapter in this textbook, do you test yourself on the list of new terms and on the review questions?

4. After you read a short section (roughly a page in length), do you make yourself summarize what you have just read—using your own words?

5. Do you reread a portion when it doesn't make sense or when you realize that you haven't been paying attention?

6. Do you try to draw connections among the ideas in your textbook?

7. Do you try to draw connections between the ideas in your textbook and information you have learned in class?

8. When you read a term you do not know, do you try to determine its meaning by looking it up in a dictionary or in the glossary of this textbook?

9. When you review material prior to a test, do you spend more time reviewing the reading that you consider difficult than the reading you consider easy?

10. When reading through several journal articles to see whether they might be relevant for a paper you are writing, do you try to assess—without reading every word—the general scope or findings of each article?

◎ Section Summary: *Metacognition*

1. Metacognition is your knowledge, awareness, and control of your cognitive processes; three important components of metacognition are metamemory, the tip-of-the-tongue phenomenon, and metacomprehension.

2. People's metamemories are quite accurate when they are judging which items they will remember best, but they are often overconfident about their overall performance.

3. In general, students are not sufficiently aware that some memory strategies are more effective than others.

4. When the task is easy, students spend somewhat more time studying difficult material, rather than easy material; when the task is difficult—and time is limited—they study material that they are likely to master.

5. The research on the tip-of-the-tongue phenomenon shows that—even when people cannot remember the word for which they are searching—they often can identify important attributes such as the first letter, the number of syllables, and similar-sounding words.

6. Studies on metacomprehension suggest that students are often overconfident in judging whether they understand the material they have read.

7. Students' metacomprehension can be improved if they take a pretest, if they wait a few minutes and think of phrases that summarize the material, and if they use deep processing during reading; good readers also use a variety of strategies to regulate their reading.

CHAPTER REVIEW QUESTIONS

1. One theme that occurred throughout the chapter is that memory is enhanced by deep levels of processing and by elaborative processing. Review the material in the section on memory strategies, identifying how almost every strategy makes use of deep processing. Also explain why deep processing would be important in metacognition.

2. Discuss as many of the memory-improvement techniques from this chapter as you can remember. In each case, tell how you can use each one to remember some information from this chapter for your next examination in cognitive psychology.

3. Why are some current memory researchers critical of the traditional approaches to memory improvement? Why does the multimodal approach emphasize a more comprehensive and complex view of memory improvement?

4. Describe Langer's concepts of mindlessness and mindfulness. Then turn to the chapter outline on page 171. Using these topics as a guide, point out how you can be more mindful in reading and studying for your next exam in cognitive psychology.

5. Why is prospective memory both different from and similar to retrospective memory? Think of a specific elderly person you know who complains about his or her memory. Does this person have more difficulty with prospective memory or with retrospective memory? What hints can you provide to this person to encourage better prospective-memory performance?

6. In general, how accurate is our metacognition? Provide examples from various metamemory studies, the tip-of-the-tongue phenomenon, and metacomprehension. When you describe the research on metamemory, be sure to describe the situation in which people are accurate and the situation in which they are inaccurate.

7. Several parts of this chapter emphasized that people tend to be overconfident about their ability to remember material and to understand written material. Summarize this information, and then describe how you can apply this information when you are reading and studying for your next exam in your course on cognitive psychology.

8. Some parts of the section on metacognition emphasized the regulation of study strategies and reading strategies, rather than simply the awareness of cognitive processes. Describe the research on strategy regulation and point out how your own strategy regulation has improved since you began college.

9. What evidence suggests that you are reasonably accurate when you report that a word is on the tip of your tongue? Why is this topic related to metacognition? What other components of the tip-of-the-tongue phenomenon would be interesting topics for future research?

10. What kind of metacomprehension tasks are relevant when you are reading this textbook? List as many tasks as possible. Why do you suppose that metacomprehension for reading passages of text would be less accurate than metamemory for learning pairs of words (for example, refer to the 1984 study by Lovelace, described on pp. 192–193)?

NEW TERMS

metacognition
memory strategy
levels of processing
rehearsal
self-reference effect
encoding specificity principle
total time hypothesis
distribution of practice effect
spacing effect
mnemonics

imagery
keyword method
method of loci
organization
chunking
hierarchy
first-letter technique
narrative technique
multimodal approach
mindfulness

mindlessness
prospective memory
retrospective memory
external memory aid
metamemory
tip-of-the-tongue phenomenon
feeling of knowing
metacomprehension

RECOMMENDED READINGS

Herrmann, D., Raybeck, D., & Gruneberg, M. (2002). *Improving memory and study skills.* Kirkland, WA: Hogrefe & Huber. Many books on memory improvement are based on the author's whims. In contrast, this useful book is written by well-respected researchers in the area, and it approaches the topic from a comprehensive perspective.

Kvavilashvili, L., & Ellis, J. (Eds.). (2000). New perspectives in prospective memory [special issue]. *Applied Cognitive Psychology, 14* (S1). This special issue provides a representative sample of research articles about prospective memory, including topics such as prospective memory in older adults and neuroscience research about prospective memory. I would also recommend browsing through other issues of *Applied Cognitive Psychology*; as the journal's title implies, you'll find many readable articles that have practical applications.

Perfect, T. J., & Schwartz, B. L. (Eds.). (2002). *Applied metacognition.* Cambridge, England: Cambridge University Press. I highly recommend this book if you want additional information about metacognition! It includes chapters on topics such as metamemory monitoring, metacomprehension, overconfidence, and the development of metacognition.

Schwartz, B. L. (2002). *Tip-of-the-tongue states: Phenomenology, mechanism, and lexical retrieval.* Mahweh, NJ: Erlbaum. Bennett Schwartz is one of the leading researchers on the tip-of-the-tongue phenomenon; his book provides a clear and interesting review of the research, as well as potential theories to explain this phenomenon.

Tulving, E., & Craik, F. I. M. (Eds.). (2000). *The Oxford handbook of memory.* New York: Oxford University Press. Two chapters in this handbook are especially helpful in providing details about metamemory: Asher Koriat's chapter on control processes in memory and Janet Metcalfe's chapter on metamemory.

ANSWERS TO DEMONSTRATION 6.4

1. despot
2. geode
3. meridian
4. venerable
5. deciduous
6. surrogate
7. quintuplets
8. charisma
9. hemoglobin
10. pterodactyl
11. geyser
12. gizzard

CHAPTER 7

Mental Imagery and Cognitive Maps

PREVIEW

Chapters 4, 5, and 6 have emphasized how we remember verbal material. Now we shift our focus to more pictorial material as we investigate three components of mental imagery: the characteristics of mental images, neuroscience research on mental images, and cognitive maps.

Psychologists have devised some creative research techniques to examine the characteristics of mental images. In many ways, mental images and the perception of real objects are similar. For example, if you were asked to create a mental image of an elephant sitting next to a rabbit, the mental image of the elephant would be larger. The section on mental images also examines a controversy about how we store mental images in memory: Are images stored in a picture-like code or in a more abstract, language-like description?

We'll also explore the recent evidence from cognitive neuroscience research. This research suggests that mental images activate some of the same brain structures that are activated during vision, hearing, and motor movement.

A cognitive map is a representation of your external environment. For instance, you have developed a cognitive map of the town or city in which your college is located. Our cognitive maps show certain systematic distortions. For example, you may remember that two streets intersect at right angles, even when the angles are far from 90°. Because of these distortions, our mental maps are a more organized and more standardized version of reality. The In Depth feature in this chapter will consider how people can create mental models of their environment, based on verbal descriptions.

INTRODUCTION

Take a moment to create a clear mental image of the cover of this textbook, including details such as its size, shape, and color, as well as the photo of the nautilus shell. You'll probably find the task easier if you close your eyes. Next, create a "mental map" of the most direct route between your current location and the nearest grocery store. Once again, close your eyes while you try to create this mental representation. This chapter examines **imagery,** which is the mental representation of stimuli when those stimuli are not physically present (Kosslyn et al., 2002). Imagery relies exclusively on top-down processing (Kosslyn & Thompson, 2000). We discussed perceptual processes in Chapters 2 and 3 of this book. Perception—in contrast to imagery—requires you to register information through the receptors in your sensory organs, such as your eyes and ears (Kosslyn, Ganis, & Thompson, 2001). As we emphasized earlier, perception requires both bottom-up and top-down processing.

We use imagery for a wide variety of cognitive activities. Try Demonstration 7.1 to illustrate the relevance of imagery in the chapters of this book that you have already

---

⑨ **Demonstration 7.1**

The Relevance of Mental Imagery in Earlier Chapters of This Book

Look back at the Table of Contents (just before Chapter 1) to review the outlines for Chapters 2–6. How would visual imagery or auditory imagery be relevant in each of these chapters? How would imagery for the movements of your arms or legs be relevant in Chapter 5's discussion of source monitoring? For the answers, look on page 244, at the end of this chapter.

---

read. Imagery is also relevant in the cognitive processes we'll discuss later in this textbook. For example, you'll see in Chapter 11 that mental imagery is immensely helpful when you want to solve a spatial problem or work on a task that requires creativity. In addition, some professions require skilled use of mental images: Would you want to fly on an airplane if the pilot had weak spatial imagery? Imagery also plays an important role in your daily life when you try to remember where you parked your car or when you plan the quickest route home from an unfamiliar location.

What kind of imagery do we use most often? When students were asked to keep diaries about their mental imagery, they reported that about two-thirds of their images were visual (Kosslyn et al., 1990). Images for hearing, touch, taste, and smell were much less common. Psychologists show a similar lopsidedness in their research preferences. Researchers occasionally study topics such as auditory imagery or smell imagery. However, most of the studies examine visual imagery (Kosslyn & Shin, 1999).

The first psychologists considered imagery to be an important part of the discipline. For example, Wundt and his followers carefully analyzed the self-reports provided in the introspections that their trained observers provided about imagery (Anderson, 1998; Palmer, 1999).

In contrast, behaviorists such as John Watson were strongly opposed to research on mental imagery, because mental images could not be directly connected to observable behavior. As a consequence, North American psychologists seldom developed research or theories about imagery during the period between 1920 and 1960 (Palmer, 1999; Tversky, 2000b). As behaviorism declined in popularity, however, cognitive psychologists rediscovered imagery. In fact, they have made it one of the most controversial areas in contemporary cognitive psychology (Farah, 2000a; Kosslyn, Ganis, & Thompson, 2001).

This chapter explores three aspects of imagery that have intrigued contemporary researchers. First, we examine the nature of mental images, with an emphasis on the way we transform these images. Then we'll explore some of the cognitive neuroscience research on different types of mental imagery. Our final topic is cognitive maps, or the mental representation of geographic information.

THE CHARACTERISTICS OF MENTAL IMAGES

As you might expect, research on mental imagery is difficult to conduct, especially because mental images are not directly observable and because they fade so quickly (Richardson, 1999). However, during recent decades, psychologists have applied to mental imagery some of the research techniques developed for studying visual perception. As a result, the investigation of imagery has made impressive advances. Try Demonstration 7.2 on page 211, which illustrates an important research technique that we'll examine shortly.

One of the major controversies in this field is the analog/propositional debate: Do our mental images resemble perception, or do they resemble language? We'll introduce that question now, and return to discuss it in more detail once we've examined the evidence.

Many theorists argue that information about a mental image is stored in an analog code (Kosslyn et al., 2002). An **analog code** (also called a **depictive representation** or a **pictorial representation**) is a representation that closely resembles the physical object. Notice that the word *analog* suggests the word *analogy*, such as the analogy between the real object and the mental image.

According to the analog-code approach, mental imagery is a close relative of perception (Baird & Hubbard, 1992). When you look at a photograph of a triangle, the physical features of that triangle are registered in your brain in a form that preserves the physical relationship among the three lines. Those who support analog coding argue that your mental image of a triangle is registered in a similar fashion, preserving the same relationship among the lines.

In contrast to the analog-code position, other theorists argue that we store images in terms of a propositional code (Pylyshyn, 1984, 2003). A **propositional code** (also called a **descriptive representation**) is an abstract, language-like representation; storage is neither visual nor spatial, and it does not physically resemble the original stimulus.

According to the propositional-code approach, mental imagery is a close relative of language, not perception (Baird & Hubbard, 1992). For example, if you try to create a mental image of a triangle, your brain will register a language-like description of the lines and angles, though the precise nature of the verbal description has not been specified.

The controversy about analog versus propositional coding has not been resolved. The majority of people who conduct research on visual imagery support the analog position, perhaps partly because they personally experience vivid, picture-like images (Reisberg et al., 2003). Like most controversies in psychology, both the analog and the propositional approaches are probably at least partially correct. As you read the following pages, you'll find it helpful to decide which studies support each viewpoint, so that you can appreciate the summary toward the end of this section, on pages 224–225.

We noted earlier that mental imagery is a challenging topic to study. Compared with topics such as verbal memory, this mental process is elusive and inaccessible. Researchers have attacked this problem by using the following logic: If a mental image really does resemble a physical object, then people must make judgments about a

🌀 **Demonstration 7.2**

Mental Rotation.

Which of these pairs of objects are the same, and which are different?

A

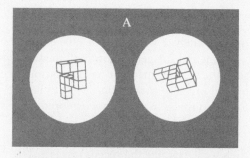

B

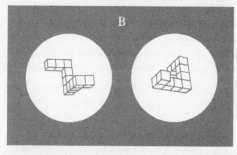

C

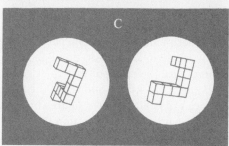

Source: Reprinted with permission from Shepard, R. N., & Metzler, J. (1971). Mental rotation of three-dimensional objects. *Science, 171,* 701–703. Copyright 1971 American Association for the Advancement of Science.

mental image in the same way that they make judgments about the corresponding physical object. For example, we should be able to rotate a mental image in the same way we can rotate a physical object. Judgments about size and shape should also be similar. In addition, a mental image should interfere with the perception of a physical object. Furthermore, we should be able to discover two interpretations of a mental image of an ambiguous figure, and we should be able to produce illusions and other vision-like effects when we construct a mental image. Let's now consider these potential parallels between imagery and perception.

Imagery and Rotation

Suppose that you are a researcher who wants to study whether people rotate a mental image in the same way they rotate a physical object. It's tempting to think that you could simply ask people to analyze their mental images and use these reports as a basis for a description of mental imagery. However, these introspective reports can be unreliable and biased because we may not have conscious access to the processes associated with our mental imagery (Anderson, 1998; Pinker, 1985). You may recall that the discussion of consciousness in Chapter 3 explored this issue.

More research has been conducted on mental imagery and rotation than on any other imagery-related topic. Let's first consider the original study by Shepard and Metzler (1971), and then we'll examine the recent research.

Shepard and Metzler's Research. It's interesting to contemplate how the research on mental imagery might have been substantially delayed if Roger Shepard hadn't had an unusual half-dream on November 16, 1968. He was just emerging from sleep on that morning when he visualized a 3-dimensional structure majestically turning in space (Shepard, 1978). This vivid image inspired the first study on imagery that used careful controls and measurement procedures—the first study that made those inaccessible mental images more accessible. It provided objective, quantitative data that could even satisfy many behaviorists (Cooper & Shepard, 1984). This study is now considered one of the classics in cognitive psychology, and it helped to earn Roger Shepard the U.S. National Medal of Science in 1995.

You tried this classic experiment by Roger Shepard and his coauthor Jacqueline Metzler (1971) when you worked on Demonstration 7.2. Notice that in the top pair of designs, the left-hand figure can be changed into the right-hand figure by keeping it flat on the page and rotating it clockwise. Suddenly, the two figures match up, and you conclude "same." You can match these two figures by using a 2-dimensional rotation. In contrast, the middle pair requires a rotation in a third dimension. You may, for example, take the two-block "arm" that is jutting out toward you and push it over to the left and away from you. Suddenly, again, the figures match up, and you conclude "same." In the case of the bottom pair, you cannot rotate the figure on the left so that it matches the figure on the right. Therefore, you conclude "different."

Shepard and Metzler (1971) asked eight participants to judge 1,600 pairs of line drawings like these. They were instructed to pull a lever with their right hand if they judged the figures to be the same, and to pull a different lever with their left hand if they judged the figures to be different. In each case, the experimenters measured the amount of time required for a decision. Notice, then, that the dependent variable is *reaction time*, in contrast to the dependent variable of *accuracy* in most of the research we have examined in this textbook.

Part A of Figure 7.1 shows the results for figures like Pair A in Demonstration 7.1. These figures require only a 2-dimensional rotation, similar to rotating a flat picture. In contrast, Part B of Figure 7.1 shows the results for figures like Pair B in Demonstration 7.1. These figures require a 3-dimensional rotation, similar to rotating an object in depth. As both graphs show, people's decision time was strongly influenced by the amount of rotation required to match a figure with its mate. For example, rotating a figure 160° requires much more time than rotating it a mere 20°. Furthermore, notice the similarity between Figures 7.1A and 7.1B; the participants in this study performed a 3-dimensional rotation just as quickly as a 2-dimensional rotation.

As you can see, the relationship between rotation and reaction time is strictly linear in both figures. This research supports the analog code, because you would take much longer to rotate an actual physical object 160° than to rotate it a mere 20°.

Recent Research on Mental Rotation. The basic findings about mental rotation have been replicated many times. Using other stimuli, such as letters of the alphabet, researchers have found a clear relationship between angle of rotation and reaction time (e.g., Bauer & Jolicoeur, 1996; Cooper & Lang, 1996; Jordan & Huntsman, 1990; Newcombe, 2002).

FIGURE 7.1

Reaction Time for Deciding That Pairs of Figures Are the Same, as a Function of the Angle of Rotation and the Nature of Rotation. Note: The centers of the circles indicate the means, and the bars on either side provide an index of the variability of those means.

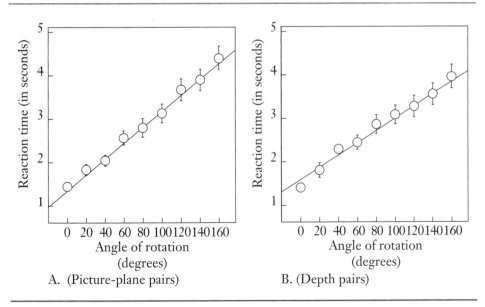

A. (Picture-plane pairs)   B. (Depth pairs)

Source: Shepard & Metzler, 1971.

We also know that elderly people perform more slowly than younger people on a mental-rotation task; in contrast, age does not influence other mental-imagery abilities, such as constructing or scanning mental images (Dror & Kosslyn, 1994). Furthermore, you won't be surprised to learn that individual differences in the rate of mental rotation are extremely large (Favreau, 1993; Kail et al., 1979).

However, practice on one mental-rotation task may not improve your performance on a different mental-rotation task (Sims & Mayer, 2002). Specifically, after students had spent 12 hours practicing the video game Tetris, they performed better than control-group students on mental-rotation tasks in which the stimuli resembled Tetris-game figures. When the mental-rotation task used visually different stimuli, all those hours of practice had no effect.

Other research shows that deaf individuals who are fluent in American Sign Language (ASL) are especially skilled in looking at an arrangement of objects in a scene and rotating that scene by 180° (Emmorey et al., 1998). Individuals who use sign language have extensive experience in watching a narrator produce a sign and rotating this sign 180°. This rotation is necessary in order to match the perspective that they would use when producing this sign. (If you are not fluent in ASL, stand in front of a mirror and notice how you and a viewer would have entirely different perspectives on your hand movements.)

Still other research has examined whether people can actually use the motor cortex of their brain when they imagine themselves rotating one of the geometric figures. Kosslyn, Thompson, and their coauthors (2001) instructed some participants to rotate—with their own hands—one of the geometric figures that had been used in Shepard and Metzler's (1971) study. They instructed other participants to simply watch as an electric motor rotated this same figure.

Next, the people in both groups performed the matching task you tried in Demonstration 7.2, by rotating the figures mentally. Meanwhile, the researchers conducted PET scans to see which areas of the brain the participants used during the mental-rotation task. The PET-scan results were clear-cut. Those participants who had rotated the original geometric figure with their hands now showed activity in the primary motor cortex—the same part of the brain that was active during the manual rotation task. In contrast, participants showed no activity in the primary motor cortex if they had simply watched as the electric motor rotated the figure.

In general, then, the research on rotating geometric figures provides some of the strongest support for the analog-coding approach. We seem to treat mental images the same way we treat physical objects when we rotate them through space.

Imagery and Size

As we have seen, the first systematic research on imagery demonstrated the similarity between rotating mental images and rotating physical objects. Researchers immediately began to examine other attributes of mental images, such as their size and shape. Try Demonstration 7.3 before you read further. Then we will discuss Kosslyn's classic research on visual imagery and size, as well as recent research on the topic.

---

⑨ **Demonstration 7.3**

Imagery and Size

    A. Imagine an elephant standing next to a rabbit. Now answer this question: *Does a rabbit have eyelashes?*

    B. Imagine a fly standing next to a rabbit. Now answer this question: *Does a rabbit have eyebrows?*

In which picture was the rabbit the largest—A or B? Which picture seemed to have more detail in the area you were examining for the eyelashes or the eyebrows—A or B?

Kosslyn's Research. Questions like those in Demonstration 7.3 were part of a carefully planned series of experiments conducted by Stephen Kosslyn, who is one of the most important researchers in the field of mental imagery. Kosslyn (1975) wanted to discover whether people would make faster judgments about large images than about small images. You can probably anticipate a major problem with this research area: How can we control the size of someone's mental image? Kosslyn reasoned that a mental image of an elephant next to a rabbit would force people to imagine a relatively small rabbit. In contrast, a mental image of a fly next to a rabbit would produce a relatively large rabbit.

When you look at real-life pictures of animals, you can see all the details quite clearly on a large picture. However, when you look at a small picture, the details are squeezed in so close together that it is difficult to make judgments about them. Suppose that this same rule for real-life pictures also holds true for the pictures in our heads. Then people should make judgments more quickly with a large mental image (such as a rabbit next to a fly) than with a small mental image (such as a rabbit next to an elephant). In Kosslyn's experiment, people made judgments about objects—for example, whether a rabbit had legs. Kosslyn's (1975) results support his prediction; judgments were significantly faster when the target mental image was large, rather than small.

Recent Research on Imagery and Size. In other research on the relationship between size and response time, Kosslyn and his colleagues (1978) showed that people required a long time to scan the distance between two widely separated points on a mental map that they had created. In contrast, they scanned the distance between two nearby points quite rapidly.

Additional research on imagery and size was designed to examine an important issue concerning research methods. Could the previous results be explained by experimenter expectancy, rather than a genuine influence from the size of the mental image? In **experimenter expectancy,** the researchers' biases and expectations influence the outcomes of the experiment. For example, researchers who conduct research in mental imagery know that longer distances should require longer search times. Perhaps these researchers could somehow transmit their expectations to the participants in the study. These participants might—either consciously or unconsciously—adjust their search speeds according to the expectations (Denis & Kosslyn, 1999a; Intons-Peterson, 1983).

To answer this criticism, Jolicoeur and Kosslyn (1985a, 1985b) repeated Kosslyn and his coauthors' (1978) mental-map experiment. However, the two research assistants who actually administered the new study were not familiar with the research on mental imagery. Instead, they were given elaborate and convincing (but incorrect) explanations about why their results should show a U-shaped relationship between distance and scanning time, rather than the typical linear relationship found in the previous research. The research assistants obtained results in this experiment that—once again—demonstrated the standard linear relationship, in which participants took longer to scan a large mental distance. Experimenter expectancy therefore cannot account for the obtained results (Denis & Kosslyn, 1999b). Additional research, summarized by Denis and Kosslyn (1999b) confirms the finding that people require more time to travel large mental distances.

Monique Smeets and Stephen Kosslyn (2001) conducted a study about women's judgments of body size that has important implications for clinical psychology. Some participants in their study were identified as having **anorexia nervosa,** a disorder in which a person is significantly underweight and has an intense fear of gaining weight (American Psychiatric Association, 2000). The participants in the control group were slender, but they were not experiencing anorexia nervosa. Each woman in both groups participated in a visual task in which she saw a brief video of herself, dressed in a leotard. In some cases, the image in the video was distorted to look either fatter or thinner, and in other cases, the woman saw an undistorted version. In each case, the woman had to judge whether this image was thinner, fatter, or equal to her real body size. The results showed that the women with anorexia nervosa were likely to judge the "distorted fatter" image as being equal to their own body size. In contrast, the women in the control group did not show any systematic distortion in their body image. Therapists need to keep this point in mind: Clients with anorexia have a mental image of their body size that is a distorted representation of their actual body size.

Up to this point, we have considered only visual images, asking questions about the sizes of imagined animals, distances on imagined maps, and the size of people's own bodies. Other research has examined auditory imagery. This research shows that people can quickly "travel" the distance between two musical notes that are similar in pitch. In contrast, people require more travel time if the two notes are widely separated on the musical scale (Intons-Peterson et al., 1992).

Imagery and Shape

So far, we've seen that our mental images resemble real, physical images in the research on rotation and in the research on size (although women with anorexia nervosa have distorted body-size imagery). The research on shape shows the same relationship.

Consider, for example, another classic study on visual imagery. Allan Paivio (1978) asked participants to make judgments about the angle formed by the two hands on a mental clock. For example, try to visualize the two hands on a standard, nondigital clock, and create a mental image of the angle formed by the two hands if the time were 3:20. Now create a mental image of the angle if the time were 7:25. Which of these two "mental clocks" has the smaller angle between the two hands?

Paivio also gave the participants several standardized tests for mental-imagery ability. As you can see in Figure 7.2, the high-imagery participants made decisions much more quickly than the low-imagery participants. As Figure 7.2 also shows, participants in both groups made decisions very slowly when they compared the angle formed by the hands at 3:20 with the angle of the hands at 7:25. After all, these two angles are quite similar. In contrast, their decisions were relatively fast if the two angles were very different in size. With real objects, people take a long time to make decisions when the objects are similar; when the objects are different, they respond quickly. People show the same pattern with their mental images of objects. According to Paivio (1978), this study offers strong support for the proposal that people use analog codes, rather than propositional codes.

Additional support for analog codes comes from research with mental images representing more complex shapes. Shepard and Chipman (1970) asked people to construct mental images of the shapes of various U.S. states, such as Colorado and Oregon. For example—without looking at a map—how similar in shape do Colorado and

FIGURE 7.2

The Influence of Angle Difference on Reaction Time, for High-Imagery and Low-Imagery People.

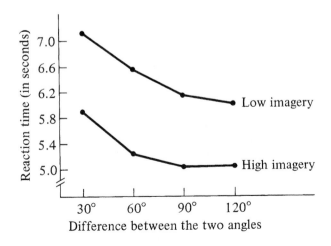

Oregon seem to you? How about Colorado and West Virginia? The same participants also made shape-similarity judgments about pairs of states in which they saw a physical sketch of each state, rather than only its name. The participants' judgments were highly similar in the two conditions. Once again, people's judgments about the shape of mental images are similar to their judgments about the shape of physical stimuli.

Let's review our conclusions about the characteristics of mental images, based on the research we have discussed so far:

1. When people *rotate* a mental image, a large rotation takes them longer, just as they take longer when making a large rotation with a physical stimulus.
2. People make *size* judgments in a similar fashion for mental images and physical stimuli; this conclusion holds true for both visual and auditory images.
3. People make decisions about *shape* in a similar fashion for mental images and physical stimuli; this conclusion holds true for both simple shapes (angles formed by hands on a clock) and complex shapes (geographic regions, like Colorado or West Virginia).

Now, let's consider some additional research that demonstrates some similarity between mental images and physical stimuli—specifically, the research on interference. As we will see, the research shows that the correspondence is strong, but it is less than perfect.

Imagery and Interference

A number of studies show that mental images and physical images can interfere with one another (e.g., Baddeley & Andrade, 1998; Brooks, 1968; Craver-Lemley & Reeves, 1987, 1992; Richardson, 1999). Let's consider two topics related to interference, specifically demonstrating that (1) a visual image interferes with visual perception, and (2) motor movement interferes with motor imagery.

Visual Images and Visual Perception. Try to create a mental image of a close friend's face, and simultaneously let your eyes wander over this page. You will probably find the task to be difficult, because you are trying to look (with your mind's eye) at your friend, and—at the same time—you are trying to look at the words on the page (a physical stimulus). In other words, you experience interference. Research has confirmed that visual imagery can indeed interfere with visual perception.

Consider the research of Segal and Fusella (1970), who asked participants to create either a visual image (for example, an image of a tree) or an auditory image (for example, the sound of an oboe). As soon as each person had formed the requested image, the experimenters presented a real physical stimulus—either a sound on a harmonica (auditory stimulus) or a small blue arrow (visual stimulus). The researchers measured the participants' ability to detect the physical stimulus.

Segal and Fusella's (1970) results showed that people were much less likely to detect the physical stimulus when the image and the signal were in the same sensory mode. For example, participants often failed to report the arrow when they had been imagining the shape of a tree; the visual image interfered with the real visual stimulus. In contrast, they had no trouble reporting that they saw the arrow when they had been imagining the sound of an oboe (that is, two different sensory modes). Similarly, they had more difficulty hearing the harmonica when they had been imagining the sound of an oboe than when they had been imagining the shape of a tree.

In a more recent study on visual interference, Mast and his colleagues (1999) instructed participants to lie on their side. Then the participants were told to imagine a set of narrow parallel lines. They were also told to rotate their mental image of this set of lines, so that the lines were in a diagonal orientation. Meanwhile, they tried to make judgments about a short line segment, specifically, whether it was presented in an exactly vertical orientation. The results showed that the imagined set of lines had the same effect as a real, physical set of lines. Both the imagined and the real set of lines produced a distortion in the participants' judgments about the line segment's vertical orientation.

Motor Movement and Motor Images. So far, the research we've discussed has emphasized visual images, though we've occasionally mentioned auditory images. However, in our daily lives we also create images of motor movements. For example, if you are taking a tennis class, you might imagine yourself serving the ball. Interestingly, if you are performing an actual motor movement at the same time (perhaps rotating the steering wheel while driving), you may have more difficulty creating an appropriate motor image.

Some research on motor imagery has been conducted by Wexler, Kosslyn, and Berthoz (1998), using a modification of the mental-rotation task. These researchers selected a motor-movement task that required participants to rotate a motor-controlled joystick at a steady rate, in either a clockwise or a counterclockwise direction. The joystick was positioned so that the participants could not see their hand movements; as a result, this task required motor movement but no visual perception.

At the same time as this motor task, participants were instructed to look at a geometric figure. Each figure was a simplified, 2-dimensional version of the figures in Demonstration 7.2. In Demonstration 7.2, you saw both members of each geometric pair at the same time. However, in the study by Wexler and his colleagues (1998), the participants first saw one member of the pair. Then they saw an arrow indicating whether they should rotate this figure clockwise or counterclockwise. Finally, they saw the second member of the pair, and they judged whether the two members matched.

As you can see from Figure 7.3, the participants made the judgments about their mental images relatively quickly when their hand was moving in the same direction that their mental image was moving. In contrast, their judgments were slower when the two movements were in opposite directions (for example, with the hand moving clockwise and the mental image moving counterclockwise).

FIGURE 7.3

Reaction Time, as a Function of the Amount of Mental Rotation and Whether the Mental Rotation Was in the Same Direction as the Hand Movement or in the Opposite Direction.

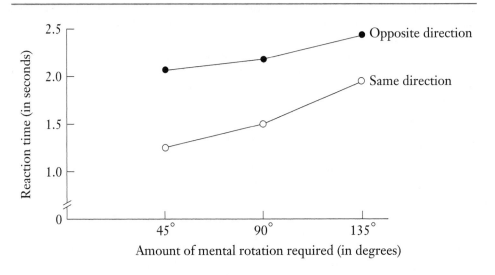

Source: Based on Wexler et al., 1998.

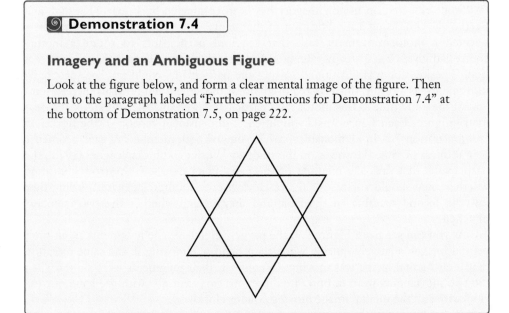

⦿ Demonstration 7.4

Imagery and an Ambiguous Figure

Look at the figure below, and form a clear mental image of the figure. Then turn to the paragraph labeled "Further instructions for Demonstration 7.4" at the bottom of Demonstration 7.5, on page 222.

The research by Wexler and his colleagues (1998) showed that an actual motor movement can interfere with a mental image of movement. Related research by Wohlschläger (2001) demonstrated that *planning* a motor movement can interfere with trying to rotate a mental image. Specifically, participants were instructed to get ready to rotate their hand in a particular direction, and then they performed a mental-rotation task similar to the Shepard and Metzler (1971) task you tried in Demonstration 7.2. Participants performed the mental-rotation task much more slowly if they had been planning to rotate their hand in the opposite direction, rather than the same direction. Clearly, then, interference effects can be found for motor imagery as well as for visual imagery.

Imagery and Ambiguous Figures

Before you read further, try Demonstration 7.4 and note whether you were able to re-interpret the figure. Most people have difficulty with tasks like this. Reed (1974) was interested in people's ability to decide whether a pattern was a portion of a design they had seen earlier. He therefore presented a series of paired figures: first a pattern like the Star of David in Demonstration 7.4, and then—after a brief delay—a second pattern (for example, a parallelogram). In half of the cases, the second pattern was truly part of the first one. In the other half, it was not (for example, a rectangle).

If people store mental images in their heads that correspond to the physical objects they have seen, then they should be able to create a mental image of the star and quickly discover the parallelogram shape hidden within it. However, the participants in Reed's (1974) study were correct only 14% of the time on the star/parallelogram example. Across all stimuli, they were correct only 55% of the time, hardly better than chance.

According to Reed (1974), this poor performance suggests that people could not have stored mental pictures. Instead, Reed proposed that people store pictures as descriptions, in propositional codes. You may have stored the description in Demonstration 7.4 as "two triangles, one pointing up and the other pointing down, placed on top of each other." When asked whether the figure contained a parallelogram, you may have searched through that verbal description and found only triangles, not parallelograms. Notice that Reed's research supports the propositional-code approach, rather than the analog-code approach.

Similar research has examined whether people can provide re-interpretations for a mental image of an ambiguous figure. For example, you can interpret the ambiguous stimulus in Figure 7.4 in two ways: a rabbit facing to the right or a duck facing to the left. Chambers and Reisberg (1985) asked participants to create a clear mental image of this figure, and then they removed the figure. Participants were then asked to give a second, different interpretation of the figure. None of the 15 people could do so. Next, the participants were asked to draw the figure from memory. Could they re-interpret this physical stimulus? All 15 looked at the figure they had drawn and supplied a second interpretation. Chambers and Reisberg's research suggests that a strong verbal propositional code can dominate over an analog code.

🌀 **Demonstration 7.5**

Reinterpreting Ambiguous Stimuli

Imagine the capital letter **H.** Now imagine the capital letter **X** superimposed directly on top of the **H,** so that the four corners of each letter match up exactly. From this mental image, what new shapes and objects do you see in your mind's eye?

(Further instructions for Demonstration 7.4: Without glancing back at the figure in Demonstration 7.4, consult your mental image. Does that mental image contain a parallelogram?)

Notice that both Reed (1977) and Chambers and Reisberg (1985) used fairly complex figures. In both cases, the researchers also presented the figure and then removed it. In contrast, research supporting the analog code often uses fairly simple figures (like the two hands of a clock), or researchers may ask participants to create *their own* images of elephants, clocks, or West Virginia. Tasks using more complex shapes may encourage a propositional code requiring verbal labels, rather than an analog code. For example, when I work on a jigsaw puzzle, I often find that I've attached a verbal label—such as "angel with outstretched wings"—to aid my search for a missing piece. In the case of these complex shapes, storage may be predominantly propositional.

In other research, Finke and his colleagues (1989) asked people to combine two mental images, as in Demonstration 7.5. The participants in this study were indeed

FIGURE 7.4

An Example of an Ambiguous Figure from Chambers and Reisberg's Study.

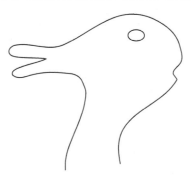

Source: Chambers & Reisberg, 1985.

able to come up with new interpretations for these ambiguous stimuli. In addition to a combined **X** and **H** figure, they reported some new geometric shapes (such as a right triangle), some new letters (such as **M**), and some objects (such as a bow tie). Other research confirms that observers can locate similar, unanticipated shapes in their mental images (Brandimonte & Gerbino, 1996; Cooper & Lang, 1996; Rouw et al., 1997).

In summary, the research on ambiguous figures shows that people create mental images using both propositional and analog codes (Reisberg, 1998). That is, we often use analog codes to provide picture-like representations to capture our mental images. However, when the stimuli and situations make it difficult to use analog codes, we may use a propositional code to create a language-like representation.

Imagery and Other Vision-Like Processes

So far, we have reviewed a variety of characteristics related to vision: rotation, size, shape, interference, and ambiguous figures. Let's briefly consider other less obvious characteristics of visual perception. We'll see that each visual characteristic has a mental-imagery counterpart.

For example, people can see a visual target more accurately if the target is presented with masking stimuli on each of the target's sides. Mental imagery produces the same masking effect; people can see a visual target more accurately if they create mental images of masks on each side of the target (Ishai & Sagi, 1995).

This study on the masking effect has additional significance in terms of demand characteristics. **Demand characteristics** are all the cues that might convey the experimenter's hypothesis to the participant. Experimenter expectancy—the process by which the researcher's expectations might be transmitted to participants in an experiment (see pp. 215–216)—is one source of these cues. However, experiments provide numerous other demand characteristics. Some critics of the analog approach have proposed that the experimental results in imagery experiments might be traceable to one or more of these demand characteristics. For example, in many cases, participants may be able to guess the results that the experimenter wants. Perhaps they might guess that an auditory image is supposed to interfere with an auditory perception. However, the masking effect is virtually unknown to people without a background in the field of perception. The participants in that study would never have guessed that targets are especially easy to see if they are surrounded by masking stimuli. Demand characteristics, therefore, cannot account for the masking effect with mental images.

Researchers have also examined whether mental images resemble visual perception in other respects. For example, people have especially good acuity for mental images that are visualized in the center of the retina, rather than in the periphery; visual perception operates the same way (Kosslyn, 1983). People can even create illusory conjunctions—like the ones we discussed on page 88—by combining features of visual images and mental images (Craver-Lemley et al., 1999). Other studies demonstrate additional parallels between mental images and visual perception (Finke & Schmidt, 1978; Kosslyn, 2001; Kosslyn & Thompson, 2000).

Revisiting the Imagery Controversy

The imagery controversy has been an important and long-lasting debate in cognitive psychology (Farah, 2000a; Kosslyn, Ganis, & Thompson, 2001; Phelps, 1999). At the beginning of this chapter, we introduced the analog and propositional perspectives on imagery. Now that you are familiar with the research, let's examine the two perspectives in more detail. The two viewpoints do differ in their emphasis on the similarity between mental images and physical stimuli. However, the two positions are not *completely* different from each other, and they may apply to different kinds of tasks.

The Analog Viewpoint. According to the analog perspective, we create a mental image of an object that closely resembles the actual, physical object. Take a minute to review pages 212–223, and you'll see that our reactions to mental images are frequently similar to our reactions to physical objects. Indeed, the majority of the research supports this position. Of course, no one argues that vision and mental imagery are *identical*. After all, you can easily differentiate between your mental image of your textbook's cover and your perception of that cover. However—as you'll see in the next section of this chapter—the neuropsychology research provides especially strong evidence for the analog viewpoint, because visual imagery and visual perception activate many similar structures in the cortex (Kosslyn & Thompson, 2000).

Kosslyn and Thompson (2000) have developed the analog approach to visual imagery still further by designing a model with several different subsystems that both visual imagery and visual perception share (Kosslyn, 2001; Kosslyn & Thompson, 2000; Thompson & Kosslyn, 2000). For example, one component is attention shifting. As we discussed in Chapter 3, if you are looking at a picture, you can shift your visual perception from one part of the picture to another (for example, when searching for a blue X in the picture inside the back cover of this book). Similarly, try forming a mental image of a cat. Now suppose I ask you to tell me whether the cat has curved claws on its front paws. Most people say that the original mental image did not include the claws, but their attention zooms in on this portion of the cat once they are asked about this feature (Kosslyn, 2001). A second component of Kosslyn and Thompson's (2000) model encodes properties of physical objects and mental images, such as their shape and color. A third component encodes spatial properties, such as their location and their size.

In summary, the analog viewpoint proposes that imagery resembles perception in many respects. The two processes even activate similar structures within the cerebral cortex, as we'll emphasize in the next section. In addition, mental images can be created and manipulated using several different mechanisms. As a result, our mental images can be extremely flexible and useful for a wide variety of cognitive tasks.

The Propositional Viewpoint. According to the propositional perspective, mental images are stored in an abstract, language-like form that does not physically resemble the original stimulus. Zenon Pylyshyn (1984, 1989, 2003) has been the strongest opponent of the "pictures-in-the-head" hypothesis. Pylyshyn agrees that people do experience mental images; it would be foolish to argue otherwise. However, Pylyshyn says that these images are epiphenomenal. **Epiphenomenal** means that the images are simply "tacked on" later, after an item has been recovered from (propositional) storage. The propositional perspective argues that—when we perform cognitive tasks requiring imagery—we recover these language-like propositions from storage. Then we work with these propositions. At the very end of the process, we construct the superficial mental images (Kaufmann, 1996).

Pylyshyn argues that it would be awkward—and perhaps even unworkable—to store information in terms of mental images. For instance, a huge space would be required to store all the images people claim they have.

Pylyshyn also emphasizes the differences between perceptual experiences and mental images. For example, you can re-examine and reinterpret a real photograph. However, Chambers and Reisberg's (1985) study illustrated that people usually cannot reinterpret an ambiguous mental image—such as a rabbit—even though they can easily reinterpret a visual stimulus.

As Pylyshyn also points out, when we perceive real objects, we can perform operations that are impossible with mental images. Pylyshyn (2003) suggests an informal demonstration to illustrate this last point.* Imagine that you have two flashlights. The lens of one flashlight is covered with a yellow filter. The lens of the other flashlight is covered with a blue filter (matched with the yellow filter for brightness and the saturation, or purity, of the color). Imagine that these flashlights have been turned on, and they are casting a yellow and a blue circle on a large piece of white paper. Now picture these two circles moving toward each other, until they partly overlap. What color is the specific segment where the two circles overlap? If you tried this demonstration with real flashlights and real filters, the segment of overlap would be gray or even black. However, people seldom report "gray" or "black" when they have constructed a mental image of this demonstration (Pylyshyn, 2003). As we have noted, mental images do not exactly mimic all of our perceptual experiences.

In reality, we may not be able to resolve the imagery controversy. At present, the evidence suggests that, with most stimuli and most tasks, mental images seem to be stored in an analog code (Farah, 2000a; Palmer, 1999). However, for some kinds of stimuli and several specific tasks, a propositional code may be used. The next section of this chapter explores cognitive neuroscience research. As you'll see, our mental images and our perceptual experiences employ many of the same brain structures.

---

*Pylyshyn's (2003) suggestion with the beams of colored lights requires additive color mixing, in which a yellow light and a blue light produce a gray or black color (depending on the wavelengths of the yellow and blue lights). Most of us are more familiar with subtractive color mixing, in which yellow paint mixed with blue paint produces a shade of green.

◉ Section Summary: *The Characteristics of Mental Images*

1. A major controversy in cognitive psychology focuses on mental imagery, specifically, whether information is stored in picture-like analog codes or language-like propositional codes. Research on the characteristics of mental images addresses this issue.

2. The amount of time it takes to rotate a mental image depends on the extent of the rotation, just as when we rotate a real, physical object.

3. People make faster judgments about the characteristics of large mental images than of small mental images. Also, people take longer to travel a large mental distance, whether that distance is visual or auditory. In addition, women with anorexia nervosa have distorted images of their body's size.

4. When judging shapes, people make faster decisions about two very different angles formed by the hands on a clock; they take longer to make decisions about highly similar angles, just as they would for real physical shapes.

5. Visual imagery can interfere with visual perception; auditory imagery can interfere with auditory perception; and motor movement can interfere with motor images.

6. People have difficulty identifying that a part belongs to a whole if they did not include the part in their original verbal description of the whole. Also, some ambiguous figures are difficult to reinterpret in a mental image; others can be reinterpreted fairly easily.

7. Other vision-like properties of mental images include enhanced acuity when a target is flanked by imaginary masks, enhanced acuity for stimuli seen in the center portion of the retina, and illusory conjunctions.

8. Kosslyn and Thompson (2000) have developed the analog viewpoint, so that it includes several specific operations that can be performed on both mental images and real objects. The propositional viewpoint, as expressed by Pylyshyn, argues that images are simply "tacked on" to the propositional code. At present, most—but not all—research supports the analog position.

COGNITIVE NEUROSCIENCE RESEARCH ON MENTAL IMAGERY

In Chapter 1, we discussed a variety of neuroscience research techniques that can help us understand how cognitive processes operate. This research is especially strong in the area of mental imagery. At present, almost all of the neuroscience research about imagery focuses on how the brain creates and processes various characteristics of visual images. Unfortunately, researchers know less about the neuroscience explanations for other modes, such as audition and motor movement.

Visual Imagery

We have considered many studies that illustrate how people seem to treat visual images the same way they treat visual stimuli. In general, imagery and perception seem to demonstrate similar psychological processes. But how similar are imagery and perception at the biological level? Obviously, the two processes are not identical (Kosslyn & Thompson, 2000; Miyashita, 1995). After all, mental imagery relies on top-down processing. In contrast, visual perception activates the rods and cones in the retina. When you create a mental image of an elephant, no one would suggest that the rods and cones in the back of your retina are registering an elephant-shaped pattern of stimulation.

However, numerous neuroscience studies demonstrate that brain structures at more advanced levels of visual processing—beyond the retina—do seem to be activated when we construct mental images (Kosslyn et al., 1999b; Phelps, 1999; Thompson & Kosslyn, 2000). For example, Martha Farah (2000a, 2000b) discusses some compelling evidence that the visual-processing areas of the cerebral cortex are implicated in visual mental imagery. Farah received the Troland Award from the National Academy of Sciences for her research on vision.

Farah (2000a, 2000b) examines some of the techniques presented in the discussion of cognitive neuroscience in Chapter 1. For example, researchers have studied individuals with lesions (damage) in the visual cortex and other areas of the cortex that process visual stimuli. Many of these people cannot register perceptual images, and they cannot produce mental images. Still, their other cognitive abilities are normal. Although exceptions have been reported, most individuals with these lesions show mental-imagery impairments that resemble their perceptual impairments. (Farah, 2000a, 2000b; Kosslyn, Ganis, & Thompson, 2001; Thompson & Kosslyn, 2000).

Many other studies have used PET scans, fMRIs, and other brain-imaging techniques to assess which areas of the brain show increased blood flow when people work on a variety of tasks that require visual imagery. For example, Stephen Kosslyn and his coauthors (1996) asked people to create visual images for various letters of the alphabet. Then the participants were asked a question about each letter's shape (for example, whether the letter had any curved lines). Meanwhile, a PET scan recorded the blood flow to the cortex. The researchers found that this task activated the primary visual cortex, located at the back of the brain. (See Figure 2.1 on p. 35.) This part of the cortex is the same region that is active when we perceive the shape of actual visual stimuli.

Kosslyn and his colleagues (1996) also found that the people who performed the task quickly showed an especially large increase in blood flow to the visual cortex. In contrast, those who performed the task slowly showed a much smaller increase in blood flow. Individual differences in mental imagery need to be examined more thoroughly in neuroscience research (Farah, 2000a; Kosslyn, 2002).

Other neuroscience research on imagery demonstrates that different parts of the brain are activitated for different tasks. For instance, the research confirms that the occipital visual cortex is especially active when people need to carefully inspect a visual image, as in the task we just described on features contained in letters of the alphabet (Klein et al., 2000; Sparing et al., 2002; Thompson & Kosslyn, 2000). Other regions of the brain specialize in different methods of processing visual images. For example, part of the parietal lobe—as shown in Figure 2.1 on page 35—is especially active when people need to make changes in the structure of their visual images (Newcombe, 2002).

Auditory and Motor Imagery

So far, we have emphasized neuroscience research on visual imagery. Other research demonstrates that portions of the *auditory* cortex are activated when people are instructed to imagine hearing popular songs (Zatorre et al., 1996).

Additional studies focus on *motor* imagery (Cohen et al., 1996; Kosslyn et al., 1998). Specifically, the participants in this research were instructed to perform a mental-rotation task. Meanwhile, the fMRI technique was used to record changes in blood flow in the cerebral cortex. Some of the participants who worked on this task showed increased activity in the portion of the brain (the motor cortex) that is responsible for hand movement. Apparently, these individuals performed the rotation by imagining that their hand was holding the object and turning the object around. Interestingly, other research participants did *not* show increased activity in the motor cortex. These participants must have used some other strategy (not identified in this research) to mentally rotate the figure. Neuroscience techniques will undoubtedly be used in the future to study individual differences in cognitive tasks like mental rotation.

Other research on motor imagery reveals that another brain structure is also important when we create mental images for motor movement. So far, our discussion of imagery and neuroscience has emphasized regions of the cerebral cortex, illustrated in Figure 2.1. The cerebellum is a relatively small structure that is located at the back of your head, just below the occipital lobe. The **cerebellum** controls motor movement. For example, your cerebellum helps you control your posture, it regulates your movement when you walk or dance, and it guides your fingers when you write. Researchers have now determined that the cerebellum is active when you imagine yourself making hand gestures or hitting a tennis ball with a racket or when you work on a mental-rotation task (Ivry & Fiez, 2000; Zacks et al., 2002).

The neuroscience evidence is particularly compelling because it avoids the problem of demand characteristics that we discussed earlier. As Farah (2000a) points out, people are not likely to know which parts of their brain are typically active during vision. When you mentally rotate an object, you cannot voluntarily force more blood into your visual cortex or your motor cortex! These similarities between perception and imagery are especially persuasive because they cannot be explained by social expectations.

⊚ Section Summary: *Cognitive Neuroscience Research on Mental Imagery*

1. Neuropsychological research, using case studies, has demonstrated that people with lesions in the visual cortex have the same difficulties with visual imagery that they have with visual perception.

2. Other neuropsychological research has used PET scans, fMRIs, and other brain-imaging techniques to show that visual imagery activates specific visual-processing areas of the cerebral cortex, such as the occipital visual cortex and the parietal region of the cortex.

3. Parts of the auditory cortex are activated when people imagine hearing auditory material.

4. Neuroscience research also shows that the motor cortex and the cerebellum are active when people are asked to imagine themselves performing motor tasks.

COGNITIVE MAPS

You have probably had an experience like this: You've just arrived in a new environment, perhaps for your first year of college. You ask for directions, let's say, to the library. You hear the reply, "OK, it's simple. You go up the hill, staying to the right of the Blake Building. Then you take a left, and Newton Hall will be on your right. The library will be over on your left." You struggle to recall some landmarks from the orientation tour. Was Newton Hall next to the College Union, or was it over near the Administration Building? Valiantly, you try to incorporate this new information into your discouragingly hazy mental map.

So far, this chapter has examined the general characteristics of mental images. This discussion primarily focused on a theoretical issue that has intrigued cognitive psychologists—specifically, how mental images are stored in memory. Now we consider cognitive maps, a topic that clearly relies on mental images. However, the research on cognitive maps focuses on the way we represent geographic space. More specifically, a **cognitive map** is a mental representation of the external environment that surrounds us (Laszlo et al., 1996; Tversky, 2000a). Notice, then, that the first half of this chapter emphasizes our mental images of objects. This second half emphasizes our mental images of the *relationships* among objects, such as buildings on a college campus.

Let's discuss some background information about cognitive maps, and then we'll see how distance, shape, and relative position are represented in these cognitive maps. We'll conclude this chapter with an In Depth feature that explores the way we create mental maps from verbal descriptions.

Background Information About Cognitive Maps

Research on cognitive maps has examined environmental spaces that range widely in size. These cognitive maps include classrooms, neighborhoods, cities, countries, and even larger geographic regions (Warren, 1995).

In a typical study on cognitive maps, researchers asked long-term residents of Venice, Italy, to describe the most efficient route between two landmarks (Denis et al., 1999). These descriptions were then given to a different group of people, who rated the overall quality of the directions. The raters were instructed to make judgments about the descriptions on characteristics such as clarity and inclusion of useful landmarks. In the final phase of this study, the instructions that had received the best and worst ratings were given to Italian college students who had never before visited Venice. In comparison with the students who used the good instructions, the students who used the poor instructions made more than twice as many errors and needed to ask for assistance twice as often. In other words, people can make fairly accurate judgments about whether instructions to a location will be helpful or confusing. This research, like many studies on cognitive maps, emphasizes real-world settings and ecological validity.

The study of cognitive maps is part of a larger topic called spatial cognition. **Spatial cognition** refers to our thoughts about spatial issues; it is a broad area that includes not only cognitive maps, but also how we remember the world we navigate and how we keep track of objects in a spatial array (Newcombe, 2002). Spatial cognition is interdisciplinary in its scope. For example, computer scientists try to create models of spatial knowledge. Linguists analyze how people talk about spatial arrangements. Anthropologists study how different cultures use different frameworks to describe locations. Geographers examine all of these dimensions, with the goal of creating efficient maps and other sources of information (Tversky, 1999). The topic is also relevant to architects when they are designing buildings and to urban planners when they are constructing new communities (Devlin, 2001; Tversky, 2000b).

We are often unaware just how much information we know about spatial cognition. As Laszlo and his colleagues (1996) point out, research in artificial intelligence has demonstrated the complexity of our knowledge base:

> It was discovered, much to the consternation of the programmers, that without exquisitely elaborate programs, computers made unbelievably stupid errors. A simulation of a restaurant scene, for instance, might find the patrons entering by walking directly through the walls, whereupon they might seat themselves on the floor (exactly where the computer probably has the waiter serve the food) and eventually tip the cook before leaving. To get this scene right, the programmer must supply the computer with an enormous amount of commonsense information of the kind that makes up the basic cognitive maps that guide human behavior. (p. 9)

As you might expect, individual differences in spatial cognition are quite large. However, people tend to be accurate in judging their ability to find their way to unfamiliar locations (Kitchin & Blades, 2002; Taylor et al., 1999). In other words, their metacognitions about spatial ability are reasonably correct. Furthermore, these individual differences in spatial cognition are correlated with performance on the spatial tasks that we discussed in the first half of this chapter (Newcombe, 2002).

Also, suppose that you are visiting an unfamiliar college campus. You park your car, and you set out to find a specific building. You'll increase your chances of finding your way back to your car if you periodically turn around and study the scene you'll see on your return trip (Heth et al., 2002).

Demonstration 7.6

Learning from a Map

Study the blue diagram at the bottom of this demonstration for about 30 seconds, and then cover it completely. Now answer the following questions:

1. Imagine that you are standing at Position 3, facing Position 4. Point to Position 1.

2. Now, glance quickly at the blue diagram and then cover it completely. Imagine that you are now standing at Position 1, facing Position 2. Point to Position 4.

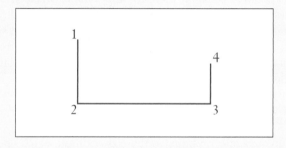

Try Demonstration 7.6 before you read further. This demonstration is based on research by Roskos-Ewoldsen and her colleagues (1998), which we will discuss shortly.

In general, researchers have not discussed the way in which cognitive maps are encoded—that is, whether the code for these maps is analog or propositional. However, most researchers who have raised this issue conclude that cognitive maps must be both analog and propositional in nature (e.g., Kitchin & Blades, 2002; Taylor et al., 1999; Tversky, 1998). Your mental map for a particular city may therefore include a series of picture-like images of the relationship among several streets and buildings. This mental map will also include propositions, such as "The Ethiopian restaurant is in downtown Toronto, northwest of the CN Tower." Information on your mental map may also include landmark knowledge and procedural knowledge (for example, "To get to the Ethiopian restaurant, go north from the hotel parking lot and turn left on Bloor").

Your mental map may also include survey knowledge, which is the relationship among locations that can be directly acquired by learning a map or by repeatedly exploring an environment. Now look back at Demonstration 7.6; which of the two tasks was easier? As you might imagine, your mental map will be easier to judge and more accurate if you acquire spatial information from a physical map that is oriented in the same direction that you are facing in your mental map. In Question 1 of this demonstration, your mental map and the physical map have the same orientation, so that task is relatively easy. In contrast, you need to perform a mental rotation in order to answer Question 2, so that task is more difficult. Research confirms that judgments are easier when your mental map and the physical map have matching orientations (Devlin, 2001; Roskos-Ewoldsen et al., 1998; Taylor et al., 1999).

The next three topics will consider how our cognitive maps represent three geographic attributes: distance, shape, and orientation. Theme 2 of this book states that our cognitive processes are generally accurate. This generalization also applies to cognitive maps. In fact, our mental representations of the environment usually reflect reality with reasonable accuracy, whether these cognitive maps depict college campuses, the city of Venice, or larger geographic regions.

According to Chapter 1's discussion of Theme 2, however, when people do make errors in their cognitive processes, those errors can often be traced to a rational strategy. The mistakes people display in their cognitive maps "make sense" because they are systematic distortions of reality (Devlin, 2001; Koriat et al., 2000; Tversky, 2000b). The mistakes reflect a tendency to base our judgments on variables that are typically relevant. They also reflect a tendency to judge our environment as being more well-organized and orderly than it really is. We will see that people tend to show systematic distortions in distance, shape, and orientation.

Cognitive Maps and Distance

How far is it from your college library to the classroom in which your cognitive psychology course is taught? How many miles separate the city in which you were born from the city where your home is currently located? When people make distance estimates like these, their estimates are often distorted by factors such as the number of intervening cities, semantic categories, and whether the destination is a landmark or a nonlandmark.

Number of Intervening Cities. In one of the first systematic studies about distance in cognitive maps, Thorndyke (1981) constructed a map of a hypothetical region with cities distributed throughout the map at varying distances from one another. Between any two cities on the map, there were 0, 1, 2, or 3 other cities along the route. Thorndyke was interested in the relationship between the number of intervening cities and distance estimation. Participants studied the map until they could accurately reconstruct it. Finally, they were instructed to estimate the distance between specified pairs of cities.

The number of intervening cities had a clear-cut influence on their estimates. For example, when the cities were really 300 miles apart on the map, people estimated that they were 280 miles apart when there were no intervening cities. In contrast, they were estimated to be 350 miles apart with three intervening cities. Notice that this error is a sensible one. In general, if cities are randomly distributed throughout a region, any two cities are indeed farther apart when there are three other cities between them; two cities with no other intervening cities are likely to be closer together.

Variations of this study confirm that the distance seems longer when the route is "cluttered" with objects along the way (Koriat et al., 2000; Tversky, 2000a).

Semantic Categories. The Fine Arts Building on my college campus seems closer to the College Union than it is to Buzzo's Music Store. The music store is actually closer. However, my distance estimate is distorted because the Fine Arts Building and the College Union are clustered together in my semantic memory under the category "college buildings." The music store does not belong to this semantic cluster, even though no physical boundary divides campus buildings from the store's located off campus.

Research by Stephen Hirtle and his colleagues illustrates how semantic factors influence distance estimates for specific locations within a town. For example, Hirtle and Mascolo (1986) constructed, in their laboratory, a hypothetical map of a town. Participants learned the locations on the map. Then the map was removed, and people estimated the distance between pairs of locations. The results showed that people tended to shift each location closer to other sites that belonged to the same cluster. For example, the courthouse might be remembered as being close to the police station and other government buildings. The shifts did not occur for members of different semantic clusters. For instance, people did not move the courthouse closer to the golf course.

The same influence of semantic categories appeared when Hirtle and Jonides (1985) asked University of Michigan students to estimate distances between pairs of locations in Ann Arbor. The students showed a clustering bias. That is, members of the same category were judged to be closer to each other than to members of different categories. In summary, these studies confirm an additional distortion in distance estimates: When two places seem semantically close, we believe that they are also geographically close (Tversky, 2000b). Once again, however, this error makes sense. In general, our real-life experience tells us that locations with similar functions are likely to be close to each other.

Landmarks Versus Nonlandmarks as Destinations. We have some friends who live in Rochester, the major city in our region of upstate New York. We sometimes invite them to come down for a meeting in Geneseo, about 45 minutes away. "But it's so far away," they complain. "Why don't you come up here instead?" They are faintly embarrassed when we point out that the distance from Geneseo to Rochester is exactly the same as the distance from Rochester to Geneseo!

The research confirms the **landmark effect,** which is the general tendency to estimate distances as being relatively short when traveling from a nonlandmark to a landmark, rather than the reverse (Devlin, 2001; Tversky et al., 1999). For example, McNamara and Diwadkar (1997) asked students to memorize a map that displayed various pictures of objects. The map included some objects that were described as landmarks, and some objects that were not landmarks. After learning the locations, the students estimated the distance between various pairs of objects.

Consistent with the landmark effect, the students showed an asymmetry in their distance estimates. In one study, for instance, they estimated that the distance was an average of 1.7 inches when traveling from the landmark to the nonlandmark. However, the estimated distance was an average of only 1.4 inches when traveling from the nonlandmark to the landmark. Prominent destinations apparently seem closer than less important destinations. This research also demonstrates the importance of context when we make decisions about distances and other features of our cognitive maps.

Cognitive Maps and Shape

Our cognitive maps represent not only distances, but shapes. These shapes are evident in map features—for example, the angles formed by intersecting streets and the curves illustrating the bends in rivers. Once again, the research shows a systematic distortion: People tend to construct cognitive maps in which the shapes are more regular than they are in reality.

Angles. Consider the research by Moar and Bower (1983), who studied people's cognitive maps of Cambridge, England. All the participants in the study had lived in Cambridge for at least 5 years. Moar and Bower wanted to determine people's estimates for the angles formed by the intersection of two streets. They were particularly interested in the angle estimates for sets of three streets that formed large triangles within the city of Cambridge. The participants showed a clear tendency to "regularize" the angles so that they were more like 90° angles. For example, three streets formed a triangle in which the "real" angles were 67°, 63°, and 50°. However, people estimated these same angles to be 84°, 78°, and 88°. In fact, this study showed that seven of the nine angles were significantly biased in the direction of a 90° angle. Furthermore, you know from your geometry class that the angles within a triangle should sum to 180°. Notice, however, that the angles in our cognitive maps of triangles do not necessarily sum to 180°. (In this particular example, for instance, the angles sum to 250°.)

What explains this systematic distortion? Moar and Bower (1983) suggest that we employ a **heuristic,** or general problem-solving strategy. In North America, when two roads meet, they generally form a 90° angle. When people use the **90°-angle heuristic,** they represent angles in a mental map as being closer to 90° than they really are. Similarly—as you may recall from Chapter 5's discussion of memory schemas on pages 157–158—it is easier to store a schematic version of an event, rather than a precise version of the event that accurately represents all the little details. This 90°-angle heuristic has also been replicated in other settings (Gauvain, 1998; Tversky, 2000b; Tversky & Lee, 1998).

Curves. The New York State Thruway runs in an east-west direction across the state, though it curves somewhat in certain areas. To me, the upward curve south of Rochester seems symmetrical, equally arched on each side of the city. However, when I checked the map, the curve is much steeper on the eastern side.

Research confirms that people tend to use a **symmetry heuristic;** people remember figures as being more symmetrical and regular than they truly are (Tversky & Schiano, 1989). According to other research, a road that is slightly curved or irregular tends to be recalled as straighter than it actually is (Tversky, 2000a). Again, these results follow the general pattern: The small inconsistencies of geographic reality are smoothed over, creating cognitive maps that are idealized and standardized.

Cognitive Maps and Relative Position

Which city is farther west—San Diego, California, or Reno, Nevada? If you are like most people—and the participants in a classic study by Stevens and Coupe (1978)—the question seems ludicrously easy. Of course San Diego is farther west, because California is west of Nevada. However, if you consult a map, you'll discover that Reno is in fact west of San Diego. Which city is farther north—Detroit or its "twin city" across the river, Windsor, in Ontario, Canada? Again, the answer seems obvious; any Canadian city must be north of a U.S. city!

Barbara Tversky (1981, 1998) points out that we use heuristics when we represent relative positions in our mental maps—just as we use heuristics to represent the angles of intersecting streets as being close to 90° angles, and just as we represent curves as being symmetrical. In particular, Tversky argues: (1) we remember a tilted geographic structure as being either more vertical or more horizontal than it really is (the rotation heuristic), and (2) we remember geographic structures as being arranged in a straighter line than they really are (the alignment heuristic).

The Rotation Heuristic. According to the **rotation heuristic,** a figure that is slightly tilted will be remembered as being either more vertical or more horizontal than it really is (Tversky, 1981, 1997, 2000b). For example, Figure 7.5 shows that the coastline of California is slanted at a significant angle. When we use the rotation heuristic for our cognitive map of California, we make the orientation more vertical by rotating the coastline. If your cognitive map suffers from the distorting effects of the rotation heuristic, you will conclude (erroneously) that San Diego is west of Reno. Similarly, the rotation heuristic encourages you to create a horizontal border between the United States and Canada. Therefore, you'll make the wrong decision about Detroit and Windsor. In reality, Windsor, in Canada, is south of Detroit.

Let us look at some research on the rotation heuristic. Tversky (1981) studied people's mental maps for the geographic region of the San Francisco Bay area. She found that 69% of the students at a Bay area university showed evidence of the rotation heuristic. In their mental maps, the coastline was rotated in a more north-south direction than is true on a geographically correct map. Keep in mind, though, that some students—in fact, 31% of them—were not influenced by this heuristic.

We also have cross-cultural evidence for the rotation heuristic. People living in Israel, Japan, and Italy also show a tendency to rotate geographic structures so that they are closer to the vertical or the horizontal than they really are (Glicksohn, 1994; Tversky et al., 1999).

FIGURE 7.5

The Correct Locations of San Diego and Reno. This figure shows that Reno is farther west than San Diego. According to the rotation heuristic, however, we tend to rotate the coastline of California into a more nearly vertical orientation, so we incorrectly conclude that San Diego is farther west than Reno.

The Alignment Heuristic. According to the **alignment heuristic,** a series of geographic structures will be remembered as being more lined up than they really are (Tversky, 1981, 2000b). To test the alignment heuristic, Tversky (1981) presented pairs of cities to students, who were asked to select which member of each pair was north (or, in some cases, east). For example, one pair was Rome and Philadelphia. As Figure 7.6 shows, Rome is actually north of Philadelphia. However, because of the alignment heuristic, people tend to line up the United States and Europe so that they are in the same latitude. We know that Rome is in the southern part of Europe and that Philadelphia is in the northern part of the United States. Therefore, we conclude—incorrectly—that Philadelphia is north of Rome.

Tversky's results indicated that the students showed a consistent tendency to use the alignment heuristic. For example, 78% judged Philadelphia to be north of Rome, and 12% judged that they were at the same latitude. Only 10% correctly answered that Rome is north of Philadelphia. On all eight pairs of items tested by Tversky, an average of 66% of participants supplied the incorrect answer. According to additional research, people's cognitive maps are most likely to be biased when northern cities in North America are compared with southern cities in Europe (Friedman et al., 2002).

The rotation heuristic and the alignment heuristic may initially sound similar. However, the rotation heuristic requires rotating a *single* coastline, country, building, or other figure in a clockwise or counterclockwise fashion so that its border is oriented in a nearly vertical or horizontal direction. In contrast, the alignment heuristic requires lining up *several separate* countries, buildings, or other figures in a straight row. Both heuristics are similar, however, because they encourage us to construct cognitive maps that are more orderly than geographic reality.

FIGURE 7.6

The Correct Locations of Philadelphia and Rome. This figure shows that Philadelphia is farther south than Rome. According to the alignment heuristic, however, we tend to line up Europe and the United States, so we incorrectly conclude that Philadelphia is north of Rome.

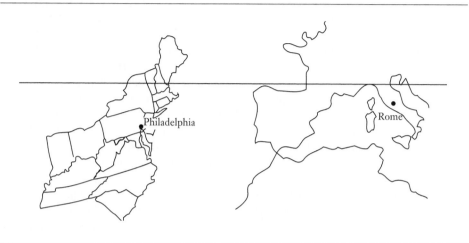

The heuristics we have examined in this chapter make sense. For example, our city streets tend to have right-angle intersections. Furthermore, pictures are generally hung on walls in a vertical orientation, rather than at a slant, and a series of houses is typically lined up evenly along the street. However, when we rely too strongly on these heuristics, we miss the important details that make each stimulus unique. When our top-down cognitive processes are too active, we fail to pay sufficient attention to bottom-up information. In fact, the angle at the intersection may really be 70°, that coastline may not run exactly north-south, and those continents are not really arranged in a neat horizontal line.

At this point, you may be reasonably skeptical about the validity of Theme 2; perhaps our cognitive processes are *not* impressively accurate. However, Mary Smyth and her coauthors (1994) place these errors in perspective:

> Bias in spatial judgments does not mean that people have a built-in tendency to get things wrong. Rather, the errors people make when they straighten edges, make junctions more like right angles, put things closer to landmarks, and remember average rather than specific positions, are indications of the way in which knowledge of spatial information is dealt with. Like the formation of concepts, the regularizing of spatial information reduces the need to maintain all the features of an environment which might possibly be relevant and allows approximate solutions to problems for which precise location is unnecessary. (p. 326)

IN DEPTH

Using Verbal Descriptions to Create Cognitive Maps

In everyday life, we often hear or read descriptions of a particular environment. For instance, a friend calls to give you directions to her house. You have never traveled there before, yet you find yourself creating a cognitive map to represent the route. Similarly, a neighbor describes the setting in which his car was hit by a truck, or you read a mystery novel explaining where the dead body was found in relation to the broken vase and the butler's fingerprints. In each case, you use verbal information to create a cognitive map. These cognitive maps allow us to simulate spatial aspects of our external environment. These representations that depict physical situations, which we derive from verbal descriptions, are called **mental models** (Millis & Cohen, 1994).

Theme 1 of this textbook emphasizes that cognitive processes are active. When we hear a description, we do not simply store these isolated statements in a passive fashion. Instead, we actively create a mental model that represents the relevant features of a scene. In fact, the mental maps that people create from a description are similar to the mental maps they create from looking at a scene (Bryant, 1998; Carr & Roskos-Ewoldsen, 1999; Tversky, 2000b). Furthermore, people integrate information from separate statements and combine them to form an integrated mental model (Newcombe & Huttenlocher, 2000).

In this In Depth feature, we will examine how people create these mental models, based on verbal description. Let us begin by considering the classic research on this topic. Then we will examine the spatial framework model, as well as other information about the characteristics of mental models.

Demonstration 7.7

Creating a Mental Model

Take a piece of paper and cover the portion of this demonstration labeled "Further Instructions." Now read the story. When you have finished reading it, cover up the story and follow the Further Instructions.

The Story

You are at the Jefferson Plaza Hotel, where you have just taken the escalator from the first to the second floor. You will be meeting someone for dinner in a few minutes. You now stand next to the top of the escalator, where you have a view of the first floor as well as the second floor. You first look directly to your left, where you see a shimmering indoor fountain about 10 yards beyond a carpeted walkway. Though you cannot see beyond the low stone wall

(continued)

Demonstration 7.7

Creating a Mental Model   (continued)

that surrounds it, you suppose that its bottom is littered with nickels and pennies that hotel guests have tossed in. The view down onto the first floor allows you to see that directly below you is a darkened, candle-lit tavern. It looks very plush, and every table you see seems to be filled with well-dressed patrons. Looking directly behind you, you see through the window of the hotel's barbershop. You can see an older gentleman, whose chest is covered by a white sheet, being shaved by a much younger man. You next look straight ahead of you, where you see a quaint little gift shop just on the other side of the escalator. You're a sucker for little ceramic statues, and you squint your eyes to try to read the hours of operation posted on the store's entrance. Hanging from the high ceiling directly above you, you see a giant banner welcoming the Elks convention to the hotel. It is made from white lettering sewn onto a blue background, and it looks to you to be about 25 feet long.

Further Instructions

Now imagine that you have turned to face the barbershop. Cover up the story above and answer the following questions:

1. What is above your head?
2. What is below your feet?
3. What is ahead of you?
4. What is behind you?
5. What is to your right?

Source: Based on Tversky, 1991, p. 133.

Franklin and Tversky's Research. Before you read further, try Demonstration 7.7, which is based on a story used in a series of studies conducted by Nancy Franklin and Barbara Tversky (1990). Franklin and Tversky presented verbal descriptions of 10 different scenes, such as a hotel lobby, an opera theater, a barn, and so forth. Each description mentioned five objects located in a plausible position in relation to the observer (either above, below, in front, in back, or to either the left or the right side). Only five objects were mentioned, so that the memory load would not be overwhelming. After reading each description, the participants were instructed to imagine that they were turning around to face a different object. They were then asked to specify which object was located in each of several directions (for example, "above your head"). In all cases, the researchers measured how long the participant took to respond to the question.

Franklin and Tversky (1990) were especially interested in discovering whether response time depended upon the location of the object that was being tested. Do we make all those decisions equally quickly? In contrast, did your experience with Demonstration 7.7 suggest that some decisions are easier than others?

Franklin and Tversky (1990) found that people could rapidly answer which objects were above and below; reaction times were short for these judgments. People required somewhat longer to decide which objects were ahead or behind. Furthermore, decisions about which objects were to the right or to the left required the longest amount of time. This research has been replicated in additional research (Bryant & Tversky, 1999; Franklin & Tversky, 1990). In all these studies, people systematically favored the vertical dimension.

Franklin and Tversky (1990) also asked participants to describe how they thought they had performed the task. All participants reported that they had constructed images of the environment as they were reading. Most also reported that they had constructed imagery that represented their own point of view as an observer of the scene. Do these reports match your own experience with Demonstration 7.7?

The Spatial Framework Model. To explain their results, Franklin and Tversky proposed the spatial framework model (Franklin & Tversky, 1990; Tversky, 1991, 1997). The spatial framework model emphasizes that certain spatial directions (such as above and below) are especially prominent in our thinking.

According to the spatial framework model, when we are in a typical upright position, the vertical or above-below dimension is especially prominent. This dimension has special significance for two reasons:

1. The vertical dimension is correlated with gravity, an advantage that neither of the other two dimensions share. Gravity has an important asymmetric effect on the world we perceive; objects fall downward, not upward. Because of its association with gravity, the above-below dimension should be particularly important and thus particularly accessible.

2. The vertical dimension on an upright human's body is physically asymmetric. That is, the top (head) and the bottom (feet) are very easy to tell apart, and so we do not confuse them with each other.

These two factors combine to help us make judgments on the above-below dimension very rapidly.

The next most prominent dimension is the front-back dimension. This dimension is not correlated with gravity in upright observers. However, we can interact with objects in front of us more readily than with objects in back of us, introducing an asymmetry. Also, the human's front half is not symmetric with the back half, again making it easy to distinguish between front and back. These two characteristics lead to judgment times for the front-back dimension that are fairly fast, although not as fast as for the above-below dimension.

The least prominent dimension is right-left. This dimension is not correlated with gravity, and we can perceive objects equally well whether they are on the right or the left. Furthermore, except for the minor preferences most of us show with our right or left hand when we manipulate objects, this dimension does not have the degree of asymmetry we find for front-back. Finally, a human's right half is roughly symmetrical with the left half. You can probably remember occasions when you confused your right and left hands, or when you told someone to turn left when you meant right. Apparently, we need additional processing time to ensure that we do not make this error. Therefore, right-left decisions take longer than either above-below or front-back decisions.

In related studies, researchers have examined how people process directions on a physical map. The results demonstrate that people can make north-south decisions significantly faster than east-west decisions (Newcombe, 2002). On a typical map in our culture, north-south corresponds to above-below, whereas right-left corresponds to east-west. In other words, these results provide further support for the spatial framework model.

In summary, then, Franklin and Tversky's spatial framework model proposes that the vertical or above-below dimension is most prominent for the upright observer (Franklin & Tversky, 1990; Tversky, 1997). The front-back dimension is next most prominent, and the right-left dimension is least prominent. Our mental models therefore reveal certain biases. These biases are based on our long-term interactions with our bodies and with the physical properties of the external world (Tversky, 1997).

Further Research on Mental Models. So far, all the research we have discussed has used scenarios written in the second person. (Notice the number of *you* sentences in Demonstration 7.7, for example.) Perhaps people can construct mental models from verbal descriptions when the text suggests that the reader is observing a scene. However, do people still construct these models when the text describes the experience of another person? If a mystery novel describes what Detective Brown sees upon arriving at the scene of the crime, do we readers jump into the scene and adopt Detective Brown's perspective? Alternately, do we remain outside the scene, like a viewer watching a movie? In fact, Bryant, Tversky, and Franklin (1992) found that readers typically prefer to adopt the perspective of an involved person.

We have seen that the mental models we derive from verbal descriptions represent both orientation and point of view. Another important feature of these mental models is landmarks. According to research by Ferguson and Hegarty (1994), we tend to establish important landmarks when we hear or read a story. Then we use those landmarks as reference points for adding other locations to our mental models.

Notice that this information about landmarks is consistent with the research described in the discussion of cognitive maps and distance on pages 232–234. Landmarks apparently have special, privileged status, whether we are constructing cognitive maps based on a physical diagram or based on a verbal narrative.

All the research on mental models provides strong testimony for the active nature of human cognitive processes. We take in information, synthesize it, and go beyond the information we have been given; we create a model to represent our knowledge (Tversky, 2000b). As you will see throughout the next chapter, this tendency to go beyond the given information is an important general characteristic of our cognitive processes.

◎ Section Summary: *Cognitive Maps*

1. A cognitive map is a mental representation of the external environment; the research on this topic often emphasizes real-world settings, and it is interdisciplinary in scope.

2. Cognitive maps often represent complex knowledge. Individual differences in spatial cognition are large. We can make judgments about spatial cognition more easily if our cognitive map matches the orientation of a physical map.

3. Cognitive maps usually represent reality with reasonable accuracy. However, systematic errors in these maps usually reflect the tendency to base our judgments on variables that are typically relevant and to judge our environment as being more regular than it really is.

4. Estimates of distance on cognitive maps can be distorted by the number of intervening cities and by the semantic categories representing the buildings on the cognitive maps. In addition, we estimate that landmarks are closer than nonlandmarks.

5. Shapes on cognitive maps can be distorted so that angles of intersecting streets are closer to 90° than they are in reality, and so that curves are more nearly symmetrical than they are in reality.

6. The relative positions of features on cognitive maps can be distorted so that a slightly tilted figure will be remembered as being more vertical or more horizontal than it really is (rotation heuristic). Furthermore, a series of figures will be remembered as being more lined up than they really are (alignment heuristic).

7. We often create mental models of environments on the basis of a verbal description. In these mental models, the up-down dimension has special prominence, followed by the front-back dimension. The right-left dimension is most difficult. Franklin and Tversky (1990) explain these data in terms of the spatial framework model.

CHAPTER REVIEW QUESTIONS

1. Summarize the two theories of the characteristics of mental images: the analog code and the propositional code. Describe the findings about mental rotation, size, shape, re-interpreting ambiguous figures, and any other topics you recall. In each case, note which theory the results support.

2. Almost all of this chapter dealt with visual imagery, because little information is available about imagery in the other senses. How might you design a study on taste imagery that would be conceptually similar to one of the studies mentioned in the section on mental imagery? See whether you can also design studies to examine smell, hearing, and touch, basing these studies on the research techniques discussed in the first half of this chapter.

3. How do the studies on imagery and interference support the viewpoint that mental images operate like actual perceptions? Answer this question with respect to research on both visual images and motor images.

4. Which areas of research provided the strongest support for the propositional storage of information about objects? I mentioned my own experience with using a propositional code for a jigsaw-puzzle piece; can you think of an occasion where you seemed to use a propositional code for an unfamiliar stimulus?

5. According to the research from cognitive neuroscience, what evidence do we have that visual, auditory, and motor imagery resemble perception in those three modes? Why does this research avoid the problem of demand characteristics, which might be relevant in other imagery research?

6. Cognitive maps sometimes correspond to reality, but sometimes they show systematic deviations. Discuss the factors that seem to produce systematic distortions when people estimate distances on mental maps.

7. What are the heuristics that cause systematic distortions in geographic shape and in relative position represented on cognitive maps? How are these related to two concepts we discussed in earlier chapters—namely, top-down processing (Chapter 2) and schemas (Chapter 5)?

8. According to Franklin and Tversky (1990), the three dimensions represented in our mental models are not created equal. Which dimension has special prominence? How does the spatial framework model explain these differences?

9. The material we discussed in the first portion of this chapter emphasized that mental imagery resembles perception. However, the material in the second portion emphasized that cognitive maps may be influenced by our concepts, as well as by our perceptions. Discuss these points, including some information about mental models.

10. In general, cognitive psychologists tend to ignore individual differences. However, this chapter examined several ways in which individuals differ with respect to mental imagery and spatial cognition. Describe this information, and speculate about other areas in which individual differences could be examined.

NEW TERMS

imagery
analog code
depictive representation
pictorial representation
propositional code
descriptive representation
experimenter expectancy

anorexia nervosa
demand characteristics
epiphenomenal
cerebellum
cognitive map
spatial cognition
landmark effect

heuristic
90°-angle heuristic
symmetry heuristic
rotation heuristic
alignment heuristic
mental models
spatial framework model

RECOMMENDED READINGS

Devlin, A. S. (2001). *Mind and maze: Spatial cognition and environmental behavior.* Westport, CT: Praeger. Ann Devlin's book explores many components of spatial cognition, including spatial cognition during childhood, neuroscience research, map reading, and environmental psychology.

Kosslyn, S. M., & Thompson, W. L. (2000). Shared mechanisms in visual imagery and visual perception: Insights from cognitive neurosciences. In M. S. Gazzaniga (Ed.), *The new cognitive neurosciences* (2nd ed., pp. 975–985). Cambridge, MA: MIT Press. This brief chapter provides a solid introduction to the neuroscience research on imagery.

Newcombe, N. S. (2002). Spatial cognition. In D. Medin (Ed.), *Stevens' handbook of experimental psychology* (3rd. ed., Vol. 2, pp. 113–163). New York: Wiley. Nora Newcombe's comprehensive chapter on spatial cognition includes information on developmental aspects and on individual differences.

Richardson, J. T. E. (1999). *Imagery.* East Sussex, England: Psychology Press. This brief book traces the history of research on imagery, and then it reviews the research on the characteristics of mental imagery, the neuropsychology of imagery, and imagery as a mnemonic strategy.

Tversky, B. (2000b). Remembering spaces. In E. Tulving & F. I. M. Craik (Eds.), *The Oxford handbook of memory* (pp. 363–378). New York: Oxford University Press. Barbara Tversky's chapter provides a clear summary of the research on mental maps, including the heuristics used in constructing mental maps and the spatial framework model.

ANSWERS TO DEMONSTRATION 7.1

In Chapter 2, people need to consult some sort of mental image to identify a shape (e.g., a letter of the alphabet) or to identify a sound (e.g., a speech sound). In Chapter 3, when people conduct a search for a target—perhaps for a blue X, as in Demonstration 3.2—they must keep a mental image in mind as they inspect the potential targets. In Chapter 4, the entire discussion of the visuospatial sketchpad is based on visual imagery. In Chapter 5, visual imagery is relevant to the material on face recognition in long-term memory. Chapter 5 also discussed source monitoring; when you are trying to decide whether you actually performed an action such as returning a book to a friend, you may try to remember the muscular effort required to walk to this destination. Chapter 6 discussed visual imagery as a helpful class of mnemonic devices for retrospective memory. In addition, you may use visual imagery or motor imagery in order to prompt your prospective memory for some action you must perform in the future.

CHAPTER 8
General Knowledge

PREVIEW

This chapter examines our background knowledge—the knowledge that informs and influences cognitive processes such as memory and spatial cognition. We will explore two major topics: semantic memory and schemas.

Semantic memory refers to our organized knowledge about the world. We will look at four categories of theories that attempt to explain how all this information could be stored. These theories are partly compatible with one another, but they emphasize different aspects of semantic memory. Suppose that you are trying to decide whether an object in the grocery store is an apple. The feature comparison model proposes that you examine a list of necessary features—such as color, size, and shape—to decide if it is an apple. The prototype approach argues that you decide whether this object is an apple by comparing it with an idealized apple most typical of the category. The exemplar approach emphasizes that you decide whether it is an apple by comparing it with some specific examples of apples with which you are familiar (perhaps a McIntosh, an Ida Red, and a Fuji apple). These three theories—feature comparison, prototype, and exemplar—are primarily concerned about category membership. In contrast, the network models examined in this chapter emphasize the interconnections among related items; for example, an apple may be related to other items such as *red*, *seed-bearing*, and *pear*. (Incidentally, the most prominent network model, the parallel distributed processing approach, was introduced in Chapter 1.)

Schemas and scripts apply to larger clusters of knowledge. A schema is a generalized kind of knowledge about situations and events. One kind of schema is called a script; scripts describe an expected sequence of events. For example, most people have a well-defined "restaurant script," which specifies all the events that are likely to occur when you dine in a restaurant. Schemas influence our memories in several ways: selecting the material we want to remember, changing our memory for visual scenes, storing the meaning of a verbal passage, interpreting the material, and forming a single, integrated representation in memory. Schemas can cause inaccuracies during these stages, but we are often more accurate than schema theory proposes.

INTRODUCTION

Consider the following sentence:

> When Lisa was on her way back from the store with the balloon, she fell and the balloon floated away.

Think about all the information you take for granted and all the reasonable inferences you make while reading this brief sentence. For instance, consider the word *balloon*. You know that balloons can be made of several lightweight substances, that they can be filled with air or a lightweight gas, that they can have a shape that is almost oval or something such as an animal or a cartoon character. However, a balloon is unlikely to be created from a sock, it is unlikely to be filled with raspberry yogurt, and it is unlikely to be shaped like a spear of broccoli.

Now reread that entire sentence about the balloon, and think about the inferences you are likely to make. For instance, Lisa is probably a child, not a 40-year-old woman. Also, she probably bought the balloon in the store. You might also guess that the balloon was attached to a string, but the other end of the string was not firmly attached to Lisa. When she fell, she probably let go of the string. She may have scraped her knee, and it may have bled. A sentence that initially seemed simple is immediately enriched by an astonishing amount of general knowledge about objects and events in our world.

To provide a context for Chapter 8, let's briefly review the topics we've considered so far in this textbook. In Chapter 2, on visual and auditory recognition, we examined how the senses gather stimuli from the outside world, and how these stimuli are then interpreted by our previous knowledge. Chapter 3 emphasized that we have difficulty paying attention to more than one message at a time; our knowledge may influence which message we choose to process and which we choose to ignore.

In Chapters 4–7, we discussed how these stimuli from the outside world are stored in memory. In many cases, we saw that our previous knowledge can influence memory. For example, it can help us chunk items together to aid working memory (Chapter 4). Furthermore, our knowledge can help us process information deeply. It also provides the kind of expertise that enhances long-term memory; and it can influence our memory for the events in our lives (Chapter 5). In addition, our knowledge can help us organize information in order to recall it more accurately (Chapter 6). Finally, when we apply general principles such as the rotation heuristic and the alignment heuristic, our knowledge can distort our memories of spatial relationships, making them more regular than they actually are (Chapter 7). All these cognitive processes rely on general knowledge, demonstrating again that our cognitive processes are interrelated (Theme 4).

For this first half of the book, then, we've emphasized how information from the outside world is taken into your cognitive system and is somehow influenced by your general knowledge. This knowledge allows you to go beyond the information in the stimulus in a useful, productive fashion (Billman, 1996; Landauer & Dumais, 1997). Now we need to focus specifically on the nature of this general knowledge by examining two of its components.

First, we'll consider semantic memory. If you are a typical adult, you know the meaning of at least 20,000 to 40,000 words (Baddeley, 1990). You also know a tremendous amount of information about each of these words. For example, you know that a cat has fur and that an apple has seeds. You also know that a car is a good example of a vehicle . . . but an elevator is a bad example.

Second, we'll consider the nature of schemas, or general knowledge about an object or event. Schemas allow us to know much more than the simple combination of words in a sentence would suggest (Eysenck & Keane, 1990).

This chapter emphasizes our impressive cognitive abilities (Theme 2). We have an enormous amount of information at our disposal, and we use this information efficiently and accurately. This chapter also confirms the active nature of our cognitive processes (Theme 1). In the last part of Chapter 7, for example, we saw that people can use the information in a verbal description to actively construct a mental model of an environment. As we'll see in the current chapter, people who are given one bit of information can go beyond that specific information to actively retrieve other stored knowledge about word relationships and other likely inferences. Let us explore the nature of general knowledge as we see how people go beyond the given information in semantic memory and in schemas.

THE STRUCTURE OF SEMANTIC MEMORY

As we discussed in earlier chapters, **semantic memory** is our organized knowledge about the world (Wheeler, 2000). We contrasted semantic memory with **episodic memory,** which contains information about events that happen to us. Chapters 4, 5, and 6 emphasized different aspects of episodic memory. As we mentioned, the distinction between semantic and episodic memory is not clear-cut (Wheeler, 2000). In general, though, semantic memory refers to knowledge or information; it does not mention how that information was acquired. An example of semantic memory would be: "Tegucigalpa is the capital of Honduras." In contrast, episodic memory always implies the phrase, "It happened to me," because episodic memory emphasizes when, where, or how this event occurred. An example of episodic memory would be: "This morning I learned that Tegucigalpa is the capital of Honduras." Let's discuss some background information about semantic memory before we examine several theoretical models of how it operates.

Background on Semantic Memory

Psychologists use the term *semantic memory* in a broad sense—much broader than the word *semantic* implies in normal conversation (Tulving & Lepage, 2000). For example, semantic memory includes encyclopedic knowledge (e.g., "Martin Luther King, Jr., was born in Atlanta, Georgia"). It also includes lexical or language knowledge (e.g., "The word *snow* is related to the word *rain*"). In addition, semantic memory includes conceptual knowledge (e.g., "A square has four sides"). As researchers in the discipline point out, semantic memory influences most of our cognitive activities. For instance, this form of memory is required to determine locations, read sentences, solve problems, and make decisions.

Categories and concepts are essential components of semantic memory. In fact, we need to divide up the world into categories in order to make sense of our knowledge (Schwarz, 1995). A **category** is a class of objects that belong together. For example, a variety of objects represent a certain category of furniture; all of these objects can be called *table*. Psychologists use the term **concept** to refer to our mental representations of a category (Wisniewski, 2002). For instance, you have a concept of "table," which refers to your mental representation of the objects in that category. (Incidentally, in this chapter I'll follow the tradition in cognitive psychology of using italics for the actual word names, and quotation marks for categories and concepts.)

Your semantic memory allows you to code the objects you encounter. Even though the objects are not identical, you can combine a wide variety of similar objects into a single, one-word concept (Wisniewski, 2002). This coding process greatly reduces the storage space, because many objects can all be stored with the same label (Sternberg & Ben-Zeev, 2001).

Your concepts also allow you to make inferences when you encounter new examples from a category. For example, even a young child may know that a member of the category "table" has the attribute "you can place things on it." When she encounters a new table, she makes the inference (usually correctly) that you can place things on this table (E. E. Smith, 1995). As we noted earlier, these inferences allow us to go beyond the given information, greatly expanding our knowledge. Otherwise—if you had no concepts—you would need to examine each new table you encountered, in order to figure out how to use it (Murphy, 2002).

We noted that semantic memory allows us to combine similar objects into a single concept. But how do we decide which objects are similar? As you'll soon see, each of four approaches to semantic memory has a slightly different perspective on the nature of similarity (Markman & Gentner, 2001). Let's now consider these four major approaches. They include the feature comparison model, the prototype approach, the exemplar approach, and network models.

Most theorists in the area of semantic memory believe that each model may be at least partly correct. Furthermore, each model can account for some aspect of semantic memory (Markman, 2002). In fact, it's unlikely that the wide variety of concepts would all be represented in the same way in our semantic memory (Haberlandt, 1999; Hampton, 1997a). Therefore, as you read about these four approaches, you do not need to choose which single approach is correct and which three must consequently be wrong.

The Feature Comparison Model

One logical way to organize semantic memory would be in terms of lists of features. According to the **feature comparison model,** concepts are stored in memory according to a list of necessary features or characteristics. People use a decision process to make judgments about these concepts. Let's first look at the structure that Smith and his colleagues (1974) propose for semantic memory, and then we'll consider the research that has been conducted on the feature comparison model. Finally, we'll evaluate this approach to semantic memory.

Structural Components of the Feature Comparison Model. Consider the concept "cat" for a moment. We could make up a list of features that are often relevant to cats:

> has fur
>
> dislikes water
>
> has four legs
>
> meows
>
> has a tail
>
> chases mice

FIGURE 8.1

The Feature Comparison Model of Semantic Memory.

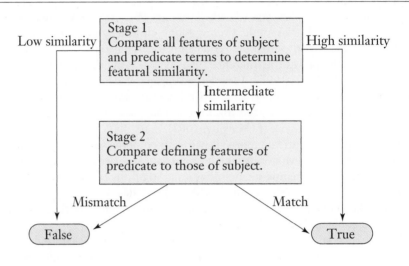

Source: Based on Smith, 1978. Courtesy of Lawrence Erlbaum Associates, Inc.

⊚ Demonstration 8.1

The Sentence Verification Technique

For each of the items below, answer as quickly as possible either "True" or "False."

1. A poodle is a dog.
2. A squirrel is an animal.
3. A flower is a rock.
4. A carrot is a vegetable.
5. A mango is a fruit.
6. A petunia is a tree.
7. A robin is a bird.
8. A rutabaga is a vegetable.

Let's consider the decision process, as described by Smith and his coauthors (1974). Imagine a study in which people must reply either, "True" or "False" to the statement, "A cat is an animal." In the first stage of the decision process, people compare all the features of the subject of the sentence, *cat*, and the predicate, which focuses on the word *animal*. Figure 8.1 shows an outline of the feature comparison model.

Three decisions are possible at Stage 1. First of all, the subject term and the predicate term may show low similarity, and so the person quickly replies, "False" to the question. For example, the statement, "A cat is a pencil" has such little similarity between the two terms that you would immediately answer, "False." In a second situation, the subject and the predicate term may show high similarity, leading to a quick "True" answer. "A cat is an animal" leads to an immediate "True." However, if the subject and the predicate terms show intermediate similarity, the decision requires a Stage 2 comparison. For example, you might need a Stage 2 comparison for a statement such as, "A bird is a mammal." As you can imagine, these decisions take longer. Now, before you read further, try Demonstration 8.1.

Smith and his coauthors (1974) propose that the features used in this model are either defining features or characteristic features. **Defining features** are those attributes that are necessary to the meaning of the item. For example, the defining features of a robin include that it is living and has feathers and a red breast. **Characteristic features** are those attributes that are merely descriptive but are not essential. For example, the characteristic features of a robin include that it flies, perches in trees, is not domesticated, and is small in size. If the distinction between defining features and characteristic features seems somewhat arbitrary, you'll be pleased to know that the research confirms this impression!

Research on the Feature Comparison Model. The sentence verification technique is one of the major tools used to explore the feature comparison model. In the **sentence verification technique,** people see simple sentences, and they must consult their stored semantic knowledge to determine whether the sentences are true or false. Demonstration 8.1 shows the kinds of items presented in the sentence verification technique. In general, people are highly accurate on this task, so it's not useful to compare the error rates across experimental conditions. Instead, researchers measure reaction times.

One common finding in research using the sentence verification technique is the typicality effect. In the **typicality effect,** people reach decisions faster when an item is a typical member of a category, rather than an unusual member. For example, in Demonstration 8.1, you probably decided quickly that a carrot is a vegetable, but you may have paused before deciding that a rutabaga is a vegetable. In a representative study, participants judged high-typicality sentences such as, "A globe is round" significantly faster than low-typicality sentences such as, "A barrel is round."

The feature comparison model can explain the typicality effect. For example, a carrot is a typical member of its category, so the features of carrots and the features of vegetables are highly similar. People quickly answer the question, "Is a carrot a vegetable?" because they require only Stage 1 processing in the model. However, a rutabaga is an example of an atypical vegetable. People require much longer to answer the question, "Is a rutabaga a vegetable?" because the decision requires Stage 2 processing as well as Stage 1 processing.

Research on another aspect of the feature comparison model clearly contradicts this approach. Specifically, a major problem with the feature comparison model is that very few of the concepts we use in everyday life can be captured by a specific list of necessary features (Burgess & Lund, 2000; Hahn & Chater, 1997; Wisniewski, 2002). For example, Sloman and his colleagues (1998) asked college students to judge whether they could imagine an example of a concept that lacked a given characteristic. When judging a robin, for example, they could imagine a robin that didn't fly, didn't eat, didn't have feathers, and didn't have a red breast! Notice, then, that the participants did not believe that any specific feature is absolutely necessary in order to qualify for the category of "robin."

Conclusions About the Feature Comparison Model. We have seen that the feature comparison model can account for the typicality effect. However, the research does not support the idea that category membership is based on a list of necessary features.

Another problem with the feature comparison model is its assumption that the individual features are independent of one another. In fact, many features are correlated for concepts found in nature. For example, objects that have leaves are unlikely to have legs or fur. In contrast, objects that have fur are highly likely to have legs (Markman, 1999, 2002). Finally, the feature comparison model does not explain how the members of categories are related to one another (Barsalou, 1992b).

Our next topic is the prototype approach to concepts. Like the feature comparison model, the prototype approach emphasizes that we ignore many details that make each item in a category unique (Heit & Barsalou, 1996). Also, like the feature comparison model, the prototype approach does not explain how the members of categories are related to one another. However, the feature comparison model is based on the similarity between an item and a list of features that are necessary for category membership. In contrast, the prototype model is based on the similarity between an item and an idealized object that represents the category (Sternberg & Ben-Zeev, 2001).

The Prototype Approach

According to a theory proposed by Eleanor Rosch, we organize each category on the basis of a **prototype,** which is the idealized item that is most typical of the category (Murphy, 2002; Rosch, 1973). According to this **prototype approach,** you decide whether an item belongs to a category by comparing that item with a prototype. If the item is similar to the prototype, you include that item in the category (Sternberg & Ben-Zeev, 2001; Wisniewski, 2002). For example, you conclude that a robin is a bird because it matches your ideal prototype for a bird. However, if the item you are judging is sufficiently different from the prototype, you place it into another category where it more closely resembles that category's prototype.

The prototype of a category does not really need to exist (Markman, 1999; Murphy, 2002). For example, if I were to ask you to describe a prototypical animal, you might tell me about a four-legged creature with fur, a tail, and a size somewhere between a large dog and a cow—something that does not precisely resemble any creature on earth. Thus, a prototype is an abstract, idealized example.

Rosch (1973) also emphasizes that members of a category differ in their **prototypicality,** or degree to which they are prototypical. A robin and a sparrow are very prototypical birds, whereas ostriches and penguins are nonprototypes. Think of a prototype, or most typical member, for a particular group of students on your campus, perhaps students with a particular academic major. Also think of a nonprototype ("You mean he's an art major? He doesn't seem at all like one!"). Now think of a prototype for a professor, a fruit, and a vehicle; then think of a nonprototype for each category. For example, a tomato is a nonprototypical fruit, and an elevator is a nonprototypical vehicle.

The prototype approach represents a different perspective from the feature comparison model that we just examined. According to the feature comparison model, an item belongs to a category as long as it possesses the necessary and sufficient features (Markman, 1999). The feature comparison perspective therefore argues that category membership is very clear-cut. For example, for the category "bachelor," the defining features are *male* and *unmarried.* However, don't you think that your 32-year-old unmarried male cousin represents a better example of a bachelor than does your 2-year-old nephew or an elderly Catholic priest? All three individuals are indeed male and unmarried, so the feature comparison model would conclude that all three deserve to be categorized as "bachelors." In contrast, the prototype approach would argue that not all members of the category "bachelor" are created equal. Instead, your cousin is a more prototypical bachelor than your nephew or the priest.

Eleanor Rosch and her coauthors, as well as other researchers, have conducted numerous studies on the characteristics of prototypes. Their research demonstrates that all members of categories are *not* created equal (Hampton, 1997b; Murphy, 2002; Whittlesea, 1997). Instead, a category tends to have a **graded structure,** beginning with the most representative or prototypical members and continuing on through the category's nonprototypical members. Let us examine several important characteristics of prototypes. Then we will discuss another important component of the prototype approach, which focuses on levels of categorization.

Characteristics of Prototypes. Prototypes differ from the nonprototypical members of categories in several respects. As you will see, prototypes have a special, privileged status.

1. *Prototypes are supplied as examples of a category.* Several studies have shown that people judge some items to be better examples of a concept than other items. In one study, for example, Mervis, Catlin, and Rosch (1976) looked at some category norms that had already been collected. The norms had been constructed by asking people to provide examples of eight different categories, such as "birds," "fruit," "sports," and "weapons." Mervis and her coauthors asked a different group of people to supply prototype ratings for each of these examples. A statistical analysis showed that the items that were rated most prototypical were the same items that people supplied most often in the category norms. For instance, for the category "bird," people considered a robin to be very prototypical, and *robin* was very frequently listed as an example of the category "bird." In contrast, people rated a *penguin* as low on the prototype scale, and

penguin was only rarely listed as an example of the category "bird." Thus, if someone asks you to name a member of a category, you will probably name a prototype.

Our earlier explanation of the feature comparison model discussed the typicality effect. As it happens, the prototype approach accounts well for the typicality effect (Murphy, 2002). That is, when people are asked to judge whether an item belongs to a particular category, they judge typical items (prototypes) faster than atypical items (nonprototypes). For instance, when judging whether items belong to the category "bird," people judge *robin* more quickly than *penguin*. This rapid judging holds true for both pictures of objects and names of objects (Hampton, 1997b; Heit & Barsalou, 1996). To summarize this first characteristic of prototypes, we can conclude that people supply prototypes more often as examples, and people also make quicker judgments about category membership when assessing prototypes.

2. *Prototypes are judged more quickly after priming.* The **priming effect** means that people respond faster to an item if it was preceded by a similar item. For example, you would make judgments about apples more quickly if you had just seen the word *fruit* than if you had just seen the word *giraffe*.

The research shows that priming facilitates the responses to prototypes more than it facilitates the responses to nonprototypes. Imagine, for example, that you are participating in a study on priming. Your task is to judge pairs of similar colors and to answer whether or not they are the same. On some occasions, the name of the color is shown to you before you must judge the pair of colors; these are the primed trials. On other occasions, no color name is supplied to you as a "warning"; these are the unprimed trials. Rosch (1975) tried this priming setup for both prototype colors (for example, a good, bright red) and nonprototype colors (for example, a muddy red).

Rosch's results showed that priming was very helpful when people made judgments about prototypical colors; they responded more quickly after primed trials than after nonprimed trials. However, priming actually *inhibited* the judgments for nonprototypical colors, even after 2 weeks of practice. In other words, if you see the word *red*, you expect to see a true, fire-engine red color. If you see, instead, a dark, muddy red color, the priming offers no advantage. Instead, you need extra time in order to reconcile your image of a bright, vivid color with the muddy color you actually see before you.

3. *Prototypes share attributes in a family resemblance category.* Before we examine this issue, let's introduce a new term, family resemblance. **Family resemblance** means that no single attribute is shared by all examples of a concept; however, each example has at least one attribute in common with some other example of the concept (Hampton, 1997b; Whittlesea, 1997). As the philosopher Wittgenstein (1953) pointed out, some concepts are difficult to describe in terms of specific defining features. For example, consider the concept of "games." Think about the games you know. What single attribute do they all have in common? How is Monopoly similar to volleyball? You might respond that both involve competition; but then what about the children's game Ring Around the Rosie? Some games require skill, but others depend upon luck. Notice how each game shares some attributes with some other game, yet no single attribute is shared by all games. In fact, all these members of the concept "games" have a family resemblance to one another.

Rosch and Mervis (1975) examined the role of prototypes in family resemblance. Specifically, they examined whether the items that people judge to be most prototypical would have the greatest number of attributes in common with other members of the category. First, they asked a group of people to provide prototype ratings for words in several categories. Table 8.1 shows three of these categories. For the category "vehicles," notice that *car* was rated as the most prototypical, whereas *sled* had a low prototype rating. Then, Rosch and Mervis asked a new group of people to list the attributes possessed by each item. Finally, from this information, the researchers calculated a number that showed what proportion of an item's attributes were also shared by other members of the same category. *Car* received a high score; like most other items on the "vehicles" list, it has wheels, moves horizontally, and uses fuel. In contrast, *sled* received a low score.

Rosch and Mervis (1975) discovered a significant correlation between the two measures—prototype rating and the attributes-in-common score. In other words, a highly prototypical item—such as "car"—usually has many attributes in common with other category members. In contrast, an item that is not prototypical—such as "sled"—has few attributes in common with other category members. See whether this relationship also holds true for the following concepts: "profession," "adventure movie," and "snack food."

TABLE 8.1

Prototype Ratings for Words in Three Categories.

| | Category | | |
Item	Vehicle	Vegetable	Clothing
1	Car	Peas	Pants
2	Truck	Carrots	Shirt
3	Bus	String beans	Dress
4	Motorcycle	Spinach	Skirt
5	Train	Broccoli	Jacket
6	Trolley car	Asparagus	Coat
7	Bicycle	Corn	Sweater
8	Airplane	Cauliflower	Underwear
9	Boat	Brussels sprouts	Socks
10	Tractor	Lettuce	Pajamas
11	Cart	Beets	Bathing suit
12	Wheelchair	Tomato	Shoes
13	Tank	Lima beans	Vest
14	Raft	Eggplant	Tie
15	Sled	Onion	Mittens

Source: Rosch & Mervis, 1975.

Most researchers in semantic memory agree that categories tend to have a structure based on family resemblance (Murphy, 2002; Pinker & Prince, 1999). That is, members of that category usually share attributes with other members of that category. However, no single attribute serves as the necessary and sufficient criterion for membership in the category.

Levels of Categorization. We have just examined three characteristics of prototypes that differentiate them from nonprototypes. The second major portion of Eleanor Rosch's prototype theory looks at the way that our semantic categories are structured in terms of different levels.

Consider these examples: Suppose that you are sitting on a wooden structure that faces your desk. You can call that structure by several different names: *furniture, chair,* or *desk chair.* You can also refer to your pet as a *dog,* a *spaniel,* or a *cocker spaniel.* You can tighten the mirror on your car with a *tool,* a *screwdriver,* or a *Phillips screwdriver.*

An object can belong to several different but related categories. Some category levels are called **superordinate-level categories,** which means they are higher-level or more general categories. "Furniture," "animal," and "tool" are all examples of superordinate-level categories. **Basic-level categories** are moderately specific. "Chair," "dog," and "screwdriver" are examples of basic-level categories. Finally, **subordinate-level categories** refer to lower-level or more specific categories. "Desk chair," "collie," and "Phillips screwdriver" are examples of subordinate categories. Try reviewing these terms by thinking of some other superordinate terms you use often, such as *vehicle, clothing,* and *musical instrument.* Can you think of basic-level and subordinate-level examples for each of these?

As you continue to read the rest of this description of prototype theory, keep in mind that a prototype is *not* the same as a basic-level category. A prototype is the best example of a category. In contrast, a basic-level category refers to a category that is neither too general nor too specific.

Basic-level categories seem to have special status (Biederman et al., 1999; Rosch et al., 1976; Wisniewski, 2002). In general, they are more useful than either superordinate-level categories or subordinate-level categories. Let's examine how these basic-level categories seem to have special privileges, in contrast to the other two category levels.

1. *Basic-level names are used to identify objects.* Try naming some of the objects that you can see from where you are sitting. You are likely to use basic-level names for these objects. You will mention *pen,* for example, rather than the superordinate *writing instrument* or the subordinate *Bic fine-point pen.* Rosch and her colleagues (1976) asked people to look at pictures and identify the objects; they found that people preferred to use basic-level names. Apparently, the basic-level name gives enough information without being overly detailed (Biederman et al., 1999; Medin et al., 2000; Wisniewski, 2002). Furthermore, people produce basic-level names faster than superordinate or subordinate names (Kosslyn et al., 1995). In other words, the basic level does have special, privileged status.

2. *Basic-level names are more likely to produce the priming effect.* Members of the same basic-level category share the same general shape (Biederman et al., 1999; Mur-

phy, 2002). For example, members of the category "chair" look roughly the same. We would expect, therefore, that when people hear the word *chair*, they would form a mental image that would resemble most chairs.

The mental image is relevant because Rosch and her colleagues (1976) wanted to see whether priming with basic-level names would be helpful. In one variation of the priming technique, the experimenter gives the name of the object, and the participant decides whether two pictures that follow are the same as one another. For example, you might hear the word *apple* and see pictures of two identical apples. Presumably, priming is effective because the presentation of the word allows you to create a mental image of this word, which helps when you make the later decision.

At any rate, the results showed that priming with basic-level names was helpful— participants made faster judgments if they saw a basic-level term like *apple* before judging the apples. However, priming with superordinate names (such as *fruit*) was not helpful. Apparently, when you hear the word *fruit*, you create a rather general representation of fruit, rather than a representation that is specific enough to prepare you for judging apples.

3. *Different levels of categorization activate different parts of the brain.* Neuroscience research using PET scans has examined whether different levels of categorization are processed in different regions of the brain (Kosslyn et al., 1995). On a typical trial, a participant might be asked to judge whether a word (e.g., *toy, doll,* or *rag doll*) matched a particular picture. This research showed that superordinate terms (e.g., *toy*) are more likely than basic-level terms (e.g., *doll*) to activate part of the prefrontal cortex. That finding makes sense, because this part of the cortex processes language and associative memory. To answer whether the picture of the doll qualifies as a toy, you must consult your memory about category membership.

In contrast, the research showed that subordinate terms (e.g., *rag doll*) are more likely than basic-level terms (e.g., *doll*) to activate areas of the brain involved when we shift visual attention. Again, this finding makes sense. To answer this question, you must shift your attention from the general shape of the object to determine if the fabric and style of the doll indeed permit it to be categorized as a "rag doll."

4. *Experts use subordinate categories differently.* So far, we have seen that people use basic-level names to identify objects, and that basic-level names produce the priming effect. We have also seen that basic-level names are less likely than other names to require the activation of additional regions of the cortex. So far, however, we have considered only the performance of novices, people who do not have expertise in the topic being studied. The research shows that basic-level categories may indeed have special status if you are not an expert in an area. However, if you *do* have expertise, the more specialized categories may also have "privileged" status (Medin et al., 2000; Tanaka & Taylor, 1991; Wisniewski, 2002).

Let's consider the research of Johnson and Mervis (1997), who studied individuals with differing levels of expertise in identifying songbirds. These researchers studied 12 undergraduate students who were novices with respect to bird names. Johnson and Mervis also located 12 advanced-level experts on birds. Each participant was shown a series of color photos of birds, as well as irrelevant items such as fruit and fish. The participant was instructed to look at each photo and provide a correct name for the item.

The novices uniformly supplied the basic-level term *bird*, as we would expect. However, the advanced-level experts rarely produced either the basic-level term (e.g., *bird*) or the subordinate-level term (e.g., *warbler*). Instead, on 87% of the trials, these experts gave a sub-subordinate term, such as *yellow-throated warbler*. In short, the basic level has privileged status for nonexperts in a discipline. In contrast, experts usually prefer a very specific level of categorization.

Conclusions About the Prototype Approach. One advantage of the prototype approach is that it can account for our ability to form concepts for groups that are loosely structured. For example, we can create a concept for stimuli that merely share a family resemblance, such as games. Prototype models work especially well when the members of a category have no single characteristic in common (Barsalou, 1992b).

However, some researchers have located categories for which the prototype is not the idealized item that is most typical of the category. Lynch and her colleagues (2000) studied tree prototypes. They asked both tree novices and tree experts to rate the names of 48 trees for "goodness of example." The tree novices (undergraduate students) gave the highest ratings to trees with familiar names, such as maple trees and oak trees, rather than trees that look typical. The tree experts were tree researchers and other professionals who specialize in trees. These experts gave the highest ratings to the tallest trees, even though these trees are much taller than "typical" trees. The prototype model should be able to predict when the prototype for a category is really not a typical item.

An ideal prototype model must also acknowledge that concepts can be unstable and variable. For example, our notions about the ideal prototype can shift as the context changes (Barsalou, 1993). Novick (2003) found that American college students rated *airplane* as being a prototypical vehicle during the period immediately following the terrorist attack of September 11, 2001. In contrast, *airplane* was considered a nonprototypical vehicle in studies that had been gathering norms on vehicles during the 5 years prior to this date. As the media coverage decreased after the attack, *airplane* decreased in prototypicality. In fact, 4½ months after the attack, *airplane* was no longer a prototypical vehicle.

Another problem with the prototype approach is that it suggests that categories have fuzzy boundaries. However, most people strongly believe that some categories do have clear-cut boundaries, not fuzzy ones (Komatsu, 1992). For example, we feel strongly that a Pomeranian is a dog and should be categorized with German shepherds, rather than with the fluffy Persian cats that it physically resembles.

Furthermore, the prototype approach explains how we can reduce all the information about a wide variety of stimuli into a single, idealized abstraction. This approach says that we do not need to retain a vast amount of information about an enormous number of category members. However, the reality is that we often *do* store specific information about these individual examples of a category. An ideal model of semantic memory would therefore need to include a mechanism for storing this specific information, as well as abstract prototypes (Barsalou, 1990, 1992b).

In summary, to account for the complexity of the concepts we store in semantic memory, an ideal theory must explain how concepts can be altered by factors such as context. Furthermore, this ideal theory must account for our intuitions that some concepts seem to be defined by clear-cut boundaries. The prototype theory clearly accounts for a number of phenomena such as family resemblance. Unfortunately, however, research on prototype theory has decreased since the 1980s, and it has not been developed to account for some additional complexities of the categories we use in our daily lives.

The Exemplar Approach

The **exemplar approach** argues that we first learn some specific examples of a concept; then we classify each new stimulus by deciding how closely it resembles those specific examples (Wisniewski, 2002). Each of those examples stored in memory is called an **exemplar.** The exemplar approach emphasizes that your concept of "dog" would be represented by numerous examples of dogs you have known (Murphy,

---

⊚ Demonstration 8.2

Exemplars and Typicality

A. For the first part of this demonstration, take out a sheet of paper and write the numbers 1 through 7 in a column. Then, next to the appropriate number, write the first example that comes to mind for each of the following categories:

1. amphibian
2. bird
3. fish
4. insect
5. mammal
6. microorganism
7. reptile

B. For the second part of the demonstration, look at each of the items you wrote on the sheet of paper. Rate how typical each item is for the category "animal." Use a scale where 1 = not at all typical, and 10 = very typical. For example, if you wrote *barracuda* on the list, supply a number between 1 and 10 to indicate the extent to which *barracuda* is typical of an animal.

C. For the final part of this demonstration, rate each of the seven categories in Part A, in terms of how typical each category is for the superordinate category "animal." Use the same rating scale as in Part B.

Source: Partly based on a study by Heit & Barsalou, 1996.

2002). In contrast, your *prototype* of a dog would be an idealized representation of a dog, with average size for a dog and average other features—but not necessarily like any particular dog you've ever seen.

Consider another example. Suppose that you are taking a course in abnormal psychology. You have just read four case studies, each describing a depressed individual. You then decide to read a fifth case study, and you find that this individual also fits into the category "depressed person" because this description closely resembles one of the earlier four exemplars. Furthermore, this individual does not resemble any exemplars in a set of case studies you read last week when you were learning about anxiety disorders.

A Representative Study on the Exemplar Approach. Before you read further, try Demonstration 8.2, which is based on a study by Evan Heit and Lawrence Barsalou (1996). These researchers wanted to determine whether the exemplar approach could explain the structure of several superordinate categories, such as "animal." When people make judgments about animals, do they think about specific exemplars or about prototypes?

Heit and Barsalou (1996) asked a group of undergraduates to supply the first example that came to mind for each of the seven basic-level categories in Part A of Demonstration 8.2. Then a second group of undergraduates rated the typicality of each of those examples, with respect to the superordinate category "animal." For instance, this second group would rate examples—such as *frog* or *salamander*—in terms of whether it was typical of the concept "animal." That second group also rated the seven basic-level categories. (To make the demonstration simpler—though not as well controlled—you performed all three tasks.)

Heit and Barsalou (1996) then assembled all the data. They wanted to see whether they could create an equation that would accurately predict—for the category "animal"—the typicality of the rating of the seven categories ("amphibian," "bird," "fish," and so on), based on the exemplars generated in a task like Task A of Demonstration 8.2. Specifically, they took into account the frequency of each of those exemplars; for example, the basic-level category "insect" frequently produced the exemplar *bee* but rarely produced the exemplar *Japanese beetle*. They also took into account the typicality ratings, similar to those you provided in Task B of the demonstration.

The information about exemplar frequency and exemplar typicality accurately predicted which of the seven categories were most typical for the subordinate category "animal" (Task C). In fact, the correlation between the predicted typicality and the actual typicality was $r = +.92$, indicating an extremely strong relationship. In case you are curious, mammals were considered the most typical animals, and microorganisms were the least typical.

The prototype approach suggests that our categories consider only the most typical items (Wisniewski, 2002). If this proposal is correct, then we can forget about the less typical items, and our categories would not be substantially changed. In another part of their study, Heit and Barsalou (1996) tried eliminating the less typical exemplars from the equation. The correlation between predicted typicality and actual typicality decreased significantly. Notice the implications: Suppose that you are asked a question such as, "How typical is an insect, with respect to the category 'animal'?" To make that judgment, you don't just take into account a very prototypical insect—

perhaps a combination of a bee and a fly. Instead, you also include some information about a caterpillar, a grasshopper, and maybe even a Japanese beetle.

Comparing the Exemplar Approach with Other Approaches. Notice that the exemplar approach resembles the prototype approach in one important respect: To make decisions about category membership, we compare a new item we are currently considering against some stored representation of the category (Markman, 1999; Murphy, 2002). If the similarity is strong enough, we conclude that this new item does indeed belong to the category. However, the prototype approach says that this stored representation is a typical member of the category. In contrast, the exemplar approach says that the stored representation is a collection of numerous specific members of the category (J. D. Smith, 2002).

In addition, the exemplar approach avoids an important problem associated with the feature comparison approach—that people usually cannot create a list of necessary and sufficient features for a category (Hahn & Chater, 1997). The exemplar approach proposes that we do not need any list of features, because all the necessary information is stored in the specific exemplars.

According to the exemplar approach, people do not need to perform any kind of abstraction process (Heit & Barsalou, 1996; Hintzman, 1986; Knowlton, 1997). That is, while reading those four case studies about depressed people, you did not figure out a list of necessary and sufficient features that the individuals had in common, as the feature comparison model would suggest. You also did not devise a prototype—an ideal, typical person with depression. The exemplar approach argues that creating a list of characteristics or creating an ideal person would force you to discard useful, specific data about individual cases.

One problem with the exemplar approach, however, is that our semantic memory would quickly become overpopulated with numerous exemplars for numerous categories (Nosofsky & Palmieri, 1998; Sternberg & Ben-Zeev, 2001). The exemplar approach may therefore be more suitable when considering a category that has relatively few members (Knowlton, 1997). For instance, the exemplar approach might operate for the category "tropical fruit," unless you happen to live in a tropical region of the world. In contrast, the prototype approach may be more suitable when considering a category that has numerous members. For example, a prototype may be the most efficient approach for a large category such as "fruit" or "animal." Despite the encouraging results from Heit and Barsalou's (1996) study, the exemplar approach may be simply too bulky for some purposes. In many situations, it is not effective to use a classification strategy based purely on exemplars (Erickson & Kruschke, 1998, 2002).

Individual differences may be substantial in the way people represent categories. Perhaps some people store information about specific exemplars, especially for categories in which they have expertise. Other people may construct categories that do not include information about specific exemplars (Thomas, 1998). These individuals may construct categories based on more generic prototypes.

In reality, the prototype approach and the exemplar approach may coexist, so that a concept includes information about both prototypes and specific exemplars (Murphy, 2002; Ross & Makin, 1999; Wisniewski, 2002). In fact, one possibility is that the brain uses both prototype processing and exemplar processing, but each is handled by a different hemisphere. Specifically, the left hemisphere may store prototypes and the right hemisphere may store exemplars (Gazzaniga et al., 2002; Kosslyn, Gazzaniga, Galaburda, & Rabin, 1999). Furthermore, different kinds of categories may require different strategies for category formation (E. E. Smith et al., 1998; J. D. Smith, 2002). People may in fact use a combination of prototype strategies and exemplar strategies when they form categories in everyday life.

Network Models

The feature comparison model, the prototype approach, and the exemplar approach all emphasize whether an item belongs to a category. In contrast, network theories are less concerned with categorization and more concerned about the interconnections among related items.

Think for a moment about the large number of associations you have to the word *apple*. How can we find an effective way to represent the different aspects of meaning for *apple* that are stored in memory? A number of theorists favor network models. Originally, the word *network* referred to an arrangement of threads in a net-like structure, with many connections among these threads. Similarly, a **network model** of semantic memory proposes a net-like organization of concepts in memory, with many interconnections. The meaning of a particular concept, such as "apple," depends on the concepts to which it is connected.

Here, we will briefly consider the network model developed by Collins and Loftus (1975), as well as Anderson's (1983, 1990, 2000) ACT theory. We'll conclude our section on the structure of semantic memory with a third network theory, the parallel distributed processing (PDP) approach. The PDP approach, which we introduced in Chapter 1, argues that cognitive processes can be understood in terms of networks that link together neuron-like units.

The Collins and Loftus Network Model. Collins and Loftus (1975) developed a theory in which meaning is represented by hypothetical networks. The **Collins and Loftus network model** proposes that semantic memory is organized in terms of net-like structures, with many interconnections; when we retrieve information, activation spreads to related concepts.

In this model, each concept can be represented as a **node,** or location in the network. Each **link** connects a particular node with another concept node. The collection of nodes and links forms a network. Figure 8.2 shows a small portion of the network that might surround the concept "apple."

How does this network model work? When the name of a concept is mentioned, the node representing that concept is activated. The activation expands or spreads from that node to other nodes with which it is connected, a process called **spreading activation.** The activation requires longer to spread to the more remote nodes in the network (Markman, 2002).

Let's consider how the Collins and Loftus (1975) model would explain what happens in a sentence verification task, such as the one you tried in Demonstration 8.1, on page 250. Suppose you hear the sentence, "A McIntosh is a fruit." This model

FIGURE 8.2

An Example of a Network Structure for the Concept "Apple," as in the Collins and Loftus Network Model.

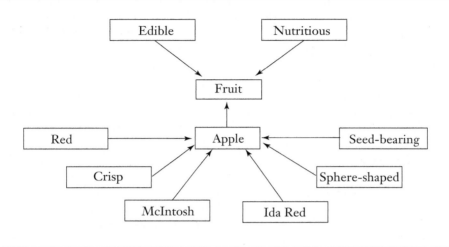

proposes that activation will spread from "McIntosh" and "fruit" to the node "apple." A search of memory notes the intersection of these two activation patterns. As a consequence, the sentence, "A McIntosh is a fruit" deserves a "yes" answer. However, suppose you hear the sentence, "An apple is a mammal." Activation spreads outward from both "apple" and "mammal," but no intersection can be found. This sentence deserves a "no" answer.

Collins and Loftus (1975) also propose that frequently used links have greater strengths. As a result, activation travels faster between the nodes. Therefore, it is easy to explain the typicality effect, in which people reach decisions faster when an item is a typical member of a category, rather than an unusual one. Specifically, the link between "vegetable" and "carrot" is stronger than the link between "vegetable" and "rutabaga."

The concept of spreading activation is an appealing one. However, Collins and Loftus's (1975) model has been superseded by more complex theories that attempt to explain broader aspects of general knowledge. Two theories that have superseded the Collins and Loftus model are Anderson's ACT theory and the parallel distributed processing approach.

Anderson's ACT Theory. John Anderson of Carnegie Mellon University has constructed a series of network models, which he calls ACT (Anderson, 1983, 1993, 1996; Anderson & Schooler, 2000; Anderson & Schunn, 2000). **ACT,** an acronym for "adaptive control of thought," attempts to account for all of cognition. The models we've considered so far have a limited goal: to explain how we organize our cognitive concepts. In contrast, ACT and its variants are designed to explain memory, learning, spatial cognition, language, reasoning, and decision making—most of the topics in this book.

Obviously, a theory that attempts to explain all of cognition is extremely complex. However, we will focus on the model's more specific view of declarative knowledge, which is responsible for semantic memory. **Declarative knowledge** is knowledge about facts and things—the essence of this current chapter. Consider several examples of declarative knowledge that might be represented on a new digital watch (Black, 1984). The declarative network contains an interconnected set of informational statements (for example, "The watch has three buttons"); visual images (for example, "The date button is on the left"); and information about the order of events (for example, "Set the date first, then hours, then minutes, then the seconds").

As you saw on pages 262–263, the network model devised by Collins and Loftus (1975) focuses on networks of individual words. Anderson, in contrast, designed a model based on larger units of meaning. According to Anderson (1990), the meaning of a sentence can be represented by a *propositional network*, or pattern of interconnected propositions.

We discussed propositions in Chapter 7, in connection with the storage of mental images. Anderson's definition of a proposition, however, is somewhat more precise: A **proposition** is the smallest unit of knowledge that can be judged either true or false. For instance, the phrase *white cat* does not qualify as a proposition because we cannot find out whether it is true or false unless we know something more about the white cat. The model proposes that each of the following three statements is a proposition:

1. Susan gave a cat to Maria.
2. The cat was white.
3. Maria is the president of the club.

These three propositions can appear by themselves, but they can also be combined into a sentence, such as the following:

Susan gave a white cat to Maria, who is the president of the club.

Figure 8.3 shows how this sentence could be represented by a propositional network. As you can see, each of the three propositions in the sentence is represented by a node, and the links are represented by arrows. Notice, too, that the network represents the important relations in the three propositions, but not the exact wording. Propositions are abstract; they do not represent a specific set of words. (Later in the chapter, we will discuss research that demonstrates how we typically remember the gist or general message of language, rather than the specific wording of sentences.)

Furthermore, Anderson suggests that each of the concepts in a proposition can be represented by its own individual network. Figure 8.4 illustrates just a small part of the representation of the word *cat* in memory. Try to imagine what the propositional network in Figure 8.3 would look like if each of the concepts in that network were to be replaced by an expanded network representing the richness of meanings you have acquired. Obviously, these networks need to be complicated in order to accurately represent the dozens of associations we have for each item in semantic memory (Miller, 1999).

FIGURE 8.3

A Propositional Network Representing the Sentence "Susan gave a white cat to Maria, who is the president of the club."

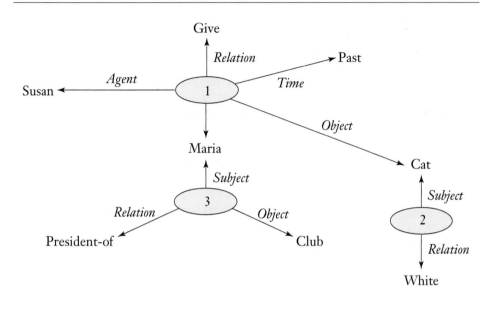

FIGURE 8.4

A Partial Representation of the Word *Cat* in Memory.

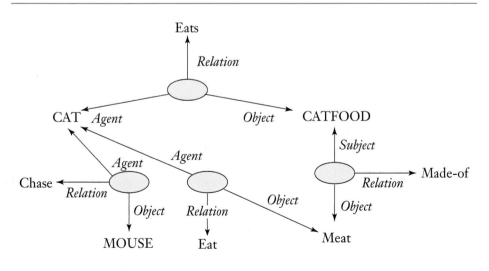

Anderson's model of semantic memory makes some additional proposals. For example, similar to Collins and Loftus's (1975) model, the links vary in strength. Suppose that you see the word *night.* Strongly associated concepts like "dark" will be activated more quickly than weakly associated concepts like "pillow." Furthermore, these links become stronger as they are used more often (Anderson, 2000; Anderson & Schunn, 2000; Sternberg & Ben-Zeev, 2001). Practice is vitally important in developing more extensive semantic memory (Anderson & Schooler, 2000). This mechanism for strengthening the links can therefore account for long-term learning.

Also, the model assumes that, at any given moment, as many as 10 nodes are represented in your working memory. In addition, the model proposes that activation can spread. However, Anderson argues that the spread of activation has a limited capacity because of the limits of working memory. Thus, if many links are activated simultaneously, each link receives relatively little activation (Anderson, Reder, & Lebiere, 1996; Markman, 2002). As a consequence, this knowledge will be retrieved relatively slowly (Anderson, 2000).

Anderson's model has been highly praised for its skill in integrating cognitive processes and for its scholarship. However, others have objected that the model has not yet integrated the findings from neuroscience into the theoretical explanations of memory. Nevertheless, the theory could be compatible with the brain's neural connections (Haberlandt, 1999; Roediger et al., 2001). In contrast, the parallel distrib-

---

⊙ Demonstration 8.3

Parallel Distributed Processing

For each of the two tasks below, read the set of clues and then guess as quickly as possible what thing is being described.

Task A

1. It is orange.
2. It grows below the ground.
3. It is a vegetable.
4. Rabbits characteristically like this item.

Task B

1. Its name starts with the letter *p.*
2. It inhabits barnyards.
3. It is typically yellow in color.
4. It says, "Oink."

uted processing approach—which we discuss next—is specifically designed in terms of the neural networks found in the cerebral cortex.

The Parallel Distributed Processing Approach. The **parallel distributed processing (PDP) approach** argues that cognitive processes can be represented by a model in which activation flows through networks that link together a large number of simple, neuron-like units (Markman, 1999; McClelland, 1995). Two other names—**connectionism** and **neural networks**—are often used interchangeably with *PDP approach.* The researchers who designed it tried to construct their model by taking into account the physiological and structural properties of human neurons (McClelland, 2000). We briefly introduced the PDP approach in Chapter 1; now let's consider it in more detail.

Before you read further, try Demonstration 8.3, which illustrates some features of the PDP approach.

Each of the clues in Task A of Demonstration 8.3 probably reminded you of several possible candidates. Perhaps you thought of the correct answer after just a couple of clues, even though the description was not complete. Notice, however, that you did not conduct a complete search of all orange objects before beginning a second search of all below-ground objects, then all vegetables, then all rabbit-endorsed items. In other words, you did not conduct a **serial search** for *carrot,* processing each attribute one at a time. Instead, you used a **parallel search,** in which you considered all attributes simultaneously. The word *parallel* is reflected in the name *parallel distributed processing.* The information-processing approach emphasizes serial processing, as we saw in Chapter 1. In contrast, the PDP approach argues that many cognitive processes take place in a parallel fashion. In other words, activation can flow through many pathways at the same time (Protopapas, 1999; Sternberg & Ben-Zeev, 2001).

Furthermore, notice that your memory can cope quite well, even if one of the clues is incorrect (Shanks, 1997). For instance, in Task B you searched for a barnyard-dwelling, oink-producing creature whose name starts with *p.* The word *pig* emerged, despite the misleading clue about the yellow color. Similarly, if someone describes a classmate from Saratoga Springs who is a tall male in your child development course, you can identify the appropriate student, even if he is from Poughkeepsie.

Before we proceed, note three characteristics of the memory searches you performed in Demonstration 8.3:

1. If a machine has one faulty part, it typically will not work, even if all the other parts function well. If your car's battery is dead, the cooperative effort of all the functioning parts still cannot make your car move forward. Human memory is much more flexible, active, and impressive, consistent with Themes 1 and 2 of this book. Memory can still work well, even with some inappropriate input.

2. Memory storage is **content addressable;** that is, we can use attributes (such as an object's color) to locate material in memory. PDP theory argues that, if we enter the network with an attribute such as a color, we'll activate the appropriate neural unit or units (Shanks, 1997).

3. Some clues are more effective than others in helping us locate material in memory. For example, in Task B, most people would find the information

about "oink" noises to be more useful than, for instance, information about the number of legs, the animal has.

James McClelland is one of the major developers of the PDP approach. McClelland (1981) described how our knowledge about a group of individuals might be stored by connections that link these people with their personal characteristics. His original example portrayed members of two gangs of small-time criminals, the Jets and the Sharks. We'll use a simpler and presumably more familiar example that features five college students. Table 8.2 lists these students, together with their college majors, years in school, and political orientation. Figure 8.5 shows how this information could be represented in network form. Notice that this figure represents only a fraction of the number of people a college student is likely to know and also just a fraction of the characteristics associated with each person. Take a minute to imagine how large a piece of paper you would need to represent all the people you know, together with all the characteristics you consider relevant.

According to the PDP approach, each individual's characteristics are connected in a mutually stimulating network. If the connections among the characteristics are well established through extensive practice, then an appropriate clue allows you to locate the characteristics of a specified individual (McClelland, 1995; McClelland et al., 1986; Rumelhart et al., 1986).

Imagine that you want to locate the characteristics of Roberto, who is the only Roberto in the system. If you enter the network with the name *Roberto*, you can discover that he is a psychology major, a senior, and politically liberal. However, as we noted earlier, some clues are more effective than others. If you enter the network with the characteristic *psychology major*, your search produces ambiguity, because you would locate two names—Marti and Roberto.

One advantage of the PDP model is that it allows us to explain how human memory can help us when some information is missing. Specifically, people can make a **spontaneous generalization** by drawing inferences about general information based on individual cases (Protopapas, 1999).

For example, suppose that your memory stores the information in Figure 8.5 and similar information on other college students. Suppose, also, that someone were to ask you whether engineering students tend to be politically conservative. PDP theory suggests that the clue *engineering student* would activate information about all the engineering students you know, including information about their political orientation. You would reply that they do tend to be politically conservative, even though this statement is not directly stored in memory. (Our ability to make inferences will be discussed in more detail later in this chapter, and also in Chapters 9 and 12.) Notice, then, that the structure of the PDP model makes some predictions about human cognitive processes, and these predictions can then be tested by researchers.

Spontaneous generalization accounts for some of the memory errors and distortions we discussed in Chapter 5, on long-term memory. Spontaneous generalization can also help to explain stereotyping, a complex cognitive process discussed later in this chapter and also in Chapter 12, on decision making. The PDP model argues that we do not simply retrieve a memory in the same fashion that we might retrieve a

TABLE 8.2

Attributes of Representative Individuals Whom a College Student Might Know.

Name	Major	Year	Political Orientation
1. Joe	Art	Junior	Liberal
2. Marti	Psychology	Sophomore	Liberal
3. Sam	Engineering	Senior	Conservative
4. Liz	Engineering	Sophomore	Conservative
5. Roberto	Psychology	Senior	Liberal

FIGURE 8.5

A Sample of the Units and Connections That Represent the Individuals in Table 8.2.

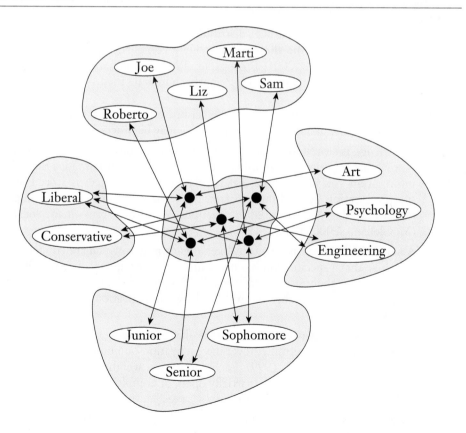

book from a library. Instead, we reconstruct a memory, and that memory sometimes includes inappropriate information (McClelland, 1999).

We just noted that spontaneous generalization allows us to make inferences about a category (for example, "engineering student"). PDP models also allow us to fill in missing information about a particular person or a particular object by making a best guess; we can make a **default assignment** based on information from similar people or objects. Suppose, for example, that you meet Christina, who happens to be an engineering student. Someone asks you about Christina's political preferences, but you have never discussed politics with her. This question will activate information about the political leanings of other engineers. Based on a default assignment, you will reply that she is probably conservative.

Incidentally, students sometimes confuse the terms *spontaneous generalization* and *default assignment*. Remember that spontaneous generalization means that we draw a conclusion about a general category (for example, "engineering students"), whereas default assignment means that we draw a conclusion about a specific member of a category (for example, a particular engineering student).

Notice, however, that both spontaneous generalization and default assignment can produce errors. For example, Christina may really be the president of your university's Anti-War Coalition.

So far, our discussion of parallel distributed processing has been concrete and straightforward. In reality, the theory is extremely complex, sophisticated, and abstract (e.g., Gluck & Myers, 2001; Protopapas, 1999; Rumelhart et al., 1986). The most important characteristics of the PDP approach include the following:

1. Cognitive processes are based on parallel operations, rather than serial operations. Therefore, many patterns of activation may be proceeding simultaneously.

2. Knowledge is stored in the association of connections among the basic units. Notice that this view is very different from the commonsense idea that all the information you know about a particular person or object is stored in one specific location in the brain. In fact, the term *distributed processing* suggests that knowledge is distributed in a pattern of activity across many locations (McClelland, 2000; Shanks, 1997).

3. A network contains basic neuron-like units or nodes, which are connected together so that a specific unit has many links to other units (hence the alternate name for the theory: *connectionism*). PDP theorists argue that all cognitive processes can presumably be explained by the activation of these networks (Markman, 1999).

4. The connections between these neuron-like units are weighted, and the **connection weights** determine how much activation one unit can pass on to another unit (McClelland, 1999). Each connection weight operates like a valve that can be completely open, partially open, or completely shut.

5. When a unit reaches a critical level of activation, it may affect another unit, either by exciting it (if the connection weight is positive) or by inhibiting it (if the connection weight is negative). Notice that this design resembles the exci-

tation and inhibition of neurons in the human brain (Gluck & Myers, 2001; Markman, 1999). Incidentally, Figure 8.5 shows only excitatory connections, but you can imagine additional, inhibitory connections. For example, the characteristic *polite* might have a negative connection weight associated with some of the less civilized students in this figure.

6. Every new event changes the strength of connections among relevant units by adjusting the connection weights (McClelland, 1995; Sternberg & Ben-Zeev, 2001). As a consequence, you are likely to respond differently the next time you experience a similar event. For example, while you have been reading about the PDP approach, you have been changing the strength of connections between the name *PDP approach* and such terms as *content addressable* and *spontaneous generalization.* The next time you encounter the term *PDP approach*, all these related terms are likely to be activated. The neural networks are specifically designed to "learn from experience" (Hahn & Chater, 1997).

7. Sometimes we have only partial memory for some information, rather than complete, perfect memory. The brain's ability to provide partial memory is called **graceful degradation.** For example, Chapter 6 discussed the **tip-of-the-tongue phenomenon,** which occurs when you know which target you are seeking; however, you cannot retrieve the actual target. Consistent with graceful degradation, you may know the target's first letter and the number of syllables—even though the word itself refuses to leap into memory. Graceful degradation also explains why the brain continues to work somewhat accurately, even when an accident or stroke has destroyed portions of the cortex (Baddeley, 1997).

We've examined some of the most important characteristics of the PDP approach. Let's now briefly discuss the current status of this theory. Clearly, the PDP perspective is one of the most important shifts in cognitive psychology in recent decades (Haberlandt, 1999; Levine, 2002). However, the approach is relatively new, and we cannot yet evaluate whether it can accommodate actual data about a wide variety of cognitive processes.

Some supporters are enthusiastic that the PDP approach seems generally consistent with the neurological design of neurons and the brain (Bressler, 2002; Gluck & Myers, 2001; Protopapas, 1999). Many are therefore hopeful that PDP research may provide important links between psychology and neuroscience.

Theorists argue that the PDP approach works better for some kinds of cognitive tasks than for others. As you might expect, parallel distributed processing works better for tasks in which several processes typically operate at the same time, as in pattern recognition, categorization, and memory search. However, other cognitive tasks demand primarily serial processing. Language use, problem solving, and reasoning—cognitive tasks we consider later in this book—often require serial processing, rather than parallel operations. For these "higher" mental processes, artificial intelligence approaches and other models may be more effective (Baddeley, 1997; Bechtel, 1997; Pinker, 1997).

So, what are some of the cognitive tasks that can be explained by the PDP approach? These include the use of past-tense verbs (O'Reilly & Munakata, 2000), the word superiority effect (Markman, 2002), speech perception (Protopapas, 1999), retroactive interference (McClelland, 2000), acquisition of information about different geographic regions (Kitchin & Blades, 2002), category formation (Levine, 2002; McClelland, 2000), and complex decision making (Levine, 2002; Lord et al., 2003).

The PDP approach has also been used to explain cognitive disorders, such as the reading problems experienced by people with dyslexia (Levine, 2002; O'Reilly & Munakata, 2000). It can also account for the cognitive difficulties found in people with schizophrenia (Chen & Berrios, 1998), and memory deficits associated with Alzheimer's disease (Tippett et al., 1995; Wallenstein & Hasselmo, 1998).

Researchers believe that the PDP approach works quite well for certain memory tasks, such as recovering from memory an item for which we have only partial information. Also, the current PDP models can explain situations where learning accumulates gradually across trials (Goschke, 1997; McClelland, 1995).

However, PDP models cannot yet provide a satisfactory account for our memory of a single episode. The PDP approach also has trouble explaining the rapid forgetting of extremely well-learned information that occurs when we learn additional information (McCloskey & Cohen, 1989; Ratcliff, 1990). Finally, the models cannot account for our ability to recall earlier material when it has been replaced by more current material (Lewandowsky & Li, 1995).

Earlier in the chapter, we discussed the feature comparison model, the prototype approach, the exemplar approach, and two other network theories. All of those theoretical approaches also generated enthusiasm when they were first proposed. However, the PDP approach is broader than most of these theories because it addresses perception, language, and decision making, as well as numerous aspects of memory. Will the enthusiasm initially generated by this approach eventually fade as it did for some of the earlier approaches? At present, many of the features of connectionism are highly speculative (Goschke, 1997). It is possible, however, that the PDP approach will eventually become the standard framework for analyzing human memory.

🌀 Section Summary: *The Structure of Semantic Memory*

1. The previous chapters emphasized how our general knowledge influences our cognitive processes; this chapter examines both the extent of our general knowledge and the active processing of our general knowledge.

2. A category is a class of objects that belong together; a concept is your mental representation of that category.

3. The feature comparison model proposes that concepts are stored in terms of a list of necessary features. Some decisions about semantic memory can be made rapidly, whereas more subtle decisions require two stages.

4. According to prototype theory, people compare new stimuli with an idealized prototype in order to categorize them. People frequently supply prototypes when they are asked to give an example of a category; prototypes are judged more quickly after priming; and prototypes share a large number of attributes with other items that belong to the same family-resemblance category.

5. Prototype theory also proposes that basic-level categories are more likely than subordinate- or superordinate-level categories to be used to identify objects. In addition, basic-level names produce the priming effect, and different levels of categorization activate different regions of the brain. However, experts are more likely to use subordinate and sub-subordinate terms, rather than basic-level terms.

6. The prototype approach can account for family resemblance among category members, but it cannot account for situations in which the best example is not the most typical item, for the influence of context on concepts, and for the observation that we sometimes do have clear-cut boundaries for category membership. It also cannot account for the storage of specific information about category members.

7. The exemplar approach proposes that we classify a new stimulus by deciding how closely it resembles specific examples (or exemplars) that we have already learned; research suggests that our concepts may indeed include information about less typical exemplars. The exemplar approach may be most suitable when we have relatively small categories. It's possible that people may use both prototypes and exemplars to represent concepts.

8. Three important network models include one proposed by Collins and Loftus (1975), in which concepts are interconnected in semantic memory and activation spreads to related concepts.

9. A second network model is Anderson's ACT approach, which attempts to explain a wide variety of cognitive processes. In Anderson's model of declarative memory, both sentences and concepts can be represented by a network structure.

10. The third network model is the parallel distributed processing (PDP) approach, in which memory can function—even with some inappropriate input—and some clues are more effective than others in helping us locate material in memory. We can also make spontaneous generalizations about a category, and we can make default assignments to fill in missing information about a particular member of a category.

11. The PDP approach argues that cognitive processes are based on parallel operations, with knowledge distributed across many locations in the brain. Also, memory consists of networks of neuron-like units; the activation of one unit may excite or inhibit a neighboring unit. We sometimes have partial memory for some information—for example, with the tip-of-the-tongue phenomenon.

12. The PDP approach works best for pattern recognition, categorization, and certain memory tasks in which several processes must operate simultaneously; it may be less relevant for higher mental processes.

SCHEMAS AND SCRIPTS

So far, our discussion of general knowledge has focused on words, concepts, and—occasionally—sentences. However, our cognitive processes also handle knowledge units that are much larger. For example, our knowledge includes information about familiar situations, events, and other "packages" of things we know. This generalized knowledge about a situation or an event is called a **schema.** (The plural form is either *schemas* or *schemata*; we will use *schemas*.) For example, you have a schema for the interior of a hardware store. It should have wrenches, cans of paint, garden hoses, and lightbulbs—but not psychology textbooks, DVDs of Verdi operas, or birthday cakes.

Schema theories are especially helpful when psychologists try to explain how people process complex situations and events (Markman, 1999). In this section of the chapter, we'll consider some background information on schemas and a subcategory called *scripts*. Then we'll discuss how schemas can influence various phases of memory. First, however, try Demonstration 8.4.

Background on Schemas and Scripts

Schema theories propose that people encode, in their memory, "generic" information about a situation. Then they use this information to understand and remember new examples of the schema. Specifically, schemas guide our recognition and understanding of new examples by providing expectations about what should occur. Schemas therefore emphasize top-down processing, a principle of cognitive processes high-

---

🌀 **Demonstration 8.4**

The Nature of Scripts

Read the following paragraph, which is based on a paragraph from Trafimow and Wyer (1993, p. 368):

> After doing this, he found the article. He then walked through the doorway and took a piece of candy out of his pocket. Next, he got some change and saw a person he knew. Subsequently, Joe found a machine. He realized he had developed a slight headache. After he aligned the original, Joe put in the coin and pushed the button. Thus, Joe had copied the piece of paper.

Now turn to the list of new terms for Chapter 8, on page 293. Look at the first column of terms and write out the definition for as many of these terms as you know. Take about 5 minutes on the task. Then look at the paragraph labeled "Further instructions for Demonstration 8.4," which appears at the bottom of Demonstration 8.5, on page 277.

lighted in Theme 5. Schemas also allow us to predict what will happen in a new situation. These predictions will usually be correct. Schemas are **heuristics,** or general rules that are typically accurate.

However, schemas can sometimes lead us astray, and we make errors. Still, these errors usually make sense within the framework of that schema. Consistent with Theme 2, our cognitive processes are generally accurate, and our mistakes are typically rational.

The concept of schemas has had a long history in psychology. For example, Piaget's work in the 1920s investigated schemas in infants, and Bartlett (1932) tested memory for schemas in adults. Schemas were not popular during the behaviorist era, because they emphasize unseen cognitive processes. However, cognitive psychologists have conducted numerous studies on this topic, so that *schema* is a standard term in contemporary cognitive psychology (Brewer, 1999, 2000).

Schemas are also important in areas other than cognitive psychology, such as social psychology. For instance, Honneycutt and Cantrill (2001) explore how schemas are relevant in romantic relationships. Furthermore, Hong and her coauthors (2000) examine how bicultural individuals develop a different set of schemas for each of their two cultures. A young boy may see the world through U.S.-based schemas while at school, but he uses Mexican-based schemas when he returns to his home. In addition, schemas are becoming more important in clinical psychology, which is using techniques such as schema therapy (Young et al., 2003). In **schema therapy,** the clinician works together with the client in order to create appropriate new schemas that can replace the maladaptive schemas developed during childhood, adolescence, and earlier adulthood.

One common kind of schema is a script. A **script** is a simple, well-structured sequence of events—in a specified order—that are associated with a highly familiar activity (Anderson & Conway, 1993; Markman, 2002; Schank & Abelson, 1995). A script is an abstraction, a prototype of a series of events that share an underlying similarity. The terms *schema* and *script* are often used interchangeably. However, *script* is actually a narrower term, referring to a sequence of events that happens across a period of time. Scripts help us understand that many everyday events unfold in a specified order (Woll, 2002; Zacks et al., 2001).

Consider a typical script, describing the standard sequence of events that a customer might expect in a restaurant (Abelson, 1981; Schank & Abelson, 1977). The "restaurant script" includes events such as sitting down, looking at the menu, eating the food, and paying the bill. We could also have scripts for visiting a dentist's office, for how a board meeting should be run, and for the first day of class in a college course. Much of our education consists of learning the scripts that we are expected to follow in our culture (Schank & Abelson, 1995).

The research demonstrates that people recall a script much more accurately if the script has been clearly identified in advance. For example, Trafimow and Wyer (1993) developed four different scripts, each describing a familiar sequence of actions: photocopying a piece of paper, cashing a check, making tea, and taking the subway. Some details irrelevant to the script (such as taking a piece of candy out of a pocket) were also added. In some cases, the script-identifying event was presented first. In other cases, the script-identifying event was presented last. For instance, in Demonstration 8.4, you saw the information about copying the piece of paper after you had read the script.

After reading all four descriptions, the participants were given a 5-minute filler task, which required recalling the names of U.S. states and their capitals. Then they were asked to recall the events from the four original descriptions. When the script-identifying event had been presented first, participants recalled 23% of those events. In contrast, they recalled only 10% when the script-identifying event had been presented last. As you might expect, the events in a sequence are much more memorable if you can appreciate—from the very beginning—that these events are all part of a standard script. With this kind of background information, the events in the sequence make sense.

For the remainder of the chapter, let's examine how schemas—and their subcategory, scripts—operate in several phases of memory (Alba & Hasher, 1983; Intraub et al., 1998). As you'll see, schemas have an important influence on these five components of memory:

1. During the selection of material to be remembered;
2. In boundary extension (when you store a scene in memory);
3. During abstraction (when you store the meaning, but not the specific details of the material);
4. During interpretation (when you make inferences about the material); and
5. During integration (when you form a single memory representation of the material).

Schemas and Memory Selection

The research on schemas and memory selection has produced contradictory findings. Sometimes people remember material best when it is *consistent* with a schema; other times they remember material best when it is *inconsistent* with the schema (Hirt et al., 1998). Let's first consider a classic study that favors schema-consistent memory.

Enhanced Memory for Schema-Consistent Material. Try Demonstration 8.5 when you have the opportunity. This demonstration is based on a study by Brewer and Treyens (1981). These authors asked participants in their study to wait, one at a time, in the room pictured in the demonstration. Each time, the experimenter explained that this was his office, and he needed to check the laboratory to see if the previous participant had completed the experiment. After 35 seconds, the experimenter asked the participant to move to a nearby room. Here, each person was given a surprise memory test: Recall everything in the room in which he or she had waited.

The results showed that people were highly likely to recall objects consistent with the "office schema": Nearly everyone remembered the desk, the chair next to the desk, and the wall. However, few recalled the wine bottle and the coffee pot, and only one remembered the picnic basket. These items were not consistent with the office schema.

In this particular study by Brewer and Treyens (1981), people accurately recalled information *consistent* with the "office schema." Notice, however, that people did not

🌀 Demonstration 8.5

Schemas and Memory

After reading these instructions, cover them and the rest of the text in this demonstration so that only the picture shows. Present the picture to a friend, with the instructions, "Look at this picture of a psychologist's office for a brief time." Half a minute later, close the book and ask your friend to list everything that was in the room.

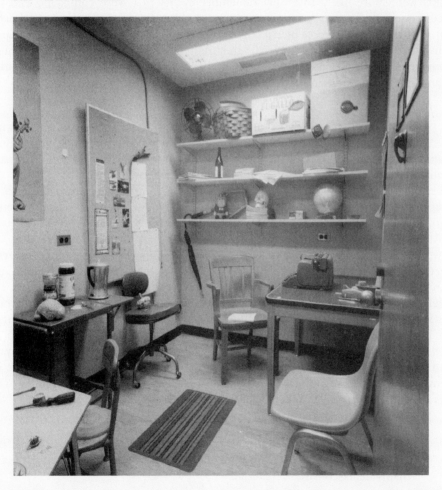

(Further instructions for Demonstration 8.4: Now without looking back at Demonstration 8.4, write down the story from that demonstration, being as accurate as possible.)

Source: Based on Brewer & Treyens, 1981.

realize that they were going to be asked to remember the items; in other words, the task involved **incidental learning.** Incidental learning conditions may encourage us to be more casual about processing the objects we see. As a consequence, we may recall objects more accurately when they match our expectations.

In addition, some people in Brewer and Treyens's (1981) study "remembered" items that were not in the room. For example, nine said they remembered books, though none had been in sight. This tendency to supply schema-consistent items represents an interesting reconstruction error. Similarly, Neuschatz and his coauthors (2002) instructed students to watch a video of a man giving a lecture. The students were more likely to falsely remember events that were consistent with the "lecture schema," rather than inconsistent with that schema. If you try to recall what happened during your most recent cognitive psychology class, you are likely to report schema-consistent activities—even if they didn't happen. For instance, you might "remember" your professor referring to a concept from the previous lecture, rather than eating a sandwich or dancing across the floor.

Enhanced Memory for Schema-Inconsistent Material. As you might imagine, we sometimes show better recall for material that violates our expectations (e.g., Lampinen et al., 2000; Neuschatz et al., 2002; Schützwohl, 1998). People are especially likely to recall schema-*inconsistent* material when that material is vivid, and when it interrupts the ongoing schema (Brewer, 2000). For instance, Davidson (1994) asked participants to read a variety of stories, describing well-known schemas such as "going to the movies." The results demonstrated that people were especially likely to recall events that interrupted the normal, expected story. For example, one story described a woman named Sarah who was going to the movies. The participants were very likely to remember a schema-inconsistent sentence such as, "A child runs through the theater and smashes head-on into Sarah." In contrast, they were less likely to remember a schema-consistent sentence such as, "The usher tears their tickets in half and gives them the stubs" (p. 773). Incidentally, before you read further, try Demonstrations 8.6 and 8.7.

Rojahn and Pettigrew (1992) conducted a meta-analysis of the research on memory and schemas. Most of the studies included in the meta-analysis seemed to require **intentional learning,** situations where people realized that they were going to be asked to remember the items. This meta-analysis produced three general trends:

1. When memory was assessed in terms of recall—as in Davidson's (1994) study—people were likely to remember schema-inconsistent material better than schema-consistent material.

2. When memory was assessed in terms of recognition and the results had been corrected for guessing, schema-inconsistent material was still favored.

3. However, when memory was assessed in terms of recognition and the results had *not* been corrected for guessing, schema-consistent material was favored.

Demonstration 8.6

Memory for Objects

Look at the objects below very carefully. Then turn to page 281, just above the rectangle, where you will find further instructions for this demonstration.

In other words, suppose that you cannot remember whether you've seen a sentence on a recognition test about a movie schema. Then you're more likely to guess that you saw a sentence about an usher tearing up tickets, rather than a sentence that violates the schema, such as our example about the child who collides with the woman.

Why should we often remember schema-*inconsistent* material so accurately? A plausible explanation is that we are especially likely to remember material that attracts attention and requires more effort to process. With effortful, deep processing, we'll recall that unusual material (Erdfelder & Bredenkamp, 1998; Lampinen et al., 2000).

The Current Status of Schemas and Memory Selection. Ironically, we cannot establish any clear schema for the research on people's recall of events that actually happened. Apparently, we seem to remember schema-consistent material more accurately if the task uses incidental learning or if memory is assessed by recognition—with no correction for guessing. In most cases of intentional learning, however, schema-inconsistent material appears to be more memorable. Still, the research does seem to support another component of the schema approach to memory selection: When people "remember" events that never actually happened, they are more likely to produce schema-consistent events, (e.g., a professor's reference to a previous lecture), rather than schema-inconsistent events (e.g. the professor dancing across the floor).

Demonstration 8.7

Constructive Memory

Part 1
Read each sentence, count to five, answer the question, and go on to the next sentence.

Sentence	Question
The girl broke the window on the porch.	Broke what?
The tree in the front yard shaded the man who was smoking his pipe.	Where?
The cat, running from the barking dog, jumped on the table.	From what?
The tree was tall.	Was what?
The cat running from the dog jumped on the table.	Where?
The girl who lives next door broke the window on the porch.	Lives where?
The scared cat was running from the barking dog.	What was?
The girl lives next door.	Who does?
The tree shaded the man who was smoking his pipe.	What did?
The scared cat jumped on the table.	What did?
The girl who lives next door broke the large window.	Broke what?
The man was smoking his pipe.	Who was?
The large window was on the porch.	Where?
The tall tree was in the front yard.	What was?
The cat jumped on the table.	Where?
The tall tree in the front yard shaded the man.	Did what?
The dog was barking.	Was what?
The window was large.	What was?

Part 2
Cover the preceding sentences. Now read each of the following sentences and decide whether it is a sentence from the list in Part 1.

1. The girl who lives next door broke the window.   (old _____, new _____)

2. The tree was in the front yard.   (old _____, new _____)

3. The scared cat, running from the barking dog, jumped on the table.   (old _____, new _____)

4. The window was on the porch.   (old _____, new _____)

5. The tree in the front yard shaded the man.   (old _____, new _____)

6. The cat was running from the dog.   (old _____, new _____)

(continued)

⑨ Demonstration 8.7

Constructive Memory   (*continued*)

7. The tall tree shaded the man who was
    smoking his pipe.   (old _____, new _____)
8. The cat was scared.   (old _____, new _____)
9. The girl who lives next door broke the
    large window on the porch.   (old _____, new _____)
10. The tall tree shaded the girl who broke
    the window.   (old _____, new _____)
11. The cat was running from the barking dog.   (old _____, new _____)
12. The girl broke the large window.   (old _____, new _____)
13. The scared cat ran from the barking dog
    that jumped on the table.   (old _____, new _____)
14. The girl broke the large window on the porch. (old _____, new _____)
15. The scared cat which broke the window on
    the porch climbed the tree.   (old _____, new _____)
16. The tall tree in the front yard shaded the
    man who was smoking his pipe.   (old _____, new _____)

*(Further instructions for Demonstration 8.6: In the box below, draw from memory the
scene you saw in Demonstration 8.6. Do not look back at that photo!)*

Source: Parts 1 and 2 of this demonstration are based on an example created by Jenkins, 1974;
the original research was conducted by Bransford and Franks, 1971.

Schemas and Boundary Extension

Now take a moment to examine the objects you drew for Demonstration 8.7, and compare your sketch with the original photo. Does your sketch include the bottom edge of the garbage can lid—which was not present in the original photo? Does your sketch show more background surrounding each garbage can, including the top of the picket fence? If so, you've demonstrated boundary extension. **Boundary extension** refers to the tendency to remember having viewed a greater portion of a scene than was actually shown. We have a schema for the scene depicted in Demonstration 8.6, which we could call "a photo of a backyard garbage area." Notice that the other topics in this discussion of schemas are verbal; in boundary extension, however, the material is visual. Still, our schemas help us fill in missing material during a memory task.

The boundary-extension phenomenon has been explored by Helene Intraub and her colleagues (e.g., Intraub, 1997; Intraub & Berkowits, 1996; Intraub et al., 1998). For example, Intraub and Berkowits (1996) showed college students a series of slides like the photo of the garbage scene in Demonstration 8.6. Each slide was shown briefly, for 15 seconds or less. Immediately afterward, the students were instructed to draw an exact replica of the original photo. The participants consistently produced a sketch that extended the boundaries beyond the view presented in the original photo. As a result, they drew more of the background that surrounded the central figure, and they also depicted a complete figure, rather than a partial one.

According to Intraub and her coauthors (1998), we comprehend a photograph by activating a *perceptual schema*. This schema features a complete central figure in the photo, and it also includes a mental representation of visual information that is just outside the boundaries of the photo. We use perceptual schemas when we look at real-life scenes, as well as photos of a scene. Notice why schemas are relevant in boundary extension: Based on our expectations, we create perceptual schemas that extend beyond the edges of the photograph and beyond the scope of our retinas.

The boundary-extension phenomenon also has important implications for eye-witness testimony, a topic we discussed in Chapter 5. Eyewitnesses may recall having seen portions of a suspect's face that were not really visible at the scene of the crime (Foley & Foley, 1998). In addition, after people search for a target in a crowded scene, they recall having viewed a complete target—even if it had been partially blocked by other figures (Foley et al., 2002). Apparently, the incomplete figure activates our imagery processes, so that we "fill in the blanks." Consequently, our memory stores more idealized, schema-consistent images, rather than partial figures.

Schemas and Memory Abstraction

Abstraction is a memory process that stores the meaning of a message without storing the exact words and grammatical structures. For example, you can recall much of the information about the concept "family resemblance," without recalling a single sentence in its exact, original form. In some cases, people have good word-for-word recall, or **verbatim memory.** For instance, professional actors can recite the exact words from a Shakespeare play. More often, our verbatim memory is far from spec-tacular even a few minutes after a passage has been presented (e.g., Koriat et al.,

2000; Sachs, 1967). However, we tend to recall the gist or general meaning with impressive accuracy. Therefore, our abstracted version of the passage is consistent with the original schema. Let's consider two approaches to the abstraction issue: the constructive approach and the pragmatic approach.

The Constructive Approach. Be sure to try Demonstration 8.7 on pages 280 and 281 before reading further. This is a simpler version of a classic study by Bransford and Franks (1971). How many sentences in Part 2 of the demonstration had you seen before? The answer is at the end of the chapter, on page 294.

Bransford and Franks (1971) asked the participants in their study to listen to sentences from several different stories. Then the participants were given a recognition test that also included new items, many of which were combinations of the earlier sentences. Nonetheless, people were convinced that they had seen these new items before. This kind of error is called a false alarm. In memory research, a **false alarm** occurs when people "remember" an item that was not originally presented. Bransford and Franks's study showed that false alarms were particularly likely for complex sentences that were consistent with the original schema, for example, "The tall tree in the front yard shaded the man who was smoking his pipe." Furthermore, the participants did not make false alarms for sentences that violated the meaning of the earlier sentences—for example, "The scared cat that broke the window on the porch climbed the tree." This research has also been more recently replicated by Holmes and his colleagues (1998).

Bransford and Franks (1971) proposed a constructive model of memory for prose material. According to the **constructive model of memory,** people integrate information from individual sentences in order to construct larger ideas. People therefore think that they have already seen those complex sentences because they have combined the various facts in memory. Once sentences are fused in memory, we cannot untangle them into their original components and recall those components verbatim.

Notice that the constructive view of memory emphasizes the active nature of our cognitive processes, consistent with Theme 1 of this book. Sentences do not passively enter memory, where each is stored separately. Instead, we try to make sense out of sentences that seem to be related to one another. We combine the sentences into a coherent story, fitting the pieces together.

Constructive memory also illustrates Theme 2. Although memory is generally accurate, the errors in cognitive processing can often be traced to generally useful strategies. In real life, a useful heuristic is to fuse sentences together. However, this heuristic can lead us astray if it is applied inappropriately. As it turns out, participants in Bransford and Franks's (1971) study used a constructive memory strategy that is useful in real life but inappropriate in a study that tests verbatim memory.

The Pragmatic Approach. Murphy and Shapiro (1994) have developed a different view of memory for sentences, which they call the pragmatic view of text memory. The **pragmatic view of memory** proposes that people pay attention to the aspect of a message that is most relevant to their current goals. In other words, people can strategically control their attention. In everyday life, you realize that you should pay attention to the general meaning of a story. As a consequence, you recall the gist quite accurately but ignore the specific sentences. However, if you realize that you should pay attention to the exact words in a sentence, then your verbatim memory can be accurate.

In one of their experiments, Murphy and Shapiro (1994) instructed participants to pay attention to the specific words in each of several sentences. These participants were highly accurate in recognizing the correct words on a later test. In contrast, they were not misled into believing they had seen close synonyms that had not appeared in the earlier sentences.

In another experiment, Murphy and Shapiro (1994) speculated that people are particularly likely to pay attention to the specific words in a sentence if the words are part of a criticism or an insult. After all, from the pragmatic view, the exact words do matter if you are being insulted. In this study, participants read one of two letters that presumably had been written by a young woman named Samantha. One letter, supposedly written to her cousin Paul, chatted about her new infant in a bland fashion and included a number of neutral sentences such as, "It never occurred to me that I would be a mother so young" (p. 91). The other letter was supposedly written by Samantha to her boyfriend, Arthur. Ten of the sentences that had been neutral in the bland letter to cousin Paul now appeared in a sarcastic context, though the exact words were identical. For example, the sentence, "It never occurred to me that I would be a mother so young" now referred to Arthur's infantile behavior.

Memory was later assessed with a 14-item recognition test that included five of the original sentences, five paraphrased versions of those sentences with a slightly different form (for example, "I never thought I would be a mother at such a young age"), and four irrelevant sentences. Table 8.3 shows the results. As you can see, people rarely made the mistake of falsely "recognizing" the irrelevant sentences. However, they correctly recognized ("Hits") the sarcastic sentences more often than the bland sentences. Furthermore, there were more false alarms for the paraphrases of the bland sentences than for the paraphrases of the sarcastic sentences. When we compare the overall accuracy for the two versions (by subtracting the false alarms from the correct responses), we see that people were much more accurate in their

TABLE 8.3

Percentage of "Old" Judgments Made to Test Items in Murphy and Shapiro's (1994) Study.

	Story Condition	
	Bland	**Sarcastic**
Irrelevant sentences	4%	5%
Hits (original sentences)	71%	86%
False alarms (paraphrases)	54%	43%
Hits minus false alarms	17%	43%

Source: Murphy & Shapiro, 1994.

verbatim memory for the sarcastic version (43%) than for the bland version (17%). Perhaps we are especially sensitive about emotionally threatening material, so we make an effort to recall the exact words of the sentences.

The Current Status of Schemas and Memory Abstraction. Some theorists prefer the constructive approach to memory abstraction, whereas others prefer the pragmatic approach. However, the two approaches are actually quite compatible. Specifically, in many cases, we do integrate information from individual sentences so that we can construct large schemas, especially when the situation suggests that the exact words are not crucial. However, in other cases, we know that the specific words do matter, and so we allocate extra attention to the precise wording. An actor rehearsing for a play or two people quarreling will need to remember more than just the gist of a verbal message. Notice that this conclusion about remembering both general descriptions and specific information is similar to our previous conclusions about semantic memory. Specifically, your semantic memory stores both general prototypes and specific exemplar-based information.

IN DEPTH

Schemas and Inferences in Memory

In many cases, people add their own general knowledge to the material they encounter, and they "remember" that this information was present in the original material. Thus, recall can contain **inferences,** or logical interpretations and conclusions that were not part of the original stimulus material. In this In Depth discussion, we will consider both the classic research on this topic and new research demonstrating that people make inferences based on stereotypes. We'll then briefly consider the power of inferences in persuading other people.

The Classic Research on Inferences. Research in this area began with the studies of Sir Frederick Bartlett (1932), a memory researcher who used natural language material. As we've mentioned before, his theories and techniques foreshadowed the approaches of contemporary cognitive psychologists. Bartlett believed that the most interesting aspect of memory was the complex interaction between the prior knowledge of the participants in the experiment and the material presented during the experiment. In particular, he argued that an individual's unique interests and personal background can shape the contents of memory.

In Bartlett's (1932) best-known series of studies, he asked British students to read a Native American story called "The War of the Ghosts." They were then asked to recall the story 15 minutes later. Bartlett found that the participants tended to omit material that did not make sense from the viewpoint of a British student (for example, a portion of the story in which a ghost had attacked someone, who did not feel the wound). They also tended to shape the story into a more familiar framework, often more similar to British fairy tales.

Most relevant to our current topic, Bartlett's participants often added extra material to the story, making inferences so that the story made more sense from the British perspective. For example, part of the story describes a man who says he will not go off to war because "My relatives do not know where I have gone. But you [another man] may go with them" (Bartlett, 1932, p. 65). Participants often inserted inferences such as, "But you have no one to expect you" to explain the puzzling relationship between those two sentences (Brewer, 2000).

Bartlett also asked his participants to recall the story again, after a delay of several days. He reported that, as time passed after hearing the original story, the recalled story borrowed more heavily from previous knowledge, and less from the information in the original story.

Subsequent research confirms that schemas can influence our inferences when we are reading ambiguous or unclear material (Bransford et al., 1972; Groome, 1999; Schacter, 2001). As Brewer (2000) emphasizes, the research on schemas and inferences demonstrates how our cognitive processes actively work to make sense out of puzzling information (Theme 1). Specifically, our top-down processes often shape our memory for complex material (Theme 5).

The research shows that background knowledge can mislead people, causing them to make systematic errors and "remember" inferences that were not actually stated. In our daily lives, however, background information is usually helpful, rather than counterproductive. For instance, our background knowledge can help us recall stories. Simple stories have definite, regular structures (Schank & Abelson, 1995). People become familiar with the basic structure of stories from their prior experiences in their cultures. They use this structure in sorting out any new stories they hear. Once again, when background information is consistent with the stimulus materials, this background information is clearly helpful.

Research on Inferences Based on Gender Stereotypes. Related research on inferences about schema-consistent material examines gender stereotypes. **Gender stereotypes** are organized, widely shared sets of beliefs about the characteristics of females and males (Golombok & Fivush, 1994). Even when a gender stereotype is partially accurate, it cannot be applied to every individual of the specified gender (Kunda, 1999). When people know someone's gender, they often make inferences about that individual's personal characteristics. In many cases, these inferences may not be accurate.

Let's consider a representative study that assessed gender-based inferences by means of a recognition-memory task. Dunning and Sherman (1997) instructed participants to read sentences such as, "The women at the office liked to talk around the water cooler." Later, the participants were tested for recognition memory. Specifically, participants saw a series of sentences, and they were told to respond "old" if they had previously read *exactly* the same version of the sentence earlier in the session. Otherwise, they should respond "new."

Let's look at the results for new sentences that were *consistent* with a widely held gender stereotype: "The women at the office liked to gossip around the water cooler." Participants responded "old" to 29% of these sentences. Other new sentences were *inconsistent* with another widely held stereotype: "The women at the office liked to talk sports around the water cooler." Participants responded "old" to only 18% of these sentences. Apparently, when people saw the original sentence, they sometimes made the stereotype-consistent inference that the women must have been gossiping. They were less likely to make a gender-inconsistent inference about the women's discussing sports.

Dunning and Sherman's (1997) recognition test is an example of an explicit memory task. As you learned in Chapter 5 (p. 146), an **explicit memory task** instructs participants to remember information. The participants in this study knew that their memory was being tested when they judged whether the sentences were old or new. However, people might guess that the researcher is measuring their gender stereotypes, and they may be aware that it's not appropriate to hold rigid stereotypes. Therefore, other researchers have designed implicit memory tasks.

As Chapter 5 described, in an **implicit memory task,** people perform a cognitive task that does not directly ask for recall or recognition. In Chapter 5, we examined implicit tasks that assessed episodic memory, typically people's memory for words that they had seen earlier in the session. When researchers use implicit memory tasks to assess gender stereotypes, they assess people's semantic memory, their general knowledge about gender in our culture, and their tendency to make gender-consistent inferences. Let's consider two implicit memory tasks which demonstrate that gender stereotypes influence inferences in implicit memory, as well as in explicit memory.

1. *Using neuroscience techniques to assess gender stereotypes.* Osterhout, Bersick, and McLaughlin (1997) assessed gender stereotypes by using a neuroscience technique. As you learned in Chapter 1, the **event-related potential (ERP) technique** records tiny fluctuations in the brain's electrical activity, in response to a stimulus. Previous researchers had tested people who were instructed to read sentences such as, "I like my coffee with cream and *dog*" (p. 273). The researchers had discovered that the ERPs quickly changed in response to the surprising word.

To examine gender stereotypes, Osterhout and his colleagues (1997) presented some sentences that are consistent with gender stereotypes, such as, "The nurse prepared herself for the operation." These stereotype-consistent sentences did not elicit a change in the ERPs. In contrast, the ERPs changed significantly for stereotype-inconsistent sentences such as, "The nurse prepared himself for the operation." In reading the word *nurse*, people had made the gender-stereotyped inference that the nurse must be female. Consequently, the unexpected, stereotype-inconsistent word *himself* produced changes in the ERPs. In summary, this neuroscience task demonstrated implicit gender stereotypes.

2. *Using the Implicit Association Test to assess gender stereotypes.* Nosek, Banaji, and Greenwald (2002) used a very different method to assess implicit gender stereotypes, specifically the gender stereotype that mathematics is associated with males and that the arts are associated with females. Suppose that they had asked their college-student participants (at Yale University) an explicit question: "Is math more strongly associated with males than with females?" Research with students like these

has demonstrated that the dominant response would be "No." After all, when students are asked an explicit question like this, they have time to be thoughtful and to recall that this answer would not be socially appropriate.

Instead of an explicit measure, Nosek and his colleagues used the Implicit Association Test (Greenwald & Nosek, 2001; Greenwald et al., 1998). The **Implicit Association Test (IAT)** is based on the principle that people can mentally pair related words together much more easily than they can pair unrelated words.

Specifically, when taking the IAT, participants sat in front of a computer screen that presented a series of words. On a typical trial—where the pairings were consistent with gender stereotypes—the participant would be told to press the key on the left if the word was related to math (e.g., *calculus* or *numbers*) or if the word was related to males (e.g., *uncle* or *son*). This same participant would press the key on the right if the word was related to the arts (e.g., *poetry* or *dance*) or if the word was related to females (e.g., *aunt* or *daughter*). Then the instructions shifted so that the pairings were inconsistent with gender stereotypes. Now, on a typical trial, the participant would press the left key for a word related to math or a word related to females. The participant would press the right key for a word related to the arts or a word related to males. In all cases, participants were urged to respond as quickly as possible, so that they would not consciously consider their responses.

The results showed that the participants responded significantly faster to the stereotype-consistent pairings than to the stereotype-inconsistent pairings. In other words, math and males seem to go together, whereas the arts and females seem to go together. In other research discussed in the same journal article, Nosek and his coauthors (2002) used the IAT to measure attitudes, as well as stereotypes. For example, one component of the study focused on women who strongly considered themselves to be feminine and strongly associated math with being masculine. These women specifically did *not* associate themselves with mathematics, and this anti-math tendency was found even among women who were math majors! In summary, gender stereotypes are far from innocent cognitive tendencies that add yet another example of schema-consistent inferences. Instead, these stereotypes can have the power to influence people's self-images and their sense of academic competence.

If you are interested in additional information about social categories other than gender, and attitudes as well as stereotypes, you can pursue these topics in the following resources: Banaji (2001), Banaji and Bhaskar (1999), Blair (1998), and Greenwald and his colleagues (2002). When you have the opportunity, try Demonstration 8.8.

Implications for Persuasion. This material on schemas and memory interpretations can be applied to advertising and other areas that require persuasion. Suppose that an ad says, "Four out of five doctors recommend the ingredients in Gonif's brand medication." You might reasonably infer, therefore, that four out of five doctors would also recommend Gonif's medication itself—even though the ad doesn't say so.

◎ **Demonstration 8.8**

Using the Implicit Association Test to Assess Implicit Attitudes Toward Social Groups

Log onto the World Wide Web and visit a site sponsored by an organization called Teaching Tolerance: <http://www.tolerance.org/hidden_bias/02.html>

You can examine your own attitudes about gender, ethnicity, sexual orientation, people with disabilities, and elderly people. Be certain to follow the caution to make your responses as quickly as possible. More leisurely responses might assess explicit attitudes, rather than implicit attitudes.

Research suggests that people who read advertisements may jump to conclusions, "remembering" inferences that were never actually stated. Harris and his colleagues (1989) asked college students to read stories that contained several advertising slogans. Some slogans made a direct claim (for example, "Tylenol cures colds"). Other slogans merely implied the same claim (for example, "Tylenol fights colds"). On a multiple-choice task that followed, people who had seen the implied-claim version often selected the direct-claim version instead. You can see why these results suggest that consumers should be careful. If an advertiser implies that a particular product has outstanding properties, make certain that you do not jump to inappropriate conclusions. You are likely to "remember" those inferences, rather than the actual, stated information.

The information about inferences and persuasion can be related to politics as well as to advertising. On January 28, 2003, President George W. Bush included this sentence in his State of the Union address: "The British government has learned that Saddam Hussein recently sought significant quantities of uranium from Africa." Months later, when the public discovered that this statement was not correct, National Security Adviser Condoleezza Rice said that Bush's remark had been technically accurate. After all, Bush had correctly stated that the British government had reported this information (Truthout, 2003). In reality, however, most of us had made the *incorrect* inference that "Saddam Hussein did indeed recently seek uranium from Africa."

After reading about the experimental evidence for humans' tendencies to draw inappropriate inferences, you might conclude that people inevitably draw conclusions based on inferences from their daily experience. However, inference making is not an obligatory process (Alba & Hasher, 1983; Wynn & Logie, 1998). Several researchers have found that inference making occurs only in certain situations. In fact, people often recall material in its original form. Consistent with Theme 2, memory is often highly accurate.

Schemas and Integration in Memory

The final process in memory formation is integration. Schema theories argue that a single, integrated representation is created in memory from the information that was selected in the first phase, abstracted in a later phase, and interpreted in a still later phase (Koriat et al., 2000). In fact, some researchers argue that schemas exert a more powerful effect during the integration phase than during the earlier phases of memory (e.g., Hirt et al., 1998). Once again, however, schemas do not always operate. As we'll see, schema-consistent integration is more likely when recall is delayed and when people are performing a second, simultaneous task during recall.

Integration and Delayed Recall. A number of studies show that background knowledge does not encourage schema-consistent integration if people are tested immediately after the material is learned. However, after a longer delay, the material becomes integrated with existing schemas, and the recall is now altered. For instance, Harris and his colleagues (1989) asked college students in Kansas to read a story that was consistent with either U.S. culture or traditional Mexican culture. A representative story about planning a date in the traditional Mexican culture included a sentence about the young man's older sister accompanying the couple as a chaperone; the U.S. version had no chaperone. When story recall was tested 30 minutes after reading the material, the students showed no tendency for the Mexican-schema stories to shift in the direction consistent with U.S. schemas. After a 2-day delay, however, the students had shifted a significant number of story details.

Integration and Limited Memory Capacity. Research also suggests that schemas are more likely to influence memory integration when memory capacity is strained during recall, but not on a relatively simple task. For example, Sherman and Bessenoff (1999) found that people committed many schema-consistent errors when they had to work on two memory tasks simultaneously. Specifically, they misremembered that pleasant words had been used to describe a priest, whereas unpleasant words had been used to describe a skinhead. In contrast, people who worked on just one memory task did not show this schema-consistent tendency. In summary, people often integrate material in memory, especially when there is a long delay prior to recall and when memory capacity is limited. However, memory integration is certainly not inevitable.

CONCLUSIONS ABOUT SCHEMAS

In summary, schemas can influence memory in the initial selection of material, in remembering visual scenes, in abstraction, in interpretation, and even in the final process of integration. However, we must note that schemas often fail to operate in the expected fashion. For instance:

1. We often select material that is *inconsistent* with our schemas.

2. We may indeed remember that we saw only part of an object, rather than the complete object.

3. We frequently recall the exact words of a passage as it was originally presented—otherwise, chorus directors would have resigned long ago.

4. We often avoid making inappropriate inferences.

5. We may keep the elements in memory isolated from each other, rather than integrated together.

6. When people are recalling information from their real-life experiences—rather than information created by researchers—they may be more accurate (Wynn & Logie, 1998).

Yes, schemas clearly can influence memory. However, the influence is far from complete. After all, as Theme 5 states, our cognitive processes are guided by bottom-up processing, as well as top-down processing. Therefore, we select, recall, interpret, and integrate many unique features of each stimulus, in addition to the schema-consistent features that match our background knowledge.

◎ Section Summary: *Schemas and Scripts*

1. A schema is generalized knowledge about a situation or an event; a script is a kind of schema that describes a simple, well-structured sequence of events associated with a highly familiar activity.

2. According to research on scripts, we can recall the elements in a script more accurately if the script is identified at the outset.

3. Schemas may operate in the selection of memories; for example, people recall items consistent with an office schema. However, schema-inconsistent information is often favored when the task requires intentional learning, when memory is assessed by recall, and when results are corrected for guessing.

4. When we remember a scene, we often extend the boundaries of the objects that had partially appeared in the scene by "remembering" them as complete objects.

5. According to the constructive model of memory, schemas encourage memory abstraction, so that the general meaning of a message is retained, even if the details are lost. According to the pragmatic view of memory, people can shift their attention to remember the exact words—when the specific words really matter. Both perspectives seem to operate, depending on the circumstances.

6. Schemas influence the inferences we make in memory; people may recall inferences that never really appeared in the original material. The research on gender stereotypes shows that people make schema-consistent inferences in explicit memory (e.g., a recognition test) and in implicit memory (e.g., the ERP technique and the Implicit Association Test). People often "recall" incorrect inferences from advertisements and political messages.

7. Schemas encourage an integrated representation in memory. Research shows that people may misremember material during the integration process, so that the material is more consistent with their schemas, especially if recall is delayed and people are performing another task at the same time.

CHAPTER REVIEW QUESTIONS

1. Suppose that you read the following question on a true/false examination: "A script is a kind of schema." Describe how you would process that question in terms of the feature comparison model, the exemplar approach, the Collins and Loftus network model, and Anderson's ACT network model.

2. Think of a prototype for the category "household pet," and contrast it with a nonprototypical household pet. Compare these two animals with respect to (a) whether they would be supplied as examples of the category; (b) how quickly they could be judged after priming; and (c) the attributes that each would share with most other household pets.

3. Consider the basic-level category "dime," in contrast to the superordinate-level category "money" and the subordinate-level category "1986 dime." Discuss how basic-level terminology is used to identify objects. Compared to basic-level categories, which part of the brain is more likely to be activated by the superordinate-level category, and which is more likely to be activated by the subordinate-level category? Finally, discuss how an expert coin collector might identify a dime.

4. Describe the prototype approach and the exemplar approach to semantic memory. How are they similar, and how are they different? In light of the discussion in this chapter, when would you be likely to use a prototype approach in trying to categorize an object? When would you be most likely to use the exemplar approach? In each case, give an example from your daily experience.

5. Think of some kind of information that could be represented in a diagram similar to the one in Figure 8.5 (for example, popular singers, famous novelists, or people you know at your college). Provide an example of spontaneous generalization and an example of default assignment that could be applied to this body of information. How might the terms *content addressable* and *graceful degradation* be applied to this example?

6. Suppose that a friend is taking a course in introductory psychology, and the course briefly mentions the PDP approach. How would you describe the characteristics of this approach to your friend, in a 5-minute overview? Include examples, and also be sure to describe why the approach is called *parallel distributed processing*.

7. Describe three scripts with which you are very familiar. How would these scripts be considered heuristics, rather than exact predictors of what will happen the next time you find yourself in one of the situations described in the script?

8. You probably have a fairly clear schema of the concept "dentist's office." Focus on the discussion titled "Schemas and Memory Selection" (pp. 276–279) and point out the circumstances in which you would be likely to remember (a) schema-consistent material and (b) schema-inconsistent material. How might boundary extension operate when you try to reconstruct the scene you see from the dentist's chair?

9. What evidence do we have from explicit memory tasks that gender stereotypes encourage us to draw inferences that are consistent with those stereotypes? How would the demand characteristics mentioned in Chapter 7 (p. 223) be relevant to explicit memory tasks? Then discuss the two implicit memory tasks described in the In Depth discussion on inferences, and explain why they may be more effective than explicit tasks in assessing people's stereotypes.

10. Think of a schema or a script with which you are especially familiar. Explain how that schema or script might influence your memory during four different phases: selection, abstraction, interpretation, and integration. Be sure to consider how memory sometimes favors schema-consistent information and sometimes favors schema-inconsistent information, as well as the cases when memory accurately reflects bottom-up processing.

NEW TERMS

semantic memory
episodic memory
category
concept
feature comparison model
defining features
characteristic features
sentence verification
  technique
typicality effect
prototype
prototype approach
prototypicality
graded structure
priming effect
family resemblance
superordinate-level categories
basic-level categories
subordinate-level categories
exemplar approach
exemplar
network model

Collins and Loftus network
  model
node
link
spreading activation
ACT
declarative knowledge
proposition
parallel distributed processing
  (PDP) approach
connectionism
neural networks
serial search
parallel search
content addressable
spontaneous generalization
default assignment
connection weights
graceful degradation
tip-of-the-tongue
  phenomenon
schema

heuristics
schema therapy
script
incidental learning
intentional learning
boundary extension
abstraction
verbatim memory
false alarm
constructive model of
  memory
pragmatic view of memory
inferences
gender stereotypes
explicit memory task
implicit memory task
event-related potential (ERP)
  technique
Implicit Association Test
  (IAT)

RECOMMENDED READINGS

Markman, A. B. (1999). *Knowledge representation*. Mahwah, NJ: Erlbaum. I strongly recommend this book, because it provides a well-organized overview of the research and theories about semantic memory and schemas. In a field where the writing is often difficult to understand, this book is relatively accessible.

Murphy, G. L. (2002). *The big book of concepts*. Cambridge, MA: MIT Press. Topics in this book include theories of concepts, the development of conceptual knowledge, and word meaning. The tongue-in-cheek title of this book is consistent with the author's sense of humor throughout the chapters.

Pashler, H. (Ed.). (2002). *Stevens' handbook of experimental psychology* (3rd ed.). New York: Wiley. The chapters on knowledge representation and on concepts and categorization are especially relevant to the topic of general knowledge; they contain current, comprehensive information that will be useful for advanced-level students.

Saito, A. (Ed.). (2000). *Bartlett, culture and cognition*. East Sussex, England: Psychology Press. Frederick Bartlett's innovative work on schemas inspired this book, which examines anthropology issues, as well as schematic memory.

ANSWER TO DEMONSTRATION 8.7

Every sentence in Part 2 is new.

CHAPTER 9

Language I: Introduction to Language and Language Comprehension

PREVIEW

In Chapters 9 and 10, we'll examine the psychological aspects of language. Specifically, Chapter 9 emphasizes language comprehension in the form of listening and reading. In contrast, Chapter 10 will emphasize language production (speaking and writing), as well as bilingualism—a topic that encompasses both language comprehension and language production.

We'll begin Chapter 9 by exploring the nature of language. In particular, we'll look at the structure of language, a brief history of psycholinguistics, several factors that influence comprehension, and some neuroscience research on language.

Then, the chapter will explore basic reading processes, beginning with a comparison of written and spoken language. Context is important when we need to understand the meaning of an unfamiliar word, and working memory also plays an important role in understanding sentences. This section will also examine the role of sound in word recognition, as well as important implications for teaching reading to children.

The last part of Chapter 9 moves beyond small linguistic units to consider how we understand discourse, or language units that are larger than a sentence. Some important components of discourse comprehension include forming a coherent representation of a passage and drawing inferences that were not actually stated in the passage. Researchers in the field of artificial intelligence have designed programs that attempt to comprehend language; this research emphasizes the impressive competence of humans in understanding language.

INTRODUCTION

Try to imagine a world without language. In fact, think how your life would change if you woke up tomorrow and language were forbidden. Your interactions with all other people would be limited to gestures. Telephones, televisions, radios, newspapers, and books would all be useless. Almost all college courses would disappear. You wouldn't even be able to talk to yourself, so it would be impossible to reminisce, remind yourself what you need to accomplish right now, or make plans for your future.

Like many cognitive skills, language rarely receives the credit it deserves. After all, you simply listen to someone with a moving mouth and vocal equipment, and you understand the message they are trying to convey. Equally effortlessly, you open your own mouth and sentences emerge almost instantaneously—an impressive testimony to the efficiency of our cognitive processes (Theme 2).

Another equally impressive characteristic of our language skills is our extraordinary ability to master thousands of words. For instance, the average college-educated North American has a speaking vocabulary in the range of 75,000 to 100,000 words (Bock & Garnsey, 1998; Wingfield, 1993).

Furthermore, human language is probably one of the most complex behaviors to be found anywhere on our planet (Gleitman & Liberman, 1995). The domain of language includes an impressive diversity of skills. Consider just a few of the skills that you need in order to understand a sentence: encoding the sound of a speaker's voice, encoding the visual features of printed language, accessing the meaning of words, understanding the rules that determine word order, and appreciating from a speaker's intonation whether a sentence is a question or a statement. Furthermore, you manage to accomplish all these tasks while listening to a speaker who is probably producing three words each *second* (Levelt et al., 1999; Vigliocco & Hartsuiker, 2002). In fact, talking is so difficult that it should be an Olympic event—except that most humans have mastered this athletic achievement (Bock & Garnsey, 1998).

In addition, the productivity of language is unlimited. For example, if we consider only the number of 20-word sentences that you could potentially generate, you would need 10,000,000,000,000 years—or 2,000 times the age of the earth—to say them all (Miller, 1967; Pinker, 1993).

In Chapters 9 and 10, we will discuss **psycholinguistics,** an interdisciplinary field that examines how people use language to communicate ideas (Clark & Van Der Wege, 2002). We use language in thousands of different settings, from courtrooms to comic strips. Furthermore, language provides an excellent example of Theme 4 of this textbook, the interrelatedness of the cognitive processes. In fact, virtually every topic discussed so far in this book makes some contribution to language processing. To illustrate this point, try Demonstration 9.1.

The two chapters on language should also convince you that humans are active information processors (Theme 1). Rather than passively listening to language, we actively consult our previous knowledge, use various strategies, form expectations, and draw conclusions. When we speak, we must determine what our listeners already know and what other information must be conveyed. Language is not only our most remarkable cognitive achievement, but it is also the most social of our cognitive processes.

---

⑨ Demonstration 9.1

How Other Cognitive Processes Contribute to Language

Look below at the list of chapters you have read so far. For each chapter, list at least one topic that is connected to language. The answers appear at the end of this chapter, on page 330.

Chapter 2: Perceptual Processes I: Visual and Auditory Recognition
Chapter 3: Perceptual Processes II: Attention and Consciousness
Chapter 4: Working Memory
Chapter 5: Long-Term Memory
Chapter 6: Memory Strategies and Metacognition
Chapter 7: Mental Imagery and Cognitive Maps
Chapter 8: General Knowledge

The first of our two chapters on language focuses on language comprehension. After an introductory discussion about the nature of language, we will examine basic reading, as well as the more complex process of understanding discourse. In Chapter 10, we will switch our focus from understanding to the production of language. Chapter 10 considers two production tasks: speaking and writing. With a background in both language comprehension and language production, we can then consider bilingualism. Bilinguals—certainly the winners in any Olympic language contest—manage to communicate easily in more than one language.

THE NATURE OF LANGUAGE

Psycholinguists have developed a specialized vocabulary for language terms; let's now consider these terms. A **phoneme** (pronounced "*foe*-neem") is the basic unit of spoken language, such as the sounds *a*, *k*, and *th*. The English language has 40 phonemes (Groome, 1999). In contrast, a **morpheme** (pronounced "*more*-feem") is the basic unit of meaning. For example, the word *reactivated* actually contains four morphemes: *re-*, *active*, *-ate*, and *-ed*. Each of those segments conveys meaning. Many morphemes can stand on their own (like *giraffe*). In contrast, some morphemes must be attached to other morphemes in order to convey their meaning. For instance, *re-* indicates a repeated action.

Semantics is the area of psycholinguistics that examines the meanings of words and sentences (Carroll, 2004). The related term, **semantic memory,** refers to our organized knowledge about the world. We have discussed semantic memory throughout earlier chapters of this book, but especially in Chapter 8.

Another major component of psycholinguistics is syntax. **Syntax** refers to the grammatical rules that govern how we organize words into sentences (Owens, 2001). An additional important term is **pragmatics,** which is our knowledge of the social rules that underlie language use (Carroll, 2004). For example, think how you would define the word *syntax* to a 12-year-old child, as opposed to a college classmate. Pragmatics is an especially important topic when we consider the production of language (Chapter 10), but pragmatic factors also influence comprehension.

As you can see from reviewing the terms in this section, psycholinguistics encompasses a broad range of topics, including sounds, several levels of meaning, grammar, and social factors. We begin by noting a problem with the current research in psycholinguistics. Then we'll consider additional aspects of the nature of language: some background about the structure of language, a brief history of psycholinguistics, factors affecting comprehension, and neurolinguistics.

A Caution: Psycholinguistics Is English-Centered

In an important article, Elizabeth Bates and her coauthors (2001) emphasize a bias that operates in research about psycholinguistics. Specifically, most researchers in this discipline focus on how people understand and use English. As a result, some of the findings may apply only to English speakers, rather than to all humans. If your own first language is English, your ideas about language are probably English-centered. Therefore, you may react with surprise if you travel to another language community. For instance, I recall visiting Grenada, Spain, and hearing the tour guide (who appeared to be Spanish) describing the sights in Spanish and in Japanese to the tourists in her group. I'm embarrassed to report that I was startled to hear her translating Spanish into Japanese, without first passing through English.

Bates and her colleagues (2001) point out some differences among languages. For example, in Chinese, voice pitch is used to distinguish between two words composed of the same phonemes, but pitch is not distinctive in English. Furthermore, Sesotho—a language spoken in southern Africa—uses the passive voice more than English does. In many languages, the nouns have a grammatical gender, though English does not. Throughout the world, people speak between 2,500 and 3,000 different languages. Psycholinguists will need to conduct additional research in many other languages, if they want to determine which linguistic principles apply universally.

Background on the Structure of Language

Before we consider the history of psycholinguistics, we need to discuss a central concept in understanding language, called phrase structure. **Phrase structure** emphasizes that we construct a sentence by using a hierarchical structure that is based on grammatical building blocks called **constituents** (Carroll, 2004). For example, suppose we have the following sentence:

The young woman carried the heavy painting.

We can divide this sentence into two broad constituents: (1) the phrase that focuses on the noun—"the young woman"—and (2) the phrase that focuses on the verb—"carried the heavy painting." Each of these constituents can be further subdivided, creating a hierarchy of constituents with a diagram resembling an upside-down tree. These diagrams, like the one in Figure 9.1, help us appreciate that a sentence is not simply a chain of words, strung together like beads on a necklace. Instead, we appreciate more complicated relationships among the elements of a sentence (Gibson & Pearlmutter, 1998; Owens, 2001).

Why should English speakers bother with constituents? Why shouldn't we simply process the words one at a time? As it turns out, we often need the entire constituent to give us cues about the meaning of the words. For example, consider the word *painting* in the sentence we just analyzed. *Painting* could be either a verb or a noun. However, from the context in which *painting* appears in the constituent *the heavy painting*, we know that the noun version is appropriate. The research indicates that people maintain a complete constituent in working memory while they process its meaning (Jarvella, 1971).

FIGURE 9.1

An Example of Constituents.

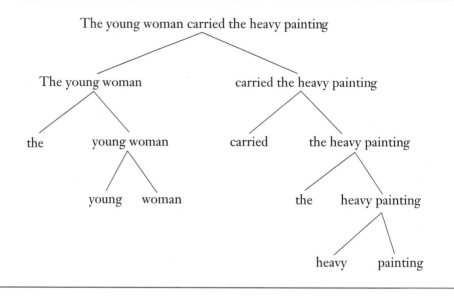

A Brief History of Psycholinguistics

Now that we have identified some central concepts in psycholinguistics, let's consider some highlights in the history of this field. Early philosophers in Greece and India debated the nature of language (Chomsky, 2000). Centuries later, both Wilhelm Wundt and William James also speculated about our impressive abilities in this area (Carroll, 2004; Levelt, 1998). However, the current discipline of psycholinguistics can be traced to the 1960s, when psycholinguists began to test whether the theories of Noam Chomsky could be supported by psychological research (McKoon & Ratcliff, 1998). Let's consider Chomsky's theory, the reactions to his theory, and subsequent theories about language.

Chomsky's Transformational Grammar. People usually think of a sentence as an orderly sequence of words that are lined up in a row on a sheet of paper. Noam Chomsky (1957) caused great excitement among psychologists and linguists by proposing that there is more to a sentence than meets the eye (or the ear). Chomsky's work on the psychology of language was mentioned in Chapter 1 of this textbook as one of the forces that led to decreased interest in behaviorism. The behaviorists emphasized the observable aspects of language behavior (Harley, 2001). In contrast, Chomsky argued that human language abilities could be explained only in terms of a complex system of rules and principles represented in the minds of speakers. Chomsky is clearly one of the most influential theorists in modern linguistics (N. Smith, 2000; Williams, 1999).

Chomsky proposed that humans have innate language skills. That is, we have an inborn understanding of the abstract principles of language. As a result, children do not need to learn the basic, generalizable concepts that are universal to all languages (Belletti & Rizzi, 2002; N. Smith, 2000). Of course, many more superficial characteristics require learning. Children in Portugal and Brazil learn Portuguese, and children in Japan learn Japanese. Also, Spanish-speaking children will need to learn the difference between *ser* and *estar*. Spanish linguistic space is carved up somewhat differently from that of English, where children learn only one form of the verb *to be* (Agassi, 1997). Still, Chomsky argues that all children have a substantial, inborn language ability. This ability allows them to produce and understand sentences they have never heard before (Belletti & Rizzi, 2002; Chomsky, 2000).

Chomsky (1975) also proposed that language is **modular;** people have a set of specific linguistic abilities that do not follow the principles of other cognitive processes, such as memory and decision making. (We discussed a related concept, the phonetic module, in connection with speech perception on pp. 62–63.) Because language is modular, Chomsky (2002) argues, young children learn complex linguistic structures many years before they master other, simpler tasks, such as mental arithmetic.

In contrast to Chomsky's theory, the standard cognitive approach to language argues that language is interconnected with cognitive processes such as working memory. According to this alternative approach, we are skilled at language because our powerful brains can master many cognitive tasks. Language is just one of those tasks, having the same status as tasks such as memory and problem solving (Bates, 2000; Carroll, 2004).

In addition, Chomsky (1957) argued that we must move beyond phrase-structure grammar if we want to describe people's linguistic competence (Harley, 2001). Chomsky therefore devised a model of **transformational grammar** to convert underlying, deep structure into the surface structure of a sentence. **Surface structure** is represented by the words that are actually spoken or written. In contrast, **deep structure** (or **underlying structure**) is the underlying, more abstract meaning of a sentence. Let us examine transformational grammar in more detail.

Chomsky pointed out that we need transformational grammar in order to explain why two sentences may have very different surface structures, but very similar deep structures. Consider these two sentences: (1) "Sara threw the ball" and (2) "The ball was thrown by Sara." Notice that the two surface structures are different. None of the words occupies the same position in the two sentences, and three of the words in the second sentence do not even appear in the first sentence. The phrase-structure diagrams would also represent these two sentences differently. However, "deep down," speakers of English feel that the sentences have identical core meanings (Harley, 2001).

Chomsky (1957) also pointed out that two sentences may have very similar surface structures but very different deep structures. Consider these two sentences: (1) "John is easy to please" and (2) "John is eager to please." These sentences differ by only a single word, yet their meanings are quite different.

Two sentences can even have *identical* surface structures but very different deep structures; these are called **ambiguous sentences.** Here are three ambiguous sentences, each of which has two meanings:

The shooting of the hunters was terrible.
They are cooking apples.
The lamb is too hot to eat.

Notice that each sentence can be represented by two very different phrase-structure diagrams. In fact, try making two diagrams like the one in Figure 9.1 to represent the two underlying meanings for the sentence "They are cooking apples." We will discuss ambiguity in more detail later in the chapter.

Chomsky (1957) proposed that people understand sentences by transforming the surface structure into a basic, deep structure or **kernel** form. He argues that we use **transformational rules** to convert surface structure to deep structure during understanding. We also use transformational rules to convert deep structure to surface structure when we speak or write.

Reactions to Chomsky's Theory. Initially, psychologists responded enthusiastically to Chomsky's ideas about transformational grammar (Bock et al., 1992; Williams, 1999). Not all the evidence for Chomsky's theory was favorable, however. For example, the research failed to support Chomsky's prediction that people would take longer to process sentences that required numerous transformations (Carroll, 2004; Slobin, 1966). Furthermore, some of Chomsky's theories have not been tested. For example, Chomsky argued that the underlying, deep structure is identical for two equivalent sentences from two different languages, such as English and Korean. However, no research has explored this proposal (Agassi, 1997).

Chomsky's later theories have provided more sophisticated linguistic analyses. For example, Chomsky has placed constraints on the possible hypotheses that the language learner can make about the structure of language (Chomsky, 1981, 2000; Harley, 2001). Chomsky's newer approach also emphasizes the information contained in the individual words of a sentence. For example, the word *discuss* not only conveys information about the word's meaning, but it also specifies the requirement that *discuss* must be followed by a noun, as in the sentence, "Rita discussed the novel" (Ratner & Gleason, 1993).

Psycholinguistic Theories Emphasizing Meaning. Beginning in the 1970s, many psychologists became discouraged with transformational grammar's emphasis on syntax, or the grammatical rules about organizing words into sentences (McKoon & Ratcliff, 1998). These psychologists began to develop theories that emphasized semantics, or the *meaning* of language. In recent years, this focus on semantics has led psychologists to explore how people understand the meaning of paragraphs and stories. We'll look at some of that research later in this chapter.

Several theories have been developed that emphasize meaning (e.g., Kintsch, 1998; Newmeyer, 1998). Here, we will briefly describe a representative theory, the cognitive-functional approach to language. The **cognitive-functional approach** emphasizes that the function of human language is to communicate meaning to other individuals. As a result, we structure our language in order to focus our listeners' attention on the information we wish to emphasize. As Michael Tomasello (1998a, 1998b) points out, this approach examines how people use language in a natural setting, in order to accomplish their goals. As the name suggests, the cognitive-functional approach also emphasizes how cognitive processes—such as attention and memory—are intertwined with our language comprehension and production.

For instance, look at Demonstration 9.2, which illustrates a concrete example of the cognitive-functional approach (Tomasello, 1998a). Notice how each of those sentences emphasizes a somewhat different perspective on the same event. You'll probably find that these different perspectives are reflected in the variety of questions you generated. In short, the cognitive-functional approach argues that people can use language creatively, in order to communicate subtle shades of meaning. We'll explore the social use of language more thoroughly in Chapter 10.

Factors Affecting Comprehension

Chomsky's theory of transformational grammar sparked an interest in the factors that can influence our understanding of sentences. Psychologists soon began to conduct research on these factors. Let's now discuss why people have more difficulty

---

⑨ Demonstration 9.2

The Cognitive-Functional Approach to Language

Imagine that you recently saw an event in which a man named Fred broke a window, using a rock. A person who was not present at the time asks you for information about the event. For each of the sentences below, construct a question that this person might have asked that would prompt you to reply with that specific wording for the sentence. For example, the brief response, "Fred broke the window" might have been prompted by the question, "What did Fred do?"

1. Fred broke the window with a rock.
2. The rock broke the window.
3. The window got broken.
4. It was Fred who broke the window.
5. It was the window that Fred broke.
6. What Fred did was to break the window.

Source: Based on Tomasello, 1998a, p. 483.

understanding sentences (1) if they contain negatives, such as *not;* (2) if they are in the passive rather than the active voice; (3) if they contain nested structures, with a descriptive clause in the middle of the sentence; and (4) if they are ambiguous.

Negatives. A headline in a newspaper read, "Judge Denies Bid to Stop Retirement by Professor." This sentence requires several readings to understand the basic message: Will the professor continue to teach? The research on negatives is clear-cut. If a sentence contains a negative word, such as *no* or *not,* or an implied negative (such as *denies*), the sentence almost always requires more processing time than a similar, affirmative sentence (Williams, 1999).

In a classic study, Clark and Chase (1972) asked people to verify statements, such as the following:

Star is above plus. $\begin{array}{c}*\\+\end{array}$

The participants responded quickly if the sentence was affirmative. They responded more slowly if the sentence contained the negative form *isn't* (for example, "Plus isn't above star"). The participants also made fewer errors with affirmative sentences than with negative sentences. Notice that these results are consistent with Theme 3 of this textbook: Our cognitive processes handle positive information better than negative information.

As you can imagine, readers' understanding decreases as the number of negative terms increases. For example, people perform only slightly better than chance when they judge sentences such as, "Few people strongly deny that the world is not flat" (Sherman, 1976, p. 145).

Sometimes our difficulty in processing negative terms can have serious social consequences. Consider a national survey that had been commissioned by the American Jewish Committee. One question read: "Does it seem possible or does it seem impossible to you that the Nazi extermination of the Jews never happened?" (Kifner, 1994, p. A14). According to the survey, 33% of the respondents replied that it was possible the Nazi extermination never happened. As you can imagine, these results were widely publicized, and commentators were dismayed at the ignorance of so many American citizens. In reality, however, most of the respondents had simply been puzzled by the double negative. If they indeed believed that the Holocaust had occurred, they had to respond, "It is impossible to me that the Nazi extermination never happened."

The Passive Voice. As we discussed earlier, Chomsky (1957, 1965) pointed out that the active and passive forms of a sentence may differ in their surface structure, even though they have similar deep structures. However, the active form is more basic; the transformation to the passive form requires additional words. The active form is also easier to understand (Obler et al., 1991; Williams, 1999). For example, Ferreira and her coauthors (2002) asked participants to determine whether each sentence in a series was plausible or likely. The participants were highly accurate in responding "No" to sentences in the active voice, such as, "The man bit the dog." In contrast, their accuracy dropped to about 75% when the same sentences were converted to the passive voice, for example, "The dog was bitten by the man" (p. 13).

The current writing style manuals now recommend the active voice. For example, the current manual of the American Psychological Association (2001) points out that the active-voice sentence such as "Nuñez (2000) designed the experiment," is much more direct and vigorous than "The experiment was designed by Nuñez (2000)."

Nested Structures. A **nested structure** is a phrase that is embedded within another sentence. For example, we can take the simple sentence, "The plane leaves at 9:41," and insert the nested structure "that I want to take." We create a more structurally complex sentence: "The plane that I want to take leaves at 9:41." However, readers experience a "memory cost" when they try to read a sentence that contains a nested structure (Gibson, 1998, 1999; Rayner & Clifton, 2002). You need to remember the first part of the sentence, "the plane," while you process the nested structure. Afterward, you can process the remainder of the sentence. The memory cost becomes excessive when the sentence contains multiple nested structures. For example, you might find yourself stranded when you try to understand the following sentence:

The plane that I want to take when I go to Denver after he returns from Washington leaves at 9:41.

The next time you write a paper, remember how these three factors can influence comprehension. Whenever possible, follow these guidelines: (1) Use linguistically positive sentences, rather than negative ones; (2) use active sentences, rather than passive ones; and (3) use simple sentences, rather than nested structures.

Ambiguity. Suppose that you saw the following headline in your local newspaper: "Bombing Rocks Hope for Peace." As you might imagine, sentences are difficult to understand if they contain an ambiguous word or an ambiguous sentence structure. Recall that we mentioned ambiguous sentences in connection with Chomsky's transformational grammar. Now let's consider how people manage to understand these sentences.

Psychologists have designed several methods of measuring the difficulty of understanding a sentence (MacDonald, 1999; Rodd et al., 2002). For example, one method measures variables such as the amount of time that the reader pauses on a word before moving his or her eyes to the next words in the sentence (Rayner & Clifton, 2002). People typically pause longer when they are processing an ambiguous word.

Psychologists have proposed many theories to explain how listeners process ambiguous material (Rayner & Clifton, 2002; Simpson, 1994). Current research supports the following explanation: When people encounter a potential ambiguity, the activation builds up for all the well-known meanings of the ambiguous item. Furthermore, the degree of activation for a particular meaning depends on that meaning's relative frequency and on the context provided by the rest of the sentence (Morris & Binder, 2001; Rayner & Clifton, 2002; Sereno et al., 2003).

Consider this potentially ambiguous sentence: "Pat took the money to the bank." Here, the "financial institution" interpretation of *bank* would receive the most activation. After all, this is the most common interpretation of *bank*, and the context of *money* also suggests this meaning. Some minimal activation also builds up for other meanings of *bank* (as in *riverbank* and *blood bank*). However, just a fraction of a second later, these alternative meanings are suppressed, and they are no longer active (Gernsbacher et al., 2001; Rayner & Clifton, 2002). This explanation of ambiguity would be consistent with the parallel distributed processing approach.

As Rueckl (1995) observes, "Ambiguity is a fact of life. Happily, the human cognitive system is well-equipped to deal with it" (p. 501). Indeed, we can understand ambiguous sentences, just as we can understand negative sentences, sentences using the passive voice, and sentences with complex nesting. However, we typically respond more quickly and more accurately when the language we encounter is more straightforward. Now that you are familiar with the concept of ambiguity, try Demonstration 9.3.

⊚ Demonstration 9.3

Searching for Ambiguous Language

Ambiguity occurs quite often in the English language (Rodd et al., 2002). Perhaps the best source of ambiguous words and phrases is newspaper headlines. After all, these headlines must be very brief, so they often omit the auxiliary words that could resolve the ambiguity. Here are some actual newspaper headlines that colleagues, students, and I have seen:

1. "Eye drops off shelf"
2. "Squad helps dog bite victims"
3. "British left waffles on Falkland Islands"
4. "Stolen painting found by tree"
5. "Clinton wins budget; more lies ahead"
6. "Miners refuse to work after death"
7. "Kids make nutritious snacks"
8. "Local high school dropouts cut in half"

For the next few weeks, search the headlines of the newspapers you normally read. Keep a list of any that seem to be ambiguous. Try to notice whether your first interpretation of the ambiguous portion was a correct or incorrect understanding of the phrase. If you find any particularly intriguing ambiguities, please send them to me! My address is: Department of Psychology, SUNY Geneseo, Geneseo, NY 14454.

IN DEPTH

Neurolinguistics

Neurolinguistics is the discipline that examines how the brain processes language (Treiman et al., 2003). Research in this area has become increasingly active in recent years, and it demonstrates that the neurological basis of language is impressively complex. Let's consider three topics: aphasia, hemispheric specialization in language processing, and neuroimaging research with normal individuals.

Individuals with Aphasia. The initial investigations in neurolinguistics began in the 1800s, when early researchers studied individuals who had lanaguage disorders. In fact, until recently, almost all the information that scientists had acquired about neurolinguistics was based on people with aphasia. A person with **aphasia** has difficulty communicating, caused by damage to the speech areas of the brain. This damage is typically caused by a stroke or a serious infection (Pinker, 1999; Small, 2002). Figure 9.2 illustrates two especially relevant regions of the brain.

FIGURE 9.2

Broca's Area and Wernicke's Area: Two Regions of the Brain That Are Commonly Associated with Aphasia.

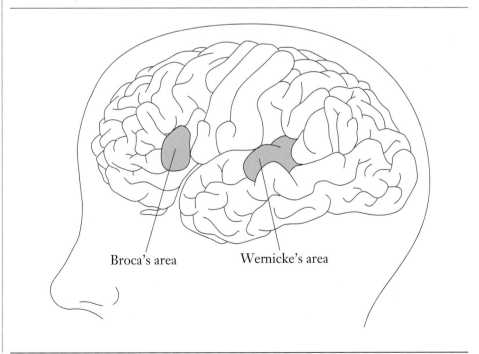

Broca's area   Wernicke's area

Damage to **Broca's area** (toward the front of the brain) typically produces speech that is hesitant, effortful, and grammatically simple (Dick et al., 2001; Gazzaniga et al., 2002). For example, one person with Broca's aphasia tried to describe the circumstances of his stroke:

> Alright . . . Uh . . . stroke and uh . . . I . . . huh tawanna guy . . . h . . . h . . . hot tub and . . . And the . . . two days when uh . . . Hos . . . uh . . . huh hospital and uh . . . amet . . . am . . . ambulance. (Dick et al., 2001, p. 760)

Broca's aphasia is primarily characterized by an expressive-language deficit—or trouble producing language. However, people with Broca's aphasia may also have some trouble understanding language (Dick et al., 2001; Dronkers, 1999). For example, they may be unable to tell the difference between "He showed her baby the pictures" and "He showed her the baby pictures" (Jackendoff, 1994, p. 149).

The other major aphasia is called Wernicke's aphasia (pronounced either "*Ver*-nih-kee" or "*Wer*-nih-kee"). Damage to **Wernicke's area** (toward the back of the brain) typically produces serious difficulties in understanding speech, as well as language production that is too wordy and confused (Harley, 2001). For example, people with Wernicke's aphasia have such severe receptive-language problems that they cannot understand basic instructions like "Point to the telephone" or "Show me the picture of the watch." In contrast to the quotation above, here's how a person with Wernicke's aphasia tried to describe the circumstances of his stroke:

> It just suddenly had a feffert and all the feffort had gone with it. It even stepped my horn. They took them from earth you know. They make my favorite nine to severed and now I'm a been habed by the uh stam of fortment of my annulment which is now forever. (Dick et al., 2001, p. 761)

The basic information about Broca's aphasia and Wernicke's aphasia has been known for about a century. However, the distinction between these two aphasias is not as clear-cut as researchers had once believed (Dronkers, 1999; Gazzaniga et al., 2002; Grodzinsky, 2000).

For example, remember the caution emphasized earlier in the chapter on pages 298–299: We should not rely exclusively on English-based psycholinguistic research (Bates et al., 2001). For instance, researchers who examined aphasia in English speakers concluded that individuals with Broca's aphasia made many grammatical errors. However, these same researchers concluded that individuals with Wernicke's aphasia typically produced grammatically correct sentences.

But here is a complication: English speakers use the same grammatical form for a noun, whether it is the subject or the object of a sentence. In contrast, languages such as German and Czech add letters to the end of a noun if it is the object of a sentence, rather than the subject. Interestingly, people with Wernicke's aphasia who speak languages like German and Czech often fail to add the appropriate endings to the nouns. In short, we see that *both* kinds of aphasia can decrease a person's grammatical accuracy—once we examine some languages other than English (Dick et al., 2001).

Hemispheric Specialization. We noted at the beginning of this In Depth section that the early researchers examined people with aphasia. These scientists also noticed that individuals with speech disorders typically had more severe damage in the left hemisphere of the brain, rather than the right hemisphere. During the mid-1900s, researchers began a more systematic study of lateralization. **Lateralization** means that each hemisphere of the brain has somewhat different functions.

You may have heard a statement such as this: "Language is localized in the left hemisphere of the brain." However, this statement is too strong. Yes, most neurolinguistic studies find greater activation in the left hemisphere than in the right (Bates, 2000; Grodzinsky, 2000). Still, for about 5% of right-handers and about 50% of left-handers, language is either localized in the *right* hemisphere or is processed equally by both hemispheres (Blumstein, 1995; Kinsbourne, 1998; Maratsos & Matheny, 1994).

The left hemisphere does indeed perform most of the work in language processing, for the majority of people. The left hemisphere is especially skilled at speech perception; it quickly selects the most likely interpretation of a sound (Gernsbacher & Kaschak, 2003). The left hemisphere also divides complex words into their simpler meanings—for example, dividing the word *talking* into the two morphemes *talk* and *-ing* (Kosslyn et al., 1999a). Furthermore, the left hemisphere determines cause-and-effect relationships (Gazzaniga et al., 2002). It also excels at reading, as well as at understanding meaning and grammar (Ben-Schachar et al., in press; Gernsbacher & Kaschak, 2003).

For many years, people thought that the right hemisphere did not play a role in language processing. However, we now know that this hemisphere does perform some tasks. For example, the right hemisphere interprets the emotional tone of a message (Gernsbacher & Kaschak, 2003; Vingerhoets et al., 2003). It also plays a role in appreciating humor (Shammi & Stuss, 1999). Furthermore, the right hemisphere helps to interpret metaphors. A person with a damaged right hemisphere might think that the phrase "sour grapes" literally refers to the acidity of grapes, rather than to a particular form of jealousy (Springer & Deutsch, 1998). In general, then, the right hemisphere is responsible for more abstract language tasks (Gernsbacher & Kaschak, 2003).

The left and right hemispheres often work together on tasks such as interpreting subtle word meanings, resolving ambiguities, and combining the meaning of several sentences (Beeman & Chiarello, 1998b; Beeman et al., 2000; Fischler, 1998). For example, suppose that you are one of the majority of individuals for whom the left hemisphere is dominant for language. Imagine that you see this ambiguous message that I once spotted on a bumper sticker:

SOMETIMES I WAKE UP GRUMPY.
OTHER TIMES I LET HIM SLEEP IN.

On seeing the phrase, "SOMETIMES I WAKE UP GRUMPY," your left hemisphere immediately constructs a meaning in which *GRUMPY* refers to "I" (that is, the owner of the car). After reading the next sentence, "OTHER TIMES I LET HIM SLEEP IN," your right hemisphere searches for a less obvious interpretation, in which *GRUMPY* refers to another person. Fortunately, when people have normal brain functions, both hemispheres work together in a complementary fashion (Gazzaniga et al., 2002).

Neuroimaging Research with Normal Individuals. During the past 15 years, researchers have increasingly used neuroimaging to investigate language in the human brain (Gernsbacher & Kaschak, 2003). Let's examine the results of research using the **positron emission tomography (PET scan)** technique, which measures the changes in blood flow within regions of the brain in order to understand the pattern of brain activity.

Several researchers have provided an elegant analysis of brain activity by using PET scans (Buckner & Petersen, 1998; Posner & McCandliss, 1999; Posner & Raichle, 1994). Their technique used the following procedure: (1) Present an increasingly complex series of language tasks; and (2) "subtract" the blood flow pattern created by the simpler tasks from the blood flow pattern created by the next most complex task. This technique therefore identifies the brain activity associated with each specific component of language.

Figure 9.3 shows the typical setup for this kind of PET-scan approach. During the simplest task, at the first level, the participant simply looks at the crosshair (+) on the television monitor. During the second-level visual task, the participant passively views a word. During the second-level auditory task, the participant passively hears a word. During the third-level task, the participant is instructed to speak the word that was seen. Finally, during the fourth-level task, the participant is told to provide a verb that describes the function of the word that was seen. (For example, if the word is *hammer*, the participant might say, "Pound.")

Now turn to Color Figure 4, inside the back cover of this textbook. Here you can see the PET scans that were generated after subtracting the blood flow pattern associated with the simpler tasks. For example, Part A of Color Figure 4 shows the PET scan for passively viewing a word, after subtracting the blood flow patterns associated with simply looking at the crosshair. The red and yellow colors indicate the greatest brain activity in a PET scan.

Notice what happens when people passively look at words (Part A). The most active region is the occipital cortex—the rear part of the brain that processes visual stimuli. When people passively listen to words (Part B), their temporal cortex—near the ear—is most active. The task of speaking words activates the motor regions in the parietal portion of the cortex (Part C). Finally, the task of generating meaning (thinking of a related verb, as shown in Part D) activates both the frontal cortex and the temporal cortex (Buckner & Petersen, 1998). Take a moment to look at Figure 9.3 and Color Figure 4 simultaneously. Imagine that you are participating in each phase of this study, and place your hand on the portion of your head near the brain region activated by each task. As you can see from the color figure, one of the most impressive findings in these PET-scan studies is the variety of brain regions that process language (Rayner & Clifton, 2002).

Similar findings have been reported when researchers use the fMRI technique to see how people process complete sentences. As Chapter 1 pointed out, **functional magnetic resonance imaging (fMRI)** is based on the principle that oxygen-

FIGURE 9.3

**The Setup for Posner and Raichle's Series of Linguistic Tasks.
See page 310 for explanation.**

Source: Based on Posner and Raichle, 1994.

rich blood is an index of brain activity (Raichle, 2000). According to research by Keller and his coauthors (2001), sentence comprehension activates many different brain regions. In addition, some brain regions handle several different linguistic processes. Furthermore, Michael and her coauthors (2001) found that fMRI patterns were fairly similar, whether people listened to sentences or read them.

However, fMRIs showed more activity in the left hemisphere when people read the sentences, rather than listened to them. In summary, the neuroimaging research highlights the complex coordination of brain regions that allow us to understand language.

In the first part of this chapter, we have examined the basic structure of language, the history of psycholinguistics, factors affecting comprehension, and neurolinguistics. Let's summarize this background knowledge and then turn our attention to the important topic of reading.

Section Summary: *The Nature of Language*

1. Some of the central concepts in psycholinguistics are the phoneme, the morpheme, semantics, syntax, and pragmatics.

2. Because most psycholinguistics research focuses on English, we cannot draw conclusions about whether the results can be applied to other languages.

3. People use the information in constituents to determine meaning; working memory stores the constituent that people are currently processing, until its meaning can be determined.

4. Chomsky proposed that language skills are innate in humans, and that language is modular.

5. Chomsky's theory of transformational grammar proposed that deep structure is converted to surface structure via transformational rules; research partially supports Chomsky's theory.

6. Many current psychologists favor the cognitive-functional approach to language, which emphasizes that we structure our language so that listeners will pay attention to the information we want to emphasize.

7. Sentences are more difficult to understand if they contain negatives, if they are in the passive voice, if they include nested structures, and if they are ambiguous.

8. Neurolinguistic research on adults with aphasia suggests that damage in Broca's area leads to difficulty in producing language, whereas damage in Wernicke's area leads to difficulty in understanding language; however, the distinction is not clear-cut.

9. The left hemisphere typically performs most aspects of language processing, such as speech perception, syntax processing, and reading; however, the right hemisphere interprets a message's emotional tone, decodes metaphors, and resolves ambiguities.

10. Research using PET scans and fMRIs highlights a variety of brain regions that are responsible for language-related activities.

BASIC READING PROCESSES

Reading seems so simple to competent adult readers that we forget how challenging the task is for most children (Rayner et al., 2001). Take a minute to think about the impressive variety of cognitive tasks you perform when reading a paragraph like this one. Reading requires you to use many cognitive processes we have discussed in previous chapters. For example, you must recognize letters (Chapter 2), move your eyes across the page (Chapter 3), use working memory to remember material from the sentence you are currently processing (Chapter 4), and recall earlier material that is stored in long-term memory (Chapters 5 and 6). You also need to use metacomprehension to think about the reading comprehension process (Chapter 6). In some cases, you must also construct a mental image to represent the scene of the action in the passage you are reading (Chapter 7). In addition, you must consult your semantic memory, your schemas, and your scripts when you try to understand the paragraph (Chapter 8).

In Demonstration 9.1 and throughout this book, we emphasize that the cognitive processes are interrelated (Theme 4). Reading is an important activity that requires virtually every cognitive process discussed in this textbook. Despite the complexity of the reading process, however, we are usually blissfully unaware of the cognitive effort that reading requires (Gorrell, 1999; Pressley et al., 1996). For example we can identify an isolated word in 200 milliseconds, which is $\frac{1}{5}$ of a second. In addition, we manage to read with impressive efficiency, typically at the rate of about 250 to 300 words per minute (Rayner et al., 2003; Wagner & Stanovich, 1996). Consistent with Theme 2, reading is remarkably efficient and accurate.

Here's an additional reason that you should be impressed with your reading skills: In English, we do not have a one-to-one correspondence between letters of the alphabet and speech sounds. Try Demonstration 9.4 on page 314 to illustrate this point.

Let's begin this section on basic reading processes by comparing written language with spoken language. Then we'll explore how we discover the meaning of an unfamiliar word. We'll also see how working memory plays a role in reading, and then we'll consider some theories about word recognition. A separate section in this chapter, on discourse processing, will examine how we understand larger units of language—such as sentences and stories—in both written and spoken language.

Comparing Written and Spoken Language

In Chapter 2, we explored several components of spoken language comprehension. In this section on *written* language comprehension, we encounter a somewhat different set of challenges. Reading and the comprehension of spoken language differ in important ways (Cornoldi & Oakhill, 1996; Rapp et al., 2001; Rayner & Clifton, 2002; Underwood & Batt, 1996):

1. Reading is visual and is spread out across space, whereas speech is auditory and is spread out across time.

⊙ Demonstration 9.4

Noticing That Letters of the Alphabet Do Not Have a One-to-One Correspondence with Speech Sounds

Each of the words below has a somewhat different pronunciation for the letter sequence *ea*. Read each word aloud and notice the variety of phonemes that can be produced with those two letters.

beauty	bread	clear
create	deal	great
heard	knowledgeable	react
seance	bear	dealt

As you have demonstrated, this two-letter sequence can be pronounced in 12 different ways. Furthermore, each phoneme in the English language can be spelled in a variety of ways. Go back over this list of words and try to think of another word that has a different spelling for that phoneme. For example, the *ea(u)* phoneme in *beauty* is like the *iew* phoneme in *view*.

Source: Based on Underwood & Batt, 1996.

---

2. Readers can control the rate of input, whereas listeners usually cannot.

3. Readers can re-scan the written input, whereas listeners must rely much more heavily on their working memory.

4. Writing shows discrete boundaries between words, whereas speech does not.

5. Writing is confined to the words on a page, whereas speech is supplemented by additional auditory cues—such as stressed words and variations in pace—that enrich the linguistic message.

6. Children require elaborate teaching to master written language, whereas they learn spoken language very easily.

As you can imagine, these characteristics of written language have important implications for our cognitive processes. For example, we can consult the words on a page when we want to make sense out of a passage in a book—a luxury we seldom have with spoken language. Despite the differences between written and spoken language, however, both processes require us to understand words and appreciate the meaning of sentences. In fact, this similarity is highlighted by studies of individual differences. For adults, scores on reading comprehension tests are highly correlated with scores on oral comprehension tests; typically the correlation is about +.90 (Rayner et al., 2001).

Demonstration 9.5

Figuring Out the Meaning of a Word from Context

Read the paragraph below. Then define, as precisely as possible, the words that are italicized.

> Two ill-dressed people—the one a tired woman of middle years and the other a tense young man—sat around a fire where the common meal was almost ready. The mother, Tanith, peered at her son through the *oam* of the bubbling stew. It had been a long time since his last *ceilidh* and Tobar had changed greatly; where once he had seemed all legs and clumsy joints, he now was well-formed and in control of his hard, young body. As they ate, Tobar told of his past year, re-creating for Tanith how he had wandered long and far in his quest to gain the skills he would need to be permitted to rejoin the company. Then all too soon, their brief *ceilidh* over, Tobar walked over to touch his mother's arm and quickly left.

Source: Based on Sternberg & Powell, 1983.

Discovering the Meaning of an Unfamiliar Word

Chapter 2 examined how context aids both the visual recognition of letters and the auditory recognition of phonemes. Context also helps you recognize words. Specifically, you perceive familiar words more accurately when they are embedded within the meaningful context of a sentence (Kintsch, 1998; Rayner & Clifton, 2002). We also saw, earlier in this chapter, that context helps to resolve the meaning of an ambiguous word.

In addition, context is vitally important when people want to discover the meanings of *unfamiliar* words. Try Demonstration 9.5, which is an example of the passages used by Sternberg and Powell (1983) in their work on verbal comprehension.

When we read, we often come upon a word whose meaning is unfamiliar. We then typically attempt to use a word's context to figure out its meaning. Sternberg and Powell (1983) propose that context can provide several kinds of information cues about meaning. For instance, context can help us understand how often X (the unknown word) occurs and where it is located. Consider the following sentence: "At dawn, the *blen* arose on the horizon and shone brightly."

This sentence contains several contextual cues that make it easy to infer the meaning of *blen*. For instance, the phrase "at dawn" provides a cue about the time at which the arising of the *blen* occurred. The word *arose* limits the possible candidates for *blen* to those things that move or appear to move. Other words and phrases in the sentence are equally helpful. With all these cues, an experienced reader can easily understand that the nonsense word *blen* is a synonym for the familiar word *sun*.

Contextual cues are especially useful if the unknown word appears in several different contexts. According to the research, words that appear in a rich context of different cues are more likely to be accurately defined (Sternberg & Powell, 1983).

As you might expect, the students in Sternberg and Powell's study showed large individual differences in their ability to use contextual cues and to provide accurate definitions for the unfamiliar words. The students who were particularly good at this task were also found to have higher scores on tests of vocabulary, reading comprehension, and general intelligence. (Incidentally, in the passage in Demonstration 9.5, *oam* means "steam" and a *ceilidh* is a "visit.")

Reading and Working Memory

Working memory plays an important role during reading, especially because working memory has a limited capacity (Carpenter et al., 1995; Carroll, 2004). The research shows that readers who have a relatively large working-memory span can quickly process ambiguous sentences (Miyake et al., 1994). In addition, researchers have demonstrated that people with large working-memory spans are especially skilled in guessing the meaning of unusual words on the basis of sentence context (Daneman & Green, 1986). Apparently, the large memory span allows them to read efficiently, so that they have more attention "left over" to remember the important contextual cues.

Working memory also helps us to understand complicated sentences (Carpenter et al., 1994, 1995; Just et al., 1996). People who can maintain many items in memory—while they unravel a sentence—are quick and accurate in understanding complex sentences such as "The reporter whom the senator attacked admitted the error."

All this research on reading and working memory is an excellent illustration of Theme 4. The cognitive processes do not operate in isolation. Instead, reading skill depends heavily on other cognitive abilities, such as working memory.

The Role of Sound in Word Recognition

So far, our examination of reading in this textbook has emphasized how we identify alphabetical letters (Chapter 2), how our sacccadic eye movements scan a line of text (Chapter 3), how we discover the meaning of an unfamiliar word, and how working memory plays a role in reading. Now we'll address a difficult and controversial question about reading: How do we look at a pattern of letters and actually recognize that word? For example, how do you manage to look at the 11 letters in the last word of the title just above this paragraph and realize that it says *recognition?*

Three different hypotheses have been developed to explain how readers recognize printed words when they read to themselves. One hypothesis, which we will call the **direct-access hypothesis,** states that readers can recognize a word directly from the printed letters. That is, you look at the word *recognition*, and the visual pattern is sufficient to let you locate information about the meaning of the word in semantic memory (Rayner et al., 2003).

Another hypothesis, which we will call the **indirect-access hypothesis** or the **phonologically mediated hypothesis,** states that we must translate the ink marks on the page into some form of sound before we can locate information about a word's meaning (Perfetti, 1996). Notice that this process is indirect because, according to this hypothesis, we must go through the intermediate step of converting the visual stimulus into a phonological (sound) stimulus. Think about whether you seem to use this intermediate step when you read. As you read this sentence, for example, do you have a speech-like representation of the words? You probably don't actually move your lips when you read, and you certainly don't say the words out loud. But do you seem to have an auditory image of what you are reading?

The third hypothesis, called the **dual-route hypothesis,** states that we can use either of two routes (Coltheart & Rastle, 1994; Perfetti, 1999):

1. Sometimes we recognize a word directly through the visual route, especially if the word has an irregular spelling and cannot be "sounded out"—for example, the words *one* or *through.*

2. Other times, we recognize a word indirectly through the sound route, especially if the word has a regular spelling and can be sounded out—for example, the words *ten* and *cabinet.*

At present, this flexible dual-route hypothesis seems like the most appropriate approach. Let's discuss the research supporting both parts of the dual-route hypothesis, and then we'll consider the implications for teaching reading to children.

Research on the Dual-Route Hypothesis. We'll begin with a classic study that supports the direct-access hypothesis, which argues that people directly recognize a word through the visual route. Bradshaw and Nettleton (1974) showed people pairs of words that were similar in spelling, but different in sound, such as *mown–down, horse–worse,* and *quart–part.* In one condition, the participants were instructed to read the first word silently and then pronounce the second word out loud. Now, if they had been translating the first member of a pair into sound, the sound of *mown* would interfere with saying *down* out loud. However, the results showed that the participants experienced no hesitation in pronouncing the second word. This finding suggests that we do not silently pronounce each word during normal reading.

Now let's shift to the research on the indirect-access hypothesis. Many studies suggest that visual stimuli are often translated into sound during reading. Word sounds may be especially important when children begin to read. Numerous studies demonstrate that children with high phonological awareness have superior reading skills. That is, the children who are able to identify sound patterns in a word also receive higher scores on reading achievement tests (Levy, 1999; Stothard & Hulme, 1996; Wagner & Stanovich, 1996). Furthermore, Byrne and Fielding-Barnsley (1991) trained some preschool children in phoneme skills, and they trained other preschool children in semantic skills. The phoneme-trained children performed better on a word-identification test.

Perhaps you're thinking that children may need to translate the printed word into sound—after all, children even move their lips when they read—but adults usually do not. Try Demonstration 9.6 and see whether you change your mind. Adults read "tongue twisters" very slowly, which indicates that—at least in some circumstances—they are indeed translating the printed words into sounds (Harley, 2001; Keller et al., 2003; Perfetti, 1996).

Other evidence for the indirect-access hypothesis in adult readers comes from research by Luo and his coauthors (1998). These researchers instructed college students to read a series of pairs of words and decide whether the two words were related or unrelated in meaning. A typical pair in the experimental condition was *LION–BARE*. As you can see, the word *BARE* sounds the same as the word *BEAR*, which is semantically related to *LION*. The students frequently made errors on these pairs; they incorrectly judged the two words as being semantically related. This error pattern suggests that they were silently pronouncing the word pairs when they made the judgments. In contrast, they made relatively few errors on control-condition word pairs, such as *LION–BEAN*. Additional support for the indirect-access hypothesis comes from studies demonstrating that readers activate phonological information early in a fixation pause (Rayner et al., 1998).

As we noted earlier, the dual-route hypothesis has the definite advantage of flexibility. This hypothesis argues that the characteristics of the reading material determine whether access is indirect or direct. For instance, you may use indirect access the first time you see a long, uncommon word; you may use direct access for a common word (Bernstein & Carr, 1996; Seidenberg, 1995).

---

⑨ Demonstration 9.6

Reading Tongue Twisters

Read each of the following tongue twisters silently to yourself:

1. The seasick sailor staggered as he zigzagged sideways.
2. Peter Piper picked a peck of pickled peppers. A peck of pickled peppers Peter Piper picked.
3. She sells seashells down by the seaside.
4. Congressional caucus questions controversial CIA-*Contra*-Crack connection.
5. Sheila and Celia slyly shave the cedar shingle splinter.

Now be honest. Could you "hear" yourself pronouncing these words as you were reading? Did you have to read them more slowly than other sentences in this book?

The dual-route hypothesis also argues that characteristics of the reader determine whether access is indirect or direct. Beginning readers would be especially likely to sound out the words, using indirect access; experienced readers would be especially likely to recognize the words directly from print. Adults also vary in their reading styles. College students who are good readers typically use direct access, whereas college students who are relatively poor readers typically use indirect access (Jared et al., 1999).

At present, the dual-route hypothesis seems like an intelligent compromise. Readers can identify words either directly or indirectly, depending on the characteristics of both the text and the reader.

Implications for Teaching Reading to Children. The debate about theories of word recognition has some important implications for teaching reading. Those who favor the direct-access hypothesis typically suggest that educators should use the whole-word approach. The **whole-word approach** argues that readers can directly connect the written word—as an entire unit—with the meaning that the word represents (Chialant & Caramazza, 1995; Crowder & Wagner, 1992; Rayner et al., 2001). The whole-word approach emphasizes that the correspondence between the written and spoken codes in English is notoriously complex, as we saw in Demonstration 9.4. Supporters therefore argue against emphasizing the way a word sounds. Instead, the whole-word approach encourages children to identify words in terms of the context in which the words appear.

In contrast, people who favor the indirect-access hypothesis typically support the phonics approach. The **phonics approach** states that readers recognize words by trying to pronounce the individual letters in the word. If your grade school teachers told you to "sound it out" when you stumbled on a new word, they championed the phonics approach. This approach argues that speech sound is a necessary intermediate step in reading. The phonics approach emphasizes developing young children's awareness of phonemes. Phonics training helps children who have reading problems (Rayner et al., 2001). In addition, children who have received phonics training are better spellers than those with no training (Pressley et al., 1996).

The debate between the whole-word supporters and the phonics supporters is feverish. However, most of the evidence supports the phonics approach (de Jong & van der Leij, 1999; Rayner et al., 2001; Tunmer & Chapman, 1998). For example, a meta-analysis of 34 studies showed that phonological training programs had a major impact on children's reading skills (Bus & van IJzendoorn, 1999). Children should be taught to use phonics to guess the pronunciation of a word; they should also use context as a backup to confirm their initial hypothesis.

This debate among educators is further complicated by a prominent movement within education called whole language. The **whole-language approach** suggests that reading instruction should emphasize meaning; children should read storybooks, experiment with writing before they are expert spellers, try to guess the meaning of a word from the sentence's context, and use reading throughout the classroom (Adams & Bruck, 1995; Pressley et al., 1996; Rayner et al., 2001). Those who favor this perspective typically support the whole-word approach, rather than the phonics approach. Notice, however, that supporters of the phonics approach might admire many components of the whole-language approach, even though they may reject the specific emphasis on the whole-word approach (Rayner et al., 2001).

The reading debate is far from resolved. Even if the phonics approach is supported by recent research, the whole-word approach may also provide benefits. For example, this approach seems to increase children's enthusiasm for learning to read (Rayner et al., 2001). In addition, individual differences may operate. Most children may learn best with the phonics method, but some may thrive with the whole-word method. Some combination of both approaches may turn out to be especially effective. In any event, reading practice clearly improves reading skills because it increases familiarity with both vocabulary words and syntax.

Section Summary: *Basic Reading Processes*

1. Reading is a challenging cognitive task that differs from understanding spoken language in several respects; for example, readers can control the rate of input and they can re-scan the text.

2. Readers often use a variety of contextual cues to determine the meaning of an unfamiliar word.

3. Working memory helps readers decode ambiguous sentences and unravel the meaning of a complex sentence.

4. The dual-route hypothesis argues that readers sometimes recognize a word directly from the printed letters (i.e., direct access), and they sometimes convert the printed letters into a phonological code in order to access the word (i.e., indirect access).

5. Educators who use the whole-word approach typically agree with the direct-access hypothesis, whereas educators who use the phonics approach typically agree with the indirect-access hypothesis; the research usually supports the phonics approach, but we cannot draw firm conclusions about this controversial topic.

6. The whole-*language* approach emphasizes the meaning of words; this approach is endorsed by those who favor the whole-word approach, and parts of the whole-language approach are endorsed by those who emphasize phonics.

UNDERSTANDING DISCOURSE

We began this chapter with an overview of the nature of language; we considered both linguistic theory and the biological basis of language. Then we explored basic reading processes. You'll notice that these topics all focus on the way we process small units of language, such as a phoneme, a letter, a word, or an isolated sentence. In your daily life, however, you are continually processing connected **discourse,** or language units that are larger than a sentence (Bamberg & Moissinac, 2003; Treiman et al., 2003). You listen to the news on the radio, you hear a friend telling a story, you follow the instructions for assembling a bookcase . . . and you read your cognitive psychology textbook.

Frederick Bartlett (1932) was concerned about these larger linguistic units when he conducted research about 70 years ago on memory for stories. However, for the next few decades, psychologists and linguists concentrated primarily on words and isolated sentences. The topic of discourse processing was not revived until the mid-1970s (Butcher & Kintsch, 2003; Graesser et al., 2003b).

During the past decade, research on discourse processing has branched out into new areas. Some representative recent topics include the following: readers' ability to access background information relevant to the story (Cook et al., 1998; O'Brien et al., 1998), readers' memory for portions of the story's plot (Butcher & Kintsch, 2003; Gerrig & McKoon, 1998), the role of long-term working memory in understanding discourse (Butcher & Kintsch, 2003), readers' inferences about a character's emotional state (Gernsbacher et al., 1998), and the use of negation in a novel (Hidalgo Downing, 2000).

So far in this chapter, we've emphasized how context can help us understand sounds, letters, and words. Now we'll see that context is also important when we consider larger linguistic units. As Chapter 8 explained, general background knowledge and expertise help to facilitate our conceptual understanding. Research on discourse comprehension also emphasizes the importance of expertise, scripts, and schemas (e.g., Moravcsik & Kintsch, 1993; van den Broek et al., 1999). At all levels of language comprehension, we see additional evidence of Theme 5. That is, the processing of the physical stimuli (bottom-up processing) interacts with the context provided by our expectations and previous knowledge (top-down processing). This interaction is especially prominent when we form a coherent representation of the text and when we draw inferences during reading.

Our exploration of discourse comprehension focuses on the following selected topics: forming a coherent representation of the text, drawing inferences during reading, and artificial intelligence and reading.

Forming a Coherent Representation of the Text

Reading comprehension is enormously more complicated than simply fitting words and phrases together. In addition, readers must gather information together and remember the various concepts so that the message is both cohesive and stable. We should note that listeners—as well as readers—form coherent representations, remember the material, and draw inferences when they hear spoken language (e.g., Butcher & Kintsch, 2003; Marslen-Wilson et al., 1993). However, virtually all the research examines discourse processing during reading.

In order to form a coherent representation, we often construct mental models of the material we are reading (Zwaan, 1999). In Chapter 7, we saw that people construct mental models based on a written description of an environment. Similarly, readers construct internal representations that include descriptions of the characters in a story. This descriptive information may include the characters' occupations, relationships, emotional states, personal traits, goals, and actions (Carpenter et al., 1995; Trabasso et al., 1995).

Readers may need to maintain this representation in long-term memory for many pages of a novel, while the author pursues a secondary plot (Gerrig & McKoon, 2001).

Walter Kintsch, one of the pioneers in the research on discourse processing, describes the processing cycles we use when we understand a passage (Butcher & Kintsch, 2003; Kintsch, 1998). According to the concept of **processing cycles,** we understand each new sentence within the context of the previous text. We quickly process the information in a new sentence and integrate the important information within the general representation of the text. Schemas also play a major role in creating a coherent representation, consistent with our discussion in Chapter 8. At this point, working memory no longer stores the specific words of the sentence. We then move on to a new sentence—and a new cycle. When people try to form a coherent representation of the text they are reading, they often make inferences that go beyond the information supplied by the writer. Let's consider this topic in more detail.

Inferences in Reading

I recently read a novel called *The God of Small Things* by Arundhati Roy (1997). The novel follows young twins named Rahel and Estha, as they grow up in the Kerala region of India. The twins watch their educated mother, Ammu, falling in love with Velutha, a handsome and talented man from the untouchable class. Readers do not need to have a sophisticated knowledge of social class in India in order to draw an important inference:

Demonstration 9.7

Reading a Passage of Text

Read the following passage, and notice whether it seems to flow smoothly and logically:

1. Dick had a week's vacation due
2. and he wanted to go to a place
3. where he could swim and sunbathe.
4. He bought a book on travel.
5. Then he looked at the ads
6. in the travel section of the Sunday newspaper.
7. He went to his local travel agent
8. and asked for a plane ticket to Alaska.
9. He paid for it with his charge card.

Source: Based on Huitema et al., 1993, p. 1054.

Sadly, this relationship must have a tragic ending. Whenever we read, we activate important mental processes by going beyond the information presented on the printed page.

When we make an **inference** during reading, we draw on our world knowledge in order to activate information that is not explicitly stated in a written passage (van den Broek, 1994; Zwaan & Singer, 2003). We discussed inferences in Chapter 8 in connection with the influence of schemas on memory. People combine their information about the world with the information presented in a passage, and they draw a reasonable conclusion based on that combination. Consistent with Theme 1, people are active information processors.

Let's explore several issues that have been raised in connection with inferences during reading. First, we'll consider the constructionist view. Then we'll discuss factors that encourage inferences. Our final topic is higher-level inferences. Incidentally, try Demonstration 9.7 before you read further.

The Constructionist View of Inferences. According to the widely accepted **constructionist view of inferences,** readers usually draw inferences about the causes of events and the relationships between events. When you read a novel, for instance, you construct inferences about a character's motivations, personality, and emotions. You develop expectations about new plot developments, about the writer's point of view, and so forth (Huitema et al., 1993; Sternberg & Ben-Zeev, 2001). This perspective is a "constructionist view" because readers actively construct explanations as they integrate the current information with all the relevant information from the previous parts of the text, as well as their background knowledge (O'Brien & Myers, 1999; Zwaan & Singer, 2003). The constructionist view argues that people can draw inferences, even when the related topics are separated by several irrelevant sentences.

Let's consider some research by John Huitema and his coauthors (1993), who studied brief stories like the one you read in Demonstration 9.7. The introductory material in this demonstration leads you to believe that Dick will soon be lounging on a sunny beach. You drew this inference on line 3, and this inference is contradicted five lines later, rather than in the very next sentence.

Huitema and his colleagues (1993) tested four conditions. You saw the far/inconsistent version of the story, in which several lines of text separated the sentence stating the goal from the inconsistent statement. In the near/inconsistent version, the goal and the inconsistent statement were in adjacent sentences. In the far/consistent version, several lines of text separated the goal and a consistent statement (in which Dick asked for a plane ticket to Florida—a place consistent with swimming). In the near/consistent version, the goal and the consistent statement were in adjacent sentences.

The dependent measure in this experiment was the amount of time that participants had taken to read the crucial line about Dick's travel destination (line 8). This variable could be easily measured, because participants pressed a key after reading each line in order to advance the text to the next line.

As you can see from Figure 9.4, in the near condition, participants read the inconsistent version significantly more slowly than the consistent version. This finding is not surprising. However, you'll notice that participants also read the inconsistent version significantly more slowly than the consistent version in the far condition, when the relevant portions of the task were separated by four intervening lines.

FIGURE 9.4

Amount of Time Taken to Read the Crucial Line in the Study by Huitema and His Colleagues (1993), as a Function of the Amount of Separation Between the Goal and the Crucial Line and the Compatibility Between the Goal and the Crucial Line (consistent vs. inconsistent).

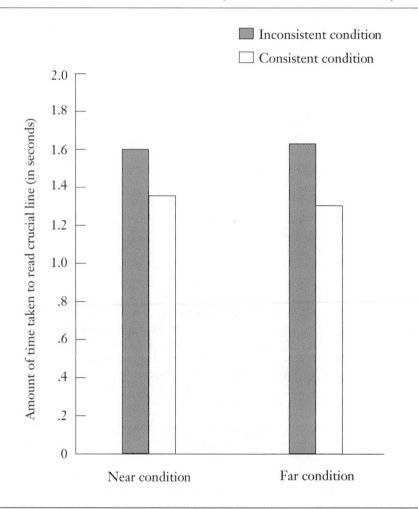

Source: Based on Huitema et al., 1993.

The data from Huitema and his colleagues (1993) support the constructionist view. Readers clearly try to connect material within a text passage, and they consult information stored in long-term memory. During discourse processing, we try to construct a representation of the text that is internally consistent—even when irrelevant material intervenes (Klin et al., 1999; Rayner & Clifton, 2002; Underwood & Batt, 1996).

Other support for the constructionist view comes from research by Soyoung Suh and Tom Trabasso. These researchers instructed participants to talk out loud as they were reading text passages, in order to explain their interpretations of the stories (Suh & Trabasso, 1993; Trabasso & Suh, 1993). In these stories, the main character had an initial goal that was blocked. When the goal was fulfilled in the last line of the story, about 90% of the participants specifically mentioned the original goal when they were commenting on the last line. Suh and Trabasso argue that readers create causal inferences in order to integrate discourse and construct a well-organized story.

Factors That Encourage Inferences. Naturally, we do not always draw inferences when we read a passage. Individual differences among readers are important. For example, people are likely to synthesize information and draw inferences if they have a large working-memory capacity (Butcher & Kintsch, 2003; Carpenter et al., 1995). They are also likely to draw inferences if they have excellent metacomprehension skills, so that they are aware that they must search for connections between two seemingly unrelated sentences (Ehrlich, 1998; Graesser et al., 1996).

People are also likely to draw inferences if they have background information or expertise about the topic described in the text. In fact, expertise in an area can compensate for a relatively small working-memory capacity (Butcher & Kintsch, 2003; Kintsch, 1998). In addition, people who are depressed are *less* likely to draw inferences (Ellis et al., 1997).

Other research shows that people often fail to construct inferences when they are reading scientific texts (Millis & Graesser, 1994; Noordman et al., 1992). In addition, people who are reading a sequence of newspaper articles on the same topic are not likely to make backward inferences (van Oostendorp & Bonebakker, 1999). In other words, they do not re-interpret their earlier inferences about a topic, once they have learned contradictory information in a later news release.

This part of our discussion has focused on factors that affect inferences, and we have seen that some inferences are more probable than others. In explaining these factors, however, let's recall an important point from Chapter 8: We are sometimes just as likely to remember our inferences as to remember statements that actually occurred in the text. Our inferences blend with the text, forming a cohesive story. We often retain the gist or general meaning of a passage, forgetting that we constructed some elements that did not actually appear in the story.

Higher-Level Inferences. Researchers are beginning to explore higher-level inferences, beyond the level of the paragraph. One kind of higher-level inference is based on our own preferences about the way we want a story to turn out. Perhaps you've turned the pages of a fast-paced spy novel and mentally shouted to your favorite character, "Watch out!" In fact, Allbritton and Gerrig (1991) found that readers did generate what they called *participatory responses* when the readers became involved in a story. These mental preferences for the story's outcome can be so strong that they can actually interfere with readers' ability to judge how the story turned out, making us pause as we try to decide whether that unhappy ending really did occur (Gerrig, 1998). You may even find yourself so hopeful about a happy ending you've constructed that you read the final sentences several times, trying to convince yourself that the hero or heroine didn't die!

In summary, people often draw inferences when they read. They integrate material into a cohesive unit, and they are puzzled if they encounter something that contradicts the inferences they drew. People are especially likely to draw inferences if they have a large working-memory capacity or expertise. Inferences may be less common with material such as scientific texts and news articles. However, when people read a novel, they often draw higher-level inferences based on their own plot preferences.

Artificial Intelligence and Reading

As discussed in Chapter 1, **artificial intelligence (AI)** is the area of computer science that attempts to construct computers that can execute human-like cognitive processes. The goal of AI is to develop computer programs that will perform tasks—such as language comprehension—that appear to be intelligent. When developing AI models of language, the basic assumption is that computers start off with no knowledge whatsoever about natural language. **Natural language** is ordinary human language with all its sloppiness, ambiguities, and complexities. The researcher has to write into the program all the information that is necessary to make the computer behave as if it understands sentences typed on its keyboard. The program must be in the form of detailed instructions, and the computer must be given specific programming operations for analyzing all input (Harley, 2001; Sobel, 2001).

For example, researchers' theories about language can then be tested by running a specific program and determining whether it responds correctly to the linguistic input (Harley, 2001). The researchers might test whether a computer "understands" a story by seeing whether it can provide a summary, using phrases that were not in the original text.

Some programs have been designed to recognize human speech, a component of language comprehension that we often take for granted. These speech recognition systems are much less competent than humans (Sobel, 2001). For example, we emphasized in Chapter 2 that humans can typically discover the location of boundaries between spoken words, even when no boundaries exist. The only way a computer can solve this problem is to require the speaker to pause between words—something that speakers rarely do in natural language (Bock & Garnsey, 1998).

The FRUMP Project. Let's consider a classic example of a computer program designed to perform reading tasks. One script-based program was given the unattractive name of **FRUMP,** an acronym for Fast Reading Understanding and Memory Program (De Jong, 1982). The goal of FRUMP was to summarize newspaper stories, written in ordinary language. When it was developed, FRUMP could interpret about 10% of news releases issued by United Press International (Butcher & Kintsch, 2003; Kintsch, 1984). FRUMP used a bottom-up approach at only one point—when it searched the words to decide which script to use. Otherwise, it worked in a top-down fashion by applying world knowledge, based on 48 different scripts. FRUMP summarized only the main points of the script; everything else was disregarded.

Consider, for example, the "vehicle accident" script, which is activated when the text contains information about some kind of vehicle striking some physical object in some location. The script contains information about the number of people killed, the number of people injured, and the cause of the accident. On the basis of the "vehicle accident" script, FRUMP summarized a news article as follows: "A vehicle accident occurred in Colorado. A plane hit the ground. 1 person died." FRUMP did manage to capture the facts of the story. However, it missed the major reason that the item was newsworthy: Yes, 1 person was killed, but 21 people actually survived!

Studies with script-based programs like FRUMP have demonstrated that human language uses scripts in a very flexible fashion and in ever-changing contexts (Kintsch, 1998). Humans also draw numerous inferences that artificial intelligence systems cannot access. We can be impressed that FRUMP managed to process a reasonable number of newspaper stories, but its errors highlight the wide-ranging capabilities of human readers (Theme 2).

Subsequent Projects. Cognitive scientists continue to develop programs designed to understand language (Moore & Wiemer-Hastings, 2003). For example, a program called HAL has processed about 300 million words of text in order to determine which words typically occur together in the English language. This model predicts which word combinations in a sentence would be easiest to understand (Burgess, 1998; Burgess et al., 1998; McKoon & Ratcliff, 1998).

One of the most useful artificial intelligence programs was created by cognitive psychologist Thomas Landauer and his colleagues (Foltz, 2003; Landauer et al., 1998). Their program, called **latent semantic analysis (LSA),** is designed to assess the amount of semantic similarity between two words or two discourse segments. LSA can even be used to grade essays.

For example, suppose a textbook contains the following sentence: "The phonological loop responds to the phonetic characteristics of speech but does not evaluate speech for semantic content" (Butcher & Kintsch, 2003, p. 551). Imagine that two students are writing a short essay for a cognitive psychology exam. With reference to this passage, Chris writes, "The rehearsal loop that practices speech sounds does not pick up meaning in words. Rather, it just reacts whenever it hears something that sounds like language." On the same exam, Pat writes, The loop that listens to the words does not understand anything about the phonetic noises that it hears. All it does is listen for noise and then respond by practicing that noise." If you recall the material from Chapter 4, you would agree with LSA's analysis that Chris's essay is a more accurate summary of the original text than Pat's essay is.

LSA is indeed impressive, but even its developers note that it cannot match a human grader. For instance Landauer told a reporter, "We're not pretending you can use this to score essays that are supposed to be creative about a new topic" (Murray, 1998, p. 43). Furthermore, all the current programs master just a small component of language comprehension. For example, LSA ignores syntax, whereas humans can easily detect syntax errors. In addition, LSA learns only from written text, whereas humans learn from spoken language, facial expressions, and physical gestures (Butcher & Kintsch, 2003). Once again, the artificial intelligence approach to language illustrates humans' tremendous breadth of knowledge, cognitive flexibility, understanding of syntax, and sources of information.

⑨ Section Summary: *Understanding Discourse*

1. Psycholinguistics researchers are increasingly focusing on discourse processing, or language units that are larger than a sentence.

2. Readers try to form coherent representations of discourse, by using context, long-term memory, mental models, schemas, and inferences.

3. According to the constructionist view, people actively draw inferences that connect parts of the text, even though the parts may be widely separated.

4. Inferences are especially likely when people have large working-memory capacity, excellent metacomprehension skills, and expertise in the area. Finally, people also draw higher-level inferences beyond the level of the paragraph.

5. An artificial intelligence program called FRUMP was designed to summarize newspaper stories. A more recent program called latent semantic analysis (LSA) can assess the similarity between two passages of text. The relatively narrow scope of this research highlights humans' competence in a wide variety of reading tasks.

CHAPTER REVIEW QUESTIONS

1. Why is language one of the most impressive human accomplishments, and in what ways does it illustrate the interrelatedness of the cognitive processes?

2. Construct a simple sentence and divide it into constituents. Explain how these constituents are important in language comprehension. Next, construct a different sentence, one that has the same deep structure as your original sentence, but different surface structure. From the perspective of the cognitive-functional approach, do these two versions of the sentence communicate different messages?

3. What does the information on aphasia, hemispheric specialization, and brain-imaging techniques tell us about the regions of the brain that play a role in understanding and producing language?

4. In the section about the factors affecting comprehension, one factor was ambiguity. Create several ambiguous sentences, and then add a few words of context to clarify each ambiguity. Next, recall the three other factors in this section that can influence comprehension. Begin with the easy-to-comprehend sentence, "The students are wasting their time." Then use each of these factors to transform that sentence into difficult-to-comprehend sentences.

5. Context is an important concept throughout this chapter. Explain how context is important in (a) processing ambiguous words; (b) discovering the meaning of an unfamiliar word; (c) background knowledge in understanding discourse; and (d) artificial intelligence approaches to language comprehension.

6. Throughout this chapter, we emphasized that memory contributes to language comprehension. Using the chapter outline as your guide, specify how both working memory and long-term memory are essential when we try to understand language.

7. Describe how the dual-route hypothesis explains how you recognize the words you are reading. If you can recall how you were taught to read, figure out whether that method emphasized the whole-word approach or the phonics approach.

8. Describe the constructionist view of inference discussed in the last section of this chapter. Think about several kinds of reading tasks you have performed in the last 2 days. Be sure to include examples other than reading your textbook. Point out how the constructionist perspective would be relevant during each discourse-processing task.

9. Many parts of this chapter emphasized individual differences. Summarize this information, and speculate how individual differences might also be relevant in other aspects of language comprehension.

10. This chapter discussed both listening and reading. Compare these two kinds of language tasks. Which processes are similar, and which are different? In preparation for Chapter 10, compare speech production and writing in a similar fashion.

NEW TERMS

psycholinguistics
phoneme
morpheme
semantics
semantic memory
syntax
pragmatics
phrase structure
constituents
modular (language)
transformational grammar
surface structure
deep structure
underlying structure
ambiguous sentences
kernel

transformational rules
cognitive-functional approach
nested structure
neurolinguistics
aphasia
Broca's area
Wernicke's area
lateralization
positron emission
    tomography (PET scan)
functional magnetic
    resonance imaging (fMRI)
direct-access hypothesis
indirect-access hypothesis
phonologically mediated
    hypothesis

dual-route hypothesis
whole-word approach
phonics approach
whole-language approach
discourse
processing cycles
inference
constructionist view of
    inferences
artificial intelligence (AI)
natural language
FRUMP
latent semantic analysis
    (LSA)

RECOMMENDED READINGS

Carroll, D. W. (2004). *Psychology of language* (4th ed.). Belmont, CA: Wadsworth. I strongly recommend this psycholinguistics textbook, which is clearly written and comprehensive.

Graesser, A. C., Gernsbacher, M. A., & Goldman, S. R. (2003a). *Handbook of discourse processes.* Mahwah, NJ: Erlbaum. Here's an excellent handbook that includes 13 chapters on a variety of topics related to discourse processing.

Healy, A. F., & Proctor, R. W. (Eds.). (2003). *Handbook of psychology* (Vol. 4). Hoboken, NJ: Wiley. Two chapters in this handbook are especially relevant for the current chapter, one by Rayner and his colleagues on reading and one by Butcher and Kintsch on text comprehension.

Rayner, K., et al. (2001). How psychological science informs the teaching of reading. *Psychological Science in the Public Interest, 2,* 31–74. Keith Rayner and his colleagues have prepared this special issue of a journal; it's especially useful for teachers who would like to know how to apply psychology research to the classroom.

Williams, J. D. (1999). *The teacher's grammar book.* Mahwah, NJ: Erlbaum. Most books on the psychology of language are difficult to understand; this was the most reader-friendly description I found for information on topics such as phrase-structure grammar and transformational-generative grammar.

ANSWERS TO DEMONSTRATION 9.1

Chapter 2: Visual recognition allows you to see letters and words, and auditory recognition allows you to hear phonemes and words. Chapter 3: Divided attention can permit you to take in information about two simultaneous verbal messages, whereas selective attention encourages you to pay attention to one message and ignore the other; saccadic eye movements are important in reading. Chapter 4: Working memory helps you store the stimuli (either visual or auditory) long enough to process and interpret them. Chapter 5: Long-term memory allows you to retrieve information you processed long ago. Chapter 6: The tip-of-the-tongue phenomenon means that you will sometimes be unable to access certain words, whereas metacomprehension allows you to determine whether you understand a verbal message. Chapter 7: You create mental models when you process a description about a spatial layout. Chapter 8: Semantic memory is responsible for the meaning of words and the relationships between concepts, whereas schemas and scripts provide background knowledge for processing language. *Note:* Other answers are also possible.

CHAPTER 10

Language II:
Language Production
and Bilingualism

Introduction

Speaking

Writing

Bilingualism and Second-Language Acquisition

PREVIEW

Whereas Chapter 9 examined language comprehension (listening and reading), Chapter 10 focuses on language production. The specific topics to be covered include speaking, writing, and bilingualism.

Our ability to produce spoken words and sentences is an impressive accomplishment. For example, we need to plan how to arrange the words in an orderly sequence within a sentence. Most of our spoken language is linguistically accurate, but we sometimes make speech errors such as slips-of-the-tongue. When we tell a story, the narrative typically follows a specific structure. The social context of speech is also crucial; for example, speakers must be certain that their conversational partners share the same background information.

Writing is an important activity for college students and many professionals. However, psychologists have only recently begun to develop a cognitive model of writing, which emphasizes the importance of working memory. Writing consists of three tasks that often overlap in time: planning, sentence generation, and revision. One clinical application of the research focuses on writing about emotional problems.

Bilingualism is a topic that demonstrates how humans can master listening, reading, speaking, and writing—in at least two languages. Therefore, bilingualism is an appropriate conclusion to our two-chapter exploration of language. Bilingual people seem to have a number of advantages over those who are monolingual. For example, they are more aware of language structure, and they perform better on tests measuring concept formation and problem solving. Compared with adults, children may learn to speak a second language with a less pronounced accent. However, adults and children are similar in their acquisition of vocabulary in that second language. There are also no consistent differences between adults and children with respect to their mastery of grammar in a second language.

INTRODUCTION

Consider the number of ways in which you have produced language today. Unless you are reading this chapter very early in the morning, you may have greeted a friend, talked to someone at breakfast, spoken on the telephone, taken notes on a reading assignment, sent an e-mail, or written a reminder to yourself.

Language is probably the most social of all our cognitive processes, and its social nature is especially obvious when we consider language production. Except for the notes and comments we make to ourselves, we are usually producing language in interactions with other people. Here's a question you may not have considered before: *Why* do we produce language in our interpersonal relationships? According to Guerin's (2003) analysis, most of our speech production is designed to accomplish at least one of the following goals:

1. To persuade someone to do something.
2. To persuade someone to say something (e.g., to establish a fact).
3. To influence someone to remain in a relationship, by keeping this person's attention or by entertaining this person.
4. To influence someone to remain in a relationship, by encouraging this person to like you.

Now consider another aspect of language production: Every sentence that is comprehended by one person must have been produced by somebody else. If psychologists distributed their research equitably, we would know just as much about language production as we know about language comprehension. Furthermore, Chapter 10 would be just as long as Chapter 9.

However, psychologists have tended to study language comprehension, rather than language production One reason researchers ignore language production is that they cannot typically manipulate the ideas that an individual wishes to say or write. In contrast, they can easily manipulate the text that a person hears or reads (Carroll, 2004; Fromkin & Bernstein Ratner, 1998). In addition, some cognitive psychology researchers may avoid studying language production because it is action oriented, and therefore reminiscent of the behaviorist approach (Bock & Griffin, 2000). Fortunately, however, psychologists are becoming somewhat more interested in the components of language production (e.g., Bock & Griffin, 2000; Clark & Van Der Wege, 2002; Fowler, 2003; Rapp & Goldrick, 2000; Wheeldon, 2000a).

Let us begin by examining spoken language, and then we'll consider written language. Our final topic, bilingualism, employs all the impressive skills of both language comprehension and language production, so it will serve as the final section of these two chapters on language.

SPEAKING

Every day, most of us spend several hours telling stories, chatting, quarreling, talking on the telephone, and speaking to ourselves. Even when we listen, we produce supportive comments such as "yeah" and "mm hm" (Gardner, 2001). Indeed, speaking is one of our most complex cognitive and motor skills (Bock & Griffin, 2000; Levelt, 1998). In this section of the chapter, we will first examine how we produce both individual words and sentences. Then we'll examine some common speech errors. Finally, we'll move beyond the sentence as we examine the production of discourse and the social context of speech.

Producing a Word

Like many cognitive processes, word production does not initially seem remarkable. After all, you simply open your mouth and a word emerges effortlessly. Word production becomes impressive, however, once we analyze the dimensions of the task. As we noted in Chapter 9, we can produce about two or three words each second (Levelt et al., 1999; Vigliocco & Hartsuiker, 2002). Furthermore, the average college-educated North American has a speaking vocabulary in the range of 75,000 to 100,000 words (Bock & Garnsey, 1998; Wingfield, 1993). When you are talking, then, you must select at least two words every second from your extensive storehouse of at least 75,000 words!

Furthermore, you must choose a word accurately, so that its grammatical, semantic, and phonological information are all correct (Cutting & Ferreira, 1999; Rapp & Goldrick, 2000). As Bock and Griffin (2000) point out, many factors "complicate the journey from mind to mouth" (p. 39).

Word production is the most active topic of research within the area of language production. An important, unresolved controversy focuses on the process of retrieving grammatical, semantic, and phonological information. Some researchers argue that speakers retrieve all three kinds of information at the same time (Damian & Martin, 1999; O'Seaghdha & Marin, 1997). According to this approach, for example, you look at an apple and simultaneously access the grammatical properties of *apple*, the meaning of *apple*, and the phonemes in the word *apple*.

Other researchers argue that we access each kind of information independently, with little interaction among them (Levelt et al., 1998, 1999; Pickering & Branigan, 1998; Roelofs & Baayen, 2002). For example, van Turennout and her colleagues (1998) conducted research with Dutch-speaking individuals. As in many languages—such as Spanish, French, and German—Dutch nouns have a grammatical gender. These researchers presented pictures of objects and animals, and the participants were asked to name the object as quickly as possible. Using the event-related potential technique (see p. 16), the researchers demonstrated that the speakers accessed the grammatical gender of the word about 40 milliseconds before the phonological properties of the word. These results suggest that the different kinds of information are not accessed exactly simultaneously, but with literally split-second timing.

When we produce a word, we execute elaborate motor movements of the mouth and other parts of the vocal system (Fowler, 2003). Interestingly, however, motor movements of your hands can sometimes help you remember the word you want to produce (Carroll, 2004; Goldin-Meadow, 1999). Frick-Horbury and Guttentag (1998) read the definitions for 50 low-frequency, concrete English nouns. For example, the definition "a pendulum-like instrument designed to mark exact time by regular ticking" (p. 59) was supposed to suggest the noun *metronome*. Notice, then, that this technique resembles the tip-of-the-tongue research described in Chapter 6.

In Frick-Horbury and Guttentag's (1998) study, however, half of the participants had their hand movements restricted; they had to hold a rod with both hands. These individuals produced an average of 19 words. In contrast, the participants with unrestricted hand movements produced an average of 24 words. According to the researchers, when our verbal system is unable to retrieve a word, gestures may sometimes activate relevant information.

Producing a Sentence

Every time you produce a sentence, you must overcome the limits of your memory and attention in order to plan and deliver that sentence (Bock, 1999; Bock & Huitema, 1999). Speech production requires a series of stages. We begin by mentally planning the **gist,** or the overall meaning, of the message we intend to generate. In other words, we begin by producing speech in a top-down fashion (Clark & Van Der Wege, 2002). During the second stage, we devise the general structure of the sentence, without selecting the exact words. In the third stage, we choose both the words and their specific forms (for example, not just the word *eat*, but the form *am eating*). In the fourth and final stage, we convert these intentions into speech by articulating the phonemes (Carroll, 2004; Yeni-Komshian, 1998). As you might expect, these stages of sentence production typically overlap in time. We often begin to plan the final part of a sentence before we have pronounced the first part of that sentence (Fowler, 2003; M. Smith, 2000).

Under ideal circumstances, a speaker moves rapidly through these four stages. For instance, Griffin and Bock (2000) showed college students a simple cartoon. In less than 2 seconds, the students began to produce a description such as, "The turtle is squirting the mouse with water."

Typically, we pause as we plan what we intend to say, with the pauses being longer for lengthy utterances. In general, these pauses occupy about half of our speaking time (Bock, 1995, 1999). When we are talking for an extended period (for example, telling a friend about a recent vacation), we alternate between hesitant phases and fluent phases. We therefore speak haltingly as we plan what we will say. Then, during the fluent phase, we are rewarded for our earlier planning, and the words flow more easily (Carroll, 2004; Clark & Wasow, 1998; Harley, 2001).

We often tackle an important problem when we are planning a sentence. We may have a general thought that we want to express, or we may have a mental image that needs to be conveyed verbally. These rather shapeless ideas must be translated into a statement that has a disciplined, linear shape, with words following one another in time. This problem of arranging words in an ordered, linear sequence is called the **linearization problem** (Fox Tree, 2000; Levelt, 1994). Try noticing how linearization usually occurs quite effortlessly. Consistent with Theme 2, you typically speak both rapidly and accurately. However, you may occasionally find yourself struggling, trying to describe several ideas simultaneously, at the very beginning of a description.

The speech-production process is more complex than you might initially imagine. For example, we must also plan the **prosody** of an utterance, or the "melody" of its intonation and stress (Fowler, 2003; Roelofs & Meyer, 1998; Wheeldon, 2000b). When you actually speak a sentence, more than 100 different muscles must coordinate their interactions (Levelt, 1994). Let's now consider the nature of the speech errors we occasionally make, as well as the production of discourse that is longer than a sentence.

Speech Errors

The speech that most people produce is generally very accurate and well formed, consistent with Theme 2. In spontaneous language samples, people make an error less than once every 500 sentences (Dell, Burger, & Svec, 1997; Vigliocco & Hartsuiker, 2002). However, we may pause in the middle of a sentence or start a new sentence before finishing the previous one. Naturally, the circumstances of the conversation can influence the number of speech errors. For example, people using the telephone to make airline reservations made errors that they later corrected at the rate of one error every 10 to 20 sentences (Nakatani & Hirschberg, 1994).

Even high-status speakers—including U.S. presidents—can sometimes make speech errors. For instance, the speech errors of President George W. Bush have been widely reported (e.g., Miller, 2001). In a talk in LaCrosse, Wisconsin, he announced, "Families is where our nation finds hope, where wings take dream" (October 18, 2000). In a speech to the Hispanic Scholarship Fund Institute in Washington, DC, President Bush said, "If a person doesn't have the capacity that we all want that person to have, I suspect hope is in the far distant future, if at all" (May 22, 2001).

Researchers have been particularly interested in the kind of speech errors called slips-of-the-tongue. **Slips-of-the-tongue** are errors in which sounds or entire words are rearranged between two or more different words. Let's look at these errors in more detail.

Types of Slip-of-the-Tongue Errors. Gary Dell (1986, 1995) proposes that three kinds of slips-of-the-tongue are especially common:

1. Sound errors, which occur when sounds in nearby words are exchanged—for example, *snow flurries→flow snurries.*
2. Morpheme errors, which occur when **morphemes** (the smallest meaningful units in language, such as *-ly* or *in-*) are exchanged in nearby words—for example, *self-destruct instruction→self-instruct destruction.*
3. Word errors, which occur when words are exchanged—for example, *writing a letter to my mother→writing a mother to my letter.*

Each of these three kinds of errors can take several forms, in addition to the exchange errors listed above. For example, people make anticipation errors (*reading list→leading list*), perseveration errors (*waking rabbits→waking wabbits*), and deletions (*same state→same sate*). Anticipatory errors are especially common, because we are likely to be planning ahead, rather than reflecting on the words we have already said. Furthermore, we are likely to create a word (e.g., *leading*), rather than a nonword (e.g., *wabbit*) when we make a slip-of-the-tongue error (Rapp & Goldrick, 2000). Finally, we seldom create a word that begins with an unlikely letter sequence; an English speaker rarely creates a slip-of-the-tongue such as *dlorm* when trying to say *dorm* (Dell et al., 2000).

In almost all cases, the errors occur across items from the same category (Carroll, 2004; Clark & Van Der Wege, 2002; Fowler, 2003). For instance, in sound errors, initial consonants interchange with other initial consonants (as in the *flow snurries* example). In morpheme errors, prefixes interchange with other prefixes (as in the *self-instruct* example). In word errors, people interchange members of the same grammatical category (as in the *mother to my letter* example). The pattern of these errors suggests that the words we are currently pronouncing are influenced by both the words we have already spoken and the words we are planning to speak (Dell, Burger, & Svec, 1997).

Dell and his colleagues propose an elaborate and comprehensive theory for speech errors that is similar to the parallel distributed processing approach and includes the concept of spreading activation (Dell, 1986, 1995; Dell, Burger & Svec, 1997; Dell et al., 1997). Let us consider a brief overview of what might happen to encourage a sound error. As Dell argues, when you are constructing a sentence, you construct a representation at the word-meaning level. Your word-meaning representation is fairly complete before you begin to represent the sentence at the sound level. When you begin to speak, each element of the word you are planning to say will activate the sound elements to which they are linked. For example, Figure 10.1 shows how the words in the tongue twister "She sells seashells" might activate each of the six sounds in the last word, *seashells.*

Usually, we utter the sounds that are most highly activated, and usually these sounds are the appropriate ones. However, each sound can be activated by several different words. Notice, for example, that the *sh* sound in the sound-level representation of *seashells* (that is, *seshelz)* is highly "charged" because it receives activation from the first word in the sentence, *she*, as well as the *sh* in *seashells.* As Dell (1986, 1995) emphasizes, errors are a natural result from the theory's assumptions. Incorrect items can sometimes have activation levels that are just as high as (or higher than) the correct items. In Figure 10.1, the activation level for *sh* is just as high as the level for *s.* By mistake, a speaker may select an incorrect item in a sentence, such as "She sells sheashells." Notice that the rhythm of the sentence also encourages the speaker to say "sheashells."

In recent research, Dell and his colleagues have developed parallel distributed processing models to explain speech errors (Dell, Burger, & Svec, 1997; Dell et al., 1997; Foygel & Dell, 2000). The model argues that word selection can be explained by spreading activation throughout a lexical network. This model has successfully predicted the pattern of errors in both normal and aphasic speakers; speakers sometimes produce sounds that have high activation levels, even though these sounds may not be correct.

Try Demonstration 10.1 to determine the form and function of the slips-of-the-tongue that you typically make or hear. Incidentally, listeners often fail to detect slips-of-the-tongue, thereby committing what we could call "slips-of-the-ear" (Ferber, 1991; Meyer, 2000). As you know from the material on context and phonemic restoration in Chapter 2, we often fail to notice speech errors because context effects and top-down processing (Theme 5) are often so strong.

FIGURE 10.1

An Example of Dell's Model of Sound Processing in Sentence Production (simplified). See text for explanation.

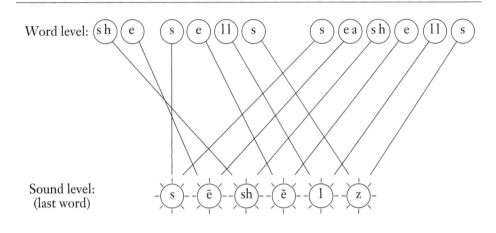

🐚 **Demonstration 10.1**

Slips-of-the-Tongue

Keep a record of all the slips-of-the-tongue that you either hear or make your-self in the next 2 days. Classify each slip as a sound error, morpheme error, or word error. Furthermore, decide whether the mistake is an exchange error, an anticipation error, or some other type. Also note whether the mistake occurs across items from the same category. Finally, see if you can determine why the mistake occurred, using an analysis similar to Dell's.

Producing Discourse

When we speak, we typically produce **discourse,** or language units that are larger than a sentence (Bamberg & Moissinac, 2003; Treiman et al., 2003). Psycholinguists have paid the most attention to the **narrative,** the type of discourse in which some-one describes a series of events. Some narratives describe actual events, and some are fictional. The events in a narrative are conveyed in a time-related sequence, and they are often emotionally involving (H. H. Clark, 1994; Guerin, 2003; Schiffrin, 1994). Storytellers have a specific goal that must be conveyed, but the organization is not fully preplanned at the beginning of the story (H. H. Clark, 1994). To achieve their goal, storytellers often choose their words carefully in order to present their actions in a favorable light (Berger, 1997; Edwards, 1997).

The format of a narrative is unusual, because it allows the speaker to "hold the floor" for an extended period. During that time, six parts of the narrative are usually conveyed: (1) a brief overview of the story, (2) a summary of the characters and setting, (3) an action that made the situation complicated, (4) the point of the story, (5) the resolution of the story, and (6) the final signal that the narrative is complete (for example, ". . . and so that's how I ended up traveling to Colorado with a complete stranger"). These features tend to make the story cohesive and well organized (H. H. Clark, 1994). Now that you know something about the function and structure of narratives, try Demonstration 10.2.

The Social Context of Speech

When we speak, we need to plan the content of our language. We must produce relatively error-free speech, and we must also plan the message of our discourse. In addition to these challenging assignments, we need to be attuned to the social context of speech. Language is really a social instrument (Clark & Van Der Wege, 2002; Guerin, 2003; Schober & Brennan, 2003). In fact, conversation is like a complicated dance (Clark, 1985, 1994). Speakers cannot simply utter words aloud and expect to be understood. Instead, speakers must consider their conversation partners, make numerous assumptions about those partners, and design appropriate utterances.

This complicated dance requires precise coordination. When two people enter a doorway simultaneously, they need to coordinate their motor actions. Similarly, two speakers must coordinate turn taking, they must agree on the meaning of ambiguous terms, and they must understand each other's intentions (Clark & Van Der Wege, 2002). When Helen tells Sam, "The Bakers are on their way," both participants in the conversation need to understand that this is an indirect invitation for Sam to start dinner, rather than to call the police for protection (Clark, 1985).

The knowledge of the social rules that underlie language use is called **pragmatics** (Carroll, 2004). Pragmatics focuses on how speakers successfully communicate

---

⊙ **Demonstration 10.2**

The Structure of Narratives

During the next few weeks, try to notice—in your daily conversations—what happens when someone you know begins to tell a story. First, how does the storyteller announce that she or he is about to begin the narrative? Does the structure of the narrative match the six-part sequence we discussed? Does the storyteller attempt to check whether the listeners have the appropriate background knowledge? What other characteristics do you notice that distinguish this kind of discourse from a normal conversation in which people take turns speaking?

messages to their audience. Two important topics in the research on pragmatics are common ground and an understanding of directives.

Common Ground. Suppose that a young man named Andy asks his friend Lisa, "How was your weekend?" and Lisa answers, "It was like being in Conshohocken again." Andy will understand this reply only if they share a similar understanding about the characteristics or events that took place in Conshohocken. In fact, we would expect Lisa to make this remark only if she is certain that she and Andy share the appropriate common ground (Clark & Van Der Wege, 2002; Gerrig & Littman, 1990; Krauss & Chiu, 1998).

Common ground means that the conversationalists share the similar background knowledge, schemas, and experiences that are necessary for mutual understanding (Clark & Van Der Wege, 2002; Fox Tree, 2000). To guarantee conversational coherence, the speakers need to collaborate to make certain that they share common ground. For instance, the listener should provide positive evidence of understanding, such as the comment "uh-huh" or perhaps a nod of the head (Gardner, 2001). Speakers should also monitor their conversational partners to make certain that they are paying attention, and they must clarify any misunderstandings if their listeners look puzzled.

One day, our plumber called me from the hardware store, where he was trying to locate some handles for our washbowl faucet. As he described the various models over the telephone, I instantly realized that we were replicating a classic study by Clark and Wilkes-Gibbs (1986) on the collaboration process involved in establishing common ground. Demonstration 10.3 is a modification of their study, in which people worked together to arrange complex figures.

The participants in Clark and Wilkes-Gibbs's (1986) study played this game for six trials; each trial consisted of arranging all 12 figures in order. On the first trial, the director required an average of nearly four turns to describe each figure and make certain that the matcher understood the reference. (A typical "turn" consisted of a statement from the director, followed by a question or a guess from the matcher.) As Figure 10.2 shows, however, the director and the matcher soon developed a mutual shorthand, and the number of required turns decreased rapidly over trials. Just as two dancers become more skilled as they practice together at coordinating their movements, conversational partners become more skilled in communicating efficiently.

The term **lexical entrainment** refers to this pattern that two communicators use when they create and adopt a standard term to refer to an object (Brennan & Clark, 1996). According to the research, people who work together can quickly and efficiently develop lexical entrainment (Garrod, 1999; Markman & Makin, 1998; Schober & Brennan, 2003).

To study lexical entrainment in more detail, Bortfeld and Brennan (1997) used photos of 15 different kinds of chairs. In some cases, a student whose first language was English was paired with a student whose first language was Japanese, Chinese, or Korean. In other cases, both students spoke English as their first language. Interestingly, both kinds of student pairs showed the same degree of lexical entrainment. Both kinds of pairs soon developed names for the chairs such as "the flowered lounge

⑨ Demonstration 10.3

Collaborating to Establish Common Ground

For this demonstration, you need to make two photocopies of the figures below. Then cut the figures apart, keeping each sheet's figures in a separate pile and making certain the dot is at the top of each figure. Now locate two volunteers and a watch that can measure time in seconds. Your volunteers should sit across from each other or at separate tables, with their figures in front of them. Neither person should be able to see the other's figures.

Appoint one person to be the "director" and the other the "matcher." The director should arrange the figures in random order in two rows of six figures each. This person's task is to describe the first figure in enough detail so that the "matcher" is able to identify that figure and place it in Position 1 in front of him or her. The goal is for the matcher to place all 12 figures in the same order as the director's figures. They may use any kind of verbal descriptions they choose, but no gestures or imitation of body position. Record how long it takes them to reach their goal, and then make sure that the figures do match.

Ask them to try the game two more times, with the same person serving as director. Record the times again, and note whether the time decreases on the second and third trials; are the volunteers increasingly efficient in establishing common ground? Do they tend to develop a standard vocabulary (for example, "the ice skater") to refer to a given figure?

chair" or "the wooden high chair." Lexical entrainment is apparently a fairly natural kind of pragmatic skill. Speakers clearly work collaboratively to agree on the names they will use in a conversation.

We have been discussing how people can establish common ground, even with strangers. However, this process is far from perfect. For example, speakers often

FIGURE 10.2

Average Number of Turns That Directors in Clark and Wilkes-Gibbs's Study Required for Each Figure, as a Function of Trial Number.

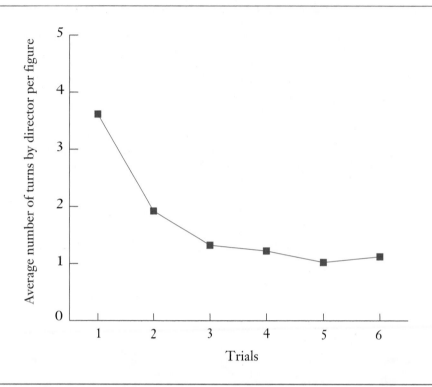

Trials

Source: Clark & Wilkes-Gibbs, 1986.

overestimate their listeners' ability to understand a message (Keysar & Henly, 2002; Schober & Brennan, 2003). In addition, speakers tend to assume that listeners need and want the same things the speakers themselves do (Nickerson, 2001). Also, as you might imagine, people are less likely to effectively establish common ground if they are under time pressure (Clark & Van Der Wege, 2002; Horton & Keysar, 1996).

Directives. A **directive** is a sentence that requests someone to do something. In general, the most polite directives require more words (Brown & Levinson, 1987). For example, "Could you possibly by any chance lend me your car for just a few minutes?" would be considered more polite than, "Could you lend me your car?" However, some of these elaborate directives are perceived to be overly polite—even ironic—and so they may actually seem insulting (Kumon-Nakamura et al., 1995).

Gibbs (1986) investigated the hypothesis that speakers will state their directives in a format that anticipates potential obstacles to compliance. Participants in this study read scenarios of everyday situations. They were asked to imagine themselves in each situation, and to write down one sentence that they might say. A typical scenario described going to a restaurant and ordering something that might not be available.

The results showed that people were most likely to frame their requests in terms of a possible obstacle that might create a problem. In the restaurant scenario, for example, 68% of the sentences began, "Do you have . . ."; requests such as "I'd like . . ." were much less common. Try noticing how you word your own requests. Do you tend to address a potential obstacle?

Many other directives are asked in the form of an indirect request. An **indirect request** is stated like a request for information, even though it's really a request for someone to do something or to *stop* doing something (Clark & Van Der Wege, 2002; Gibbs, 2003). For example, a teacher might ask a class, "What are you laughing at?" The teacher is not really wondering about the source of the laughter. Instead, he or she is requesting silence. Other indirect requests take the form of hints. You probably know someone who asks vague questions like, "I wonder if there's any butter in the refrigerator?" instead of the more direct question, "Would you get me some butter, please?" Obviously, indirect requests offer numerous opportunities for misunderstandings!

In short, speakers are typically attuned to the social context of speech. They usually work to achieve common ground, and they take care in selecting suitable directives.

✺ Section Summary: *Speaking*

1. Researchers are much less likely to conduct studies on language production than studies on language comprehension, but some components of production are now being examined.

2. Word production is an impressive accomplishment; researchers disagree about whether grammatical, semantic, and phonological information about a word is accessed simultaneously or at different times.

3. Four stages in producing a sentence include working out the gist, formulating the general structure of the sentence, making the word choice, and articulating the phonemes; these processes overlap in time.

4. Speaking also requires speakers to overcome the linearization problem and to plan the prosody of their messages.

5. According to Dell and his colleagues, slips-of-the-tongue occur because a speech sound other than the intended one is highly activated; to explain these errors, these researches have developed a parallel distributed processing model with spreading activation.

6. A narrative is a kind of discourse that typically includes certain specified story components.

7. The pragmatic rules of speech regulate social components of speech production such as common ground (often including lexical entrainment) and the skillful use of directives (often including indirect requests).

WRITING

Writing is a task that requires virtually every cognitive activity described in this textbook (Theme 4). Think about the last writing project you completed, and consider how that project required attention, memory, imagery, background knowledge, metacognition, reading, problem solving, creativity, reasoning, and decision making (Kellogg, 1994, 1996).

Writing is also an important component of many people's occupations. For example, technical and professional people report that writing occupies about 30% of their typical working day (Faigley & Miller, 1982; Kellogg, 1989).

However, writing is one of the least understood linguistic tasks; research in this area is relatively limited (Harley, 2001; Levy & Ransdell, 1995). For example, several major handbooks in cognitive psychology and cognitive science do not even include the term *writing* in their indexes (Bechtel & Graham, 1998a; Healy & Proctor, 2003; Pashler, 2002; Wheeldon, 2000a; Wilson & Keil, 1999). We noted earlier in this chapter that research on understanding speech is more prevalent than research on speech production. The contrast is even more dramatic when we compare written language. Reading inspires hundreds of books and research articles each year, whereas writing inspires only a handful. Even a widespread activity like composing an e-mail is seldom studied (Daiute, 2000; Finch, 2003; Olson & Olson, 2003).

Writing and speaking share many cognitive components. However, writing is more likely to be performed in isolation, with more complex syntax and more extensive revisions. Writing also requires more time (Ellis & Beattie, 1986; Harley, 2001). When you speak, you are more likely to refer to yourself. When speaking, you are also more interactive with your audience, and you have a better opportunity to establish common ground with this audience (Chafe & Danielewicz, 1987; Gibbs, 1998).

Writing consists of three phases: planning, sentence generation, and revising. However—like the similar stages we discussed in terms of understanding and producing spoken language—these tasks often overlap in time (Kellogg, 1994, 1996; Ransdell & Levy, 1999). For example, you may be planning your overall writing strategy while generating parts of several sentences. All components of the task are complex, and they strain the limits of attention (Kellogg, 1994, 1998; Torrance & Jeffery, 1999). In fact, a classic article on writing emphasizes that a person working on a writing assignment is "a thinker on full-time cognitive overload" (Flower & Hayes, 1980, p. 33). Still, consistent with Theme 2, we generally manage to coordinate these tasks quite skillfully when we produce written language.

Let's begin our exploration of writing by considering a cognitive model of the writing process. Then we'll examine the three phases of writing: planning, sentence generation, and revising. Finally, we'll discuss several examples of writing in real-world settings.

A Cognitive Model of Writing

Several leading researchers in the area of writing have devised a model that emphasizes the importance of cognitive processes and also includes other psychological factors (Chenoweth & Hayes, 2001; Hayes, 1996; Kellogg, 1994, 2001a, 2001b). For instance, writing is influenced by social factors, such as the audience who will read your paper (Hayes, 1996). Motor factors also influence your writing. You may write differently when using a computer rather than a pen and paper (Kellogg, 2001a).

Motivational factors are also important. For example, **self-efficacy** is your own assessment of your capabilities in a certain area. If two students are similar in writing ability, the student with high writing self-efficacy will typically produce a better paper for an academic course (Hayes, 1996; Pajares, 2003).

Working memory plays a central role in the cognitive approach to writing. In Chapter 4, we discussed Alan Baddeley's model of working memory. **Working memory** refers to the brief, immediate memory for material we are currently processing, as well as the coordination of our ongoing mental activities. One component of working memory, the **phonological loop,** stores a limited number of sounds for a short period of time. People often talk to themselves as they generate sentences during writing—a procedure that requires the phonological loop (Kellogg, 1996). Another component of working memory, the **visuospatial sketchpad,** stores both visual and spatial information. The visuospatial sketchpad is useful when writers try to visualize the order of the sections of a paper and when they need to include figures and graphs in their paper (Kellogg, 1996).

As you may recall, the most important component of Baddeley's model of working memory is called the central executive. The **central executive** integrates information from the phonological loop, the visuospatial sketchpad, and the episodic buffer. The central executive also plays a role in attention, planning, and coordinating other cognitive activities. Because writing is such a complex task, the central executive is active in virtually every phase of the writing process (Kellogg, 1996, 1998, 2001a). For example, it coordinates the planning phase, and it is essential when we generate sentences. It also oversees the revision process. The limited capacity of the central executive makes the writing task especially challenging.

So far, we have discussed how writing is influenced by the social environment, the physical environment, motivational factors, and several components of working memory. A final important cognitive factor is long-term memory. Some important components of long-term memory include the writer's semantic memory, specific expertise about the topic, general schemas, knowledge about the audience for whom the paper is intended, and knowledge about the writing style to be used for the particular assignment (Hayes, 1996; Kellogg, 2001b). As you can see, our summary of the cognitive approach to writing provides an opportunity to review practically every topic we have discussed in the earlier chapters of this textbook!

Planning the Writing Assignment

The first stage in planning to write is to generate a list of ideas, a process called **prewriting.** Prewriting is difficult and strategic—much different from many relatively automatic language tasks (Collins, 1998; Torrance et al., 1996). As you can imagine, students differ enormously in the quality of the ideas generated during this phase (Bruning et al., 1999). Research has shown that good writers spend more high-quality time in planning during prewriting (Hayes, 1989).

Research strongly supports the value of outlining a paper before you begin to write (Kellogg, 1988, 1994, 1998; Rau & Sebrechts, 1996). An outline may help you avoid overloaded attention. It may also help you resolve the linearization problem, which occurs in writing as well as in speaking. You've probably had the experience of beginning to write a paper, only to find that each of several interrelated ideas needs to be placed first! An outline can help you sort these ideas into an orderly, linear sequence.

◎ Demonstration 10.4

Producing Sentences

For this exercise, you should be alone in a room, with no one else present to inhibit your spontaneity. Take a piece of paper on which you will write two sentences as requested below. For this writing task, however, say out loud the thoughts you are considering while you write each sentence. Then read the next section, on sentence generation.

1. Write one sentence to answer the question, "What are the most important characteristics that a good student should have?"
2. Write one sentence to answer the question, "What do you consider to be your strongest personality characteristics—the ones that you most admire in yourself?"

Sentence Generation During Writing

Before you read further, try Demonstration 10.4, which requires you to generate some sentences. During sentence generation, the writer must translate the general ideas developed during planning, thus creating the actual sentences of the text.

An important characteristic of sentence generation is that hesitant phases tend to alternate with fluent phases, just as we discussed for spoken language (Chenoweth & Hayes, 2001). Think about your own pattern when you were writing the sentences in Demonstration 10.4. Did you show a similar pattern of pauses alternating with fluent writing?

Earlier in this chapter, we discussed slips-of-the-tongue. People also make errors when they write, whether they use a keyboard or a pen. However, writing errors are usually confined to a spelling error within a single word, whereas speaking errors often reflect switches between words (Berg, 2002).

The Revision Phase of Writing

The revision phase of writing should emphasize the importance of organization and coherence, so that the parts of your paper are interrelated (Britton, 1996). In order to revise what you have written, you need to reconsider whether your paper accomplishes the goals of the assignment. The revision task *should* be time consuming. As Kellogg (1998) points out, there are numerous opportunities for writers to make mistakes!

The most effective writers use flexible revision strategies, and they make substantial changes if their paper doesn't accomplish its goal (Harley, 2001). However, college students typically devote little time to revising a paper (Torrance et al., 1999). For instance, college students in one study estimated that they had spent 30% of their writing time on revising their papers, but observation of their actual writing behavior showed that they consistently spent less than 10% of their time on revisions (Levy & Ransdell, 1995). We have seen that students' metacognitions about reading comprehension are not very accurate (Chapter 6); their metacognitions about the writing process also seem to be inaccurate.

As you can imagine, expert writers are especially skilled at making appropriate revisions. Hayes and his colleagues (1987) compared the revision strategies of seven first-year college students and seven expert writers. Everyone was given the same poorly written two-page letter and was asked to revise it for an audience of young college students.

The results showed that the first-year students typically approached the text one sentence at a time. They fixed relatively minor problems with spelling and grammar, but they ignored problems of organization, focus, and transition between ideas. The students were also more likely to judge some defective sentences as being appropriate. For example, several students found no fault with the sentence, "In sports like fencing for a long time many of our varsity team members had no previous experience anyway." Finally, the students were less likely than the expert writers to diagnose the source of a problem in a sentence. A student might say, "This sentence just doesn't sound right," whereas an expert might say, "The subject and the verb don't agree here."

In other situations, however, expertise can be a drawback. Specifically, if you know too much, you may not recognize that the text could be unclear to readers with little background knowledge (Hayes, 1989). Writing—like speaking—requires us to establish common ground with our audience.

One final caution about the revision process focuses on the proofreading stage. Daneman and Stainton (1993) confirmed what many of us already suspected: You can proofread someone else's writing more accurately than your own. Our extreme familiarity with what we have written helps us overlook the errors in the text. Top-down processing (Theme 5) triumphs again! Many of my students also seem to assume that the spell-check feature on their word processors will locate every mistake, but it identifies the nonwords only. It doesn't protest when you've entered the word *line*, rather than the word *life*. Furthermore, you've probably found that you cannot proofread your paper for spelling when you are focusing on the paper's content.

Writing in Real-World Settings

We noted earlier that writing occupies about 30% of many people's workday. However, researchers have generally ignored how we write in real-world settings. Fortunately, we do have some information on three topics: (1) How psychologists write for professional journals; (2) how people write in selected occupations; and (3) how the writing process helps many people make sense out of their psychological problems.

Psychologists' Professional Writing Style. As you have undoubtedly discovered, writing style in psychology courses and in the natural sciences is generally different from the writing style used in humanities courses. The best way to examine these differences is to read a style manual like the *Publication Manual of the American Psychological Association* (American Psychological Association, 2001).

Robert Madigan and his colleagues (1995) explored the characteristics of articles that had been published in psychology journals. Like most psychology journals, the journals in their sample required that writers complied with the guidelines specified in the *Publication Manual*. The *Manual* requires journal articles to follow a specific schema, a formula that includes an introduction, a methods section, a results section, and a discussion section.

Madigan and his coauthors (1995) also noted a particular writing style in the psychology journal articles. For instance, psychologists try to avoid overgeneralizations by using "hedges"—phrases such as *tend to*, *suggest that*, and *in this case*. In addition, psychologists writing a journal article typically avoid flowery language or vivid metaphors. The goal is to draw attention to the research, not to the language used to describe the research.

Most psychologists spend hours each week on various writing tasks. Ironically, however, very few have conducted empirical research on this extremely complex cognitive activity.

Writing on the Job. Dias and his colleagues (1999) have studied the differences between writing for college courses and writing in workplace settings, such as a business or a social work agency. When you write a paper for a psychology course, you are writing for the professor. You know that your writing will be positively evaluated if it demonstrates qualities such as originality and critical thinking. In the workplace, those qualities are seldom valued. Instead, your writing must be consistent with the goals of your employer. For instance, the report you write may have legal or financial consequences for an organization. If you work in a school setting or a social work agency, your report may affect people's lives. When you write a document in the workplace, you may also need to revise it several times, based on suggestions from a supervisor. This phase is seldom relevant in the college classroom. In summary, when college students make the transition from the classroom to the workplace, they must adopt a different perspective, because their writing will now be evaluated in terms of its contributions to an organization.

Writing About Emotional Problems. James Pennebaker and his colleagues have discovered an important new application of the writing process (Pennebaker & Graybeal, 2001; Pennebaker et al., 2003). Specifically, when people write about a personally upsetting experience, their mental and physical health often improves. In a series of studies, these researchers invited people to come to their laboratory and write for 15 to 20 minutes a day on 3 to 4 consecutive days. The participants in the experimental group were instructed to write about a previous traumatic experience. In contrast, the participants in the control group wrote about trivial topics for the same amount of time.

Pennebaker and his coauthors (2003) discovered that students who had been in the experimental condition began to earn better grades than those in the control condition. Furthermore, unemployed people in the experimental condition were more likely to find employment. The researchers also found that the participants in the experimental condition were more likely than those in the control condition to show improvements in their immune function, measures of stress, and other indexes of good physical health.

Interestingly, an analysis of the writing samples showed that the best predictor of physical health was the number of words that revealed cognitive activity (e.g., *understand* and *think*). In contrast, the number of words revealing emotions (e.g., *joyful* and *angry*) was not a strong predictor of physical health. Apparently, the benefits from the writing experience can be traced to creating an understanding of the painful experience. The words we write can therefore have an important effect on our future well-being.

Section Summary: *Writing*

1. Writing requires numerous other cognitive activities, but it has received little research attention.

2. The cognitive model of writing emphasizes the importance of social factors, motivational factors, working memory, and long-term memory.

3. Good writers spend high-quality time in planning; outlining also improves one's writing.

4. When people generate sentences during writing, their fluent phases alternate with hesitant phases.

5. Expert writers are more likely than beginning college students to revise a paper thoroughly, and they are also more likely to diagnose defective sentences. Finally, people proofread others' writing more accurately than their own.

6. According to the research on writing in the real world: (a) The writing style in psychology is different from the style used in other disciplines; (b) writing in the workplace emphasizes the goals of the employer, rather than originality or critical thinking; and (c) when people write about a personally upsetting experience, their mental and physical health often improves.

BILINGUALISM AND SECOND-LANGUAGE ACQUISITION

So far, these two chapters on language have considered four impressively complicated cognitive tasks: understanding spoken language, reading, speaking, and writing. These tasks require the simultaneous coordination of cognitive skills and social knowledge. We can marvel that human beings can manage all these tasks in one language. But then we must remind ourselves that many people master two or more languages.

A **bilingual** speaker is a person who—in everyday life—uses two languages that differ (Francis, 1999). Technically, we should use the term **multilingual** to refer to someone who uses more than two languages, but psycholinguists often use the term *bilingual* to include multilinguals as well. Some bilinguals learn two languages simultaneously during childhood, an arrangement called **simultaneous bilingualism.** Other bilinguals experience **sequential bilingualism;** this person's native language is referred to as the **first language,** and the nonnative language that he or she acquires is the **second language.**

In this section on bilingualism, let's first discuss some background information. Then we'll note some advantages that people experience when they are bilingual. Our final topic will be an In Depth feature exploring the relationship between age of acquisition of a second language and proficiency in that second language.

Background on Bilingualism

About half of the people in the world are at least somewhat bilingual (Fabbro, 1999). Some people live in bilingual regions, such as Quebec, Northern Wales, Belgium, or Switzerland. Others become bilingual because their home language is not the language used for school and business. For example, Zulu speakers in South Africa must learn English. People also become bilingual because colonization has imposed another language upon them (Bialystok, 2001). Still others become bilingual because they have studied another language in school, or because they grew up in homes where two languages were used routinely. In addition, immigrants moving to a new country usually need to master the language of that culture.

English may be the most common language in both Canada and the United States, but many other languages are also widely used in these countries. Table 10.1 shows the 10 languages most frequently "spoken at home" in the United States. Table 10.2 shows the 10 languages most frequently listed as a person's "mother tongue" in Canada. As you can see from both tables, bilingualism is an important issue in the lives of many North Americans.

When children in North America speak a language other than English in their homes, the educational system typically pressures them to acquire English at school. However, schools seldom appreciate the value of keeping a child fluent in a first language such as Korean, Arabic, or Spanish (Bialystok, 2001; García et al., 1998; Snow, 1998).

TABLE 10.1

Ten Languages Most Frequently Spoken at Home in the United States, Based on the 2000 U.S. Census (for people aged 5 and older).

Language	Estimated Number of Speakers[1]
English	215,200,000
Spanish	28,100,000
Chinese	2,000,000
French	1,600,000
German	1,400,000
Tagalog[2]	1,200,000
Vietnamese	1,000,000
Italian	1,000,000
Korean	900,000
Russian	700,000

Notes: (1) The number of speakers is estimated to the nearest 100,000.

(2) Tagalog is a language spoken in the Philippines.

Source: Shin & Bruno, 2003.

TABLE 10.2

Ten Languages Most Frequently Identified as the "Mother Tongue" in Canada, Based on the 2001 Statistics Canada Census.

Language	Estimated Number of Speakers
English	17,352,315
French	6,703,325
Chinese	853,745
Italian	469,485
German	438,080
Punjabi[1]	271,220
Spanish	245,495
Portuguese	213,815
Polish	208,375
Arabic	199,940

Note: (1) Punjabi is a language spoken in India and Pakistan.

Source: Statistics Canada, 2001.

As you can imagine, the topic of bilingualism has important political and social psychological implications, especially when educators and politicians make statements about various ethnic groups (Genesee & Gándara, 1999; Phillipson, 2000). These same social psychological forces are important when an individual wants to become bilingual. Two important predictors of success in acquiring a second language are a person's motivation and his or her attitude toward the people who speak that language (Gass & Selinker, 2001; Leather & James, 1996; Tokuhama-Espinosa, 2001). In fact, researchers have tried to predict how well English Canadian high school students will learn French. Research showed that the students' attitude toward French Canadians was just as important as their cognitive, language-learning aptitude (Gardner & Lambert, 1959; Lambert, 1992).

As you might expect, the relationship between attitudes and language proficiency also works in the reverse direction. Specifically, elementary school English Canadians who learned French developed more positive attitudes toward French Canadians than did children in a monolingual control group of English Canadian children (Genesee & Gándara, 1999; Lambert, 1987).

In the last decade, bilingualism has become an increasingly popular topic in psychology and linguistics. For instance, this interdisciplinary area now has its own journal, *Bilingualism: Language & Culture*. Several books published in the current decade explore bilingualism and second-language learning. These books address issues such as political aspects of bilingualism (Phillipson, 2000), bilingualism during childhood (Cenoz & Genesee, 2001; Döpke, 2001; Hall & Verplaetse, 2000; Nelson et al., 2001; Tokuhama-Espinosa, 2001), and teaching a second language to college students (Gass & Mackey, 2000; Gass & Selinker, 2001; Ohta, 2001; Rosenthal, 2000; Silva & Matsuda, 2001).

Now that you have some background on bilingualism, let's consider two topics that are especially important for cognitive psychologists: (1) the advantages of bilingualism and (2) the relationship between age of acquisition and language mastery.

Advantages of Bilingualism

Early-twentieth-century theorists proposed that bilingualism produced cognitive deficits because the brain must store two linguistic systems (Carroll, 2004; García et al., 1998). However, in the 1960s, researchers began to discover that bilinguals often scored higher than monolinguals on a variety of tasks. In one of the best-known studies, for example, bilinguals were more advanced in school, they scored better on tests of first-language skills, and they showed greater mental flexibility (Lambert, 1990; Peal & Lambert, 1962).

Bilingual people have one tremendous advantage over monolinguals: They can communicate in two languages. Even 10-year-olds can translate spoken and written language with impressive accuracy (Bialystok, 2001).

In addition to gaining fluency in a second language, bilinguals seem to have a number of other advantages over monolinguals, including the following:

1. Bilinguals actually acquire more expertise in their native (first) language (van Hell & Dijkstra, 2002). For example, English-speaking Canadian children whose classes are taught in French gain greater understanding of English-language structure (Diaz, 1985; Lambert et al., 1991). Bilingual children are also more likely to realize that a word such as *rainbow* can be divided into two morphemes, *rain* and *bow* (Campbell & Sais, 1995). In addition, preschool bilingual children are more likely to appreciate that a printed symbol stands for a word (Bialystok, 1997).

2. Bilinguals excel at paying selective attention to relatively subtle aspects of a language task, ignoring more obvious linguistic characteristics (Bialystok, 1992, 2001; Bialystok & Majumder, 1998; Cromdal, 1999). For example, Bilaystok and Majumder gave third-grade children sentences that were grammatically correct but semantically incorrect (for example, "The dog meows"). The bilingual children were more likely than the monolingual children to recognize that the sentence was grammatically correct.

3. Bilinguals are more aware that the names assigned to concepts are arbitrary (Bialystok, 1987, 1988; Cromdal, 1999; Hakuta, 1986). For example, monolingual children cannot imagine that a cow could just as easily have been assigned the name *dog*. A number of studies have examined **metalinguistics,** or knowledge about the form and structure of language. On many measures of metalinguistic skill—but not all of them—bilinguals outperform monolinguals (Bialystok, 1988, 1992, 2001; Campbell & Sais, 1995; Galambos & Goldin-Meadow, 1990; Galambos & Hakuta, 1988).

4. Bilingual children are more sensitive to some pragmatic aspects of language (Comeau & Genesee, 2001). For example, English-speaking children whose classes are taught in French are more aware than monolinguals that, when you speak to a blindfolded child, you need to supply additional information (Genesee et al., 1975).

5. Bilingual children are better at following complicated instructions and performing tasks where the instructions change from one trial to the next (Bialystock, 1999; Hamers & Blanc, 1989; Powers & López, 1985).

7. Bilingual children perform better than monolinguals on tests of creativity, such as thinking of a wide variety of uses for a paper clip (Hamers & Blanc, 1989; Ricciardelli, 1992; Scott, 1973).

8. Bilinguals perform better on concept-formation tasks and on tests of nonverbal intelligence that require reorganization of visual patterns (Peal & Lambert, 1962). Bilinguals also score higher on problem-solving tasks that require them to ignore irrelevant information (Bialystok, 2001; Bialystok & Codd, 1997; Bialystok & Majumder, 1998).

Ellen Bialystok (2001) examined a wide range of bilingual advantages. She concluded that most advantages can be traced to an important factor: Bilingual children are especially skilled in selective-attention tasks where they must inhibit the most obvious response. This experience with selective attention may facilitate the development of selected regions in the frontal lobe.

The disadvantages of being bilingual are trivial. People who use two languages extensively may subtly alter how they pronounce some speech sounds in both languages (Caramazza et al., 1973; Sancier & Fowler, 1997). Bilinguals are also slightly slower in making some kinds of decisions about language, though these are unlikely to inhibit communication (Amrhein, 1999). For example, an English-French bilingual may be momentarily uncertain whether a passage is written in English or in French (Taylor & Taylor, 1990). Bilinguals may also experience a slight disadvantage in language-processing speed, in comparison to monolinguals, but this disadvantage is far outweighed by the advantages of being able to communicate effectively in two languages.

IN DEPTH

Second-Language Proficiency as a Function of Age of Acquisition

A number of years ago, I met a family who had moved to the United States from Iceland and had been in their new country only a week. Both of these highly intelligent and highly educated parents had studied English in school for at least 10 years. However, they clearly struggled to understand and produce conversational speech. In contrast, their 4-year-old son had already picked up a good deal of English with no formal training. When the time came to leave, the parents haltingly said their good-byes. The 4-year-old—in unaccented English—shouted enthusiastically, "See you later, alligator!"

This anecdote raises some important questions about the relationship between the age at which you begin to learn a second language (or **age of acquisition**) and your eventual proficiency in that language. Some theorists have proposed a critical period hypothesis. According to the **critical period hypothesis,** your ability to acquire a second language is strictly limited to a specific period. In fact, individuals who have already reached a specified age—perhaps early puberty—will no longer be able to acquire a new language with native-like fluency.

However, the current research evidence does not support a clear-cut, biologically based "deadline" for learning a second language. For example, several studies demonstrate that adults and older adolescents can indeed learn to speak a new language very fluently (Bialystok 2001; Birdsong, 1999; Birdsong & Molis, 2000). Many studies do report a *gradual* decline in a variety of second-language skills, as a function of age of acquisition. However, these studies do not show an abrupt drop—as predicted by the critical period hypothesis—when language learners reach a certain age (Bialystok, 2001; Hakuta et al., 2003).

Even if we reject the critical period hypothesis, we still need to explore a more general issue: Do older people have more difficulty than younger people in mastering a second language? Like so many psychological controversies, the answer varies as a function of the dependent variable. As you'll see, researchers draw different conclusions, depending on whether they measure phonology, vocabulary, or grammar. This discussion emphasizes a study by Flege and his colleagues (1999), who examined two of these topics—phonology and grammar.

Phonology. Research suggests that age of acquisition does influence the mastery of **phonology,** or speech sounds. Specifically, people who acquire a second language during early childhood are more likely to pronounce words like a native speaker of that language. In contrast, those who acquire a second language during adulthood will be more likely to have a foreign accent when they speak their new language (Bialystok, 2001; Flege et al., 1999; Kilborn, 1994).

Let's consider in some detail a study conducted by James Flege, Grace Yeni-Komshian, and Serena Liu (1999). These researchers located 240 individuals whose native language was Korean and who immigrated to the United States when they were between the ages of 1 and 23 years. At the time of the study, all participants had lived in the United States for at least 8 years.

To test phonology, Flege and his colleagues asked the participants to listen to an English sentence, wait about 1 second, and then repeat it. The researchers recorded five sentences that each participant produced. The phonology of each sentence was then judged by 10 speakers whose native language was English. The judges used a 9-point rating scale, in which 9 represented "no accent." The judges also rated the phonology of 24 speakers whose native language was English; you can see their scores, clustered at the upper-left corner of Figure 10.3.

Now look at the corresponding data for the Korean participants. As you can see, people who had arrived in the United States during childhood typically had minimal accents when speaking English. In contrast, those who had arrived as adolescents or adults usually had stronger accents. However, you'll notice a fairly regular decline with age of acquisition, rather than the abrupt drop predicted by the critical period hypothesis (Bialystok, 2001).

Vocabulary. When the measure of language proficiency is vocabulary, age of acquisition does not seem to be related to language skills (Bialystok, 2001). Several studies reviewed by Bialystok and Hakuta (1994) reported that adults and children are equally skilled in learning words in their new language. This finding makes sense, because people continue to learn new terms in their own language throughout their lifetimes. For example, you have already learned several hundred new vocabulary words in cognitive psychology since you began this course!

Grammar. The controversy about age of acquisition is strongest when we consider mastery of grammar (e.g., Bialystok, 2001; Johnson & Newport, 1989). Let's focus on the study by Flege and his coauthors (1999), which we initially discussed at the top of the page. These researchers also examined how native speakers of Korean had mastered English grammar. The people who were tested for phonology were also tested for their ability to detect errors in English grammar. Specifically, the researchers asked the participants to judge nine different categories of English sentences, noting whether each sentence was grammatical. Here are three representative categories, together with examples of ungrammatical sentences:

FIGURE 10.3

The Average Rating for Foreign Accent, as a Function of the Individual's Age of Arrival in the United States. Note: A rating of 9 = no accent.

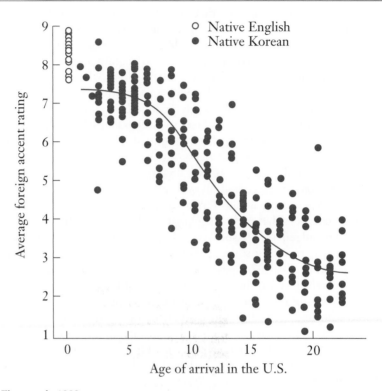

Source: Flege et al., 1999.

1. Yes/no questions: *Should have Timothy gone to the party?*
2. Pronouns: *Susan is making some cookies for we.*
3. Plurals: *Todd has many coat in his closet.*

In the initial analysis of the data, this study demonstrated once again that those who had learned English during childhood had better mastery of English grammar. However, Flege and his colleagues (1999) then discovered that people who had arrived in the United States at an early age had much more education in U.S. schools, in contrast to people who had arrived as teenagers or adults. As a consequence, the "early arrivers" had much more experience with formal training in the English language.

The researchers therefore conducted a second analysis, comparing early arrivers with late arrivers. These two subgroups had been carefully matched with respect to education; both had an average of 10.5 years of U.S. education. In this second analysis, the early arrivers received an average score of 84% correct on the grammar test. This score was not significantly different from the average score of 83% for the late arrivers. In short, once we control for years of education in the United States, age of acquisition is not related to an individual's mastery of English grammar. (Incidentally, a similar subgroup analysis for phonology, which we discussed on p. 355, showed that age of arrival still had a significant effect on pronunciation.)

The research we have cited up until now in this In Depth feature examined only the grammatical performance of people with an Asian first language. These languages are very different from English. Other research has been conducted on grammatical competence with bilinguals whose first language is Spanish or Dutch—two languages that are more similar to English. These studies do not show any consistent relationship between age of arrival and mastery of English grammar (Bahrick et al., 1994; Birdsong & Molis, 2001; Jia et al., 2002; Snow & Hoefnagel-Hohle, 1978).

To understand how age of acquisition is related to competence in a second language, we will need to wait until additional research has been performed on a wider variety of first- and second-language combinations. In addition, we need research in which the second language is something other than English. As we noted at the beginning of Chapter 9, the research in psycholinguistics focuses on English. At present, though, the results suggest that age of acquisition of a second language seems to be related to the speaker's accent in this new language. However, age of acquisition does not affect the speaker's mastery of vocabulary. Finally, age of acquisition affects knowledge about grammar if the two languages are very different

---

⑨ Demonstration 10.5

Exploring Bilingualism

If you are fortunate enough to be bilingual or multilingual, you can answer these questions yourself. If you are not, locate someone you know well enough to ask the following questions:

1. How old were you when you were first exposed to your second language?
2. Under what circumstances did you acquire this second language? For example, did you have formal lessons in this language?
3. When you began to learn this second language, did you find yourself becoming any less fluent in your native language? If so, can you provide any examples?
4. Do you think you have any special insights about the nature of language that a monolingual may not have?
5. Does the North American culture (including peer groups) discourage bilinguals from using their first language?

from each other, and if the speaker has not been educated in English. However, older learners may not face a disadvantage if the two languages are similar.

As a final exercise in helping you understand bilingualism, try Demonstration 10.5 at your next opportunity. Quite clearly, bilinguals and multilinguals provide the best illustration of how Theme 2 applies to language, because they manage to master accurate and rapid communication in two or more languages.

⊚ Section Summary: *Bilingualism and Second-Language Acquisition*

1. Many residents of Canada and the United States speak a first language other than English; motivation and attitudes are important determinants of bilingual skills.

2. Bilinguals have an advantage over monolinguals in their understanding of first-language structure, their ability to pay attention to subtle aspects of language, their awareness of the arbitrary nature of concept names, and their sensitivity to pragmatics. Bilinguals also show superior performance on measures of their ability to follow instructions, their creativity, their concept formation, and their problem solving.

3. In general, bilinguals excel on selective-attention tasks in which they must inhibit the most obvious response.

4. People who acquire a second language during early childhood are less likely than adult learners to speak their new language with an accent, but adults and children are equally skilled in acquiring vocabulary. Age of acquisition is not consistently related to competency in grammar.

CHAPTER REVIEW QUESTIONS

1. To some extent, the cognitive tasks required for language production (Chapter 10) are similar to the cognitive tasks required for language comprehension (Chapter 9). Describe some of the more complex cognitive tasks that are specifically necessary for language production, but not language comprehension.

2. Recall several conversations you have had in the last day or two. Describe how these conversations reflected three components of speech production: (a) pragmatics; (b) common ground; and (c) directives.

3. What is the linearization problem? In what way is it more relevant in language production (either speaking or writing) than it would be when you create a mental image (Chapter 7)?

4. Think of a slip-of-the-tongue that you recently made or heard in a conversation. What kind of error is this, according to Dell's classification, and how would Dell's theory explain this particular error? What slips-of-the-tongue would you be *least* likely to make?

5. Analyze the next conversation you overhear, from the viewpoint of the social context of speech. Pay particular attention to (a) establishing common ground, (b) lexical entrainment, (c) directives, and (d) indirect requests.

6. How does writing differ from speaking? What cognitive tasks do these two activities share?

7. Based on the material in the section on writing, what hints could you adopt to produce a better paper the next time you are given a formal writing assignment? Describe how at least one aspect from the section "Writing in Real-World Settings" might be relevant to your own life.

8. Think of another language that you would like to speak with some fluency; what factors would facilitate your mastery of that language? Describe several tasks in which bilinguals are likely to perform better than monolinguals. Which tasks would monolinguals probably perform better than bilinguals?

9. The section on bilingualism mentioned metalinguistics, or knowledge of the form and structure of language. Review this chapter, noting several topics that would be interesting to explore, with respect to metalinguistics. Suggest several specific research projects, and describe how you would devise a test of metalinguistics. (For example, how would you devise a test of people's knowledge about the social context of speech?)

10. Language is perhaps the most social of our cognitive activities. Describe how social factors are relevant in our speaking and writing, as well as bilingual interactions.

NEW TERMS

gist	directive	simultaneous
linearization problem	indirect request	bilingualism
prosody	self-efficacy	sequential bilingualism
slips-of-the-tongue	working memory	first language
morphemes	phonological loop	second language
discourse	visuospatial sketchpad	metalinguistics
narrative	central executive	age of acquisition
pragmatics	prewriting	critical period
common ground	bilingual	hypothesis
lexical entrainment	multilingual	phonology

RECOMMENDED READINGS

Bialystok, E. (2001). *Bilingualism in development: Language, literacy, and cognition.* New York: Cambridge University Press. Ellen Bialystok is one of the most prominent researchers on the topic of bilingualism; this book provides an excellent summary of the complexity of the research on bilingual issues.

Graesser, A. C., Gernsbacher, M. A., & Goldman, S. R. (2003a). *Handbook of discourse processes.* Mahwah, NJ: Erlbaum. This handbook includes chapters on topics such as spoken discourse, indirect requests, and discourse development.

Pennebaker, J. W., Mehl, M. R., & Niederhoffer, K. G. (2003). Psychological aspects of natural language use: Our words, ourselves. *Annual Review of Psychology, 54,* 547–577. This chapter provides an interesting perspective on how people's word usage is related to their mental and physical health.

Wheeldon, L. (Ed.). (2000a). *Aspects of language production.* Philadelphia: Psychology Press. Here is an excellent book for students who want to explore advanced-level discussions of topics such as word production, prosody, and coordination in conversational speech.

Problem Solving and Creativity

PREVIEW

You use problem solving when you want to reach a particular goal, but you cannot immediately figure out the appropriate pathway to that goal. This chapter considers four aspects of problem solving: (1) understanding the problem, (2) problem-solving strategies, (3) factors that influence problem solving, and (4) creativity.

In order to understand a problem, you need to pay attention to its relevant information. Then you can represent the problem using many alternate methods, such as symbols, diagrams, and visual images. In their daily lives, people sometimes understand complex problems, even though they might fail to solve these same problems if they appeared on a standardized examination.

After you understand a problem, you must figure out how to solve it. Many problem-solving approaches are based on heuristics. A heuristic is a shortcut that typically produces a correct solution. One heuristic is the hill-climbing heuristic; at every choice point, you simply choose the alternative that seems to lead most directly toward your goal. A second approach is the means-ends heuristic, in which you break a problem into subproblems and then solve these individual subproblems. A third heuristic is the analogy approach, in which you solve the current problem, based on your experience with similar previous problems.

The section on factors that influence problem solving emphasizes how top-down processing and bottom-up processing are both important in effective problem solving. Experts make good use of their well-developed top-down skills. In contrast, overactive top-down processing can sometimes interfere with effective problem solving, as we'll see in the discussions of mental set and functional fixedness. An additional problem occurs when overactive top-down processing encourages stereotype threat. For example, if gender is emphasized when a woman is about to take a mathematics test, thoughts about her lack of math ability may cause her to make more errors. Finally, top-down processing may prevent you from solving insight problems, but it may help you solve noninsight problems.

Creativity can be defined as finding solutions that are novel, high quality, and useful. We'll discuss both a classic and a contemporary approach to creativity, and then we'll see how your motivation for working on a task may influence your creativity. Finally, we'll examine the topic of incubation, which shows that you can sometimes be more creative if you take a break while you are working on a problem that requires creativity.

INTRODUCTION

Every day, you solve dozens of problems. For example, think about all the problems you solved just yesterday. Perhaps you wanted to leave a note in a professor's mailbox, but you had no pen or pencil. Maybe you began to solve the problem of trying to organize your resources for a literature-review paper in your cognitive psychology course. Although you spent most of the day solving problems, you may have decided to relax late at night—by solving even more problems. Maybe you played a card game or watched a mystery on television or tried to help a friend who is struggling with a personal problem.

You use **problem solving** when you want to reach a certain goal, but the solution is not immediately obvious because obstacles are blocking your path (Leighton & Sternberg, 2003; Robertson, 2001). Most jobs require some kind of problem solving. For example, clinical psychologists must develop wise problem-solving strategies to help their clients solve real-life problems (Sternberg, 1998). Foreign-service officers often need to resolve life-threatening problems, keeping in mind the values and general knowledge of different cultural groups engaged in a conflict. Scientists must use problem solving in order to design, conduct, and interpret research (Tweney, 1998).

Every problem contains three features: (1) the initial state, (2) the goal state, and (3) the obstacles. For example, suppose you want to go shopping in a nearby town. The **initial state** describes the situation at the beginning of the problem. In this case, your initial state might be, "I am in my room, 10 miles from that town, with no car and no access to public transportation." The **goal state** is reached when you solve the problem. Here, it would be, "I am shopping in that town." The **obstacles** describe the restrictions that make it difficult to proceed from the initial state to the goal state (Davidson et al., 1994). The obstacles in this hypothetical problem might include the following: "I can't borrow a car from a stranger," "I can't drive a stick-shift car," and "I cannot walk 10 miles." Take a moment to recall a problem you have recently solved. Determine the initial state, the goal state, and the obstacles, so that you are familiar with these three concepts. Then try Demonstration 11.1.

In Chapter 1, we defined the term *cognition* as the acquisition, storage, transformation, and use of knowledge. So far in this textbook, we have paid the least attention to the transformation of knowledge. However, in this chapter and in the next chapter on reasoning and decision making, we focus on how people must take the information they have acquired and transform it to reach an appropriate answer. Furthermore, both Chapters 11 and 12 can be included in the general category called "thinking." **Thinking** requires you to go beyond the information you were given; thinking also has a goal such as a solution, a decision, or a belief (Baron, 2000).

Throughout this chapter, we will note the active nature of cognitive processes in problem solving, consistent with Theme 1. When people solve problems, they seldom take a random, trial-and-error approach, blindly trying different options until they find

---

⑨ Demonstration 11.1

Attention and Problem Solving

Suppose you are a bus driver. On the first stop you pick up 6 men and 2 women. At the second stop 2 men leave and 1 woman boards the bus. At the third stop 1 man leaves and 2 women enter the bus. At the fourth stop 3 men get on and 3 women get off. At the fifth stop, 2 men get off, 3 men get on, 1 woman gets off, and 2 women get on. What is the bus driver's name?

Source: Halpern, 2003, p. 389.

a solution. Instead, they typically show extraordinary flexibility (Hinrichs, 1992). They plan their attacks, often breaking a problem into its component parts and devising a plan for solving each part. In addition, people frequently use certain kinds of strategies that are likely to produce a solution relatively quickly. As this textbook emphasizes, humans do not passively absorb information from the environment. Instead, we plan our approach to problems, choosing strategies that are likely to provide useful solutions.

The first step in problem solving is understanding the problem, so let's consider this topic first. Once you understand a problem, the next step is to select a strategy for solving it; we will consider several problem-solving approaches in the second section of this chapter. Then we will examine several factors that influence effective problem solving; for example, expertise is clearly helpful, but a mental set is counterproductive. Our final topic is creativity—an area that requires finding novel solutions to challenging problems.

UNDERSTANDING THE PROBLEM

Some years ago, the companies located in a New York City skyscraper faced a major problem. The people in the building were continually complaining that the elevators moved too slowly. Numerous consultants were brought in, but the complaints only increased. When several companies threatened to move out, plans were drawn up to add an extremely expensive new set of elevators. Before reconstruction began, however, someone decided to add mirrors in the lobbies next to the elevators. The complaints stopped. Apparently, the original problem solvers had not properly understood the problem. In fact, the real problem wasn't the speed of the elevators, but the boredom of waiting for them to arrive (Thomas, 1989).

In problem-solving research, the term **understanding** means that you have constructed a mental representation of the problem, based on the information provided in the problem and your own previous experience (Robertson, 2001). In order to understand a problem, you need to construct an accurate mental representation (Greeno, 1977, 1991). Think about an occasion when you noticed that your mental representation did not correspond to the situation you needed to understand. I recall my mother giving her friend a recipe for homemade yogurt, which included the sentence, "Then you put the yogurt in a warm blanket." The friend looked quite pained and asked, "But isn't it awfully messy to wash the blanket out?" Unfortunately, the friend's internal representation had omitted the fact that the yogurt was in a container.

In this section of the chapter, we'll consider several topics related to understanding a problem: (1) the importance of paying attention; (2) methods of representing the problem; and (3) situated cognition, a perspective that emphasizes the role of context in understanding a problem.

Paying Attention to Important Information

To understand a problem, you must decide which information is most relevant to the problem's solution and then attend to that information. Notice, then, that one cognitive task—problem solving—relies on other cognitive activities such as attention, memory, and decision making. This is another example of the interrelatedness of our cognitive processes (Theme 4).

Attention is important in understanding problems because attention is limited, and competing thoughts can produce divided attention (Bruning et al., 1999). For instance, Bransford and Stein (1984) presented algebra "story problems" to a group of college students. You'll remember these problems—a typical one might ask about a train traveling in one direction and a car driving in another direction. In this study, the students were asked to record their thoughts and emotions as they inspected the problem. Many students had an immediate negative reaction to the problem, such as, "Oh no, this is a mathematical word problem—I hate those things." These negative thoughts occurred frequently throughout the 5 minutes allotted to the task. Clearly, they distracted the students' attention away from the central task of problem solving.

Consider, too, the number of problems we face in everyday life in which the major challenge is discovering what information deserves attention and what is irrelevant. For instance, a problem on a statistics test may include many details about experimental design that are really not important for solving the problem. The challenge in a problem like this may really be to decide which information merits attention.

Another major challenge in understanding a problem is focusing on the appropriate part (Dunbar, 1998). Researchers have found that effective problem solvers read the description of a problem very carefully, paying particular attention to inconsistencies (Mayer & Hegarty, 1996). Incidentally, if you paid attention to the bus driver riddle on page 363, you could solve it without rereading it. However, if you didn't pay attention, you can locate the answer in the first sentence of Demonstration 11.1. In summary, then, attention is a necessary initial component of understanding a problem.

Methods of Representing the Problem

As soon as the problem solver has decided which information is essential and which can be disregarded, the next step is to find a good method to represent the problem. If you choose an inappropriate method, you might not reach an effective solution to the problem (Robertson, 2001). If you can find an effective representation, you can organize the information efficiently and reduce the strain on your limited working memory (Davidson & Sternberg, 1998). This concrete representation must show the essential information that is necessary for the problem's solution. Some of the most effective methods of representing problems include symbols, matrices, diagrams, and visual images.

---

⑨ Demonstration 11.2

Using Symbols in Problem Solving

Solve the following problem: Mary is 10 years younger than twice Susan's age. Five years from now, Mary will be 8 years older than Susan's age at that time. How old are Mary and Susan? (You can find the answer in the discussion of "Symbols" a little later in the text.)

Symbols. Sometimes the most effective way to represent an abstract problem is by using symbols, as students learn to do in high school algebra. Consider Demonstration 11.2. The usual way of solving this problem is to let a symbol such as *m* represent Mary's age and a symbol such as *s* represent Susan's age. We can then "translate" each sentence into a formula. The first sentence becomes "$m = 2s - 10$" and the second sentence becomes "$m + 5 = s + 5 + 8$." We can then substitute for *m* in the second sentence and perform the necessary arithmetic. We then learn that Susan must be 18 and Mary must be 26.

⊚ Demonstration 11.3

Representations of Problems

Read the following information, fill in the information in the matrix, and then answer the question, "What disease does Ms. Anderson have, and in what room is she?" (The answer is at the end of the chapter.)

Five people are in a hospital. Each person has only one disease, and each has a different disease. Each person occupies a separate room; the room numbers are 101 through 105.

1. The person with asthma is in Room 101.
2. Ms. Lopez has heart disease.
3. Ms. Green is in Room 105.
4. Ms. Smith has tuberculosis.
5. The woman with mononucleosis is in Room 104.
6. Ms. Thomas is in Room 101.
7. Ms. Smith is in Room 102.
8. One of the patients, other than Ms. Anderson, has gall bladder disease.

	Room Number				
	101	102	103	104	105
Anderson					
Lopez					
Green					
Smith					
Thomas					

Source: Based on Schwartz, 1971.

Of course, a major challenge is that problem solvers often make mistakes when they try to translate words into symbols. For example, Schoenfeld (1982) describes how calculus students were asked to rephrase simple algebra problem statements so that they were more understandable. About 10% of the rephrasings included information that directly contradicted the input, and 20% contained confusing or unintelligible information. If you misunderstand a problem, you will not translate it accurately into symbols. (And, remember that even a proper understanding of a problem does not guarantee an appropriate translation into symbols!)

One common problem in translating sentences into symbols is that the problem solver may simplify the sentence, thereby misrepresenting the information (Reed, 1999). For example, Mayer and Hegarty (1996) asked college students to read a series of algebra word problems, and then to recall them later. The students often misremembered the problems that contained relational statements such as, "The engine's rate in still water is 12 miles per hour more than the rate of the current." A common error was to represent this statement in a simpler form, such as, "The engine's rate in still water is 12 miles per hour."

Matrices. A **matrix** is a chart that shows all possible combinations of items. A matrix is an excellent way to keep track of items, particularly when the problem is complex and the relevant information is categorical (Halpern, 2003). For example, you can solve Demonstration 11.3 most effectively by using a matrix like the one at the bottom of that demonstration.

Demonstration 11.3 is based on research by Steven Schwartz and his colleagues (Schwartz, 1971; Schwartz & Fattaleh, 1972; Schwartz & Polish, 1974). Schwartz and his coworkers found that students who represented the problem by a matrix were more likely to solve the problem correctly, compared to students who used alternative problem representations. Now try Demonstration 11.4 before you read further.

---

⑨ Demonstration 11.4

The Buddhist Monk Problem

Exactly at sunrise one morning, a Buddhist monk set out to climb a tall mountain. The narrow path was not more than a foot or two wide, and it wound around the mountain to a beautiful, glittering temple at the mountain peak.

　　The monk climbed the path at varying rates of speed. He stopped many times along the way to rest and to eat the fruit he carried with him. He reached the temple just before sunset. At the temple, he fasted and meditated for several days. Then he began his journey back along the same path, starting at sunrise and walking, as before, at variable speeds with many stops along the way. However, his average speed going down the hill was greater than his average climbing speed.

　　Prove that there must be a spot along the path that the monk will pass on both trips at exactly the same time of day. (The answer is found in Figure 11.1.)

Diagrams. We know that diagrams are helpful when we want to assemble an object. For example, Novick and Morse (2000) asked students to construct origami objects—such as a miniature piano—using folded paper. People who received both a verbal description and a step-by-step diagram were much more accurate than people who received only a verbal description.

Diagrams can be useful in representing a large amount of information. For example, a **hierarchical tree diagram** is a figure that uses a tree-like structure to specify various possible options in a problem. (Figure 6.3 on p. 182 shows a hierarchical tree diagram, in a different context.) Diagrams can represent complicated information in a clear, concrete form, so that you have more "mental space" in working memory for other problem-solving activities (Halpern, 2003; Wheatley, 1997). Furthermore, students can master these aids with relatively little effort. For example, Novick and her colleagues (1999) found that, after a brief training session on matrices and hierarchical diagrams, students were able to choose the most appropriate method for representing a variety of problems.

A diagram can also provide an additional advantage. Grant and Spivey (2003) found that diagrams attracted people's eye movements to relevant areas of the diagram, helping them solve problems more successfully.

A graph is sometimes the most effective kind of diagram for representing visual information during problem solving. Consider, for example, the Buddhist monk problem you solved in Demonstration 11.4. As Figure 11.1 illustrates, we can use one line to show the monk going up the mountain on the first day. We can then use a second line to show the monk coming down the mountain several days later. The point at which the lines cross tells us the spot that the monk will pass at the same time on each of the 2 days. I have arbitrarily drawn the lines so that they cross at a point 900 feet up the mountain at 12 noon. However, the two paths must always cross at *some* point, even if you vary the monk's rate of ascent and descent.

Visual Images. Other people prefer to solve problems like the one about the Buddhist monk by using visual imagery. One young woman who chose a visual approach to this problem reported the following:

> I tried this and that, until I got fed up with the whole thing, but the image of that monk in his saffron robe walking up the hill kept persisting in my mind. Then a moment came when, superimposed on this image, I saw another, more transparent one, of the monk walking down the hill, and I realized in a flash that the two figures must meet at some point some time—regardless at what speed they walk and how often each of them stops. Then I reasoned out what I already knew: whether the monk descends two days or three days later comes to the same; so I was quite justified in letting him descend on the same day, in duplicate so to speak. (Koestler, 1964, p. 184)

Notice that a visual image can let us escape from the boundaries of traditional, concrete representations. Good visual-imagery skills also provide an advantage when a problem requires you to construct a figure (Adeyemo, 1994).

FIGURE 11.1

A Graphic Representation of the Buddhist Monk Problem in Demonstration 11.4.

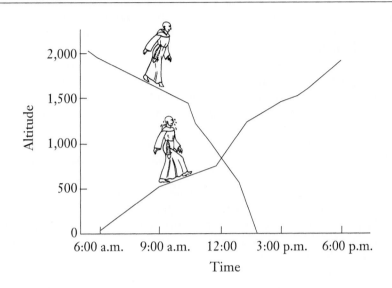

Furthermore, some imagery representations may be more effective than others. For example, Adeyemo (1990) asked college students to construct an innovative coatrack, given only specified equipment. Students who had been instructed to create a visual image of an imaginary structure were much more successful in solving the problem than were students who had been instructed to create an image of a familiar coatrack.

So far, we have considered the importance of attention in understanding problems. We've also seen that problems can be represented according to several different formats, including symbols, matrices, diagrams, and visual images. Our final topic in this section moves into a new dimension because it emphasizes the rich environmental and social context in which we understand the problems we must solve.

Situated Cognition: The Importance of Context

In the streets of several large cities in Brazil, 10-year-old boys were selling candy to people passing by. Researchers studied these children, who had no formal education, yet they demonstrated a sophisticated understanding of mathematics. In addition, during that era, they were using an inflated monetary system in which a box of candy bars could sell for 20,000 Brazilian cruzeiros. Also, a seller might offer two candy bars for 500 cruzeiros, and five candy bars for 1,000 cruzeiros, so he needed to understand how to compare two ratios (Carraher et al., 1985; Robertson, 2001; Woll, 2002).

How can children understand ratio comparisons—a concept that 10-year-olds seldom learn in North American schools? Many psychologists and educators emphasize situated cognition. Supporters of the **situated-cognition approach** argue that our ability to solve a problem is tied into the specific context in which we learned to solve that problem (Lave, 1997; Robertson, 2001; Seifert, 1999).

The research on situated cognition demonstrates that ordinary people succeed in figuring out which brand of a particular product is cheaper in the grocery store, even though they would fail to understand the same problem on a standardized mathematics test (Kirshner & Whitson, 1997a; Lave, 1988). It is important, however, not to overstate the advantages of situated cognition; we obviously do transfer much of our classroom knowledge to our everyday problem solving (Reed, 1999).

An important concept in the situated-cognition perspective is that we gather useful information from the stimulus-rich settings of everyday life. This information helps us understand a problem more quickly and more completely (Agre, 1997; Wilson, 2002). In everyday life, we also interact with other people, who provide information and help us clarify our cognitive processes. All these factors help us learn to become more competent in understanding and solving problems (Glaser, 2001; Greeno et al., 1998; Seifert, 1999).

The traditional cognitive approach to thinking emphasizes the processes that take place inside an individual person's head. The situated-cognition approach argues that the traditional cognitive approach is too simplistic, because in real life, our cognitive processes take advantage of an information-rich environment, supplemented by complex social interactions with other people (Greeno et al., 1998; Olson & Olson, 2003).

As you can imagine, the situated-cognition perspective has important implications for education, beginning in kindergarten and extending beyond graduate school. For example, this perspective suggests that college students can learn especially effectively during internships and other practice settings (Hakel, 2001).

This situated-cognition perspective is consistent with the idea that psychologists should emphasize ecological validity if they want to accurately understand cognitive processes. As noted in Chapter 1 and in Chapter 5's discussion of autobiographical memory, a study has **ecological validity** if the conditions in which the research is conducted are similar to the natural setting in which the results will be applied. For example, a study of children's mathematical skills in selling candy would have greater ecological validity than a study of children's mathematical skills on a paper-and-pencil, standardized examination.

One important principle of the situated-cognition perspective is that people learn skills within the context of a specific situation, such as a grocery store. As a consequence, they may fail to transfer these skills and use them effectively in another situation, such as a standardized math test (Anderson, Reder, & Simon, 1996; Bereiter, 1997). We will return to this problem later in the chapter when we examine how people often fail to appreciate an analogy between previous problem-solving tasks and the problem they are currently trying to solve.

◎ Section Summary: *Understanding the Problem*

1. When you engage in problem solving, you begin with the initial state and try to deal with obstacles in order to reach the goal state.

2. Understanding the problem requires constructing an accurate mental representation of the problem.

3. Attention is relevant in problem solving because attention is limited, because competing thoughts can produce divided attention, and because problem solvers must focus their attention on the appropriate part of the problem.

4. Methods for representing problems include symbols, matrices, diagrams, and visual images.

5. According to the situated-cognition approach, we must emphasize the context for problem solving. People understand problems within a rich environmental context, combined with complex social interactions. They can solve problems in real-life settings that they might not be able to solve in a school setting.

PROBLEM-SOLVING STRATEGIES

Once you have represented the problem, you can use many different strategies to attack it. Some strategies are very time consuming. For instance, an **algorithm** is a method that will always produce a solution to the problem, although the process can sometimes be inefficient (Sternberg & Ben-Zeev, 2001). One example of an algorithm is a method called an **exhaustive search,** in which you try out all possible answers using a specified system. For instance, a high school student might be faced with the algebra problem in Demonstration 11.2 on an examination. The student could begin with $m = 0$ and $s = 0$ and try all possible values for m and s until the solution is reached. With such an inefficient algorithm, however, the exam would probably be over before this one problem is solved.

Algorithms are often inefficient and unsophisticated. Other, more sophisticated methods reduce the possibilities that must be explored to find a solution. For example, suppose that you have been working on some anagrams, rearranging the letters to create an English word. The next anagram is LSSTNEUIAMYOUL. You might begin to solve that lengthy anagram by trying to identify the first two letters of your target word; you decide to pick out only pronounceable two-letter combinations. Perhaps you would reject combinations such as *LS, LT,* and *LN,* but you consider *LE, LU,* and—ideally—*SI.* This strategy would probably lead you to a solution much faster than an exhaustive search of all the more than 87 billion possible arrangements of the 14 letters in SIMULTANEOUSLY.

The strategy of looking only for pronounceable letter combinations is an example of a heuristic. As you know from other chapters, a **heuristic** is a general rule that is usually correct. In problem solving, a heuristic is a strategy in which you ignore some alternatives and explore only those alternatives that are most likely to produce a solution. However, a heuristic does not guarantee that you will solve a problem correctly (Hertwig & Todd, 2002; Robertson, 2001).

We noted that algorithms such as an exhaustive search will always produce a solution, although you may grow a few years older in the process. Heuristics, in contrast, do not guarantee a solution. For instance, suppose you were given the anagram IPMHYLOD, and you use the heuristic of rejecting unlikely combinations of letters at the beginning of the target word. If you reject words beginning with LY, you would fail to find the correct solution, LYMPHOID. When solving a problem, you'll need to weigh the benefits of an algorithm's speed against the costs of possibly missing the correct solution.

Psychologists have conducted more research on problem solvers' heuristics than on their algorithms. One reason is that most everyday problems cannot be solved by algorithms. For example, no algorithm can be applied to the problem of getting to a nearby town when you don't own a car. Furthermore, people are more likely to use heuristics than algorithms. Three of the most widely used heuristics are the hill-climbing heuristic, the means-ends heuristic, and the analogy.

The Hill-Climbing Heuristic

One of the most straightforward problem-solving strategies is called the hill-climbing heuristic. To understand this heuristic, imagine that your goal is to climb to the top of a hill. Just ahead, you see a fork in the path. Unfortunately, you cannot see far into the distance on either path. Because your goal is to climb upward, you select the path that has the steepest incline. Similarly, when you reach a choice point when using the **hill-climbing heuristic,** you simply select the alternative that seems to lead most directly toward your goal state (Lovett, 2002).

The hill-climbing heuristic can be useful when you cannot discover sufficient information about your alternatives—when you can see only the immediate next step (Dunbar, 1998). However, like many heuristics, the hill-climbing heuristic can lead you astray. The biggest drawback to this heuristic is that problem solvers must consistently choose the alternative that appears to lead most directly toward the goal. In doing so, they may fail to choose a less direct alternative, which may have greater long-term benefits. For example, a hillside path that seems to lead upward may quickly come to an abrupt end. The hill-climbing heuristic certainly does not guarantee that you'll end up on the top of the very highest hill (Robertson, 2001).

Similarly, a student whose goal is to earn a high salary may decide to take a job immediately after graduating from college, although a graduate degree may yield greater long-term benefits. Sometimes the best solution to a problem requires us to move temporarily backward—away from the goal (Lovett, 2002). We'll reconsider the "moving backward" issue in the discussion of the means-ends heuristic that follows. However, the important point to remember about the hill-climbing heuristic is that it encourages short-term goals, rather than long-term solutions. (Try Demonstration 11.5 before you read further.)

🌀 Demonstration 11.5

The Hobbits-and-Orcs Problem

Try solving this problem. (The answer is at the end of the chapter.)

Three Hobbits and three Orcs arrive at the right side of a riverbank, and they all wish to cross to the left side. Fortunately, there is a boat—but unfortunately, the boat can hold only two creatures at one time. There is another problem: Orcs are vicious creatures, and whenever there are more Orcs than Hobbits on one side of the river, the Orcs will immediately attack the Hobbits and eat them up. Consequently, you should be certain that you never leave more Orcs than Hobbits on any riverbank. How should the problem be solved? (It must be added that the Orcs, though vicious, can be trusted to bring the boat back!)

The Means-Ends Heuristic

The **means-ends heuristic** has two important components: (1) First you divide the problem into a number of **subproblems,** or smaller problems, and (2) then you try to reduce the difference between the initial state and the goal state for each of the subproblems. The name *means-ends heuristic* is appropriate because it requires you to identify the "ends" you want and then figure out the "means" you will use to reach those ends. The means-ends heuristic focuses the problem solver's attention on the difference between the initial problem state and the goal state. This heuristic is more sophisticated than the hill-climbing heuristic, and it is one of the most effective and flexible problem-solving strategies (Dunbar, 1998; Lovett, 2002).

Every day we all solve problems by using means-ends analysis. For example, several years ago, a student I knew well came running into my office saying, "Can I use your stapler, Dr. Matlin?" When I handed her the stapler, she immediately inserted the bottom edge of her skirt and deftly tacked up the hem. As she explained in a more leisurely fashion later that day, she had been faced with a problem: At 11:50, she realized that the hem of her skirt had come loose, and she was scheduled to deliver a class presentation in 10 minutes. Using the means-ends heuristic, she divided the problem into two subproblems: (1) identifying some object that could fix the hem, and (2) locating that object.

When you use the means-ends heuristic to solve a problem, you can proceed in either the forward direction, from the initial state to the goal state, or backward from the goal state to the initial state (Robertson, 2001). Thus, you may solve the second subproblem prior to the first subproblem. Try noticing the kinds of problems you might solve using means-ends analysis, such as writing a term paper for a history course, solving a problem in a statistics class, or figuring out the solution to numerous everyday dilemmas. Let's now examine some research showing how people use means-ends analysis in solving problems, as well as computer-simulation investigations of this heuristic.

Research on the Means-Ends Heuristic. Research demonstrates that people do organize problems in terms of subproblems. For example, Greeno (1974) examined how people solve the Hobbits-and-Orcs problem in Demonstration 11.5. His study showed that people pause at points in the problem when they begin to tackle a subproblem and need to organize a sequence of moves. Working memory is especially active when people are planning one of these move sequences (Simon, 2001; Ward & Allport, 1997).

Sometimes the correct solution to a problem depends on moving backward and temporarily *increasing* the difference between the initial state and the goal state. For example, how did you solve the Hobbits-and-Orcs problem in Demonstration 11.5? Maybe you concentrated on *reducing* the difference between the initial state (all creatures on the right side) and the goal state (all creatures on the left side), and you therefore moved them only from right to left. If you did, you would have ignored some steps that were crucial for solving the problem, such as in Step 6 where you must move *two* creatures backward across the river to the riverbank on the right. (See the steps in the answer on p. 398.)

Research confirms that people are reluctant to move away from the goal state—even if the correct solution depends on making this temporary detour (Robertson, 2001; Thomas, 1974). In real life, as in the Hobbits-and-Orcs problem, the most effective way to move forward is sometimes to move backward temporarily. Think about an occasion when you were working on one of the later subproblems within a problem, and you discovered that your solution to an earlier subproblem had been inadequate. For example, when you are writing a paper based on library research, you might discover that the resources you gathered during an earlier stage were not appropriate. Now you need to move backward to that earlier subproblem and revisit the library. My students tell me that this situation is particularly frustrating, especially because it seems to increase the difference between the initial state and the goal state. In short, if we want to solve a problem effectively, using means-ends analysis, we must sometimes violate a strict difference-reduction strategy.

Computer Simulation. One of the most widely discussed examples of computer simulation was devised to account for the way humans use means-ends analysis in solving problems (Baron, 1994; Stillings et al., 1995). Specifically, Allen Newell and Herbert Simon developed a theory that featured subgoals and reducing the difference between the initial state and the goal state (Newell & Simon, 1972; Simon, 1995, 1999). Let's first consider some general characteristics of computer simulation, when applied to problem solving. Then we'll briefly discuss Newell and Simon's approach, as well as more recent developments in computer simulation.

As discussed earlier in the book, when researchers use **computer simulation,** they write a computer program that will perform a task the same way that a human would. For example, a researcher might try to write a computer program for the Hobbits-and-Orcs problem. The program should make some false starts, just as a human would. The program should be no better at solving the problem than a human would be, and it also should be no worse. The researcher tests the program by having it solve a problem and noting whether the steps it takes match the steps that humans would take in solving the problem.

In studying problem solving, computer simulation forces the theorist to be clear and unambiguous about the components of the theory (Gilhooly, 1996). If the computer program's performance does not match the performance of human problem solvers, then the theory needs to be revised.

In 1972, Newell and Simon developed a now-classic computer simulation called General Problem Solver. **General Problem Solver (GPS)** is a program whose basic strategy is means-ends analysis. The goal of the GPS is not simply to solve problems in the most efficient way. Instead, it mimics the processes that normal humans use when they tackle these problems (Lovett, 2002; Simon, 1996). GPS has several different methods of operating. For example, the GPS may search for a process that would help reduce the difference between the initial state and the goal state. Then that process is applied to the initial state to produce a new state, which is presumably closer to the goal.

The General Problem Solver was the first program to simulate a variety of human symbolic behaviors (Sobel, 2001; Sternberg & Ben-Zeev, 2001). As a result, GPS has had an important impact on the history of cognitive psychology. It was used to simulate how humans solve transport problems like that of the Hobbits and Orcs. In addition, researchers used the GPS to simulate human performance on a wide variety of tasks, such as the grammatical analysis of sentences, proofs in logic, and problems in physics and trigonometry.

The GPS was eventually discarded by Newell and Simon because its generality was not as great as they had wished (Gardner, 1985). Contemporary cognitive scientists also acknowledge that people often solve **ill-defined problems,** where the goal is not obvious; means-ends analysis is therefore not useful (Sobel, 2001).

John Anderson and his colleagues have directed many computer simulations of problem solving (Anderson & Gluck, 2001; Anderson et al., 1995). These projects are an outgrowth of Anderson's ACT theory, which was summarized in Chapter 8. Anderson and his coworkers have now developed programs for solving problems in algebra, geometry, and computer science. These programs were developed originally in order to learn more about how students acquire skills in problem solving. However, these researchers have also developed "cognitive tutors" that can be used in high school mathematics classes (Anderson et al., 1995). Notice, then, that a project initially designed to examine theoretical questions can be applied to real-life situations.

The Analogy Approach

Every day you use analogies to solve problems. When confronted with a problem in a mathematics course, for example, you refer to previous examples in your textbook. When you write a paper for your cognitive psychology course, you use many of the same strategies that were helpful when you wrote a previous paper for social psychology. Analogies also figure prominently in creative breakthroughs in domains such as art, science, and politics (Blanchette & Dunbar, 2000; Dunbar, 2001; Robertson, 2001). When we use the **analogy approach** in problem solving, we use a solution to a similar, earlier problem to help solve a new one. Let's consider the general structure of the analogy approach, and then we'll look at some of the factors that can encourage problem solvers to use the analogy approach most effectively.

The Structure of the Analogy Approach. The major challenge for people who use the analogy strategy is to determine the real problem—that is, the abstract puzzle underneath all the details. In the section on understanding the problem, we emphasized that problem solvers must peel away the irrelevant information in order to reach the core of the problem. For example, when you attacked Demonstration 11.5, you did not really need to know anything about Hobbits and Orcs—except for any characteristics that were relevant for getting them across the river. The story could just as well have described residents of different countries traveling between two cities. The term **problem isomorphs** is used to refer to a set of problems that have the same underlying structures and solutions, but different specific details.

The major barrier to using the analogy approach, however, is that people tend to focus more on the superficial content of the problem than on its abstract, underlying meaning (Reeves & Weisberg, 1993, 1994; VanderStoep & Seifert, 1994). In other words, they pay more attention to the obvious **surface features,** the specific objects and terms used in the question. Unfortunately, these problem solvers may fail to emphasize the **structural features,** the underlying core that must be understood in order to solve the problem correctly.

For example, Rutgers University was trying to design a system that would allow prospective students to keep track of the status of their college applications. At first, Rutgers staff members looked only at the systems used by other universities, which were similar to their existing system in terms of surface features. Then the Rutgers staff shifted their attention to structural features; they realized that they actually had a tracking problem. So they examined the system that the Federal Express company uses to track the location of its packages, which provided a highly effective solution to their college-application problem (Ruben, 2001).

Numerous studies have demonstrated that people often fail to see the analogy between a problem they have solved and a new problem isomorph that has similar structural features (e.g., Barnett & Ceci, 2002; Hakel, 2001; Lovett, 2002; Novick, 1988; Reed, 1977, 1999). As emphasized by the situated-cognition perspective (pp. 369–370), people often have trouble solving the same problem in a new setting; they fail to transfer their knowledge. They may also have trouble solving the same problem when it is "dressed up" with a superficially different cover story (Bassok et al., 1995). People with limited problem-solving skills and limited metacognitive ability are especially likely to have difficulty using analogies (Davidson & Sternberg, 1998).

Factors Encouraging Appropriate Use of Analogies. In many cases, problem solvers can overcome the influence of context, and they can appropriately apply the analogy method. For instance, suppose that two problems initially seem unrelated because they have different surface characteristics. However, these two problems *do* have the same structural characteristics. If someone gives you a hint to compare the two problems, you are likely to discover the structural similarities and use the analogy approach properly (Lovett, 2002; Vander Stoep & Seifert, 1994).

People are also more likely to use the analogy strategy correctly when they try several structurally similar problems before they tackle the target problem (Davidson & Sternberg, 1998; Needham & Begg, 1991). Furthermore, students solve statistics problems more accurately if they have been trained to sort problems into categories on the basis of structural similarities (Quilici & Mayer, 2002).

The research on using analogies to solve problems suggests that this technique can be extremely useful. Furthermore, people can become more effective problem solvers if they are encouraged to emphasize structural similarities.

◎ Section Summary: *Problem-Solving Strategies*

1. With algorithms, such as exhaustive search, the problem solver eventually reaches a solution, but this method is often very time consuming. In contrast, heuristics are faster because they examine only a few of the alternatives; however, they do not guarantee a solution.

2. One of the simplest problem-solving strategies is the hill-climbing heuristic; at every choice point, you select the alternative that seems to lead most directly to the goal. However, the answer may not be the best long-term solution.

3. The means-ends heuristic requires dividing a problem into subproblems and trying to reduce the difference between the initial state and the goal state for each of the subproblems. The General Problem Solver (GPS) is a computer program designed to use means-ends analysis.

4. Another heuristic is the analogy approach, in which people solve a new problem by referring to an earlier problem. They may be distracted by superficial similarity, but several precautions can encourage people to emphasize structural similarity.

FACTORS THAT INFLUENCE PROBLEM SOLVING

Theme 5 of this book focuses on the interplay between bottom-up processing and top-down processing. **Bottom-up processing** emphasizes the information about the stimulus, as registered on our sensory receptors. In contrast, **top-down processing** emphasizes our concepts, expectations, and memory, which we have acquired from past experience.

As you'll see in this section, these two kinds of processing help us understand how several important factors can affect our ability to solve a problem. For example, experts use top-down processing effectively when they solve problems; they take advantage of their accumulated memory, concepts, and knowledge. In contrast, both mental set and functional fixedness can interfere with solving a problem; both of these factors rely too heavily on top-down processing. This chapter's In Depth section also shows how stereotypes may encourage people to have overactive top-down processing, which leads to poor problem-solving ability. Finally, if the problem requires insight, we must also overcome overactive top-down processing in order to approach the problem from an unfamiliar perspective. Thus, effective problem solving requires an ideal blend of both top-down and bottom-up processing (Theme 5).

Expertise

An individual with **expertise** demonstrates consistently exceptional performance on representative tasks for a particular area (Ericsson & Lehmann, 1996). You may recall that we discussed how expertise in a particular area influences people's working memory (Chapter 4) and their long-term memory (Chapters 5 and 6), as well as their concepts (Chapter 8). Now we'll explore how expertise facilitates problem solving. Specifically, experts have top-down processes that allow them to perform well on many different components of problem solving in their area of expertise.

Most cognitive psychologists specify that it takes at least 10 years of intense practice to gain expertise in a specific area (Ericsson & Charness, 1997; Robertson, 2001). Expertise does not come easily. For example, Lehmann and Ericsson (1998) estimated that a group of 20-year-old expert musicians had each devoted more than 10,000 hours to deliberate practice! However, experts excel primarily in their own domain of expertise (Ericsson, 1999; Robertson, 2001). You wouldn't expect an expert musician to excel at the problem of designing an experiment in cognitive psychology!

Let's trace how experts differ from novices during many phases of problem solving. We'll begin with some of the advantages that operate in the early phases of problem solving, then explore differences in problem-solving strategies, and finally consider more general abilities, such as metacognition.

Knowledge Base. Novices and experts differ substantially in their knowledge base, or schemas (Bransford et al., 2000; Ericsson, 1999; Robertson, 2001). For example, Chi (1981) found in her study of physics problem solving that the novices simply lacked important knowledge about the principles of physics. As we discussed in previous chapters, you need the appropriate schemas in order to understand a topic properly. Experts may perform especially well if they have had training in a variety of relevant settings (Barnett & Koslowski, 2002).

Memory. Experts differ from novices with respect to their memory for information related to their area of expertise (Bransford et al., 2000; Glaser & Chi, 1988; Robertson, 2001). In Chapter 4, for example, we saw that memory experts can use retrieval cues from their "regular" short-term working memory in order to access a large, stable body of information in long-term working memory (Ericsson & Delaney, 1999).

The memory skills of experts seem to be very specific. For example, expert chess players have much better memory than novices for various chess positions. According to one estimate, chess experts can remember about 50,000 "chunks," or familiar arrangements of chess pieces (Gobet & Simon, 1996a). However, chess experts are only slightly better than novices at remembering random arrangements of the chess pieces (Gobet & Simon, 1996b). In other words, experts' memory is substantially better only if the chess arrangement fits into a particular schema (Lovett, 2002).

Representation. Novices and experts also represent the problems differently. Larkin (1983, 1985) asked people to solve a variety of physics problems. She found that the novices in her study were likely to use naive problem representations, which depicted real-world objects such as blocks, pulleys, and toboggans. That is, the novices focused on *surface features*. In contrast, the experts were able to construct physical representations about abstract ideas such as force and momentum; these experts focused on *structural features*. Other researchers have found similar results (e.g., Ferguson-Hessler & De Jong, 1987; Lovett, 2002; Robertson, 2001).

Problem-Solving Strategies. When experts encounter a novel problem in their area of expertise, they are more likely than novices to use the means-ends heuristic effectively (Sternberg & Ben-Zeev, 2001). That is, they divide a problem into several subproblems, which they solve in a specified order (Schraagen, 1993). Experts and novices also differ in the way they use the analogy approach. When solving physics problems, experts typically appreciate the structural similarity between problems. In contrast, novices are more likely to be distracted by surface similarities, and they therefore often choose an inappropriate source problem (Gilhooly, 1996; Leighton & Sternberg, 2003). Notice that these findings resemble our earlier conclusions about analogies; skilled problem solvers are more likely to select a source problem on the basis of structural similarity.

Speed and Accuracy. As you might expect, experts are much faster than novices, and they solve problems very accurately (Bédard & Chi, 1992; Carlson, 1997; Custers et al., 1996). Their operations become more automatic, and a particular stimulus situation also quickly triggers a response (Bransford et al., 2000; Glaser & Chi, 1988; Robertson, 2001).

On some tasks, experts may solve problems faster because they use parallel processing, rather than serial processing. As the discussion on attention in Chapter 3 noted, **parallel processing** handles two or more items at the same time. In contrast, **serial processing** handles only one item at a time. Novick and Coté (1992) examined experts, who reported that they could solve anagrams quickly, and novices, who said their anagram-solving skills were "awful." The experts solved the anagrams so

---

⊙ Demonstration 11.6

Mental Set

Try these two examples to see the effects of mental set.

A. Luchins's Water-Jar Problem

Imagine that you have three jars, A, B, and C. For each of the seven problems below, the capacity of the three jars is listed. You must use these jars in order to obtain the amount of liquid specified in the Goal column. You may obtain the goal amount by adding or subtracting the quantities listed in A, B, and C. (The answers can be found a little later in the text, in the discussion of mental set.)

Problem	A	B	C	Goal
1	24	130	3	100
2	9	44	7	21
3	21	58	4	29
4	12	160	25	98
5	19	75	5	46
6	23	49	3	20
7	18	48	4	22

B. A Number Puzzle

You are no doubt familiar with the kind of number puzzles in which you try to figure out the pattern for the order of numbers. Why are these numbers arranged in this order?

$$8, \quad 5, \quad 4, \quad 9, \quad 1, \quad 7, \quad 6, \quad 3, \quad 2, \quad 0$$

The answer appears at the end of the chapter.

Source: Part A of this demonstration is based on Luchins, 1942.

quickly that they must have been considering several alternate solutions at the same time. To experts, the solution to anagrams such as DNSUO, RCWDO, and IASYD seemed to "pop out" in less than 2 seconds. In contrast, the novices were probably using serial processing. (Incidentally, are you a novice or an expert anagram solver?)

Metacognitive Skills. Experts are better than novices at monitoring their problem solving; you may recall that Chapter 6 discussed how self-monitoring is a component of metacognition. For example, experts seem to be better at judging the difficulty of a problem. They are also more aware when they are making an error or oversimplifying the problem, and they are more skilled at allocating their time appropriately when solving problems (Bransford et al., 2000; Carlson, 1997; Glaser & Chi, 1988).

In short, experts are more skilled at numerous phases of problem solving and are also more skilled at monitoring their progress while working on a problem. However, experts perform poorly on one task related to metacognition. Specifically, experts underestimate the amount of time that novices will require to learn a task in the experts' area of specialization (Hinds, 1999). In contrast, the novices are more accurate in acknowledging that the task will be difficult!

Mental Set

Before you read further, be sure to try the two parts of Demonstration 11.6, which illustrate a mental set. When problem solvers have a **mental set,** they keep trying the same solution they have used in previous problems, even though the problem could be solved by a different, easier method. A mental set is a mental rut that prevents us from carefully thinking about a problem and solving it effectively (Langer, 1997; Langer & Moldoveanu, 2000; Lovett, 2002).

We noted earlier that problem solving demands both top-down and bottom-up processing (Theme 5). Expertise makes *appropriate* use of top-down processing, because experts can employ their previous knowledge to solve problems both quickly and accurately. In contrast, both mental set and functional fixedness—which we'll discuss in a moment—represent *overactive* top-down processing. In these two cases, problem solvers are so strongly guided by their previous experience that they fail to consider more effective solutions to their problems.

The classic experiment on mental set is Abraham Luchins's (1942) water-jar problem, illustrated in Part A of Demonstration 11.6. The best way to solve Problem 1 is to fill up jar B and remove one jarful with jar A and two jarsful with jar C. Problems 1 through 5 can all be solved in this fashion, so they create a mental set for the problem solver. Most people will keep using this method when they reach Problems 6 and 7. Unfortunately, their previous learning will actually hinder their performance, because these last two problems can be solved by easier, more direct methods. For example, Problem 6 can be solved by subtracting C from A, and Problem 7 can be solved by adding C to A.

Luchins (1942) gave one group of participants a series of complex problems such as Problems 1 through 5 that we just discussed. He found that almost all of them persisted in using the same complex solution on later problems. In contrast, participants in a control group began right away with problems such as 6 and 7 in the demonstration.

These people almost always solved these problems in the easier fashion. The same findings have been replicated in a series of three experiments by McKelvie (1990). Similarly, college students designed less creative toys if they had already seen toys that had been made by other people (Smith, 1995b; Smith et al., 1993).

A mental set is an example of a more general tendency that Ellen Langer (1997, 2002) calls mindlessness. The term **mindlessness** refers to a kind of automatic thinking in which we are entrapped in old categories, without being aware of new information available in the environment. In mindlessness, we look at a problem from only one point of view. In contrast, when we demonstrate **mindfulness,** we create new categories, we are eager to learn new information, and we are willing to look at the world from a different point of view. We can use mindfulness in approaching a variety of everyday problems, from studying for an examination, to buying a birthday present, to searching for a summer job.

Functional Fixedness

Like a mental set, functional fixedness occurs when our top-down processing is overactive; we rely too heavily on our previous concepts, expectations, and memory. However, mental set refers to our problem-solving strategies, whereas functional fixedness refers to the way we think about physical objects. Specifically, **functional fixedness** means that the functions or uses we assign to objects tend to remain fixed or stable. As a result, we fail to look at features of a stimulus that might be useful in helping us solve a problem (Lovett, 2002; Robertson, 2001).

To overcome functional fixedness, we need to think flexibly about new ways that objects can be used. My sister, for example, described a creative solution to a problem she faced on a business trip. She had purchased a take-out dinner from a wonderful Indian restaurant. Back in her hotel, she discovered that the bag contained no plastic spoons or forks, and the hotel dining room had closed several hours earlier. How could she solve this problem? She searched the hotel room, discovered an attractive new shoehorn in the "complimentary packet," washed it thoroughly, and enjoyed her chicken biriyani. She conquered functional fixedness by realizing that an object designed for one particular function (fitting a foot into a shoe) could also serve another function (conveying some food into the mouth).

The classic study in functional fixedness is called Duncker's candle problem (Duncker, 1945). Imagine that you have been led to a room that contains a table. On the table are three objects: a candle, a box of matches, and a box of thumbtacks. Your task is to find a way to attach a candle to the wall of the room so that it burns properly, using no other objects than those on the table. Most people approach this problem by trying to tack the candle to the wall or by using melted wax to try to glue it up. Both tactics fail miserably! The solution requires overcoming functional fixedness by realizing that the matchbox can be used for a different purpose, holding a candle, rather than holding some matches. In fact, you can tack the empty matchbox to the wall to serve as a candle holder.

In our everyday life, most of us have access to a variety of tools and objects, so functional fixedness does not create a significant handicap. In contrast, consider the quandary of Dr. Angus Wallace and Dr. Tom Wong. These physicians had just left on a plane for Hong Kong when they learned that another passenger was experiencing a collapsed lung. The only surgical equipment they had brought onboard was a segment of rubber tubing and a scalpel. Still, they operated on the woman and saved her life, using only this modest equipment and objects in the airplane that normally have fixed functions—a coathanger, a knife, a fork, and a bottle of Evian water (Adler & Hall, 1995).

Functional fixedness and mental sets are two more examples of part of Theme 2: Mistakes in cognitive processing can often be traced to a strategy that is basically very rational. Objects in our world normally have fixed functions. For example, we use a screwdriver to tighten a screw, and we use a coin to purchase something. In general, the strategy of using one object for one task and a second object for a different task is appropriate. After all, each was specifically designed for its own task. Functional fixedness occurs, however, when we apply that strategy too rigidly. For example, we fail to realize that—if we don't have a screwdriver—a coin may provide a handy substitute. Similarly, it is generally a wise strategy to use the knowledge you learned in solving earlier problems to solve the present dilemma. If an old idea works well, keep using it! However, in the case of a mental set, we apply the strategy gained from past experience too rigidly and fail to notice more efficient solutions.

IN DEPTH

Stereotypes and Problem Solving

So far, we have examined two situations in which top-down processes are overactive. In a mental set, we keep trying to solve a problem the way we have in the past, even though we could use an easier method. In functional fixedness, we think that an object can be used in only one way, even though we could use that object for other purposes.

In this third situation, however, our top-down processes may be overactive because of our beliefs about our own abilities, as based on stereotypes. Some research on this topic has been conducted about ethnic-group stereotypes and social-class stereotypes. However, the most widely researched topic is gender stereotypes. As we noted in Chapter 8, **gender stereotypes** are organized, widely shared sets of beliefs about the characteristics of females and males (Golombok & Fivush, 1994). A typical stereotype is that men are more skilled than women in solving mathematics problems. Gender stereotypes may be partially accurate, but they do not apply to every person of the specified gender. For instance, many women will score higher than the average man on any test of math problem-solving ability.

To provide a context for our discussion here, glance back at the research about inferences based on gender stereotypes. Pages 286–288 of Chapter 8 reported, for example, that women do not associate themselves with mathematics, and this tendency holds true even for women who are math majors.

The Nature of Stereotype Threat. Imagine two high school students—Jennifer and Matthew—who are about to begin the math portion of the Scholastic Assessment Test (SAT) for the first time. Both are excellent students, with A averages in their math courses. They know that this will probably be the most important test they will ever take, because the results could determine which college they will attend. Both students are anxious, but Jennifer has an additional source of anxiety: She must struggle with the stereotype that, because she is a female, she should score lower than male students (Quinn & Spencer, 2001). This additional anxiety may in fact lead her to solve math problems less effectively and to earn a relatively low score on the math portion of the SAT. This additional "evidence" of poor performance strengthens her stereotype about females' low math performance. In this example, Jennifer is experiencing **stereotype threat:** If you belong to a group that is hampered by a negative stereotype—and you think about your membership in that group—your performance may suffer (Jussim et al., 2000; Steele, 1997).

Research with Asian American Females. Consider some research by Shih and her coauthors (1999), in which all of the participants were Asian American women. In North America, one stereotype is that Asian Americans are "good at math," compared to those from other ethnic groups. In contrast, as we just discussed, another stereotype is that women are "bad at math," compared to men.

Shih and her coworkers (1999) divided the Asian-American women into three different conditions:

1. *Ethnicity-emphasis condition:* One group of participants were asked to indicate their ethnicity and then answer several questions about their ethnic identity. Then they took a challenging math test. These women answered 54% of the questions correctly.

2. *Control-group condition:* A second group of participants did not answer any questions beforehand. They simply took the challenging math test. These women answered 49% of the questions correctly.

3. *Gender-emphasis condition:* A third group of participants were asked to indicate their gender and then answer several questions about their gender identity. Then they took the challenging math test. These women answered only 43% of the questions correctly.

Apparently, when Asian-American women are reminded of their ethnicity, they perform relatively well. However, when Asian-American women are reminded of their gender, they experience stereotype threat, and their problem-solving ability declines.

Stereotype threat also operates for children. For example, Ambady and her coauthors (2001) replicated the study we just described. Specifically, they tested Asian-American girls in early elementary school (kindergarten through second grade) and in middle school (sixth through eighth grade). As in the study with college women, these girls performed best when their Asian ethnicity was emphasized, intermediate in the control condition, and worst when their gender was emphasized.

Research with European American Women. The effects of stereotype threat have also been replicated in samples where most of the women are European American (O'Brien & Crandall, 2003; Quinn & Spencer, 2001; Spencer et al., 1999). For instance, O'Brien and Crandall (2003) studied a group of college women taking a difficult math test. Some women were told that they would take a math test that was known to show gender differences. These women performed significantly worse than women in a second group, who were told that the math test was known to show no gender differences.

Potential Explanations. Why should stereotype threat lead to poorer performance? Two factors probably contribute to the problem. One factor is that stereotype threat probably produces arousal, especially because other research reported elevated blood pressure when people experienced stereotype threat (Blascovich et al., 2001; O'Brien & Crandall, 2003). High arousal is likely to interfere with working memory, especially on difficult tasks. Another factor is that females who are taking a difficult math test may work hard to suppress the thought that they should perform poorly (Quinn & Spencer, 2001). As you may recall from Chapter 3, thought suppression requires great effort, which further reduces the capacity of working memory.

In what way do the increased arousal and reduced cognitive capacity actually decrease women's ability to solve math problems? Quinn and Spencer (2001) proposed that these factors decrease women's abilities to construct problem-solving strategies. They studied female and male undergraduates. Half of each group completed a test with word problems; these items required strategies in order to convert the words into algebraic equations. The other half of each group completed a test with algebra problems (presented as numerical equations); these items did not require any conversion strategies. As Figure 11.2 shows, the men performed significantly better than the women on the word problems, but men and women performed similarly on the algebra problems. In an additional study, Quinn and Spencer (2001) found that women were much less likely to formulate a problem-solving strategy if they were in the stereotype-threat condition, rather than in the gender-fair condition.

At this point, you may be wondering whether gender differences appear on real-world tests, in addition to the psychology laboratory. The short answer to this question is that females tend to earn higher grades in math classes, and most standardized math tests show no substantial gender differences. During high school, however, males score higher on difficult word problems and on the math portion of the SAT (Matlin, 2004b). These two kinds of strategy-based math questions are precisely the kind of problems that are most influenced by stereotype threat.

The research on stereotype threat and problem solving tends to focus on gender comparisons. However, Black students perform more poorly when their ethnicity is emphasized (Steele & Aronson, 1995). Also, low socioeconomic-class students perform more poorly when socioeconomic class is emphasized (Crozet & Claire, 1998). When people are reminded that they belong to a group which is not expected to perform well on a test, top-down processing can lead to decreased performance on that test.

FIGURE 11.2

Average Performance by Men and Women on Word Problem Test and Numerical Test.

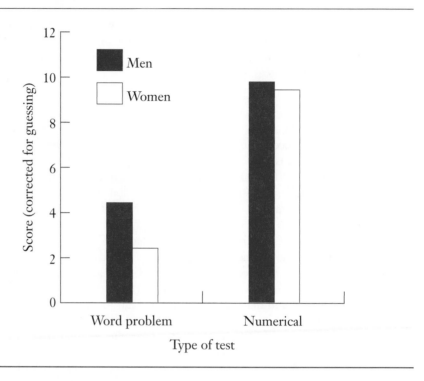

⬡ **Demonstration 11.7**

Two Insight Problems

A. The Sahara Problem (based on Perkins, 2001)

Suppose that you are driving a Jeep through the Sahara Desert. You see someone lying facedown in the sand. Exploring further, you see that it's a dead man. You see no tracks anywhere nearby, and there have been no recent winds to erase the tracks. You look in a pack on the man's back. What do you find?

B. The Triangle Problem

With six matches, construct four equilateral triangles. One complete match must make up one side of each triangle.

The answers to these two problems appear at the end of the chapter.

Insight Versus Noninsight Problems

Demonstration 11.7 illustrates two typical insight problems. When you solve an **insight problem,** the problem initially seems impossible to solve, but an alternative approach suddenly bursts into your consciousness; you immediately realize that your new solution is correct (Fiore & Schooler, 1998; Lovett, 2002; Robertson, 2001). In contrast, when you work on a **noninsight problem,** you solve the problem gradually, using your memory, reasoning skills, and a routine set of procedures (J. E. Davidson, 1995; Schooler et al., 1995). For example, Demonstration 11.2 was a noninsight problem, because you pursued the answer in a logical, step-by-step fashion, gradually solving the algebra problem.

Let's examine the nature of insight in somewhat more detail. Then we'll consider people's metacognitions when working on insight and noninsight problems.

The Nature of Insight. The concept of insight was very important to Gestalt psychologists (Lovett, 2002). As Chapters 1 and 2 noted, Gestalt psychologists emphasized organizational tendencies, especially in perception and in problem solving. They argued that the parts of a problem may initially seem unrelated to one another, but a sudden flash of insight could make the parts instantly fit together into a solution. If you solved the problems successfully in Demonstration 11.7, you experienced this feeling of sudden success.

Behaviorists rejected the concept of insight because the idea of a sudden cognitive reorganization was not compatible with their emphasis on observable behavior. Furthermore, some psychologists prefer to think of people solving problems in a gradual, orderly fashion. These psychologists are uneasy about the sudden transformation that is suggested by the concept of insight (Metcalfe, 1998b). Despite these objections, insight is a popular concept with many cognitive psychologists.

According to cognitive psychologists who favor the concept of insight, people who are working on an insight problem usually hold some inappropriate assumptions when they begin to solve the problem. For example, when you began to solve Part B of Demonstration 11.7, at first you probably assumed that the six matches needed to be arranged on a flat surface. In other words, top-down processing inappropriately dominated your thinking, and you were considering the wrong set of alternatives (Schooler & Melcher, 1994; Schooler et al., 1995). To solve an insight problem correctly, you may need to take a break so that the misleading information no longer dominates your thinking (Perkins, 2001; Schooler et al., 1995; Smith, 1995a).

In addition, the research on insight problems shows that it is not helpful to talk to yourself while working on the problem, explaining why you are pursuing certain strategies. Apparently, language interferes with insightful problem solving (Fiore & Schooler, 1998; Schooler et al., 1993).

In contrast, noninsight problems typically do benefit from top-down processing. The strategies you learned in high school math classes offer guidance as you work, step-by-step, toward the proper conclusion of an algebra problem. In addition, the research is mixed about whether it is helpful to talk to yourself while working on noninsight problems. Some researchers find that self-explanation is helpful (e.g., Berardi-Colletta et al., 1995; Chi, 2000; Chi et al., 2001). Other researchers find that self-explanation has no consistent effects—either helpful or harmful (Schooler & Melcher, 1994; Schooler et al., 1993).

Metacognition During Problem Solving. When you are working on a problem, how confident are you that you are on the right track? Janet Metcalfe (1986) argues that the pattern of your metacognitions differs for noninsight and insight problems. Specifically, people's confidence builds gradually for problems that do not require insight, such as standard high school algebra problems. In contrast, when people work on insight problems, they experience a sudden leap in confidence when they are close to a correct solution. In fact, the sudden rise in confidence can be used to distinguish insight from noninsight problems (Metcalfe & Wiebe, 1987).

Let us examine Metcalfe's (1986) research on metacognitions about insight problems. Metcalfe presented students with problems like this one:

> A stranger approached a museum curator and offered him an ancient bronze coin. The coin had an authentic appearance and was marked with the date 544 B.C. The curator had happily made acquisitions from suspicious sources before, but this time he promptly called the police and had the stranger arrested. Why? (p. 624)

As students worked on this kind of insight problem, they supplied ratings every 10 seconds on a "feeling-of-warmth" scale. A rating of 0 indicated that they were completely "cold" about the problem, with no glimmer of a solution. A score of 10 meant that they were certain they had a solution.

As you can see from Figure 11.3, the warmth ratings initially showed only gradual increases for the insight problems. However, these warmth ratings soared dramatically when the correct solution was discovered. If you figured out the answer to the coin question, did you experience this same sudden burst of certainty? (Incidentally, the answer to this problem is that someone who had actually lived in 544 B.C. could not possibly have used the designation "B.C." to indicate the birth of Christ half a millennium later.) Metcalfe's results have been replicated (J. E. Davidson, 1995), confirming that problem solvers typically experience a dramatic increase in their confidence when they believe they have located the correct solution to an insight problem.

The difference between noninsight problems and insight problems suggests that people solve the two kinds of problems differently. You might begin to solve a problem by contemplating whether you have had previous experience with similar problems. Top-down processing will be useful when you approach a noninsight problem, and you should consider trying to explain your strategies to yourself. From time to time, however, you should also consider whether the problem might need insight. Insight problems require a different approach, and it's difficult to learn how to solve insight problems more effectively. However, you might try to represent the problem in a different way (Lovett, 2002; Perkins, 2001). An insight problem forces you to search for the answer "outside the box" by abandoning your customary assumptions and looking for novel solutions.

FIGURE 11.3

"Warmth Ratings" for Answers That Were Correct, as a Function of Time of Rating Prior to Answering.

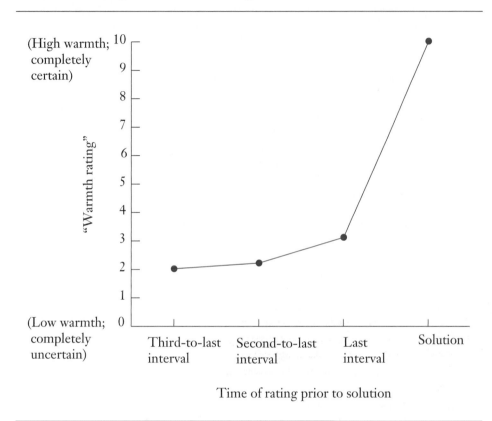

Source: Based on Metcalfe, 1986.

🌀 Section Summary: *Factors That Influence Problem Solving*

1. Experts differ from novices with respect to their knowledge base, memory for task-related material, method of problem representation, problem-solving approaches, speed and accuracy, and metacognitive skills.

2. Problem solving is also influenced by your mental set (in which you keep trying the same solution strategy, although another strategy would be more effective) and functional fixedness (in which you assign a fixed use to an object, although the object could be used for other tasks). In both cases, top-down processing is overactive; however, these strategies are basically rational.

3. Stereotype threat can occur when people belong to a group that is associated with a negative stereotype; if these people think about this group membership, their performance on a test may suffer.

4. The research shows that stereotype threat is associated with Asian-American and European American women; an explanation for stereotype threat may be that problem-solving strategies are hindered by factors such as high arousal and thought suppression

5. Insight problems are solved when the answer appears suddenly; noninsight problems are solved gradually, using reasoning skills and standardized procedures. Top-down processing is overactive in the case of insight problems but is appropriately helpful in the case of noninsight problems.

6. Research on metacognition shows that your confidence builds gradually for *noninsight* problems; in contrast, your confidence on *insight* problems is initially low, but it suddenly increases when you solve the problem.

CREATIVITY

Perhaps you breathed a sigh of relief when you finished the sections on problem solving and prepared to read a section on creativity. Problem solving sounds so routine; people who solve problems plug along as they work out their means-ends analyses. In contrast, creativity sounds inspired; people who think creatively often experience moments of genius, and lightbulbs frequently flash above their heads.

Truthfully, however, creativity is an area of problem solving. Creativity—like the problem-solving tasks we have already considered—requires moving from an initial state to a goal state. However, creativity is more controversial because we have no standardized definition of creativity, and the theoretical approaches are so diverse.

In recent years, creativity has become a popular topic, both within and beyond psychology. Numerous books on the topic have been published since the mid-1990s (e.g., Csikszentmihalyi, 1996; Levesque, 2001; Nettle, 2001; Perkins, 2001; Perry, 1999; Runco & Pritzker, 1999; Shavinina, 2003; Sternberg, 1999b; Torrance, 2000; Ward et al., 1997). Unfortunately, however, the amount of actual research on creativity has lagged behind the quantity of research on most other topics in cognitive psychology (Mayer, 1999). One reason may be that cognitive psychologists rarely explore individual differences, a popular approach in research on creativity.

Let's begin our exploration of creativity by discussing definitions, as well as two different approaches to creativity. Then we'll consider the relationship between task motivation and creativity. Our final topic focuses on incubation: Can your creativity be enhanced if you take a break while working on a challenging project?

Definitions

An entire chapter could be written on the variety of definitions for creativity. However, most theorists agree that novelty or originality is a necessary component of creativity (Mayer, 1999). But novelty is not enough. The answer we seek must also allow us to reach some goal; it must be useful and appropriate. Suppose I asked you to creatively answer the question, "How can you roast a pig?" The nineteenth-century essayist Charles Lamb observed that one way to roast a pig would be to put it into a house and then burn down the house. The answer certainly meets the criterion of novelty, but it does not fulfill the usefulness requirement. To most theorists, then, **creativity** requires finding solutions that are novel, high quality, and useful (e.g., Boden, 1999; Mayer, 1999; Sternberg & Ben-Zeev, 2001).

Although many theorists agree on the basic definition of creativity, their views differ on other characteristics. For instance, some psychologists argue that creativity is based on ordinary thinking, something related to our everyday problem solving (e.g., Halpern, 2003; Ruscio & Amabile, 1999; Weisberg, 1999). In contrast, other psychologists argue that ordinary people seldom produce creative products. Instead, certain exceptional people are extraordinarily creative in their specific area of expertise, such as music, literature, or science (e.g., Feldman et al., 1994; Simonton, 1997, 1999).

Approaches to Creativity

Theorists have devised many different approaches to studying creativity. Let's consider two contrasting viewpoints. The first is Guilford's (1967) classic description of divergent production, and the second is a contemporary perspective that emphasizes the multiple necessary components of creativity (e.g., Sternberg & Lubart, 1995).

Divergent Production. Researchers have been interested in measuring creativity for more than a century. However, the initial scientific research is typically traced to J. P. Guilford (Plucker & Renzulli, 1999). Guilford (1967) proposed that creativity should be measured in terms of **divergent production,** or the number of varied responses made to each test item. Contemporary researchers still tend to emphasize that creativity requires divergent thinking, rather than one single best answer (Mayer, 1999; Russ, 2001). Demonstration 11.8 shows several ways in which Guilford measured divergent production. These test items allow the problem solver to explore in many different directions from the initial problem state. Notice that some items require test takers to overcome functional fixedness.

Research on tests of divergent production has found moderate correlations between people's test scores and other judgments of their creativity (Guilford, 1967; Sternberg & O'Hara, 1999). However, the number of different ideas may not be the best measure of creativity (Nickerson et al., 1985). After all, this measure does not assess whether the solutions meet the three criteria for creativity—that solutions should be novel, high quality, and useful.

⑨ Demonstration 11.8

Divergent Production Tests

Try the following items, which are similar to Guilford's divergent production tests.

1. Many words begin with an *L* and end with an *N*. In 1 minute, list as many words as possible that have the form *L_____N*. (The words can have any number of letters between the *L* and the *N*.)

2. Suppose that people reached their final height at the age of 2, and so normal adult height would be less than 3 feet. In 1 minute, list as many consequences as possible that would result from this change.

3. Below is a list of names. They can be classified in many ways. For example, one classification would be in terms of the number of syllables: SALLY, MAYA, and HAROLD have two syllables, whereas BETH, GAIL, and JUAN have one syllable. Classify them in as many other ways as possible in 1 minute.

    BETH   HAROLD   GAIL   JUAN   MAYA   SALLY

4. Below are four shapes. In 1 minute, combine them to make each of the following objects: a face, a lamp, a piece of playground equipment, and a tree. Each shape may be used once, many times, or not at all in forming each object, and it may be expanded or shrunk to any size. Each shape may also be rotated.

Source: Based on Guilford, 1967.

Investment Theory of Creativity. Financial experts tell us that wise investors should buy low and sell high. Similarly, Robert Sternberg and his colleagues propose that creative people, who deal in the world of ideas, also buy low and sell high (Sternberg & Lubart, 1995, 1996; Sternberg & O'Hara, 1999). That is, they produce a creative idea when no one else is interested in the "investment." At a later time, when the idea has become popular, they move on to a new creative project.

What are the characteristics of these people who are wise creative investors? According to Sternberg and Lubart's **investment theory of creativity,** the essential attributes are intelligence, knowledge, motivation, an encouraging environment, an appropriate thinking style, and an appropriate personality. To work creatively, you'll need all six of these attributes. Suppose, for example, that a person qualifies in five of the characteristics, but he or she may lack intelligence. This person will probably not produce anything creative (Sternberg, 2001). Notice that this approach to creativity also emphasizes factors in the environment *outside* the individual. People may have creative personal attributes. However, if they lack a supportive work environment, they will not be creative in the workplace.

The investment theory of creativity is inherently appealing, particularly because it emphasizes the complex prerequisites for creative achievements. Let's now focus on one of these six prerequisites: motivation. As you'll see, some kinds of motivation are particularly likely to enhance creativity.

Task Motivation and Creativity

Physicist Arthur Schawlow won the Nobel Prize in physics in 1981. He was once asked what factors distinguished highly creative from less creative scientists. He answered that the creative scientists are especially motivated by a curiosity that compels them to pursue the answers to a scientific puzzle (Schawlow, 1982).

The research of Teresa Amabile and her coauthors confirms that an important component of creativity is **intrinsic motivation,** or the motivation to work on a task for its own sake, because you find it interesting, exciting, or personally challenging (Amabile, 1997; Collins & Amabile, 1999; Eliott & Mapes, 2002). Intrinsic motivation can be contrasted with **extrinsic motivation,** or the motivation to work on a task, not because you find it enjoyable, but in order to earn a promised reward or to win a competition. As you'll see, intrinsic motivation can enhance creativity, whereas some kinds of extrinsic motivation can decrease creativity.

The Relationship Between Intrinsic Motivation and Creativity. Teresa Amabile, Beth Hennessey, and their colleagues have developed theories and conducted research on the importance of intrinsic motivation (e.g., Amabile, 1990, 1996, 1997; Hennessey, 2000; Hennessey & Amabile, 1984, 1988; Ruscio, Whitney, & Amabile, 1998). Basically, they argue that people are likely to be most creative when they are working on a task that they truly enjoy. In one study, Ruscio and his coauthors (1998) administered a standardized test of intrinsic motivation to college students. The test asked participants to rate their level of interest in three different kinds of activities: writing, art, and problem solving. Several weeks later, the students came to the laboratory, where they were asked to perform tasks in these three areas. Demonstration 11.9 is similar to the writing task, for example.

While the students worked on the projects, the researchers videotaped their progress and recorded comments that the students provided about their strategies. After the students had left, each creative project was rated by trained judges. The results showed that the students with high intrinsic-motivation scores on the standardized test were indeed more involved in the tasks than those who had lower scores. Also, these more involved students were more likely to produce a creative project.

⊚ **Demonstration 11.9**

Writing a Creative Poem

For this demonstration, you will write an American haiku. These instructions are similar to those that Ruscio and his colleagues supplied to the participants in their study, as follows:

An American haiku is a five-line poem. As you can see from the sample poem below, the first line simply contains a noun, in this case the noun *ocean*. The second line has two adjectives describing the noun. The third line features three verbs related to the noun. The fourth line is a phrase of any length, which is related to the noun. The last line simply repeats the first line.

> Ocean
> Wavy, foamy
> Roll, tumble, crash
> All captured in this shell at my ear.
> Ocean

Now your task is to write a similar American haiku, featuring the noun *summer*. Take 5 minutes to write this poem.

Source: Based on Ruscio et al., 1998, p. 249.

The Relationship Between Extrinsic Motivation and Creativity. Many studies have demonstrated that students tend to produce less creative projects if they are working on these projects for external reasons (Amabile, 1990, 1994, 1997; Hennessey, 2000). For example, the American haiku you wrote in Demonstration 11.9 would probably have been less creative if you had been told that it would be evaluated by a panel of judges. When people view a task as being just a means of earning a reward, a good grade, or a positive evaluation, their extrinsic motivation is high. As a result, their intrinsic motivation often decreases. Consequently, their creativity is also likely to decrease (Hennessey, 2000).

In a representative study, for example, college students wrote less creative poems when they were told that their poems would be evaluated by a group of professional poets (Amabile, 1996). Other research confirms these findings. The effect holds true for both adults and children, and for both artistic creativity and verbal creativity (Amabile, 1990, 1996; Hennessey, 2000; Hennessey & Amabile, 1988).

Additional research has explored other extrinsic factors that can decrease creativity. For example, you may be less creative if someone is watching you while you are working, if you must compete for prizes, and if someone restricts your choices about how you can express your creativity (Amabile, 1990, 1994; Hennessey, 2000).

For many years, researchers had adopted a simple perspective: Intrinsic motivation is good, and extrinsic motivation is bad. You've probably studied psychology long enough to know that no conclusions in our discipline could be that straightforward. A more detailed analysis suggests that some kinds of extrinsic motivation can actually enhance creativity (Eisenberger & Rhoades, 2001). For example, extrinsic motivation can be helpful when it is in the form of useful information and when it can help you complete a task more effectively (Amabile, 1997; Collins & Amabile, 1999).

In general, however, extrinsic motivation reduces your creativity when it controls and limits your options. These findings have important implications for education and for the workplace: Encourage people to work on tasks they enjoy, and select a system of external rewards that will not undermine people's creative efforts.

Incubation and Creativity

So far, we have examined the definitions for creativity, as well as two theoretical approaches. We've also seen that creativity can be increased or reduced by motivational factors. One additional factor—called incubation—is more difficult to document.

Have you ever worked on a creative project and come to an impasse—then found that the solution leapt into your mind after you took a break? Many artists, scientists, and other creative people testify that incubation helps them solve problems creatively. **Incubation** is defined as a situation in which you are initially unsuccessful in solving a problem, but you are more likely to solve the problem after taking a break, rather than continuing to work on the problem without interruption (Perkins, 2001; Smith, 1995b). For example, Frank Offner is a highly creative inventor of medical equipment. In an interview, he argued that incubation is an essential phase of creative problem solving:

> I will tell you one thing that I found in both science and technology: If you have a problem, don't sit down and try to solve it. Because I will never solve it if I am just sitting down and thinking about it. It will hit me maybe in the middle of the night, while I am driving my car or taking a shower, or something like that. (Csikszentmihalyi, 1996, p. 99)

Incubation sounds plausible, and some research shows that incubation does improve creative problem solving (e.g., Csikszentmihalyi, 1996; Houtz & Frankel, 1992). However, in well-controlled laboratory research, incubation is not consistently helpful (Gilhooly, 1996; Nickerson, 1999; Perkins, 2001). Of course, the psychology laboratory is an artificial environment. Consequently, this laboratory research may not be generalizable to real-world creativity (Ward, 2001).

In those cases in which incubation *does* work, what would be a likely mechanism? One possibility, currently favored by cognitive psychologists, is that top-down factors—such as mental set and functional fixedness—may temporarily block you from going beyond the traditional strategies. If you keep working on the problem in those circumstances, you'll keep retrieving the same unproductive ideas. However, if you wait a while or change the location in which you are working, you are likely to represent the problem differently. With a different problem representation, you may now solve the problem creatively (Nickerson, 1999; Perkins, 2001; Smith, 1995b).

Undergraduate students in psychology often think that all the interesting research questions have already been answered. In the area of creativity, we certainly have not answered all the questions. We do not know, for instance, whether incubation really does promote creativity. Some other important questions about creativity also remain unanswered. For example, researchers have not carefully examined how creativity can be enhanced when a group of people is attempting to solve a problem (Kurtzberg & Amabile, 2000–2001).

⑨ Section Summary: *Creativity*

1. Numerous definitions have been proposed for creativity; one common definition is that creativity requires finding a solution that is novel, high quality, and useful.

2. Two approaches to creativity include (a) Guilford's measurements of divergent production and (b) Sternberg's multifactor investment theory, which proposes that creativity requires intelligence, knowledge, motivation, an encouraging environment, an appropriate thinking style and personality.

3. According to Amabile, Hennessey, and their coauthors, intrinsic motivation promotes high levels of creativity; in contrast, extrinsic motivation can reduce creativity if it controls you and limits your options.

4. Some theorists argue that incubation encourages creative problem solving, but well-controlled research in the psychology laboratory often fails to support this concept.

CHAPTER REVIEW QUESTIONS

1. This chapter examined several different methods of representing a problem. Return to the description of these methods, and point out how each method could be used to solve a problem you have faced either in college classes or in your personal life during recent weeks. In addition, identify how the situated-cognition perspective can be applied to your understanding of a problem.

2. In problem solving, how do algorithms differ from heuristics? When you solve problems, what situations encourage each of these two approaches? Describe a situation in which the means-ends heuristic was more useful than an algorithm. Identify a time when you used the hill-climbing heuristic, and note whether it was effective in solving the problem.

3. What barriers prevent our successful use of the analogy approach to problem solving? Think of an area in which you are an expert (an academic subject, a hobby, or work-related knowledge) and point out whether you are skilled in recognizing the structural similarities shared by problem isomorphs.

4. Think of a different area in which you have expertise, and explain the six cognitive areas in which you are likely to have an advantage over a novice. Does your expertise cause you to have trouble estimating the difficulty of a task in this area?

5. How are mental set and functional fixedness related to each other, and how do they limit problem solving? Why would incubation—when it works—help in overcoming these two barriers to effective problem solving?

6. Metacognition was mentioned twice in this chapter. Discuss these two applications, and point out how metacognitive measures can help us determine which problems require insight and which do not.

7. Imagine that you are teaching seventh grade, and your students are about to take a series of standardized tests of cognitive ability. Assume that your students hold the stereotype that boys are better at math and science, whereas girls are better at grammar and creative writing. During the period before the tests begin, you hear the children discussing which gender will perform better on each kind of test. Predict how stereotype threat might influence their performance, and suggest the specific ways in which stereotype threat could influence the students' cognitive processes.

8. Think of an example of an insight problem and a noninsight problem that you have solved recently. Based on the discussing of this topic, how would these two problems differ with respect to (a) the way in which you made progress in solving the problem, (b) the nature of your metacognitions about your progress in problem solving, and (c) the role of language in problem solving.

9. The influence of the environment on problem solving was discussed in several places—in connection with situated cognition, the analogical approach, one of the approaches to creativity, and factors influencing creativity. Using this information, point out why environmental factors are important in problem solving.

10. Imagine that you are a supervisor of 10 employees in a small company. Describe how you might use the material in this chapter to encourage more effective problem solving and greater creativity. Then describe the activities you would want to avoid because they would hinder problem solving and creativity.

NEW TERMS

problem solving
initial state
goal state
obstacles
thinking
understanding
matrix
hierarchical tree
  diagram

situated-cognition
  approach
ecological validity
algorithm
exhaustive search
heuristic
hill-climbing heuristic
means-ends heuristic
subproblems

computer simulation
General Problem Solver
  (GPS)
ill-defined problems
analogy approach
problem isomorphs
surface features
structural features
bottom-up processing

top-down processing
expertise
parallel processing
serial processing
mental set
mindlessness
mindfulness

functional fixedness
gender stereotypes
stereotype threat
insight problem
noninsight problem
creativity
divergent production

investment theory of
creativity
intrinsic motivation
extrinsic motivation
incubation

RECOMMENDED READINGS

Halpern, D. F. (2003). *Thought and knowledge: An introduction to critical thinking* (4th ed.). Mahwah, NJ: Erlbaum. Diane Halpern writes clearly and engagingly about critical thinking and higher mental processes; her book includes chapters on problem solving and creativity, and she also provides a cognitive psychology approach to critical thinking.

Lovett, M. C. (2002). Problem solving. In D. Medin (Ed.), *Stevens' handbook of experimental psychology* (Vol. 2, pp. 317–362). New York: Wiley. Marsha Lovett's chapter on problem solving provides an excellent overview of the topic, and it also includes topics such as research methods and models of problem solving.

Perkins, D. (2001). *The Eureka Effect: The art and logic of breakthrough thinking.* New York: Norton. David Perkins has written extensively about the topics of insight and creativity. This book blends research and anecdotes about these topics. It also includes many examples of puzzles and riddles, together with their answers.

Runco, M. A., & Pritzker, S. R. (Eds.). (1999). *Encyclopedia of creativity.* San Diego: Academic Press. This two-volume encyclopedia includes discussion of central psychological issues such as giftedness and creativity, interdisciplinary topics such as political science and creativity, and essays on creative individuals throughout Western history.

ANSWER TO DEMONSTRATION 11.3

In the hospital room problem, Ms. Anderson has mononucleosis, and she is in Room 104.

ANSWER TO DEMONSTRATION 11.5

In the Hobbits-and-Orcs problem (with R representing the right bank and L representing the left bank), here are the steps in the solution:

1. Move 2 Orcs, R to L.
2. Move 1 Orc, L to R.
3. Move 2 Orcs, R to L.
4. Move 1 Orc, L to R.
5. Move 2 Hobbits, R to L.
6. Move 1 Orc, 1 Hobbit, L to R.
7. Move 2 Hobbits, R to L.
8. Move 1 Orc, L to R.
9. Move 2 Orcs, R to L.

10. Move 1 Orc, L to R.
11. Move 2 Orcs, R to L.

ANSWER TO DEMONSTRATION 11.6, PART B

The numbers are in alphabetical order; your mental set probably suggested that the numbers were in some mathematical sequence, not a language-based sequence.

ANSWER TO DEMONSTRATION 11.7, PART A

The pack on the man's back contained an unopened parachute. (Other solutions would also be possible.)

ANSWER TO DEMONSTRATION 11.7, PART B

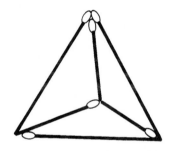

CHAPTER 12
Deductive Reasoning and Decision Making

PREVIEW

This chapter considers how people perform two complex cognitive tasks: deductive reasoning and decision making. The topic of thinking includes problem solving (Chapter 11), as well as deductive reasoning and decision making.

In deductive reasoning tasks, you must draw some logical conclusions, based on the information supplied to you. This chapter focuses on conditional reasoning, using statements such as, "If today is Saturday, then Abyssinia Restaurant is open." People make several systematic errors on conditional reasoning tasks; for example, their conclusions may be influenced by their prior beliefs, and they may fail to test whether their hypotheses could be incorrect.

In decision making, we assess and choose among several alternatives; we often use heuristics, or general strategies, to make decisions. Heuristics usually lead to the correct decision, but we sometimes apply them inappropriately. One heuristic is representativeness, in which we judge a sample to be likely because it looks similar to the population from which it was selected. For example, if you toss a coin six times, an outcome of six heads in a row looks very unlikely. However, sometimes we pay so much attention to representativeness that we ignore other important information such as sample size. We use a second strategy, the availability heuristic, when we estimate frequency in terms of how easily we think of examples of something. For instance, you estimate the number of students from Illinois at your college to be large if you can easily think of examples of people who meet these criteria. Unfortunately, availability is often influenced by two irrelevant factors—recency and familiarity—and so we sometimes make decision errors when we use this heuristic. We use the third heuristic, the anchoring and adjustment heuristic, when we begin by guessing a first approximation (an anchor) and then make an adjustment, based on other information. This strategy is reasonable, except that our adjustments are typically too small. Other topics we'll discuss in this chapter include how context and wording influence decisions, why people are often overconfident, and why our hindsight is often inaccurate. We'll complete this chapter by exploring some new, more optimistic interpretations of human decision making.

INTRODUCTION

You use deductive reasoning every day, although you might not spontaneously choose such a formal-sounding label. For example, a friend tells you, "If I finish my paper before noon, I'll call you and we can meet for lunch." A glance at your watch reveals that it is now 12:43, and you received no phone call. Therefore, you draw the logical conclusion, "My friend did not finish that paper before noon." Every day, you also make dozens of decisions. Should you ask Professor Adams for the letter of recommendation, or should you try Professor Sanchez?

Problem solving (as discussed in the previous chapter), deductive reasoning, and decision making are all interrelated, and we will note several similarities among these tasks throughout this chapter. All three topics are included in the general category called thinking. **Thinking** requires you to go beyond the information you were given; thinking also has a goal such as a solution, a decision, or a belief (Baron, 2000). In other words, you begin with several pieces of information, and you must mentally manipulate that information to solve a problem, to draw a conclusion on a deductive reasoning task, or to make a decision (Waltz et al., 1999).

Furthermore, as Theme 2 argues, we often take a heuristic that is typically helpful, and we overgeneralize it to inappropriate situations. Consequently, when we are engaged in a thinking task, we are likely to make a "smart mistake."

Our two topics for this chapter—deductive reasoning and decision making—are clearly related. In **deductive reasoning,** you are given some specific premises, and you are asked whether those premises allow you to draw a particular conclusion, based on the principles of logic (Evans, 2000; Halpern, 2003). In deductive reasoning, the premises are either true or false, and formal logic specifies the rules you must use in order to draw conclusions.

Our second topic in this chapter, **decision making,** refers to assessing and choosing among several alternatives. In contrast to deductive reasoning, decision making is much more ambiguous. Much of the information may be missing or contradictory. In addition, no clear-cut rules tell us how to proceed from the information to the conclusions. Furthermore, the consequences of that decision won't be immediately apparent (Evans et al., 1993; Simon et al., 2001). In fact, you may never know whether you would have been wiser to choose Professor Adams or Professor Sanchez.

In real life, the uncertainty of decision making is more common than the certainty of deductive reasoning. However, we have trouble on both kinds of tasks, and we do not always reach the appropriate conclusions.

DEDUCTIVE REASONING

One of the most common kinds of deductive reasoning tasks is called conditional reasoning. **Conditional reasoning** (or **propositional reasoning**) problems tell us about the relationship between conditions. Here's a typical conditional reasoning task:

If a student at my college is enrolled in a course in cognitive psychology,
then the student must have completed a course in research methods.
Chris has not completed a course in research methods.
Therefore, Chris is not taking a course in cognitive psychology.

Notice that this problem tells us about the relationship between conditions, such as the relationship between enrollment in a class and the need for a prerequisite. The kind of conditional reasoning we consider in this section explores reasoning problems that have an "if . . . then . . ." kind of structure. When researchers study conditional reasoning, they instruct people to judge whether the conclusion is valid or invalid. In the example above, the conclusion, "Chris is not taking a course in cognitive psychology" is indeed valid.

Another common kind of deductive reasoning task is called a syllogism. A **syllogism** consists of two statements that we must assume to be true, plus a conclusion. Syllogisms refer to quantities, so they use the words *all*, *none*, *some*, and other similar terms. Here's a typical syllogism:

> Some psychology majors are friendly people.
> Some friendly people are concerned about poverty.
> Therefore, some psychology majors are concerned about poverty.

When researchers study syllogisms, they instruct people to judge whether the conclusion is valid, invalid, or indeterminate. In this case, the answer is indeterminate. In fact, those psychology majors who are friendly people and those friendly people who are concerned about poverty could really be two separate populations, with no overlap whatsoever. Notice that our everyday experience encourages us to say, "Yes, the conclusion is valid," because we know that the world must contain many psychology majors who are concerned about poverty! In the abstract world of deductive reasoning, however, we must conclude, "The conclusion is indeterminate."

You could take a philosophy course in logic that would spend an entire semester teaching you about the structure and solution of deductive reasoning problems like these. However, we will emphasize the cognitive factors that influence deductive reasoning. Furthermore, we will limit ourselves to conditional reasoning, a kind of deductive reasoning that students typically find more approachable. Fortunately, researchers have found that conditional reasoning tasks and syllogisms are influenced by virtually the same set of cognitive factors (Gilhooly, 1996; Klauer et al., 2000; Matlin, 1994; Stanovich, 1999). In addition, people's performance on conditional reasoning tasks is correlated with their performance on syllogism tasks (Stanovich & West, 2000).

Let's first explore the four basic kinds of conditional reasoning tasks. Next we'll see how reasoning is influenced by two factors: whether the statements include negative information and whether the problem is concrete or abstract. Then we'll discuss three different cognitive tendencies that people typically show when they solve these reasoning problems.

An Overview of Conditional Reasoning

Conditional reasoning situations occur frequently in daily life, yet these problems are surprisingly difficult to solve correctly. Let's examine the formal principles that have been devised for solving these problems.

Table 12.1 illustrates **the propositional calculus,*** which is a system for categorizing the kinds of reasoning used in analyzing propositions or statements. Let's first

---

*By tradition, the word *the* is inserted here, forming the phrase *the propositional calculus*, rather than simply *propositional calculus*.

TABLE 12.1

The Propositional Calculus: The Four Kinds of Reasoning, with Examples for the Statement, "If this is an apple, then this is a fruit."

Action taken	Portion of the statement	
	Antecedent	**Consequent**
Affirm	Affirming the antecedent (valid)	Affirming the consequent (invalid)
	This is an apple; therefore this a fruit.	*This is a fruit; therefore this is an apple.*
Deny	Denying the antecedent (invalid)	Denying the consequent (valid)
	This is not an apple; therefore this is not a fruit.	*This is not a fruit; therefore this is not an apple.*

introduce some basic terminology. The word **antecedent** means the proposition or statement that comes first; the antecedent is contained in the "if . . ." part of the sentence. The word **consequent** refers to the proposition that follows; it is the consequence. The consequent is contained in the "then . . ." part of the sentence. When we work on a conditional reasoning task, we can perform two possible actions: (1) we can affirm part of the sentence, saying that it is true; or (2) we can deny part of the sentence, saying that it is false.

By combining the two parts of the sentence with the two actions, we have four conditional reasoning situations:

1. **Affirming the antecedent** means that you say the "if . . ." part of the sentence is true. As shown in the upper-left corner of Table 12.1, this kind of reasoning leads to a valid, or correct, conclusion.

2. The fallacy (or error) of **affirming the consequent** means that you say the "then . . ." part of the sentence is true. This kind of reasoning leads to an invalid conclusion. Notice the upper-right corner of Table 12.1; the conclusion "This is an apple" is incorrect. After all, the item could be a pear, or a mango, or numerous other kinds of non-apple fruit.

We can easily see why people are tempted to affirm the consequent: In real life, we are often correct when we make this kind of reasoning error (Evans, 2000; Nickerson et al., 1985). For example, consider the two propositions "If a person is a talented singer, then he or she has musical abilities" and "Paula has musical abilities." It is a good bet that we can conclude Paula is indeed a talented singer. However, in logical reasoning we cannot rely on statements such as, "It's a good bet that. . . ." (Furthermore, I remember a student whose musical skills as a violinist were exceptional, yet she sang off-key. The conclusion about her talented singing would have been incorrect.) As Theme 2 emphasizes, many cognitive errors can be traced to a strategy that usually works well. In this case, however, "it's a good bet that" is not the same as "always."

3. The fallacy of **denying the antecedent** means that you say the "if . . ." part of the sentence is false. Denying the antecedent also leads to an invalid conclusion, as you can see from the lower-left corner of Table 12.1. Again, the item could be some fruit other than an apple.

4. **Denying the consequent** means that you say the "then . . ." part of the sentence is false. In the lower-right corner of Table 12.1, notice that this kind of reasoning leads to a correct conclusion.*

Now test yourself on the four kinds of conditional reasoning tasks by trying Demonstration 12.1. Make certain that you understand these four examples, and review Table 12.1 if you have any difficulty.

Try noticing how often you use the two correct kinds of reasoning. For example, a street sign might read, "Parking permitted only between 6 p.m. and 7 a.m." This sign could be translated into the "if . . . then . . ." form: "If it is between 6 p.m. and 7 a.m., then parking is permitted." You know that it is now 6:30 p.m. By the method of affirming the antecedent, you conclude that you may park on the street. Similarly, a judge says, "If I find Tom Smith guilty, he is going to jail." You learn that Tom Smith did not go to jail. Therefore, you conclude, by the method of denying the consequent, that Tom was judged not guilty.

Also, watch out for conclusions that are *not* valid. For example, Halpern (2003) reported an incident she heard on the evening news:

> Viewers were told that if the President of the United States handled a tense situation with China well, then a tense international situation would be resolved without escalation of hostilities. The situation was resolved well (hostilities did not escalate), so the commentators concluded that the President handled the tense situation well. (p. 149)

Notice that this invalid conclusion was reached by affirming the consequent.

As you might guess, the easiest kind of conditional reasoning task is affirming the antecedent. The most difficult is denying the consequent (García Madruga et al., 2000).

According to Theme 4, the cognitive processes are interrelated. Our ability on conditional reasoning tasks certainly illustrates this theme. For example, conditional reasoning requires language skills (Rips, 2002; Schaeken et al., 2000b), and it often uses mental imagery (Evans, 2002). In addition, Chapter 9 discussed how people

---

*If you have taken courses in research methods or statistics, you will recognize that scientific reasoning is based on the strategy of denying the consequent—that is, ruling out the null hypothesis.

⊚ Demonstration 12.1

The Propositional Calculus

Decide which of the following conclusions are valid and which are invalid. The answers are at the end of the chapter.

1. *Affirming the antecedent.*

   If today is Tuesday, then I have my bowling class.
   Today is Tuesday.
   Therefore, I have my bowling class.

2. *Affirming the consequent.*

   If Nereyda is a psychology major, then she is a student.
   Nereyda is a student.
   Therefore, Nereyda is a psychology major.

3. *Denying the antecedent.*

   If I am a first-year student, then I must register for next semester's classes today.
   I am not a first-year student.
   Therefore, I must not register for next semester's classes today.

4. *Denying the consequent.*

   If the judge is fair, then Susan is the winner.
   Susan is not the winner.
   Therefore, the judge is not fair.

---

often draw logical conclusions when they are reading a story. Furthermore, research confirms that conditional reasoning relies upon working memory—primarily the central-executive component of working memory that we discussed in Chapter 4 (Gilhooly, 1998; Rips, 1995). We would expect the burden on working memory to be especially heavy when some of the propositions contain negative terms (rather than just positive ones) and when people are trying to solve abstract reasoning problems (rather than concrete ones). Let's examine these two topics before we consider several cognitive tendencies that are revealed on conditional reasoning tasks.

Difficulties with Negative Information

Theme 3 of this book states that people can handle positive information better than negative information. As you may recall from Chapter 9, people have trouble processing sentences containing words such as *no* or *not*. This same theme is also true for conditional reasoning tasks. For example, try the following reasoning problem:

> If today is not Friday, then we will not have a quiz today.
> We will not have a quiz today.
> Therefore, today is not Friday.

This problem is much more challenging than a similar problem that begins, "If today is Friday . . ."

Research shows that people take longer to evaluate problems that contain negative information, and they are also more likely to make errors on these problems (Garnham & Oakhill, 1994; Halpern, 2003; Noveck & Politzer, 1998). Working memory is especially likely to be strained when the problem involves denying the antecedent or denying the consequent. Most of us squirm when we see a reasoning problem that includes a statement like, "It is not true that today is not Friday." We are likely to make an error in translating either the initial statement or the conclusion into more accessible, positive forms.

Difficulties with Abstract Reasoning Problems

In general, people are more accurate when they solve reasoning problems that use concrete examples about everyday categories, rather than abstract, theoretical examples. For instance, you probably worked through the items in Demonstration 12.1 quite easily. In contrast, even short reasoning problems are difficult if they refer to abstract items where the characteristics are arbitrary (Manktelow, 1999; Oaksford & Chater, 1998; Wason & Johnson-Laird, 1972). For example, try this problem about geometric objects:

> If an object is red, then it is rectangular.
> This object is not rectangular.
> Therefore, it is not red. (Valid or invalid?)

Incidentally, the answer to this item is at the bottom of Demonstration 12.2 (p. 410). Other related research demonstrates that performance is better if the propositions are high in imagery (Clement & Falmagne, 1986). Furthermore, accuracy increases when people use diagrams to make the problem more concrete (Bauer & Johnson-Laird, 1993; Halpern, 2003). However, reasoning can sometimes be more difficult when the problems are concrete if our everyday knowledge interferes with logical principles. Let's see how this principle operates in the following discussion of the belief-bias effect.

The Belief-Bias Effect

In our lives outside the psychology laboratory, our background knowledge helps us function well. Inside the psychology laboratory—and in a course on logic—this background information encourages us to make errors. For example, try the following problem (Cummins et al., 1991, p. 276):

> If my finger is cut, then it bleeds.
> My finger is bleeding.
> Therefore, my finger is cut.

In everyday life, that conclusion is likely to be correct; if your finger is bleeding, then the most likely explanation is some variation on a cut. However, in the world of logic, this cut finger problem commits the error of affirming the consequent, so it cannot be correct (Cummins et al., 1991). Similarly, your common sense encouraged you to decide that the conclusion was valid for the syllogism on page 404, about the psychology majors who are concerned about poverty.

The **belief-bias effect** occurs in reasoning when people make judgments based on prior beliefs and general knowledge, rather than on the rules of logic (Evans, 2002, 2004; Quinn & Markovits, 1998; Rips, 1995). In general, people are likely to make errors when the logic of a reasoning problem conflicts with their background knowledge (Holyoak & Simon, 1999; Klauer et al., 2000; Manktelow, 1999). For example, when a conditional reasoning task is difficult, people search for additional information relevant to the situation. If the conclusion *seems* sensible, they argue that the reasoning process was correct.

The belief-bias effect is one more example of top-down processing (Theme 5). Our prior expectations help us organize our experiences and understand the world. When we see a statement that looks familiar in a reasoning problem, we do not pay enough attention to the specific reasoning process that generated this statement (M. S. Cohen, 1993). As a result, we fail to question an invalid conclusion.

Some researchers have identified substantial individual differences in people's susceptibility to the belief-bias effect. Specifically, people are likely to be influenced by the belief-bias effect if they score low on a test of flexible thinking (Stanovich, 1999; Stanovich & West, 1997, 1998). These people are likely to agree with statements such as, "No one can talk me out of something I know is right."

In contrast, people who are flexible thinkers agree with statements such as "People should always take into consideration evidence that goes against their beliefs." These people typically solve the reasoning problems correctly, without being distracted by the belief-bias effect. In general, they also tend to look more carefully at a reasoning problem, trying to determine whether the logic is faulty (Stanovich & West, 2000). When people use this kind of active, open-minded thinking, they ask questions about their initial conclusions, and they seek out new alternative solutions (Baron, 2000; Byrne et al., 2000; Johnson-Laird et al., 2000).

---

⑨ **Demonstration 12.2**

The Confirmation Bias

Imagine that each square below represents a card. Imagine that you are participating in a study in which the experimenter has told you that every card has a letter on one side and a number on the other side.

    You are then given this rule about these four cards: "If a card has a vowel on one side, then it has an even number on the other side."

    Your task is to decide which card or cards you would need to turn over in order to find out whether this rule is valid or invalid. What is your answer? The correct answer is discussed in the text.

E	**J**	**6**	**7**

(Incidentally, the answer to the problem about the objects on p. 408 is "valid.")

Source: The confirmation-bias task in this demonstration is based on Wason, 1968.

The Confirmation Bias

Try Demonstration 12.2 (above) before reading further. Peter Wason's (1968) selection task has inspired more research than any other deductive reasoning problem— and it has also raised many questions about whether humans are basically rational (Ahn & Graham, 1999; Evans, 2002, 2004; Oswald & Grosjean, 2004). Let's first examine the original version of the selection task, and then we'll see how people typically perform better on more realistic variations of this task.

    The Standard Wason Selection Task. Demonstration 12.2 shows the original version of the selection task. Wason (1968) found that people show a **confirmation bias;** they would rather try to confirm a hypothesis than try to disprove it (Klayman & Ha, 1996; Manktelow, 1999; Woll, 2002). Most people working on this classical selection task choose to turn over the *E* card. For example, one review of the literature showed than an average of 89% of research participants selected this appropriate strategy (Oaksford & Chater, 1994). This strategy allowed them to confirm the hypothesis by the valid method of affirming the antecedent, because this card has a vowel on it. If this card has an even number on the other side, the rule is correct. If the number is odd, the rule is incorrect.

The other valid method in deductive reasoning is to deny the consequent. To accomplish this goal, you must choose to turn over the 7 card. The information about the other side of the 7 is very valuable— just as valuable as the information about the other side of the *E*. Remember that the rule is: "If a card has a vowel on its letter side, then it has an even number on its number side."

To deny the consequent in this Wason task, we need to check out a card that does *not* have an even number on its number side. (In this case, then, we must check out the 7 card.) We saw that most people—that is, 89% of the participants—are eager to affirm the antecedent. However, they are reluctant to deny the consequent by searching for counterexamples. This strategy would be a wise attempt to reject a hypothesis, but people avoid this option. In a review of the literature, only 25% of research participants selected this appropriate strategy (Oaksford & Chater, 1994).

You may wonder why we did not need to check on the J and the 6. If you reread the rule, you will notice that the rule did not say anything about consonants, such as J. The other side of the J could show an odd number, an even number, or even a Vermeer painting, and we wouldn't care. A review of the literature showed that most people appropriately avoided this option; they chose it only 16% of the time (Oaksford & Chater, 1994).

The rule also does not specify what must appear on the other side of the even numbers, such as *6*. However, many people select the 6 to turn over. In fact, in a review of the literature, 62% chose this option (Oaksford & Chater, 1994). People often assume that the two parts of the rule can be switched, so that it reads, "If a card has an even number on its number side, then it has a vowel on its letter side." Thus, they make an error by choosing the 6.

Perhaps you notice that this preference for confirming a hypothesis—rather than disproving it—corresponds to Theme 3 of this book. On the selection task, we see that people who are given a choice would rather seek out positive information than negative information. We would rather know what something *is* than what it *is not*. This preference is very strong. However, people who take time to inspect the problem carefully are more likely than impulsive people to select the two correct cards in this task (Toplak & Stanovich, 2002). Furthermore, people with high scores on the SAT exams are also more likely to answer this selection task correctly (Stanovich & West, 2000).

Variations on the Wason Selection Task. In recent years, researchers have tested numerous versions of the classic selection task. Even a subtle change in the wording of the problem can change the results dramatically (Evans, 2002, 2004; Jackson & Griggs, 1990). Careful instructions about conditional reasoning strategies can also have an impact (Griggs, 1995; Griggs & Jackson, 1990; Platt & Griggs, 1995).

However, most of the research has focused on versions in which the numbers and letters on the cards are replaced by concrete information and situations that we encounter in our everyday lives. As you might guess, performance is much better when the task is concrete, familiar, and realistic (e.g., Evans, 2002, 2004; Hogarth, 2001; Woll, 2002).

Let's consider a classic study that demonstrates how well people can do on a concrete version of this task, rather than the standard, abstract version you saw in

Demonstration 12.2. Griggs and Cox (1982) tested college students in Florida using a variation of the selection task. This task focused on the drinking age, which was then 19 in the state of Florida. The problem was much more concrete and relevant to most college students. The participants in this study saw the following problem:

> On this task imagine that you are a police officer on duty. It is your job to ensure that people conform to certain rules. The cards in front of you have information about four people sitting at a table. On one side of a card is a person's age and on the other side of the card is what the person is drinking. Here is a rule: IF A PERSON IS DRINKING BEER, THEN THE PERSON MUST BE OVER 19 YEARS OF AGE. Select the card or cards that you definitely need to turn over to determine whether or not the people are violating the rule. (p. 415)

Four cards were presented, each with one label: DRINKING A BEER, DRINKING A COKE, 16 YEARS OF AGE, and 22 YEARS OF AGE.

Griggs and Cox (1982) found that 73% of the students who tried the drinking age problem made the correct selections, in contrast to 0% who tried the standard, abstract form of the selection task. The difference in performance between concrete and abstract tasks is especially dramatic when the wording of the selection task implies some kind of social contract designed to prevent people from cheating (Gigerenzer & Hug, 1992; Leighton & Sternberg, 2003; Platt & Griggs, 1993b; Rips, 2002).

Some theorists argue that evolution may have favored people who developed specialized skills in understanding important, adaptive problems (Cosmides, 1989; Cosmides & Tooby, 1995). As a result, we humans may be especially competent in understanding the kinds of rules that are necessary for cooperative interactions in a society. For example, people can understand the societal rule that alcohol consumption is limited to individuals who are at least 19 years of age. In contrast, we may be less skilled in understanding rules that have no implications for social interactions such as abstract problems about cards, letters, and numbers (Evans & Over, 1996).

How can we translate the confirmation bias into real-life experiences? Try noticing your own behavior when you are searching for evidence. Do you consistently look for information that will confirm that you are right, or do you valiantly pursue ways in which your conclusion can be wrong?

The confirmation bias also operates in international politics. For example, if Country A wants to start a war in Country B, Country A will keep seeking support for its position. Country A will also *avoid* seeking information that its position may not be correct. Myers (2002) points out a remedy for the confirmation bias: Try to explain why another person might hold the *opposite* view. In an ideal world, the leaders of Country A should sincerely try to construct arguments against attacking Country B.

Failing to Transfer Knowledge to a New Task

So far, we have seen that people struggle with conditional reasoning problems that include negative or abstract information. Their accuracy is also reduced because of the belief-bias effect. In addition, they mainly try to confirm their hypotheses.

Perhaps you could have predicted the final source of errors that we will discuss here, based on the information on problem solving in Chapter 11. In that chapter, we saw that people have trouble seeing that the math problem they are currently working on is similar to a problem that they correctly solved at an earlier time. Similarly, people have trouble appreciating the similarity between two versions of the selection task illustrated in Demonstration 12.2 (Klaczynski et al., 1989). As a result, they fail to transfer their knowledge, and they make mistakes on the second task.

This overview of conditional reasoning does not provide much evidence for Theme 2 of this book. At least in the psychology laboratory, people are not especially accurate when they try to solve "if . . . then . . ." kinds of problems. However, the circumstances are usually more favorable in our daily lives, where problems are concrete and situations are consistent with our belief biases. Deductive reasoning is such a difficult task that we are not as efficient and accurate as we are in perception and memory—two areas in which humans are generally very competent.

◉ **Section Summary:** *Deductive Reasoning*

1. Conditional reasoning focuses on "if . . . then . . ." relationships; performance is most accurate for affirmative (rather than negative) statements, and for concrete (rather than abstract) problems.

2. The belief-bias effect interferes with accurate conditional reasoning; top-down processing encourages people to trust their prior knowledge, rather than the principles of logic.

3. Furthermore, people often fall victim to the confirmation bias; they try only to confirm a hypothesis, rather than try to reject it.

4. A variety of factors influence performance on the Wason selection task (which assesses the confirmation bias); for example, accuracy is enhanced when the task describes a concrete situation that is governed by societal rules.

5. People often fail to transfer their knowledge to a new reasoning task.

6. Although people do not perform well on these reasoning tasks in the laboratory, their accuracy may be greater in real-life situations.

DECISION MAKING

As you have just seen, reasoning uses established rules to draw clear-cut conclusions. In contrast, when we make decisions, we have no established rules, and we also do not even know whether our decisions are correct (Klein, 1997; Tversky & Fox, 1995). You may be missing some critical information, and you may not trust other information. Should you apply to graduate school or get a job after college? Should you take social psychology in the morning or in the afternoon? Decision making does not provide a list of rules (such as the propositional calculus) that can help you assess the relative merits of each option. In addition, emotional factors usually influence our everyday decision making (Markman & Medin, 2002).

Decision making is an interdisciplinary field that includes researchers in economics, consumer research, political science, history, sociology, statistics, philosophy, medicine, and law—as well as psychology (Markman & Medin, 2002; Simonson et al., 2001; Tetlock & Mellers, 2002). Within the discipline of psychology, decision making inspires numerous books and articles each year. For example, several recent books provide a general overview of decision making (e.g., Connolly et al., 2000; Gigerenzer & Selten, 2001; Gigerenzer et al., 1999; Gilovich et al., 2002; Jaeger et al., 2001; Juslin & Montgomery, 1999; Kahneman & Tversky, 2000).

Other recent books consider more specific issues, such as moral decision making (Baron, 1998), political decision making (McDermott, 1998; Vertzberger, 1998), public policy decisions (Gowda & Fox, 2002), decisions about dangerous events (Glassner, 1999), judgment during stressful situations (Hammond, 2000), intuition and decision making (Hogarth, 2001; Myers, 2002), and unwise decisions made by intelligent people (Sternberg, 2002). In general, the research on decision making examines concrete, realistic scenarios, rather than the abstract situations used in research on deductive reasoning.

This section on decision making emphasizes decision-making heuristics. As you'll recall from previous chapters, **heuristics** are general strategies that typically produce a correct solution. However, we humans often fail to appreciate the limitations of these heuristics, and so we do not always make wise decisions. Throughout this section, you will often see the names of two researchers, Daniel Kahneman and Amos Tversky. These two individuals proposed that a small number of heuristics guide human decision making. As they emphasized, the same strategies that normally guide us toward the correct decision may sometimes lead us astray (Kahneman & Frederick, 2002, Kahneman & Tversky, 1996). Notice that this heuristics approach is consistent with Theme 2 of this book: Our cognitive processes are usually efficient and accurate, and our mistakes can often be traced to a rational strategy.

In this part of the chapter, we will discuss many studies that illustrate errors in decision making. These errors should not lead us to conclude that humans are limited, foolish creatures. Instead, people's decision-making heuristics are well adapted to handle a wide range of problems (Hertwig & Todd, 2002; Kahneman & Tversky, 1996). However, these same heuristics become a liability when they are applied too broadly, for example, when we emphasize heuristics rather than other important information.

Let us explore three classic decision-making heuristics: representativeness, availability, and anchoring and adjustment. Then, in a discussion of framing, we will consider how wording and context influence decisions. Next, the In Depth feature explores how we are often overconfident when we make decisions. We'll also consider hindsight bias, a phenomenon related to overconfidence. Finally, we will examine some of the new approaches to decision making.

The Representativeness Heuristic

Here's a remarkable coincidence: Three early U.S. presidents—Adams, Jefferson, and Monroe—all died on the Fourth of July, although in different years (Myers, 2002). You have probably noticed many more personal coincidences. For example, while categorizing the books on decision making for the list on page 414, I was pleased to locate two books on political decision making. While recording the citations, I noticed an amazing coincidence: One was published by Stanford University Press, and the other by the University of Michigan Press; I had earned my bachelor's degree from Stanford and my PhD from the University of Michigan.

When we experience coincidences like these, we may have the sense of mystical harmony in the universe (Myers, 2002). Somehow these coincidences do not look random enough to be explained away by chance. Deaths of three presidents, for example, should be scattered randomly throughout the year, rather than occurring on the same day.

Now consider this example. Suppose that you have a regular penny with one head (H) and one tail (T), and you toss it six times. Which outcome seems most likely, T H H T H T or H H H T T T?

If you are like most people, you would guess that T H H T H T would be the most likely outcome of those two possibilities (Teigen, 2004). After all, you know that coin tossing should produce heads and tails in random order, and the order T H H T H T looks much more random than H H H T T T.

A sample looks **representative** if it is similar in important characteristics to the population from which it was selected. For instance, if a sample was selected by a random process, then that sample must look random in order for people to say it looks representative. Thus, T H H T H T is a sample that would be judged representative because it has an equal number of heads and tails (which would be the case in random coin tosses). Furthermore, T H H T H T would be judged representative because the order of the T's and H's looks random rather than orderly.

---

⑨ Demonstration 12.3

Sample Size and Representativeness

A nearby town is served by two hospitals. About 45 babies are born each day in the larger hospital. About 15 babies are born each day in the smaller hospital. Approximately 50% of all babies are boys, as you know. However, the exact percentage of babies who are boys will vary from day to day. Some days it may be higher than 50%, some days it may be lower. For a period of 1 year, both the larger hospital and the smaller hospital recorded the number of days on which more than 60% of the babies born were boys. Which hospital do you think recorded more such days?

_____ The larger hospital
_____ The smaller hospital
_____ About the same (say, within 5% of each other)

The research shows that we often use the **representativeness heuristic;** we judge that a sample is likely if it is similar to the population from which this sample was selected (Kahneman & Frederick, 2002; Kahneman & Tversky, 1972). Our cognitive processes are exceptionally skilled at assessing similarity, so it typically makes sense for us to exploit that ability by using the representativeness heuristic (Sloman, 1999).

According to the representativeness heuristic, we believe that random-looking outcomes are more likely than orderly outcomes—as long as the outcome has been produced by a random process. In reality, however, a random process occasionally produces an outcome that seems nonrandom. Has a cashier ever added up your bill, and the sum looked *too* orderly—say, $22.22? You might even be tempted to check the arithmetic, because addition is a process that should yield a random-looking outcome. You would be less likely to check the bill if it were $21.97, because that very random-looking outcome is a more representative kind of answer. But chance alone often produces an orderly sum like $22.22, just as chance alone often produces orderly patterns like the three presidents dying on the Fourth of July.

Kahneman and Tversky (1972) conducted several experiments that emphasize the importance of representativeness. In one study, for example, they asked people to make judgments about families with six children. People judged the sequence G B B G B G to be more likely than the sequence B B B G G G. People base their decisions on representativeness, rather than on actual probability. Be sure to try Demonstration 12.3 on page 415 before you read further.

When we make judgments about a series of coin tosses and the birth order of children, we emphasize whether the sequence looks random. On other occasions, we may judge similarity in terms of several different characteristics. For example, the representativeness heuristic often encourages us to make errors when we make more complex decisions, such as judgments about human beings. A person who is European American, wealthy, and tough on crime may seem like a "representative" U.S. Republican. However, you can probably name many Democrats who also fit that description (Kunda, 1999).

Perhaps the major problem with using the representativeness heuristic is this: The heuristic is so persuasive that we often ignore statistical information that we should consider (Fischhoff, 1999; Hertwig & Todd, 2002; Kunda, 1999). Two kinds of useful statistical information are the sample size and the base rate.

Sample Size and Representativeness. When we make a decision, representativeness is such a compelling heuristic that we often fail to pay attention to sample size. For example, how did you respond to Demonstration 12.3 on page 415? When Kahneman and Tversky (1972) asked college students this question, 56% responded, "About the same." In other words, the majority of students thought that a large hospital and a small hospital were equally likely to report having at least 60% baby boys born on a given day. Thus, they ignored sample size.

In reality, however, sample size is an important characteristic that should be considered whenever you make decisions. A large sample is statistically likely to reflect the true proportions in a population. In contrast, a small sample will often reveal an extreme proportion (e.g., at least 60% boy babies). However, people are often unaware that deviations from a population proportion are more likely in these small samples (Teigen, 2004).

Tversky and Kahneman (1971) point out that we *should* believe in the **law of large numbers,** which states that large samples will be representative of the population from which they are selected. The law of large numbers is a correct law. However, we often commit the **small-sample fallacy** by assuming that small samples will be representative of the population from which they are selected (Poulton, 1994). Unfortunately, the small-sample fallacy leads us to incorrect decisions.

We often commit the small-sample fallacy in social situations, as well as in relatively abstract statistics problems. For example, we may draw unwarranted stereotypes about a group of people on the basis of a small number of group members (Hamilton & Sherman, 1994). One effective way of combating inappropriate stereotypes is to become acquainted with a large number of people from the target group— for example, through exchange programs with groups of people from other countries. More generally, people can also be trained to appreciate the importance of the law of large numbers (Fong et al., 1986; Sedlmeier, 1999).

---

⑨ Demonstration 12.4

Base Rates and Representativeness

Imagine that some psychologists have administered personality tests to 30 engineers and 70 lawyers, all people who are successful in their fields. Brief descriptions were written for each of the 30 engineers and the 70 lawyers. A sample description follows. Judge that description by indicating the probability that the person described is an engineer. Use a scale from 0 to 100.

> Jack is a 45-year-old man. He is married and has four children. He is generally conservative, careful, and ambitious. He shows no interest in political and social issues and spends most of his free time on his many hobbies, which include home carpentry, sailing, and mathematical puzzles.

The probability that the man is one of the 30 engineers in the sample of 100 is _____ %.

Source: Kahneman and Tversky, 1973, p. 241.

Base Rate and Representativeness. Representativeness is such a compelling heuristic that people also ignore the **base rate,** or how often the item occurs in the population (Teigen, 2004). Be sure you have tried Demonstration 12.4 on page 417 before we proceed. Using problems like the one in this demonstration, Kahneman and Tversky (1973) showed that people rely on representativeness when they are asked to judge category membership. We focus almost exclusively on whether a description is representative of members of each category. By emphasizing representativeness, we commit the **base-rate fallacy,** underemphasizing important information about base rate (Dawes, 1998; Johnson-Laird et al., 1999; Woll, 2002).

In one study, students read the following description of a man named Rudy:

Rudy is a bit on the peculiar side. He has unusual tastes in movies and art, he is married to a performer, and he has tattoos on various parts of his body. In his spare time Rudy takes yoga classes and likes to collect 78 rpm records. An outgoing and rather boisterous person, he has been known to act on a dare on more than one occasion. What do you think Rudy's occupation most likely is? A) Farmer B) Librarian C) Trapeze Artist D) Surgeon E) Lawyer (Swinkels, 2003, p. 120).

If people pay attention to base rates, they should select a profession that has a high base rate in the population, such as a lawyer. However, most students in Swinkels's (2003) study used the representativeness heuristic, and they guessed that Rudy was a trapeze artist. The description of Rudy was highly similar to (that is, representative of) the stereotype of a trapeze artist.

You might argue, however, that the study with Rudy was unfair. After all, the base rates of the various professions were not even mentioned in the problem. Maybe the students failed to consider that lawyers are more common than trapeze artists. Well, the base rate was made very clear in Demonstration 12.4; you were told that the base rate was 30 engineers and 70 lawyers in the population. Did you make use of this base rate and guess that Jack was highly likely to be a lawyer? In one study using this kind of setup, most people ignored this base-rate information and judged on the basis of representativeness (Kahneman & Tversky, 1973). In fact, this description for Jack is highly representative of our stereotype for engineers, and so people tend to guess a high percentage for the answer to the question.

Kahneman and Tversky (1973) point out how their studies are related to Bayes' theorem. **Bayes' theorem** states that judgments should be influenced by two factors: base rate and the likelihood ratio. The **likelihood ratio** assesses whether the description is more likely to apply to Population A or Population B. For example, the description in Demonstration 12.4 is probably much more representative of a typical engineer than of a typical lawyer. We seem to base our decision on this likelihood ratio, and so we reply, "Engineer." Meanwhile, we ignore the useful information contained in the base rates. Because people often ignore base rates, they are not obeying Bayes' theorem, and they can make unwise decisions.

The base-rate issue has some real-life consequences. A clinical psychologist may diagnose a client's disorder by emphasizing the similarity between this client's symptoms and the prototype person with that disorder. Meanwhile, the psychologist may ignore the fact that this disorder is actually very rare.

We should emphasize, however, that people vary widely in the way they tackle problems. Furthermore, some problems—and some alternative wordings of problems—produce more accurate decisions (Gigerenzer, 1998a; Kunda, 1999; Shafir & LeBoeuf, 2002). Training sessions also encourage students to use base-rate information appropriately (Gebotys & Claxton-Oldfield, 1989; Hammond, 1996; Kruschke, 1996).

You should also be alert for other everyday examples of the base-rate fallacy. For instance, one study of pedestrians killed at intersections showed that 10% were killed when crossing at a signal that said "walk." In contrast, only 6% were killed when crossing at a signal that said "stop" (Poulton, 1994). Does that mean that—for your own safety—you should cross the street only when the signal says "stop"? But think about the base rates: Many more people cross the street when the signal says "walk."

⊙ **Demonstration 12.5**

The Conjunction Fallacy

Read the following paragraph:

> Linda is 31 years old, single, outspoken, and very bright. She majored in philosophy. As a student, she was deeply concerned with issues of discrimination and social justice, and she also participated in antinuclear demonstrations.

Now rank the following options in terms of the probability of their describing Linda. Give a ranking of 1 to the most likely option and a ranking of 8 to the least likely option:

_____ Linda is a teacher at an elementary school.
_____ Linda works in a bookstore and takes yoga classes.
_____ Linda is active in the feminist movement.
_____ Linda is a psychiatric social worker.
_____ Linda is a member of the League of Women Voters.
_____ Linda is a bank teller.
_____ Linda is an insurance salesperson.
_____ Linda is a bank teller and is active in the feminist movement.

Source: From Tversky and Kahneman, 1983.

The Conjunction Fallacy and Representativeness. Be sure to try Demonstration 12.5 on page 419 before you read further. Now inspect your answers. Which did you rank more likely—that Linda is a bank teller, or that Linda is a bank teller and is active in the feminist movement? Demonstration 12.5 is one of the questions that Tversky and Kahneman (1983) tested in their study on the conjunction fallacy. Let us examine their experiment and then discuss the nature of the conjunction fallacy.

Tversky and Kahneman (1983) presented the "Linda" problem and another similar problem to three groups of people. One was a statistically naive group of undergraduates. The second group consisted of first-year graduate students who had taken one or more courses in statistics; this group had intermediate knowledge about the principles of probability. The third group consisted of doctoral students in a decision science program of a business school who had taken several advanced courses in probability and statistics; they were labeled the sophisticated group. In each case, the participants were asked to rank all eight statements according to their probability, with the rank of 1 assigned to the most likely statement.

Figure 12.1 shows the average rank for each of the three groups for the two critical statements: (1) "Linda is a bank teller" and (2) "Linda is a bank teller and is active in the feminist movement." Notice that the people in all three groups thought that the second statement would be more likely than the first.

Think for a moment why this conclusion is mathematically impossible. The **conjunction rule** states that the probability of the conjunction of two events cannot be larger than the probability of either of its constituent events. In the Linda problem, the conjunction of the two events—bank teller and feminist—cannot occur more often than either event by itself—for instance, being a bank teller. (Consider some other situations in which the conjunction rule operates; for example, the number of U.S. college students who were born in the state of Iowa cannot be greater than the number of U.S. college students.)

As we saw earlier in this section, representativeness is such a powerful heuristic that people often ignore useful statistical information, such as sample size and base rate. Apparently, they also ignore the mathematical implications of the conjunction rule.

Tversky and Kahneman (1983) discovered that most people commit the **conjunction fallacy:** They judge the probability of the conjunction of two events to be greater than the probability of a constituent event. Tversky and Kahneman trace the conjunction fallacy to the representativeness heuristic. They argue that people judge the conjunction of "bank teller" and "feminist" to be more likely than the simple event "bank teller," because "feminist" is a characteristic that is very representative of (that is, similar to) someone who is single, outspoken, bright, a philosophy major, concerned about social justice, and an anti-nuclear activist. A person with these characteristics doesn't seem very likely to become a bank teller. However, she seems highly likely to be a feminist. By adding the extra detail of "feminist" to "bank teller," we have made the description seem more representative and plausible—even though that description is statistically less likely. The conjunction fallacy is especially strong when the first characteristic in the conjunction (e.g., "bank teller") is unlikely, but the second characteristic (e.g., "feminist") is more likely (Swoyer, 2002).

FIGURE 12.1

The Influence of Type of Statement and Level of Statistical Sophistication on Likelihood Rankings. Low numbers on the ranking indicate that people think the event is more likely, an incorrect decision.

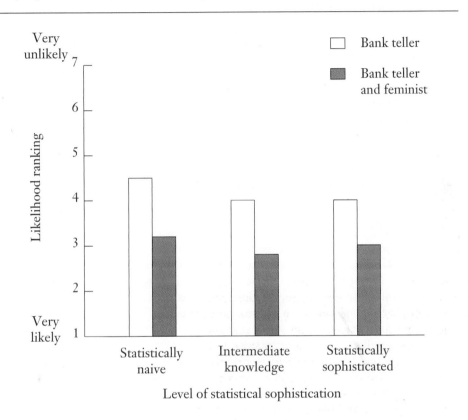

Source: Based on Tversky & Kahneman, 1983.

Psychologists have been intrigued with the conjunction fallacy, especially because it demonstrates that people can ignore one of the most basic principles of probability theory. The results for the conjunction fallacy have been replicated many times, with generally consistent findings (D. Davidson, 1995; Dougherty et al., 1999; Osherson, 1995). For example, the probability of "spilling hot coffee" seems greater than the probability of "spilling coffee" (Moldoveanu & Langer, 2002) . . . until you identify the conjunction fallacy.

Some skeptics have wondered whether the conjunction fallacy can be traced to a simple verbal misunderstanding. For example, perhaps people interpret the statement, "Linda is a bank teller" to mean that Linda is a bank teller who is *not* active in the feminist movement. However, we do not have much evidence for this explanation

(Agnoli & Krantz, 1989; Dawes, 1998). Other research shows that people are more accurate if the problem is described in terms of actual numbers, rather than probabilities (Gigerenzer, 1998b; Hertwig & Gigerenzer, 1999; Mellers et al., 2001). Still, the conjunction fallacy does not disappear, even under these favorable conditions (Ben-Zeev, 2002; Richardson, 1998).

Before we discuss a second decision-making heuristic, let's briefly review the representativeness heuristic. We use the representativeness heuristic when we make decisions based on whether a sample looks similar in important characteristics to the population from which it is selected. The representativeness heuristic is so appealing that we tend to ignore other important characteristics that we *should* consider, such as sample size and base rate. We also fail to realize that the probability of two events occurring together (for example, bank teller and feminist) needs to be smaller than the probability of just one of those events (for example, bank teller). In summary, the representativeness heuristic is basically helpful in our daily lives, but we sometimes use it inappropriately (Ben-Zeev, 2002).

The Availability Heuristic

A second important heuristic that people use in making decisions is availability. You use the **availability heuristic** whenever you estimate frequency or probability in terms of how easy it is to think of examples of something (Dawes, 1998; Tversky & Kahneman, 1973). In other words, people judge frequency by assessing whether relevant examples can be easily retrieved from memory or whether this memory retrieval requires great effort.

The availability heuristic is generally helpful in everyday life. For example, suppose that someone asked you whether your college had more students from Illinois or more from Idaho. You have probably not memorized the geography statistics, so you would be likely to answer the question in terms of the relative availability of examples of Illinois students and Idaho students. Perhaps your memory has stored the names of dozens of Illinois students, and so you can easily retrieve their names ("Cynthia, Akiko, Bob . . ."). Perhaps your memory has stored only one name of an Idaho student, so it's difficult to think of examples of this category. Because examples of Illinois students were relatively easy to retrieve, you conclude that your college has more Illinois students. In general, then, this availability heuristic is a relatively effective method for making decisions about frequency.

As you'll recall, a heuristic is a general strategy that is typically accurate. The availability heuristic is accurate as long as availability is correlated with true, objective frequency—and it usually is. However, the availability heuristic can lead to errors. As we will see in a moment, several factors that can bias memory retrieval are not correlated with true, objective frequency (Kunda, 1999). These factors can influence availability and therefore decrease the accuracy of our decisions. We will see that recency and familiarity—both factors that influence memory—can potentially distort availability. Figure 12.2 illustrates how these two factors can contaminate the relationship between true frequency and availability.

FIGURE 12.2

The Relationship Between True Frequency and Estimated Frequency, with Recency and Familiarity as "Contaminating" Factors.

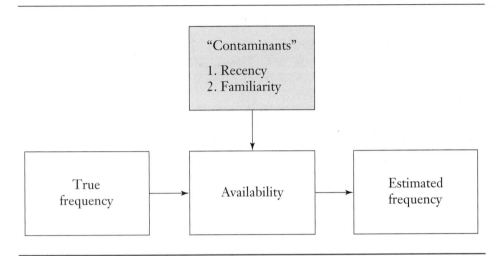

We mentioned at the beginning of the chapter that deductive reasoning and decision making are interrelated. The availability heuristic is related to the belief-bias effect in reasoning, in which people base their conclusions on their prior beliefs that come readily to mind. People seem to treat the reasoning task as a decision-making problem, and the logically correct answer is so unbelievable that it does not come readily to mind (Rips, 1994). As a result, people give the incorrect answer.

Let's make certain that you understand how availability differs from representativeness. When we use the representativeness heuristic, we are given a specific example (such as T H H T H T or Linda the bank teller). We then make judgments about whether the specific example is *similar* to the general category it is supposed to represent (such as coin tosses or philosophy majors concerned about social justice). In contrast, when we use the availability heuristic, we are given a general category, and we must *remember* the specific examples (such as examples of Illinois students). Then we make decisions based on whether the specific examples come easily to mind. So here is a way to remember the two heuristics:

1. If the problem is based on a judgment about the *similarity*, you are dealing with the representativeness heuristic.
2. If the problem requires you to *remember examples*, you are dealing with the availability heuristic.

We'll begin our exploration of availability by considering two factors that influence availability—recency and familiarity. Then we will examine a consequence of availability, called illusory correlations. Finally, we will see how availability operates when people try to imagine an event in the future.

Recency and Availability. As you know from Chapters 4, 5, and 6, memory for items generally declines with the passage of time. Thus, you recall the more recent items more accurately. In other words, more recent items are more available. As a result, we judge recent items to be more likely than they really are. For example, take yourself back to the spring of 1999, following several widely publicized school shootings. If you had been asked to estimate the frequency of violence in the schools, your estimate would probably have been high.

The availability heuristic plays an important role in a variety of professions. For example, physicians are more likely to select a particular diagnosis if they have recently diagnosed a similar case (Weber et al., 1993).

Other research suggests implications for clinical psychology. MacLeod and Campbell (1992) found that when people were encouraged to recall pleasant events from their past, they judged pleasant events to be more likely in their future. In contrast, when people were encouraged to recall unpleasant events, they judged unpleasant events to be more likely in their future. Psychotherapists might be able to encourage depressed clients to envision a more hopeful future by having them recall and focus on previous pleasant events. In short, the availability heuristic suggests many practical applications.

Familiarity and Availability. The familiarity of the examples—as well as their recency—can also produce a distortion in frequency estimation. For instance, people who know many divorced individuals often provide higher estimates of national divorce rates than do people who have rarely encountered divorce (Kozielecki, 1981).

Familiarity also contaminates medical judgments. For example, physicians often have distorted ideas about the dangers of various diseases that are discussed frequently in medical journals. Specifically, the number of medical-journal articles about a disease is highly correlated with physicians' estimates about whether that disease is likely to be fatal (Christensen-Szalanski et al., 1983). This correlation holds true, regardless of what the articles actually said about the disease.

Journalists and news reporters overexpose us to some events and underexpose us to others (Dougherty et al., 1999; Fox & Farmer, 2002; Glassner, 1999; Reber, 2004). For example, they tell us about violent events such as fires and murders much more often than less dramatic (and more common) causes of death. One hundred times as many people die from diseases as are murdered, yet the newspapers carry three times as many articles about murders.

According to research conducted in Canada, the United States, and China, the media can even influence people's estimates of a country's population (Brown & Siegler, 1992; Brown, Cui & Gordon, 2002). Brown and Siegler (1992) found that students estimated the population of El Salvador as 12 million, though its actual population was only 5 million. In contrast, their estimate for Indonesia was 19.5 million, though its actual population was 180 million. At the time the study was conducted, El Salvador was frequently in the news because of U.S. intervention in Latin America. Because students in the early 1990s had not heard recent news about Indonesia, they severely underestimated that country's population. Try asking a friend to estimate the population of Israel (population = 6,000,000) and Bulgaria (population = 7,600,000). How about Iraq (population = 24,000,000) and Nepal (population = 25,900,000)? Are your friend's estimates for these two pairs of countries distorted by the frequency of media coverage?

The media can also influence viewers' ideas about the prevalence of different points of view (Ivins, 1999). For instance, in December 1999, approximately 35,000 people went to Seattle to protest the troublesome policies of the World Trade Organization (WTO). Union organizers pointed out the problems that WTO policies raised for U.S. workers. Human rights advocates carried signs condemning countries that violated international policies. Students urged people to consider the problem of slave labor in international sweatshops. However, the newspaper and television coverage paid little attention to these and other groups that were peacefully protesting the WTO policies. The media simply called them "just a bunch of people worried about turtles." Who was featured in their coverage? They focused on the relatively small number of anarchists who chose to trash some of the local stores. Notice whether you can spot the same tendency in current news broadcasts. Do the media still create our cognitive realities?

◉ Demonstration 12.6

Familiarity and Availability

Read this list of names to several friends. After you have finished the entire list, ask your friends to estimate whether there were more men or women listed. Do not allow them to answer, "About the same." (In reality, 14 women's names and 15 men's names are listed.)

Louisa May Alcott	Maya Angelou
John Dickson Carr	Virginia Woolf
Alice Walker	Robert Lovett
Thomas McGuane	Judy Blume
Laura Ingalls Wilder	George Nathan
Frederick Rolfe	Allan Nevins
Edward George Lytton	Jane Austen
Danielle Steel	Henry Crabb Robinson
Michael Drayton	Joseph Lincoln
Toni Morrison	Emily Brontë
Hubert Selby, Jr.	Arthur Hutchinson
Sue Grafton	James Hunt
Agatha Christie	Joyce Carol Oates
Richard Watson Gilder	Brian Hooker
Harriet Beecher Stowe	

Try Demonstration 12.6, which is a modification of a highly influential study by Tversky and Kahneman (1973). See whether your friends respond according to the familiarity of the examples, rather than true frequency. Tversky and Kahneman presented people with lists of 39 names. A typical list might contain the names of 19 famous women and 20 less famous men. After hearing the list, participants were asked to judge whether the list contained more men's names or more women's names. About 80% of the participants in this condition erroneously guessed that there were more women's names on the list. The relatively familiar names were apparently more available, even though women's names were objectively less frequent. Similar results have been obtained in replications (Manis et al., 1993; McKelvie, 1997; Reber, 2004).

Illusory Correlation and Availability. So far, we have seen that availability—or the ease with which examples come to mind—is typically a useful heuristic. However, this heuristic can become "contaminated" by factors such as recency and frequency, leading to inappropriate decisions about an event's frequency. Now we turn to a third topic, to see how the availability heuristic can contribute to a cognitive error called an illusory correlation.

As you know, a correlation is a statistical relationship between two variables, and *illusory* means deceptive or unreal. Therefore, an **illusory correlation** occurs when people believe that two variables are statistically related, even though there is no real evidence for this relationship. According to numerous studies, we often believe that a certain group of people tends to have certain kinds of characteristics, even though an accurate tabulation would show that the relationship is not statistically significant (Fiedler, 2004; Hamilton et al., 1993; Stroessner & Plaks, 2001).

Think of some examples of stereotypes that arise from illusory correlations. These illusory correlations may either have no basis in fact or much less basis than is commonly believed. For example, consider the following illusory correlations: females are unskilled at math, blondes are not very bright, gay males and lesbians have psychological problems, and so forth. According to the **social cognition approach,** we form stereotypes by means of our normal cognitive processes, which rely on strategies such as the availability heuristic (Reber, 2004; Stroessner & Plaks, 2001).

An early investigation of illusory correlation was performed by Chapman and Chapman (1967), who tried to see whether people reported systematic patterns in situations that were really completely random. In brief, these researchers asked people in a psychiatric hospital to draw some human figures. These figures were then paired *completely at random* with six psychiatric symptoms, such as suspiciousness and dependence. College students then examined these drawings, which had been labeled with the symptoms of the people who had supposedly drawn them. Afterward, the students were asked to report what features of the drawings were most often paired with each symptom. Remember, now, that the stimuli had been arranged so that the drawings were not systematically related to the symptoms. Nonetheless, the college students reported that paranoid people had frequently drawn exaggerated eyes, whereas dependent people had frequently drawn exaggerated mouths. Chapman and Chapman (1969) also found that students formed an illusory correlation between people's reported sexual orientation and their responses on an inkblot test.

Theorists have proposed a variety of alternate explanations for illusory correlations, including unevenly distributed attention and characteristics of the memory trace (e.g., Kunda, 1999; Stroessner & Plaks, 2001). However, let's explore in more detail how the availability heuristic could be used to explain illusory correlations.

When we try to determine whether two variables are related to each other, we really ought to consider four kinds of information. For example, suppose that we want to determine whether people who are lesbians or gay males are more likely than heterosexuals to have psychological problems. Incidentally, some people seem to believe in this illusory correlation, even though the research shows no consistent relationship between sexual orientation and psychological problems (e.g., Gonsiorek, 1996; Peplau & Garnets, 2000; Rothblum & Factor, 2001). To do the research properly, we need to pay attention to the frequency of four possible combinations: (1) gay people who have psychological problems, (2) gay people who do not have psychological problems, (3) straight people who have psychological problems, and (4) straight people who do not have psychological problems. Imagine, for example, that researchers gathered the data in Table 12.2. Their decision should be based on a comparison of two ratios:

$$\frac{\text{gay people with psychological problems}}{\text{total number of gay people}} \quad \text{versus} \quad \frac{\text{straight people with psychological problems}}{\text{total number of straight people}}$$

Using the data from Table 12.2, for example, we would find that 6 out of 60 gay people (or 10%) have psychological problems, and 8 out of 80 straight people (also 10%) have psychological problems. We should therefore conclude that sexual orientation is not related to psychological problems.

Unfortunately, however, people often pay attention to only one cell in the matrix, especially if the two characteristics are statistically less frequent (Hamilton et al., 1993; Kunda, 1999; Stroessner & Plaks, 2001). In this example, some people notice

TABLE 12.2

A Matrix Showing Hypothetical Information About Sexual Orientation and Psychological Problems.

	Number in each category	
	Gay people	**Straight people**
People with psychological problems	6	8
People without psychological problems	54	72
Totals	60	80

only the gay people who have psychological problems, ignoring the important information in the other three cells. People with a bias against gay people might be especially likely to pay attention to this cell, and they will continue to look for information that confirms their hypothesis that gay people have problems. You'll recall from the discussion of conditional reasoning that people would rather try to confirm a hypothesis than try to disprove it. Consistent with Theme 3 of this book, we favor positive information and handle it more efficiently.

Try applying the information about illusory correlations to some stereotype that you hold. Notice whether you have tended to focus on only one cell in the matrix, ignoring the other three. Have you specifically tried to *disconfirm* the stereotypes? Also, notice how politicians and the media often base their arguments on illusory correlations (Myers, 2002). For example, they may focus on the number of welfare recipients with fraudulent claims. This number is meaningless unless we also know the number of welfare recipients *without* fraudulent claims, or else the number of people who do not receive welfare who make other kinds of fraudulent claims.

The Simulation Heuristic and Availability. So far, we have discussed decisions you can make by thinking of examples and judging the relative frequency of those examples. The correct answer to these decisions could be obtained by counting an unbiased list of the examples. For instance, you could answer the question about the number of male and female authors in Demonstration 12.6 by counting the names on the list.

In real life, however, we often judge probabilities in situations that cannot be evaluated by simply counting the list of examples. For instance, what is the probability that Bill and Jane will get divorced? What is the probability that you will become a clinical psychologist? Each marriage and each career are unique, so we cannot provide an answer by counting examples of other people's marriages or careers.

Kahneman and Tversky (1982) proposed that the simulation heuristic is a special example of the availability heuristic. However, the availability heuristic refers to the ease with which we can recall *examples*, whereas the **simulation heuristic** refers to the ease with which we can think of a particular *scenario*, or series of events (Poulton, 1994).

For example, suppose that you want to judge the likelihood of your becoming a clinical psychologist. You might construct a scenario in which you do extremely well in your course work, achieve superb scores on the Graduate Record Exams, receive strong letters of recommendation from your professors, get accepted into the graduate school of your choice, receive your PhD, complete your internship, and set up your practice. If you have no difficulty imagining each event in this scenario, then you may judge the entire scenario as being likely. On the other hand, constructing a scenario for your becoming the president of the United States or the prime minister of Canada may be more difficult, and so you would judge the scenario as being unlikely.

The simulation heuristic explains why we are especially frustrated when we just miss reaching a goal (Goldinger et al., 2003). Kahneman and Tversky (1982) asked students to judge which of two individuals should be more upset, a man who missed his plane by 5 minutes or a man who missed it by 30 minutes. You won't be surprised to learn that 96% of the respondents answered that the more upsetting experience would be to miss the flight by 5 minutes. Kahneman and Tversky propose that we can envision this individual constructing a simulation in which he didn't stop to buy a newspaper or some other trivial event—thereby arriving on time. In contrast, we have trouble seeing how a person could construct a simulation that would save 30 minutes.

In recent research, people were more likely to blame a person who was hurt in an accident if they could easily generate a simulation in which the person had *avoided* the accident. You'll be more likely to blame Mr. Smith for his car accident if you can easily visualize him *not* quitting work 15 minutes earlier than usual to go to a movie (Goldinger et al., 2003). Furthermore, people are more likely to think that a person is relatively normal if they can create a simulation that links psychiatric symptoms together (Ahn et al., 2003). For example, they judged a woman to be relatively normal if her insomnia caused her memory problems, which caused her anxiety. In contrast, they judged her to be disturbed if the insomnia, memory problems, and anxiety were described as unconnected problems.

Let us review what we've discussed about the availability heuristic, in which we estimate frequency or probability in terms of how easily we can think of examples of something. This heuristic is generally accurate in our daily lives, and people are able to estimate relative frequency with impressive accuracy (Sedlmeier et al., 1998). However, availability can be contaminated by two factors that are not related to objective frequency—recency and familiarity. This information suggests a specific precaution for situations in which you make frequency judgments: Ask yourself whether you are giving a special advantage to a category of items that occurred more recently or that are somehow more familiar (Kunda, 1999).

In this discussion, we also saw that availability helps create illusory correlations, another error in decision making. Finally, we often judge likelihood in terms of the simulation heuristic, in which we imagine a series of possible events, rather than recalling examples of them. We apparently use the simulation heuristic when we judge our performance, figure out whether a victim is to be blamed for an accident, or judge whether someone is normal or psychologically disturbed.

The Anchoring and Adjustment Heuristic

Has this kind of experience happened to you? You're shopping for a jacket, and you describe to the salesperson what you are looking for. He shows you a jacket that is clearly the top of the line—and very expensive. After gulping and asking to see some other styles, you find that you walk out of the store with a jacket that is less expensive than the first one, but more costly than you had intended to purchase. The clever clerk may have encouraged you to fall for the anchoring and adjustment heuristic (Mussweiler et al., 2004; Poulton, 1994).

According to the **anchoring and adjustment heuristic**—also known as the **anchoring effect**—we begin with a first approximation—an **anchor**—and then we make adjustments to that number on the basis of additional information (Mussweiler et al., 2004; Slovic et al., 1974; Tversky & Kahneman, 1982). This heuristic often leads to a reasonable answer, just as the representativeness and availability heuristics often lead to reasonable answers. However, the anchoring effect is especially powerful; people typically rely too heavily on the anchor, and their adjustments are too small. Notice, incidentally, that the anchoring and adjustment heuristic is often based on the availability heuristic, because highly available information is likely to serve as an anchor.

The anchoring and adjustment heuristic illustrates once more that we humans tend to endorse our current hypotheses or beliefs, rather than trying to question them (Baron, 2000). We've seen several other examples of this tendency in the present chapter:

1. *The belief-bias effect:* We rely too heavily on our established beliefs.
2. *The confirmation bias:* We prefer to confirm a current hypothesis, rather than to reject it.
3. *The illusory correlation:* We rely too strongly on one well-known cell in a data matrix, failing to seek information about the other three cells.

These three tendencies—as well as the anchoring and adjustment heuristic—are all examples of Theme 5, which emphasizes top-down processing.

Let's begin by considering some research on the anchoring and adjustment heuristic. Then we will see how this heuristic can be applied to estimating confidence intervals. Finally, we'll examine several applications to areas beyond cognitive psychology.

◉ Demonstration 12.7

The Anchoring and Adjustment Heuristic

Copy the two multiplication problems listed below on separate pieces of paper. Show Problem A to at least five friends, and show Problem B to at least five other friends. In each case, ask the participants to estimate the answer within 5 seconds.

A. $8 \times 7 \times 6 \times 5 \times 4 \times 3 \times 2 \times 1$

B. $1 \times 2 \times 3 \times 4 \times 5 \times 6 \times 7 \times 8$

Now tally the answers separately for the two problems, listing the answers from smallest to largest. Calculate the median for each problem. (If you have an uneven number of participants, the median is the answer in the middle of the distribution—with half larger and half smaller. If you have an even number of participants, take the average between the two answers in the middle of the distribution.)

Research on the Anchoring and Adjustment Heuristic. Demonstration 12.7 illustrates the anchoring and adjustment heuristic. In a classic study, high school students were asked to estimate the answers to these two multiplication problems (Tversky & Kahneman, 1982). The students were allowed only 5 seconds to respond. The results showed that the two problems generated widely different answers. Some students started with a relatively large number—8—and the median of their estimates was 2,250. (That is, half the students estimated higher than 2,250, and half estimated lower.) In contrast, other students started with a small number—1—and their median estimate

---

⑨ Demonstration 12.8

Estimating Confidence Intervals

For each of the following questions, answer in terms of a range, rather than a single number. Specifically you should supply a 98% confidence interval, which is the range within which you expect the correct answer to fall. For example, suppose you answer a question by supplying a 98% confidence interval that is 2,000 to 7,000. This means that you think there is only a 2% chance that the real answer is either less than 2,000 or more than 7,000. The correct answers can be found at the end of the chapter on page 449.

1. What percentage of the voting-age population in Canada did *not* vote in the 2000 federal election?
2. What percentage of the voting-age population in the United States did *not* vote in the 2000 presidential election?
3. What percentage of U.S. college graduates report that they smoked at least one cigarette during the previous month?
4. What was the estimated population of California in 2001?
5. What is the size of Sweden, in square miles?
6. How many full-time undergraduates were enrolled in Canadian universities in 1999?
7. How many people in the world speak Mandarin Chinese as their first language?
8. What is the current literacy rate in Cuba?
9. What was the year of birth for Sojourner Truth, the Black female abolitionist?
10. How many political refugees were reported worldwide, as of 2001?

Source: All questions are based on information in the *World Almanac and Book of Facts* (2003) and Statistics Canada (2003).

was only 512. Interestingly, both groups seem to have anchored too heavily on the initial impression formed by the series of single-digit numbers in each question, because both estimates are far too low: The correct answer for both problems is 40,320. Were the people you tested influenced by the anchoring and adjustment heuristic?

The anchoring and adjustment heuristic is so powerful that it operates even when the anchors are obviously arbitrary or impossibly extreme (e.g., a person living to the age of 140). It also operates for both novices and experts (Englich & Mussweiler, 2001; Mussweiler et al., 2004; Tversky & Kahneman, 1974). Furthermore, it operates whether the anchor is provided by the researcher or by the participant (Epley & Gilovich, 2001). Although the precise explanations for the anchoring and adjustment heuristic have not yet been identified, one likely mechanism is that the anchor restricts the search for relevant information in memory. Specifically, people concentrate their search on information relatively close to the anchor (Pohl et al., 2003).

Let's consider some applications of the basic anchoring and adjustment heuristic. Then we'll see how the anchoring and adjustment heuristic encourages us to make errors when we estimate confidence intervals.

Applications of the Anchoring and Adjustment Heuristic. The anchoring and adjustment heuristic is not confined to situations in which we estimate numbers. In fact, it often operates when we make judgments about other people (Kunda, 1999). For example, let's suppose that you hold a stereotype about people who belong to a particular group, such as people who live in a region of the United States or students who have a particular major. When you meet someone from that group, you are likely to rely on your stereotype in order to create an initial anchor. Then you consider the unique characteristics of that particular individual, and you make some adjustments. However, you may not make sufficiently large adjustments away from that initial anchor. To use another familiar framework, you probably rely too heavily on top-down processing, and not enough on bottom-up processing.

The anchoring and adjustment heuristic has numerous applications in everyday life. For example, Englich and Mussweiler (2001) studied anchoring effects in courtroom sentencing. Trial judges with an average of 15 years of experience listened to a typical legal case. The role of the prosecutor was played by a person who was introduced as a computer science student. When the "prosecutor" demanded a sentence of 34 months, these experienced judges recommended a sentence of 36 months. When the same "prosecutor" demanded a sentence of 12 months, the judges recommended 28 months. Other research shows that the anchoring and adjustment heuristic operates when assessing environmental risk (Holtgrave et al., 1994), during genetic counseling (Shiloh, 1994), and in establishing real estate prices (Northcraft & Neale, 1987). Be sure to try Demonstration 12.8 on page 431 before you read further.

Estimating Confidence Intervals. We use anchoring and adjustment when we estimate a single number. We also use this heuristic when we estimate **confidence intervals,** or ranges within which we expect a number to fall a certain percentage of the time. (For example, you might guess that the 98% confidence interval for the number of students at a particular college is 3,000 to 5,000. This guess would mean that you think there is a 98% chance that the population is between 3,000 and 5,000.)

Demonstration 12.8 tested the accuracy of your estimates for various kinds of almanac information. Check page 449 to see how many of your confidence-interval estimates included the correct answer. Suppose that a large number of people were to answer a large number of questions. Then we would expect their confidence intervals to include the correct answer about 98% of the time—assuming that their estimation techniques are correct. However, studies have shown that people provide 98% confidence intervals that actually include the correct answer only about 60% of the time (Block & Harper, 1991; Fischhoff, 1982; Tversky & Kahneman, 1974). In other words, the confidence intervals that we estimate are definitely too narrow (Hoffrage, 2004).

Tversky and Kahneman (1974) point out how the anchoring and adjustment heuristic is relevant when we make confidence-interval estimates. We first provide a best estimate and use this figure as an anchor. Then we make adjustments upward and downward from this anchor to construct the confidence-interval estimate. However, our adjustments are often too small. For example, perhaps you initially guessed that the percentage of U.S. nonvoters in the 2000 elections was 25%. You might then say that your confidence interval was between 15% and 35%. This range is too narrow, because you may have made a large error in your original estimate. Again, we establish our anchor and we do not wander far from it in the adjustment process.

Try applying the anchoring and adjustment heuristic to your own life. Suppose that you are trying to guess how much you will make in tips in your summer job. You will probably make a first guess and then base your range on this figure. However, your final answer will depend too heavily on that first guess, which may not have been carefully chosen. Your adjustments will not adequately reflect all the additional

---

⑨ Demonstration 12.9

The Framing Effect and Background Information

Try the following two problems:

Problem 1
Imagine that you decided to see a play and you paid $20 for the admission price of one ticket. As you enter the theater, you discover that you have lost the ticket. The theater keeps no record of ticket purchasers, so the ticket cannot be recovered. Would you pay $20 for another ticket for the play?

Problem 2
Imagine that you have decided to buy a ticket for a play where the admission price of one ticket is $20. As you enter the theater, you discover that you have lost a $20 bill. Would you still pay $20 for a ticket for the play?

Source: Based on Tversky & Kahneman, 1981.

factors that you should consider after you made your first guess. When we shut our eyes to new evidence, we rely too heavily on top-down processing.

Let's review the last of the three major decision-making heuristics. When we use the anchoring and adjustment heuristic, we begin by guessing a first approximation or anchor. Then we make adjustments to that anchor. This heuristic is generally useful, but we typically fail to make large enough adjustments. The anchoring and adjustment heuristic can be applied to a variety of areas, such as stereotyping, legal studies, risk assessment, genetic counseling, and real estate. The anchoring and adjustment heuristic also accounts for our errors when we estimate confidence intervals; we usually supply ranges that are far too narrow, given the degree of uncertainty they should reflect. In order to overcome potential biases from the anchoring and adjustment heuristic, think carefully about your initial estimate. Then ask yourself whether you are paying enough attention to the unique features of this specific situation that might require large adjustments away from your initial anchor.

The Framing Effect

While I was proofreading this chapter on decision making, I took a break to read the mail that had just arrived. I opened an envelope from an organization I support, called "The Feminist Majority." The letter pointed out that in a previous year, right-wing organizations had introduced legislation in 17 state governments that would eliminate affirmative action programs for women and people of color. This figure surprised and saddened me; apparently the anti–affirmative action supporters had more influence than I had imagined! And then I realized that the framing effect might be operating. Perhaps, at that very moment, other people throughout the United States were opening their mail from organizations that endorsed the other perspective. Perhaps their letter pointed out that their organization—and others with a similar viewpoint—had *failed* to introduce legislation in 33 state governments. Yes, a fairly subtle change in the wording of a sentence can produce a very different emotional reaction! Are political organizations perhaps hiring cognitive psychologists?

The **framing effect** demonstrates that the outcome of a decision can be influenced by two factors: (1) the background context of the choice and (2) the way in which a question is worded (or framed). However, before we discuss these two factors, be sure you have tried Demonstration 12.9.

Background Information and the Framing Effect. If you reread Demonstration 12.9, you'll notice that the amount of money is $20 in both cases. If decision makers were perfectly "rational," they would respond identically to both problems (Shafir & Tversky, 1995; Stanovich, 1999). However, the decision frame differs for the two situations; they seem "psychologically different."

As Kahneman and Tversky (1984) point out, we frequently organize our mental expense accounts according to topics. Specifically, we view going to the theater as a transaction in which the cost of the ticket is exchanged for the experience of seeing a play. If you buy another ticket, the cost of seeing that play has increased to a level that many people find unacceptable. When Kahneman and Tversky asked people what they would do in the case of Problem 1, only 46% said that they would pay for another ticket. In contrast, in Problem 2, we don't tally the lost $20 bill in the same account as the cost of a ticket. In this second case, we view the lost $20 as being generally irrelevant to the ticket. In Kahneman and Tversky's study, 88% of the participants said that they would purchase the ticket in Problem 2. In other words, the background information provides different frames for the two problems, and the frame strongly influences the decision. Now, before you read further, try Demonstration 12.10.

⊚ Demonstration 12.10

The Framing Effect and the Wording of a Question

Try the following two problems:

Problem 1
Imagine that the United States is preparing for the outbreak of an unusual Asian disease, which is expected to kill 600 people. Two alternative programs to combat the disease have been proposed. Assume that the exact scientific estimate of the consequences of the programs are as follows:

> If Program A is adopted, 200 people will be saved.
> If Program B is adopted, there is a one-third probability that 600 people will be saved, and a two-thirds probability that no people will be saved.

> Which program would you favor?

Problem 2
Now imagine the same situation, with these two alternatives:

> If Program C is adopted, 400 people will die.
> If Program D is adopted, there is a one-third probability that nobody will die, and a two-thirds probability that 600 people will die.

> Which program would you favor?

Source: Based on Tversky & Kahneman, 1981.

The Wording of a Question and the Framing Effect. In Chapter 11, we saw that people often fail to realize that two problems may share a deep-structure similarity. In other words, people are distracted by the surface-structure differences. We will see that people are also distracted by surface-structure differences when they make decisions between various options.

Tversky and Kahneman (1981) tested college students in both Canada and the United States, using Problem 1 in Demonstration 12.10; notice that both choices emphasize the number of lives that would be *saved*. They found that 72% of their participants chose Program A, and only 28% chose Program B. Notice that the participants in this group were "risk averse." That is, they preferred the certainty of saving 200 lives, rather than the risky prospect of a one-in-three possibility of saving 600 lives. Notice, however, that the benefits of Programs A and B in Problem 1 are statistically identical.

Now inspect your answer to Problem 2, in which both choices emphasize the number of lives that would be *lost* (that is, the number of deaths). Tversky and Kahneman (1981) presented this problem to a different group of students from the same college. Only 22% favored Program C, but 78% favored Program D. Here the participants were "risk taking"; they preferred the two-in-three chance that 600 would die, rather than the guaranteed death of 400 people. Again, however, the benefits of the two programs are statistically equal. Furthermore, notice that Problem 1 and Problem 2 have identical deep structures. The only difference is that the outcomes are described in Problem 1 in terms of the lives saved, but in Problem 2 in terms of the lives lost.

The way that the question is framed—lives saved or lives lost—has an important effect on people's decisions. This framing changes people from focusing on the possible gains (lives saved) to focusing on the possible losses (lives lost). In the case of Problem 1, we tend to prefer having 200 lives saved for sure; we avoid the option where it's possible that no lives will be saved. In the case of Problem 2, we tend to prefer the risk that nobody will die (even though there is a good chance that 600 will die) rather than choose the option where 400 face certain death. Keep in mind this important distinction:

1. When dealing with possible *gains* (for example, lives saved), people tend to *avoid* risks.

2. When dealing with possible *losses* (for example, lives lost), people tend to *seek* risks.

The influence of framing on decision making is both pervasive and robust. Numerous studies have replicated the general framing effect (Halpern, 2003; Isen, 2000; Rohrbaugh & Shanteau, 1999; Shafir & Tversky, 1995; Stanovich, 1999). For instance, the framing effect is common among statistically sophisticated people as well as statistically naive people, and the magnitude of the effect is relatively large. Furthermore, framing effects are found in older adults, as well as students in their 20s (Mayhorn et al., 2002). The framing effect also has an important impact on consumer behavior. In one classic study, for example, Johnson (1987) discovered that people are much more likely to prefer ground beef that is labeled "80% lean," rather than "20% fat."

Numerous studies have also examined how framing can influence medical decisions (e.g., Linville et al., 1993; Rothman & Salovey, 1997). For example, Jasper and his colleagues (2001) discovered an important application of the framing effect when health-care professionals provide information about drug-related risks. These researchers monitored a telephone counseling service in Toronto, Canada, which provided information to women who were already pregnant or planned to become pregnant. As you know, women need to be careful to avoid taking certain medications during pregnancy. When a woman called the counseling service with a question about taking a drug to counteract allergies, she was randomly assigned to one of two groups. Women in one group heard a message that was framed in terms of a possible problem: "In every pregnancy, there is a 1–3% chance that a woman will give birth to a child who has a major birth defect. This drug has not been shown to change that." Women in the other group heard a message that was framed in terms of a healthy outcome: "In every pregnancy, there is a 97–99% chance that a woman will give birth to a child who does not have a major birth defect. This drug has not been shown to change that" (p. 1237).

Several days after calling, the women were contacted, and they were asked to rate their likelihood of taking the allergy medication. The women in the first group (birth defect) rated their own personal risk as being relatively high, compared to women in the second group (no birth defect).

As Huber and her colleagues (1987) concluded in connection with the general framing effect, decision making often depends on whether the choice is presented as "Is the pitcher half empty, or is the pitcher half full?" This area of research confirms Theme 4 of this textbook; the cognitive processes are indeed interrelated. In this case, descriptive language has an important influence on decision making.

Let's review the framing effect. Background information can influence decisions; we do not make choices in a vacuum, devoid of knowledge about the world. In addition, the wording of the question can influence decisions. Specifically, people avoid risks when the wording implies gains, and they seek risks when the wording implies losses. Furthermore, these framing effects have been replicated in a variety of laboratory and real-world situations. The research suggests some practical advice: When you are making an important decision, try rewording the description of this decision. For example, suppose that you need to decide whether to accept a particular job offer. Ask yourself how you would feel about having this job, and then ask yourself how you would feel about *not* having this job.

IN DEPTH

Overconfidence in Decisions

So far, we have seen that decisions can be influenced by three decision-making heuristics: the representativeness heuristic, the availability heuristic, and the anchoring and adjustment heuristic. Furthermore, the framing effect demonstrates that both background information and wording can influence decision making inappropriately. Given these sources of error, people should realize that their decision-making skills are nothing to boast about. Unfortunately, however, the research shows that people are often overconfident (Dougherty, 2001; Hoffrage, 2004; Myers, 2002; Shafir & LeBoeuf, 2002). **Overconfidence** means that people's confidence judgments are higher than they should be, based on their actual performance on the task.

We have already discussed two examples of overconfidence in decision making in this chapter. In the discussion of illusory correlations, we emphasized that people are confident that two variables are related, when in fact the relationship is either weak or nonexistent. In the discussion of anchoring and adjustment, we saw that people are so confident in their estimation abilities that they supply very narrow confidence intervals for their estimates.

Overconfidence is a characteristic of other cognitive tasks, in addition to decision making. For example, Chapter 5 noted that people are often overconfident when they provide eyewitness testimony. Furthermore, Chapter 6 pointed out that people are typically overconfident about how well they understood material they had read, even though they had answered many questions incorrectly. Let's consider research on several aspects of overconfidence; then we'll discuss several factors that help to create overconfidence.

General Studies on Overconfidence. A variety of studies show that humans are overconfident in many decision-making situations. For example, people are overconfident about how long a person with a fatal disease will live, which firms will go bankrupt, and whether the defendant is guilty in a court trial (Kahneman & Tversky, 1995). People consistently have more confidence in their own decisions than in predictions that are based on statistically objective measurements.

People are also overconfident in estimating their future performance, based on judgments about their current performance (Bjork, 1999). People also tend to overestimate their social skills, creativity, leadership abilities, and a wide range of academic skills (Kruger, 1999; Matlin, 2004a; Matlin & Stang, 1978). In addition, physicists, economists, and other researchers are overconfident that their theories are correct (Trout, 2002).

Furthermore, people are overconfident about their assessment of other people. For example, employers who decide which applicants to hire for a job, based on an interview, are overconfident about the wisdom of their decisions (Bishop & Trout, 2002). Also, clinical psychologists are overconfident in diagnosing a mental disorder in their clients (Bishop & Trout, 2002; Ridley, 1995). In addition, physicians tend to be overconfident that a patient has one specific disease, rather than two separate diseases (McKenzie, 1998).

We should note, however, that some researchers are more optimistic about humans' ability to predict the accuracy of their decisions. These researchers admit that people are likely to be overconfident when they answer selected "trick questions" that have counterintuitive answers. However, the studies show that people usually provide more accurate confidence estimates when they are asked to make a large, unselected set of judgments, such as estimating the population of each of the 50

U.S. states (Gigerenzer et al., 1991; Hoffrage, 2004; Juslin et al., 2000; Mellers et al., 1998).

We also need to emphasize the substantial individual differences in overconfidence. For example, a large-scale study on students' decision-making abilities showed that 77% of the participants were overconfident about their accuracy in answering general-knowledge questions like those in Demonstration 12.8. However, these results tell us that 23% were either on target or underconfident (Stanovich, 1999). Other research demonstrates that males are more likely than females to be overconfident about the accuracy of their decisions (Eccles et al., 1998; Pulford & Colman, 1997).

Let's consider two research areas in which overconfidence has been extensively documented. As you'll see, politicians are often overconfident about the decisions they make. Furthermore, if we explore an area that is personally more familiar, students are usually overconfident that they will complete their academic projects on time.

Overconfidence in Political Decision Making. Even very bright politicians can make extremely unwise decisions. Former U.S. President Bill Clinton had a sexual relationship with White House intern Monica Lewinsky, even though most ordinary citizens could have predicted a disastrous outcome (Halpern, 2002; Sternberg, 2002). As Sternberg argues, powerful politicians such as Clinton often believe that they are all-knowing and that they can do almost anything they want, even in their personal lives.

Let's shift to the decisions that politicians make about international policy—decisions that can affect thousands of people. Unfortunately, political leaders seldom think systematically about the risks involved in important decisions. For instance, they often fail to consider the risks involved in invading another country (Vertzberger, 1998). As Kahneman and Tversky (1995) noted, in an international conflict, each side tends to overestimate its chances of success.

When politicians need to make a decision, they are also overconfident that their data are accurate. I wrote this chapter in December 2003, when U.S. citizens were gradually learning that our country went to war with Iraq because our political leaders were overconfident that Iraq had owned weapons of mass destruction. For instance, Vice President Dick Cheney had stated on August 26, 2002, "There is no doubt that Saddam Hussein now has weapons of mass destruction." President George W. Bush had declared on March 17, 2003, "Intelligence gathered by this and other governments leaves no doubt that the Iraq regime continues to possess and conceal some of the most lethal weapons ever devised." However, it is becoming clear that crucial information had been forged, and these weapons do not exist (Pitt, 2003; Press, 2004; Remnick, 2003).

Consider the following example of a disastrous political decision that occurred some time ago. In 1988, the U.S.S. *Vincennes* was patrolling in the Persian Gulf during the war between Iran and Iraq. The ship's radar had just detected an unknown aircraft, and Captain Will Rogers needed to decide whether the aircraft was simply a civilian airplane or whether it was actually attacking his ship. Rogers decided to shoot down the aircraft. As both Rogers and the rest of the world soon learned, the aircraft was only an Iranian civilian airplane, and all 290 passengers aboard the plane died. Unfortunately, the captain had been overconfident about his original judgment and had failed to verify critical characteristics of the situation (Bales, 1988; Klein, 1998).

The *Vincennes* incident inspired an applied research program for the U.S. Navy. This program, called Tactical Decision Making Under Stress, was designed to encourage military decision makers to carefully consider alternative hypotheses (Cannon-Bowers & Salas, 1998). One suggestion is a strategy called the crystal-ball technique (M. S. Cohen et al., 1998). The **crystal-ball technique** asks decision makers to imagine that a completely accurate crystal ball has determined that their favored hypothesis is actually *incorrect*; the decision makers must therefore search for alternative explanations for the event. They must also find reasonable evidence to support these alternative explanations. If Captain Rogers had used the crystal-ball technique, for example, he would have been asked to describe several reasons why the mystery aircraft might simply be a commercial airplane carrying civilians.

Unfortunately, political leaders are apparently not currently using methods like the crystal-ball technique to make important political decisions. As Griffin and Tversky (2002) point out,

> It can be argued that people's willingness to engage in military, legal, and other costly battles would be reduced if they had a more realistic assessment of their chances of success. We doubt that the benefits of overconfidence outweigh its costs. (p. 249)

Students' Overconfidence About Completing Projects on Time. Are you surprised to learn that students are often overly optimistic about how quickly they can complete a project (Buehler et al., 1994, 2002)? In reality, this overconfidence applies to most humans. According to the **planning fallacy,** people typically underestimate the amount of time (or money) required to complete a project; they also estimate that the task will be relatively easy to complete (Buehler et al., 2002). Notice why this fallacy is related to overconfidence: If you are overconfident in decision making, you will estimate that your paper for cognitive psychology will take only 10 hours to complete, and you can easily finish it on time if you start next Tuesday.

Shelley Taylor and her colleagues (1998) explored the planning fallacy by studying how college students worked on academic projects. They asked students at the University of California at Los Angeles to select an academic project—such as a short paper—that needed to be completed during the next week. One group of students received instructions in "process simulation"; they were told to envision every step in the process of completing the project, such as gathering the materials, organizing the project's basic structure, and so forth. A second group received instructions in "outcome simulation"; they were told to imagine that the project was completed and that they were very satisfied with the outcome. Students in these two groups were instructed to rehearse the simulations for 5 minutes each day during

TABLE 12.3

The Influence of Instructions on Students' Progress on Academic Projects.

	Group		
	Process simulation	**Outcome simulation**	**Control**
% who began on time	24%	26%	14%
% who finished on time	41%	33%	14%

Source: Taylor et al., 1998.

the following week. A third group served as the control condition; they did not use any simulation.

Table 12.3 shows the results of the study. A statistical analysis demonstrated that the three groups did not differ significantly with respect to beginning on time. (The students in the control group were somewhat less likely to begin on time, but the difference was not statistically significant.) As you can see, however, the simulation instructions had a statistically significant influence on the percentage who finished on time. The students in the process-simulation condition finished significantly faster than those in the outcome-simulation condition, who in turn finished significantly faster than those in the control group.

The planning fallacy has been replicated in several studies in the United States, Canada, and Japan. How can we explain people's overconfidence that they will complete a task on time? One factor is that people create an optimistic scenario that represents the ideal way in which they will make progress on a project. This scenario fails to consider the large number of problems that can arise (Buehler et al., 2002). In other words, people use the anchoring and adjustment heuristic, and they do not make large enough adjustments to their original scenario. When students use process simulation—as in the study by Taylor and her coauthors (1998)—they apparently regulate their behavior so that it is somewhat more consistent with their original overconfident estimation of the completion time. As these researchers point out, however, only 41% of students in the most productive condition actually completed the project on time. Even process simulation cannot come close to eliminating the planning fallacy!

Reasons for Overconfidence. We have seen many examples demonstrating that people tend to be overconfident about the correctness of their decisions. This overconfidence arises from errors during many different stages in the decision-making process:

1. People are often unaware that their knowledge is based on very tenuous and uncertain assumptions and on information from unreliable or inappropriate sources (Bishop & Trout, 2002; Carlson, 1995; Greenberg et al., 1994).

2. Examples confirming our hypotheses are readily available, whereas we resist searching for counterexamples (Baron, 1998; Idson et al., 2001; Sanbonmatsu et al., 1998). You'll recall from the discussion of deductive reasoning that people persist in confirming their current hypothesis, rather than looking for negative evidence. Incidentally, when people are encouraged to seek other hypotheses, their overconfidence is substantially reduced (Sanbonmatsu et al., 1998; Sloman, 1999).

3. People have difficulty recalling the other possible hypotheses, and decision making depends on memory (Theme 4). If you cannot recall the competing hypotheses, you will be overly confident about the hypothesis you have endorsed (Trout, 2002).

4. Even if people manage to recall the other possible hypotheses, they do not treat them seriously. The choice once seemed ambiguous, but the alternatives now seem trivial (Simon et al., 2001).

5. A self-fulfilling-prophecy effect operates (Einhorn & Hogarth, 1981). For example, admissions officers who judge that a candidate is particularly well qualified for admission to a program may feel that their judgment is supported when their candidate does well. However, the candidate's success may be due primarily to the positive effects of the program itself. Even the people who had been rejected might have been successful if they had been allowed to participate in the program.

Ulrich Hoffrage (2004) points out that we should consider a possible bright side to the grim information about our human tendency to be overconfident. Suppose that we could indeed accurately estimate the probability that we would learn to speak another language fluently, finish a paper on time, win an election, or accomplish another challenging task. Many of these probabilities would be so discouragingly low that we would never attempt them! We overestimate the probability of success, and then we attack the task with (over)confidence. Furthermore, the self-fulfilling prophecy provides additional encouragement toward success.

Realistically, however, when people face a highly risky situation and they are overconfident, the outcome can often produce disasters, deaths, and widespread destruction. Jonathan Baron (1998) uses the term **my-side bias** to describe the overconfidence that one's own view is correct in a confrontational situation. Baron points out that conflict often arises when individuals (or groups or nations) each fall victim to my-side bias. They are so confident that their position is correct that they cannot consider the possibility that their opponent's position may be at least partially correct. If you find yourself in conflict with someone, try to overcome my-side bias and determine whether some part of the other person's position may have merit. More generally, try to reduce the overconfidence bias when you face an important decision. Review the five points listed above, and determine whether your confidence is appropriately justified.

The Hindsight Bias

In the preceding In Depth feature, we discussed how people are overconfident about predicting events that will happen in the future. In contrast, **hindsight** refers to our judgments about events that have already happened. The **hindsight bias** occurs when an event has happened, and we say that we had in fact "known it all along." In other words, the hindsight bias reflects our overconfidence that we could have predicted a particular outcome (Hom & Ciaramitaro, 2001; Pohl, 2004b; Winman & Juslin, 1999). The hindsight bias demonstrates that we often reconstruct the past so that it matches our present knowledge (Schacter, 2001).

Research About the Hindsight Bias. Demonstration 12.11 is based on research about the hindsight bias (Hawkins & Hastie, 1990; Pohl, 2004b; Winman et al., 1998). Notice whether your friends who had been given the answer were more confident than those who did not have the benefit of hindsight.

The hindsight bias operates not only for factual information, but also for the judgments we make about people. For example, Linda Carli (1999) asked students to read a two-page story about a young woman named Barbara and her relationship with Jack, a man she had met in graduate school. The story, told from Barbara's viewpoint, provided background information about Barbara, her interactions with Jack, and their growing relationship. Half of the students read a version that had a tragic ending, in which Jack rapes Barbara. The other half read a version with a happy ending, in which Jack proposes marriage to Barbara. The two versions were identical, except for the ending.

After reading the story, each student then completed a true/false memory test. This test examined recall for the facts of the story, but it also included items about information that had not been mentioned in the story. Some items were consistent with a stereotyped version of a rape scenario (e.g., "Barbara met many men at parties"), and some items were consistent with a marriage-proposal scenario (e.g., "Barbara wanted a family very much").

The results of Carli's (1999) study confirmed the hindsight bias. People who read the version about the rape said that they could have predicted Barbara would be raped. Similarly, people who read the marriage-proposal version said that they could have predicted Jack would propose to Barbara. (Remember that the two versions were actually identical, except for the final ending.) Furthermore, each group committed systematic errors on the memory test; each group recalled items that were consistent with the ending they had read, even though the information had not appeared in the story.

Carli's (1999) research helps us understand why many people "blame the victim" following a tragic event such as a rape. In reality, that individual's earlier actions may have been perfectly appropriate. However, people often search the past for reasons why a victim deserved that outcome. As we've seen in Carli's research, people may even "reconstruct" some reasons that did not occur.

The hindsight bias has been demonstrated in a number of different situations, though the effect is not always strong (e.g., Agans & Shaffer, 1994; Cannon & Quinsey,

⊚ Demonstration 12.11

The Hindsight Bias

Locate some friends who have time to answer several questions. Ask half of them the following four questions, together with the information about the correct answer.

1. Which of these two cities has a larger population, as of 2002?
　　a. Montreal, Quebec
　　b. Toronto, Ontario

The correct answer is Toronto. Give the probability estimates (in terms of percentages adding up to 100%) that you would have given to both alternatives, if the correct answer had *not* been indicated.

2. The residents of which of these two countries have the longer life expectancy?
　　a. Israel
　　b. Ireland

The correct answer is Israel. Give the probability estimates you would have given to both alternatives, if the correct answer had not been indicated.

3. Which of these two U.S. states is larger, in terms of square miles?
　　a. Maine
　　b. Indiana

The correct answer is Indiana. Give the probability estimates you would have given to both alternatives, if the correct answer had not been indicated.

4. Which country had the higher infant mortality rate in 2002, in terms of percentage of children who die before their first birthday?
　　a. United States
　　b. Holland

The correct answer is the United States. Give the probability estimates you would have given to both alternatives, if the correct answer had not been indicated.

Now ask the other half of your participants the same four questions, but do not supply the correct answers. In each case, however, ask them, "Give the probability estimates that each of the two possibilities could be the correct answer."

Source: All questions are based on information in the *World Almanac and Book of Facts* (2003) and Statistics Canada (2003).

1995; Christensen-Szalanski & Willham, 1991; Creyer & Ross, 1993; Pohl 2004b). The bias has also been documented in North America, Europe, Asia, and Australia (Pohl et al., 2002). According to the research, doctors show the hindsight bias when guessing a medical diagnosis (Dehn & Erdfelder, 1998). We also demonstrate this bias in our everyday experiences. For example, people display the hindsight bias when making judgments about the amount of sugar, butter, and fruit juice in a variety of foods (Pohl et al., 2003).

Explanations for the Hindsight Bias. Despite all the research, the explanations for the hindsight bias are not clear (Pohl, 2004b). We noted in discussing Carli's (1999) study that people may misremember past events so that the events are consistent with current information; these events help to justify the outcome. Another likely cognitive explanation is that people might use anchoring and adjustment (Hawkins & Hastie, 1990; Pohl, 2004b). After all, they have been told that a particular outcome actually happened—that it was 100% certain. Therefore, they use this 100% value as the anchor in estimating the likelihood that they would have predicted the answer, and then they do not adjust their certainty downward as much as they should.

An additional explanation is motivational, rather than cognitive. Perhaps people simply want to look good in the eyes of the experimenter or other people who may be evaluating them (Hawkins & Hastie, 1990). Did the results of Carli's study about the tragic versus the upbeat story ending surprise me? Of course not . . . I knew it all along!

Two Perspectives on Decision Making: The Optimists Versus the Pessimists

So far, the material on decision making has provided little evidence for Theme 2. We can admire our impressive perceptual, memory, and linguistic capabilities, but our decision-making skills aren't worth bragging about. We rely too heavily on three decision-making heuristics, and we are plagued by framing effects, overconfidence, and the hindsight bias. This is the admittedly pessimistic view presented by researchers such as Kahneman and Tversky (1996, 2000). However, these researchers have argued that the three heuristics usually serve us well in our everyday life.

Since the 1990s, however, several optimistic decision theorists have emerged. Among the most prominent are Gerd Gigerenzer and his colleagues (e.g., Gigerenzer, 1998a; Gigerenzer et al., 1999; Goldstein & Gigerenzer, 2002; Todd & Gigerenzer, 2000). These theorists argue that people are not perfectly rational decision makers; still, researchers such as Kahneman and Tversky have not given people a fair chance. Specifically, the pessimists' research has not tested people fairly and has not used naturalistic settings (Hammond, 1996; Henrich et al., 2001; Manktelow, 1999). For example, the optimists point out that people's decision-making abilities are reasonably accurate when researchers eliminate trick questions that encourage decision makers to ignore important information like base rate. They also point out that people perform better when the question is asked in terms of frequencies, rather than probabilities (e.g., Brase et al., 1998; Cosmides & Tooby, 1996; Gigerenzer, 1998b).

The optimists also note that research participants may interpret the decision-making task differently from what the experimenters had intended. For example, participants might consider that the experimenters are lying about information such as the relative frequency of engineers and lawyers in Demonstration 12.4 (M. S. Cohen, 1993). In addition, participants bring their world knowledge into the research laboratory, where researchers often design the tasks to contradict this world knowledge (Frisch, 1993).

As in most controversies, both positions are probably at least partially correct. The optimists may have a point; the methods used by Kahneman and Tversky—and others who emphasize decision-making heuristics—may underestimate our potential. However, the pessimists may also have a point; they have always argued that the heuristics usually serve us well, and we can become more effective decision makers by realizing the limitations of these important strategies (Kahneman & Tversky, 1996, 2000).

◉ Section Summary: *Decision Making*

1. Decision-making heuristics are typically helpful in our daily lives; we can make errors in decision making when we overemphasize heuristics and underemphasize the unique features of the current decision.

2. According to the representativeness heuristic, we judge that a sample is likely if it resembles the population from which it was selected (for example, the sample should look random if it was gathered by random selection).

3. We are so impressed by representativeness that we tend to ignore important statistical information such as the size of the sample and the base rates; the representativeness heuristic also produces the conjunction fallacy.

4. According to the availability heuristic, we estimate frequency or probability in terms of how easily we can remember examples of something.

5. The availability heuristic produces errors when biasing factors such as recency and familiarity influence availability. The availability heuristic also helps explain the phenomenon of illusory correlation. Furthermore, when we use the simulation heuristic (which is related to availability), we judge likelihood in terms of how easily we can imagine a sequence of possible events.

6. According to the anchoring and adjustment heuristic, we establish an anchor and then make adjustments based on other information; the problem is that these adjustments are usually too small.

7. We also use the anchoring and adjustment heuristic when we estimate confidence intervals. We begin with a single best estimate, and then we make very small adjustments on either side of that estimate to establish a confidence interval that often is too narrow.

8. The way in which a question is framed can influence our decisions; background information can influence our decisions inappropriately. Also, when the wording implies gains, we tend to avoid risks; when the wording implies losses, we tend to seek out risks.

9. People are frequently overconfident about their decisions. For instance, political decision makers may risk lives when they are overconfident. In addition, college students tend to be overconfident about the estimated completion time for projects, but they can use process stimulation to reduce their overconfidence.

10. In the hindsight bias, people know the outcome of an event, and they are overly optimistic that they could have predicted that specific outcome before it actually happened.

11. Gigerenzer and other optimistic decision-making theorists argue that humans are reasonably skilled at making decisions; they propose that researchers who emphasize heuristics have not tested people fairly.

12. Kahneman, Tversky, and other relatively pessimistic theorists argue that the heuristics usually lead to accurate decisions; however, we can make even more accurate decisions by acknowledging the limitations of the heuristics.

CHAPTER REVIEW QUESTIONS

1. Describe the basic differences between deductive reasoning and decision making. Provide at least one example from your daily life that illustrates each of these cognitive processes. Why can both of them be categorized as "thinking"?

2. To make certain that you understand conditional reasoning, begin with this sentence: "If I want to pass this course in cognitive psychology, I must hand in my paper by next Friday." Apply the four conditional reasoning situations (the propositional calculus) to this sentence, and point out which are valid and which are invalid.

3. What factors influence our accuracy when we work on conditional reasoning tasks? Give an example of each of these factors, based on your own experience.

4. Many of the errors that people make in reasoning can be traced to overreliance on previous knowledge or overactive top-down processes. Discuss this point, and then relate it to the anchoring and adjustment heuristic.

5. Throughout this chapter, you have seen many examples of a general cognitive tendency: We tend to accept the status quo (or the currently favored hypothesis), without sufficiently exploring other options. Describe how this statement applies to both deductive reasoning and several kinds of decision-making tasks.

6. Decide which heuristic is represented in each of the following everyday errors: (a) You decide that you will be more likely to live in Massachusetts than in New Mexico, because you can more easily envision a sequence of events that brings you to Massachusetts. (b) Someone asks you whether cardinals or robins are more common, and you make this decision based on the number of birds of each kind that you have seen this winter. (c) One of your classes has

30 students, including two people named Matthew and three named Jessica, which seems too coincidental to be due to chance alone. (d) You estimate the number of bottles of soda you will need for the Fourth of July picnic based on the Christmas party consumption, taking into account the fact that the weather will be warmer in July.

7. In the case of the representativeness heuristic, people fail to take into account two important factors that should be *emphasized*. In the case of the availability heuristic, people take into account two important factors that should be *ignored*. Discuss these two statements, with reference to the information in this chapter. Give examples of each of these four kinds of errors.

8. Describe the variety of ways in which people tend to be overconfident in their decision making. Think of relevant examples from your own experience. Then point out how you can avoid the planning fallacy when you face a deadline for a class assignment. Finally, point out how your knowledge of the my-side bias could help you resolve your next interpersonal conflict.

9. Think of a recent example from the news in which a politician made a decision for which he or she was criticized by news commentators. How could overconfidence have led to this unwise decision? Why might the hindsight bias be relevant here? What cognitive processes might the news commentators be using to make the decision seem more foolish than it might actually have been?

10. Imagine that you have been hired by your local high school district to create a course in critical thinking. Review the chapter and make 15 to 20 suggestions (each only a sentence long) about precautions that should be included in such a program.

NEW TERMS

thinking
deductive reasoning
decision making
conditional reasoning
propositional reasoning
syllogism
the propositional calculus
antecedent
consequent
affirming the antecedent
affirming the consequent
denying the antecedent
denying the consequent
belief-bias effect
confirmation bias

heuristics
representative
representativeness
  heuristic
law of large numbers
small-sample fallacy
base rate
base-rate fallacy
Bayes' theorem
likelihood ratio
conjunction rule
conjunction fallacy
availability heuristic
illusory correlation
social cognition approach

simulation heuristic
anchoring and
  adjustment heuristic
anchoring effect
anchor
confidence intervals
framing effect
overconfidence
crystal-ball technique
planning fallacy
my-side bias
hindsight
hindsight bias

RECOMMENDED READINGS

Gigerenzer, G., & Selten, R. (Eds.). (2001). *Bounded rationality: The adaptive toolbox.* Cambridge, MA: MIT Press. In this book, Gigerenzer and his colleagues provide a representative view of the "optimist" viewpoint of decision making; the chapters critique the Kahneman and Tversky focus on heuristics and argue that people perform reasonably well on many kinds of decision-making tasks.

Gilovich, T., Griffin, D., & Kahneman, D. (Eds.). (2002). *Heuristics and biases: The psychology of intuitive judgment.* New York: Cambridge University Press. This book features 42 chapters on a wide range of topics related to decision making; some chapters are reprints of classic articles, and other chapters were written specifically for this volume.

Myers, D. G. (2002). *Intuition: Its powers and perils.* New Haven, CT: Yale University Press. David Myers has written an informative and interesting book on intuitions in everyday life; the book blends the psychology research with well-chosen everyday examples.

Pohl, R. (2004a). *Cognitive illusions: Handbook on fallacies and biases in thinking, judgment, and memory.* Hove, England: Psychology Press. I strongly recommend this book, which is designed for students enrolled in courses in cognitive psychology. It includes 22 chapters on topics such as the confirmation bias, the availability heuristic, and overconfidence.

Schaeken, W., DeVooght, G., Vandierendonck, A., & d'Ydewalle, G. (Eds.). (2000a). *Deductive reasoning and strategies.* Mahwah, NJ: Erlbaum. Articles and books on deductive reasoning are typically difficult to understand. This book is relatively accessible for students who want to know more about the research on topics such as strategies in reasoning problems and the effectiveness of counterexamples in conditional reasoning.

ANSWERS TO DEMONSTRATION 12.1

1. valid
2. invalid
3. invalid
4. valid

ANSWERS TO DEMONSTRATION 12.8

1. 28% nonvoters
2. 49% nonvoters
3. 14% of college graduates
4. 34,501,130 people
5. 158,000 square miles
6. 580,376 full-time undergraduates
7. 874,000,000 people
8. 96% literacy rate
9. 1797 was her year of birth.
10. 14,921,000 political refugees

(Did most of your confidence intervals include the correct answers, or were these confidence intervals too broad?)

CHAPTER 13
Cognitive Development Throughout the Lifespan

PREVIEW

This chapter examines how cognitive processes develop in several areas that you've learned about in earlier chapters. Rather than discussing many topics briefly, we will explore three topics in detail: memory, metacognition, and language. One purpose of this chapter is to inform you about the development in these three important abilities. You'll see that some skills improve as children mature to adulthood, and some decline as adults reach old age. However, many skills show less change than you might expect. A second purpose of this chapter is to encourage you to review some important concepts that were introduced earlier in the book. As you know from Chapter 6, people learn more effectively if their learning is spread over time. You can now refresh your memory about concepts that you initially learned several weeks ago.

According to recent research, even young infants can remember people, objects, and events. For example, young infants can remember how to activate a mobile, using a kicking motion that they learned several weeks earlier. Children's long-term recognition memory is surprisingly accurate, but their working memory and long-term recall memory are considerably less accurate than in adults. Young children also fail to use memory strategies spontaneously when they want to remember something. Elderly adults are somewhat similar to young adults on several working memory and long-term memory tasks. However, other kinds of memory (for example, memory for pairs of unrelated English words) may decline.

Studies on metacognition reveal that children change in their metamemory as they grow older. For example, young children wildly overestimate their own memory span, whereas older children are more accurate. Older children are also more skilled in knowing whether they have understood a passage they have read. However, young adults and elderly adults are generally comparable in their metamemory.

With respect to language development, young infants are remarkably competent in perceiving speech sounds and other important components of language. As children mature, their skills increase dramatically in areas such as word meaning, grammatical relationships, and the social aspects of language.

INTRODUCTION

Consider the following conversation between a mother and her 2½-year-old child:

Child: Why that boy go home?
Mother: Because his mother thought he was tired.
Child: Why he tired?
Mother: Because he hasn't slept all day.
Child: Why he not sleep?

Mother: Because they went to a party.
Child: Why they go to party?
Mother (exasperated): Because! (Karmiloff & Karmiloff-Smith, 2001, p. 102)

This interaction captures the considerable language skills of young children. It also illustrates Theme 1 of this textbook, because children actively pursue information (Gauvain, 2001; Gelman & Lucariello, 2002). In fact, parents—such as this mother—may occasionally wish that children were considerably less persistent in their pursuit of knowledge. However, the interaction also illustrates that children's syntax is not yet fully developed. As a 4-year-old boy remarked to his mother one morning, "You know, I thought I'd be a grown-up by now. . . . It sure is taking a long time!" (Rogoff, 1990, p. 3). As we will see in this chapter, the boy is certainly correct. Four-year-olds have mastered some components of memory and language. However, they still need to develop their skills in memory performance, memory strategies, metacognition, syntax, and pragmatics.

Most cognitive psychology textbooks limit their discussion of cognitive development to infancy and childhood. I prefer the **lifespan approach to development,** which argues that developmental changes are not complete when people reach young adulthood; instead, we continue to change and adapt throughout our entire lives (Smith & Baltes, 1999; Whitbourne, 2005). As you will see, some cognitive skills decline during the aging process, but many other capabilities remain stable. A lifespan approach to cognitive development is important in North America, because about 12% of Canadian and U.S. residents are 65 years of age or older (*Canadian Global Almanac*, 2001; *World Almanac and Book of Facts*, 2003). Fortunately, an increasing number of psychologists are focusing their research on elderly individuals (Birren & Schroots, 2001).

When we study the cognitive abilities of the very young and the very old, the research problems are even more complex than when we study young adults. For example, how can young infants convey what they know, given their limited language and motor skills? With creative research techniques, however, researchers can overcome these limitations and discover that even young infants have a solid head start in understanding information about the people and objects in their world (e.g., Baillargeon, 2002; Mandler, 2003; Rovee-Collier & Barr, 2002).

Research with elderly individuals presents a different set of methodological problems (Rabbitt, 2002; Salthouse, 2000; Smith & Baltes, 1999; Whitbourne, 2005). Hundreds of studies have compared the cognitive performance of young, healthy college students with the performance of elderly people whose health, self-confidence, education, and familiarity with technology are relatively poor. Furthermore, college students have had extensive recent experience with memorizing material and taking tests, whereas elderly people have not. Notice the problem: Suppose that a poorly controlled memory study determines that young adults recall 25% more items than elderly adults. Perhaps the superior performance of the young adults should be attributed to confounding variables—such as health or education—rather than to the aging process itself. In general, researchers believe that confounding variables can explain a substantial portion of the differences in cognitive performance. However, researchers have identified some age-related differences that persist, even when confounding variables have been eliminated (Baltes et al., 1999; Rabbitt, 2002; Whitbourne, 2005).

This chapter focuses on cognitive development in three areas: memory, metacognition, and language.* I specifically organized this textbook so that the final chapter would encourage you to review the major concepts from three important areas within cognitive psychology. In addition, you will learn that infants and young children possess cognitive skills you might not have suspected. You'll also see that elderly people are much more cognitively competent than the popular stereotype suggests.

THE LIFESPAN DEVELOPMENT OF MEMORY

We have examined memory in many parts of this textbook. Chapters 4, 5, and 6 focused specifically on memory, and the remaining chapters discussed the contribution of memory to other cognitive processes. Now we will examine how memory develops from infancy—the first 2 years of life—and childhood through old age.

Memory in Infants

Try to picture an infant who is about 4 months old—not yet old enough to sit upright without support. Would you expect that this baby would recognize his or her mother or remember how to make a mobile move? Several decades ago, psychologists believed that infants as young as 4 months of age could not really see or hear, and they certainly could not be counted on to remember anything (Gelman, 2002). Naturally, we cannot expect sophisticated memory feats from a young infant. Some synaptic connections in the portions of the cortex most relevant to long-term memory are not fully developed in infants (Bauer, 2002).

Furthermore, researchers will underestimate infants' memory capacities unless they can create a task that depends upon a response the infant has already mastered. Fortunately, developmental psychologists have recently devised several methods to test infants' ability to remember people and objects. This research shows that infants have greater memory capabilities than you might expect. Indeed Theme 2—which emphasizes cognitive competence—can be applied even to infants.

Researchers have measured infants' memory using methods such as inspecting their attention patterns (e.g., Courage & Howe, 2001; Luo et al., 2003; Rovee-Collier et al., 2001) and their ability to imitate an action after a delay (e.g., Barr et al.,

---

*This chapter does not cover theoretical approaches to cognitive development, such as the approach of Jean Piaget. The complex and controversial theoretical issues would require a lengthy discussion (e.g., Aguiar & Baillargeon, 2002; Baillargeon, 2002; Cohen, 2002; DeHart et al., 2004). Furthermore, many students who read this book are likely to have learned about theories of cognitive development in previous courses.

2001; Mandler & McDonough, 1997; Rovee-Collier & Barr, 2002). Let's consider two other research approaches in greater detail: (1) recognizing mother and (2) conjugate reinforcement with a mobile. As you'll see, babies can demonstrate substantial memory ability, even during their first month of life.

Recognizing Mother. In our North American culture, infants generally spend more time with their mothers than with any other person. Research on visual recognition shows that even 3-day-olds can distinguish their mother from a stranger (Bushnell & Sai, 1987; Rovee-Collier et al., 2001; Slater & Butterworth, 1997). In a representative study, Walton and her coauthors (1992) found that infants younger than 3 days of age made significantly more sucking responses in order to produce a video of their mother's face, rather than a video of a visually similar stranger's face.

Infants' ability to recognize their mother's voice is especially remarkable (Siegler et al., 2003). For example, Kisilevsky and her coauthors (2003) tested infants about 1 or 2 weeks *before* they were born. Specifically, these researchers approached women who were receiving prenatal care at a hospital in China, to ask about testing their infants' voice-recognition ability. If the mother agreed, the researchers presented either the mother's voice reading a Chinese poem or a female stranger's voice reading the same poem. Impressively, the infant's heart rate changed more when hearing their mother's voice than when hearing the stranger's voice.

Infants can even become accustomed to characteristics of their mother's spoken message, while still in the uterus. For example, DeCasper and Spence (1986) demonstrated that newborns preferred a particular Dr. Seuss passage that their mother had read aloud each day during the last 3 months of pregnancy, rather than a similar passage that had never been read. Young infants must therefore recognize specific intonations or phrases.

Conjugate Reinforcement with a Mobile. The most extensive program of research on infant memory has been conducted by Carolyn Rovee-Collier and her colleagues, using the conjugate reinforcement technique. In the **conjugate reinforcement technique,** a mobile is placed above an infant's crib; a ribbon connects the infant's ankle and the mobile, so that the infant's kicks will make the mobile move. (See Figure 13.1.) This game is especially appealing to 2- to 6-month-old infants. After several minutes, they begin to kick rapidly and pump up the mobile; then they lie quietly and watch parts of the mobile move. As the movement dies down, they typically shriek and then kick vigorously, thereby pumping it up again. In operant conditioning terms, the response is a foot kick, and the reinforcement is the movement of the mobile (Rovee-Collier & Barr, 2002; Rovee-Collier & Boller, 1995; Rovee-Collier et al., 2001).

Let's see how the conjugate reinforcement technique can be used to assess infant memory. All the training and testing take place in the infant's crib at home, so that measurements are not distorted by the infant's reactions to the new surroundings. For a 3-minute period at the beginning of the first session, the experimenter takes a baseline measure. During this time, the ribbon is connected from the infant's ankle to

FIGURE 13.1

The Conjugate Reinforcement Setup in Rovee-Collier's Research.

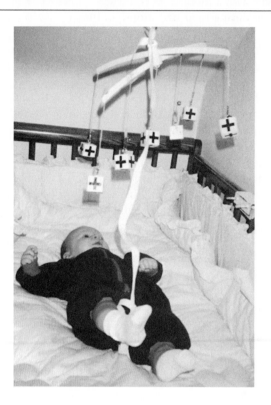

an "empty" mobile stand, rather than to the mobile. Thus, the experimenters can measure the amount of spontaneous kicking that occurs in the presence of the mobile, before the infant learns how to make the mobile move (Rovee-Collier, 1999; Rovee-Collier & Barr, 2002).

Next, the experimenter moves the ribbon so that it runs from the baby's ankle to the stand from which the mobile is hung. The babies are allowed 9 minutes to discover that their kicks can activate the mobile; this is the acquisition phase. The infants typically receive two training sessions like this, spaced 24 hours apart (Rovee-Collier, 1999). At the end of the second training session, the ribbon is unhooked and returned to the empty stand for 3 minutes in order to measure what the infants remember; this is the immediate retention test.

Long-term memory is then measured after 1 to 42 days have elapsed. The mobile is once again hung above the infant's crib, with the ribbon hooked to the empty stand. If the infant recognizes the mobile and recalls how kicking had produced movement, then he or she will soon produce the foot-kick response. Notice, then, that Rovee-Collier has devised a clever way to "ask" infants if they remember how to activate the mobile. She has also devised an objective method for assessing long-term memory, because she can compare two measures: (1) the number of kicks produced in the immediate retention test, and (2) the number of kicks produced following the delay.

Rovee-Collier has also devised a second operant conditioning task that would be more appealing to infants between the ages of 6 and 18 months. In this second task, older infants learn to press a lever in order to make a miniature train move along a circular track. By combining information from the two tasks, researchers can trace infant memory from 2 months through 18 months of age (Rovee-Collier, 1999; Rovee-Collier & Barr, 2002). Figure 13.2 shows how much time can pass

FIGURE 13.2

The Maximum Duration for Which Different Groups of Infants Demonstrated Significant Retention. In this study, 2- to 6-month-old infants kicked to activate a mobile, and 6- to 18-month-old infants pressed a lever to activate a train.

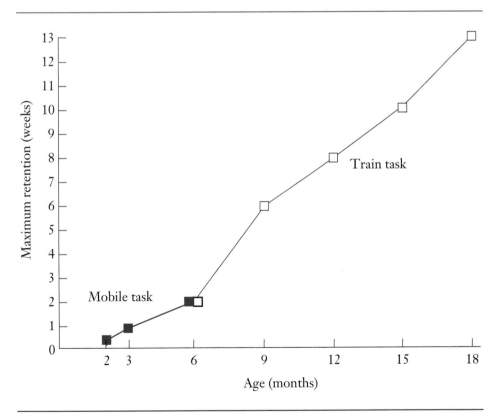

Source: Rovee-Collier, 1999.

before infants no longer show significant recall for the relevant task. For example, 6-month-olds can recall how to move the mobile and also how to move the train, even after a 2-week delay. This research demonstrates that long-term retention shows a steady improvement during the first 18 months of life (Rovee-Collier et al., 2001).

Several decades ago, researchers thought that infant memory was extremely limited. However, Rovee-Collier and her coworkers have demonstrated that infants can remember actions, even after a substantial delay. Furthermore, infant memory and adult memory are influenced by many of the same factors (Rovee-Collier & Barr, 2002; Rovee-Collier & Hayne, 2000; Rovee-Collier et al., 2001).

For example, you saw in Chapter 5 that context sometimes influences adult memory. Context effects are even stronger for infants. Rovee-Collier and her colleagues (1985) used the conjugate reinforcement technique to test 3-month-old infants whose cribs were lined with a fabric that had a distinctive, colorful pattern. The infants' recall was excellent when they were tested after a 7-day delay. However, another group of infants was tested with the same mobile and the same delay—but with a different crib liner. This second group of infants showed no retention whatsoever! Without the proper environmental context, infants' memories decline sharply (Rovee-Collier & Hayne, 2000).

You'll also recall from Chapter 5 (pp. 160–161) that young adults' eyewitness testimony for details of an accident was less accurate if they learned new information—about a stop sign, rather than a yield sign—after witnessing the events. Similarly, Rovee-Collier and her coauthors (1993) measured "eyewitness testimony" in 3-month-olds. Immediately after the infants had learned how to produce movement in one particular mobile, they were shown a different mobile for just 3 minutes. When their long-term memory was later tested, infants showed significantly less recall for the original mobile than did infants in a control group, who had seen no second mobile. Infants—like adults—recall an event less accurately if they have been exposed to postevent information (Gulya et al., 2002).

In additional research, Rovee-Collier and her associates have discovered numerous other similarities between infant and adult memory. For example, you may recall the **spacing effect** from Chapter 6; students learn most effectively if their practice is distributed over time, rather than if they learn the material all at once (p. 177). A number of studies have now demonstrated that infants also remember better if their practice is distributed (Rovee-Collier, 1995; Rovee-Collier et al., 2001). Furthermore, infants show a levels-of-processing effect, with better recall for items that were processed at a deep level (Adler et al., 1998; Rovee-Collier et al., 2001). As you can see, researchers have designed creative techniques which allow them to discover that many principles of adult memory are also relevant for infants who have not yet reached their first birthday.

In summary, infants demonstrate memory on a number of tasks. Newborns can recognize the face and voice of their mothers, and 6-month-olds can remember how to activate a mobile after a 2-week delay. By the age of 14 months, babies can remember how to imitate actions they had seen 3 months earlier.

Memory in Children

We have seen that researchers need to be extremely inventive when they study infant memory. By using the conjugate reinforcement technique, imitation tasks, and other creative methods, they have concluded that infants' memory is reasonably impressive.

Assessing children's memory is much easier, because children can respond verbally. However, the task is still far from simple. Young children may have trouble understanding task instructions, and they may not be able to identify certain stimuli (for example, letters of the alphabet). Let's consider three topics: (1) children's working memory, (2) their long-term memory, and (3) their memory strategies.

Children's Working Memory. Working memory is often measured in terms of memory span, or the number of items that can be correctly recalled in order immediately after presentation. Memory spans improve dramatically during childhood (Gathercole, 1998; Schneider, 2002; Swanson, 1999). According to one estimate, for example, a 2-year-old can recall an average of two numbers in a row, whereas a 9-year-old can recall six (Kail, 1992). Factors such as speed of pronunciation help to explain why older children can recall a greater number of words (Kail, 1997). As you may recall from Chapter 4, pronunciation time is related to the capacity of adults' working memory.

In Chapter 4, we also noted that working memory coordinates our ongoing mental activities, in addition to briefly storing information. Nelson Cowan and his colleagues created a measure of working memory that emphasizes this ongoing mental activity as well as the memory span (Cowan et al., 2002; Cowan et al., 2003). Specifically, 7- and 8-year-old children were instructed to read a series of sentences and to supply the missing word. A typical set of two sentences might be "Mary got home and unlocked the ____" and "Ben laughed and then clapped his____." The child would presumably say "door" to the first sentence and "hands" to the second one. After responding to the series of sentences, the children were asked to recall the words they had supplied. If they answered correctly (in this case, "door, hands"), they were then given a series of three sentences. Children who could quickly and accurately recall more than two of these words typically scored higher than other children on standardized tests of reading ability.

Now let's turn our attention to long-term memory in children. Later, we'll see how older children's use of memory strategies helps to explain the improvement in their memory performance.

Children's Long-Term Memory. Children typically have excellent recognition memory but poor recall memory (e.g., Flavell et al., 2002; Howe, 2000; Howe et al., 2000; Schneider & Bjorklund, 1998). In a classic study, Myers and Perlmutter (1978) performed studies similar to those in Demonstration 13.1, using 2- and 4-year-old children. To test recognition, the researchers showed children 18 objects. Then they presented 36 items, including the 18 previous objects and 18 new objects. The 2-year-olds recognized an impressive 80% of the items, and the 4-year-olds recognized about 90% of the items. When different groups of children were tested for their ability

---

⑨ Demonstration 13.1

Age Differences in Recall and Recognition

In this experiment you will need to test a college-age person and a preschool child. You should reassure the child's parents that you are simply testing memory as part of a class project.

You will be examining both recall and recognition in this demonstration. First, assemble 20 common objects, such as a pen, pencil, piece of paper, leaf, stick, rock, book, key, apple, and so on. Place the objects in a box or cover them with a cloth.

You will use the same testing procedure for both people, although the preschool child will require more extensive explanation. Remove 10 objects in all, 1 at a time. Show each object for about 5 seconds and then conceal it again. After all 10 objects have been shown, ask each person to recall as many of the objects as possible. Do not provide feedback about the correctness of the responses. After recall is complete, test for recognition. Remove one object at a time, randomly presenting the old objects mixed in sequence with new objects. In each case, ask whether the object is old or new.

Count the number of correct recalls and the number of correct recognitions for each person. You should find that they both show a similarly high level of performance on the recognition measures. However, the college student will recall far more than the child.

---

to *recall* nine objects, the 2-year-olds recalled only about 20% of the items, and the 4-year-olds recalled about 40% of the items. Recall memory seems to require the active use of memory strategies. As you'll see later in this section, these strategies are not developed until middle childhood (Schneider & Bjorklund, 1998). Let's now consider several more specific issues: (1) autobiographic memory for events from childhood; (2) source monitoring; and (3) eyewitness testimony.

1. *Autobiographical memory and early childhood.* When older children and adults think back on their early experiences, they typically cannot recall events that had occurred in their own lives before they were about 2 or 3 years old, a phenomenon called **childhood amnesia** (Bruce et al., 2000; Carver & Bauer, 1999; Howe, 2000, 2003). Childhood amnesia is surprising, given the impressive memory skills that infants demonstrate. We also know that 2-year-old children frequently describe an event that occurred several weeks or months ago, so they must be able to store verbal memories for substantial periods of time (Eacott, 1999; Gauvain, 2001; Ornstein & Haden, 2001).

In a representative study of childhood amnesia, Eacott and Crawley (1998) located college students who had a sibling who was 2 to 3 years younger than themselves. Each student was asked a series of questions about the birth of the younger sibling, and the answers were confirmed by checking with each student's mother. The results showed that students were much more likely to answer the questions correctly if they had been 3 years old at the time of the sibling's birth. In contrast, they recalled few details if they had been only 2 years old.

In a related study, Rubin (2000) located previous research in which adolescents and adults had been instructed to recall autobiographical memories from the first 10 years of their lives. As you can see in Figure 13.3, people seldom recall events that happened when they were younger than 3.

Many researchers have documented childhood amnesia. However, they have not reached consensus about explaining the phenomenon (Eacott & Crawley, 1998; Gathercole, 1998; Howe, 2003). Neurological factors may provide a partial explanation. Specifically, the prefrontal cortex may not be sufficiently developed to encode these memories so that they can be retrieved years later, during adulthood (Newcombe et al., 2000). Another factor is that children younger than 2 do not have a well-organized sense of who they are (Conway & Pleydell-Pearce, 2000; Howe, 2000, 2003). Therefore, they may have difficulty encoding and retrieving a series of events connected with themselves (Newcombe et al., 2000).

FIGURE 13.3

The Proportion of Memories Supplied by Adolescents and Adults That Occurred for Each Year, 1 to 10 Years of Age.

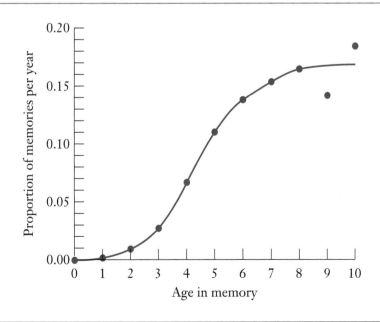

Source: Based on studies examined by Rubin (2000).

2. *Children's source monitoring.* You may recall that Chapter 5 discussed **source monitoring,** which is the process of trying to decide which memories or beliefs are real and which are simply imagined. In general, children below the age of 7 have more difficulty than adults in distinguishing between reality and fantasy (Foley, 1998; Foley & Ratner, 1998; Ratner et al., 2000; Ratner et al., 2001). For example, I know an extremely bright child who had participated in an imaginary trip to the moon one day at school. Later that day, she insisted to her parents that she really had visited the moon.

Research by Mary Ann Foley, Hilary Horn Ratner, and their colleagues has systematically clarified the conditions in which young children are most likely to make source-monitoring errors. For example Foley and Ratner (1998) asked one group of 6-year-olds to perform specific physical activities, such as making a motion like an airplane. A second group of 6-year-olds was instructed to imagine how specific physical activities would feel (for example: "Try to imagine what it would actually feel like to do that"). A third group was instructed to visualize themselves performing each specific physical activity (for example: "Try to picture what you look like . . ."). The results showed that children seldom reported that a performed action had actually just been imagined. In contrast, they were fairly likely to report that an imagined action had actually been performed. This bias was especially likely for children in the second group. In other words, the children who made the most source-monitoring errors were those who had imagined how it would feel to make airplane movements; they often convinced themselves that they had actually circled around the room.

Other research on source monitoring shows that children sometimes recall that they performed a task, when the task had actually been performed by another person with whom they had been collaborating (Foley, Ratner & House, 2002; Ratner et al., 2002). Apparently, children between the ages of 4 and 6 can watch another person at work, and they anticipate the steps in the project. Later, they become confused, and they transform *thinking* about the project into actually *completing* the project.

3. *Children's eyewitness testimony.* A third important topic related to children's memory concerns the accuracy of their eyewitness testimony. As you might guess, older children provide much more accurate eyewitness testimony than younger children (Ornstein, Baker-Ward, et al., 1997; Powell et al., 2003; Schneider, 2002).

An actual court case inspired Michelle Leichtman and Stephen Ceci (1995) to conduct an experiment. In this court case, a 9-year-old girl had provided eyewitness testimony, and it seemed likely that both stereotypes and suggestions could have influenced her report. Leichtman and Ceci's study therefore explored the impact of these two factors. They tested 176 preschoolers, assigning each child to one of four conditions. In the control condition, a stranger named Sam Stone visited the classroom, strolling around and making several bland comments for a period of about 2 minutes. In the stereotype condition, a research assistant presented one story each week to the children for 3 weeks prior to Sam Stone's visit; each story emphasized that Sam Stone was nice but very clumsy and bumbling. In the suggestion condition, children had no information about Sam Stone prior to his visit. However, during interviews after his visit, the interviewer provided two incorrect suggestions—that Sam Stone had ripped a book and that he had spilled chocolate on a white teddy bear.

Finally, in the stereotype-plus-suggestion condition, children were exposed to both the stereotype before Sam Stone's visit and the incorrect suggestions afterward.

Ten weeks after Sam Stone's classroom visit, a new interviewer—whom no child had previously met—asked what Sam Stone had done during his visit. As a key part of the interview, the children were asked whether they had actually seen Sam Stone tear up the book and pour chocolate on the teddy bear. Figure 13.4 shows the percentage of children in each condition who said they had witnessed at least one of these events.

Notice, first of all, that children in the control group were highly accurate; only 5% of the younger children and none of the older children claimed to have witnessed something that Sam Stone had not actually done. Therefore, we must emphasize that children's eyewitness testimony can be highly accurate when conditions are ideal and

FIGURE 13.4

The Effects of Stereotypes and Suggestions on Young Children's Eyewitness Testimony. Graph shows the percentage who reported actually seeing events that had not occurred.

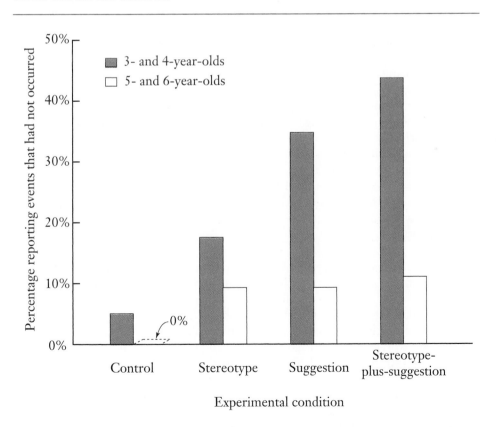

Source: Based on Leichtman & Ceci, 1995.

no misleading information is provided either before or after the target event (Bruck & Ceci, 1999; Bruck et al., 1997; Schneider, 2002).

As Figure 13.4 also shows, however, a worrisome number of children claimed that they had witnessed these actions if a previous stereotype had been established. Even more of the younger children claimed they had witnessed the actions when inaccurate suggestions had been made after the event. Most alarming is that nearly half the younger children claimed to have witnessed the actions when they had received both the stereotype and the suggestions.

As we've seen, the accuracy of children's eyewitness testimony is influenced by the child's age, stereotyping, and misleading suggestions (Bjorklund et al., 2002). We also saw—in the discussion of source monitoring—that children have trouble deciding which memories are real and which are simply imagined. Several additional factors influence the accuracy of children's testimonies. For example, children make more errors when interviewers ask questions in a highly emotional tone or when the interviewer uses complex language (Bruck & Ceci, 1999; Imhoff & Baker-Ward, 1999). Children also make more errors when interviewed by a stranger, rather than a parent (Jackson & Crockenberg, 1998). Furthermore, children are extremely reluctant to say, "I don't know" when an adult asks a question (Bruck & Ceci, 1999).

Research by Peter Ornstein, Lynne Baker-Ward, and their colleagues provides further information on the accuracy of children's eyewitness testimony. These researchers have studied children's ability to recall events that occurred during visits to their doctor's office. Interestingly, children's recall can be impressively accurate, for example, when they are questioned about a medical procedure that had been painful (Ornstein, Shapiro et al., 1997). Furthermore, children are relatively accurate in recalling typical events from a routine physical exam, such as having their heart listened to. In contrast, they are less accurate in recalling unusual events that occurred only during the most recent visit, such as having their head circumference measured (Ornstein et al., 1998).

The topic of children's eyewitness testimony is too complicated to construct any simple formula for when to trust children and when to suspect their reports (e.g., Bruck & Ceci, 1999; Bruck et al., 1998; Flavell et al., 2002). In general, though, the reports of younger children may be questionable when factors such as stereotypes and suggestive comments can reduce their accuracy. However, older children are reasonably trustworthy.

Children's Memory Strategies. So far, our exploration of children's memory has demonstrated that children are fairly similar to adults in recognizing items, but children are much less accurate in recalling them. When adults want to remember something that must be recalled at a later time, they often use memory strategies. One important reason children have relatively poor recall is that they are not able to use memory strategies effectively (Bransford et al., 2000; DeHart et al., 2004).

Memory strategies are deliberate, goal-oriented activities we use to improve our memories (Kail, 2004). Young children may not realize that strategies can be helpful. Furthermore, children may not use the strategies effectively, a problem called **utilization deficiency.** As a result, the strategies may not improve their recall (Bjorklund et al., 1997; Flavell et al., 1993; Schneider, 2002). In contrast, older children typically realize that strategies are helpful. In addition, they choose their strategies more carefully and use them more consistently. Also, older children often use a variety of strategies when they need to learn several items, and they may monitor how they use these strategies (Coyle & Bjorklund, 1997; Schneider, 1998). As a result, older children can recall items with reasonable accuracy. Let's survey three major kinds of memory strategies: rehearsal, organization, and imagery.

1. *Rehearsal*, or merely repeating items over and over, is not a particularly effective strategy, but it may be useful for maintaining items in working memory. Research suggests that 4- and 5-year-olds do not spontaneously rehearse material they want to remember (Flavell et al., 1966; Gathercole et al., 1994). However, 7-year-olds do use rehearsal strategies, often silently rehearsing several words together (Gathercole, 1998; Schneider & Bjorklund, 1998).

Another important point is that younger children often benefit from rehearsal strategies, even though they do not use these strategies spontaneously (e.g., Bjorklund et al., 1997; Flavell et al., 2002; Gathercole, 1998). As we will see later in the chapter, in the section on metacognition, young children often fail to realize that they could improve their memory performance by using strategies.

2. *Organizational strategies*, such as categorizing and grouping, are frequently used by adults, as we saw in Chapter 6. However, young children do not spontaneously group similar items together to aid memorization (Bransford et al., 2000; Flavell et al., 2002; Schneider & Bjorklund, 1998). Try Demonstration 13.2 on page 466 and see whether children are reluctant to adopt an organizational strategy.

This demonstration is based on a classic study by Moely and her colleagues (1969), in which children studied pictures from four categories: animals, clothing, furniture, and vehicles. During the 2-minute study period, they were told that they could rearrange the pictures in any order they wished. Younger children rarely moved the pictures next to other similar pictures, but older children frequently organized the pictures into categories. The researchers specifically urged other groups of children to organize the pictures. This training procedure encouraged even the younger children to adopt an organizational strategy, and this strategy increased their recall. Thus, children often have the ability to organize, though they are not aware that organization will enhance recall. Other research has shown that 10- and 12-year-old children often spontaneously organize items by category—for example, by recalling all the kinds of furniture they have in their home (Plumert, 1994).

3. *Imagery*, a topic discussed in Chapters 6 and 7, is an extremely useful device for improving memory in adults. Research shows that children as young as 6 can also effectively use visual imagery on memory tasks (Foley et al., 1993; Kosslyn, 1976). Furthermore, after just 5 minutes of training, 6-year-olds were able to use imagery to improve both their working memory and long-term memory (Yuille & Catchpole, 1977). However, young children usually do not use imagery spontaneously. In fact, the spontaneous use of imagery does not develop until adolescence, and even most college students do not use this helpful strategy often enough (Schneider & Bjorklund, 1998).

⑨ Demonstration 13.2

Organizational Strategies in Children

Make a photocopy of the pictures on this page and use scissors to cut them apart (or, alternatively, cut four different categories of pictures out of magazines). In this study you will test a child between the ages of 4 and 8; ideally, it would be interesting to test children of several different ages. Arrange these pictures in random order in a circle facing the child. Instruct him or her to study the pictures so that they can be remembered later. Mention that the pictures can be rearranged in any order. After a 2-minute study period, remove the pictures and ask the child to list as many items as possible. Notice two things in this demonstration: (1) Does the child rearrange the items at all during the study period? (2) Does the child show clustering during recall, with similar items appearing together?

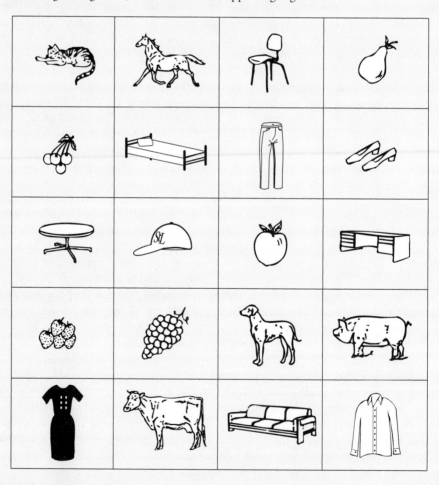

In short, preschool children are unlikely to use memory strategies in a careful, consistent fashion. In fact, as we have suggested here—and will further discuss in connection with metamemory—young children are not likely to appreciate that they need to use memory strategies (Schneider, 1999). However, as children develop, they learn how to use memory strategies such as rehearsal, organization, and (eventually) imagery. Furthermore, they become increasingly aware that—if they want to remember something—they would be wise to use these memory strategies, rather than merely trusting that they will remember important material (Bransford et al., 2000; Kuhn, 2000).

IN DEPTH

Memory in Elderly People

The popular stereotype for elderly people is that they may be pleasant, but they are typically forgetful and cognitively incompetent (Cuddy & Fiske, 2002; Hummert, 1999; Levy & Banaji, 2002). Consider the following example of the way people judge cognitive errors made by elderly people (Hulicka, 1982). A 78-year-old woman served a meal to her guests, and the meal was excellent, except that she had used Clorox instead of vinegar in the salad dressing. Her concerned relatives attributed the error to impaired memory and general intellectual decline, and they discussed placing her in a nursing home. As it turned out, someone else had placed the Clorox in the cupboard where the vinegar was kept. Understandably, the woman had reached for the wrong bottle, which was similar in size, shape, and color to the vinegar bottle.

Some time later, the same people were guests in another home. A young woman in search of hair spray reached into a bathroom cabinet and found a can of the right size and shape. She proceeded to drench her hair with Lysol. In this case, however, no one suggested that the younger woman be institutionalized; they merely teased her about her absentmindedness. Apparently, people are so convinced that elderly people have cognitive deficits that an incident considered humorous in a younger person provides proof of incompetence in an older person.

During the last decade, research on age-related changes in memory has increased dramatically, and a wide variety of review articles and books have been published (e.g., Birren & Schaie, 2001; Cavanaugh & Whitbourne, 1999; Dixon & Cohen, 2003; Graf & Ohta, 2002; Light, 2000; Park & Schwarz, 2000; Swanson, 1999; Tulving & Craik, 2000; Whitbourne, 2005). The picture that emerges suggests large individual differences and complex developmental trends in various components of memory (Fabiani & Wee, 2001; Light, 2000; Whitbourne, 2005). Let us consider the research on working memory and long-term memory in elderly people; then we will examine some potential explanations for the memory changes during aging.

Working Memory in Elderly People. How well do elderly people perform on tasks requiring working memory, when material must be retained in memory for less than a minute? If you have taken several previous psychology courses, you know that your professors and your textbooks frequently use the phrase, "It all depends on . . . ." In the case of working memory, factors such as the nature of the task determine whether we find age similarities or age differences. In general, we find age similarities when the task is relatively straightforward and requires simple storage. In contrast, we typically find age differences when the task is complicated and requires manipulation of information (Bäckman et al., 2001; Balota et al., 2000; Fabiani & Wee, 2001; Park et al., 2002; Whitbourne, 2005).

For example, younger and older adults perform similarly on a standard digit-span test, where people are instructed to recall a list of numbers in order (Bäckman et al., 2001; Dixon & Cohen, 2003; Fabiani & Wee, 2001). This finding is consistent with the proposal that the phonological loop functions relatively well in elderly people (Baddeley, 1999). (As you learned in Chapter 4, the **phonological loop** stores a limited number of sounds for a short period of time.) However, age differences are substantial for a task in which people must ignore irrelevant information or perform two simultaneous tasks (Li, 2002; Lustig, Hasher, & Tonev, 2001; Lustig, May, & Hasher, 2001; Oberauer et al., 2003). For instance, in one study, people were given short lists of unrelated words, with the instructions to report the words in correct alphabetical order (Craik, 1990). On this complex task, the average young participant reported 3.2 correct items on the alphabetical-order task, whereas the average elderly participant reported only 1.7 correct items.

Another example of the complex nature of working memory comes from Stine and her coauthors (1989), who tested people's recall for spoken English. When the sentences had normal syntax and were spoken at a normal rate, the younger and older participants performed similarly. In contrast, when the words were in random order and the speech rate was much faster than normal, the younger participants recalled about twice as many items. We should keep in mind, then, that elderly people often perform well on the tasks they are most likely to encounter in everyday life. In general, however, the phonological loop and the visuospatial sketchpad decline at roughly the same gradual rate during the aging process (Park et al., 2002).

Long-Term Memory in Elderly People. Do elderly people differ from younger adults in their long-term memory? Once again, the answer is, "It all depends on . . . ." In general, the age differences are smallest on tasks that test recognition memory and on tasks that can be performed relatively automatically. However, age differences emerge on more complex tasks. In this discussion of long-term memory, let's consider three topics: (1) implicit memory, (2) explicit recognition memory, and (3) explicit recall memory.

1. *Implicit Memory.* Chapter 5 discussed the difference between explicit and implicit memory tasks. As explained in that chapter, participants in an **explicit memory task** are specifically instructed to remember information that they have previously learned (for example, to recognize or recall information). In contrast, an

implicit memory task requires the participants to perform a perceptual or cognitive task (for example, to complete a series of word fragments); past experience with the material facilitates their performance on the task.

In a representative study, Light and her colleagues (1995) measured implicit memory in terms of the time participants required to say a letter sequence that was formed by combining two familiar one-syllable words (for example, *fishdust*). Implicit memory is demonstrated when people perform more quickly on letter sequences that they have seen on previous trials, compared to letter sequences formed by recombining words from the previous trials (for example, when they had seen *artmale* and *pointinch*, and then they see the recombined item *artinch*). In other words, people demonstrate memory by showing that they read a familiar sequence faster than an unfamiliar sequence. On this implicit memory task, adults between the ages of 64 and 78 performed as well as did the younger adults, who were between the ages of 18 and 24.

Other research on implicit memory shows either similar performance by older and younger adults, or else just a slight deficit for older adults (e.g., Bäckman et al., 2001; Balota et al., 2000; Grady & Craik, 2000; Light, 1996, 2000; Whitbourne, 2005). Thus, age differences are minimal when the memory task does not require effortful remembering.

2. Explicit Recognition Memory. A number of research papers and reviews of the literature argue that long-term recognition memory declines either slowly or not at all as people grow older (Baddeley, 1999; Fabiani & Wee, 2001; Kester et al., 2002; Stine-Morrow & Miller, 1999). For example, one study on recognition memory found that 20-year-olds correctly recognized 67% of words that had been presented earlier; the 70-year-olds recalled a nearly identical 66% of the words (Intons-Peterson et al., 1999).

3. Explicit Recall Memory. So far, our discussion of long-term memory has shown that elderly people perform reasonably well on two kinds of long-term memory tasks: implicit memory tests and explicit recognition tests. Let us now turn to performance on explicit *recall* tasks. In general, performance on these measures decreases slowly throughout later adulthood, and the age differences are more substantial (Bäckman et al., 2001; Dixon & Cohen, 2003; Wingfield & Kahana, 2002). In a representative study, Dunlosky and Hertzog (1998a) asked participants to learn pairs of unrelated English words. They reported that the 20-year-old participants recalled an average of 20% more of the items than did the 70-year-old participants. In other research, older people made more errors in recalling names, recalling details of historical events, and remembering stories (Cohen, 1993; Cohen et al., 1994; Zelinski & Gilewski, 1988).

However, elderly individuals differ widely in their performance on long-term recall tasks. For example, people with low verbal ability and little education are especially likely to show a decline in recall during the aging process. In contrast, age differences are minimal for people who have high verbal ability and are highly educated (Bäckman et al., 2001; Hertzog & Dunlosky, 1996; Rabbitt, 2002). We also have some evidence that elderly people are less likely to show a decline in recall memory if they live in an Asian culture or some other community in which elderly individuals are highly valued (Langer, 1997; Levy & Langer, 1994). These findings suggest that elderly people in mainstream North American culture may be somewhat influenced by our stereotype about forgetful older people (Kester et al., 2002).

We have seen that verbal ability, education, and culture can influence whether elderly people have more memory problems than young people. Lynn Hasher and her coauthors have explored another variable to add to the list of "It all depends on . . ." factors: the time of day when people's memory is tested (Hasher et al., 2002; Winocur & Hasher, 2002; Yoon, May, & Hasher, 2000). Specifically, older adults tend to function most effectively in the morning, whereas younger adults tend to function most effectively in the late afternoon or evening. In a representative study, Hasher and her colleagues (2002) located older adults who were "morning people" and younger adults who were "evening people," as measured by a standardized test. Half of each group was tested from 8:00 to 9:15 a.m., and half was tested from 4:30 to 5:15 p.m. Every individual saw three lists of 10 English words, displayed one word at a time on a computer screen.

Hasher and her coauthors' (2002) results are shown in Figure 13.5. When the participants were tested in the morning, the older adults remembered almost as many words as the young adults. During the afternoon testing, however, the older adults remembered significantly fewer words than the young adults.

Interestingly, an occasional study even shows that elderly adults have more accurate recall than younger adults. For instance, Park and her coauthors (1999) examined people who were taking medication for rheumatoid arthritis. Using current technology, these researchers were able to install a microchip in every participant's bottle of medication. Only 28% of the younger participants (ages 34 to 54) remembered to take their medication every day for the 1-month period of the study. In contrast, 47% of the older participants (ages 55 to 84) had perfect scores on this measure. The explanation for this unusual finding isn't clear, but several studies confirm that elderly individuals can show impressively accurate memory in real-life settings (Park & Hedden, 2001).

Notice how the research on long-term memory obeys the "It all depends on . . ." principle. Elderly people are fairly similar to younger people in implicit memory and explicit recognition memory. Even when we examine an area in which age differences are more prominent—such as explicit recall—we cannot draw a simple conclusion, because highly verbal, well-educated elderly people are less likely to show deficits. Elderly people can also perform relatively well when tested in the morning. In other words, memory deficits are far from universal among elderly people.

Explanations for Age Differences in Memory. As one theorist in the area of memory and aging concluded, this research reveals a "bewildering mass of contradictory findings" (Sharps, 1998, p. 284). As you probably suspected, a complex pattern of results requires a complex explanation. Also, we must emphasize that we are seeking explanations for memory changes that accompany the normal aging process; disorders such as Alzheimer's disease require different explanations (e.g., Hodges, 2000).

FIGURE 13.5

Average Number of Words Recalled on Each of Three Lists of Words (maximum score = 10), as a Function of the Participant's Age and the Time of the Test (morning or afternoon).

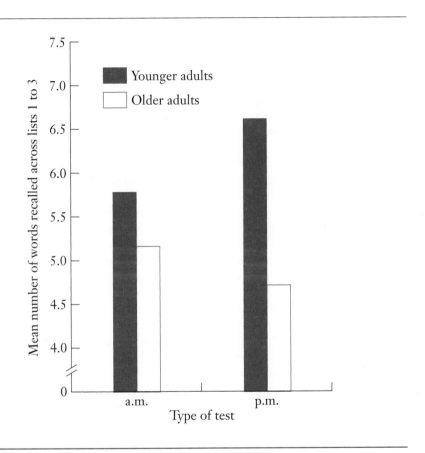

Research in cognitive neuroscience demonstrates clear-cut changes in brain structures as people grow older. Remember that explicit recall memory is especially likely to show a deficit. From a neuroscience perspective, this makes sense, because explicit recall relies on a complex network of many different brain structures, including the frontal and parietal regions of the cortex and many subcortical structures. Because these parts of the brain must work together, explicit recall memory can be disrupted if one of the components of the network is not functioning appropriately. Furthermore, many of these brain structures are known to decrease in volume during normal aging (Fabiani & Wee, 2001).

However, it is not yet clear how these biological changes in the brain actually correspond to psychological processes (Grady & Craik, 2000). Let's look at several psychological processes that might be responsible for the pattern of changes in memory performance during normal aging. To account for these changes, we probably need to rely on several mechanisms, because no single explanation is sufficient (Bäckman et al., 2001).

1. *Ineffective use of memory strategies and metamemory.* Elderly people could have impaired memory because they use memory strategies and metamemory less effectively. Some research suggests that elderly individuals are less likely to use organizational strategies and imagery (e.g., Carney & Levin, 1998). However, numerous studies conclude that elderly and young adults use similar memory strategies (Dunlosky & Hertzog, 1998a; Light, 2000). Furthermore—as we will see later in this chapter—age differences in metamemory are not consistent enough to explain differences in memory performance.

Notice that these results with elderly people are different from the results with children. We noted earlier that children's memory problems can probably be traced to a deficit in memory strategies. In addition, children's metamemory skills are not well developed, so that they do not appreciate that they need to use memory strategies. In contrast, elderly adults resemble younger adults in both strategy use and metamemory. As a result, we will need to search elsewhere to learn why elderly adults have memory problems.

2. *The contextual-cues hypothesis.* As we saw earlier, elderly people perform relatively well on recognition tasks, where contextual cues are present. In contrast, contextual cues are absent on explicit recall tasks; instead, these recall tasks require people to use effortful, deliberate processing. Young adults are relatively skilled in remembering contextual cues, for example, where they were and what date it was when they heard a particular news item (Craik & Anderson, 1999; Grady & Craik, 2000; Light, 2000). These contextual cues may boost the accuracy of a young adult's explicit recall. In contrast, elderly adults recall fewer contextual cues. Therefore, elderly adults must rely on effortful, deliberate processing in order to retrieve the information, and the explicit-recall task is more difficult for them.

3. *Reduced processing resources and processing speed.* The hypothesis that has been most extensively researched in the past decade is that elderly people process information less effectively. One reduced-processing-resources explanation is that working memory is diminished in elderly people; we discussed this age-related difference in working memory on page 468. A second reduced-processing explanation is that elderly people often experience **cognitive slowing,** or a slower rate of responding on cognitive tasks (e.g., Balota et al., 2000; Bashore & Ridderinkhof, 2002; Salthouse, 2002). The reduced-processing explanation can account for some of the age-related differences in memory, but not all of them (Light, 1996, 2000).

At present, some variant of the reduced-resources explanation seems most promising. However, none of these mechanisms completely accounts for the pattern of age-related differences in memory (Bäckman et al., 2001; Light, 1996, 2000). Perhaps a more refined version of several of these hypotheses will be developed, or additional hypotheses will be proposed. At this point, we currently have a complex set of findings about memory in elderly individuals, but no satisfying explanation for these results.

⑨ Section Summary: *The Lifespan Development of Memory*

1. The lifespan approach to development emphasizes that developmental changes and adaptations continue throughout the lifespan.

2. Psychologists interested in the development of cognition encounter methodological problems in their research, particularly when they study infants and elderly people.

3. Research demonstrates that 3-day-olds can recognize their mothers. Older infants can recall how to move a mobile—following a delay of several days—when they are tested with the conjugate reinforcement technique; infant memory is influenced by many factors that are also important in adulthood.

4. Compared to adults, children have reduced working memory; children have reasonably strong recognition memory, but poor recall memory.

5. The research on childhood amnesia suggests that older children and adults cannot recall events that occurred prior to the age of 2 or 3. In general, children have poor source monitoring.

6. Under ideal circumstances, children's eyewitness reports can be trustworthy, but their reports may be unreliable when they are young or when they have been supplied with stereotypes and suggestive questions.

7. Children's eyewitness testimony is also influenced by characteristics of the interview; however, children recall the events of a doctor's visit reasonably accurately.

8. As children grow older, they increasingly use memory strategies such as rehearsal and organization; by adolescence, they can also use imagery appropriately.

9. As adults grow older, their working memory remains intact for some tasks, but it is limited if the task is complicated or it requires manipulation of information.

10. With respect to long-term memory in adulthood, age differences are relatively small for implicit memory tasks and for explicit recognition tasks.

11. Age differences on explicit recall tasks are more substantial. However, elderly individuals perform relatively well if they have high verbal ability, if they are

highly educated, or if they are tested early in the day. Furthermore, in a few situations, elderly people have *more* accurate memory than younger adults.

12. Cognitive neuroscience research shows clear-cut changes in the brain structure of elderly individuals. Potential psychological explanations for age-related memory changes during adulthood include (a) ineffective use of memory strategies and metamemory, (b) the contextual-cues hypothesis, and (c) reduced processing resources and processing speed.

THE LIFESPAN DEVELOPMENT OF METACOGNITION

As we discussed in Chapter 6, **metacognition** is your knowledge about your cognitive processes—or your thoughts about thinking. Two important kinds of metacognition are metamemory (for example, realizing that you need to use a strategy to remember someone's name) and metacomprehension (for example, trying to decide whether you understood that definition of *metacognition*). In this section of the chapter, we will look at metacognition in children and in elderly adults.

Metacognition in Children

Research on metacognition in children has been thriving for more than 30 years. In fact, the first major research in metacognition focused on children rather than on college students (Flavell, 1971). Flavell argued that young children have limited metacognition; they seldom monitor their memory, language, problem solving, or decision making (Flavell, 1979). More recent research about children's metacognition has focused on a topic called **theory of mind**—or children's ideas on how their minds work and on their beliefs about other people's thoughts (e.g., Flavell et al., 2000; Kuhn, 2000; Schneider, 1999). Our discussion of children's metacognition will focus on several components of children's metamemory, as well as the topic of metacomprehension.

Children's Metamemory: How Memory Works. An important component of metamemory is your knowledge about how memory works. Demonstration 13.3 includes some questions about this aspect of metamemory. Even young children, 3 and 4 years of age, know that a small set of pictures can be remembered better than a large set (Schneider & Pressley, 1997). However, children often have unsophisticated ideas about how their memories work. For example, 7-year-olds are not yet aware that words are easier to remember when they are related to one another, rather than randomly selected (Joyner & Kurtz-Costes, 1997; Moynahan, 1978; Schneider & Pressley, 1997). If children don't know how their memories work, they won't know how to plan effective study strategies (Bransford et al., 2000; Schneider, 1999, 2002).

Children's Metamemory: Realizing the Necessity of Effort. Another important component of metamemory is the awareness that, if you really want to remember something, you must make an effort (Joyner & Kurtz-Costes, 1997; Schneider, 2002). However, young children do not appreciate this principle. In addition, they are even

---

ⓢ Demonstration 13.3

Metamemory in Adults and Children

Ask a child the questions listed below. (Ideally, try to question several children of different ages.) Compare the accuracy and/or the completeness of the answers with your own responses. Note that some questions should be reworded to a level appropriate for the individuals you are testing.

1. A child will be going to a party tomorrow, and she wants to remember to bring her skates. What kinds of things can she do to help her remember them?

2. Suppose that I were to read you a list of words. How many words do you think you could recall in the correct order? (Then read the following list and count the number of words correctly recalled. Use only part of the list for the child.)

   cat rug chair leaf sky book apple pencil house teacher

3. Two children want to learn the names of some flowers. One child learned the names last month but forgot them. The other child never learned the names. Who will have an easier time in learning the names?

4. Suppose that you memorize somebody's address. Will you remember it better after 2 minutes have passed or after 2 days have passed?

5. Two children want to remember some lists of words. One child has a list of 10 words, and the other has a list of 5 words. Which child will be more likely to remember all the words on the list correctly?

6. Two children are reading the same paragraph. The teacher tells one child to remember all the sentences in the paragraph and repeat them word for word. The teacher tells the other child to remember the main ideas of the paragraph. Which child will have an easier job?

---

more likely than adults to keep studying information that they already know (Schneider & Bjorklund, 1998). Furthermore, they are not accurate in judging whether something has been committed to memory. They typically report to the experimenter that they have satisfactorily memorized a list, yet they recall little on a test (Siegler, 1998).

Older children also have naive ideas about the effort required in memorization (Schneider, 1999). I recall a visit from a sixth grader in our neighborhood who had been memorizing some information about the U.S. Constitution. My husband asked her how she was doing and whether she would like him to quiz her on the material. She replied that she knew the material well, but he could quiz her if he wanted. Her recall turned out to be minimal for both factual and conceptual information. She had assumed that by allowing her eyes to wander over the text several times, the material had magically worked its way into her memory.

Of course, magical thinking is not limited to children. If your high school courses were relatively easy for you, perhaps you reached college before you realized that you need effortful processing in order to retain difficult material. As we saw in Chapter 6, adolescents and adults often fail to appreciate the usefulness of memory strategies (Kuhn, 2000; Schneider, 2002).

Children's Metamemory: Accuracy of Predictions. In general, young children are unrealistically optimistic in predicting their memory performance. In contrast, older children, adolescents, and adults are reasonably accurate (Flavell et al., 2002; Joyner & Kurtz-Costes, 1997; Schneider, 1998).

In a classic study, Yussen and Levy (1975) studied preschool children (mean age of 4.6 years), third graders (mean age of 8.9), and college students (mean age of 20.2). Each person was first asked to estimate the number of picture names that he or she would be able to recall in correct order. Notice that this question measures metamemory because it asks people to think about their memory abilities. Next, Yussen and Levy measured everyone's true memory span on this task.

Figure 13.6 shows both memory estimates and actual memory spans for the three age groups. Notice that the preschoolers are wildly optimistic when estimating their memory. Unfortunately, this optimism may encourage a false sense of security. They may not believe that they need to spend any effort or use any strategies to memorize material (Kail, 1990). However, as children grow older, their estimates become more modest while their actual memory spans increase. Consequently, college students are fairly realistic in their memory-span estimates.

Children's Metamemory: The Relationship Between Metamemory and Memory Performance. Let us summarize several observations related to memory in young children: (1) Their metamemory is faulty—they do not realize that they need to put effort into memorizing, and they do not realize how little they can remember; (2) they do not spontaneously use helpful memory strategies; and (3) relative to older children, their memory performance is poor.

Does a causal relationship link these three observations? Perhaps the three are related in this fashion:

Metamemory → Strategy use → Memory performance

According to this argument, when children have poor metamemory, they won't be aware that they must use strategies to commit material to memory. If they do not use strategies, then their memory performance will suffer.

We have some evidence that metamemory is related to strategy use (Flavell et al., 2002; Schneider, 1999). For example, children with more sophisticated metacognitive

FIGURE 13.6

Estimated Versus Actual Memory Span, as a Function of Age.

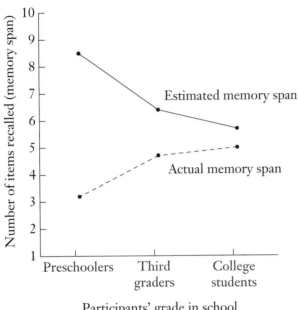

Source: Based on Yussen & Levy, 1975.

abilities are more likely to report using memory strategies (Alexander & Schwanenflugel, 1994). They are also more likely to use these strategies effectively (Justice et al., 1997). In addition, we have extensive evidence to support the second link in the chain. As we saw on pages 465–467, children's strategy use is related to memory performance.

So, metamemory is linked to strategy use and strategy use is linked to memory performance. Are the two ends in that chain—that is, metamemory and memory performance—related to each other? Analysis of the research shows that the correlation between metamemory and memory performance is moderate, $r = +.41$ (Schneider, 2002; Schneider & Pressley, 1997). It makes sense that the correlation is not stronger. An important limiting factor is that it's difficult to test children's metamemory, because they haven't yet developed sophisticated vocabulary, and their knowledge about their memory may be implicit, rather than explicit (Joyner & Kurtz-Costes, 1997; Schneider, 1999; Schneider & Pressley, 1997).

In summary, we can conclude that metamemory is moderately related to memory performance (Schneider, 2002). Consequently, the proposed causal sequence (Metamemory → Strategy use → Memory performance) could account for a substantial portion of the improvement in memory performance as children grow older.

Children's Metacomprehension. As you learned in Chapter 6, **metacomprehension** refers to your thoughts about language comprehension. During a metacomprehension task, you assess whether you understand what you are reading or what is being said to you. Metacomprehension also includes your knowledge and thoughts about comprehension. As children grow older, they become increasingly skilled in noticing when a passage is difficult to understand (Schneider, 1999). However, as you saw in Chapter 6, even college students are not highly accurate in monitoring their comprehension (Schneider & Pressley, 1997).

Children gradually learn several important components of metacomprehension. Flavell and his coauthors (1997) asked children to watch as a woman performed a number of tasks (for example, silently reading a book). They asked children a series of questions, such as, "She's still reading. Is she saying any story words to herself right now, or not?" (p. 42). Only 30% of 4-year-olds answered "yes," in contrast to 95% of 6- to 7-year-olds.

Young children often fail to identify that a paragraph may contain contradictory information (Schneider & Pressley, 1997). In a representative study, for example, children were instructed to read a paragraph in which a boy caught a fish with a fishing pole and—only one sentence later—the boy felt sad that he forgot to pack his fishing pole (Zabrucky & Ratner, 1986). Eight-year-olds told the researcher that the paragraph made sense, so their verbal reports were not accurate. However, other measures of metacomprehension demonstrated that the children had in fact detected the contradiction. For instance, they were likely to read the puzzling passages more slowly. Apparently young children *do* monitor their reading, but they cannot verbally describe their metacognitive activities (Schneider & Pressley, 1997).

Metacognition in Elderly People

Research on metacognition in elderly people is limited almost exclusively to the topic of metamemory (Dixon & Cohen, 2003). Many other components of metacognition are still unexplored. For example, we know little about elderly people's thoughts about their comprehension (that is, their metacomprehension) or their thoughts about problem solving. Our discussion of metacognition in elderly individuals is therefore restricted to the area of metamemory.

Actually, an earlier part of this chapter already revealed the major conclusions about age comparisons in metamemory. On pages 472–473, we discussed possible explanations for age differences in some areas of memory. However, we noted that young and elderly adults do not differ substantially in their metamemory. Let us consider the evidence in more detail.

1. *Beliefs about memory.* Older and younger adults share similar beliefs about the properties of memory tasks (Light, 1996; Salthouse, 1991). Both groups have the same fundamental knowledge about how memory works, which strategies are most effective, and what kinds of material can be remembered most readily (Hertzog et al., 1999).

2. *Memory monitoring.* Older and younger adults have similar abilities to monitor their memory performance (Bieman-Copland & Charness, 1994; Hertzog & Dixon, 1994). For example, the two groups are similar in their ability to predict—on an item-by-item basis—which items they can recall at a later time (Connor et al., 1997). Older and younger adults are also similar with respect to selecting the most difficult items for further study (Dunlosky & Hertzog, 1997). However, it's not clear whether older adults are more likely than younger adults to underestimate the difficulty of a memory task (e.g., Dunlosky & Hertzog, 1998b; Herrmann, 1990; Salthouse, 1991). One possibility is that older adults in their 60s and 70s may be reasonably accurate in estimating memory performance; metamemory may be less accurate among very elderly adults (Perfect, 1997).

3. *Awareness of memory problems.* Elderly people are likely to report problems with their everyday memory, especially on explicit recall tasks such as remembering phone numbers (Dunlosky & Hertzog, 1998b; Kester et al., 2002). They are also likely to say that their memory failures have increased over the years. Based on the research we reviewed on memory in elderly individuals, these reports are probably accurate.

The problem is that the popular stereotype about elderly people's poor memory may encourage elderly individuals to think that memory decline is inevitable. As a result, many elderly people will not try to develop helpful memory strategies (Hertzog et al., 1999; Kester et al., 2002). In contrast, some elderly people are high in **memory self-efficacy,** or the belief in your own potential to perform well on memory tasks. They think that it's important to keep developing their memory. As a result, they are likely to perform relatively well, especially on verbal-memory tasks (Dixon & Cohen, 2003; Hertzog et al., 1999).

In summary, our examination of metamemory has revealed that elderly adults and young adults are similar in many respects (Craik et al., 1995; Light, 2000; Salthouse, 1991). We saw earlier in this section that young children's metamemory is less accurate than young adults' metamemory. In contrast, elderly adults do not experience an overwhelming metamemory impairment.

Section Summary: *The Lifespan Development of Metacognition*

1. Young children have some knowledge of the factors that influence memory, and their knowledge increases as they mature.

2. Young children are not aware that they must make an effort to learn a list of items, and they cannot accurately judge when they have mastered the material.

3. Older children and adults are much more accurate than younger children in predicting their memory performance; young children are very overconfident.

4. To some extent, children's deficits in metamemory partly explain their poor performance on memory tasks: As children grow older, their metamemory

improves, leading to increased strategy use, in turn producing better memory performance.

5. As they grow older, young children gradually improve their metacomprehension. In addition, they may reread puzzling passages, thereby revealing that they do not understand the material; however, they may still report that the passage made sense.

6. Elderly adults and young adults have similar knowledge about their memory. They also have a similar ability to monitor their memory on an item-by-item basis; age is not consistently related to people's estimates about the difficulty of a memory task.

7. Elderly people report an increase in the frequency of some memory problems, an assessment that is probably correct. When elderly people believe that a memory decline is inevitable, they do not try to develop useful memory strategies.

THE DEVELOPMENT OF LANGUAGE

"Mama!" (8 months old)

"Wash hair." (1 year, 4 months old)

"Don't tickle my tummy, Mommy!" (1 year, 11 months old)

"My Grandma gave me this dolly, Cara. My Grandma is my Mommy's Mommy. I have another Grandma, too. She's my Daddy's Mommy. And Aunt Elli is my Daddy's sister." (2 years, 9 months old)

These selections from the early language of my daughter Sally are typical of children's remarkable achievements during language acquisition. Individual children differ in the rate at which they master language (e.g., Bloom & Gleitman, 1999; Boysson-Bardies, 1999). Still, within a period of 2 to 3 years, all normal children progress from one-word utterances to complex discourse. In fact, by the age of 5, most children produce sentences that resemble adult speech (Gleitman & Bloom, 1999; Kuhl, 2000).

Language acquisition is often said to be the most spectacular of human accomplishments, and children's linguistic skills clearly exemplify Theme 2. For instance, the average 6-year-old can speak between about 10,000 and 14,000 words. To acquire a vocabulary this large, children must learn about seven new words each day from the time they start speaking until their sixth birthday (Carroll, 2004; Wellman, 2000). If you are not impressed by a 14,000-word vocabulary, consider how much effort high school students must exert to acquire 1,000 words in a foreign language—and those 6-year-old language learners are only waist-high!

However, language acquisition includes much more than the simple acquisition of new words. For example, children combine these words into phrases that they have never heard before, such as, "My dolly dreamed about toys" (2 years, 2 months).

Researchers have typically ignored developmental changes in language during late adulthood, although some new research is beginning to emerge (e.g., Charness et al., 2001; Hillis, 2002; Kemper & Mitzner, 2001; Nussbaum et al., 2000; Stine-Morrow & Miller, 1999; Whitbourne, 2005; Wingfield & Stine-Morrow, 2000). Our discussion of language development will therefore be limited to infancy and childhood.

Language in Infants

Let's begin by considering how young infants perceive the sounds of speech. Then we will look at their early skill in understanding language, as well as their language production. Finally, we'll see how infants' language acquisition is encouraged by the language that adults use in interacting with them.

Speech Perception in Infancy. To acquire language, infants must be able to distinguish between **phonemes,** or the smallest sound units in a language. However, the ability to make distinctions is only half of the struggle; infants must also be able to group together the sounds that are phonetically equivalent. For example, language acquisition requires the ability to recognize that the sounds *b* and *p* are different from each other, whereas the sound *b* spoken by the deepest bass voice, in the middle of a word, is the same as the sound *b* spoken by the highest soprano voice, at the end of a word (Jusczyk & Luce, 2002).

If you have recently seen a baby who is younger than 6 months old, you might have been tempted to conclude that the baby's mastery of language was roughly equivalent to that of a tennis shoe. Until the early 1970s, psychologists were not much more optimistic. However, more than 30 years of research have demonstrated that infants' speech perception is surprisingly advanced. Infants can perceive almost all the speech-sound contrasts used in language, either at birth or within the first few weeks of life (Cheour, 1998; Jusczyk & Luce, 2002). They can also recognize similarities, an important early stage in the understanding of language. Infants' abilities are highly conducive to language learning (Carroll, 2004; Flavell et al., 2002; Werker & Tees, 1999).

Peter Eimas and his coauthors (1971) were among the first to discover infants' capacity for speech perception. They used a method called **nonnutritive sucking,** in which babies suck on nipples to produce a particular sound. No liquid is delivered through the nipple, but the infant is required to suck at least two times each second to maintain the sound. Typically, babies begin each session by sucking frequently to maintain the sound. However, they gradually show habituation. As you may have learned in other psychology courses, **habituation** occurs when a stimulus is presented frequently, and the response rate decreases. Presumably, the sound is now too boring, and it is not worth the hard work of frequent sucking.

How can the nonnutritive sucking technique be used to provide insight into infant speech perception? Eimas and his colleagues (1971) presented a specific speech sound to the 1- to 4-month-old infants in their study. After the infant had habituated to the first sound, the researchers presented a second speech sound. For example, an infant who had shown habituation to *bah* was suddenly presented with a highly similar sound, *pah*. These infants showed dishabituation. That is, when *pah* was presented, they suddenly started sucking vigorously once more. In contrast, a different group of infants showed no dishabituation when they continued to hear the *bah* sound; their response rate continued to decrease. Thus, the nonnutritive sucking technique revealed that infants respond at different rates to different sounds, and so they must be able to perceive the difference between them.

In some cases, young infants are even better than older infants and adults in making phonemic distinctions. For example, infants raised in English-speaking homes can make distinctions between phonemic contrasts that are important in Hindi, a language spoken in India. In Hindi, the *t* sound is sometimes made by placing the tongue against the back of the teeth and sometimes by placing the tongue farther back along the roof of the mouth. In contrast, English does not distinguish between these two *t* sounds. However, Werker and Tees (1984) demonstrated that English-speaking infants can distinguish between these phonemes with about 95% accuracy when they are 6 to 8 months old. Accuracy drops to about 70% at 8 to 10 months of age, and to about 20% at 10 to 12 months of age. Young infants may be able to appreciate phonetic distinctions in all languages. Later, however, they reorganize their perceptual categories so that they focus on the important distinctions they hear in their own language (Cheour et al., 1998; Kuhl, 2000; Plunkett & Schafer, 1999).

According to other research on speech perception, 4-month-old infants respond relatively quickly to their native language, by turning their head toward a loudspeaker. In contrast, they respond more slowly to an unfamiliar language (Bosch & Sebastián-Gallés, 1997). Furthermore, infants as young as 8 months of age can appreciate that word boundaries separate each pair of words in a sequence (Jusczyk, 2002; Saffran, 2001).

Language Comprehension in Infancy. The research on speech perception in infancy has been active for several decades. In contrast, researchers have been slower to explore how infants master the more complex aspects of language comprehension, beyond the level of the phoneme. However, we now have information about young infants' comprehension skills in a variety of areas: (1) recognizing important words, (2) appreciating semantic concepts, (3) discriminating between grammatical words and words that emphasize meaning, and (4) understanding the correspondence between a speaker's facial expression and the emotional tone of the speaker's voice.

1. *Recognizing important words.* Interestingly, infants between the ages of 4 and 5 months can already recognize the sound patterns in their own name. Specifically, Mandel and her colleagues (1995) found that infants are likely to turn their heads to look at a location from which their own name is spoken. In contrast, they seldom turn their heads when a different name is spoken that is similar in length and accented syllable (e.g., *Megan* for an infant named *Rachel*).

Young infants also understand a few selected words. For example, Tincoff and Jusczyk (1999) showed 6-month-olds two videos placed next to each other. One video showed the infant's mother, and the other showed the infant's father. Meanwhile, the researchers presented either the word *mommy* or the word *daddy*. When *mommy* was presented, the infants looked longest at the video of their mother; when *daddy* was presented, they looked longest at the video of their father. However, the infants' concepts are not yet generalized to other adults. In a second study, these researchers used videos of other males and females. The infants showed no preference for looking at the gender-appropriate stranger when hearing the words "mommy" and "daddy" (Tincoff & Jusczyk, 1999).

2. *Appreciating semantic concepts.* So far, we've seen that infants recognize their own names, and they also associate familiar names with the faces of their caregivers. Jean Mandler and her colleagues have shown that infants have more sophisticated concepts about objects than we might have expected. For example, by the age of 9 months, infants can distinguish between toy birds and toy airplanes that are visually very similar (Mandler, 1997, 2002; Mandler & McDonough, 1993). They can also distinguish between animate and inanimate objects (Mandler, 2003).

In other research, McDonough and Mandler (1998) showed 9-month-old infants a dog drinking from a cup and a car giving a doll a ride. The researchers then handed the infants some new objects from two categories—such as a cat and an anteater for the animal category and a truck and a forklift for the vehicle category. The infants showed the appropriate imitation patterns for the new objects, even for the relatively unfamiliar ones. That is, they showed the anteater drinking, whereas they had the forklift giving the doll a ride. Infants therefore have the ability to generalize across a category such as "animal" or "vehicle" (Mandler, 2003).

3. *Discriminating between grammatical words and meaning words.* Infants can even distinguish between more abstract categories of words (Shi & Werker, 2001). Specifically, 6-month-olds prefer to listen to nouns and verbs that convey meaning (e.g., *mommy*, *play*, and *cookie*), rather than words that serve a grammatical function (e.g., *in*, *the*, and *that's*).

4. *Understanding the correspondence between sound and sight.* Infants also appreciate another component of language comprehension: the emotional tone of spoken language (Flavell et al., 2002). For example, Walker-Andrews (1986) played recordings of either a happy voice or an angry voice to 7-month-old infants. Meanwhile, the infants saw a pair of films—one of a happy speaker and one of an angry speaker—projected side-by-side. The mouth region of the faces was covered so that the infants could not rely on lip movements to match the voice with the film. Consequently, the infants had to look for emotional cues in the speaker's cheeks and eyes, rather than their mouths. The results showed that infants who heard a happy voice tended to watch the happy face, whereas infants who heard an angry voice tended to watch the angry face. As Walker-Andrews (1997) summarizes this matching tendency, "Infants appear to experience a world of perceptual unity" (p. 449). As a result, even young infants appreciate that facial expression must correspond with vocal intonation.

The word *infant* originally meant "not speaking." In a moment we'll see that the language production of infants is certainly limited. However, their speech perception and language comprehension are impressively sophisticated, even when they are only a few months old.

Language Production in Infancy. The early vocalizations of infants pass through a series of stages. By about 2 months of age, infants begin to make **cooing** noises, sounds that involve vowels such as *oo*. By about 6 months they have developed **babbling,** a vocalization that uses both consonants and vowels, often repeating sounds in a series such as *dadada* (Flavell et al., 2002). By about 10 months of age, these vocalizations begin to sound like the infant's native language (Bates et al., 2001; DeHart et al., 2004; Kuhl, 2000). This observation coincides with infants' decreased ability to discriminate between phonemes that are irrelevant in their native language (Jusczyk, 1997; Kuhl & Meltzoff, 1996; Werker & Tees, 1999); we discussed this phenomenon on page 482. Interestingly, deaf infants who have been exposed to sign language also begin at about this time to "babble" with their hands, producing systematic but meaningless actions that are not found in hearing children (Bonvillian, 1999; Jusczyk, 1997).

The first attempts at intentional communication occur at about 8 months of age, when babies begin to produce actions designed to capture the attention of other people. They may hand an object to an adult, or they may repeat an action—such as clapping—that has attracted attention in the past (Reddy, 1999). Let's now consider the nature of the language that adults provide to infants.

Adults' Language to Infants. Infants learn language quickly because of their impressive auditory skills, their memory capacity, and their receptivity to language. In addition, infants receive superb assistance from their parents and other adults. Adults who raise children tend to make language acquisition somewhat simpler by adjusting their language when speaking with the children. The term **child-directed speech** is used to refer to the language spoken to children. Child-directed speech uses repetition, simple vocabulary and syntax, a focus on the here and now, clear pronunciation, slow pace, a high pitch, exaggerated changes in pitch, and exaggerated facial expressions (Kellman & Arterberry, 1998; Menyuk et al., 1995; Trainor et al., 2000). Demonstration 13.4 illustrates child-directed speech (DeHart, 1989).

Motherese is a term that was previously used for child-directed speech. However, this gender-biased term neglects the fact that many fathers, other adults, and older children speak "motherese" to infants and young children (DeHart et al., 2004; Gleitman & Bloom, 1999). In reality, though, many fathers who are secondary caregivers do seem to be less "tuned in" to their offspring's communication needs, and their speech to infants tends to be more like their speech to adults. Also, when fathers do not understand something spoken by their children, they usually respond with a nonspecific question, such as, "What?" In contrast, mothers make more specific requests for clarification, such as, "Where should I put the Raggedy Andy?" (DeHart et al., 2004; Tomasello et al., 1990). Obviously, it would be interesting to study the

---

◎ Demonstration 13.4

Producing Child-Directed Speech

Locate a doll that resembles an infant as closely as possible in features and size. Select a friend who has had experience with infants, and ask him or her to imagine that the doll is a niece or nephew who just arrived with parents for a first visit. Encourage your friend to interact with the "baby" in a normal fashion. Observe your friend's language for qualities such as pitch, variation in pitch, vocabulary, sentence length, repetition, and intonation. Also observe any nonverbal communication. What qualities are different from the language used with adults?

---

language patterns of fathers who are primary caregivers, as well as mothers who are secondary caregivers. Most psychological gender differences are minimal when researchers eliminate confounding variables such as the number of hours spent in caregiving (Crawford & Unger, 2004; Matlin, 2004b).

Research in a variety of language communities throughout the world shows that adults use a different language style when speaking to infants and young children than when speaking to older people (Kuhl et al., 1997; Mazuka, 1998; Trainor et al., 2000). The features of child-directed language help young language learners understand the meaning and structure of language.

However, mothers who are psychologically depressed do not use all the useful features of child-directed language, such as the exaggerated changes in pitch. Babies of depressed mothers may therefore have a disadvantage in terms of language-learning opportunities, unless other caretakers provide sufficient child-directed language (Kaplan et al., 2002).

Language in Children

Sometime around their first birthday, most infants throughout the world speak their first word (Waxman, 2002). Let's look at the characteristics of these initial words, as well as the words spoken by older children. Then we will consider children's grammar, specifically morphology and syntax. Finally, we will examine how children master pragmatics, or the social rules of language.

Words. Although children typically produce their first word when they are about 1 year of age, the vocabulary size for normal 1-year-old children ranges from 0 to about 50 words (Bates et al., 2001; Fenson et al., 1991). A child's first words usually refer to people, objects, and their own activities (Bloom, 2001; de Villiers & de Villiers, 1999; Waxman, 2002).

Word production increases rapidly. By the time children are 20 months old, they produce an average of about 180 words. By 28 months, the average is about 380 words (Boysson-Bardies, 1999; Fenson et al., 1991; Woodward & Markman, 1998). Children's vocabulary growth is especially rapid if caregivers frequently read to them and if caregivers frequently talk about activities they are doing with the child (Patterson, 2002; Rollins, 2003).

Children's comprehension of words also increases rapidly (Rollins, 2003). For example, when they hear a particular word, they quickly direct their attention to the appropriate object (Fernald et al., 1998). Children can also learn the meaning of some words by overhearing them in other people's conversations (Akhtar et al., 2001). In general, children understand more words than they can produce (Boysson-Bardies, 1999). Children's memory skills also improve rapidly during this period, which boosts both their language production and their language comprehension (Baddeley et al., 1998; MacWhinney, 1998). This interrelationship between memory and language is an example of Theme 4 of this textbook.

Another factor that helps children learn new words is called **fast mapping,** or using context to make a reasonable guess about a word's meaning after just one or two exposures (Bloom, 2001; Flavell et al., 2003; Kuczaj, 1999). Chapter 9 emphasized that adults are guided by the context in which a word appears. Fast mapping demonstrates that context is also critically important for young children.

In a study on fast mapping, Heibeck and Markman (1987) showed preschoolers pairs of objects and asked the children to select one of them. The request specifically used one familiar term and one unfamiliar term, such as, "Bring me the chartreuse one. Not the blue one, the chartreuse one." Other requests used familiar and unfamiliar terms for shape and texture, as well as color. The children understood the requests, bringing the appropriate object with the unfamiliar label. When tested several minutes later, even 2-year-olds remembered the unfamiliar terms. Children with large vocabularies are especially skilled in using fast mapping (Kuczaj, 1999).

Young children may apply a newly learned label to a category that is either too broad or too narrow. An **overextension** is the use of a word to refer to other objects in addition to objects that adults would consider appropriate (Bloom, 2000; Dromi, 1999; Flavell et al., 2003). For example, my daughter Beth used the word *baish* to refer initially to her blanket. Then she later applied the term to a diaper, a diaper pin, and a vitamin pill. Often an object's shape or function is important in determining overextensions, but sometimes (as in the case of the vitamin pill) overextensions defy adult explanation. Incidentally, they frequently occur for properly pronounced English words, as well as for children's own invented words. You've probably heard of children who call every adult male—including the mailman—"Daddy."

Children around the age of 2 often produce overextensions for words such as *dog* and *ball*. For example, one child produced the name *dog* for nine species of dog and one toy dog—all correct answers. However, he also used the word *dog* for two bears, a wolf, a fox, a doe, a rhinoceros, a hippopotamus, and a fish—all overextensions. Overextensions are especially common when a child does not yet know the correct word for an unfamiliar item (Bloom, 2000). Few 2-year-olds are well acquainted with a rhinoceros or a hippopotamus.

Children may also supply an **underextension,** using a word in a narrower sense than adults do (Bloom, 2000; Dromi, 1999). For example, they may apply the name *doggie* only to the family pet. Older children may refuse to believe that the word *animal* could apply to a praying mantis (Anglin, 1997).

Morphology. Children initially use the simple form of a word in every context—for example, "girl run," rather than "girl runs." However, they soon begin to master how to add on **morphemes** (basic units of meaning, which include endings such as *-s* and *-ed*, as well as simple words such as *run*). **Morphology** is the study of these basic units of meaning.

English-speaking children acquire morphemes in a fairly regular order between the ages of 1½ and 3½. For example, the first morpheme to develop is *-ing* (for example, *running*). Plurals develop next, using the morpheme *-s* (for example, *girls*). The regular past tense develops still later (for example, *kicked*) (Brown, 1973; Kuczaj, 1977; Pinker, 1999).

Children appreciate morphology at a young age. For example, 15-month-olds pay significantly greater attention to phrases with appropriate morphology, such as, "Grandma is singing," than to phrases with inappropriate morphology, such as, "Grandma can singing" (Santelmann & Jusczyk, 1998).

After children have learned many words with regular plurals and past tenses—like *girls* and *kicked*—they progress to a more advanced understanding of morphology. At this point, they sometimes create their own regular forms, such as *mouses* and *runned*, although typically children are surprisingly accurate (Bates et al., 2001). These errors show that language acquisition is not simply a matter of imitating the words produced by parents, because parents seldom produce mistakes such as *mouses* and *runned* (Stromswold, 1999).

The tendency to add the most customary morphemes to create new forms of irregular words is called **overregularization.** (Keep in mind, then, that *overextension* refers to the tendency to broaden a word's meaning inappropriately, whereas *overregularization* refers to the tendency to add regular morphemes inappropriately.) Later still, children learn that many words have regular plurals and past tenses, but some words have irregular forms, such as *mice* and *ran* (Flavell et al., 2002; McDonald, 1997).

Theorists have developed several different explanations of children's overregularizations. One approach is based on parallel distributed processing, which we discussed in previous chapters. According to the **parallel distributed processing (PDP)** framework, cognitive processes can be understood in terms of networks that link groups of neuron-like units. This framework proposes that the language system keeps a tally of the morpheme patterns for forming past tenses (McClelland & Seidenberg, 2000; Rumelhart & McClelland, 1986, 1987). The language system notes that *-ed* is the statistically most likely pattern, and so this ending is generalized to new verbs. The child therefore forms inappropriate past tenses, such as *runned, growed, goed,* and *eated*. The PDP approach argues that a child does not need to consult an internal set of rules to make these overregularizations. Instead, patterns of excitation within neural networks can account for the phenomenon.

Gary Marcus (1996) has proposed an alternative explanation for overregularization. According to Marcus's **rule-and-memory theory,** children learn a general rule for past-tense verbs, which specifies that they must add *-ed;* however, they also store in memory the past tenses for many irregular verbs. English has about 180 verbs with irregular past tenses, so young children would store only the most common of these irregular verbs (Marcus, 1996). Marcus's theory also proposes that people will consistently use an irregular form—assuming that they remember it—rather than the default "add *-ed*" rule. As children gather more expertise about language, they gradually replace the overregularized words with the appropriate past-tense verbs. Marcus (1996) applied his theory to a sample of more than 11,000 past-tense verbs generated by children, and he found that specific components of the theory predicted the patterns of overregularization. He also observed a regular decrease in the number of overregularizations, from 4% among preschoolers, to 1% among fourth graders.

Syntax. At about 18 to 24 months of age, the average child begins to combine two words—usually after acquiring between 50 and 100 words (Boysson-Bardies, 1999; Flavell et al., 2002; Stromswold, 1999). An important issue that arises at this point is **syntax,** or the grammatical rules that govern how words can be combined into sentences (Pinker, 1995). As children struggle with syntax, their rate of combining words is initially slow. However, it increases rapidly after the age of 2 (de Villiers & de Villiers, 1999). Another factor that probably contributes to this rapid increase in word combinations is the growing capacity of working memory.

Children's two-word utterances express many different kinds of relationships, such as possessor–possession ("Mama dress"), action–object ("Eat cookie"), and agent–action ("Teddy fall"). Furthermore, a two-word phrase can have different meanings in different contexts. "Daddy sock" may signify that the father is putting the child's sock on her foot, or that a particular sock belongs to the father (de Villiers & de Villiers, 1999).

Children learning many languages—not just English—use telegraphic speech (de Villiers & de Villiers, 1999; Slobin, 1979). **Telegraphic speech** is language that includes content words, such as nouns and verbs, but omits the extra words that serve only a grammatical function, such as prepositions and articles. The name *telegraphic speech* is appropriate because when adults need to conserve words (for example, when sending a telegram—several decades ago—or placing an advertisement in a newspaper), they also omit the extra words. Similarly, a child who wants to convey, "The puppy is sitting on my blanket," will say, "Puppy blanket." Notice that this telegraphic phrase is more sophisticated than an arbitrary grouping of words (DeHart et al., 2004; Karmiloff & Karmiloff-Smith, 2001).

After children have reached the two-word stage, they begin to fill in the missing words and word endings, and they also improve their word order. "Baby cry" becomes "The baby is crying," for example. By 3½ years of age, most children are reasonably accurate with respect to both morphology and syntax (Bates & Goodman, 1997). Their sentences also express more complex concepts such as causality and time sequences (Bloom, 1998).

We need to emphasize that language learning is an active process, consistent with Theme 1 of this book. Children learn language by actively constructing their own speech. They produce phrases that adults would never say, such as "Allgone sticky," "Bye-bye hot," and "More page" (Rogers, 1985). Children's speech is far richer than a simple imitation of adult language.

Another example of the active nature of children's language is **crib speech,** or monologues that children produce when they are alone in their cribs. In fact, 1- and 2-year-old children often practice their linguistic skills when they are alone (Kuczaj, 1983). One frequent pattern is to build longer phrases, as in the sequence, "Block. Yellow block. Look at all the yellow blocks." Substitutions are common, too: "What color blanket? What color map? What color glass?"

As children grow increasingly skilled in producing sophisticated language, they also grow increasingly skilled in understanding it. Consider, for example, how a child comes to understand the sentence, "Pat hit Chris." How does the child know who is the actor in that sentence and who is the recipient of the action? In English, the word order of the sentence is the most important cue, and children use this information appropriately (Hirsh-Pasek & Golinkoff, 1996). We might be tempted to assume that word order is similarly helpful in all languages. However, young children learning Turkish or Polish use the endings of words—rather than word-order information—to decode the meaning of sentences (Weist, 1985). Children seem to be clever strategists who can use whatever syntax cues are available in their language.

Pragmatics. As we discussed in Chapter 10, the term **pragmatics** refers to the social rules of language. Children must learn what should be said (and what should not be said) in certain circumstances. They need to learn how two speakers coordinate conversation. They must also master how to behave as listeners, as well as speakers. In addition, children learn the rules of polite conversation, for instance, during a mealtime conversation (Pan et al., 2000). Most important, children learn that a major purpose of language is to accomplish goals (Snow, 1999).

Every family has its stories about children's wildly inappropriate remarks to elderly relatives, friendly neighbors, and complete strangers. A student in my child development class shared an example of a pragmatic violation. Her family was attending a church service, and her 4-year-old brother noticed that their father was starting to fall asleep during the sermon. So the little boy stood up on the church pew and announced in a loud voice, "Be quiet everyone! My daddy is trying to sleep!" As you can imagine, everyone reacted more strongly to the fact that the child had broken a pragmatic rule than to the fact that he had tried to help his dozing daddy.

One pragmatic skill that children learn is to adapt their language to the listener. For instance, they must determine whether their listener has the appropriate background information about a topic (Pan & Snow, 1999; Siegal, 1996). Until the early 1970s, psychologists believed that children's language ignored the listener's level of understanding. However, an important study by Shatz and Gelman (1973) showed that children often make appropriate adjustments. These researchers found that 4-year-olds modified their speech substantially when the listener was a 2-year-old rather than a peer or an adult. Specifically, the 4-year-olds described a toy to their

2-year-old listeners using short, simple utterances. However, when describing the toy to another 4-year-old or an adult, their utterances were much longer and more complex. Even 2-year-olds tend to modify their language when speaking to their infant siblings (Dunn & Kendrick, 1982). If you know any young preschoolers, you may wish to repeat Demonstration 13.4 with them; children clearly understand some of the social aspects of language before they enter kindergarten.

Children also learn to take turns in a conversation. Sophisticated turn taking requires each speaker to anticipate when the conversational partner will complete his or her remark—a requirement that demands an impressive knowledge of language structure (Siegal, 1996; Snow, 1999). Young children have longer gaps in turn taking than adults do, perhaps because they are not as skilled in anticipating the completion of a remark. As children mature, they also learn how to use phrases such as "and then" to signal that they plan to continue talking, so that the listener must not interrupt (Pan & Snow, 1999).

The next time you observe two adults conversing, notice how the listener responds to the speaker by smiling, gazing, and other gestures of interest. In one study, researchers recorded these kinds of listener responses in young children who were discussing with an adult such topics as toys, a popular film, and siblings (Miller et al., 1985). All these listener responses were more abundant in the older children. For example, 8% of 3-year-olds said "uh-hum" at some point while the adult was speaking, in contrast to 50% of 5-year-olds. Furthermore, only 67% of 3-year-old listeners nodded their heads, in contrast to 100% of 5-year-olds. Thus, children learn how to be pragmatically skilled listeners, as well as speakers (Snow, 1999).

Infants and children seem to be specially prepared to notice and interact socially (Wellman & Gelman, 1992). Children are eager to master language and to become active participants in ongoing conversations. This enthusiasm about learning language encourages children to master the words, morphemes, syntax, and pragmatics of speech.

Throughout this chapter, we have seen examples of the early competence of infants and children. For instance, young infants are remarkably skilled at remembering faces and distinguishing speech sounds. These early skills foreshadow the impressive cognitive skills that adults exhibit (Theme 2). Furthermore, children's active, inquiring interactions with the people, objects, and concepts in their world (Theme 1) help them develop memory, metamemory, and language. Finally, the research on the cognitive skills of elderly people reveals some specific deficits. However, many cognitive abilities remain both accurate and active throughout the life span.

Section Summary: *The Development of Language*

1. Studies with infants reveal remarkable speech perception abilities; for example, infants can perceive differences between similar phonemes, differentiate their native language from an unfamiliar language, and establish word boundaries in a sequence of sounds.

2. During late infancy, babbling begins to resemble the language in the infant's environment, and the infant attempts intentional communication. The language that parents use with infants encourages their verbal development.

3. Young children rapidly acquire new words from context (fast mapping), but their word usage shows both overextensions and underextensions.

4. During language acquisition, children show overregularization, adding regular morphemes to words that have irregular plurals and past tenses; this phenomenon has been explained in terms of parallel distributed processing and in terms of the rule-and-memory theory.

5. Children's early word combinations are telegraphic; children also make active efforts to master syntax.

6. Young children often violate pragmatic rules; as children mature, however, they adapt their language to the listener, and they develop turn-taking strategies. They also learn how listeners are supposed to respond to speakers.

CHAPTER REVIEW QUESTIONS

1. For most of the twentieth century, psychologists were pessimistic about the cognitive skills of infants and young children. Since the 1970s, however, psychologists have discovered that children are much more cognitively competent than had been expected. If you wanted to impress someone with infants' and children's cognitive abilities, what would you describe about their memory, metacognition, and language abilities?

2. Part of the difficulty with infant research is designing experiments that reveal an infant's true abilities. Describe how experimental procedures have been developed to discover infants' skills in memory and language.

3. Compare children, young adults, and elderly people with respect to working memory, implicit memory, explicit recognition memory, and explicit recall memory. Be sure to list factors that might influence your conclusions.

4. Describe the proposed explanation for children's memory performance, which focuses on memory strategies and metamemory. Discuss the evidence for this explanation, including information on the correlation between metamemory and memory performance.

5. Imagine that the outcome of an important court case in your community depends on the testimony of a young child. What kind of factors would encourage you to trust the child's report, and which ones would make you suspicious?

6. In general, what kinds of memory tasks are especially difficult for elderly people? What explanations can best explain memory deficits in elderly individuals? Can metamemory account for these problems?

7. This chapter describes children's metamemory and strategy use. What could a third-grade teacher do to encourage students' memory skills? What should this teacher know about children's metacognitive ability?

8. Branthwaite and Rogers (1985) remark that being a child is like being a spy, trying to break a code to discover the way in which the world works. Apply this idea to the development of word meaning, morphology, word order, and pragmatic rules.

9. Describe some of the pragmatic rules of language that are important in our culture. How does the mastery of these rules change with development?

10. Considering the information about cognitive processes in this chapter, are infants as different from young adults as you had originally thought? Do the findings on elderly people surprise you, or do they match your original impressions?

ONE LAST TASK

To review this book as comprehensively as possible, try this final task: On separate sheets of paper, list each of the five themes of this book. Then skim through each chapter, noting on the appropriate sheet each time a theme is mentioned. You can check the completeness of your lists by consulting the entries for Theme 1, 2, 3, 4, and 5 in the subject index. After completing your lists, try to synthesize the material within each of the five themes.

NEW TERMS

lifespan approach to development
conjugate reinforcement technique
spacing effect
childhood amnesia
source monitoring
memory strategies
utilization deficiency
phonological loop
explicit memory task
implicit memory task
cognitive slowing

metacognition
theory of mind
metacomprehension
memory self-efficacy
phonemes
nonnutritive sucking
habituation
cooing
babbling
child-directed speech
motherese
fast mapping
overextension

underextension
morphemes
morphology
overregularization
parallel distributed processing (PDP)
rule-and-memory theory
syntax
telegraphic speech
crib speech
pragmatics

RECOMMENDED READINGS

Bloom, P. (2000). *How children learn the meanings of words*. Cambridge, MA: MIT Press. Many books about the psychology of language are written in a complex, lifeless style. This refreshing book examines children's growing mastery of words, including such topics as fast mapping, pronouns, and number words; he also includes interesting anecdotes about children's language.

Craik, F. I. M., & Salthouse, T. A. (Eds.). (2000). *The handbook of aging and cognition* (2nd ed.). Mahwah, NJ: Erlbaum. I highly recommend this volume for college libraries. It includes 13 chapters on topics discussed in this chapter, such as memory and metacognition in elderly people; other useful topics include attention and aging, language in elderly people, and emotional components of aging.

DeHart, G. B., Sroufe, L. A., & Cooper, R. G. (2004). *Child development: Its nature and course* (5th ed.). New York: McGraw Hill. This textbook provides a well-written, interesting, and comprehensive overview of children's lives; Chapters 5, 9, and 11 are especially relevant to the cognitive development of infants and children.

Goswami, U. (Ed.). (2002). *Blackwell handbook of childhood cognitive development*. Malden, MA: Blackwell. This handbook explores two topics addressed in this chapter—infant cognition and childhood memory. It also includes chapters on numerous other topics such Piagetian approaches, pretend play, and autism.

Pashler, H. (Ed.). (2002). *Stevens' handbook of experimental psychology*. New York: Wiley. Many chapters in this four-volume set focus on cognitive development. The topics include speech perception in Volume 1, cognitive development in Volume 2, learning and cognitive development in Volume 3, and infant cognition and cognition in elderly individuals in Volume 4.

Whitbourne, S. K. (2005). *Adult development and aging: Biopsychosocial perspectives* (2nd ed.). Hoboken, NJ: Wiley. Susan Whitbourne, a prominent gerontologist, provides a clear overview of the research on cognitive aging; she also explores related topics such as perception, health, and social interactions in elderly individuals.

Glossary

abstraction A memory process that stores the meaning of a message without storing the exact words and grammatical structures.

ACT (adaptive control of thought) A model, designed by John Anderson, that attempts to account for all of cognition, including memory, learning, spatial cognition, language, reasoning, and decision making.

adaptive control of thought (ACT) *See* ACT (adaptive control of thought).

affirming the antecedent In conditional reasoning, this phrase means that one is saying that the "if . . ." part of the sentence is true. This kind of reasoning leads to a valid, or correct, conclusion.

affirming the consequent In conditional reasoning, this phrase means that one is saying that the "then . . ." part of the sentence is true. This kind of reasoning leads to an incorrect conclusion.

age of acquisition In psycholinguistics, the age at which a person begins to learn a second language.

AI *See* artificial intelligence (AI).

algorithm A method that will always produce a solution to the problem, although the process may be very inefficient.

alignment heuristic In cognitive maps, a heuristic by which people tend to remember a series of geographic structures as being more lined up than they really are.

ambiguous figure-ground relationship In Gestalt psychology, the situation in which the figure and the ground reverse from time to time, so that the figure becomes the ground and then becomes the figure again.

ambiguous sentences Sentences that have identical surface structures but very different deep structures.

analog code In imagery, a mental representation that closely resembles the physical object. Also called a depictive representation or a pictorial representation.

analogy approach In problem solving, the approach that uses a solution to a similar, earlier problem to help solve a new one.

anchor In decision making, the first approximation in the anchoring and adjustment heuristic.

anchoring and adjustment heuristic A decision-making heuristic in which people begin with a first approximation (an anchor) and then make adjustments

to that number on the basis of additional information. Typically, people rely too heavily on the anchor, and their adjustments are too small.

anchoring effect *See* anchoring and adjustment heuristic.

anorexia nervosa A disorder in which a person is significantly underweight and has an intense fear of gaining weight.

antecedent In conditional reasoning, the proposition or statement that comes first; the antecedent is contained in the "if . . ." part of the sentence.

anterior attention network An area in the frontal lobe of the cortex responsible for attention tasks that focus on word meaning.

anterograde amnesia A loss of memory for events that occurred after brain damage.

aphasia Damage to the speech area of the brain, which produces difficulty in communication.

artificial intelligence (AI) The branch of computer science that seeks to explore human cognitive processes by creating computer models that exhibit "intelligent" behavior.

Atkinson-Shiffrin model The proposal that memory can be understood as a sequence of discrete steps, in which information is transferred from one cognitive storage area to another.

attention A concentration of mental activity.

attentional blink The inability to detect the second stimulus in a series when the series of stimuli is presented rapidly and one's attention becomes overloaded.

autobiographical memory Memory for events and issues related to oneself.

automatic processing The kind of parallel information processing used on easy tasks and on tasks that use highly familiar items.

availability heuristic A decision-making heuristic in which frequency or probability is estimated in terms of how easy it is to think of examples of something.

babbling The early vocalization of infants that uses both consonants and vowels, often repeating sounds in a series (for example, *dadada*).

base rate The frequency of occurrence of an item in the population.

base-rate fallacy In decision making, an error in which people underemphasize important information about base rate.

basic-level categories In the prototype approach to semantic memory, a moderately specific category level.

Bayes' theorem The rule that judgment should be influenced by two factors: base rate and the likelihood ratio. In decision making, people tend to overemphasize the likelihood ratio and underemphasize the base rate.

behaviorist approach A theoretical perspective that focuses only on objective, observable reactions. Behaviorism emphasizes the environmental stimuli that determine behavior.

belief-bias effect A situation in reasoning when people make judgments based on prior beliefs and general knowledge, rather than on the rules of logic.

betrayal trauma A child's adaptive response when a trusted parent or caretaker betrays him or her by sexual abuse. The child depends on this adult and must actively forget about the abuse in order to maintain an attachment to the adult.

bilingual A term describing a person who uses two different languages in his or her everyday life.

binding problem A problem in human vision that stems from the fact that important features of an object are not represented as a unified whole by the visual system.

blindsight The condition in which an individual with a damaged visual cortex claims not to be able to see an object, yet can accurately report some characteristics of that object.

bottleneck theories The theories of attention that propose that there is a narrow passageway in human information processing that limits the quantity of information to which people can pay attention. When one message is flowing through the bottleneck, other messages must be left behind.

bottom-up processing The kind of cognitive processing that emphasizes the importance of information from the stimuli registered on sensory receptors.

boundary extension The tendency to "remember" having seen a greater portion of a scene than was actually shown.

brain lesions The destruction of brain tissue caused by strokes, tumors, or accidents.

Broca's area An area in the front of the brain; damage to this area produces speech that is hesitant, effortful, and grammatically simple.

categorical perception A phenomenon in which people report hearing a clear-cut phoneme (e.g., a clear-cut *b* or a clear-cut *p*), even though they actually heard a range of sounds within a gradual continuum between two speech sounds (e.g., the continuum between *b* and *p*).

category A class of objects that belong together.

central executive In Baddeley's working-memory model, the component of memory that integrates information from the phonological loop, the visuospatial sketchpad, and the episodic buffer. The central executive also plays a major role in attention, planning strategies, and coordinating behavior, as well as suppressing irrelevant information.

cerebellum A relatively small structure in the brain that controls motor movement. The cerebellum is located at the back of the head, just below the occipital lobe.

cerebral cortex The outer layer of the brain that is responsible for cognitive processes.

change blindness The inability to detect change in an object or a scene.

characteristic features In semantic memory, the features of an item that are descriptive but are not essential.

child-directed speech The kind of language used by adult caretakers when speaking to children, including repetition, simple vocabulary and syntax, a focus on the here and now, clear pronunciation, slow pace, a high pitch, exaggerated changes in pitch, and exaggerated facial expressions.

childhood amnesia The inability of older children and adults to recall events that had occurred in their own lives before they were about 2 or 3 years old.

chunk The basic unit of short-term memory, consisting of several components that are strongly associated with one another.

chunking A memory organizational strategy in which several small units are combined into larger units.

coarticulation The variability in phoneme pronunciation that occurs because the shape of the mouth is influenced by the previous phoneme and the following phoneme.

cocktail party effect The situation in which, when paying close attention to one conversation, a person can often notice if his or her name is mentioned in a nearby conversation.

cognition A term for the mental activities involving the acquisition, storage, transformation, and use of knowledge.

cognitive approach A theoretical orientation that emphasizes people's knowledge and their mental processes.

cognitive-functional approach A theory that the function of human language is to communicate meaning to other individuals.

cognitive map A mental representation of the external environment that surrounds a person.

cognitive neuroscience The field that examines how cognitive processes can be explained by the structure and function of the brain.

cognitive psychology (1) A synonym for cognition. (2) The cognitive approach to psychology; a theoretical approach that emphasizes people's knowledge and their mental processes.

cognitive science An interdisciplinary field that examines questions about the mind. Cognitive science includes the disciplines of cognitive psychology, neuroscience, and computer science, as well as philosophy, linguistics, anthropology, sociology, and economics.

cognitive slowing In elderly people, a slower rate of responding on cognitive tasks.

Collins and Loftus network model The proposal that semantic memory is organized in terms of net-like structures with many interconnections; when information is retrieved, activation spreads to related concepts.

common ground A situation in which conversational partners share similar background knowledge, schemas, and experiences, which is necessary for mutual understanding.

computer metaphor The perspective that cognitive processes work like a computer—in other words, like a complex, multipurpose machine that processes information quickly and accurately.

computer simulation A computer system that resembles human performance on a specific cognitive task.

concept The mental representation of a category.

conditional reasoning A kind of deductive reasoning that concerns the relationship between conditions, using an "if . . . then . . ." format. Also known as propositional reasoning.

confidence intervals In decision making, the estimated range within which a number is expected to fall a certain percentage of the time.

confirmation bias In reasoning, the phenomenon that people would rather try to confirm a hypothesis than try to disprove it.

conjugate reinforcement technique An infant-memory research technique in which a mobile is placed above an infant's crib with a ribbon connecting the infant's ankle and the mobile, so that the infant's kicks make the mobile move.

conjunction fallacy In decision making, the erroneous judgment that the probability of the conjunction of two events is greater than the probability of either constituent event occurring alone.

conjunction rule In decision making, a rule stating that the probability of a conjunction of two events cannot be larger than the probability of either of its constituent events.

connection weights In the parallel distributed processing approach, the weighted connections (links) between neuron-like units, or nodes, of a network.

connectionism The model proposing that cognitive processes can be understood in terms of networks that link together neuron-like units, and that many operations can proceed simultaneously rather than one step at a time. Also known as the parallel distributed processing (PDP) approach.

consciousness An awareness of the external world, as well as thoughts and emotions about one's internal world.

consequent In conditional reasoning, the proposition that follows the antecedent; it is the consequence.

consistency bias During recall, the tendency to exaggerate the consistency between past and present feelings and beliefs. As a consequence, memory of the past may be distorted.

constituents In psycholinguistics, the grammatical building blocks on which the hierarchical structure of sentence construction is based.

constructionist view of inferences A concept stating that readers usually draw inferences about the causes of events and the relationship between events.

constructive model of memory The model by which people integrate information from individual sentences in order to construct larger ideas.

constructivist approach In memory, the argument that recollections change as people revise the past to satisfy their present concerns and knowledge.

content addressable In the parallel distributed processing approach, the characteristic of memory by which people use attributes (such as color) to locate material in memory.

context-dependent memory The principle stating that recall is better if the retrieval context is similar to the encoding context. In contrast, forgetting often occurs when the two contexts do not match.

control processes In the Atkinson-Shiffrin model, strategies—such as rehearsal—that people use to improve their memory.

controlled processing The kind of serial information processing used on difficult tasks or on tasks that use unfamiliar terms.

cooing The early vocalization of infants that involves vowels such as *oo*.

creativity In problem solving, the process of finding a solution that is novel, high quality, and useful.

crib speech The monologues that children produce when they are alone in their cribs.

critical period hypothesis The argument that the ability to acquire a second language is strictly limited to a specific period. Individuals who have already reached a specified age (e.g., early puberty) will no longer be able to acquire a new language with native-like fluency.

cross-modal task In research on selective attention, a task using two different perceptual systems (e.g., vision and hearing).

cross-race effect *See* own-race bias.

crystal-ball technique A decision-making technique in which people imagine that a completely accurate crystal ball has determined that their favored hypothesis is actually incorrect; the decision makers must therefore search for alternative explanations for the event.

decision making The thought process for assessing and choosing among several alternatives.

declarative knowledge One's knowledge about facts and things.

deductive reasoning The reasoning process in which specific premises are given, and a person decides whether those premises allow a particular logical conclusion to be drawn. In reasoning, the premises are either true or false, and formal logic specifies the rules for drawing conclusions.

deep structure In language, the underlying, more abstract meaning of a sentence.

default assignment In parallel distributed processing, the act of filling in missing information about a particular person or a particular object by making a best guess, based on information from similar people or objects.

defining features In semantic memory, the features that are essential to the meaning of the item.

demand characteristics The cues that might convey the experimenter's hypothesis to a participant in research.

denying the antecedent In conditional reasoning, this phrase means that one is saying that the "if . . ." part of the sentence is false. Denying the antecedent leads to an incorrect conclusion.

denying the consequent In conditional reasoning, this phrase means that one is saying that the "then . . ." part of the sentence is false. This kind of reasoning leads to a correct conclusion.

dependent variable The behavior—performed by research participants—that is measured by the researchers.

depictive representation In imagery, a mental representation that closely resembles the physical object. Also called a pictorial representation or analog code.

depth-of-processing approach The proposal that deep, meaningful kinds of information processing lead to more permanent retention than shallow, sensory kinds of processing. Also known as the levels-of-processing approach.

descriptive representation In imagery, an abstract, language-like mental representation, in a form that is neither visual nor spatial; this mental representation does not physically resemble the original stimulus. Also called a propositional code.

dichotic listening (pronounced "die-*kot*-ick") The experience of listening simultaneously to two different stimuli, one in each ear.

direct-access hypothesis In language, the hypothesis that readers can recognize words directly from printed letters. That is, the visual pattern of the word is sufficient to locate information about the meaning of the word from semantic memory.

directive In language, a sentence that requests someone to do something; polite directives usually require more words.

discourse Long passages of spoken and written language; language units that are larger than a sentence.

dissociation In cognitive neuroscience, a pattern that occurs when a variable has large effects on Test A performance, but little or no effect on Test B performance. A dissociation also occurs when a variable has one kind of effect if measured by Test A, and exactly the opposite effect if measured by Test B. Dissociation is similar to the concept of statistical interaction.

distal stimulus In perception, the actual object that is "out there" in the environment—for example, a telephone sitting on a desk.

distinctive feature A characteristic, or component, of a visual stimulus.

distinctiveness In memory recall, the term describing a stimulus that is different from all other memory traces.

distributed attention The kind of perceptual processing that allows people to register features automatically, using parallel processing across the field. Roughly equivalent to automatic processing, this kind of processing is so effortless that a person is not even aware when it happens.

distribution of practice effect In memory, the research finding that people learn more if they spread their learning trials over time, rather than learn the material all at once. Also known as the spacing effect.

divergent production A measurement of creativity in terms of the number of varied responses made to each test item.

divided-attention tasks Tasks in which people must attend to two or more simultaneous messages, responding to each as needed.

dual-route hypothesis In language, the hypothesis that readers sometimes recognize a word directly through the visual route, and sometimes recognize a word indirectly through the sound route.

dysphoric (person) A person at risk for depression.

ecological validity A principle stating that the conditions in which research is conducted should be similar to the natural setting to which the results will be applied.

elaboration A processing style in memory acquisition that requires rich processing in terms of meaning and interconnected concepts.

emotion In psychological terms, a reaction to a specific stimulus.

empirical evidence Scientific evidence obtained by careful observation and experimentation.

encoding The initial acquisition of information. During encoding, information is placed into storage.

encoding specificity principle The principle stating that recall is better if the retrieval context is similar to the encoding context. In contrast, forgetting often occurs when the two contexts do not match.

epiphenomenal In imagery, the term describing a mental image that is simply "tacked on" later, after an item has been recovered from (propositional) storage.

episodic buffer In Baddeley's working-memory model, the episodic buffer serves as a temporary storehouse for gathering and combining information from the phonological loop, the visuospatial sketchpad, and long-term memory. The episodic buffer actively manipulates information in order to interpret an earlier experience, solve new problems, and plan future activities.

episodic memory People's memory for events that happened to them; the memories describe episodes in life.

ERP *See* event-related potential (ERP) technique.

event-related potential (ERP) technique A neuroscience technique that records the tiny fluctuations (lasting just a fraction of a second) in the brain's electrical activity, in response to a stimulus.

exemplar In semantic memory, the specific examples of a concept stored in memory.

exemplar approach In semantic memory, the argument that people first learn some specific examples of a concept, and then classify a new stimulus by deciding how closely it resembles those specific examples.

exhaustive search In semantic memory, the specific type of algorithm, in which all possible answers are tried, using a specified system.

experimenter expectancy The situation in which the experimenter's biases and expectations can influence the outcome of an experiment.

expertise Consistently superior performance on a set of tasks for a domain, achieved by deliberate practice over a period of at least 10 years.

explicit memory task A memory task in which participants are specifically instructed to remember information that they have previously learned (for example, to recognize or recall information).

external memory aid Any device, external to the person, that facilitates memory in some way.

extrinsic motivation The motivation to work on a task in order to earn a promised reward or to win a competition.

false alarm In memory research, the phenomenon in which people "remember" an item that was not originally presented.

false-memory perspective The approach whose supporters argue that many recovered memories are actually incorrect memories; that is, they are constructed stories about events that never occurred.

family resemblance In the prototype approach to semantic memory, the notion that each example has at least one attribute in common with some other example of the concept.

fast mapping The ability of children, when learning new words, to use context to make a reasonable guess about a word's meaning after just one or two exposures.

feature-analysis theories Object-recognition theories proposing that a visual stimulus is composed of a small number of characteristics or components, each of which is called a distinctive feature.

feature comparison model An approach to semantic memory in which concepts are stored in memory according to a list of necessary features or characteristics.

feature-integration theory A theory of attention proposing that people sometimes look at a scene using distributed attention, with all parts of the scene processed at the same time; on other occasions, they use focused attention, with each item in the scene processed one at a time.

feeling of knowing In memory, the prediction about whether one could correctly recognize the correct answer to a question.

figure In Gestalt psychology, when two areas share a common boundary, the figure has a distinct shape with clearly defined edges. In contrast, the ground forms the background.

first language A bilingual person's native language.

first-letter technique A memory strategy in which the first letter of each word to be remembered is used to compose a word or sentence.

fixations The period between saccadic movements in which the visual system acquires the information that is useful for reading.

flashbulb memory Memory for the situation in which a person first learned of a very surprising and emotionally arousing event.

fMRI *See* functional magnetic resonance imaging (fMRI).

focused attention In feature-integration theory, the kind of perceptual processing that requires serial processing, in which objects are identified one at a time.

fovea In vision, the center of the retina, which has better acuity than other retinal regions.

framing effect A phenomenon in which the outcome of a decision is influenced by either of two factors: (1) the background context of the choice or (2) the way in which a question is worded (framed).

FRUMP (Fast Reading Understanding and Memory Program) A script-based computer program designed to perform reading tasks.

functional fixedness In problem solving, a phenomenon in which top-down processing is overactive; the functions or uses assigned to objects tend to remain fixed or stable.

functional magnetic resonance imaging (fMRI) A neuroscience procedure in which a research participant reclines with his or her head surrounded by a large magnet. This magnetic field produces changes in the oxygen atoms. A scanning device records these oxygen atoms while the participant performs a cognitive task.

gender stereotypes The organized, widely shared set of beliefs about the characteristics of females and males. Gender stereotypes may be partially accurate, but they do not apply to every person of the specified gender.

general mechanism approaches In psycholinguistics, the proposal that humans use the same neural mechanisms to process both speech sounds and nonspeech sounds, and that speech perception is a learned ability.

General Problem Solver (GPS) A computer program whose basic problem-solving strategy is means-ends analysis. The goal of the GPS is to mimic the processes that normal humans use when they tackle a problem.

geons In vision, a shortened version of the phrase "geometrical ions." In the recognition-by-components theory, the basic assumption is that a given view of an object can be represented as an arrangement of simple 3-D shapes or geons.

Gestalt (pronounced "Geh-*shtahlt*") The term for recognition that is based on an overall quality that transcends the individual elements.

Gestalt psychology (pronounced "Geh-*shtahlt*") The theoretical approach which emphasizes that humans have basic tendencies to organize what they see, and that the whole is greater than the sum of its parts.

gist The overall meaning of the message that is intended.

goal state In problem solving, the state reached when the problem is solved.

GPS *See* General Problem Solver (GPS).

graceful degradation In the parallel distributed processing approach, the brain's ability to provide partial memory.

graded structure In the prototype approach to semantic memory, the organization of members within a category, beginning with the most representative or prototypical members and continuing on through the category's nonprototypical members.

ground In Gestalt psychology, the ground is the region that is behind the figure, forming the background.

habituation A decrease in response rate that occurs when a stimulus is presented frequently.

heuristic A general problem-solving strategy that typically produces a correct solution.

hierarchical tree diagram A figure that uses a tree-like structure to specify various possible options in a problem.

hierarchy A memory organizational strategy in which items are arranged in a series of classes, from the most general classes to the most specific.

hill-climbing heuristic In problem solving, a strategy of choosing—at each choice point—the alternative that seems to lead most directly toward the goal.

hindsight Judgments about events that have already happened.

hindsight bias The tendency for people to falsely report that they would have accurately predicted an outcome, even if they had not been told about that outcome in advance.

holistic A term describing recognition based on overall shape and structure, rather than on individual elements.

IAT *See* Implicit Association Test (IAT).

iconic memory The kind of memory that allows an image of a visual stimulus to persist for about 200 to 400 milliseconds after the stimulus has disappeared. Also known as visual sensory memory.

ill-defined problems Problems in which the goal is not obvious.

illusory conjunction An inappropriate combination of features (for example, combining one object's shape with a nearby object's color).

illusory contours A visual illusion, in which people see edges even though they are not physically present in the stimulus. Also called subjective contours.

illusory correlation A situation in which people believe that two variables are statistically related, even though there is no real evidence for this relationship.

imagery Mental representations of stimuli that are not physically present.

Implicit Association Test (IAT) A test of stereotyping, based on the principle that people can mentally pair related words together much more easily than they can pair unrelated words.

implicit memory task A memory task in which participants see the material; later, during the test phase, people are instructed to complete a cognitive task that does not directly ask for recall or recognition. Previous experience with the material facilitates performance on the task.

inattentional blindness The inability to notice a new object that appears suddenly and unexpectedly when a person is paying attention to other events in a scene.

incidental learning Learning that occurs when people are not aware that they are going to be asked to remember items.

incubation A situation in which a person is initially unsuccessful in solving a problem, but he or she becomes more likely to solve the problem after taking a break, rather than continuing to work on the problem without interruption.

indirect-access hypothesis A hypothesis about reading, which states that people must translate the letters on the page into some form of sound before they can locate information about a word's meaning. This process is indirect because people must take the intermediate step of converting the visual stimulus into a phonological (sound) stimulus. Also known as the phonologically mediated hypothesis.

indirect request In language, a request for someone to do something or to *stop* doing something, presented like a request for information.

infantile amnesia *See* childhood amnesia.

inferences Logical interpretations and conclusions that were never part of the original stimulus material. In reading, the activation of information that is not explicitly stated in a written passage.

information-processing approach An approach in cognitive psychology that argues that (1) a mental process can best be understood by comparison with the operations of a computer, and (2) a mental process can be interpreted as information progressing through the system in a series of stages, one step at a time.

initial state In problem solving, a description of the situation at the beginning of a problem.

insight problem A problem that initially seems impossible to solve, but an alternative approach suddenly enters a person's mind; the problem solver immediately realizes that the solution is correct.

intentional learning Learning that occurs when people are aware that they are going to be asked to remember items.

intrinsic motivation The motivation to work on a task for its own sake, because it is interesting, exciting, or personally challenging.

introspection The process of systematically analyzing one's own sensations and reporting them as objectively as possible.

investment theory of creativity A theory, proposed by Robert Sternberg and T. I. Lubart, in which the essential attributes of creativity are intelligence, knowledge, motivation, an encouraging environment, an appropriate thinking style, and an appropriate personality.

ironic effects of mental control The way people's efforts backfire when they attempt to control their consciousness or try to eliminate a particular thought.

kernel In psycholinguistics, a term describing the basic, deep structure of sentences.

keyword method A memory strategy in which the learner identifies an English word (the keyword) that sounds similar to the new word; then an image is created that links the keyword with the meaning of the new word.

landmark effect In a mental map, the general tendency to estimate distances as being relatively short when traveling from a nonlandmark to a landmark, rather than the reverse.

Latent Semantic Analysis (LSA) An artificial intelligence program designed to assess the amount of semantic similarity between two words or two discourse segments. LSA can be used to grade essays.

lateralization The concept indicating that each hemisphere of the brain has somewhat different functions.

law of large numbers In decision making, the proposition that large samples will be representative of the population from which they are selected.

levels of processing The observation that recall accuracy is improved when information is processed at a deep level, rather than at a shallow level.

levels-of-processing approach The proposal that deep, meaningful kinds of information processing lead to more permanent retention than shallow, sensory kinds of processing. Also known as the depth-of-processing approach.

lexical entrainment In language, the word choice that two communicators develop when they create and adopt a standard term to refer to an object.

lifespan approach to development The perspective that developmental changes are not complete when people reach young adulthood; instead, people continue to change and adapt throughout their entire lives.

likelihood ratio In decision making, the assessment of whether a description is more likely to apply to population A or population B.

linearization problem In language, the problem of arranging words in an ordered, linear sequence.

link In the Collins and Loftus network model, the element that connects a particular concept node with another concept node.

long-term memory The large-capacity memory that contains one's memory for experiences and information that have accumulated over a lifetime.

long-term working memory A set of acquired strategies that allow memory experts to expand their memory performance for specific types of material within their domain of expertise.

LSA *See* Latent Semantic Analysis (LSA).

matrix In problem solving, a chart that shows all possible combinations of items.

McGurk effect A phenomenon in which visual information influences speech perception; for example, when a speaker's lips have a shape appropriate for *ga* yet the auditory information is *ba*, the listener may report hearing *da*.

means-ends heuristic A problem-solving strategy in which a person first divides the problem into a number of subproblems and then tries to reduce the difference between the initial state and the goal state for each subproblem.

memory The process of maintaining information over time.

memory self-efficacy A person's belief in his or her potential to perform well on memory tasks.

memory span The number of items that can be correctly recalled in the appropriate order.

memory strategies Deliberate, goal-oriented behaviors used to improve memory.

mental models Representations—derived from verbal descriptions—that depict specific situations (for example, a mental model of the layout of a room, derived from a description in a novel).

mental set A mental rut or mindless rigidity that blocks effective problem solving.

meta-analysis technique A statistical method for combining the results of numerous previous studies into one statistical index that tells whether a variable has a statistically significant effect.

metacognition Knowledge about one's own cognitive processes.

metacomprehension Thoughts about one's own reading comprehension and language comprehension.

metalinguistics Knowledge about the form and structure of language.

metamemory Knowledge, awareness, and control of one's own memory.

method of loci (pronounced "*low*-sigh") A memory strategy in which items to be learned are associated with a series of physical locations, arranged in a specific sequence. During recall, a person reviews the locations in order to retrieve the items.

mindfulness The creation of new categories, receptivity to new information, and a willingness to look at the world from a different point of view.

mindlessness A kind of automatic thinking, in which people approach everything in the same, routine fashion that they have used in the past.

misinformation effect A phenomenon that occurs after people first view an event, and then receive misleading information about it; later, they mistakenly recall the misleading information, rather than what they actually saw.

mnemonics (pronounced "ni-*mon*-icks") The use of a strategy to help memory.

modular In language, a term describing the proposal that people have a set of specific linguistic abilities that do not follow the principles of other cognitive processes, such as memory and decision making.

mood A general, long-lasting emotional experience.

mood congruence A phenomenon demonstrating that memory is better when the material to be remembered is congruent with a person's current mood.

mood-dependent memory A principle stating that people are more likely to remember material if their mood at the time of retrieval matches the mood they were in when they originally learned the material.

morpheme (pronounced "*more*-feem") The basic unit of meaning in language.

morphology The study of the basic units of meaning in language.

motherese The kind of language used by adult caretakers when speaking to children, more often known as child-directed speech.

multilingual A term describing someone who uses more than two languages.

multimodal approach A theory of memory improvement that emphasizes a comprehensive approach to memory problems (for example, attention to physical and mental problems, as well as a variety of memory strategies).

my-side bias In decision making, the general tendency to be overconfident that one's own view is correct in a confrontational situation.

narrative The type of discourse in which someone describes a series of events, either actual or fictional. The events in a narrative are described in a time-related sequence, and they are often emotionally involving.

narrative technique A memory organizational method that creates stories to link a series of words together.

natural language Ordinary human language, as found in everyday life, which includes errors and ambiguities.

nested structure In language, a phrase that is embedded within another sentence.

network model A model of semantic memory that proposes a net-like organization of concepts in memory, with many interconnections. The meaning of a particular concept depends on the concepts to which it is connected.

neural networks The model proposing that cognitive processes can be understood in terms of networks that link together neuron-like units; in addition, many operations can proceed simultaneously rather than one step at a time. Also known as the parallel distributed processing (PDP) approach.

neurolinguistics The discipline that examines how the brain processes language.

neuron The basic cell in the nervous system.

90°-angle heuristic In mental maps, the heuristic that angles in a mental map are remembered as being closer to 90° than they really are.

node In the parallel distributed processing approach, the location of each neural activity. Nodes are interconnected in a complex fashion with many other nodes. In the Collins and Loftus network model of semantic memory, each concept can be represented as a node, or location in the network. Links connect nodes to form a network.

noninsight problem A problem that is solved gradually, using memory, reasoning skills, and a routine set of procedures.

nonnutritive sucking A research method for assessing speech perception, in which a baby sucks on a nipple to produce a particular sound.

object permanence The knowledge that an object exists, even when it is temporarily out of sight.

object recognition The process of identifying a complex arrangement of sensory stimuli.

obstacles In problem solving, the restrictions that make it difficult to proceed from the initial state to the goal state.

operational definition A precise definition that specifies exactly how researchers will measure a concept.

organization In memory, the attempt to bring systematic order to the material to be learned; often used to refer to a category of memory strategies.

other-race effect *See* own-race bias.

overconfidence People's tendency to be overly optimistic about the accuracy of their judgments, based on their actual performance.

overextension Children's use of a word to refer to other objects, in addition to objects that adults would consider appropriate.

overregularization The tendency to add regular morphemes inappropriately (for example, *mouses* or *runned*).

own-race bias Phenomenon in which people are generally more accurate in identifying members of their own ethnic group than members of another ethnic group.

parallel distributed processing (PDP) approach The model proposing that cognitive processes can be understood in terms of networks that link together neuron-like units; in addition, the model states that many operations can proceed simultaneously rather than one at a time. Also known as connectionism and neural networks.

parallel processing A type of cognitive processing in which many signals are handled at the same time, as opposed to serial processing.

parallel search A type of information processing in which all attributes are considered simultaneously.

pattern recognition The process of identifying a complex arrangement of sensory stimuli.

PDP *See* parallel distributed processing (PDP) approach.

perception The use of previous knowledge to gather and interpret the stimuli registered by the senses.

perceptual span In reading, the number of letters and spaces that can be perceived during a fixation (the pause between saccadic movements).

PET scan *See* positron emission tomography (PET scan).

phobic disorder An excessive fear of a specific object.

phoneme (pronounced "*foe*-neem") The basic unit of spoken language.

phonemic restoration The phenomenon in which people fill in sounds that are missing by using context as a cue.

phonetic module A hypothetical special-purpose neural mechanism in humans that specifically facilitates speech perception, rather than other kinds of auditory perception. Proposed by psycholinguists who favor the modular approach to language.

phonics approach An approach to reading that states that people recognize words by trying to pronounce the individual letters in the word. The phonics approach emphasizes that speech sound is a necessary intermediate step in reading.

phonological loop In Baddeley's working-memory model, the storage device for a limited number of sounds for a short period of time.

phonologically mediated hypothesis In reading, the hypothesis that people must translate the letters on the page into some form of sound before they can locate information about a word's meaning. This process is indirect because people go through the intermediate step of converting the visual stimulus into a phonological (sound) stimulus. Also known as the indirect-access hypothesis.

phonology Speech sounds of a language.

phrase structure In psycholinguistics, an approach that emphasizes the hierarchical structure of sentences, based on grammatical building blocks called constituents.

PI *See* proactive interference (PI).

pictorial representation A mental representation that closely resembles the physical object. Also called a depictive representation or an analog code.

planning fallacy In decision making, people's underestimation of the amount of time or money required to complete a project; they also incorrectly estimate that the task will be relatively easy to complete.

Pollyanna Principle In memory and other cognitive processes, the principle that pleasant items are usually processed more efficiently and more accurately than less pleasant items.

positron emission tomography (PET scan) A procedure in which researchers measure blood flow by injecting the participant with a radioactive chemical just before the participant performs a cognitive task.

posterior attention network Located in the parietal lobe of the cortex, the network responsible for attention tasks such as visual search.

pragmatic view of memory In language comprehension, the proposition that people pay attention to the aspect of a message that is most relevant to their current goals. In other words, people can strategically control their attention.

pragmatics The social rules that underlie language use. Pragmatics focuses on how speakers successfully communicate messages to their audience.

prefrontal cortex The region of the brain in the front portion of the frontal lobe.

prewriting The first stage in planning to write, which requires generating a list of ideas.

primacy effect In a serial-position curve, the enhanced recall for items at the beginning of a list, which presumably occurs because early items are rehearsed more than other items.

primary visual cortex The portion of the cerebral cortex that is concerned with basic processing of visual stimuli. Located in the occipital lobe of the brain.

priming effect A term referring to the faster response to an item if it is preceded by a similar item.

proactive interference (PI) A concept stating that people have trouble learning new material because previously learned material keeps interfering with new learning.

problem isomorphs In problem solving, a set of problems with the same underlying structures and solutions, but with different specific details.

problem solving The use of strategies to reach a goal in which the solution is not immediately obvious because obstacles are blocking the path.

procedural memory A person's memory about how to do something.

processing cycles In language comprehension, understanding each new sentence within the context of the previous text.

proposition The smallest unit of knowledge that can be judged either true or false.

propositional calculus In logical reasoning, a system for categorizing the kinds of reasoning used in analyzing propositions or statements.

propositional code In imagery, an abstract, language-like mental representation, in a form that is neither visual nor spatial; this mental representation does not physically resemble the original stimulus. Also called a descriptive representation.

propositional reasoning A kind of deductive reasoning that concerns the relationship between conditions, using an "if . . . then . . ." format. Also known as conditional reasoning.

prosody The "melody," or intonation and stress of speech.

prosopagnosia (pronounced "pro-soap-ag-*know*-zhia") A condition in which people cannot recognize human faces visually, though they perceive other objects normally.

prospective memory Remembering to do things in the future.

prototype In semantic-memory theory, the idealized item that is most typical of the category.

prototype approach An approach to semantic memory in which one decides whether an item belongs to a category by comparing that item with a prototype.

prototypicality The degree to which members of a category are prototypical.

proximal stimulus In perception, the information registered on one's sensory receptors (for example, the image on the retina created by the telephone sitting on a desk).

psycholinguistics An interdisciplinary field that examines how people use language to communicate ideas.

pure AI The branch of computer science that seeks to accomplish a task as efficiently as possible.

recall In memory, the reproduction of items that had been learned at an earlier time.

recency effect In a serial-position curve, the enhanced accuracy for the final items in a series of stimuli, which presumably occurs because the items are still in working memory.

recognition In memory, the identification of items that had been presented at an earlier time.

recognition-by-components theory In perception, the proposal that a given view of an object can be represented as an arrangement of simple 3-D shapes called geons. Also known as the structural theory.

recovered-memory perspective The approach whose supporters argue that memories of childhood abuse can be forgotten and then recovered.

regressions In reading, the eye movements in which the eye returns to earlier material in the sentence.

rehearsal Repetition of information to be learned.

release from proactive interference A phenomenon in which proactive interference is reduced when a person switches to a new stimulus category, which produces increased recall.

repetition priming task A memory task in which recent exposure to a word increases the likelihood that this word will later come to mind, when one is given a cue that could evoke many words.

replications Experiments in which a phenomenon is tested under a variety of different conditions.

representative In decision making, a type of sample that is similar in important characteristics to the population from which it was selected; for example, if one tosses a coin six times, the outcome THHTHT seems representative.

representativeness heuristic A decision-making heuristic by which a sample is judged likely if it is similar to the population from which it was selected.

retrieval In memory, the process of locating information in storage in one's mind and accessing that information.

retroactive interference In memory, the process in which people have trouble recalling old material because recently learned, new material keeps interfering with old memories.

retrograde amnesia A loss of memory for events that occurred prior to brain damage.

retrospective memory A memory task in which one recalls previously learned information.

rotation heuristic In cognitive maps, the heuristic by which a figure that is slightly tilted will be remembered as being either more vertical or more horizontal than it really is.

rule-and-memory theory In language development, the theory that children learn a general rule for past-tense verbs that specifies that they must add -*ed*; however, they also store in memory the past tenses for irregular verbs.

saccadic eye movement (pronounced "suh-*kah*-dik") The kind of eye movement that brings the center of the retina into position of the words to be read.

schema (pronounced "*skee*-muh") Generalized knowledge or expectation, which is distilled from past experiences with an event, an object, or a person. Schemas are used to guide memory recall.

schema therapy In clinical psychology, an approach to help a client develop appropriate, new schemas that can replace the maladaptive schemas developed during childhood, adolescence, and earlier adulthood.

schizophrenia A pychological disorder characterized by severely disordered thoughts. People with schizophrenia have particular difficulty controlling their attention.

script A simple, well-structured sequence of events associated with a highly familiar activity; a script is one category of schema.

second language A bilingual individual's nonnative language.

selective-attention task A task in which people must respond selectively to certain sources of information while ignoring other sources of information.

self-efficacy A self-assessment of one's own capabilities in a certain area.

self-reference effect The enhancement of long-term memory by relating the material to personal experiences.

semantic memory A person's organized knowledge about the world, including knowledge about word meanings and other factual information.

semantics The area of psycholinguistics that examines the meanings of words and sentences.

sensory memory A large-capacity storage system that records information from each of the senses with reasonable accuracy.

sentence verification technique A research method in which people see simple sentences, and they must consult their stored semantic knowledge to determine whether the sentences are true or false.

sequential bilingualism A term referring to bilinguals who acquire a second, nonnative language after they have learned their native language.

serial position effect The U-shaped relationship between a word's position in a list and its probability of recall.

serial processing A type of cognitive processing in which only one item is handled at a given time, and one step must be completed before proceeding to the next step.

serial search A type of information processing in which one attribute is processed at a time.

shadow In attention research, the process of repeating a message heard in one ear during a dichotic listening task.

short-term memory The kind of memory that contains only the small amount of information that a person is actively using. Short-term memory is also called working memory.

simulation heuristic A decision-making heuristic in which judgment is based on the ease with which

people can think of a particular scenario, or series of events.

simultaneous bilingualism A term referring to bilinguals who learn two languages simultaneously during childhood.

single-cell recording technique A neuroscience technique in which researchers study the characteristics of an animal's brain and nervous system by inserting a thin electrode next to a single neuron.

situated-cognition approach An approach that examines how the ability to solve a problem is tied to the specific context in which a person learned to solve that problem.

situative perspective *See* situated-cognition approach.

slips-of-the-tongue Speech errors in which sounds or entire words are rearranged between two or more different words.

small-sample fallacy The incorrect assumption that small samples will be representative of the population from which they were selected.

social cognition approach The perspective that stereotypes are formed by means of normal cognitive processes, which rely on strategies such as the availability heuristic.

source monitoring The process of trying to identify the origin of memories and beliefs in order to decide which memories or beliefs are real and which are simply imagined.

source problem In problem solving, a problem that was solved in the past, and is similar to the current, target problem.

spacing effect The research phenomenon that people learn more if they spread their learning trials over time, rather than learn the material all at once. Also known as the distribution of practice effect.

spatial cognition A broad area that includes how people construct cognitive maps, how people remember the world they navigate, and how they keep track of objects in a spatial array.

spatial framework model In spatial cognition, a model emphasizing that the above-below dimension is more prominent in spatial thinking than the right-left dimension.

special-mechanism approach In psycholinguistics, an approach stating that humans have a specialized cognitive device for decoding speech stimuli. As a result, people process speech sounds more quickly and accurately than other auditory stimuli. Also known as the speech-is-special approach.

speech-is-special approach In psycholinguistics, an approach stating that humans have a specialized cognitive device for decoding speech stimuli. As a result, people process speech sounds more quickly and accurately than other auditory stimuli. Also known as the special-mechanism approach.

speech perception In hearing, the translation of sound vibrations into a string of sounds that the listener perceives to be speech.

spontaneous generalization In parallel distributed processing, the inferences that people draw about general information that they have never learned, based on specific examples.

spreading activation In semantic memory, the process in which, when the name of a concept is mentioned, the node representing that concept is activated, and the activation expands from that node to other nodes to which it is connected.

stereotype threat A source of anxiety involving membership in a group that is hampered by a negative stereotype, producing performance problems.

Stroop effect The observation that people take much longer to name the color of a stimulus when it is used in printing an incongruent word than when it appears as a solid patch of color.

structural features In problem solving, the abstract, underlying core of a problem.

structural theory In perception, the proposal that a given view of an object can be represented as an arrangement of simple 3-D shapes called geons. Also known as the recognition-by-components theory.

subjective contours A visual illusion, in which people see edges even though they are not physically present in the stimulus. Also called illusory contours.

subordinate-level categories In the prototype approach to semantic memory, the lower-level or more specific category levels.

subproblems The smaller problems into which a target problem is divided, to facilitate problem solving.

superordinate-level categories In the prototype approach to semantic memory, the higher-level or more general category levels.

surface features In problem solving, the superficial content of the problem to be solved.

surface structure In language, the words that are actually spoken or written.

syllogism A deductive reasoning task consisting of two statements that are assumed to be true, plus a conclusion.

symmetry heuristic In cognitive maps, the heuristic that figures are remembered as more symmetrical and regular than they truly are.

syntax The grammatical rules that govern how words can be organized into sentences.

target problem In problem solving, the current problem to be solved.

telegraphic speech In the development of language, the kind of early speech that includes content words, such as nouns and verbs, but omits the extra words that serve only a grammatical function, such as prepositions and articles.

template A specific perceptual pattern stored in memory.

template-matching theory In pattern recognition, the theory stating that a stimulus is compared with a set of templates, or specific patterns stored in memory. After comparing stimuli to a number of templates, a person notes the template that matches most closely.

Theme 1 Cognitive processes are active, rather than passive.

Theme 2 Cognitive processes are remarkably efficient and accurate.

Theme 3 Cognitive processes handle positive information better than negative information.

Theme 4 Cognitive processes are interrelated with one another; they do not operate in isolation.

Theme 5 Many cognitive processes rely on both bottom-up and top-down processing.

theory of mind In cognitive development, children's ideas of how their minds work and their beliefs about other people's thoughts.

thinking The cognitive process of going beyond the information given; thinking also has a goal, such as a solution, a decision, or a belief.

tip-of-the-tongue phenomenon The subjective feeling that people have of being confident that they know the target word for which they are searching, yet they cannot recall it.

top-down processing The kind of cognitive processing that emphasizes the influence of concepts, expectations, and memory.

total time hypothesis In memory, the proposition that the amount learned depends on the total time devoted to learning.

transfer-appropriate processing A principle stating that recall is better if the retrieval context is similar to the encoding context. In contrast, forgetting often occurs when the two contexts do not match. Also known as the encoding specificity principle.

transformational grammar In psycholinguistics, the conversion of underlying, deep structure into the surface structure of a sentence.

transformational rules In transformational grammar, the rules that are used to convert surface structure to deep structure during understanding and to convert deep structure to surface structure when speaking or writing.

typicality effect Using the sentence verification technique, a research finding that people reach decisions faster when an item is a typical member of a category, rather than an unusual member.

underextension The use of words, by children, in a narrower sense than adults would use them.

underlying structure In psycholinguistics, the underlying, abstract meaning of a sentence. Also known as deep structure.

understanding In problem solving, the internal representation of a problem, based on the information provided in the problem and one's own previous experience.

unilateral neglect In perception, a spatial deficit for one-half of the visual field.

utilization deficiency The lack of application of memory strategies, especially common in children.

verbatim memory Word-for-word memory, as opposed to recall of the "gist" or general meaning.

viewer-centered approach In perception, the model proposing that a small number of views of 3-D objects are stored in memory, rather than just one view.

visual sensory memory The kind of memory that allows an image of a visual stimulus to persist for about 200 to 400 milliseconds after the stimulus has disappeared. Also known as iconic memory.

visuospatial sketchpad In Baddeley's working-memory model, the component that stores visual and spatial information. It also stores visual information that has been encoded from verbal stimuli.

weapon focus A phenomenon in eyewitness testimony in which the witness's attention had been distracted at the time of the event by a weapon.

Wernicke's area (pronounced "*Ver*-nih-keez" or "*Wer*-nih-keez") An area toward the back of the brain; damage to this area causes serious difficulties in understanding speech, as well as language production that is too wordy and confused.

whole-language approach A movement within education suggesting that reading instruction should emphasize meaning; in addition, children should read storybooks, experiment with writing before they are expert spellers, try to guess the meaning of a word from the sentence's context, and use reading throughout the classroom.

whole-word approach An approach to reading stating that people can directly connect the written word—as an entire pattern—with the meaning that the word represents. The whole-word approach emphasizes that the correspondence between the written and spoken codes in English is complex, and it argues against emphasizing the way a word sounds. Instead, readers are encouraged to identify words in terms of the context in which they appear.

word superiority effect In perception, a phenomenon in which a single letter can be identified more accurately and more rapidly when it appears in a meaningful word than when it appears by itself or in a meaningless string of unrelated letters.

working memory The brief, immediate memory for material that is currently being processed; a portion of working memory also coordinates ongoing mental activities; working memory was previously called short-term memory.

working-memory approach According to Baddeley, immediate memory is a multipart system that temporarily holds and manipulates information during performance of cognitive tasks.

References

Abelson, R. P. (1981). Psychological status of the script concept. *American Psychologist, 36*, 715–729.

Abrams, R. A. (1992). Planning and producing saccadic eye movements. In K. Rayner (Ed.), *Eye movements and visual cognition* (pp. 66–88). New York: Springer-Verlag.

Adams, M. J., & Bruck, M. (1995, Summer). Resolving the great debate. *American Educator*, pp. 7, 10–20.

Adeyemo, S. A. (1990). Thinking imagery and problem solving. *Psychological Studies, 35*, 179–190.

Adeyemo, S. A. (1994). Individual differences in thinking and problem solving. *Personality and Individual Differences, 17*, 117–124.

Adler, J., & Hall, C. (1995, June 5). Surgery at 33,000 feet. *Newsweek*, p. 36.

Adler, S. A., Gerhardstein, P., & Rovee-Collier, C. (1998). Levels-of-processing effects in infant memory? *Child Development, 69*, 280–294.

Adler, T. (1991, July). Memory researcher wins Troland award. *APA Monitor*, pp. 12–13.

Agans, R. P., & Shaffer, L. S. (1994). The hindsight bias: The role of the availability heuristic and perceived risk. *Basic and Applied Social Psychology, 15*, 439–449.

Agassi, J. (1997). The novelty of Chomsky's theories. In D. M. Johnson & C. E. Erneling (Eds.), *The future of the cognitive revolution* (pp. 136–148). New York: Oxford University Press.

Agnoli, F., & Krantz, D. H. (1989). Suppressing natural heuristics by formal instruction: The case of the conjunction fallacy. *Cognitive Psychology, 21*, 515–550.

Agre, P. E. (1997). Living math: Lave and Walkerdine on the meaning of everyday arithmetic. In D. Kirshner & J. A. Whitson (Eds.), *Situated cognition: Social, semiotic, and psychological perspectives* (pp. 71–82). Mahwah, NJ: Erlbaum.

Aguiar, A., & Baillargeon, R. (2002). Developments in young infants' reasoning about occluded objects. *Cognitive Psychology, 45*, 267–336.

Ahn, W-k., & Graham, L. M. (1999). The impact of necessity and sufficiency in the Wason four-card selection task. *Psychological Science, 10*, 237–242.

Ahn, W-k., Novick, L. R., & Kim, N. S. (2003). Understanding behavior makes it more normal. *Psychonomic Bulletin & Review, 10*, 746–752.

Akhtar, N., Jipson, J., & Callanan, M. A. (2001). Learning words through overhearing. *Child Development, 72*, 416–430.

Alba, J. W., & Hasher, L. (1983). Is memory schematic? *Psychological Bulletin, 93*, 203–231.

Alexander, J. M., & Schwanenflugel, P. J. (1994). Strategy regulation: The role of intelligence, metacognitive attributions, and knowledge base. *Developmental Psychology, 30*, 709–723.

Allbritton, D. W., & Gerrig, R. J. (1991). Participatory responses in text understanding. *Journal of Memory and Language, 30*, 603–626.

Alter, J. (2000, July 3). A reckoning on death row. *Newsweek*, p. 31.

Amabile, T. M. (1990). Within you, without you: The social psychology of creativity, and beyond. In M. A. Runco & R. S. Albert (Eds.), *Theories of creativity* (pp. 61–91). Newbury Park, NY: Sage.

Amabile, T. M. (1994). The "atmosphere of pure work": Creativity in research and development. In W. R. Shadish & S. Fuller (Eds.), *The social psychology of science* (pp. 316–328). New York: Guilford.

Amabile, T. M. (1996). Creativity in context: Update to the social psychology of creativity. Boulder, CO: Westview.

Amabile, T. M. (1997). Motivating creativity in organizations: On doing what you love and loving what you do. *California Management Review, 40*, 39–58.

Ambady, N., Shih, M., Kim, A., & Pittinsky, T. L. (2001). Stereotype susceptibility in children: Effects of identity activation on quantitative performance. *Psychological Science, 12*, 385–390.

American Psychiatric Association. (2000). *Diagnostic and statistical manual of mental disorders* (4th ed., text revision). Washington, DC: Author.

American Psychological Association. (2001). *Publication manual of the American Psychological Association* (5th ed.). Washington, DC: Author.

Amrhein, P. C. (1999). On the functional equivalence of monolinguals and bilinguals in "monolingual mode": The bilingual anticipation effect in picture-word processing. *Psychological Science, 10*, 230–236.

Anastasi, J. S., & Rhodes, M. G. (2003). *Evidence for a same-age bias in face recognition.* Manuscript submitted for publication.

Anderson, J. R. (1983). *The architecture of cognition.* Cambridge, MA: Harvard University Press.

Anderson, J. R. (1990). *The adaptive character of thought.* Hillsdale, NJ: Erlbaum.

Anderson, J. R. (1993). Problem solving and learning. *American Psychologist, 48,* 35–44.

Anderson, J. R. (1996). ACT: A simple theory of complex cognition. *American Psychologist, 51,* 355–365.

Anderson, J. R. (2000). *Learning and memory: An integrated approach* (2nd ed.). New York: Wiley.

Anderson, J. R., Corbett, A. T., Koedinger, K. R., & Pelletier, R. (1995). Cognitive tutors: Lessons learned. *The Journal of the Learning Sciences, 4,* 167–207.

Anderson, J. R., & Gluck, K. A. (2001). What role do cognitive architectures play in intelligent tutoring systems? In S. M. Carver & D. Klahr (Eds.), *Cognition and instruction: Twenty-five years of progress* (pp. 227–261). Mahwah, NJ: Erlbaum.

Anderson, J. R., Reder, L. M., & Lebiere, C. (1996). Working memory: Activation limitations on retrieval. *Cognitive Psychology, 30,* 221–256.

Anderson, J. R., Reder, L. M., & Simon, H. A. (1996). Situated learning and education. *Educational Researcher, 25,* 5–11.

Anderson, J. R., & Schooler, L. J. (2000). The adaptive nature of memory. In E. Tulving & F. I. M. Craik (Eds.), *The Oxford handbook of memory* (pp. 557–581). New York: Oxford University Press.

Anderson, J. R., & Schunn, C. D. (2000). Implications of the ACT-R learning theory: No magic bullets. In R. Glaser (Ed.), *Advances in instructional psychology* (Vol. 5, pp. 1–33). Mahwah, NJ: Erlbaum.

Anderson, M. C. (2001). Active forgetting: Evidence for functional inhibition as a source of memory failure. In J. J. Freyd & A. P. DePrince (Eds.), *Trauma and cognitive science* (pp. 185–210). New York: Haworth.

Anderson, R. E. (1998). Imagery and spatial representation. In W. Bechtel & G. Graham (Eds.), *A companion to cognitive science* (pp. 204–211). Malden, MA: Blackwell.

Anderson, S. J., & Conway, M. A. (1993). Investigating the structure of autobiographical memories. *Journal of Experimental Psychology: Learning, Memory, and Cognition, 19,* 1178–1196.

Anglin, J. M. (1997). *Word, object, and conceptual development.* New York: Norton.

Anthony, T., Cooper, C., & Mullen, B. (1992). Cross-racial facial identification: A social cognitive integration. *Personality and Social Psychology Bulletin, 18,* 296–301.

Archambault, A., O'Donnell, C., & Schyns, P. (1999). Blind to object changes: When learning the same object at different levels of categorization modifies its perception. *Psychological Science, 10,* 249–255.

Ashby, F. G., Prinzmetal, W., Ivry, R., & Maddox, W. T. (1996). A formal theory of feature binding in object perception. *Psychological Review, 103,* 165–192.

Atkins, P. W. B., & Baddeley, A. D. (1998). Working memory and distributed vocabulary learning. *Applied Psycholinguistics, 19,* 537–552.

Atkinson, R. C., & Shiffrin, R. M. (1968). Human memory: A proposed system and its control processes. In K. W. Spence & J. T. Spence (Eds.), *The psychology of learning and motivation: Advances in research and theory* (Vol. 2, pp. 89–105). New York: Academic Press.

Awh, E., & Jonides, J. (1999). Spatial working memory and spatial selective attention. In R. Parasuraman (Ed.), *The attentive brain* (pp. 353–380). Cambridge, MA: MIT Press.

Awh, E., Jonides, J., & Reuter-Lorenz, P. A. (1998). Rehearsal in spatial working memory. *Journal of Experimental Psychology: Human Perception and Performance, 24,* 780–790.

Baars, B. J. (1997). *In the theater of consciousness.* New York: Oxford University Press.

Baars, B. J., & Newman, J. B. (Eds.). (2002). *Essential sources in the scientific study of consciousness.* Cambridge, MA: MIT Press.

Baars, B. J., Newman, J., & Taylor, J. G. (1998). Neuronal mechanisms of consciousness: A relational global-workplace framework. In S. R. Hameroff, A. W. Kaszniak, & A. C. Scott (Eds.), *Toward a science of consciousness II: The second Tucson discussion and debates* (pp. 269–278). Cambridge, MA: MIT Press.

Bäckman, L., Small, B. J., & Wahlin, A. (2001). Aging and memory: Cognitive and biological perspectives. In J. E. Birren & K. W. Schaie (Eds.), *Handbook of the psychology of aging* (5th ed., pp. 349–377). San Diego: Academic Press.

Baddeley, A. D. (1986). *Working memory.* Oxford, England: Clarendon.

Baddeley, A. D. (1990). *Human memory: Theory and practice.* Boston: Allyn and Bacon.

Baddeley, A. D. (1994). The magical number seven: Still magic after all these years? *Psychological Review, 101,* 353–356.

Baddeley, A. D. (1995a). The psychology of memory. In A. D. Baddeley, B. A. Wilson, & F. N. Watts (Eds.), *Handbook of memory disorders* (pp. 3–25). Chichester, England: Wiley.

Baddeley, A. D. (1995b). Working memory. In M. S. Gazzaniga (Ed.), *The cognitive neurosciences* (pp. 755–764). Cambridge, MA: MIT Books.

Baddeley, A. D. (1997). *Human memory: Theory and practice* (Rev. ed.). East Sussex, England: Psychology Press.

Baddeley, A. D. (1999). *Essentials of human memory.* East Sussex, England: Psychology Press.

Baddeley, A. D. (2000a). The episodic buffer: A new component of working memory? *Trends in Cognitive Sciences, 4,* 417–423.

Baddeley, A. D. (2000b). The magic number and the episodic buffer. *Behavioral and Brain Sciences, 24,* 117–118.

Baddeley, A. D. (2000c). Short-term and working memory. In E. Tulving & F. I. M. Craik (Eds.), *The Oxford handbook of memory* (pp. 77–92). New York: Oxford University Press.

Baddeley, A. D. (2001a). Is working memory still working? *American Psychologist, 56,* 849–864.

Baddeley, A. D. (2001b). Levels of working memory. In M. Naveh-Benjamin, M. Moscovitch, & H. L. Roediger, III (Eds.), *Perspectives on human memory and cognitive aging* (pp. 111–123). New York: Psychology Press.

Baddeley, A. D., & Andrade, J. (1998). Working memory and consciousness: An empirical approach. In M. A. Conway, S. E. Gathercole, & C. Cornoldi (Eds.), *Theories of memory II* (pp. 1–24). Hove, England: Psychology Press.

Baddeley, A. D., Gathercole, S., & Papagno, C. (1998). The phonological loop as a language learning device. *Psychological Review, 105,* 158–173.

Baddeley, A. D., Grant, S., Wight, E., & Thomson, N. (1973). Imagery and visual working memory. In P. M. A. Rabbitt & S. Dornic (Eds.), *Attention and performance V* (pp. 205–217). London: Academic Press.

Baddeley, A. D., & Hitch, G. J. (1974). Working memory. In G. Bower (Ed.), *Recent advances in learning and memory* (Vol. 8, pp. 47–90). New York: Academic Press.

Baddeley, A. D., Thomson, N., & Buchanan, M. (1975). Word length and the structure of short-term memory. *Journal of Verbal Learning and Verbal Behavior, 14,* 575–589.

Baddeley, A. D., Wilson, B. A., & Watts, F. N. (Eds.). (1995). *Handbook of memory disorders.* Chichester, England: Wiley.

Bahrick, H. P., & Hall, L. K. (1991). Lifetime maintenance of high school mathematics content. *Journal of Experimental Psychology: General, 120,* 20–33.

Bahrick, H. P., Hall, L. K., & Dunlosky, J. (1993). Reconstructive processing of memory content for high versus low test scores and grades. *Applied Cognitive Psychology, 7,* 1–10.

Bahrick, H. P., et al. (1994). Fifty years of language maintenance and language dominance in bilingual Hispanic immigrants. *Journal of Experimental Psychology: General, 123,* 264–283.

Baillargeon, R. (2002). The acquisition of physical knowledge in infancy: A summary in eight lessons. In U. Goswami (Ed.), *Blackwell handbook of childhood cognitive development* (pp. 47–83). Malden, MA: Blackwell.

Baird, J. C., & Hubbard, T. L. (1992). Psychophysics of visual imagery. In D. Algom (Ed.), *Psychophysical approaches to cognition* (pp. 389–440). Amsterdam: Elsevier.

Baker, K. D. (1999). Personal communication.

Balch, W. R., Myers, D. M., & Papotto, C. (1999). Dimensions of mood in mood-dependent memory. *Journal of Experimental Psychology: Learning, Memory, and Cognition, 25,* 70–83.

Baldwin, J. M. (1894). Mental development in the child and the race. New York: Macmillan.

Bales, J. (1988, December). Vincennes: Findings could have helped avert tragedy, scientists tell Hill panel. *APA Monitor,* pp. 10–11.

Balota, D. A., Dolan, P. O., & Duchek, J. M. (2000). Memory changes in healthy older adults. In E. Tulving & F. I. M. Craik (Eds.), *The Oxford handbook of memory* (pp. 395–409). New York: Oxford University Press.

Baltes, P. B., Staudinger, U. M., & Lindenverger, U. (1999). Lifespan psychology: Theory and application to intellectual functioning. *Annual Review of Psychology, 50,* 471–507.

Bamberg, M., & Moissinac, L. (2003). Discourse development. In A. C. Graesser, M. A. Gernsbacher,

& S. R. Goldman (Eds.), *Handbook of discourse processes* (pp. 395–437). Mahwah, NJ: Erlbaum.

Banaji, M. R. (2001). Implicit attitudes can be measured. In H. L. Roediger, III, J. S. Nairne, I. Neath, & A. Suprenant (Eds.), *The nature of remembering* (pp. 117–150). Washington, DC: American Psychological Association.

Banaji, M. R., & Bhaskar, M. (1999). Implicit stereotypes and memory: The bounded rationality of social beliefs. In D. L. Schacter & E. Scarry (Eds.), *Memory, brain, and belief* (pp. 139–175). Cambridge, MA: Harvard University Press.

Bar, M., & Ullman, S. (1996). Spatial context in recognition. *Perception, 25,* 343–352.

Barber, P. (1988). *Applied cognitive psychology.* London: Methuen.

Bargh, J., & Ferguson, M. J. (2000). Beyond behaviorism: On the automaticity of higher mental processes. *Psychological Bulletin, 126,* 925–945.

Barnett, S. M., & Ceci, S. J. (2002). When and where do we apply what we learn? A taxonomy for far transfer. *Psychological Bulletin, 128,* 612–637.

Barnett, S. M., & Koslowski, B. (2002). Adaptive expertise: Effects of type of experience and the level of theoretical understanding it generates. *Thinking and Reasoning, 8,* 237–267.

Baron, J. (1994). *Thinking and deciding* (2nd ed.). New York: Cambridge University Press.

Baron, J. (1998). Judgment misguided: Intuition and error in public decision making. New York: Oxford University Press.

Baron, J. (2000). *Thinking and deciding* (3rd ed.). New York: Cambridge University Press.

Barr, R., Vieria, A., & Rovee-Collier, C. (2001). Mediated imitation in 6-month-olds: Remembering by association. *Journal of Experimental Child Psychology, 79,* 229–252.

Barsalou, L. W. (1990). On the indistinguishability of exemplar memory and abstraction in category representation. In T. K. Srull & R. S. Wyer (Eds.), *Advances in social cognition* (Vol. 3, pp. 61–88). Hillsdale, NJ: Erlbaum.

Barsalou, L. W. (1992a). *Cognitive psychology: An overview for cognitive scientists.* Hillsdale, NJ: Erlbaum.

Barsalou, L. W. (1992b). Frames, concepts, and conceptual fields. In A. Lehrer & E. F. Kittay (Eds.), *Frames, fields, and contrasts* (pp. 21–74). Hillsdale, NJ: Erlbaum.

Barsalou, L. W. (1993). Flexibility, structure, and linguistic vagary in concepts: Manifestations of a compositional system of perceptual symbols. In A. F. Collins, S. E. Gathercole, M. A. Conway, & P. E. Morris (Eds.), *Theories of memory* (pp. 29–101). Hove, England: Erlbaum.

Bartlett, F. C. (1932). *Remembering: An experimental and social study.* Cambridge, England: Cambridge University Press.

Bashore, T. R., & Ridderinkhof, K. R. (2002). Old age, traumatic brain injury, and cognitive slowing: Some convergent and divergent findings. *Psychological Bulletin, 128,* 151–198.

Bassok, M., Wu, L., & Olseth, K. L. (1995). Judging a book by its cover: Interpretative effects of content on problem-solving transfer. *Memory & Cognition, 23,* 354–367.

Bates, E. (2000). On the nature and nurture of language. In R. Levi-Montalcini et al. (Eds.), *Frontiere della biologia* [Frontiers of biology]. Rome: Giovanni Trecanni.

Bates, E., Devescovi, A., & Wulfeck, B. (2001). Psycholinguistics: A cross-language perspective. *Annual Review of Psychology, 52,* 369–396.

Bates, E., & Goodman, J. C. (1997). On the inseparability of grammar and the lexicon: Evidence from acquisition, aphasia and real-time processing. *Language and Cognitive Processes, 12,* 507–584.

Bauer, B., & Jolicoeur, P. (1996). Stimulus dimensionality effects in mental rotation. *Journal of Experimental Psychology: Human Perception and Performance, 22,* 82–94.

Bauer, M. I., & Johnson-Laird, P. N. (1993). How diagrams can improve reasoning. *Psychological Science, 4,* 372–378.

Bauer, P. J. (2002). Long-term recall memory: Behavioral and neuro-developmental changes in the first 2 years of life. *Current Directions in Psychological Science, 11,* 137–141.

Beardsley, T. (1997, August). The machinery of thought. *Scientific American,* pp. 78–83.

Bechtel, W. (1997). Embodied connectionism. In D. M. Johnson & C. E. Erneling (Eds.), *The future of the cognitive revolution* (pp. 187–208). New York: Oxford University Press.

Bechtel, W., Abrahamsen, A., & Graham, G. (1998). The life of cognitive science. In W. Bechtel & G. Graham (Eds.), *A companion to cognitive science* (pp. 2–104). Malden, MA: Blackwell.

Bechtel, W., & Graham, G. (Eds.). (1998a). *A companion to cognitive science*. Malden, MA: Blackwell.

Bechtel, W., & Graham, G. (1998b). Preface. In W. Bechtel & G. Graham (Eds.), *A companion to cognitive science* (pp. xiii–xvi). Malden, MA: Blackwell.

Becker, S. (1999). Implicit learning in 3D object recognition: The importance of temporal context. *Neural Computation, 11*, 347–374.

Bédard, J., & Chi, M. T. H. (1992). Expertise. *Current Directions in Psychological Science, 1*, 135–137.

Beeman, M. J., Bowden, E. M., & Gernsbacher, M. A. (2000). Right and left hemisphere cooperation for drawing predictive and coherence inferences during normal story comprehension. *Brain and Language, 71*, 310–336.

Beeman, M. J., & Chiarello, C. (1998b). Concluding remarks: Getting the whole story right. In M. Beeman & C. Chiarello (Eds.), *Right hemisphere language comprehension: Perspectives from cognitive neuroscience* (pp. 377–389). Mahwah, NJ: Erlbaum.

Belletti, A., & Rizzi, L. (2002). Editors' introduction: Some concepts and issues in linguistic theory. In A. Belletti & L. Rizzi (Eds.), *On nature and language* (pp. 1–44). Cambridge, England: Cambridge University Press.

Bellezza, F. S. (1984). The self as a mnemonic device: The role of internal cues. *Journal of Personality and Social Psychology, 47*, 506–516.

Bellezza, F. S. (1992). Recall of congruent information in the self-reference task. *Bulletin of the Psychonomic Society, 30*, 275–278.

Bellezza, F. S. (1994). Chunking. In V. S. Ramachandran (Ed.), *Encyclopedia of human behavior* (Vol. 1, pp. 579–589). Orlando, FL: Academic Press.

Bellezza, F. S. (1996). Mnemonic method to enhance storage and retrieval. In E. Bjork & R. Bjork (Eds.), *Memory* (pp. 345–380). San Diego: Academic Press.

Bellezza, F. S., & Hoyt, S. K. (1992). The self-reference effect and mental cueing. *Social Cognition, 10*, 51–78.

Belli, R. F., & Loftus, E. F. (1996). The pliability of autobiographical memory: Misinformation and the false memory problem. In D. C. Rubin (Ed.), *Remembering our past: Studies in autobiographical memory* (pp. 157–179). New York: Cambridge University Press.

Bentin, S., et al. (2002). Priming visual face-processing mechanisms: Electrophysiological evidence. *Psychological Science, 13*, 190–193.

Ben-Zeev, T. (2002). If "ignorance makes us smart," then does reading books make us less smart?

[Review of the book *Simple heuristics that make us smart*]. *Contemporary Psychology, 47*, 653–656.

Berardi-Coletta, B., Buyer, L. S., Dominowski, R. L., & Rellinger, E. R. (1995). Metacognition and problem solving: A process-oriented approach. *Journal of Experimental Psychology: Learning, Memory, and Cognition, 21*, 205–223.

Bereiter, C. (1997). Situated cognition and how to overcome it. In D. Kirshner & J. A. Whitson (Eds.), *Situated cognition: Social, semiotic, and psychological perspectives* (pp. 281–300). Mahwah, NJ: Erlbaum.

Berg, T. (2002). Slips of the typewriter key. *Applied Psycholinguistics, 23*, 185–207.

Berger, C. R. (1997). Producing messages under uncertainty. In J. O. Greene (Ed.), *Message production* (pp. 221–224). Mahwah, NJ: Erlbaum.

Berliner, L., & Briere, J. (1999). Trauma, memory, and clinical practice. In L. M. Williams & V. L. Banyard (Eds.), *Trauma & memory* (pp. 3–18). Thousand Oaks, CA: Sage.

Bernstein, S. E., & Carr, T. H. (1996). Dual-route theories of pronouncing printed words: What can be learned from concurrent task performance? *Journal of Experimental Psychology: Learning, Memory, and Cognition, 22*, 86–116.

Bialystok, E. (1987). Words as things: Development of word concept by bilingual children. *Studies in Second Language Acquisition, 9*, 133–140.

Bialystok, E. (1988). Levels of bilingualism and levels of linguistic awareness. *Developmental Psychology, 24*, 560–567.

Bialystok, E. (1992). Selective attention in cognitive processing: The bilingual edge. In R. J. Harris (Ed.), *Language processing in bilingual children* (pp. 501–513). Amsterdam: Elsevier.

Bialystok, E. (1997). Effects of bilingualism and biliteracy on children's emerging concepts of print. *Developmental Psychology, 33*, 429–440.

Bialystok, E. (1999). Cognitive complexity and attentional control in the bilingual mind. *Child Development, 70*, 636–644.

Bialystok, E. (2001). Bilingualism in development: Language, literacy, & cognition. New York: Cambridge University Press.

Bialystok, E., & Codd, J. (1997). Cardinal limits: Evidence from language awareness and bilingualism for developing concepts of number. *Cognitive Development, 12*, 85–106.

Bialystok, E., & Hakuta, K. (1994). *In other words: The science and psychology of second-language acquisition.* New York: Basic Books.

Bialystok, E., & Majumder, S. (1998). The relationship between bilingualism and the development of cognitive processes in problem solving. *Applied Psycholinguistics, 19,* 69–85.

Bidrose, S., & Goodman, G. S. (2000). Testimony and evidence: A case study of memory for child sexual abuse. *Applied Cognitive Psychology, 14,* 197–213.

Biederman, I. (1990). Higher-level vision. In E. N. Osherson, S. M. Kosslyn, & J. M. Hollerbach (Eds.), *An invitation to cognitive science* (Vol. 2, pp. 41–72). Cambridge, MA: MIT.

Biederman, I. (1995). Visual object recognition. In S. F. Kosslyn & D. N. Osherson (Eds.), *An invitation to cognitive science* (2nd ed., pp. 121–165). Cambridge, MA: MIT Press.

Biederman, I., & Bar, M. (1999). One-shot viewpoint invariance in matching novel objects. *Vision Research, 39,* 2885–2899.

Biederman, I., & Kalocsai, P. (1997). Neurocomputational bases of object and face recognition. *Philosophical Transactions of the Royal Society of London, Series B, 352,* 1203–1219.

Biederman, I., et al. (1999). Subordinate-level objects reexamined. *Psychological Research, 62,* 131–153.

Bieman-Copland, S., & Charness, N. (1994). Memory knowledge and memory monitoring in adulthood. *Psychology and Aging, 9,* 287–302.

Billman, D. (1996). Structural biases in concept learning: Influences from multiple functions. *Psychology of Learning and Motivation, 35,* 283–321.

Binder, J., & Price, C. J. (2001). Functional neuroimaging of language. In R. Cabeza & A. Kingstone (Eds.), *Handbook of functional neuroimaging of cognition* (pp. 187–251). Cambridge, MA: MIT Press.

Birdsong, D. (1999). Introduction: Whys and whynots of the critical period hypothesis for second language acquisition. In D. Birdsong (Ed.), *Critical period hypothesis* (pp. 161–181). Mahwah, NJ: Erlbaum.

Birdsong, D., & Molis, M. (2001). On the evidence for maturational constraints in second-language acquisition. *Journal of Memory and Language, 44,* 235–249.

Birren, J. E., & Schaie, K. W. (Eds.). (2001). *Handbook of the psychology of aging* (5th ed.). San Diego, CA: Academic Press.

Birren, J. E., & Schroots, J. J. F. (2001). History of geropsychology. In J. E. Birren & K. W. Schaie (Eds.), *Handbook of the psychology of aging* (5th ed., pp. 3–28). San Diego: Academic Press.

Bishop, M. A., & Trout, J. D. (2002). 50 years of successful predictive modeling should be enough. *Lessons for Philosophy of Science, 69,* S197-S208.

Bjork, E. L., & Bjork, R. A. (1988). On the adaptive aspects of retrieval failure in autobiographical memory. In M. M. Gruneberg, P. E. Morris, & R. N. Sykes (Eds.), *Practical aspects of memory* (Vol. 2). London: Academic Press.

Bjork, R. A. (1999). Assessing our own competence: Heuristics and illusions. In D. Gopher & A. Koriat (Eds.), *Attention and performance XVII* (pp. 435–459). Cambridge, MA: MIT Press.

Bjork, R. A., & Richardson-Klavehn, A. (1987). On the puzzling relationship between environmental context and human memory. In C. Izawa (Ed.), *Current issues in cognitive processes* (pp. 313–344). Hillsdale, NJ: Erlbaum.

Bjorklund, D. F., Brown, R. D., & Bjorklund, B. R. (2002). Children's eyewitness memory: Changing reports and changing representations. In P. Graf & N. Ohta (Eds.), *Lifespan development of human memory* (pp. 101–126). Cambridge, MA: MIT Press.

Bjorklund, D. F., Miller, P. H., Coyle, T. R., & Slawinski, J. L. (1997). Instructing children to use memory strategies: Evidence of utilization deficiencies in memory training studies. *Developmental Review, 17,* 411–441.

Black, J. B. (1984). The architecture of the mind [Review of the book *The architecture of cognition*]. *Contemporary Psychology, 29,* 853–854.

Blair, I. V. (1998). Implicit stereotypes and prejudice. In G. B. Moskowitz (Ed.), *Cognitive social psychology* (pp. 359–374). Mahwah, NJ: Erlbaum.

Blanchette, I., & Dunbar, K. (2000). How analogies are generated: The roles of structural and superficial similarity. *Memory & Cognition, 28,* 108–124.

Blascovich, J., Spencer, S. J., Quinn, D., & Steele, C. (2001). African Americans and high blood pressure: The role of stereotype threat. *Psychological Science, 12,* 225–229.

Block, R. A., & Harper, D. R. (1991). Overconfidence in estimation: Testing the anchoring-and-adjustment hypothesis. *Organizational Behavior and Human Decision Processes, 49,* 188–207.

Bloom, L. (1998). Language acquisition in its developmental context. In W. Damon (Ed.), *Handbook of child psychology: Cognition, perception, and language* (5th ed., Vol. 2, pp. 309–370). New York: Wiley.

Bloom, L. C., & Mudd, S. A. (1991). Depth of processing approach to face recognition: A test of two theories. *Journal of Experimental Psychology: Learning, Memory, and Cognition, 17,* 556–565.

Bloom, P. (2000). *How children learn the meanings of words.* Cambridge, MA: MIT Press.

Bloom, P. (2001). Précis of *How children learn the meanings of words. Behavioral and Brain Sciences, 24,* 1095–1103.

Bloom, P., & Gleitman, L. (1999). Word meaning, acquisition of. In R. A. Wilson & F. C. Keil (Eds.), *The MIT encyclopedia of the cognitive sciences* (pp. 434–438). Cambridge, MA: MIT Press.

Bluck, S., & Habermas, T. (2001). Extending the study of autobiographical memory: Thinking back about life across the life span. *Review of General Psychology, 5,* 135–147.

Blumstein, S. E. (1995). The neurobiology of language. In J. L. Miller & P. D. Eimas (Eds.), *Speech, language, and communication* (pp. 339–370). San Diego: Academic Press.

Bock, K. (1995). Sentence production: From mind to mouth. In J. L. Miller & P. D. Eimas (Eds.), *Speech, language, and communication* (pp. 181–216). San Diego: Academic Press.

Bock, K. (1999). Language production. In R. A. Wilson & F. C. Keil (Eds.), *The MIT encyclopedia of the cognitive sciences* (pp. 453–456). Cambridge, MA: MIT Press.

Bock, K., & Garnsey, S. M. (1998). Language processing. In W. Bechtel & G. Graham (Eds.), *A companion to cognitive science* (pp. 226–234). Malden, MA: Blackwell.

Bock, K., & Griffin, Z. M. (2000). Producing words: How mind meets mouth. In L. Wheeldon (Ed.), *Aspects of language production* (pp. 7–47). Philadelphia: Psychology Press.

Bock, K., & Huitema, J. (1999). Language production. In S. Garrod & M. J. Pickering (Eds.), *Language processing* (pp. 365–388). East Sussex, England: Psychology Press.

Bock, K., Loebell, H., & Morey, R. (1992). From conceptual roles to structural relations: Bridging the syntactic cleft. *Psychological Review, 99,* 150–171.

Boden, M. A. (1999). Computer models of creativity. In R. J. Sternberg (Ed.), *Handbook of creativity* (pp. 351–372). New York: Cambridge University Press.

Bonvillian, J. D. (1999) Sign language development. In M. Barrett (Ed.), *The development of language* (pp. 240–264). Philadelphia: Psychology Press.

Bortfeld, H., & Brennan, S. E. (1997). Use and acquisition of idiomatic expressions in referring by native and non-native speakers. *Discourse Processes, 23,* 119–147.

Bosch, L., & Sebastián-Gallés, N. (1997). Native-language recognition abilities in 4-month-old infants from monolingual and bilingual environments. *Cognition, 65,* 33–69.

Bower, G. H. (1970). Analysis of a mnemonic device. *American Scientist, 58,* 496–510.

Bower, G. H. (1998). An associative theory of implicit and explicit memory. In M. A. Conway, S. E. Gathercole, & C. Cornoldi (Eds.), *Theories of memory* (Vol. 2, pp. 25–60). Hove, England: Psychology Press.

Bower, G. H. (2000). A brief history of memory research. In E. Tulving & F. I. M. Craik (Eds.), *The Oxford handbook of memory* (pp. 3–32). New York: Oxford University Press.

Bower, G. H., & Clark, M. C. (1969). Narrative stories as mediators for serial learning. *Psychonomic Science, 14,* 181–182.

Bower, G. H., Clark, M. C., Lesgold, A. M., & Winzenz, D. (1969). Hierarchical retrieval schemes in recall of categorized word lists. *Journal of Verbal Learning and Verbal Behavior, 8,* 323–343.

Bower, G. H., & Forgas, J. P. (2000). Affect, memory, and social cognition. In E. Eich et al. (Eds.), *Cognition and emotion* (pp. 87–168). New York: Oxford University Press.

Bower, G. H., & Springston, F. (1970). Pauses as recoding points in letter series. *Journal of Experimental Psychology, 83,* 421–430.

Bower, G. H., & Winzenz, D. (1970). Comparison of associative learning strategies. *Psychonomic Science, 20,* 119–120.

Boysson-Bardies, B. de (1999). *How language comes to children: From birth to two years.* Cambridge, MA: MIT Press.

Bradshaw, J. L., & Nettleton, N. C. (1974). Articulatory inference and the MOWN–DOWN heterophone effect. *Journal of Experimental Psychology, 102,* 88–94.

Brainerd, C. J., & Reyna, V. F. (1998). When things that were never experienced are easier to "remember" than things that were. *Psychological Science, 9*, 484–489.

Brandimonte, M. A., & Gerbino, W. (1996). When imagery fails: Effects of verbal recoding on accessibility of visual memories. In C. Cornoldi et al. (Eds.), *Stretching the imagination: Representation and transformation in mental imagery* (pp. 31–76). New York: Oxford University Press.

Brandimonte, M. A., Hitch, G. J., & Bishop, D. V. M. (1992). Influence of short-term memory codes on visual image processing: Evidence from image transformation tasks. *Journal of Experimental Psychology: Learning, Memory, and Cognition, 18*, 157–165.

Brannon, L., & Feist, J. (2000). *Health psychology: An introduction to behavior and health* (4th ed.). Belmont, CA: Wadsworth.

Bransford, J. D., Barclay, J. R., & Franks, J. J. (1972). Sentence memory: A constructive versus interpretive approach. *Cognitive Psychology, 3*, 193–209.

Bransford, J. D., Brown, A. L., & Cocking, R. R. (2000). *How people learn: Brain, mind, experience, and school* (expanded edition). Washington, DC: National Academy Press.

Bransford, J. D., & Franks, J. J. (1971). Abstraction of linguistic ideas. *Cognitive Psychology, 2*, 331–350.

Bransford, J. D., Franks, J. J., Morris, C. D., & Stein, B. S. (1979). Some general constraints on learning and memory research. In L. S. Cermak & F. I. M. Craik (Eds.), *Levels of processing in human memory* (pp. 331–354). Hillsdale, NJ: Erlbaum.

Bransford, J. D., & Stein, B. S. (1984). *The IDEAL problem solver*. New York: Freeman.

Branthwaite, A., & Rogers, D. (1985). Introduction. In A. Branthwaite & D. Rogers (Eds.), *Children growing up* (pp. 1–2). Milton, Keynes, England: Open University Press.

Brase, G. L., Cosmides, L., & Tooby, J. (1998). Individuation, counting, and statistical inference: The role of frequency and whole-object representations in judgment under uncertainty. *Journal of Experimental Psychology: General, 127*, 3–21.

Brennan, S. E., & Clark, H. H. (1996). Conceptual pacts and lexical choice in conversation. *Journal of Experimental Psychology: Learning, Memory, and Cognition, 22*, 1482–1493.

Bressler, S. L. (2002). Understanding cognition through large-scale cortical networks. *Current Directions in Psychological Science, 11*, 57–61.

Brewer, J. B., et al. (1998). Making memories: Brain activity that predicts how well visual experience will be remembered. *Science, 281*, 1185–1187.

Brewer, W. F. (1999). Schemata. In R. A. Wilson & F. C. Keil (Eds.), *The MIT encyclopedia of the cognitive sciences* (pp. 729–730). Cambridge, MA: MIT Press.

Brewer, W. F. (2000). Bartlett's concept of the schema and its impact on theories of knowledge representation in contemporary cognitive psychology. In A. Saito (Ed.), *Bartlett, culture and cognition* (pp. 69–89). East Sussex, England: Psychology Press.

Brewer, W. F., & Treyens, J. C. (1981). Role of schemata in memory for places. *Cognitive Psychology, 13*, 207–230.

Briere, J. (1997). An integrated approach to treating adults abused as children, with specific reference to self-reported recovered memories. In J. D. Read & D. S. Lindsay (Eds.), *Recollections of trauma: Scientific evidence and clinical practice* (pp. 25–47). New York: Plenum.

Brigham, T. C., & Malpass, R. S. (1985). The role of experience and context in the recognition of faces of own- and other-race. *Journal of Social Issues, 41*, 139–155.

Britton, B. K. (1996). Rewriting: The arts and sciences of improving expository instructional text. In C. Michael Levy & S. Ransdell (Eds.), *The science of writing: Theories, methods, individual differences, and applications* (pp. 323–345). Mahwah, NJ: Erlbaum.

Broadbent, D. E. (1958). *Perception and communication*. New York: Pergamon.

Brooks, L. R. (1968). Spatial and verbal components of the act of recall. *Canadian Journal of Psychology, 22*, 349–368.

Brown, A. S. (1991). A review of the tip-of-the-tongue experience. *Psychological Bulletin, 109*, 204–233.

Brown, D. P., Scheflin, A. W., & Hammond, D. C. (1998). *Memory, trauma treatment, and the law*. New York: Norton.

Brown, J. A. (1958). Some tests of the decay theory of immediate memory. *Quarterly Journal of Experimental Psychology, 10*, 12–21.

Brown, J. M. (2003). Eyewitness memory for arousing events: Putting things into context. *Applied Cognitive Psychology, 17*, 93–106.

Brown, N. R., Cui, X., & Gordon, R. D. (2002). Estimating national populations: Cross-cultural differences and availability effects. *Applied Cognitive Psychology, 16*, 811–827.

Brown, N. R., & Siegler, R. S. (1992). The role of availability in the estimation of national populations. *Memory & Cognition, 20*, 406–412.

Brown, P., & Levinson, S. C. (1987). *Politeness: Some universals of language usage.* Cambridge, England: Cambridge University Press.

Brown, R. (1973). *A first language: The early stages.* Cambridge, MA: Harvard University Press.

Brown, R., & Kulik, J. (1977). Flashbulb memories. *Cognition, 5*, 73–99.

Brown, R., & McNeill, D. (1966). The "tip of the tongue" phenomenon. *Journal of Verbal Learning and Verbal Behavior, 5*, 325–377.

Brown, S. C., & Craik, F. I. M. (2000). Encoding and retrieval of information. In E. Tulving & F. I. M. Craik (Eds.), *The Oxford handbook of memory* (pp. 93–108). New York: Oxford University Press.

Brown, T. L., Gore, C. L., & Carr, T. H. (2002). Visual attention and word recognition in Stroop color naming: Is word recognition "automatic"? *Journal of Experimental Psychology: General, 131*, 220–240.

Bruce, D., Dolan, A., & Phillips-Grant, K. (2000). On the transition from childhood amnesia to the recall of personal memories. *Psychological Science, 11*, 360–364.

Bruce, V., Henderson, A., Newman, C., & Burton, A. M. (2001). Matching identities of familiar and unfamiliar faces caught on CCTV images. *Journal of Experimental Psychology: Applied, 7*, 207–218.

Bruce, V., et al. (1999). Verification of face identities from images captured on video. *Journal of Experimental Psychology: Applied, 5*, 339–360.

Bruck, M., & Ceci, S. J. (1999). The suggestibility of children's memory. *Annual Review of Psychology, 50*, 419–439.

Bruck, M., Ceci, S. J., & Hembrooke, H. (1998). Reliability and credibility of young children's reports. *American Psychologist, 53*, 136–151.

Bruck, M., Ceci, S. J., & Melnyk, L. (1997). External and internal sources of variation in the creation of false reports in children. *Learning and Individual Differences, 9*, 289–316.

Bruner, J. (1997). Will cognitive revolutions ever stop? In D. M. Johnson & C. E. Erneling (Eds.), *The future of the cognitive revolution* (pp. 279–292). New York: Oxford University Press.

Bruning, R. H., Schraw, G. J., & Ronning, R. R. (1999). *Cognitive psychology and instruction* (3rd ed.). Upper Saddle River, NJ: Prentice Hall.

Bryant, D. J. (1998). Human spatial concepts reflect regularities of the physical world and human body. In P. Olivier & K. Gapp (Eds.), *Representation and processing of spatial expressions* (pp. 215–230). Mahwah, NJ: Erlbaum.

Bryant, D. J., & Tversky, B. (1999). Mental representations of perspective and spatial relations from diagrams and models. *Journal of Experimental Psychology: Learning, Memory, and Cognition, 25*, 137–156.

Bryant, D. J., Tversky, B., & Franklin, N. (1992). Internal and external spatial frameworks for representing described scenes. *Journal of Memory and Language, 31*, 74–98.

Buckner, R. L. (2000). Neuroimaging of memory. In M. S. Gazzaniga (Ed.), *The new cognitive neurosciences* (2nd ed., pp. 817–828). Cambridge, MA: MIT Press.

Buckner, R. L., & Logan, J. M. (2001). Functional neuroimaging methods: PET and fMRI. In R. Cabeza & A. Kingstone (Eds.), *Handbook of functional neuroimaging of cognition* (pp. 27–48). Cambridge, MA: MIT Press.

Buckner, R. L., & Petersen, S. E. (1998). Neuroimaging. In W. Bechtel & G. Graham (Eds.), *A companion to cognitive science* (pp. 413–424). Malden, MA: Blackwell.

Buehler, R., Griffin, D., & Ross, M. (1994). Exploring the "planning fallacy." Why people underestimate their task completion times. *Journal of Personality and Social Psychology, 67*, 366–381.

Buehler, R., Griffin, D., & Ross, M. (2002). Inside the planning fallacy: The causes and consequences of optimistic time predictions. In T. Gilovich, D. Griffin, & D. Kahneman (Eds.), *Heuristics and biases: The psychology of intuitive judgment* (pp. 250–270). New York: Cambridge University Press.

Burgess, C. (1998). From simple associations to the building blocks of language: Modeling meaning in memory with the HAL model. *Behavior Research Methods, Instruments, & Computers, 30*, 188–198.

Burgess, C., Livesay, K., & Lund, K. (1998). Explorations in context space: Words, sentences, discourse. *Discourse Processes, 25*, 211–257.

Burgess, C., & Lund, K. (2000). The dynamics of meaning in memory. In E. Dietrich & A. B. Markman (Eds.), *Cognitive dynamics: Conceptual and representational change in humans and machines* (pp. 117–156). Mahwah, NJ: Erlbaum.

Burgess, N., & Hitch, G. J. (1999). Memory for serial order: A network model of the phonological loop and its timing. *Psychological Review, 106*, 551–581.

Burgess, P. W., & Shallice, T. (1997). The relationship between prospective and retrospective memory: Neuropsychological evidence. In M. A. Conway (Ed.), *Cognitive models of memory* (pp. 247–272). Cambridge, MA: MIT Press.

Burt, C. D. B., Watt, S. C., Mitchell, D. A., & Conway, M. A. (1998). Retrieving the sequence of autobiographical event components. *Applied Cognitive Psychology, 12*, 321–338.

Burton, A. M., Wilson, S., Cowan, M., & Bruce, V. (1999). Face recognition in poor-quality video: Evidence from security surveillance. *Psychological Science, 10*, 243–248.

Bus, A. G., & van IJzendoorn, M. H. (1999). Phonological awareness and early reading: A meta-analysis of experimental training studies. *Journal of Educational Psychology, 91*, 403–414.

Bushman, B. J. (1998). Effects of television violence on memory for commercial messages. *Journal of Experimental Psychology: Applied, 4*, 291–307.

Bushnell, I. W. R., & Sai, F. (1987). *Neonatal recognition of the mother's face.* University of Glasgow Report, 87/1.

Butcher, K. R., & Kintsch, W. (2003). Text comprehension and discourse processing. In A. F. Healy & R. W. Proctor (Eds.), *Handbook of psychology* (Vol. 4, pp. 575–595). Hoboken, NJ: Wiley.

Byrne, B., & Fielding-Barnsley, R. (1991). Evaluation of a program to teach phonemic awareness to young children. *Journal of Educational Psychology, 83*, 451–455.

Byrne, R. M. J., Espino, O., & Santamaria, C. (2000). Counterexample availability. In W. Schaeken, G. DeVooght, A. Vandierendonck, & G. d'Ydewalle (Eds.), *Deductive reasoning and strategies* (pp. 97–110). Mahwah, NJ: Erlbaum.

Cabe, P. A., Walker, M. H., & Williams, M. (1999). Newspaper advice column letters as teaching cases for developmental psychology. *Teaching of Psychology, 26*, 128–131.

Calkins, M. W. (1894). Association: I. *Psychological Review, 1*, 476–483.

Campbell, R., & Sais, E. (1995). Accelerated metalinguistic (phonological) awareness in bilingual children. *British Journal of Developmental Psychology, 13*, 61–68.

Canadian Global Almanac. (2001). Toronto: Macmillan Canada.

Cannon, C. K., & Quinsey, V. L. (1995). The likelihood of violent behaviour: Predictions, postdictions, and hindsight bias. *Canadian Journal of Behavioral Science, 27*, 92–106.

Cannon-Bowers, J. A., & Salas, E. (Eds.). (1998). *Making decisions under stress: Implications for individuals and team training.* Washington, DC: American Psychological Association.

Caramazza, A., & Miozzo, M. (1997). The relation between syntactic and phonological knowledge in lexical access: Evidence from the "tip-of-the-tongue" phenomenon. *Cognition, 69*, 309–343.

Caramazza, A., Yenni-Komshian, G., Zurif, E., & Carbone, E. (1973). The acquisition of a new phonological contrast: The case of stop consonants in French-English bilinguals. *Journal of the Acoustical Society of America, 54*, 421–428.

Carli, L. L. (1999). Cognitive reconstruction, hindsight, and reactions to victims and perpetrators. *Personality and Social Psychology Bulletin, 25*, 966–979.

Carlson, E. R. (1995). Evaluating the credibility of sources: A missing link in the teaching of critical thinking. *Teaching of Psychology, 22*, 39–41.

Carlson, R. A. (1997). *Experienced cognition.* Mahwah, NJ: Erlbaum.

Carney, R. N., & Levin, J. R. (1998). Mnemonic strategies for adult learners. In M. C. Smith & T. Pourchot (Eds.), *Adult learning and development: Perspectives from educational psychology* (pp. 159–175). Mahwah, NJ: Erlbaum.

Carney, R. N., & Levin, J. R. (2001). Remembering the names of unfamiliar animals: Keywords as keys to their kingdom. *Applied Cognitive Psychology, 15*, 133–143.

Carpenter, P. A., & Just, M. A. (1999). Computational modeling of high-level cognition versus hypothesis testing. In R. J. Sternberg (Ed.), *The nature of cognition* (pp. 245–293). Cambridge, MA: MIT Press.

Carpenter, P. A., Just, M. A., & Reichle, E. D. (2000). Working memory and executive function: Evidence from neuroimaging. *Current Opinion in Neurobiology, 10*, 195–199.

Carpenter, P. A., Miyake, A., & Just, M. A. (1994). Working memory constraints in comprehension. In M. A. Gernsbacher (Ed.), *Handbook of psycholinguistics* (pp. 1075–1122). San Diego: Academic Press.

Carpenter, P. A., Miyake, A., & Just, M. A. (1995). Language comprehension: Sentence and discourse processing. *Annual Review of Psychology, 46,* 91–120.

Carr, W., & Roskos-Ewoldsen, B. (1999). Spatial orientation by mental transformation. *Psychological Research/ Psychologische Forschung, 62,* 36–47.

Carraher, T. N., Carraher, D. W., & Schliemann, A. D. (1985). Mathematics in the streets and in schools. *British Journal of Developmental Psychology, 3,* 21–29.

Carroll, D. W. (1999). *Psychology of language* (3rd ed.). Pacific Grove, CA: Brooks/Cole.

Carroll, D. W. (2004). *Psychology of language* (4th ed.). Belmont, CA: Wadsworth.

Carver, L. J., & Bauer, P. J. (1999). When the event is more than the sum of its parts: Nine-month-olds' long-term ordered recall. *Memory, 7,* 147–174.

Castiello, U., & Umilta, C. (1992). Orienting of attention in volleyball players. *International Journal of Sport Psychology, 23,* 301–310.

Cavanaugh, C., & Whitbourne, S. K. (Eds.). (1999). *Gerontology: An interdisciplinary perspective.* New York: Oxford University Press.

Ceballo, R. (1999). Negotiating the life narrative: A dialogue with an African American social worker. *Psychology of Women Quarterly, 23,* 309–321.

Ceci, S. J., & Liker, J. K. (1986). A day at the races: A study of IQ, expertise, and cognitive complexity. *Journal of Experimental Psychology: General, 115,* 255–266.

Ceci, S. J., & Liker, J. K. (1988). Stalking the IQ-Expertise relation: When the critics go fishing. *Journal of Experimental Psychology: General, 117,* 96–100.

Cellular Telecommunications Industry Association. (2004). Retrieved February 29, 2004, from http://www.wow-com.com/

Cenoz, J., & Genesee, F. (Eds.). (2001). *Trends in bilingual acquisition.* New York: John Benjamins.

Chafe, W., & Danielewicz, J. (1987). Properties of spoken and written language. In R. Horowitz & S. J. Samuels (Eds.), *Comprehending oral and written language* (pp. 83–113). San Diego: Academic Press.

Chambers, D., & Reisberg, D. (1985). Can mental images be ambiguous? *Journal of Experimental Psychology: Human Perception and Performance, 11,* 317–328.

Chance, J. E., & Goldstein, A. G. (1996). The other-race effect and eyewitness identification. In S. L. Sporer, R. S. Malpass, & G. Koehnken (Eds.), *Psychological issues in eyewitness identification* (pp. 153–176). Mahwah, NJ: Erlbaum.

Chapman, L. J., & Chapman, J. P. (1967). Genesis of popular but erroneous psychodiagnostic observations. *Journal of Abnormal Psychology, 72,* 193–204.

Chapman, L. J., & Chapman, J. P. (1969). Illusory correlations as an obstacle to the use of valid psychodiagnostic signs. *Journal of Abnormal Psychology, 74,* 271–280.

Chapman, P., & Underwood, G. (2000). Forgetting near-accidents: The roles of severity, culpability and experience in the poor recall of dangerous driving situations. *Applied Cognitive Psychology, 14,* 31–44.

Charness, N., Parks, D. C., & Sabel, B. A. (2001). *Communication, technology, and aging: Opportunities and challenges for the future.* New York: Springer.

Chase, W. G., & Ericsson, K. A. (1981). Skilled memory. In J. R. Anderson (Ed.), *Cognitive skills and their acquisition* (pp. 141–189). Hillsdale, NJ: Erlbaum.

Chen, E. Y. H., & Berrios, G. E. (1998). The nature of delusions: A hierarchical neural network approach. In D. J. Stein & J. Ludik (Eds.), *Neural networks and psychopathology* (pp. 167–188). Cambridge, England: Cambridge University Press.

Chenoweth, N. A., & Hayes, J. R. (2001). Fluency in writing. *Written Communication, 18,* 80–98.

Cheour, M., et al. (1998). Development of language-specific phoneme representations in the infant brain. *Nature Neuroscience, 1,* 351–353.

Cherry, C. (1953). Some experiments on the recognition of speech with one and with two ears. *Journal of the Acoustical Society of America, 25,* 975–979.

Chi, M. T. H. (1981). Knowledge development and memory performance. In M. Friedman, J. P. Das, & N. O'Connor (Eds.), *Intelligence and learning* (pp. 221–230). New York: Plenum.

Chi, M. T. H. (2000). Self-explaining expository texts: The dual processes of generating inferences and repairing mental models. In R. Glaser (Ed.), *Advances in instructional psychology* (Vol. 5, pp. 161–238). Mahwah, NJ: Erlbaum.

Chi, M. T. H., et al. (2001). Learning from human tutoring. *Cognitive Science, 25,* 471–533.

Chialant, D., & Caramazza, A. (1995). Where is morphology and how is it processed? The case of written word recognition. In L. B. Feldman (Ed.), *Morphological aspects of language processing* (pp. 55–76). Hillsdale, NJ: Erlbaum.

Chomsky, N. (1957). *Syntactic structures.* The Hague: Mouton.

Chomsky, N. (1965). *Aspects of the theory of syntax.* Cambridge, MA: MIT Press.

Chomsky, N. (1975). *Reflections on language.* New York: Pantheon.

Chomsky, N. (1981). *Lectures on government and binding.* Dordrecht, Netherlands: Foris.

Chomsky, N. (2000). *New horizons in the study of language and mind.* Cambridge, England: Cambridge University Press.

Chomsky, N. (2002). *On nature and language.* Cambridge, England: Cambridge University Press.

Christensen-Szalanski, J. J. J., & Willham, C. F. (1991). The hindsight bias: A meta-analysis. *Organizational Behavior and Human Decision Processes, 48,* 147–168.

Christensen-Szalanski, J. J. J., et al. (1983). The effect of journal coverage on physicians' perception of risk. *Journal of Applied Psychology, 68,* 278–284.

Chun, M. M., & Marois, R. (2002). The dark side of visual attention. *Current Opinion in Neurobiology, 12,* 184–189.

Chun, M. M., & Wolfe, J. M. (2001). Visual attention. In E. B. Goldstein (Ed.), *Blackwell handbook of perception* (pp. 272–310). Malden, MA: Blackwell.

Churchland, P. M., & Churchland, P. S. (1990, January). Could a machine think? *Scientific American,* pp. 32–37.

Clark, D. M., Winton, E., & Thynn, L. (1993). A further experimental investigation of thought suppression. *Behavioral Research and Therapy, 31,* 207–210.

Clark, H. H. (1985). Language use and language users. In G. Lindzey & E. Aronson (Eds.), *Handbook of social psychology* (2nd ed., Vol. 2, pp. 179–231). New York: Random House.

Clark, H. H. (1994). Discourse in production. In M. A. Gernsbacher (Ed.), *Handbook of psycholinguistics* (pp. 985–1021). San Diego: Academic Press.

Clark, H. H., & Chase, W. G. (1972). On the process of comparing sentences against pictures. *Cognitive Psychology, 3,* 472–517.

Clark, H. H., & Van Der Wege, M. M. (2002). Psycholinguistics. In D. Medin (Ed.), *Stevens' handbook of experimental psychology* (3rd ed., Vol. 2, pp. 209–259). New York: Wiley.

Clark, H. H., & Wasow, T. (1998). Repeating words in spontaneous speech. *Cognitive Psychology, 37,* 201–242.

Clark, H. H., & Wilkes-Gibbs, D. (1986). Referring as a collaborative process. *Cognition, 22,* 1–39.

Claxton, G. (1999). *Wise-up: The challenge of lifelong learning.* New York: Bloomsbury.

Cleary, M., & Pisoni, D. B. (2001). Speech perception and spoken word recognition: Research and theory. In E. B. Goldstein (Ed.), *Blackwell handbook of perception* (pp. 499–534). Malden, MA: Blackwell.

Clement, C. A., & Falmagne, R. J. (1986). Logical reasoning, world knowledge, and mental imagery: Interconnections in cognitive processes. *Memory & Cognition, 14,* 299–307.

Cohen, D. (2002). *How the child's mind develops.* Hove, England: Routledge.

Cohen, G. (1993). Memory and ageing. In G. M. Davies & R. H. Logie (Eds.), *Memory in everyday life* (pp. 419–446). Amsterdam: North-Holland.

Cohen, G., Conway, M. A., & Maylor, E. A. (1994). Flashbulb memories in older adults. *Psychology and Aging, 9,* 454–463.

Cohen, J. D., Dunbar, K. O., Barch, D. M., & Braver, T. S. (1997). Issues concerning relative speed of processing hypotheses, schizophrenic performance deficits, and prefrontal function: Comments on Schooler et al. (1997). *Journal of Experimental Psychology: General, 126,* 37–41.

Cohen, J. D., & Schooler, J. W. (1997a). Science and sentience: Some questions regarding the scientific investigation of consciousness. In J. D. Cohen & J. W. Schooler (Eds.), *Scientific approaches to consciousness* (pp. 3–10). Mahwah, NJ: Erlbaum.

Cohen, J. D., & Schooler, J. W. (Eds.). (1997b). *Scientific approaches to consciousness.* Mahwah, NJ: Erlbaum.

Cohen, J. D., Usher, M., & McClelland, J. C. (1998). A PDP approach to set size effects within the Stroop task: Reply to Kanne, Balota, Spieler, and Faust (1998). *Psychological Review, 105,* 188–194.

Cohen, M. S. (1993). The naturalistic basis of decision biases. In G. A. Klein, J. Orasanu, R. Calderwood, & C. E. Zsambok (Eds.), *Decision making in action: Models and methods* (pp. 51–99). Norwood, NJ: Ablex.

Cohen, M. S., Freeman, J. T., & Thompson, B. (1998). Critical thinking skills in tactical decision making: A model and training strategy. In J. A. Cannon-Bowers & E. Salas (Eds.), *Making decisions under stress: Implications for individual and team training* (pp. 155–189). Washington, DC: American Psychological Association.

Cohen, M. S., et al. (1996). Changes in cortical activity during mental rotation: A mapping study using functional MRI. *Brain, 119,* 89–100.

Cole, R. A., & Jakimik, J. (1980). A model of speech perception. In R. A. Cole (Ed.), *Perception and production of fluent speech* (pp. 133–163). Hillsdale, NJ: Erlbaum.

Collins, A. M., & Loftus, E. F. (1975). A spreading-activation theory of semantic memory. *Psychological Review, 82,* 407–428.

Collins, J. L. (1998). *Strategies for struggling writers.* New York: Guilford.

Collins, M. A., & Amabile, T. M. (1999). Motivation and creativity. In R. J. Sternberg (Ed.), *Handbook of creativity* (pp. 297–312). New York: Cambridge University Press.

Collins, S. C., & Kneale, P. E. (2001). *Study skills for psychology students.* New York: Oxford University Press.

Coltheart, M., & Rastle, K. (1994). Serial processing in reading aloud: Evidence for dual-route models of reading. *Journal of Experimental Psychology: Human Perception and Performance, 20,* 1197–1211.

Comeau, L., & Genesee, F. (2001). Bilingual children's repair strategies during dyadic communication. In J. Cenoz & F. Genesee (Eds.), *Trends in bilingual acquisition* (pp. 231–256). New York: John Benjamins.

Connolly, T., Arkes, H. R., & Hammond, K. R. (Eds.). (2000). *Judgment and decision making: An interdisciplinary reader* (2nd ed.). New York: Cambridge University Press.

Connor, L. T., Dunlosky, J., & Hertzog, C. (1997). Age-related differences in absolute but not relative metamemory accuracy. *Psychology and Aging, 12,* 50–71.

Connor-Greene, P. A. (2000). Making connections: Evaluating the effectiveness of journal writing in enhancing student learning. *Teaching of Psychology, 27,* 44–46.

Conte, J. R. (1999). Memory, research, and the law: Future directions. In L. M. Williams & V. L. Banyard (Eds.), *Trauma & memory* (pp. 77–92). Thousand Oaks, CA: Sage.

Conway, A. R. A., Cowan, N., & Bunting, M. F. (2001). The cocktail party phenomenon revisited: The importance of working memory capacity. *Psychonomic Bulletin & Review, 8,* 331–335.

Conway, M. A. (1995). *Flashbulb memories.* Hove, England: Erlbaum.

Conway, M. A. (Ed.). (1997). *Recovered memories and false memories.* New York: Oxford University Press.

Conway, M. A. (2001). Sensory-perceptual episodic memory and its context: Autobiographical memory. *Philosophical Transactions of the Royal Society of London, 356,* 1375–1384.

Conway, M. A., & Fthenaki, A. (2000). Disruption and loss of autobiographical memory. In F. Boller & J. Grafman (Eds.), *Handbook of neuropsychology* (2nd ed., Vol. 2, pp. 281–312). Amsterdam: Elsevier.

Conway, M. A., & Pleydell-Pearce, C. W. (2000). The construction of autobiographical memories in the self-memory system. *Psychological Review, 107,* 261–288.

Conway, M. A., Pleydell-Pearce, C. W., Whitecross, S., & Sharpe, H. (2000). Brain imaging autobiographical memory. *Psychology of Learning and Motivation, 42,* 229–263.

Conway, M. A., et al. (1994). The formation of flashbulb memories. *Memory & Cognition, 22,* 326–343.

Cook, A. E., Halleran, J. G., & O'Brien, E. J. (1998). What is readily available during reading? A memory-based view of text processing. *Discourse Processes, 26,* 109–129.

Cooper, L. A., & Hochberg, J. (1994). Objects of the mind: mental representations in visual perception and cognition. In S. Ballesteros (Ed.), *Cognitive approaches to human perception* (pp. 223–239). Hillsdale, NJ: Erlbaum.

Cooper, L. A., & Lang, J. M. (1996). Imagery and visual-spatial representations. In E. L. Bjork & R. A. Bjork (Eds.), *Memory* (pp. 129–164). San Diego: Academic Press.

Cooper, L. A., & Shepard, R. N. (1984). Turning something over in the mind. *Scientific American, 251(6),* 106–114.

Coren, S., Ward, L. M., & Enns, J. T. (1999). *Sensation and perception* (5th ed.). Fort Worth: Harcourt Brace.

Coren, S., Ward, L. M., & Enns, J. T. (2004). *Sensation and perception* (6th ed.). Hoboken, NJ: Wiley.

Corkin, S. (1984). Lasting consequences of bilateral medial temporal lobe excision. *Neuropsychologia, 6,* 255–265.

Cornoldi, C. (1998). The impact of metacognitive reflection on cognitive control. In G. Mazzoni & T. O. Nelson (Eds.), *Metacognition and cognitive neuropsychology* (pp. 139–159). Mahwah, NJ: Erlbaum.

Cornoldi, C., & Oakhill, J. (1996). Introduction: Reading comprehension difficulties. In C. Cornoldi & J. Oakhill (Eds.), *Reading comprehension difficulties: Processes and intervention* (pp. xi–xxiii). Mahwah, NJ: Erlbaum.

Corrigan, P. W., & Penn, D. L. (Eds.). (2001). *Social cognition and schizophrenia*. Washington, DC: American Psychological Association.

Cosmides, L. (1989). The logic of social exchange: Has natural selection shaped how humans reason? Studies with the Wason selection task. *Cognition, 31*, 187–276.

Cosmides, L., & Tooby, J. (1995). From function to structure: The role of evolutionary biology and computational theories in cognitive neuroscience. In M. Gazzaniga (Ed.), *The cognitive neurosciences* (pp. 1199–1210). Cambridge, MA: MIT Press.

Cosmides, L., & Tooby, J. (1996). Are humans good intuitive statisticians after all? Rethinking some conclusions from the literature on judgment under uncertainty. *Cognition, 58*, 1–73.

Courage, M. L., & Howe, M. L. (2001). Long-term retention in 3.5-month-olds: Familiarization time and individual differences in attentional style. *Journal of Experimental Child Psychology, 79*, 271–293.

Courtney, S. M., et al. (1998). An area specialized for spatial working memory in human frontal cortex. *Science, 279*, 1347–1351.

Cowan, N. (1994). Mechanisms of verbal short-term memory. *Current Directions in Psychological Science, 3*, 185–189.

Cowan, N. (1995). *Attention and memory: An integrated framework*. New York: Oxford University Press.

Cowan, N. (2001). The magical number 4 in short-term memory: A reconsideration of mental storage capacity. *Behavioral and Brain Sciences, 24*, 87–185.

Cowan, N., Saults, J. S., & Elliott, E. M. (2002). The search for what is fundamental in the development of working memory. *Advances in Child Development and Behavior, 29*, 1–49.

Cowan, N., & Wood, N. L. (1997). Constraints on awareness, attention, processing, and memory: Some recent investigations with ignored speech. *Consciousness and Cognition, 6*, 182–203.

Cowan, N., et al. (2003). Children's working memory processes: A response-timing analysis. *Journal of Experimental Psychology: General, 132*, 113–132.

Coyle, T. R., & Bjorklund, D. F. (1997). Age differences in, and consequences of, multiple- and variable-strategy use on a multitrial sort-recall task. *Developmental Psychology, 33*, 372–380.

Craik, F. I. M. (1990). Changes in memory with normal aging: A functional view. In R. J. Wurtman (Ed.), *Advances in neurology: Vol. 51. Alzheimer's disease* (pp. 201–205). New York: Raven.

Craik, F. I. M. (1999). Levels of encoding and retrieval. In B. H. Challis & B. M. Velichkovsky (Eds.), *Stratification in cognition and consciousness* (pp. 97–104). Philadelphia: John Benjamins.

Craik, F. I. M. (2002). Levels of processing: Past, present . . . and future? *Memory, 10*, 305–318.

Craik, F. I. M., & Anderson, N. D. (1999). Applying cognitive research to problems of aging. In D. Gopher & A. Koriat (Eds.), *Attention and performance XVII* (pp. 583–615). Mahwah, NJ: Erlbaum.

Craik, F. I. M., Anderson, N. D., Kerr, S. A., & Li, K. Z. H. (1995). Memory changes in normal ageing. In A. D. Baddeley, B. A. Wilson, & F. N. Watts (Eds.), *Handbook of memory disorders* (pp. 211–241). Chichester, England: Wiley.

Craik, F. I. M., & Lockhart, R. S. (1972). Levels of processing: A framework for memory research. *Journal of Verbal Learning and Verbal Behavior, 11*, 671–684.

Craik, F. I. M., & Lockhart, R. S. (1986). CHARM is not enough: Comments on Eich's model of cued recall. *Psychological Review, 93*, 360–364.

Craik, F. I. M., & Salthouse, T. A. (Eds.). (2000). *The handbook of aging and cognition* (2nd ed.). Mahwah, NJ: Erlbaum.

Craik, F. I. M., & Tulving, E. (1975). Depth of processing and the retention of words in episodic memory. *Journal of Experimental Psychology: General, 104*, 268–294.

Craik, F. I. M., et al. (1999). In search of the self: A positron emission tomography study. *Psychological Science, 10*, 26–34.

Cranberg, L. D., & Albert, M. L. (1988). The chess mind. In L. K. Obler & D. Fein (Eds.), *The exceptional brain: Neuropsychology of talent and special abilities* (pp. 156–190). New York: Guilford.

Craver-Lemley, C., Arterberry, M. E., & Reeves, A. (1999). "Illusory" illusory conjunctions: The conjoining of features of visual and imagined stimuli. *Journal of Experimental Psychology: Human Perception and Performance, 25*, 1036–1049.

Craver-Lemley, C., & Reeves, A. (1987). Visual imagery selectively reduces vernier acuity. *Perception, 16*, 599–614.

Craver-Lemley, C., & Reeves, A. (1992). How visual imagery interferes with vision. *Psychological Review, 99*, 633–649.

Crawford, M., & Unger, R. (2004). *Women and gender: A feminist psychology* (4th ed.). Boston: McGraw Hill.

Creyer, E., & Ross, W. T., Jr. (1993). Hindsight bias and inferences in choice: The mediating effect of cognitive effort. *Organizational Behavior and Human Decision Processes, 55,* 61–77.

Cromdal, J. (1999). Childhood bilingualism and metalinguistic skills: Analysis and control in young Swedish-English bilinguals. *Applied Psycholinguistics, 20,* 1–20.

Crowder, R. G. (1993). Short-term memory: Where do we stand? *Memory & Cognition, 21,* 142–155.

Crowder, R. G., & Wagner, R. K. (1992). *The psychology of reading: An introduction* (2nd ed.). New York: Oxford University Press.

Crozet, J., & Claire, T. (1998). Extending the concept of stereotype threat to social class: The intellectual underperformance of students from low socioeconomic backgrounds. *Personality and Social Psychology Bulletin, 24,* 588–594.

Csikszentmihalyi, M. (1996). *Creativity: Flow and the psychology of discovery and invention.* New York: HarperCollins.

Cuddy, A. J. C., & Fiske, S. T. (2002). Doddering but dear: Process, content, and function in stereotyping of older persons. In T. D. Nelson (Ed.), *Ageism: Stereotyping and prejudice against older persons* (pp. 3–26). Cambridge, MA: MIT Press.

Cull, W. L., & Zechmeister, E. B. (1994). The learning ability paradox in adult metamemory research: Where are the metamemory differences between good and poor learners? *Memory & Cognition, 22,* 249–257.

Cummins, D. D., Lubart, T., Alksnis, O., & Rist, R. (1991). Conditional reasoning and causation. *Memory & Cognition, 19,* 274–282.

Custers, E. J. F. M., Boshuizen, H. P. A., & Schmidt, H. G. (1996). The influence of medical expertise, case typicality, and illness script on case processing and disease probability estimates. *Memory & Cognition, 24,* 384–399.

Cutler, B. L., & Penrod, S. D. (1995). *Mistaken identification: The eyewitness, psychology, and the law.* New York: Cambridge University Press.

Cutting, J. C., & Ferreira, V. S. (1999). Semantic and phonological information flow in the production lexicon. *Journal of Experimental Psychology: Learning, Memory, and Cognition, 25,* 318–344.

Daiute, C. (2000). Writing and communication technologies. In R. Indrisano & J. R. Squire (Eds.), *Perspectives on writing* (pp. 251–276). Newark, DE: International Reading Association.

Damian, M. F., & Martin, R. C. (1999). Semantic and phonological codes interact in a single word production. *Journal of Experimental Psychology: Learning, Memory, and Cognition, 25,* 345–361.

Daneman, M., & Green, I. (1986). Individual differences in comprehending and producing words in context. *Journal of Memory and Language, 25,* 1–18.

Daneman, M., & Hannon, B. (2001). Using working memory theory to investigate the construct validity of multiple-choice reading comprehension tests such as the SAT. *Journal of Experimental Psychology: General, 130,* 208–223.

Daneman, M., & Stainton, M. (1993). The generation effect in reading and proofreading. *Reading and Writing: An Interdisciplinary Journal, 5,* 297–313.

D'Argembeau, A., Comblain, C., & Van Der Linden, M. (2003). Phenomenal characteristics of autobiographical memories for positive, negative, and neutral events. *Applied Cognitive Psychology, 17,* 281–294.

Darwin, C. J., Turvey, M. T., & Crowder, R. G. (1972). An auditory analogue of the Sperling partial report procedure: Evidence for brief auditory storage. *Cognitive Psychology, 3,* 255–267.

Davidson, D. (1994). Recognition and recall of irrelevant and interruptive atypical actions in script-based stories. *Journal of Memory and Language, 33,* 757–775.

Davidson, D. (1995). The representativeness heuristic and the conjunction fallacy effect in children's decision making. *Merrill-Palmer Quarterly, 41,* 328–346.

Davidson, J. E. (1995). The suddenness of insight. In R. J. Sternberg & J. E. Davidson (Eds.), *The nature of insight* (pp. 125–155). Cambridge, MA: MIT Press.

Davidson, J. E., Deuser, R., & Sternberg, R. J. (1994). The role of metacognition in problem solving. In J. Metcalfe & A. P. Shimamura (Eds.), *Metacognition: Knowing about knowing* (pp. 207–226). Cambridge, MA: MIT Press.

Davidson, J. E., & Sternberg, R. J. (1998). Smart problem solving: How metacognition helps. In D. J. Hacker, J. Dunlosky, & A. C. Graesser (Eds.), *Metacognition in educational theory and practice* (pp. 47–65). Mahwah, NJ: Erlbaum.

Davies, M. (1999). Consciousness. In R. A. Wilson & F. C. Keil (Eds.), *The MIT encyclopedia of the cognitive sciences* (pp. 190–193). Cambridge, MA: MIT Press.

Davis, M., & Hult, R. E. (1997). Effects of writing summaries as a generative learning activity during note taking. *Teaching of Psychology, 24*, 47–49.

Davis, M. H., Marslen-Wilson, W. D., & Gaskell, M. G. (2002). Leading up the lexical garden path: Segmentation and ambiguity in spoken word recognition. *Journal of Experimental Psychology: Human Perception and Performance, 28*, 218–244.

Dawes, R. M. (1998). Behavioral decision making and judgment. In D. T. Gilbert, S. T. Fiske, & G. Lindzey (Eds.), *The handbook of social psychology* (4th ed., Vol. 1, pp. 497–548). Boston: McGraw-Hill.

Dawson, M. R. W. (1998). *Understanding cognitive science*. Malden, MA: Blackwell.

DeCasper, A. J., & Spence, M. J. (1986). Prenatal maternal speech influences newborn's perception of speech sounds. *Infant Behavior and Development, 9*, 133–150.

Dehaene, S. (Ed.). (2001). *The cognitive neuroscience of consciousness*. Cambridge, MA: MIT Press.

Dehaene, S., & Naccache, L. (2001). Towards a cognitive neuroscience of consciousness: Basic evidence and a workspace framework. In S. Dehaene (Ed.), *The cognitive neuroscience of consciousness* (pp. 1–37). Cambridge, MA: MIT Press.

DeHart, G. B. (1989). Personal communication.

DeHart, G. B., Sroufe, L. A., & Cooper, R. G. (2004). *Child development: Its nature and course* (5th ed.). New York: McGraw Hill.

Dehn, D. M., & Erdfelder, E. (1998). What kind of bias is hindsight bias? *Psychological Research, 61*, 735–746.

De Jong, G. (1982). Skimming stories in real time: An experiment in integrated understanding. In W. Lehnert & M. H. Ringle (Eds.), *Natural language processing*. Hillsdale, NJ: Erlbaum.

de Jong, P. F., & van der Leij, A. (1999). Specific contributions of phonological abilities to early reading acquisition: Results from a Dutch latent variable longitudinal study. *Journal of Educational Psychology, 91*, 450–476.

Dell, G. S. (1986). A spreading-activation theory of retrieval in sentence production. *Psychological Review, 93*, 283–321.

Dell, G. S. (1995). Speaking and misspeaking. In L. R. Gleitman & M. Liberman (Eds.), *Language* (pp. 183–208). Cambridge, MA: MIT Press.

Dell, G. S., Burger, L. K., & Svec, W. R. (1997). Language production and serial order: A functional analysis and a model. *Psychological Review, 104*, 123–147.

Dell, G. S., Reed, K. D., Adams, D. R., & Meyer, A. S. (2000). Speech errors, phonotactic constraints, and implicit learning: A study of the role of experience in language production. *Journal of Experimental Psychology: Learning, Memory, and Cognition, 26*, 1355–1367.

Dell, G. S., et al. (1997). Lexical access in aphasic and nonaphasic speakers. *Psychological Review, 104*, 801–838.

Dempster, F. N. (1996). Distributing and managing the conditions of encoding and practice. In E. L. Bjork & R. A. Bjork (Eds.), *Memory* (pp. 318–344). San Diego: Academic Press.

Denis, M., & Kosslyn, S. M. (1999a). Does the window *really* need to be washed? More on the mental scanning paradigm. *Cahiers de Psychologie Cognitive, 18*, 593–616.

Denis, M., & Kosslyn, S. M. (1999b). Scanning visual mental images: A window on the mind. *Cahiers de Psychologie Cognitive, 18*, 409–465.

Denis, M., Pazzaglia, F., Cornoldi, C., & Bertolo, L. (1999). Spatial discourse and navigation: An analysis of route directions in the city of Venice. *Applied Cognitive Psychology, 13*, 145–174.

DeSchepper, B., & Treisman, A. (1996). Visual memory for novel shapes: Implicit coding without attention. *Journal of Experimental Psychology: Learning, Memory, and Cognition, 22*, 27–47.

D'Esposito, M., Zarahn, E., & Aguirre, G. K. (1999). Event-related functional MRI: Implications for cognitive psychology. *Psychological Bulletin, 125*, 155–164.

Deubel, H., O'Regan, J. K., & Radach, R. (2000). Attention, information processing, and eye movement control. In A. Kennedy, R. Radach, D. Heller, & J. Pyne (Eds.), *Reading as a perceptual process* (pp. 355–374). Amsterdam: Elsevier.

de Villiers, J. G., & de Villiers, P. A. (1999). Language development. In M. H. Bornstein & M. E. Lamb (Eds.), *Developmental psychology: An advanced textbook* (4th ed., pp. 313–373). Mahwah, NJ: Erlbaum.

Devlin, A. S. (2001). *Mind and maze: Spatial cognition and environmental behavior*. Westport, CT: Praeger.

deWinstanley, P. A., & Bjork, R. A. (2002). Successful lecturing: Presenting information in ways that engage effective processing. In D. F. Halpern & M. D.

Hakel (Eds.), *Applying the science of learning to university teaching and beyond* (pp. 19–31). San Francisco: Jossey-Bass.

Dias, P., Freedman, A., Medway, P., & Paré, A. (1999). *Worlds apart: Acting and writing in academic and workplace contexts*. Mahwah, NJ: Erlbaum.

Diaz, R. M. (1985). Bilingual cognitive development: Addressing three gaps in current research. *Child Development, 56*, 1376–1388.

Dick, F., et al. (2001). Language deficits, localization, and grammar: Evidence for a distributive model of language breakdown in aphasic patients and neurologically intact individuals. *Psychological Review, 108*, 759–788.

Dickinson, S. J. (1999). Object representation and recognition. In E. Lepore & Z. Pylyshyn (Eds.), *What is cognitive science?* (pp. 172–207). Malden, MA: Blackwell.

Diwadkar, V. A., Carpenter, P. A., & Just, M. A. (2000). Collaborative activity between parietal and dorsolateral prefrontal cortex in dynamic spatial working memory revealed by fMRI. *NeuroImage, 12*, 85–99.

Dixon, R. A., & Cohen, A.-L. (2003). Cognitive development in adulthood. In R. M. Lerner, M. A. Easterbrooks, & Mistry, J. (Eds.), *Handbook of psychology* (Vol. 6, pp. 443–461). Hoboken, NJ: Wiley.

Dobbins, I. G., Kroll, N. E. A., & Liu, Q. (1998). Confidence-accuracy inversions in scene recognition: A remember-know analysis. *Journal of Experimental Psychology: Learning, Memory, and Cognition, 24*, 1306–1315.

Dodd, B., & Campbell, R. (1986). *Hearing by eye: The psychology of lip reading*. London: Erlbaum.

Donovan, J. L., & Radosevich, D. J. (1999). A meta-analytic review of the distribution of practice effect: Now you see it, now you don't. *Journal of Applied Psychology, 84*, 795–805.

Döpke, S. (Ed.). (2001). *Cross-linguistic structures in simultaneous bilingualism*. New York: John Benjamins.

Dorado, J. S. (1999). Remembering incest: The complexities of this process and implications for civil statutes of limitations. In L. M. Williams & V. L. Banyard (Eds.), *Trauma & memory* (pp. 93–111). Thousand Oaks, CA: Sage.

Dougherty, M. R. P. (2001). Integration of the ecological and error models of overconfidence using a multiple-trace memory model. *Journal of Experimental Psychology: General, 130*, 579–599.

Dougherty, M. R. P., Gettys, C. F., & Ogden, E. E. (1999). MINERVA-DM: A memory processes model for judgments of likelihood. *Psychological Review, 106*, 180–209.

Downing, P. E., & Treisman, A. M. (1997). The line-motion illusion: Attention or impletion? *Journal of Experimental Psychology: Human Perception and Performance, 23*, 768–779.

Dromi, E. (1999). Early lexical development. In M. Barrett (Ed.), *The development of language* (pp. 99–131). Hove, England: Psychology Press.

Dronkers, N. F. (1999). Language, neural basis of. In R. A. Wilson & F. C. Keil (Eds.), *The MIT encyclopedia of the cognitive sciences* (pp. 448–451). Cambridge, MA: MIT Press.

Dror, I. E., & Kosslyn, S. M. (1994). Mental imagery and aging. *Psychology and Aging, 9*, 90–102.

Dunbar, K. (1998). Problem solving. In W. Bechtel & G. Graham (Eds.), *A companion to cognitive science* (pp. 289–298). Malden, MA: Blackwell.

Dunbar, K. (2001). The analogical paradox: Why analogy is so easy in naturalistic settings, yet so difficult in the psychological laboratory. In D. Gentner, K. J. Holyoak, & B. N. Kokinov (Eds.), *The analogical mind: Perspectives from cognitive science* (pp. 313–334). Cambridge, MA: MIT Press.

Duncan, J. (1993). Coordination of what and where in visual attention. *Perception, 22*, 1261–1270.

Duncan, J. (1999). Attention. In R. A. Wilson & F. C. Keil (Eds.), *The MIT encyclopedia of the cognitive sciences* (pp. 39–41). Cambridge, MA: MIT Press.

Duncker, K. (1945). On problem solving. *Psychological Monographs, 58* (Whole No. 270).

Dunlosky, J., & Hertzog, C. (1997). Older and younger adults use a functionally identical algorithm to select items for restudy during multitrial learning. *Journal of Gerontology: Psychological Sciences, 52B*, P178–P186.

Dunlosky, J., & Hertzog, C. (1998a). Aging and deficits in associative memory: What is the role of strategy production? *Psychology and Aging, 13*, 597–607.

Dunlosky, J., & Hertzog, C. (1998b). Training programs to improve learning in later adulthood: Helping older adults educate themselves. In D. J. Hacker, J. Dunlosky, & A. C. Graesser (Eds.), *Metacognition in educational theory and practice* (pp. 249–273). Mahwah, NJ: Erlbaum.

Dunlosky, J., & Nelson, T. O. (1994). Does the sensitivity of judgments of learning (JOLs) to the effects of various study activities depend on when the JOLs occur? *Journal of Memory and Language, 33,* 545–565.

Dunlosky, J., Rawson, K. A., & McDonald, S. L. (2002). Influence of practice tests on the accuracy of predicting memory performance for paired associates, sentences, and text material. In T. J. Perfect & B. L. Schwartz (Eds.), *Applied metacognition* (pp. 68–92). Cambridge, England: Cambridge University Press.

Dunn, J., & Kendrick, C. (1982). The speech of two- and three-year-olds to infant siblings: "Baby talk" and the context of communication. *Journal of Child Language, 9,* 579–595.

Dunning, D., Johnson, K., Ehrlinger, J., & Kruger, J. (2003). Why people fail to recognize their own incompetence. *Current Directions in Psychological Science, 12,* 83–87.

Dunning, D., & Sherman, D. A. (1997). Stereotypes and tacit inference. *Journal of Personality and Social Psychology, 73,* 459–471.

D'Ydewalle, G., Luwel, K., & Brunfaut, E. (1999). The importance of on-going concurrent activities as a function of age in time- and event-based prospective memory. *European Journal of Cogntiive Psychology, 11,* 219–237.

Eacott, M. J. (1999). Memory for the events of early childhood. *Current Directions in Psychological Science, 8,* 46–49.

Eacott, M. J., & Crawley, R. A. (1998). The offset of childhood amnesia: Memory for events that occurred before age 3. *Journal of Experimental Psychology: General, 127,* 22–33.

Ebbinghaus, H. (1885/1913). *Memory: A contribution to experimental psychology.* New York: Columbia Teacher's College.

Eccles, J. S., Wigfield, A., & Schiefele, U. (1998). Motivation to succeed. In W. Damon (Series Ed.) & N. Eisenberg (Vol. Ed.), *Handbook of child psychology: Vol. 4. Social, emotional, and personality development* (pp. 1017–1095). New York: Wiley.

Edwards, D. (1997). *Discourse and cognition.* London: Sage.

Egeth, H. E., & Yantis, S. (1997). Visual attention: Control, representation, and time course. *Annual Review of Psychology, 48,* 269–297.

Ehrlich, M. (1998). Metacognitive monitoring in the processing of anaphoric devices in skilled and less skilled comprehenders. In C. Cornoldi & J. Oakhill (Eds.), *Reading comprehension difficulties: Processes and interventions* (pp. 221–249). Mahwah, NJ: Erlbaum.

Eich, E. (1995a). Mood as a mediator of place dependent memory. *Journal of Experimental Psychology: General, 124,* 293–308.

Eichenbaum, H. (1997). Declarative memory: Insights from cognitive neurobiology. *Annual Review of Psychology, 48,* 547–572.

Eimas, P. D., Siqueland, E. R., Jusczyk, P., & Vigorito, J. (1971). Speech perception in infants. *Science, 171,* 303–306.

Einhorn, H. J., & Hogarth, R. M. (1981). Behavioral decision theory: processes of judgment and choice. *Annual Review of Psychology, 32,* 53–88.

Einstein, G. O., & McDaniel, M. A. (1996). Retrieval processes in prospective memory: Theoretical approaches and some new empirical findings. In M. Brandimonte, G. O. Einstein, & M. A. McDaniel (Eds.), *Prospective memory: Theory and applications* (pp. 115–141). Mahwah, NJ: Erlbaum.

Eisen, M. L., Quas, J. A., & Goodman, G. S. (Eds.). (2002). *Memory and suggestibility in the forensic interview.* Mahwah, NJ: Erlbaum.

Eisenberger, R., & Rhoades, L. (2001). Incremental effects of rewards on creativity. *Journal of Personality and Social Psychology, 81,* 728–741.

Eliott, A. J., & Mapes, R. R. (2002). Enhancing the yield. [Review of the book *Intrinsic and extrinsic motivation: The search for optimal motivation and performance*]. *Contemporary Psychology, 47,* 200–202.

Elliott, E. M., & Cowan, N. (2001). Habituation to auditory distractors in a cross-modal, color-word interference task. *Journal of Experimental Psychology: Learning, Memory, and Cognition, 27,* 654–667.

Ellis, A., & Beattie, G. (1986). *The psychology of language and communication.* New York: Guilford.

Ellis, H. C., & Moore, B. A. (1999). Mood and memory. In T. Dalgleish & M. Power (Eds.), *Handbook of cognition and emotion* (pp. 193–210). Chichester, England: Wiley.

Ellis, H. C., et al. (1997). Emotion, motivation, and text comprehension: The detection of contradictions in passages. *Journal of Experimental Psychology: General, 126,* 131–146.

Emmorey, K., Klima, E., & Hickok, G. (1998). Mental rotation within linguistic and non-linguistic domains in users of American Sign Language. *Cognition, 68,* 221–246.

Engelkamp, J. (1998). *Memory for actions*. Hove, England: Psychology Press.

Engle, R. W. (1996). Working memory and retrieval: An inhibition-resource approach. In J. T. E. Richardson et al. (Eds.), *Working memory and human cognition* (pp. 89–119). New York: Oxford University Press.

Engle, R. W. (2001). What is working memory capacity? In H. L. Roediger, III, J. S. Nairne, I. Neath, & A. M. Surprenant (Eds.), *The nature of remembering* (pp. 297–314). Washington, DC: American Psychological Association.

Engle, R. W. (2002). Working memory capacity as executive attention. *Current Directions in Psychological Science, 11*, 19–23.

Engle, R. W., & Conway, A. R. A. (1998). Working memory and comprehension. In R. H. Logie & K. J. Gilhooly (Eds.), *Working memory and thinking* (pp. 67–91). Hove, England: Psychology Press.

Engle, R. W., & Kane, M. J. (2005). Executive attention, working memory capacity, and a two-factor theory of cognitive control. *Psychology of Learning and Motivation, 44*.

Engle, R. W., & Oransky, N. (1999). Multi-store versus dynamic models of temporary storage in memory. In R. J. Sternberg (Ed.), *The nature of cognition* (pp. 515–555). Cambridge, MA: MIT Press.

Englich, B., & Mussweiler, T. (2001). Sentencing under uncertainty: Anchoring effects in the courtroom. *Journal of Applied Social Psychology, 31*, 1535–1551.

Epley, N., & Gilovich, T. (2001). Putting adjustment back into the anchoring and adjustment heuristic: Differential processing of self-generated and experimenter-provided anchors. *Psychological Science, 12*, 391–396.

Erdfelder, E., & Bredenkamp, J. (1998). Recognition of script-typical versus script-atypical information: Effects of cognitive elaboration. *Memory & Cognition, 26*, 922–938.

Erickson, M. A., & Kruschke, J. K. (1998). Rules and exemplars in category learning. *Journal of Experimental Psychology: General, 127*, 107–140.

Erickson, M. A., & Kruschke, J. K. (2002). Rule-based extrapolation in perceptual categorization. *Psychonomic Bulletin & Review, 9*, 160–168.

Ericsson, K. A. (1985). Memory skill. *Canadian Journal of Psychology, 39*, 188–231.

Ericsson, K. A. (1999). Expertise. In R. A. Wilson & F. C. Keil (Eds.), *The MIT encyclopedia of the cognitive sciences* (pp. 298–300). Cambridge, MA: MIT Press.

Ericsson, K. A., & Charness, N. (1997). Cognitive and developmental factors in expert performance. In P. J. Feltovich, K. M. Ford, & R. R. Hoffman (Eds.), *Expertise in context: Human and machine* (pp. 3–41). Cambridge, MA: MIT Press.

Ericsson, K. A., & Delaney, P. F. (1998). Working memory and expert performance. In R. H. Logie & K. J. Gilhooly (Eds.), *Working memory and thinking* (pp. 93–114). Hove, England: Psychology Press.

Ericsson, K. A., & Delaney, P. F. (1999). Long-term working memory as an alternative to capacity models of working memory in everyday skilled performance. In A. Miyake & P. Shah (Eds.), *Models of working memory: Mechanisms of active maintenance and executive control* (pp. 257–297). Cambridge, England: Cambridge University Press.

Ericsson, K. A., & Kintsch, W. (1995). Long-term working memory. *Psychological Review, 102*, 211–245.

Ericsson, K. A., & Lehmann, A. C. (1996). Expert and exceptional performance: Evidence of maximal adaptation to task constraints. *Annual Review of Psychology, 47*, 273–305.

Ericsson, K. A., & Pennington, N. (1993). The structure of memory performance in experts: Implications for memory in everyday life. In G. M. Davies & R. H. Logie (Eds.), *Memory in everyday life* (pp. 241–272). Amsterdam: Elsevier.

Evans, J. St. B. T. (2000). What could and could not be a strategy in reasoning. In W. Schaeken, G. De-Vooght, A. Vandierendonck, & G. d'Ydewalle (Eds.), *Deductive reasoning and strategies* (pp. 1–22). Mahwah, NJ: Erlbaum.

Evans, J. St. B. T. (2002). Logic and human reasoning: An assessment of the deduction paradigm. *Psychological Bulletin, 128*, 978–996.

Evans, J. St. B. T. (2004), Biases in deductive reasoning. In R. Pohl (Ed.), *Cognitive illusions: Handbook on fallacies and biases in thinking, judgment, and memory*. Hove, England: Psychology Press.

Evans, J. St. B. T., & Over, D. E. (1996). *Rationality and reasoning*. Hove, England: Psychology Press.

Evans, J. St. B. T., Over, D. E., & Manktelow, K. I. (1993). Reasoning, decision making and rationality. *Cognition, 49*, 165–187.

Eysenck, M. W. (1990). Introduction. In M. W. Eysenck (Ed.), *Cognitive psychology: An international review* (pp. 1–7). Chichester, England: Wiley.

Eysenck, M. W., & Keane, M. T. (1990). *Cognitive psychology: A student's handbook*. London: Erlbaum.

Fabbro, F. (1999). *The neurolinguistics of bilingualism.* East Sussex, England: Psychology Press.

Fabiani, M., & Wee, E. (2001). Age-related changes in working memory and frontal lobe function: A review. In C. A. Nelson & M. Luciana (Eds.), *Handbook of developmental cognitive neuroscience* (pp. 473–488). Cambridge, MA: MIT Press.

Faigley, L., & Miller, T. P. (1982). What we learn from writing on the job. *College English, 44,* 557–559.

Fan, J., et al. (2002). Testing the efficiency and indepenence of attentional networks. *Journal of Cognitive Neuroscience, 14,* 340–347.

Farah, M. J. (2000a). *The cognitive neuroscience of vision.* Malden, MA: Blackwell.

Farah, M. J. (2000b). The neural bases of mental imagery. In M. S. Gazzaniga (Ed.), *The new cognitive neurosciences* (2nd ed., pp. 961–974). Cambridge, MA: MIT Press.

Farah, M. J. (2001). Consciousness. In B. Rapp (Ed.), *The handbook of cognitive neuropsychology* (pp. 159–182). Philadelphia: Psychology Press.

Farah, M. J. (2002). Emerging ethical issues in neuroscience. *Nature Neuroscience, 5,* 1123.

Farah, M. J., Rabinowitz, C., Quinn, G. E., & Liu, G. T. (2000). Early commitment of neural substates for face recognition. *Cognitive Neuropsychology, 17,* 117–123.

Farah, M. J., Wilson, K. D., Drain, M., & Tanaka, J. N. (1998). What is "special" about face perception? *Psychological Review, 105,* 482–498.

Favreau, O. E. (1993). Do the Ns justify the means? Null hypothesis testing applied to sex and other differences. *Canadian Psychology/Psychologie Canadienne, 34,* 64–78.

Feinberg, T. E., & Farah, M. J. (2000). A historical perspective on cognitive neuroscience. In M. J. Farah & T. E. Feinberg (Eds.), *Patient-based approaches to cognitive neuroscience* (pp. 3–20). Cambridge, MA: MIT Press.

Feldman, D. H., Csikszentmihalyi, M., & Gardner, H. (1994). *Changing the world: A framework for the study of creativity.* Westport, CT: Praeger.

Fenson, L., et al. (1991). *The MacArthur Communicative Development Inventories: Technical manual.* San Diego: San Diego State University.

Ferber, R. (1991). Slip of the tongue or slip of the ear? On the perception and transcription of naturalistic slips of the tongue. *Journal of Psycholinguistic Research, 20,* 105–122.

Ferguson, E. L., & Hegarty, M. (1994). Properties of cognitive maps constructed from texts. *Memory & Cognition, 22,* 455–473.

Ferguson-Hessler, M. G. M., & De Jong, T. (1987). On the quality of knowledge in the field of electricity and magnetism. *American Journal of Physics, 55,* 492–497.

Fernald, A., et al. (1998). Rapid gains in speed of verbal processing by infants in the 2nd year. *Psychological Science, 9,* 228–231.

Fernandez-Duque, D., & Johnson, M. L. (2002). Cause and effect theories of attention: The role of conceptual metaphors. *Review of General Psychology, 6,* 153–165.

Ferreira, F., Bailey, G. D., & Ferraro, V. (2002). Good-enough representation in language comprehension. *Current Directions in Psychological Science, 11,* 11–15.

Fiedler, K. (2001). Affective states trigger processes of assimilation and accommodation. In L. L. Martin & G. L. Clore (Eds.), *Theories of mood and cognition* (pp. 85–98). Mahwah, NJ: Erlbaum.

Fiedler, K. (2004). Illusory correlation. In R. Pohl (Ed.), *Cognitive illusions: Handbook on fallacies and biases in thinking, judgment, and memory.* Hove, England: Psychology Press.

Finch, G. (2003). *Word of mouth: A new introduction to language and communication.* New York: Palgrave.

Findlay, J. M., & Gilchrist, I. D. (2001). Visual attention: The active vision perspective. In M. Jenkin & L. Harris (Eds.), *Vision and attention* (pp. 83–103). New York: Springer-Verlag.

Findlay, J. M., & Walker, R. (1999). A model of saccade generation based on parallel processing and competitive inhibition. *Behavioral and Brain Sciences, 22,* 661–721.

Finke, R. A., Pinker, S., & Farah, M. J. (1989). Reinterpreting visual patterns in mental imagery. *Cognitive Science, 13,* 51–78.

Finke, R. A., & Schmidt, M. J. (1978). The quantitative measure of pattern representation in images using orientation-specific color after-effects. *Perception & Psychophysics, 23,* 515–520.

Fiore, S. M., & Schooler, J. W. (1998). Right hemisphere contributions to creative problem solving: Converging evidence for divergent thinking. In M. Beeman & C. Chiarello (Eds.), *Right hemisphere language comprehension: Perspectives from cognitive neuroscience* (pp. 349–371). Mahwah, NJ: Erlbaum.

Fischhoff, B. (1982). Debiasing. In D. Kahneman, P. Slovic, & A. Tversky (Eds.), *Judgment under uncertainty: Heuristics and biases* (pp. 422–444). New York: Cambridge University Press.

Fischhoff, B. (1999). Judgment heuristics. In R. A. Wilson & F. C. Keil (Eds.), *The MIT encyclopedia of the cognitive sciences* (pp. 423–425). Cambridge, MA: MIT Press.

Fischler, I. (1998). Attention and language. In R. Parasuraman (Ed.), *The attentive brain* (pp. 381–399). Cambridge, MA: MIT Press.

Flavell, J. H. (1971). First discussant's comments. What is memory development the development of? *Human Development, 14,* 272–278.

Flavell, J. H. (1979). Metacognition and cognitive monitoring. *American Psychologist, 34,* 906–911.

Flavell, J. H., Beach, D. R., & Chinsky, J. M. (1966). Spontaneous verbal rehearsal in a memory task as a function of age. *Child Development, 37,* 283–299.

Flavell, J. H., Green, F. L., & Flavell, E. R. (2000). Development of children's awareness of their own thoughts. *Journal of Cognition and Development, 1,* 97–112.

Flavell, J. H., Green, F. L., Flavell, E. R., & Grossman, J. B. (1997). The development of children's knowledge about inner speech. *Child Development, 68,* 39–47.

Flavell, J. H., Miller, P. H., & Miller, S. A. (1993). *Cognitive development* (3rd ed.). Englewood Cliffs, NJ: Prentice Hall.

Flavell, J. H., Miller, P. H., & Miller, S. A. (2002). *Cognitive development* (4th ed.). Upper Saddle River, NJ: Prentice-Hall.

Flege, J. E., Yeni-Komshian, G. H., & Liu, S. (1999). Age constraints on second-language acquisition. *Journal of Memory and Language, 41,* 78–104.

Flores d'Arcais, G. B. (1988). Language perception. In F. J. Newmeyer (Ed.), *Linguistics: The Cambridge survey* (Vol. 3, pp. 97–123). Cambridge, England: Cambridge University Press.

Flower, L. S., & Hayes, J. R. (1980). The dynamics of composing: Making plans and juggling constraints. In L. W. Gregg & E. R. Steinberg (Eds.), *Cognitive processes in writing* (pp. 31–50). Hillsdale, NJ: Erlbaum.

Foley, M. A. (1998). What the study of source monitoring suggests about the role of imagery in children's thinking and remembering. In J. Rideaud &

Y. Courbois (Eds.), *Image mentale et developpement* (pp. 37–56). Paris: Presses Universitaires de France.

Foley, M. A., Belch, C., Mann, R., & McLean, M. (1999). Self-referencing: How incessant the stream? *American Journal of Psychology, 112,* 73–96.

Foley, M. A., & Foley, H. J. (1998). A study of face identification: Are people looking beyond disguises? In M. J. Intons-Peterson & D. L. Best (Eds.), *Memory distortions and their prevention* (pp. 29–47). Mahwah, NJ: Erlbaum.

Foley, M. A., Foley, H. J., & Korenman, L. M. (2002). Adapting a memory framework (source monitoring) to the study of closure processes. *Memory & Cognition, 30,* 412–422.

Foley, M. A., & Ratner, H. H. (1998). Distinguishing between memories for thoughts and deeds: The role of prospective processing in children's source monitoring. *British Journal of Developmental Psychology, 16,* 465–484.

Foley, M. A., Ratner, H. H., & House, A. T. (2002). Anticipation and source-monitoring errors: Children's memory for collaborative activities. *Journal of Cognition and Development, 3,* 385–414.

Foley, M. A., Wilder, A., McCall, R., & Van Vorst, R. (1993). The consequences for recall of children's ability to generate interactive imagery in the absence of external supports. *Journal of Experimental Child Psychology, 56,* 173–200.

Foltz, P. W. (2003). Quantitative cognitive models of text and discourse processing. In A. C. Graesser, M. A. Gernsbacher, & S. R. Goldman (Eds.), *Handbook of discourse processes* (pp. 487–523). Mahwah, NJ: Erlbaum.

Fong, G. T., Krantz, D. H., & Nisbett, R. E. (1986). The effects of statistical training on thinking about everyday problems. *Cognitive Psychology, 18,* 253–292.

Forgas, J. P. (2001). The Affect Infusion Model (AIM): An integrative theory of mood effects on cognition and judgment. In L. L. Martin & G. L. Clore (Eds.), *Theories of mood and cognition* (pp. 99–134). Mahwah, NJ: Erlbaum.

Forster, K. I. (1981). Priming and the effects of sentence and lexical contexts on naming time: Evidence for autonomous lexical processing. *Quarterly Journal of Experimental Psychology, 33A,* 465–495.

Forward, S., & Buck, C. (1988). *Betrayal of innocence: Incest and its devastation.* New York: Penguin.

Fowler, C. A. (2003). Speech production and perception. In A. F. Healy & R. W. Proctor (Eds.), *Handbook of psychology* (Vol. 4, pp. 237–266). Hoboken, NJ: Wiley.

Fox, J. C., & Farmer, R. (2002). A behavioral approach to political advertising research. In R. Gowda & J. C. Fox (Eds.), *Judgments, decisions, and public policy* (pp. 199–217). New York: Cambridge University Press.

Fox Tree, J. E. (2000). Coordinating spontaneous talk. In L. Wheeldon (Ed.), *Aspects of language production* (pp. 375–406). Philadelphia: Psychology Press.

Foygel, D., & Dell, G. S. (2000). Models of impaired lexical access in speech production. *Journal of Memory and Language, 43*, 182–216.

Francis, W. S. (1999). Cognitive integration of language and memory in bilinguals: Semantic representation. *Psychological Bulletin, 125*, 193–222.

Franklin, N., & Tversky, B. (1990). Searching imagined environments. *Journal of Experimental Psychology: General, 119*, 63–76.

Franklin, S. (1995). *Artificial minds.* Cambridge, MA: MIT Press.

Freyd, J. J. (1996). *Betrayal trauma: The logic of forgetting childhood abuse.* Cambridge, MA: Harvard University Press.

Freyd, J. J. (1998). Science in the memory debate. *Ethics & Behavior, 8*, 101–113.

Freyd, J. J., & DePrince, A. A. (Eds.). (2001). *Trauma and cognitive science.* New York: Haworth.

Freyd, J. J., & Quina, K. (2000). Feminist ethics in the practice of science: The contested memory controversy as an example. In M. M. Brabeck (Ed.), *Practicing feminist ethics in psychology* (pp. 101–123). Washington, DC: American Psychological Association.

Frick, R. W. (1988). Issues of representation and limited capacity in the auditory short-term store. *British Journal of Psychology, 79*, 213–240.

Frick, R. W. (1990). The visual suffix effect in tests of the visual short-term store. *Bulletin of the Psychonomic Society, 28*, 101–104.

Frick-Horbury, D., & Guttentag, R. E. (1998). The effects of restricting hand gesture production on lexical retrieval and free recall. *American Journal of Psychology, 111*, 43–62.

Friedman, A., Brown, N. R., & McGaffey, A. P. (2002). A basis for bias in geographical judgments. *Psychonomic Bulletin & Review, 9*, 151–159.

Friedman, W. J., & deWinstanley, P. A. (1998). Changes in the subjective properties of autobiographical memories with the passage of time. *Memory, 6*, 367–381.

Frisch, D. (1993). Reasons for framing effects. *Organizational Behavior and Human Decision Processes, 54*, 399–429.

Frishman, L. J. (2001). Basic visual processes. In E. B. Goldstein (Ed.), *Blackwell handbook of perception* (pp. 53–91). Malden, MA: Blackwell.

Fromkin, V. A., & Bernstein Ratner, N. (1998). Speech production. In J. Berko-Gleason & N. Bernstein Ratner (Eds.), *Psycholinguistics* (2nd ed., 309–346). Fort Worth, TX: Harcourt Brace.

Furnham, A., & Bradley, A. (1997). Music while you work: The differential distraction of background music on the cognitive test performance of introverts and extraverts. *Applied Cognitive Psychology, 11*, 445–455.

Galambos, S. J., & Goldin-Meadow, S. (1990). The effects of learning two languages on levels of metalinguistic awareness. *Cognition, 34*, 1–56.

Galambos, S. J., & Hakuta, K. (1988). Subject-specific and task-specific characteristics of metalinguistic awareness in bilingual children. *Applied Psycholinguistics, 9*, 141–162.

Ganellen, R. J., & Carver, C. S. (1985). Why does self-reference promote incidental encoding? *Journal of Experimental Social Psychology, 21*, 284–300.

García, G. E., Jiménez, R. T., & Pearson, D. P. (1998). Metacognition, childhood bilingualism, and reading. In D. J. Hacker, J. Dunlosky, & A. C. Graesser (Eds.), *Metacognition in education theory and practice* (pp. 193–219). Mahwah, NJ: Erlbaum.

García Madruga, J. A., Moreno, S., Carriedo, N., & Gutiérrez, F. (2000). Task, premise order, and strategies in Rip's conjunction-disjunction and conditional problems. In W. Schaeken, G. DeVooght, A. Vandierendonck, & G. d'Ydewalle (Eds.), *Deductive reasoning and strategies* (pp. 49–71). Mahwah, NJ: Erlbaum.

Gardner, H. (1985). *The mind's new science: A history of the cognitive revolution.* New York: Basic Books.

Gardner, R. (2001). *When listeners talk: Response tokens and listener stance.* Philadelphia: John Benjamins.

Gardner, R. C., & Lambert, W. E. (1959). Motivational variables in second-language acquisition. *Canadian Journal of Psychology, 13,* 266–272.

Garnham, A., & Oakhill, J. (1994). *Thinking and reasoning.* Oxford, England: Blackwell.

Garrod, S. (1999). The challenge of dialogue for theories of language processing. In S. Garrod & M. J. Pickering (Eds.), *Language processing* (pp. 389–415). East Sussex, England: Psychology Press.

Gass, S. M., & Mackey, A. (2000). *Expanding the role of stimulated recall in second language research.* Mahwah, NJ: Erlbaum.

Gass, S. M., & Selinker, L. (2001). *Second language acquisition: An introductory course* (2nd ed.). Mahwah, NJ: Erlbaum.

Gathercole, S. E. (1997). Models of verbal short-term memory. In M. A. Conway (Ed.), *Cognitive models of memory* (pp. 13–45). Cambridge, MA: MIT Press.

Gathercole, S. E. (1998). The development of memory. *Journal of Child Psychology and Psychiatry, 39,* 3–27.

Gathercole, S. E., Adams, A., & Hitch, G. J. (1994). Do young children rehearse? An individual-differences analysis. *Memory & Cognition, 22,* 201–207.

Gathercole, S. E., & Baddeley, A. D. (1993). *Working memory and language.* Hove, England: Erlbaum.

Gauvain, M. (1998). Sociocultural and practical influences on spatial memory. In M. J. Intons-Peterson & D. L. Best (Eds.), *Memory distortions and their prevention* (pp. 89–111). Mahwah, NJ: Erlbaum.

Gauvain, M. (2001). *The social context of cognitive development.* New York: Guilford.

Gazzaniga, M. S., Ivry, R. B., & Mangun, G. R. (2002). *Cognitive neuroscience: The biology of the mind* (2nd ed.). New York: Norton.

Gebotys, R. J., & Claxton-Oldfield, S. P. (1989). Errors in the quantification of uncertainty: A product of heuristics or minimal probability knowledge base? *Applied Cognitive Psychology, 3,* 237–250.

Geiselman, R. E., & Glenny, J. (1977). Effects of imagining speakers' voices on the retention of words presented visually. *Memory & Cognition, 5,* 499–504.

Geisler, W. S., & Super, B. J. (2000). Perceptual organization of two-dimensional patterns. *Psychological Review, 107,* 677–708.

Gelman, R. (2002). Cognitive development, In H. Pashler (Ed.), *Stevens' handbook of experimental psychology* (Vol. 2, pp. 533–550). New York: Wiley.

Gelman, R., & Lucariello, J. (2002). Role of learning in cognitive development. In H. Pashler (Ed.), *Stevens' handbook of experimental psychology* (Vol. 3, pp. 395–443). New York: Wiley.

Genesee, F., & Gándara, P. (1999). Bilingual education programs: A cross-national perspective. *Journal of Social Issues, 55,* 665–685.

Genesee, F., Tucker, R., & Lambert, W. E. (1975). Communication skills of bilingual children. *Child Development, 46,* 1010–1014.

Gernsbacher, M. A., Hallada, B. M., & Robertson, R. R. W. (1998). *Scientific Studies of Reading, 2,* 271–300.

Gernsbacher, M. A., & Kaschak, M. P. (2003). Neuroimaging studies of language production and comprehension. *Annual Review of Psychology, 54,* 91–114.

Gernsbacher, M. A., Robertson, R. R. W., & Werner, N. K. (2001). The costs and benefits of meaning. In D. S. Gorfein (Ed.), *On the consequences of meaning selection: Perspectives on resolving lexical ambiguity* (pp. 119–137). Washington, DC: American Psychological Association.

Gerrig, R. J. (1998). *Experiencing narrative words.* Boulder, CO: Westview Press.

Gerrig, R. J., & Littman, M. L. (1990). Disambiguation by community membership. *Memory & Cognition, 18,* 331–338.

Gerrig, R. J., & McKoon, G. (1998). The readiness is all: The functionality of memory-based text processing. *Discourse Processes, 26,* 67–86.

Gerrig, R. J., & McKoon, G. (2001). Memory processes and experiential continuity. *Psychological Science, 12,* 81–85.

Gibbs, R. W., Jr. (1986). What makes some indirect speech acts conventional? *Journal of Memory and Language, 25,* 181–196.

Gibbs, R. W., Jr. (1998). The varieties of intentions in interpersonal communication. In S. R. Fussell & R. J. Kreuz (Eds.), *Social and cognitive approaches to interpersonal communications* (pp. 19–37). Mahwah, NJ: Erlbaum.

Gibbs, R. W., Jr. (2003). Nonliteral speech acts in text and discourse. In A. C. Graesser, M. A. Gernsbacher, & S. R. Goldman (Eds.), *Handbook of discourse processes* (pp. 357–393). Mahwah, NJ: Erlbaum.

Gibson, E. J. (1969). *Principles of perceptual learning and development.* New York: Prentice Hall.

Gibson, E. J. (1998). Linguistic complexity: Locality of syntactic dependencies. *Cognition, 68,* 1–76.

Gibson, E. J. (1999). The dependency locality theory: A distance-based theory of linguistic complexity. In Y. Miyashita, A. P. Marantz, & W. O'Neil (Eds.), *Image, language, brain.* Cambridge, MA: MIT Press.

Gibson, E. J., & Pearlmutter, N. J. (1998). Constraints on sentence comprehension. *Trends in Cognitive Sciences, 2,* 262–268.

Gigerenzer, G. (1998a). Ecological intelligence: An adaptation for frequencies. In D. D. Cummins & C. Allen (Eds.), *The evolution of mind* (pp. 9–29). New York: Oxford University Press.

Gigerenzer, G. (1998b). Psychological challenges for normative models. In D. M. Gabbay & P. Smets (Eds.), *Psychological challenges for normative models* (pp. 441–467). Dordrecht, Holland: Kluwer Academic Publishers.

Gigerenzer, G., Hoffrage, U., & Kleinbolting, H. (1991). Probabilistic mental models: A Brunswickian theory of confidence. *Psychological Review, 98,* 506–528.

Gigerenzer, G., & Hug, K. (1992). Domain-specific reasoning: Social contracts, cheating, and perspective change. *Cognition, 43,* 127–171.

Gigerenzer, G., & Selten, R. (Eds.). (2001). *Bounded rationality: The adaptive toolbox.* Cambridge, MA: MIT Press.

Gigerenzer, G., Todd, P. M., & the ABC Group. (1999). *Simple heuristics that make us smart.* New York: Oxford University Press.

Gilbert, S. (2002). *Improving memory: Understanding and preventing age-related memory loss.* Boston, MA: Harvard Health Publications.

Gilhooly, K. J. (1996). *Thinking: Directed, undirected and creative* (3rd ed.). London: Academic Press.

Gilhooly, K. J. (1998). Working memory, strategies, and reasoning tasks. In R. H. Logie & K. J. Gilhooly (Eds.), *Working memory and thinking* (pp. 7–22). East Sussex, England: Psychology Press.

Gillam, B., & Chan, W. M. (2002). Grouping has a negative effect on both subjective contours and perceived occlusion at T-junctions. *Psychological Science, 13,* 279–283.

Gilovich, T., Griffin, D., & Kahneman, D. (Eds.). (2002). *Heuristics and biases: The psychology of intuitive judgment.* New York: Cambridge University Press.

Glaser, R. (2001). Progress then and now. In S. M. Carver & D. Klahr (Eds.), *Cognition and instruction: Twenty-five years of progress* (pp. 493–507). Mahwah, NJ: Erlbaum.

Glaser, R., & Chi, M. T. H. (1988). Overview. In M. T. H. Chi, R. Glaser, & M. J. Farr (Eds.), *The nature of expertise* (pp. xv–xxxvi). Hillsdale, NJ: Erlbaum.

Glassner, B. (1999). *The culture of fear: Why Americans are afraid of the wrong things.* New York: Basic Books.

Gleitman, L., & Bloom, P. (1999). Language acquisition. In R. A. Wilson & F. C. Keil (Eds.), *The MIT encyclopedia of the cognitive sciences* (pp. 434–438). Cambridge, MA: MIT Press.

Gleitman, L., & Liberman, M. (1995). The cognitive science of language: Introduction. In l. Gleitman & M. Liberman (Eds.), *Language: An invitation to cognitive science* (2nd ed., pp. xix–xxxviii). Cambridge, MA: MIT Press.

Glenberg, A. M., Sanocki, T., Epstein, W., & Morris, C. (1987). Enhancing calibration of comprehension. *Journal of Experimental Psychology: General, 116,* 119–136.

Glicksohn, J. (1994). Rotation, orientation, and cognitive mapping. *American Journal of Psychology, 107,* 39–51.

Glisky, A. L. (1995). Computers in memory rehabilitation. In A. D. Baddeley, B. A. Wilson, & F. N. Watts (Eds.), *Handbook of memory disorders* (pp. 557–575). Chichester, England: Wiley.

Gluck, M. A., & Myers, C. E. (2001). *Gateway to memory: An introduction to neural network modeling of the hippocampus and learning.* Cambridge, MA: MIT Press.

Gobet, F., & Simon, H. A. (1996a). Recall of random and distorted chess positions: Implications for the theory of expertise. *Memory & Cognition, 24,* 493–503.

Gobet, F., & Simon, H. A. (1996b). Recall of rapidly presented random chess positions is a function of skill. *Psychonomic Bulletin & Review, 3,* 159–163.

Goldberg, E. (2001). *The executive brain: Frontal lobes and the civilized mind.* New York: Oxford University Press.

Goldinger, S. D., Kleider, H. M., Azuma, T., & Beike, D. R. (2003). "Blaming the victim" under memory load. *Psychological Science, 14,* 81–85.

Goldin-Meadow, S. (1999). The role of gesture in communication and thinking. *Current Trends in Cognitive Science, 3,* 419–429.

Goldsmith, M., & Koriat, A. (1998). The strategic regulation of memory reporting: Mechanisms and performance consequences. In D. Gopher & A. Koriat (Eds.), *Attention and performance* (Vol. 17, pp. 373–400). Cambridge, MA: MIT Press.

Goldstein, D. G., & Gigerenzer, G. (2002). Models of ecological rationality: The recognition heuristic. *Psychological Review, 109,* 75–90.

Goldstein, E. B. (1999). *Sensation and perception* (5th ed.). Pacific Grove, CA: Brooks/Cole.

Goldstein, E. B. (Ed.). (2001). *Blackwell handbook of perception.* Malden, MA: Blackwell.

Goldstein, E. B. (2002). *Sensation and perception* (6th ed.). Belmont, CA: Wadsworth.

Golombok, S., & Fivush, R. (1994). *Gender development.* New York: Cambridge University Press.

Gonsiorek, J. C. (1996). Mental health and sexual orientation. In R. C. Savin-Williams & K. M. Cohen (Eds.), *The lives of lesbians, gays, and bisexuals: Children to adults* (pp. 462–478). Fort Worth: Harcourt Brace.

Goodman, G. S., et al. (2001). Effects of past abuse experiences on children's eyewitness memory. *Law and Human Behavior, 25,* 269–298.

Goodman, G. S., et al. (2003). A prospective study of memory for child sexual abuse: New findings relevant to the repressed-memory controversy. *Psychological Science, 14,* 113–118.

Gorrell, P. (1999). Sentence processing. In R. A. Wilson & F. C. Keil (Eds.), *The MIT encyclopedia of the cognitive sciences* (pp. 748–751). Cambridge, MA: MIT Press.

Goschke, T. (1997). Implicit learning and unconscious knowledge: Mental representation, computational mechanisms, and brain structure. In K. Lamberts & D. Shanks (Eds.), *Knowledge, concepts and categories* (pp. 247–333). Cambridge, MA: MIT Press.

Goswami, U. (Ed.). (2002). *Blackwell handbook of childhood cognitive development.* Malden, MA: Blackwell.

Gowda, R., & Fox, J. C. (Eds.). (2002). *Judgments, decisions, and public policy.* New York: Cambridge University Press.

Grady, C. L., & Craik, F. I. M. (2000). Changes in memory processing with age. *Current Opinion in Neurobiology, 10,* 224–231.

Graesser, A. C., Gernsbacher, M. A., & Goldman, S. R. (2003a). *Handbook of discourse processes.* Mahwah, NJ: Erlbaum.

Graesser, A. C., Gernsbacher, M. A., & Goldman, S. R. (2003b). Introduction to the handbook of discourse processes. In A. C. Graesser, M. A. Gerns-

bacher, & S. R. Goldman (Eds.), *Handbook of discourse processes* (pp. 1–23). Mahwah, NJ: Erlbaum.

Graesser, A. C., Swamer, S. S., Baggett, W. B., & Sell, M. A. (1996). New models of deep comprehension. In B. K. Britton & A. C. Graesser (Eds.), *Models of understanding text* (pp. 1–32). Mahwah, NJ: Erlbaum.

Graf, P., & Ohta, N. (2002). *Lifespan development of human memory.* Cambridge, MA: MIT Press.

Grant, E. R., & Spivey, M. J. (2003). Eye movements and problem solving: Guiding attention guides thought. *Psychological Science, 14,* 462–466.

Green, K. P., Tomiak, G. R., & Kuhl, P. K. (1997). The encoding of rate and talker information during phonetic perception. *Perception & Psychophysics, 59,* 675–692.

Greenberg, J., Pyszczynski, T., Warner, S., & Bralow, D. (1994). A prognostic utility bias in judgments of similarity between past and present instances: How available information is deemed useful for prediction. *European Journal of Social Psychology, 24,* 593–610.

Greeno, J. G. (1974). Hobbits and Orcs: Acquisition of a sequential concept. *Cognitive Psychology, 6,* 270–292.

Greeno, J. G. (1977). Process of understanding in problem solving. In N. J. Castellan, Jr., D. B. Pisoni, & G. R. Potts (Eds.), *Cognitive theory* (Vol. 2, pp. 43–84). Hillsdale, NJ: Erlbaum.

Greeno, J. G. (1991). A view of mathematical problem solving in school. In M. U. Smith (Ed.), *Toward a unified theory of problem solving* (pp. 69–98). Hillsdale, NJ: Erlbaum.

Greeno, J. G., et al. (1998). The situativity of knowing, learning, and research. *American Psychologist, 53,* 5–26.

Greenwald, A. G., McGee, D. E., & Schwartz, J. L. K. (1998). Measuring individual differences in implicit cognition: The Implicit Association Test. *Journal of Personality and Social Psychology, 74,* 1464–1480.

Greenwald, A. G., & Nosek, B. A. (2001). Health of the Implicit Association Test at age 3. *Zeitschrift für Experimentelle Psychologie, 48,* 85–93.

Greenwald, A. G., et al. (2002). A unified theory of implicit attitudes, stereotypes, self-esteem, and self-concept. *Psychological Review, 109,* 3–25.

Griffin, D., & Tversky, A. (2002). The weighing of evidence and the determinants of confidence. In T. Gilovich, D. Griffin, & D. Kahneman (Eds.), *Heuristics and biases: The psychology of intuitive judgment* (pp. 230–249). New York: Cambridge University Press.

Griffin, Z. M., & Bock, K. (2000). What the eyes say about speaking. *Psychological Science, 11,* 274–279.

Griggs, R. A. (1995). The effects of rule clarification, decision justification, and selection instruction on Wason's abstract selection task. In S. E. Newstead & J. St. B. T. Evans (Eds.), *Perspectives on thinking and reasoning: Essays in honour of Peter Wason*. Hove, England: Erlbaum.

Griggs, R. A., & Cox, J. R. (1982). The elusive thematic-materials effect in Wason's selection task. *British Journal of Psychology, 73,* 407–420.

Griggs, R. A., & Jackson, S. L. (1990). Instructional effects on responses in Wason's selection task. *British Journal of Psychology, 81,* 197–204.

Grodzinsky, Y. (2000). The neurology of syntax: Language use without Broca's area. *Behavioral and Brain Sciences, 23,* 1–71.

Grodzinsky, Y. (2002). Imaging the grammatical brain. In M. Arbib (Ed.), *Handbook of brain theory* (2nd ed.). Cambridge, MA: MIT Press.

Groninger, L. D. (1971). Mnemonic imagery and forgetting. *Psychonomic Science, 23,* 161–163.

Groninger, L. D. (2000). Face-name mediated learning and long-term retention: The role of images and imagery processes. *American Journal of Psychology, 113,* 199–219.

Groome, D. (1999). *An introduction to cognitive psychology: Processes and disorders*. East Sussex, England: Psychology Press.

Grossberg, S. (1999). Pitch-based streaming in auditory perception. In N. Griffith & P. M. Todd (Eds.), *Musical networks: Parallel distributed perception and performance* (pp. 117–140). Cambridge, MA: MIT Press.

Grossberg, S. (2000a). The complementary brain: Unifying brain dynamics and modularity. *Trends in Cognitive Sciences, 4,* 233–245.

Grossberg, S. (2000b). The imbalanced brain: From normal behavior to schizophrenia. *Biological Psychiatry, 48,* 81–98.

Grossberg, S. (2003). Filling-in the forms: Surface and boundary interactions in visual cortex. In L. Pessoa & P. DeWeerd (Eds.), *Filling-in: From perceptual completion to skill learning* (pp. 13–37). New York: Oxford University Press.

Grossberg, S., & Myers, C. W. (2000). The resonant dynamics of speech perception: Interword integration and duration-dependent backward effects. *Psychological Review, 107,* 735–767.

Gruneberg, M. M. (1998). A commentary on criticism of the keyword method of learning foreign languages. *Applied Cognitive Psychology, 12,* 529–532.

Gruneberg, M. M., & Herrmann, D. J. (1997). *Your memory for life*. London: Blanford.

Guenther, F. H. (1995). Speech sound acquisition, coarticulation, and rate effects in a neural network model of speech production. *Psychological Review, 102,* 594–621.

Guerin, B. (2003). Language use as social strategy: A review and an analytic framework for the social sciences. *Review of General Psychology, 7,* 251–298.

Guilford, J. P. (1967). *The nature of human intelligence*. New York: McGraw-Hill.

Gulya, M., Rossi-George, A., & Rovee-Collier, C. (2002). Dissipation of retroactive interference in human infants. *Journal of Experimental Psychology: Animal Behavior Processes, 28,* 151–162.

Gurung, R. A. R. (2003). Pedagogical aids and student performance. *Teaching of Psychology, 30,* 92–95.

Guynn, M. J., McDaniel, M. A., & Einstein, G. O. (1998). Prospective memory: When reminders fail. *Memory & Cognition, 26,* 287–298.

Güzeldere, G., Flanagan, O., & Hardcastle, V. G. (2000). The nature and function of consciousness: Lessons from blindsight. In M. Gazzaniga (Ed.), *The new cognitive neurosciences* (pp. 1277–1283). Cambridge, MA: MIT Press.

Haberlandt, K. (1999). *Human memory: Exploration and application*. Boston: Allyn and Bacon.

Hahn, U., & Chater, N. (1997). Concepts and similarity. In K. Lamberts & D. Shanks (Eds.), *Knowledge, concepts and categories* (pp. 43–92). Cambridge, MA: MIT Press.

Hakel, M. D. (2001). Learning that lasts. *Psychological Science, 12,* 433–434.

Hakuta, K. (1986). *Mirror of language: The debate on bilingualism*. New York: Basic Books.

Hakuta, K., Bialystok, E., & Wiley, E. (2003). Critical evidence: A test of the critical-period hypothesis for second-language acquisition. *Psychological Science, 14,* 31–38.

Hall, J. K., & Verplaetse, L. S. (Eds.). (2000). *Second and foreign language learning through classrom interaction*. Mahwah, NJ: Erlbaum.

Hall, L. K., & Bahrick, H. P. (1998). The validity of metacognitive predictions of widespread learning and long-term retention. In G. Mazzoni & T. O. Nelson (Eds.), *Metacognition and cognitive neuropsychology* (pp. 23–36). Mahwah, NJ: Erlbaum.

Halpern, D. F. (2002). Sex, lies, and audiotapes: The Clinton-Lewinsky scandal. In R. J. Sternberg (Ed.), *Why smart people can be so stupid* (pp. 106–123). New Haven, CT: Yale University Press.

Halpern, D. F. (2003). *Thought and knowledge: An introduction to critical thinking* (4th ed.). Mahwah, NJ: Erlbaum.

Halpern, D., & Hakel, M. (Eds.). (2002). *New directions in teaching and learning: Using the principles of cognitive psychology as a pedagogy for higher education.* San Francisco: Jossey-Bass.

Hameroff, S. R., Kaszniak, A. W., & Scott, A. C. (1998). *Toward a science of consciousness II: The second Tucson discussions and debates.* Cambridge, MA: MIT Press.

Hamers, J. F., & Blanc, M. H. A. (1989). *Bilinguality and bilingualism.* Cambridge, England: Cambridge University Press.

Hamilton, D. L., & Sherman, J. W. (1994). Stereotypes. In R. S. Wyer, Jr., & T. K. Srull (Eds.), *Handbook of social cognition* (2nd ed., Vol. 2, pp. 1–68). Hillsdale, NJ: Erlbaum.

Hamilton, D. L., Stroessner, S. J., & Mackie, D. M. (1993). The influence of affect on stereotyping: The case of illusory correlations. In D. M. Mackie & D. L. Hamilton (Eds.), *Affect, cognition, and stereotyping: Interactive processes in group perception* (pp. 39–61). San Diego: Academic Press.

Hammond, K. R. (1996). *Human judgment and social policy.* New York: Oxford University Press.

Hammond, K. R. (2000). *Judgment under stress.* New York: Oxford University Press.

Hampton, J. A. (1997a). Conceptual combination. In K. Lamberts & D. Shanks (Eds.), *Knowledge, concepts, and categories* (pp. 133–159). Cambridge, MA: MIT Press.

Hampton, J. A. (1997b). Psychological representation of concepts. In M. A. Conway (Ed.), *Cognitive models of memory* (pp. 81–110). Cambridge, MA: MIT Press.

Harley, T. A. (2001). *The psychology of language: From data to theory* (2nd ed.). East Sussex, England: Psychology Press.

Harris, R. J., Sardarpoor-Bascom, F., & Meyer, T. (1989). The role of cultural knowledge in distorting recall for stories. *Bulletin of the Psychonomic Society, 27,* 9–10.

Hartley, A. A. (1993). Evidence for the selective preservation of spatial selective attention in old age. *Psychology and Aging, 8,* 371–379.

Hasher, L., Chung, C., May, C. P., & Foong, N. (2002). Age, time of testing, and proactive interference. *Canadian Journal of Experimental Psychology, 56,* 200–207.

Hawkins, S. A., & Hastie, R. (1990). Hindsight: Biased judgments of past events after the outcomes are known. *Psychological Bulletin, 107,* 311–327.

Hay, J. F., & Jacoby, L. L. (1996). Separating habit and recollection: Memory slips, process dissociations, and probability matching. *Journal of Experimental Psychology: Learning, Memory, and Cognition, 22,* 1323–1335.

Hayes, J. R. (1989). Writing research: The analysis of a very complex task. In D. Klahr & K. Kotovsky (Eds.), *Complex information processing: The impact of Herbert A. Simon* (pp. 209–234). Hillsdale, NJ: Erlbaum.

Hayes, J. R. (1996). A new framework for understanding cognition and affect in writing. In C. M. Levy & S. Randsell (Eds.), *The science of writing: Theories, methods, individual differences, and applications* (pp. 1–27). Mahwah, NJ: Erlbaum.

Hayes, J. R., et al. (1987). Cognitive processes in revision. In S. Rosenberg (Ed.), *Advances in psycholinguistics: Vol. 2. Reading, writing, and languages processing.* Cambridge, England: Cambridge University Press.

Hazeltine, R. E., Prinzmetal, W., & Elliott, K. (1997). If it's not there, where is it? Locating illusory conjunctions. *Journal of Experimental Psychology: Human Perception and Performance, 23,* 263–277.

Healy, A. F., & McNamara, D. S. (1996). Verbal learning and memory: Does the modal model still work? *Annual Review of Psychology, 47,* 143–172.

Healy, A. F., & Proctor, R. W. (Eds.). (2003). *Handbook of psychology* (Vol. 4.). Hoboken, NJ: Wiley.

Hearst, E. (1991). Psychology and nothing. *American Scientist, 79,* 432–443.

Heibeck, T. H., & Markman, E. M. (1987). Word learning in children: An examination of fast mapping. *Child Development, 58,* 1021–1034.

Heit, E., & Barsalou, L. W. (1996). The instantiation principle in natural categories. *Memory, 4,* 413–451.

Henderson, J. M., & Hollingworth, A. (1999). The role of fixation position in detecting scene changes across saccades. *Psychological Science, 10,* 438–443.

Henderson, Z., Bruce, V., & Burton, A. M. (2001). Matching the faces of robbers captured on video. *Applied Cognitive Psychology, 15,* 445–464.

Henkel, L. A., Franklin, N., & Johnson, M. K. (2000). Cross-modal source monitoring confusions between perceived and imagined events. *Journal of Experi-*

mental Psychology: Learning, Memory, & Cognition, 26, 321–335.

Hennessey, B. A. (2000). Rewards and creativity. In C. Sansone & J. M. Harackiewicz (Eds.), *Intrinsic and extrinsic motivation: The search for optimal motivation and performance* (pp. 55–78). San Diego, CA: Academic Press.

Hennessey, B. A., & Amabile, T. M. (1984, April). *The effect of reward and task label on children's verbal creativity.* Paper presented at the annual meeting of the Eastern Psychological Association, Baltimore.

Hennessey, B. A., & Amabile, T. M. (1988). The conditions of creativity. In R. J. Sternberg (Ed.), *The nature of creativity: Contemporary psychological perspectives* (pp. 11–38). New York: Cambridge University Press.

Henrich, J., et al. (2001). Group report: What is the role of culture in bounded rationality? In G. Gigerenzer & R. Selten (Eds.), *Bounded rationality: The adaptive toolbox* (pp. 343–359). Cambridge, MA: MIT Press.

Hernandez-García, L., Wager, T., & Jonides, J. (2002). Functional brain imaging. In H. Pashler & J. Wixted (Eds.), *Stevens' handbook of experimental psychology* (3rd ed., Vol. 4, pp. 175–221). New York: Wiley.

Herrmann, D. J. (1990). Self-perceptions of memory performance. In W. K. Schaie, J. Rodin, & C. Schooler (Eds.), *Self-directedness and efficacy: Causes and effects throughout the life course* (pp. 199–211). Hillsdale, NJ: Erlbaum.

Herrmann, D. J. (1991). *Super memory.* Emmaus, PA: Rodale.

Herrmann, D. J. (1996). Improving prospective memory. In M. Brandimonte, G. O. Einstein, & M. A. McDaniel (Eds.), *Prospective memory: Theory and applications* (pp. 391–398). Mahwah, NJ: Erlbaum.

Herrmann, D., Plude, D., Yoder, C., & Mullin, P. (1999). Cognitive processing and extrinsic psychological systems: A holistic model of cognition. *Zeitschrift für Psychologie, 207*, 123–147.

Herrmann, D., Raybeck, D., & Gruneberg, M. (2002). *Improving memory and study skills.* Kirkland, WA: Hogrefe & Huber.

Herrmann, D., et al. (1999). Palmtop reminding devices. In J. P. Marsh, B. Gorayska, & J. L. Mey (Eds.), *Human interfaces: Questions of method and practice in cognitive technology* (pp. 327–343). Amsterdam: Elsevier.

Hertwig, R., & Gigerenzer, G. (1999). The "conjunction fallacy" revisited: How intelligent inferences look like reasoning errors. *Journal of Behavioral Decision Making, 12*, 275–305.

Hertwig, R., & Todd, P. M. (2002). Heuristics. In V. S. Ramachandran (Ed.), *Encyclopedia of the human brain* (Vol. 2, pp. 449–460). San Diego: Academic Press.

Hertzog, C., & Dixon, R. A. (1994). Metacognitive development in adulthood and old age. In J. Metcalfe and A. P. Shimamura (Eds.), *Metacognition: Knowing about knowing* (pp. 227–251). Cambridge, MA: MIT Press.

Hertzog, C., & Dunlosky, J. (1996). The aging of practical memory: An overview. In D. J. Herrmann et al. (Eds.), *Basic and applied memory research theory in context* (Vol. 1, pp. 337–358). Mahwah, NJ: Erlbaum.

Hertzog, C., Lineweaver, T. T., & McGuire, C. L. (1999). Beliefs about memory and aging. In F. Blanchard-Fields & T. M. Hess (Eds.), *Social cognition and aging* (pp. 43–68). New York: Academic Press.

Heth, C. D., Cornell, E. H., & Flood, T. L. (2002). Self-ratings of sense of direction and route reversal performance. *Applied Cognitive Psychology, 16*, 309–324.

Hidalgo Downing, L. (2000). *Negation, text worlds, and discourse: The pragmatics of fiction.* Stamford, CT: Ablex.

Higbee, K. L. (1999). 25 years of memory improvement: The evolution of a memory-skills course. *Cognitive Technology, 4*, 38–42.

Hill, R. D., Evankovich, K. D., Sheikh, J. I., & Yesavage, J. A. (1987). Imagery mnemonic training in a patient with primary degenerative dementia. *Psychology and Aging, 2*, 204–205.

Hillis, A. E. (Ed.). (2002). *The handbook of adult language disorders.* New York: Psychology Press.

Hinds, P. J. (1999). The curse of expertise: The effects of expertise and debiasing methods on predictions of novice performance. *Journal of Experimental Psychology: Applied, 5*, 205–211.

Hinrichs, T. R. (1992). *Problem solving in open worlds: A case study in design.* Hillsdale, NJ: Erlbaum.

Hintzman, D. L. (1986). "Schema abstraction" in a multiple-trace memory model. *Psychological Review, 93*, 411–428.

Hirsh-Pasek, K., & Golinkoff, R. M. (1996). *The origins of grammar: Evidence from early language comprehension.* Cambridge, MA: MIT Press.

Hirst, W., et al. (1980). Dividing attention without alternation or automaticity. *Journal of Experimental Psychology: General, 109,* 98–117.

Hirt, E. R., McDonald, H. E., & Markman, K. D. (1998). Expectancy effects in reconstructive memory: When the past is just what we expected. In S. J. Lynn & K. M. McConkey (Eds.), *Truth in memory* (pp. 62–89). New York: Guilford.

Hirtle, S. C., & Jonides, J. (1985). Evidence of hierarchies in cognitive maps. *Memory & Cognition, 13,* 208–217.

Hirtle, S. C., & Mascolo, M. F. (1986). Effect of semantic clustering on the memory of spatial locations. *Journal of Experimental Psychology: Learning, Memory, and Cognition, 12,* 182–189.

Hobson, J. A. (1997). Consciousness as a state-dependent phenomenon. In J. D. Cohen & J. W. Schooler (Eds.), *Scientific approaches to consciousness* (pp. 379–396). Mahwah, NJ: Erlbaum.

Hodges, J. R. (2000). Memory in the dementias. In E. Tulving & F. I. M. Craik (Eds.), *The Oxford handbook of memory* (pp. 441–459). New York: Oxford University Press.

Hoerl, C. (2001). The phenomenology of episodic recall. In C. Hoerl & T. McCormack (Eds.), *Time and memory: Issues in philosophy and psychology* (pp. 315–355). New York: Oxford University Press.

Hoffman, D. D. (1998). *Visual intelligence: How we create what we see.* New York: Norton.

Hoffrage, U. (2004). Overconfidence. In R. Pohl (Ed.), *Cognitive illusions: Handbook on fallacies and biases in thinking, judgment, and memory.* Hove, England: Psychology Press.

Hogarth, R. M. (2001). *Educating intuition.* Chicago: University of Chicago Press.

Hollingworth, H. (1910). The oblivescence of the disagreeable. *Journal of Philosophy, Psychology and Scientific Methods, 7,* 709–714.

Holmes, J. B., Waters, H. S., & Rajaram, S. (1998). The phenomenology of false memories: Episodic content and confidence. *Journal of Experimental Psychology: Learning, Memory, and Cognition, 24,* 1026–1040.

Holtgrave, D. R., Tinsley, B. J., & Kay, L. S. (1994). Heuristics, biases, and environmental health risk analysis. In L. Heath et al. (Eds.), *Applications of heuristics and biases to social issues* (pp. 259–285). New York: Plenum.

Holyoak, K. J., & Simon, D. (1999). Bidirectional reasoning in decision making by constraint satisfaction. *Journal of Experimental Psychology: General, 128,* 3–31.

Hom, H. L., Jr., & Ciaramitaro, M. (2001). GTIDHNIHS: I knew-it-all-along. *Applied Cognitive Psychology, 15,* 493–507.

Honeycutt, J. M., & Cantrill, J. G. (2001). *Cognition, communication, and romantic relationships.* Mahwah, NJ: Erlbaum.

Hong, Y., Morris, M. W., Chiu, C., & Benet-Martínez, V. (2000). Multicultural minds: A dynamic constructivist approach to culture and cognition. *American Psychologist, 55,* 709–720.

Honig, E. (1997). Striking lives: Oral history and the politics of memory. *Journal of Women's History, 9,* 139–157.

Horton, W. S., & Keysar, B. (1996). When do speakers take into account common ground? *Cognition, 59,* 91–117.

Houtz, J. C., & Frankel, A. D. (1992). Effects of incubation and imagery training on creativity. *Creativity Research Journal, 5,* 183–189.

Howe, M. L. (2000). *The fate of early memories.* Washington, DC: American Psychological Association.

Howe, M. L. (2003). Memories from the cradle. *Current Directions in Psychological Science, 12,* 62–65.

Howe, M. L., Courage, M. L., Vernescu, R., & Hunt, M. (2000). Distinctiveness effects in children's long-term retention. *Developmental Psychology, 36,* 778–792.

Howes, J. L., & Katz, A. N. (1992). Remote memory: Recalling autobiographical and public events from across the lifespan. *Canadian Journal of Psychology, 46,* 92–116.

Hubel, D. H. (1982). Explorations of the primary visual cortex, 1955–1978. *Nature, 299,* 515–524.

Hubel, D. H., & Wiesel, T. N. (1965). Receptive fields of single neurons in two nonstriate visual areas (18 and 19) of the cat. *Journal of Neurophysiology, 28,* 229–289.

Hubel, D. H., & Wiesel, T. N. (1979). Brain mechanisms and vision. *Scientific American, 241*(3), 150–162.

Huber, V. L., Neale, M. A., & Northcraft, G. B. (1987). Decision bias and personnel selection strategies. *Organizational Behavior and Human Decision Processes, 40,* 136–147.

Huitema, J. S., Dopkins, S., Klin, C. M., & Myers, J. L. (1993). Connecting goals and actions during reading. *Journal of Experimental Psychology: Learning, Memory, and Cognition, 19,* 1053–1060.

Hulicka, I. M. (1982). Memory functioning in late adulthood. In F. I. M. Craik & S. Trehub (Eds.), *Advances in the study of communication and affect* (Vol. 8, pp. 331–351). New York: Plenum.

Hulme, C., et al. (1999). Think before you speak: Pauses, memory search, and trace redintegration processes in verbal memory span. *Journal of Experimental Psychology: Learning, Memory, and Cognition, 25*, 447–463.

Hummert, M. L. (1999). A social cognitive perspective on age stereotypes. In T. M. Hess & F. Blanchard-Fields (Eds.), *Social cognition and aging* (pp. 175–196). San Diego: Academic Press.

Humphreys, G. W., & Riddoch, M. J. (2001). The neuropsychology of visual object and space perception. In E. B. Goldstein (Ed.), *Blackwell handbook of perception* (pp. 204–236). Malden, MA: Blackwell.

Humphreys, M. S., & Tehan, G. (1999). Cues and codes in working memory tasks. In C. Izawa (Ed.), *On human memory* (pp. 127–149). Mahwah, NJ: Erlbaum.

Hyman, I. E., Jr., Husband, T. H., & Billings, F. J. (1995). False memories of childhood experiences. *Applied Cognitive Psychology, 9*, 181–197.

Hyman, I. E., Jr., & Kleinknecht, E. E. (1999). False childhood memories: Research, theory, and applications. In L. M. Williams & V. L. Banyard (Eds.), *Trauma & memory* (pp. 175–188). Thousand Oaks, CA: Sage.

Hyman, I. E., Jr., & Loftus, E. F. (2002). False childhood memories and eyewitness memory errors. In M. L. Eisen, J. A. Quas, & G. S. Goodman (Eds.), *Memory and suggestibility in the forensic interview* (pp. 63–84). Mahwah, NJ: Erlbaum.

Iannuzzi, P., Strichart, S. S., & Mangrum, C. T., II. (1998). *Teaching study skills and strategies in college.* Boston: Allyn and Bacon.

Idson, L. C., Krantz, D. H., Osherson, D., & Bonini, N. (2001). The relation between probability and evidence judgment: An extension of support theory. *Journal of Risk and Uncertainty, 22*, 227–249.

Imhoff, M. C., & Baker-Ward, L. (1999). Preschoolers' suggestibility: Effects of developmentally appropriate language and interviewer supportiveness. *Journal of Applied Developmental Psychology, 20*, 407–429.

Inhoff, A. W., Starr, M., & Shindler, K. L. (2000). Is the processing of words during eye fixations in reading strictly serial? *Perception & Psychophysics, 62*, 1474–1484.

Intons-Peterson, M. J. (1983). Imagery paradigms: How vulnerable are they to experimenters' expectations? *Journal of Experimental Psychology: Learning, Memory, and Cognition, 10*, 699–715.

Intons-Peterson, M. J., Russell, W., & Dressel, S. (1992). The role of pitch in auditory imagery. *Journal of Experimental Psychology: Human Perception and Performance, 18*, 233–240.

Intons-Peterson, M. J., et al. (1999). Age, testing at preferred or nonpreferred times (testing optimality), and false memory. *Journal of Experimental Psychology: Learning, Memory, and Cognition, 25*, 23–40.

Intraub, H. (1997). The representation of visual scenes. *Trends in Cognitive Sciences, 1*, 217–222.

Intraub, H. (1999). Understanding and remembering briefly glimpsed pictures: Implications for visual scanning and memory. In V. Coltheart (Ed.), *Fleeting memories: Cognition of brief visual stimuli* (pp. 47–70). Cambridge, MA: MIT Press.

Intraub, H., & Berkowits, D. (1996). Beyond the edges of a picture. *American Journal of Psychology, 109*, 581–598.

Intraub, H., Gottesman, C. V., & Bills, A. J. (1998). Effects of perceiving and imagining scenes on memory for pictures. *Journal of Experimental Psychology: Learning, Memory, and Cognition, 24*, 186–201.

Irwin, D. E., & Zelinsky, G. J. (2002). Eye movements and scene perception: Memory for things observed. *Perception & Psychophysics, 64*, 882–895.

Isen, A. M. (2000). Positive affect and decision making. In M. Lewis & J. M. Haviland-Jones (Eds.), *Handbook of emotions* (2nd ed., pp. 417–435). New York: Guilford.

Ishai, A., & Sagi, D. (1995). Common mechanisms of visual imagery and perception. *Science, 268*, 1772–1774.

Isikoff, M., & Lipper, T. (2003, July 21). A spy takes the bullet. *Newsweek*, pp. 24–25.

Ivins, M. (1999, December 20). Media coverage of WTO was simplistic nonsense. *Liberal Opinion*, p. 12.

Ivry, R. B., & Fiez, J. A. (2000). Cerebellar contributions to cognition and imagery. In M. S. Gazzaniga (Ed.), *The new cognitive neurosciences* (pp. 999–1011). Cambridge, MA: MIT Press.

Izaute, M., Chambres, P., & Larochelle, S. (2002). Feeling-of-knowing for proper names. *Canadian Journal of Experimental Psychology, 56*, 263–272.

Izawa, C. (Ed.). (1999). *On human memory: Evolution, progress, and reflections on the 30th anniversary of the Atkinson-Shiffrin model.* Mahwah, NJ: Erlbaum.

Jackendoff, R. (1994). *Patterns in the mind.* New York: Basic Books.

Jackendoff, R. (1997). *The architecture of the language faculty.* Cambridge, MA: MIT Press.

Jackson, S. L., & Griggs, R. A. (1990). The elusive pragmatic reasoning schemas effect. *Quarterly Journal of Experimental Psychology, 42A*, 353–373.

Jackson, S., & Crockenberg, S. (1998). A comparison of suggestibility in 4-year-old girls in response to parental or stranger misinformation. *Journal of Applied Development Psychology, 19*, 527–542.

Jacoby, L. L., Yonelinas, A. P., & Jennings, J. M. (1997). The relation between conscious and unconscious (automatic) influences: A declaration of independence. In J. D. Cohen & J. W. Schooler (Eds.), *Scientific approaches to consciousness* (pp. 13–47). Mahwah, NJ: Erlbaum.

Jaeger, C. C., Renn, O., Rosa, E. A., & Webler, T. (2001). *Risk, uncertainty, and rational action.* London, Earthscan.

James, L. E., & Burke, D. M. (2000). Phonological priming effects on word retrieval and tip-of-the-tongue experiences in young and older adults. *Journal of Experimental Psychology: Learning, Memory, and Cognition, 26*, 1378–1391.

James, L. E., & MacKay, D. G. (2001). H.M., word knowledge, and aging: Support for a new theory of long-term retrograde amnesia. *Psychological Science, 12*, 485–492.

James, W. (1890). *The principles of psychology.* New York: Henry Holt.

Jared, D., Levy, B. A., & Rayner, K. (1999). The role of phonology in the activation of word meanings during reading: Evidence from proofreading and eye movements. *Journal of Experimental Psychology: General, 128*, 219–264.

Jarvella, R. J. (1971). Syntactic processing of connected speech. *Journal of Verbal Learning and Verbal Behavior, 10*, 409–416.

Jasper, J. D., et al. (2001). Effects of framing on teratogenic risk perception in pregnant women. *Lancet, 358*, 1237–1238.

Jenkins, J. J. (1974). Remember that old theory of memory? Well, forget it. *American Psychologist, 29*, 785–795.

Jenkins, W., & McDowall, J. (2001). Implicit memory and depression: An analysis of perceptual and conceptual processes. *Cognition and Emotion, 15*, 803–812.

Jia, G., Aaronson, D., & Wu, Y. (2002). Long-term language attainment of bilingual immigrants: Predictive variables and language group differences. *Applied Psycholinguistics, 23*, 599–621.

Johnson, J. S., & Newport, E. L. (1989). Critical effects in second language learning: The influence of maturational state on the acquisition of English as a second language. *Cognitive Psychology, 21*, 60–99.

Johnson, K. E., & Mervis, C. B. (1997). Effects of varying levels of expertise on the basic level of categorization. *Journal of Experimental Psychology: General, 126*, 248–277.

Johnson, M. H., & Bolhuis, J. J. (2000). Predispositions in perceptual and cognitive development. In J. J. Bolhuis (Ed.), *Brain, perception, memory* (pp. 68–84). New York: Oxford University Press.

Johnson, M. K. (1996). Fact, fantasy, and public policy. In D. J. Herrmann et al. (Eds.), *Basic and applied memory research theory in context* (Vol. 1, pp. 83–103). Mahwah, NJ: Erlbaum.

Johnson, M. K. (1997). Identifying the origin of mental experience. In M. S. Myslobodsky (Ed.), *The mythomanias: The nature of deception and self-deception* (pp. 133–180). Mahwah, NJ: Erlbaum.

Johnson, M. K. (1998). Individual and cultural reality monitoring. *Annals of the American Academy of Political and Social Science, 560*, 179–193.

Johnson, M. K. (2002, October). Reality monitoring: Varying levels of analysis. *APS Observer*, pp. 8, 28–29.

Johnson, M. K., & Raye, C. L. (2000). Cognitive and brain mechanisms of false memories and beliefs. In D. L. Schachter & E. Scarry (Eds.), *Memory, brain, and belief* (pp. 35–86). Cambridge, MA: Harvard University Press.

Johnson, R. D. (1987). Making judgments when information is missing: Inferences, biases, and framing effects. *Acta Psychologica, 66*, 69–72.

Johnson-Laird, P. N., Savary, F., & Bucciarelli, M. (2000). Strategies and tactics in reasoning. In W. Schaeken, G. DeVooght, A. Vandierendonck, & G. d'Ydewalle (Eds.), *Deductive reasoning and strategies* (pp. 209–240). Mahwah, NJ: Erlbaum.

Johnson-Laird, P. N., et al. (1999). Naive probability: A mental model theory of extensional reasoning. *Psychological Review, 106,* 62–88.

Johnston, W. A., & Schwarting, I. S. (1997). Novel popout: An enigma for conventional theories of attention. *Journal of Experimental Psychology: Human Perception and Performance, 23,* 622–631.

Jolicoeur, P., & Kosslyn, S. M. (1985a). Demand characteristics in image scanning experiments. *Journal of Mental Imagery, 9,* 41–50.

Jolicoeur, P., & Kosslyn, S. M. (1985b). Is time to scan visual images due to demand characteristics? *Memory & Cognition, 13,* 320–332.

Jones, J. (1999). *The psychotherapist's guide to human memory.* New York: Basic Books.

Jordan, K., & Huntsman, L. A. (1990). Image rotation of misoriented letter strings: Effects of orientation cuing and repetition. *Perception & Psychophysics, 48,* 363–374.

Jordan, T. R., & Bevan, K. M. (1994). Word superiority over isolated letters: The neglected case of forward masking. *Memory & Cognition, 22,* 133–144.

Jordan, T. R., McCotter, M. V., & Thomas, S. M. (2000). Visual and audiovisual speech perception with color and gray-scale facial images. *Perception & Psychophysics, 62,* 1394–1404.

Joyner, M. H., & Kurtz-Costes, B. (1997). Metamemory development. In N. Cowan & C. Hulme (Eds.), *The development of memory in childhood* (pp. 275–300). East Sussex, England: Psychology Press.

Jusczyk, P. W. (1997). *The discovery of spoken language.* Cambridge, MA: MIT Press.

Jusczyk, P. W. (2002). How infants adapt speech-processing capacities to native-language structure. *Current Directions in Psychological Science, 11,* 15–18.

Jusczyk, P. W., & Luce, P. A. (2002). Speech perception. In H. Pashler (Ed.), *Stevens' handbook of experimental psychology* (3rd ed., Vol. 1, pp. 493–536). New York: Wiley.

Juslin, P., & Montgomery, H. (1999). *Judgment and decision making.* Mahwah, NJ: Erlbaum.

Juslin, P., Winman, A., & Olsson, H. (2000). Naive empiricism and dogmatism in confidence research: A critical examination of the hard-easy effect. *Psychological Review, 107,* 384–396.

Jussim, L., et al. (2000). Stigma and self-fulfilling prophecies. In T. F. Heatherton, R. E. Kleck, M. R. Hebl, & J. G. Hull (Eds.), *The social psychology of stigma* (pp. 374–418). New York: Guilford.

Just, M. A., & Carpenter, P. A. (1992). A capacity theory of comprehension: Individual differences in working memory. *Psychological Review, 99,* 122–149.

Just, M. A., Carpenter, P. A., & Keller, T. A. (1996). The capacity theory of comprehension: New frontiers of evidence and arguments. *Psychological Review, 103,* 773–780.

Just, M. A., et al. (2001). Interdependence of nonoverlapping cortical systems in dual cognitive tasks. *NeuroImage, 14,* 417–426.

Justice, E. M., Baker-Ward, L., Gupta, S., & Jannings, L. R. (1997). Means to the goal of remembering: Developmental changes in awareness of strategy use-performance relations. *Journal of Experimental Child Psychology, 65,* 293–314.

Kahneman, D., & Frederick, S. (2002). Representativeness revisited: Attribute substitution in intuitive judgment. In T. Gilovich, D. Griffin, & D. Kahneman (Eds.), *Heuristics and biases: The psychology of intuitive judgment* (pp. 49–81). New York: Cambridge University Press.

Kahneman, D., & Tversky, A. (1972). Subjective probability: A judgment of representativeness. *Cognitive Psychology, 3,* 430–454.

Kahneman, D., & Tversky, A. (1973). On the psychology of prediction. *Psychological Review, 80,* 237–251.

Kahneman, D., & Tversky, A. (1982). The simulation heuristic. In D. Kahneman, P. Slovic, & A. Tversky (Eds.), *Judgment under uncertainty: Heuristics and biases* (pp. 201–208). New York: Cambridge University Press.

Kahneman, D., & Tversky, A. (1984). Choices, values, and frames. *American Psychologist, 39,* 341–350.

Kahneman, D., & Tversky, A. (1995). Conflict resolution: A cognitive perspective. In K. Arrow et al. (Eds.), *Barriers to conflict resolution* (pp. 44–60). New York: Norton.

Kahneman, D., & Tversky, A. (1996). On the reality of cognitive illusions. *Psychological Review, 103,* 582–591.

Kahneman, D., & Tversky, A. (2000). *Choice, values, and frames.* New York: Cambridge University Press.

Kail, R. (1990). *The development of memory in children* (3rd ed.). New York: Freeman.

Kail, R. (1992). Development of memory in children. In L. R. Squire (Ed.), *Encyclopedia of learning and memory* (pp. 99–102). New York: Macmillan.

Kail, R. (1997). Phonological skill and articulation time independently contribute to the development of memory span. *Journal of Experimental Child Psychology, 67,* 57–68.

Kail, R. (2004). *Children and their development* (3rd ed.). Upper Saddle River, NJ: Prentice Hall.

Kail, R., Carter, P., & Pellegrino, J. (1979). The locus of sex differences in spatial ability. *Perception & Psychophysics, 26,* 182–186.

Kalat, J. W. (2001). *Biological psychology* (7th ed.). Belmont, CA: Wadsworth.

Kane, M. J., Bleckley, K., Conway, A. R. A., & Engle, R. W. (2001). A controlled-attention view of working-memory capacity. *Journal of Experimental Psychology: General, 130,* 169–183.

Kanwisher, N., Downing, P., Epstein, R., & Kourtzi, Z. (2001). Functional neuroimaging of visual recognition. In R. Cabeza & A. Kingstone (Eds.), *Handbook of funtional neuroimaging of cognition* (pp. 110–151). Cambridge, MA: MIT Press.

Kaplan, P. S., Bachorowski, J., Smoski, M. J., & Hudenko, W. J. (2002). Infants of depressed mothers, although competent learners, fail to learn in response to their own mothers' infant-directed speech. *Psychological Science, 13,* 268–271.

Kareev, Y. (2000). Seven (indeed, plus or minus two) and the detection of correlations. *Psychological Review, 107,* 397–402.

Karmiloff, K., & Karmiloff-Smith, A. (2001). *Pathways to language: From fetus to adolescent.* Cambridge, MA: Harvard University Press.

Kasper, L. F., & Glass, A. L. (1988). An extension of the keyword method facilitates the acquisition of simple Spanish sentences. *Applied Cognitive Psychology, 2,* 137–146.

Kaufman, N. J., Randlett, A. L., & Price, J. (1985). Awareness of the use of comprehension strategies in good and poor college readers. *Reading Psychology, 6,* 1–11.

Kaufmann, G. (1996). The many faces of mental images. In C. Cornoldi et al. (Eds.), *Stretching the imagination: Representation and transformation in mental imagery* (pp. 77–118). New York: Oxford University Press.

Kelemen, W. L., & Weaver, C. A., III. (1997). Enhanced metamemory at delays: Why do judgments of learning improve over time? *Journal of Experimental Psychology: Learning, Memory, and Cognition, 23,* 1394–1409.

Keller, T. A., Carpenter, P. A., & Just, M. A. (2001). The neural bases of sentence comprehension: An fMRI examination of syntactic and lexical processing. *Cerebral Cortex, 11,* 223–237.

Keller, T. A., Carpenter, P. A., & Just, M. A. (2003). Brain imaging of tongue-twister sentence comprehension: Twisting the tongue and the brain. *Brain and Language, 84,* 189–203.

Kelley, C. M., & Jacoby, L. L. (2000). Recollection and familiarity: Process-dissociation. In E. Tulving & F. I. M. Craik (Eds.), *The Oxford handbook of memory* (pp. 215–228). New York: Oxford University Press.

Kellman, P. J., & Arterberry, M. E. (1998). *The cradle of knowledge: Development of perception in infancy.* Cambridge, MA: MIT Press.

Kellogg, R. T. (1988). Attentional overload and writing performance: Effects of rough draft and outline strategies. *Journal of Experimental Psychology: Learning, Memory, and Cognition, 14,* 355–365.

Kellogg, R. T. (1989). Idea processors: Computer aids for planning and composing text. In B. K. Britton & S. M. Glynn (Eds.), *Computer writing environments: Theory, research, and design* (pp. 57–92). Hillsdale, NJ: Erlbaum.

Kellogg, R. T. (1994). *The psychology of writing.* New York: Oxford University Press.

Kellogg, R. T. (1996). A model of working memory in writing. In C. M. Levy & S. Ransdell (Eds.), *The science of writing: Theories, methods, individual differences, and applications* (pp. 57–71). Mahwah, NJ: Erlbaum.

Kellogg, R. T. (1998). Components of working memory in text production. In M. Torrance & G. C. Jeffery (Eds.), *The cognitive demands of writing: Processing capacity and working memory effects in text production.* Amsterdam: Amsterdam University Press.

Kellogg, R. T. (2001a). Competition for working memory among writing processes. *American Journal of Psychology, 114,* 175–191.

Kellogg, R. T. (2001b). Long-term working memory in text production. *Memory & Cognition, 29,* 43–52.

Kelly, F., & Grossberg, S. (2000). Neural dynamics of 3-D surface perception: Figure-ground separation and lightness perception. *Perception & Psychophysics, 62,* 1596–1618.

Kemp, R., Towell, N., & Pike, G. (1997). When seeing should not be believing: Photographs, credit cards, and fraud. *Journal of Applied Psychology, 11,* 211–222.

Kemper, S., & Mitzner, T. L. (2001). Language production and comprehension. In J. E. Birren & K. W.

Schaie (Eds.), *Handbook of the psychology of aging* (5th ed., pp. 378–398). San Diego: Academic Press.

Kennedy, A. (2000). Attention allocation in reading: Sequential or parallel? In A. Kennedy, R. Radach, D. Heller, & J. Pyne (Eds.), *Reading as a perceptual process* (pp. 193–220). Amsterdam: Elsevier.

Kester, J. D., Benjamin, A. S., Castel, A. D., & Craik, F. I. M. (2002). Memory in elderly people. In A. D. Baddeley, M. D. Kopelman, & B. A. Wilson (Eds.), *The handbook of memory disorders* (2nd ed., pp. 543–567). New York: Wiley.

Keysar, B., & Henly, A. S. (2002). Speakers' overestimation of their effectiveness. *Psychological Science, 13*, 207–212.

Kifner, J. (1994, May 20). Pollster finds error on Holocaust doubts. *New York Times* (Late New York Edition), p. A12.

Kihlstrom, J. F. (1998). Exhumed memory. In S. J. Lynn & K. M. McConkey (Eds.), *Truth in memory* (pp. 3–31). New York: Guilford.

Kihlstrom, J. F. (1999). Conscious versus unconscious cognition. In R. J. Sternberg (Ed.), *The nature of cognition* (pp. 173–203). Cambridge, MA: MIT Press.

Kihlstrom, J. F., et al. (1990). Implicit and explicit memory following surgical anesthesia. *Psychological Science, 1*, 303–306.

Kilborn, K. (1994). Learning a language late: Second language acquisition in adults. In M. A. Gernsbacher (Ed.), *Handbook of psycholinguistics* (pp. 917–944). San Diego: Academic Press.

Kimball, D. R., & Holyoak, K. J. (2000). Transfer and expertise. In E. Tulving & F. I. M. Craik (Eds.), *The Oxford handbook of memory* (pp. 109–122). New York: Oxford University Press.

Kinsbourne, M. (1998). The right hemisphere and recovery from aphasia. In B. Stemmer & H. A. Whitaker (Eds.), *Handbook of neurolinguistics* (pp. 385–392). San Diego: Academic Press.

Kintsch, W. (1984). Approaches to the study of the psychology of language. In T. G. Bever, J. M. Carroll, & L. A. Miller (Eds.), *Talking minds: The study of language in cognitive science* (pp. 111–145). Cambridge, MA: MIT Press.

Kintsch, W. (1998). *Comprehension: A paradigm for cognition.* New York: Cambridge University Press.

Kintsch, W., & Buschke, H. (1969). Homophones and synonyms in short-term memory. *Journal of Experimental Psychology, 80*, 403–407.

Kintsch, W., et al. (1999). Models of working memory. In A. Miyake & P. Shah (Eds.), *Models of working memory: Mechanisms of active maintenance and executive control* (pp. 412–441). New York: Cambridge University Press.

Kirshner, D., & Whitson, J. A. (1997a). Editors' introduction to situated cognition: Social, semiotic, and psychological perspectives. In D. Kirshner & J. A. Whitson (Eds.), *Situated cognition: Social, semiotic, and psychological perspectives* (pp. 1–16). Mahwah, NJ: Erlbaum.

Kisilevsky, B. S., et al. (2003). Effects of experience on fetal voice recognition. *Psychological Science, 14*, 220–224.

Kitchin, R., & Blades, M. (2002). *The cognition of geographic space.* London: Tauris.

Kizilbash, A. H., Vanderploeg, R. D., & Curtiss, G. (2002). The effects of depression and anxiety on memory performance. *Archives of Clinical Neuropsychology, 17*, 57–67.

Klaczynski, P. A., Gelfand, H., & Reese, H. W. (1989). Transfer of conditional reasoning: Effects of explanations and initial problem types. *Memory & Cognition, 17*, 208–220.

Klauer, K. C., Musch, J., & Naumer, B. (2000). On belief bias in syllogistic reasoning. *Psychological Review, 107*, 852–884.

Klayman, J., & Ha, Y. (1996). Confirmation, disconfirmation, and information in hypothesis testing. In W. M. Goldstein & R. M. Hogarth (Eds.), *Research on judgment and decision making: Currents, connections, and controversies* (pp. 205–243). New York: Cambridge University Press.

Klein, G. (1997). Naturalistic decision making: Where are we going? In C. E. Zsambok & G. Klein (Eds.), *Naturalistic decision making* (pp. 383–397). Mahwah, NJ: Erlbaum.

Klein, G. (1998). *Sources of power: How people make decisions.* Cambridge, MA: MIT Press.

Klein, I., et al. (2000). Transient activity in the human calcarine cortex during visual-mental imagery: An event-related fMRI study. *Journal of Cognitive Neuroscience 12: Supplement 2*, 15–23.

Klein, S. B., & Kihlstrom, J. F. (1986). Elaboration, organization, and the self-reference effect in memory. *Journal of Experimental Psychology: General, 115*, 26–38.

Klin, C. M., Guzmán, A. E., & Levine, W. H. (1999). Prevalence and persistence of predictive inferences. *Journal of Memory and Learning, 40*, 593–604.

Knott, R., & Marslen-Wilson, W. (2001). Does the medial temporal lobe bind phonological memories? *Journal of Cognitive Neuroscience, 13,* 593–609.

Knowlton, B. (1997). Declarative and nondeclarative knowledge: Insights from cognitive neuroscience. In K. Lamberts & D. Shanks (Eds.), *Knowledge, concepts and categories* (pp. 215–246). Cambridge, MA: MIT Press.

Koestler, A. (1964). *The act of creation.* London: Hutchinson.

Komatsu, L. K. (1992). Recent views of conceptual structure. *Psychological Bulletin, 112,* 500–526.

Koriat, A. (1997). Monitoring one's own knowledge during study: A cue-utilization approach to judgments of learning. *Journal of Experimental Psychology: General, 126,* 349–370.

Koriat, A. (2000). Control processes in remembering. In E. Tulving & F. I. M. Craik (Eds.), *The Oxford handbook of memory* (pp. 333–346). New York: Oxford University Press.

Koriat, A. (2002). Metacognition research: An interim report. In T. J. Perfect & B. L. Schwartz (Eds.), *Applied metacognition* (pp. 261–286). Cambridge, England: Cambridge University Press.

Koriat, A., & Goldsmith, M. (1996). Memory metaphors and the real-life/laboratory controversy: Correspondence versus storehouse conceptions of memory. *Behavioral and Brain Science, 19,* 167–228.

Koriat, A., & Goldsmith, M. (1998). The role of metacognitive processes in the regulation of memory performance. In G. Mazzoni & T. O. Nelson (Eds.), *Metacognition and cognitive neuropsychology* (pp. 97–118). Mahwah, NJ: Erlbaum.

Koriat, A., Goldsmith, M., & Pansky, A. (2000). Toward a psychology of memory accuracy. *Annual Review of Psychology, 51,* 481–537.

Koriat, A., Sheffer, L., & Ma'ayan, H. (2002). Comparing objective and subjective learning curves: Judgments of learning exhibit increased underconfidence with practice. *Journal of Experimental Psychology: General, 131,* 147–162.

Kosslyn, S. M. (1975). Information representation in visual images. *Cognitive Psychology, 7,* 341–370.

Kosslyn, S. M. (1976). Using imagery to retrieve semantic information: A developmental study. *Child Development, 47,* 433–444.

Kosslyn, S. M. (1983). *Ghosts in the mind's machine: Creating and using images in the brain.* New York: Norton.

Kosslyn, S. M. (1999, January). *The brain and your students: How to explain why neuroscience is relevant to psychology.* Paper presented at the National Institute for the Teaching of Psychology, St. Petersburg Beach, FL.

Kosslyn, S. M. (2001). Visual consciousness. *Advances in Consciousness Research, 8,* 79–103.

Kosslyn, S. M., Alpert, N. M., & Thompson, W. L. (1995). Identifying objects at different levels of hierarchy: A positron emission tomography study. *Human Brain Mapping, 3,* 107–132.

Kosslyn, S. M., Ball, T. M., & Reiser, B. J. (1978). Visual images preserve metric spatial information: Evidence from studies of image scanning. *Journal of Experimental Psychology: Human Perception & Performance, 4,* 47–60.

Kosslyn, S. M., Ganis, G., & Thompson, W. L. (2001). Neural foundations of imagery. *Nature Reviews/Neuroscience, 2,* 635–642.

Kosslyn, S. M., Gazzaniga, M. S., Galaburda, A. M., & Rabin, C. (1999). Hemispheric specialization. In M. J. Zigmond et al. (Eds.), *Fundamental neuroscience* (pp. 1521–1542). San Diego: Academic Press.

Kosslyn, S. M., Seger, C., Pani, J. R., & Hillger, L. A. (1990). When is imagery used in everyday life? A diary study. *Journal of Mental Imagery, 14,* 131–152.

Kosslyn, S. M., & Shin, L. M. (1999). Imagery, mental. In G. Adelman & B. H. Smith (Eds.), *Elsevier's encyclopedia of neuroscience* (2nd ed., pp. 638–940). Amsterdam: Elsevier.

Kosslyn, S. M., & Thompson, W. L. (2000). Shared mechanisms in visual imagery and visual perception: Insights from cognitive neurosciences. In M. S. Gazzaniga (Ed.), *The new cognitive neurosciences* (2nd ed., pp. 975–985). Cambridge, MA: MIT Press.

Kosslyn, S. M., Thompson, W. L., Wraga, M., & Alpert, N. M. (2001). Imagining rotation by endogenous versus exogenous forces: Distinct neural mechanisms. *Cognitive Neuroscience and Neuropsychology, 12,* 2519–2525.

Kosslyn, S. M., et al. (1996). Individual differences in cerebral blood flow in Area 17 predict the time to evaluate visualized letters. *Journal of Cognitive Neuroscience, 8,* 78–82.

Kosslyn, S. M., et al. (1998). Mental rotation of objects versus hands: Neural mechanisms revealed by positron emission tomography. *Psychophysiology, 35,* 151–161.

Kosslyn, S. M., et al. (1999a). Hemispheric specialization. In M. J. Zigmond et al. (Eds.), *Fundamental neuroscience* (pp. 1521–1542). San Diego: Academic Press.

Kosslyn, S. M., et al. (1999b). The role of Area 17 in visual imagery: Convergent evidence from PET and rTMS. *Science, 284,* 167–170.

Kosslyn, S. M., et al. (2002). Bridging psychology and biology: The analysis of individuals in groups. *American Psychologist, 57,* 341–351.

Kozielecki, J. (1981). *Psychological decision theory.* Warsaw: Polish Scientific Publishers.

Krauss, R. M., & Chiu, C. (1998). Language and social behavior. In D. L. Gilbert, S. T. Fiske, & G. Lindzey (Eds.), *Handbook of social psychology* (4th ed., Vol. 2, pp. 41–88). New York: McGraw-Hill.

Krueger, L. E. (1992). The word-superiority effect and phonological recoding. *Memory & Cognition, 20,* 685–694.

Kruger, J. (1999) Lake Wobegon be gone! The "below-average effect" and the egocentric nature of comparative ability adjustments. *Journal of Personality and Social Psychology, 77,* 221–232.

Kruschke, J. K. (1996). Base rates in category learning. *Journal of Experimental Psychology: Learning, Memory, and Cognition, 22,* 3–26.

Kuczaj, S. A. (1977). The acquisition of regular and irregular past tense forms. *Journal of Verbal Learning and Verbal Behavior, 16,* 589–600.

Kuczaj, S. A. (1983). *Crib speech and language play.* New York: Springer-Verlag.

Kuczaj, S. A. (1999). The world of words: Thoughts on the development of a lexicon. In M. Barrett (Ed.), *The development of language* (pp. 133–159). Hove, England: Psychology Press.

Kuhl, P. K. (1994). Learning and representation in speech and language. *Current Opinion in Neurobiology, 4,* 812–822.

Kuhl, P. K. (2000). Language, mind, and brain: Experience alters perception. In M. Gazzaniga (Ed.), *The new cognitive neurosciences* (pp. 99–115). Cambridge, MA: MIT Press.

Kuhl, P. K., & Meltzoff, A. N. (1996). Infant vocalizations in response to speech: Vocal imitation and developmental change. *Journal of the Acoustical Society of America, 100,* 2425–2438.

Kuhl, P. K., et al. (1997). Cross-language analysis of phonetic units in language addressed to infants. *Science, 277,* 684–686.

Kuhn, D. (2000). Metacognitive development. *Current Directions in Psychological Science, 9,* 178–181.

Kumon-Nakamura, S., Glucksberg, S., & Brown, M. (1995). How about another piece of pie: The allu-sional pretense theory of discourse irony. *Journal of Experimental Psychology: General, 124,* 3–21.

Kunda, Z. (1999). *Social cognition: Making sense of people.* Cambridge, MA: MIT Press.

Kurtzberg, T. R., & Amabile, T. M. (2000–2001). From Guilford to creative synergy: Opening the black box of team-level creativity. *Creativity Research Journal, 13,* 285–294.

Kvavilashvili, L., & Ellis, J. (Eds.). (2000). New perspectives in prospective memory [special issue]. *Applied Cognitive Psychology, 14* (S1).

LaBerge, D. (1995). *Attentional processing: The brain's art of mindfulness.* Cambridge, MA: Harvard University Press.

Lambert, W. E. (1987). The effects of bilingual and bicultural experiences on children's attitudes and social perspectives. In P. Homel, M. Palij, & D. Aaronson (Eds.), *Childhood bilingualism: Aspects of linguistic, cognitive, and social development* (pp. 197–228). Hillsdale, NJ: Erlbaum.

Lambert, W. E. (1990). Persistent issues in bilingualism. In B. Harley, P. Allen, J. Cummins, & M. Swain (Eds.), *The development of second language proficiency* (pp. 201–218). Cambridge, England: Cambridge University Press.

Lambert, W. E. (1992). Challenging established views on social issues. *American Psychologist, 47,* 533–542.

Lambert, W. E., Genesee, F., Holobow, N., & Chartrand, L. (1991). *Bilingual education for majority English-speaking children.* Montreal: McGill University, Psychology Department.

Lampinen, J. M., Faries, J. M., Neuschatz, J. S., & Toglia, M. P. (2000). Recollections of things schematic: The influence of scripts on recollective experience. *Applied Cognitive Psychology, 14,* 543–554.

Landauer, T. K., & Dumais, S. T. (1997). A solution to Plato's problem: The latent semantic analysis theory of acquisition, induction, and representation of knowledge. *Psychological Review, 104,* 211–240.

Landauer, T. K., Foltz, P. W., & Laham, D. (1998). Introduction to latent semantic analysis. *Discourse Processes, 25,* 259–284.

Langer, E. J. (1997). *The power of mindful learning.* Reading, MA: Addison-Wesley.

Langer, E. J. (2000). Mindful learning. *Current Directions in Psychological Science, 9,* 220–223.

Langer, E. J. (2002). Well-being: Mindfulness versus positive evaluation. In C. R. Snyder (Ed.), *Handbook of positive psychology*. New York: Oxford University Press.

Langer, E. J., & Moldoveanu, M. (2000). The construct of mindfulness. *Journal of Social Issues, 56*, 1–9.

Lappin, J. S., & Craft, W. D. (2000). Foundations of spatial vision: From retinal images to perceived shapes. *Psychological Review, 107*, 6–38.

Larkin, J. H. (1983). The role of problem representation in physics. In D. Gentner & A. L. Stevens (Eds.), *Mental models* (pp. 75–98). Hillsdale, NJ: Erlbaum.

Larkin, J. H. (1985). Understanding, problem representations, and skill in physics. In S. F. Chipman, J. W. Segal, & R. Glaser (Eds.), *Thinking and learning skills* (Vol. 2, pp. 141–159). Hillsdale, NJ: Erlbaum.

Larsen, A., & Bundesen, C. (1996). A template-matching pandemonium recognizes unconstrained handwritten characters with high accuracy. *Memory & Cognition, 24*, 136–143.

Laszlo, E., Artigiani, R., Combs, A., & Csányi, V. (1996). *Changing visions: Human cognitive maps, past, present, and future*. Westport, CT: Praeger.

Lave, J. (1988). *Cognition in practice: Mind, mathematics, and culture in everyday life*. New York: Cambridge University Press.

Lave, J. (1997). What's special about experiments as contexts for thinking. In M. Cole, Y. Engeström, & O. Vasquez (Eds.), *Mind, culture, and activity* (pp. 56–69). New York: Cambridge University Press.

Leather, J., & James, A. (1996). Second language speech. In W. C. Ritchie & T. K. Bhatia (Eds.), *Handbook of second language acquisition* (pp. 269–316). San Diego: Academic Press.

Lehman, A. C., & Ericsson, K. A. (1998). Historical developments of expert performance: Public performance of music. In A. Steptoe (Ed.), *Genius and the mind* (pp. 67–94). Oxford, England: Oxford University Press.

Leichtman, M. D., & Ceci, S. J. (1995). The effects of stereotypes and suggestions on preschoolers' reports. *Developmental Psychology, 31*, 568–578.

Leighton, J. P., & Sternberg, R. J. (2003). Reasoning and problem solving. In A. F. Healy & R. W. Proctor (Eds.), *Handbook of psychology* (Vol. 4, pp. 623–648). Hoboken, NJ: Wiley.

Leonhard, C., & Corrigan, P. W. (2000). Social perception in schizophrenia. In P. W. Corrigan & D. L. Penn (Eds.), *Social cognition and schizophrenia* (pp. 73–95). Washington, DC: American Psychological Association.

Levelt, W. J. M. (1994). The skill of speaking. In P. Bertelson, P. Eelen, & G. d'Ydewalle (Eds.), *International perspectives on psychological science* (Vol. 1, pp. 89–103). Hove, England: Erlbaum.

Levelt, W. J. M. (1998). The genetic perspective in psycholinguistics or where do spoken words come from? *Journal of Psycholinguistic Research, 27*, 167–180.

Levelt, W. J. M., Roelofs, A., & Meyer, A. S. (1999). A theory of lexical access in speech production. *Behavioral and Brain Sciences, 22*, 1–75.

Levelt, W. J. M., et al. (1998). An MEG study of picture naming. *Journal of Cognitive Neuroscience, 10*, 553–567.

Levesque, L. C. (2001). *Breakthrough creativity: Achieving top performance using the eight creative talents*. Palo Alto, CA: Davies-Black.

Levine, D. S. (2002). Neural network modeling. In H. Pashler (Ed.), *Stevens' handbook of experimental psychology* (3rd ed., Vol. 4, pp. 223–269), New York: Wiley.

Levine, L. J. (1997). Reconstructing memory for emotions. *Journal of Experimental Psychology: General, 126*, 165–177.

Levine, L. J., & Burgess, S. L. (1997). Beyond general arousal: Effects of specific emotions on memory. *Social Cognition, 15*, 157–181.

Levy, B., & Banaji, M. R. (2002). Implicit ageism. In T. D. Nelson (Ed.), *Ageism: Stereotyping and prejudice against older persons* (pp. 49–75). Cambridge, MA: MIT Press.

Levy, B., & Langer, E. (1994). Aging free from negative stereotypes: Successful memory in China and among the American Deaf. *Journal of Personality and Social Psychology, 67*, 689–997.

Levy, B. A. (1999). Whole words, segments, and meaning: Approaches to reading education. In R. M. Klein & P. McMullen (Eds.), *Converging methods for understanding reading and dyslexia* (pp. 77–110). Cambridge, MA: MIT Press.

Levy, C. M., & Ransdell, S. (1995). Is writing as difficult as it seems? *Memory & Cognition, 23*, 767–779.

Lewandowsky, S., & Li, S.-C. (1995). Catastrophic interference in neural networks: Causes, solutions, and data. In F. N. Dempster & C. J. Brainerd (Eds.), *Interference and inhibition in cognition* (pp. 329–361). San Diego: Academic Press.

Li, S-C. (2002). Connecting the many levels and facets of cognitive aging. *Current Directions in Psychological Science, 11,* 38–43.

Liberman, A. M. (1996). *Speech: A special code.* Cambridge, MA: MIT Press.

Liberman, A. M., & Mattingly, I. G. (1989). A specialization for speech perception. *Science, 243,* 489–494.

Light, L. L. (1996). Memory and aging. In E. L. Bjork & R. A. Bjork (Eds.), *Memory* (2nd ed., pp. 443–490). San Diego: Academic Press.

Light, L. L. (2000). Memory changes in adulthood. In S. H. Qualls & N. Abeles (Eds.), *Psychology and the aging revolution* (pp. 73–97). Washington, DC: American Psychological Association.

Light, L. L., La Voie, D., & Kennison, R. (1995). Repetition priming of nonwords in young and older adults. *Journal of Experimental Psychology: Learning, Memory, and Cognition, 21,* 327–346.

Lindsay, D. S., Read, J. D., & Sharma, K. (1998). Accuracy and confidence in person identification: The relationship is strong when witnessing conditions vary widely. *Psychological Science, 9,* 215–218.

Linville, P. W., Fischer, G. W., & Fischhoff, B. (1993). AIDS risk perceptions and decision biases. In J. B. Pryor & G. D. Reeder (Eds.), *The social psychology of HIV infection* (pp. 5–38). Hillsdale, NJ: Erlbaum.

Liversedge, S. P., & Findlay, J. M. (2000). Saccadic eye movements and cognition. *Trends in Cognitive Sciences, 4,* 6–14.

Lockhart, R. S. (2000). Methods of memory research. In E. Tulving & F. I. M. Craik (Eds.), *The Oxford handbook of memory* (pp. 45–57). New York: Oxford University Press.

Lockhart, R. S. (2001). Commentary: Levels of processing and memory theory. In M. Naveh-Benjamin, M. Moscovitch, & H. L. Roediger, III (Eds.), *Perspectives on human memory and cognitive aging: Essays in honour of Fergus Craik* (pp. 99–102). New York: Psychology Press.

Loftus, E. F. (1997, September). Creating false memories. *Scientific American,* pp. 70–75.

Loftus, E. F. (2000). Remembering what never happened. In E. Tulving (Ed.), *Memory, consciousness, and the brain* (pp. 106–118). Philadelphia: Psychology Press.

Loftus, E. F., & Guyer, M. J. (2002a, May/June). Who abused Jane Doe? (Part 1). *Skeptical Inquirer,* pp. 24–32.

Loftus, E. F., & Guyer, M. J. (2002b, July/August). Who abused Jane Doe? (Part 2). *Skeptical Inquirer,* pp. 37–40.

Loftus, E. F., Miller, D. G., & Burns, H. J. (1978). Semantic integration of verbal information into visual memory. *Journal of Experimental Psychology: Human Learning and Memory, 4,* 19–31.

Logan, G. D. (2002a). An instance theory of attention and memory. *Psychological Review, 109,* 376–400.

Logan, G. D. (2002b). Parallel and serial processing. In H. Pashler & J. Wixted (Eds.), *Stevens' handbook of experimental psychology* (3rd ed., Vol. 4, pp. 271–300), New York: Wiley.

Logie, R. H. (1995). *Visuo-spatial working memory.* Hove, England: Erlbaum.

Logie, R. H., & Gilhooly, K. J. (Eds.). (1998). *Working memory and thinking.* Hove, England: Psychology Press.

Lorch, R. F., Jr., Klusewitz, M. A., & Lorch, E. P. (1995). Distinctions among reading situations. In R. F. Lorch, Jr., & E. J. O'Brien (Eds.), *Sources of coherence in reading* (pp. 375–398). Hillsdale, NJ: Erlbaum.

Lord, R. C., Hanges, P. J., & Godfrey, E. G. (2003). Integrating neural networks into decision-making and motivational theory: Rethinking VIE theory. *Canadian Psychology/Psychologie canadienne, 44,* 21–38.

Lovelace, E. A. (1984). Metamemory: Monitoring future recallability during study. *Journal of Experimental Psychology: Learning, Memory, and Cognition, 10,* 756–766.

Lovelace, E. A. (1996). *Personal communication.*

Lovett, M. C. (2002). Problem solving. In D. Medin (Ed.), *Stevens' handbook of experimental psychology* (pp. 317–362). New York: Wiley.

Luchins, A. S. (1942). Mechanization in problem solving. *Psychological Monographs, 54* (Whole No. 248).

Luck, S. J., & Girelli, M. (1998). Electrophysiological approaches to the study of selective attention in the human brain. In R. Parasuraman (Ed.), *The attentive brain* (pp. 71–94). Cambridge, MA: MIT Press.

Luck, S. J., & Vecera, S. P. (2002). Attention. In H. Pashler (Ed.), *Stevens' handbook of experimental psychology* (3rd ed., Vol. 1, pp. 235–286). New York: Wiley.

Luger, G. F. (1994). *Cognitive science: The science of intelligent systems.* San Diego: Academic Press.

Luo, C. R., Johnson, R. A., & Gallo, D. A. (1998). Automatic activation of phonological information in reading: Evidence from the semantic related-ness decision task. *Memory & Cognition, 26,* 833–843.

Luo, Y., Baillargeon, R., Brueckner, L., & Munakata, Y. (2003). Reasoning about a hidden object after a delay: Evidence for robust representations in 5-month-old infants. *Cognition, 88,* B23–B32.

Lustig, C., & Hasher, L. (2001a). Implicit memory is not immune to interference. *Psychological Bulletin, 127,* 618–628.

Lustig, C., & Hasher, L. (2001b). Implicit memory is vulnerable to proactive interference. *Psychological Science, 12,* 408–412.

Lustig, C., Hasher, L., & Tonev, S. T. (2001). In-hibitory control over the present and the past. *European Journal of Cognitive Psychology, 13,* 107–122.

Lustig, C., May, C. P., & Hasher, L. (2001). Working memory span and the role of proactive interference. *Journal of Experimental Psychology: General, 120,* 199–207.

Lynch, E. B., Coley, J. D., & Medin, D. L. (2000). Tall is typical: Central tendency, ideal dimensions, and graded category structure among tree experts and novices. *Memory & Cognition, 28,* 41–50.

Lynn, S. J., Lock, T. G., Myers, B., & Payne, D. G. (1997). Recalling the unrecallable: Should hypnosis be used to recover memories in psychotherapy? *Current Directions in Psychological Science, 6,* 79–83.

Lynn, S. J., & McConkey, K. M. (Eds.). (1998). *Truth in memory.* New York: Guilford.

MacDonald, M. C. (1999). Distributional information in language comprehension, production, and acqui-sition: Three puzzles and a moral. In B. MacWhin-ney (Ed.), *The emergence of language* (pp. 177–196). Mahwah, NJ: Erlbaum.

MacLeod, C., & Campbell, L. (1992). Memory accessi-bility and probability judgments: An experimental evaluation of the availability heuristic. *Journal of Personality and Social Psychology, 63,* 890–902.

MacLeod, C. M. (1991). Half a century of research on the Stroop effect: An integrative review. *Psychological Bulletin, 109,* 163–203.

MacLeod, C. M. (1997, March/April). Is your atten-tion under your control? The diabolic Stroop effect. *Psychological Science Agenda,* pp. 6–7.

MacLin, O. H., & Malpass, R. S. (2001). Racial catego-rization of faces: The ambiguous race face effect. *Psychology, Public Policy, and Law, 7,* 98–118.

MacWhinney, B. (1998). Models of the emergence of language. *Annual Review of Psychology, 49,* 199–227.

Madigan, R., Johnson, S., & Linton, P. (1995). The language of psychology: APA style as epistemology. *American Psychologist, 50,* 428–436.

Madigan, S., & O'Hara, R. (1992). Short-term mem-ory at the turn of the century: Mary Whiton Calkins's memory research. *American Psychologist, 47,* 170–174.

Maier, N. R. F. (1931). Reasoning in humans: II. The so-lution of a problem and its appearance in conscious-ness. *Journal of Comparative Psychology, 12,* 181–194.

Maki, R. H. (1998). Test predictions over text material. In D. J. Hacker, J. Dunlosky, & H. C. Graesser (Eds.), *Metacognition in educational theory and practice* (pp. 117–144). Mahwah, NJ: Erlbaum.

Maki, R. H., & Berry, S. L. (1984). Metacomprehen-sion of text material. *Journal of Experimental Psychol-ogy: Learning, Memory, and Cognition, 10,* 663–679.

Maki, R. H., Jonas, D., & Kallod, M. (1994). The rela-tionship between comprehension and metacompre-hension ability. *Psychonomic Bulletin & Review, 1,* 126–129.

Maki, R. H., & McGuire, M. J. (2002). Metacognition for text: Findings and implications for education. In T. J. Perfect & B. L. Schwartz (Eds.), *Applied metacognition* (pp. 39–67). Cambridge, England: Cambridge University Press.

Maki, R. H., & Serra, M. (1992). The basis of test predic-tion for text material. *Journal of Experimental Psychol-ogy: Learning, Memory, and Cognition, 18,* 116–126.

Maki, W. S., & Maki, R. H. (2000). Evaluation of a web-based introductory psychology course: II. Con-tingency management to increase use of on-line study aids. *Behavior Research Methods, Instruments & Computers, 32,* 240–245.

Mandel, D. R., Jusczyk, P. W., & Pisoni, D. B. (1995). Infants' recognition of the sound patterns of their own names. *Psychological Science, 6,* 314–317.

Mandler, G. (1985). *Cognitive psychology: An essay in cog-nitive science.* Hillsdale, NJ: Erlbaum.

Mandler, J. M. (1997). Development of categorization: Perceptual and conceptual categories. In G. Brem-ner, A. Slater, & G. Butterworth (Eds.), *Infant devel-opment: Recent advances.* Hove, England: Erlbaum.

Mandler, J. M. (2002). On the foundations of the se-mantic system. In E. Forde & G. Humphreys (Eds.), *Category-specificity in brain and mind.* Hove, England: Psychology Press.

Mandler, J. M. (2003). Conceptual categorization. In D. Rakison & L. M. Oakes (Eds.), *Early category and concept development.* New York: Oxford University Press.

Mandler, J. M., & McDonough, L. (1993). Concept formation in infancy. *Cognitive Development, 8,* 291–318.

Mandler, J. M., & McDonough, L. (1997). Nonverbal recall. In N. L. Stein, P. A. Ornstein, B. Tversky, & C. Brainerd (Eds.), *Memory for everyday and emotional events* (pp. 141–164). Mahwah, NJ: Erlbaum.

Manis, M., Shedler, J., Jonides, J., & Nelson, T. E. (1993). Availability heuristic in judgments of set size and frequency of occurrence. *Journal of Personality and Social Psychology, 65,* 448–457.

Manktelow, K. (1999). *Reasoning and thinking.* East Sussex, England: Psychology Press.

Mäntylä, T. (1997). Recollections of faces: Remembering differences and knowing similarities. *Journal of Experimental Psychology: Learning, Memory, and Cognition, 23,* 1203–1216.

Maratsos, M., & Matheny, L. (1994). Language specificity and elasticity: Brain and clinical syndrome studies. *Annual Review of Psychology, 45,* 487–516.

Marcus, G. F. (1996). Why do children say "breaked"? *Current Directions in Psychological Science, 5,* 81–85.

Markman, A. B. (1999). *Knowledge representation.* Mahwah, NJ: Erlbaum.

Markman, A. B. (2002). Knowledge representation. In D. Medin (Ed.), *Stevens' handbook of experimental psychology* (3rd ed., Vol. 2, pp. 165–208). New York: Wiley.

Markman, A. B., & Gentner, D. (2001). Thinking. *Annual Review of Psychology, 52,* 223–247.

Markman, A. B., & Makin, V. S. (1998). Referential communication and category acquisition. *Journal of Experimental Psychology: General, 127,* 331–354.

Markman, A. B., & Medin, D. L. (2002). Decision making. In D. Medin (Ed.), *Stevens' handbook of experimental psychology* (3rd. ed., Vol. 2, pp. 413–466). New York: Wiley.

Marsh, R. L., & Hicks, J. L. (1998). Event-based prospective memory and executive control of working memory. *Journal of Experimental Psychology: Learning, Memory, and Cognition, 24,* 336–349.

Marsh, R. L., Hicks, J. L., & Hancock, T. W. (2000). On the interaction of ongoing cognitive activity and the nature of an event-based intention. *Applied Cognitive Psychology, 14,* S29–S41.

Marsh, R. L., Hicks, J. L., & Landau, J. D. (1998). An investigation of everyday prospective memory. *Memory & Cognition, 26,* 633–643.

Marsh, R. L., Landau, J. D., & Hicks, J. L. (1997). Contributions of inadequate source monitoring to unconscious plagiarism during idea generation. *Journal of Experimental Psychology: Learning, Memory, and Cognition, 23,* 886–897.

Marslen-Wilson, W. D., Tyler, L. K., & Koster, C. (1993). Integrative processes in utterance resolution. *Journal of Memory and Language, 32,* 647–666.

Martin, E. (1967). Personal communication.

Martin, L. L., & Clore, G. L. (Eds.). (2001). *Theories of mood and cognition.* Mahwah, NJ: Erlbaum.

Martindale, C. (1991). *Cognitive psychology: A neural-network approach.* Pacific Grove, CA: Brooks/Cole.

Massaro, D. W. (1998). *Perceiving talking faces.* Cambridge, MA: MIT Press.

Massaro, D. W. (1999a). Speech perception. In F. Fabbro (Ed.), *Concise encyclopedia of language pathology* (pp. 42–57). Amsterdam: Elsevier.

Massaro, D. W. (1999b), Speech reading: Illusion or window into pattern recognition? *Trends in Cognitive Sciences, 3,* 310–317.

Massaro, D. W., Cohen, M. M., & Smeele, P. M. T. (1995). Cross-linguistic comparisons in the integration of visual and auditory speech. *Memory & Cognition, 23,* 113–131.

Massaro, D. W., & Cole, R. (2000, August). From "speech is special" to talking heads in language learning. *Proceedings of Integrating Speech Technology in the (Language) Learning and Assistive Interface,* pp. 153–161.

Massaro, D. W., & Cowan, N. (1993). Information processing models: Microscopes of the mind. *Annual Review of Psychology, 44,* 383–425.

Massaro, D. W., & Stork, D. G. (1998). Speech recognition and sensory integration. *American Scientist, 86,* 236–244.

Mast, F., Kosslyn, S. M., & Berthoz, A. (1999). Visual mental imagery interferes with allocentric orientation judgements. *NeuroReport, 10,* 3549–3553.

Matlin, M. W. (1994). *Cognition* (3rd ed.). Fort Worth, TX: Harcourt Brace.

Matlin, M. W. (1999). *Psychology* (3rd ed.). Fort Worth, TX: Harcourt Brace.

Matlin, M. W. (2004a) Pollyanna Principle. In R. Pohl (Ed.), *Cognitive illusions: Handbook on fallacies and biases in thinking, judgment, and memory.* Hove, England: Psychology Press.

Matlin, M. W. (2004b). *The psychology of women* (5th ed.). Belmont, CA: Wadsworth.

Matlin, M. W., & Foley, H. J. (1997). *Sensation and perception* (4th ed.). Boston: Allyn and Bacon.

Matlin, M. W., & Stang, D. J. (1978). *The Pollyanna Principle: Selectivity in language, memory, and thought.* Cambridge, MA: Schenkman.

Matlin, M. W., et al. (1979). Evaluative meaning as a determinant of spew position. *Journal of General Psychology, 100,* 3–11.

Mayer, R. E. (1999). Fifty years of creativity research. In R. J. Sternberg (Ed.), *Handbook of creativity* (pp. 449–460). New York: Cambridge University Press.

Mayer, R. E., & Hegarty, M. (1996). The process of understanding mathematical problems. In R. J. Sternberg & T. Ben-Zeev (Eds.), *The nature of mathematical thinking* (pp. 29–53). Mahwah, NJ: Erlbaum.

Mayhorn, C. B., Fisk, A. D., & Whittle, J. D. (2002). Decisions, decisions: Analysis of age, cohort, and time of testing on framing of risky decision options. *Human Factors, 44,* 515–521.

Mazuka, R. (1998). *The development of language processing strategies: A cross-linguistic study between Japanese and English.* Mahwah, NJ: Erlbaum.

Mazzoni, G., Cornoldi, C., Tomat, L., & Vecchi, T. (1997). Remembering the grocery shopping list: A study on metacognitive biases. *Applied Cognitive Psychology, 11,* 253–267.

McAdams, S., & Drake, C. (2002). Auditory perception and cognition. In S. Yantis (Ed.), *Stevens' handbook of experimental psychology* (3rd ed., Vol. 1, pp. 397–452). New York: Wiley.

McClelland, J. L. (1981). Retrieving general and specific knowledge from stored knowledge of specifics. *Proceedings of the Third Annual Conference of the Cognitive Science Society, 170–172.*

McClelland, J. L. (1995). Constructive memory and memory distortions: A parallel-distributed processing approach. In D. L. Schacter (Ed.), *Memory distortion: How minds, brains, and societies reconstruct the past* (pp. 71–89). Cambridge, MA: Harvard University Press.

McClelland, J. L. (1999). Cognitive modeling, connectionist. In R. A. Wilson & F. C. Keil (Eds.), *The MIT encyclopedia of the cognitive sciences* (pp. 137–139). Cambridge, MA: MIT Press.

McClelland, J. L. (2000). Connectionist models of memory. In E. Tulving & F. I. M. Craik (Eds.), *The Oxford handbook of memory* (pp. 583–597). New York: Oxford University Press.

McClelland, J. L., & Rumelhart, D. E. (1981). An interactive activation model of context effects in letter perception: Part 1: An account of basic findings. *Psychological Review, 88,* 375–407.

McClelland, J. L., & Rumelhart, D. E. (Eds.). (1986). *Parallel distributed processing: Explorations in the microstructure of cognition* (Vol. 2). Cambridge, MA: MIT Press.

McClelland, J. L., Rumelhart, D. E., & Hinton, G. E. (1986). The appeal of parallel distributed processing. In D. E. Rumelhart, J. L. McClelland, and the PDP Research Group (Eds.), *Parallel distributed processing* (Vol. 1, pp. 3–44). Cambridge, MA: MIT Press.

McClelland, J. L., & Seidenberg, M. S. (2000). Why do kids say *goed* and *brang*? *Science, 287,* 47–48.

McCloskey, M., & Cohen, N. J. (1989). Catastrophic interference in connectionist networks: The sequential learning problem. *The Psychology of Learning and Motivation, 24,* 109–165.

McConkey, K. M., Barnier, A. J., & Sheehan, P. W. (1998). Hypnosis and pseudomemory: Understanding the findings and their implications. In S. J. Lynn & K. M. McConkey (Eds.), *Truth in memory* (pp. 227–259). New York: Guilford.

McDaniel, M. A., & Einstein, G. O. (2000). Strategic and automatic processes in prospective memory retrieval: A multiprocess framework. *Applied Cognitive Psychology, 14,* S127–S144.

McDaniel, M. A., Waddill, P. J., & Shakesby, P. S. (1996). Study strategies, interest, and learning from text: The application of material appropriate processing. In D. J. Herrmann et al. (Eds.), *Basic and applied memory research: Practical applications* (Vol. 1, pp. 385–397). Mahwah, NJ: Erlbaum.

McDaniel, M. A., et al. (1999). Prospective memory: A neuropsychological study. *Neuropsychology, 13,* 103–110.

McDermott, R. (1998). *Risk taking in international politics: Prospect theory in American foreign policy.* Ann Arbor: University of Michigan.

McDonald, J. L. (1997). Language acquisition: The acquisition of linguistic structure in normal and special populations. *Annual Review of Psychology, 48,* 215–241.

McDonough, L., & Mandler, J. M. (1998). Inductive generalization in 9- and 11-month-olds. *Developmental Science, 1,* 227–232.

McDougall, S., & Gruneberg, M. (2002). What memory strategy is best for examinations in psychology? *Applied Cognitive Psychology, 16,* 451–458.

McGurk, H., & McDonald, J. (1976). Hearing lips and seeing voices. *Nature, 264,* 746–748.

McKelvie, S. J. (1990). Einstellung: Luchins' effect lives on. *Journal of Social Behavior and Personality, 5,* 105–121.

McKelvie, S. J. (1997). The availability heuristic: Effects of fame and gender on the estimated frequency of male and female names. *Journal of Social Psychology, 137,* 63–78.

McKelvie, S. J., Sano, E. K., & Stout, D. (1994). Effects of colored separate and interactive pictures on cued recall. *Journal of General Psychology, 12,* 241–251.

McKenzie, C. R. M. (1998). Taking into account the strength of an alternative hypothesis. *Journal of Experimental Psychology: Learning, Memory, and Cognition, 24,* 771–792.

McKoon, G., & Ratcliff, R. (1998). Memory-based language processing: Psycholinguistic research in the 1990s. *Annual Review of Psychology, 49,* 25–42.

McNally, R. J. (2003). Recovered memories of trauma: A view from the laboratory. *Current Directions in Psychological Science, 12,* 32–35.

McNamara, T. P., & Diwadkar, V. A. (1997). Symmetry and asymmetry of human spatial memory. *Cognitive Psychology, 34,* 160–190.

McNeil, J. E., & Warrington, E. K. (1993). Prosopagnosia: A face-specific disorder. *Quarterly Journal of Experimental Psychology, 46A,* 1–10.

Medin, D. L., Lynch, E. B., & Solomon, K. O. (2000). Are there kinds of concepts? *Annual Review of Psychology, 51,* 121–147.

Mellers, B., Hertwig, R., & Kahneman, D. (2001). Do frequency representations eliminate conjunction effects: An exercise in adversarial collaboration. *Psychological Science, 12,* 269–275.

Mellers, B., Schwartz, A., & Cooke, A. D. J. (1998). Judgment and decision making. *Annual Review of Psychology, 49,* 447–477.

Mendola, J. (2003). Contextual shape processing in human visual cortex: Beginning to fill-in the blanks. In L. Pessoa & P. De Weerd (Eds.), *Filling-in: From perceptual completion to cortical reorganization* (pp. 38–58). New York: Oxford University Press.

Menyuk, P., Liebergott, J. W., & Schultz, M. C. (1995). *Early language development in full-term and premature infants.* Hillsdale, NJ: Erlbaum.

Merikle, P. M., Smilek, D., & Eastwood, J. D. (2001). Perception without awareness: Perspectives from cognitive psychology. In S. Dehaene (Ed.), *The cognitive neuroscience of consciousness* (pp. 115–134). Cambridge, MA: MIT Press.

Mervis, C. B., Catlin, J., & Rosch, E. (1976). Relationships among goodness-of-example, category norms, and word frequency. *Bulletin of the Psychonomic Society, 7,* 283–284.

Metcalfe, J. (1986). Premonitions of insight predict impending error. *Journal of Experimental Psychology: Learning, Memory, and Cognition, 12,* 623–634.

Metcalfe, J. (1998a). Cognitive optimism: Self-deception or memory-based processing heuristics? *Personality and Social Psychology Review, 2,* 100–110.

Metcalfe, J. (1998b). Insight and metacognition. In G. Mazzoni & T. O. Nelson (Eds.), *Metacognition and cognitive neuropsychology* (pp. 181–197). Mahwah, NJ: Erlbaum.

Metcalfe, J. (2000). Metamemory. In E. Tulving & F. I. M. Craik (Eds.), *The Oxford handbook of memory* (pp. 197–211). New York: Oxford University Press.

Metcalfe, J. (2002). Is study time allocated selectively to a region of proximal learning? *Journal of Experimental Psychology: General, 131,* 349–363.

Metcalfe, J., & Wiebe, D. (1987). Intuition in insight and noninsight problem solving. *Memory & Cognition, 15,* 238–246.

Meyer, A. S. (2000). Form representations in word production. In L. Wheeldon (Ed.), *Aspects of language production* (pp. 49–70). Philadelphia: Psychology Press.

Meyer, D. E., & Kieras, D. E. (1997). A computational theory of executive cognitive processes and multiple-task performance: Part 1. Basic mechanisms. *Psychological Review, 104,* 3–65.

Michael, E. B., Keller, T. A., Carpenter, P. A., & Just, M. A. (2001). fMRI investigation of sentence comprehension by eye and by ear: Modality fingerprints on cognitive processes. *Human Brain Mapping, 13,* 239–252.

Miller, G. A. (1956). The magical number seven, plus or minus two: Some limits on our capacity for processing information. *Psychological Review, 63,* 81–97.

Miller, G. A. (1962). *Psychology: The science of mental life.* New York: Harper & Row.

Miller, G. A. (1967). The psycholinguists. In G. A. Miller (Ed.), *The psychology of communication* (pp. 70–92). London: Penguin.

Miller, G. A. (1979). *A very personal history.* Address to Cognitive Science Workshop, Massachusetts Institute of Technology, Cambridge, MA.

Miller, G. A. (1999). On knowing a word. *Annual Review of Psychology, 50,* 1–19.

Miller, J. L. (1999). Speech perception. In R. A. Wilson & F. C. Keil (Eds.), *The MIT encyclopedia of the cognitive sciences* (pp. 787–790). Cambridge, MA: MIT Press.

Miller, J. L., & Eimas, P. D. (1995b). Speech perception: From signal to word. *Annual Review of Psychology, 46,* 467–492.

Miller, L. C., Lechner, R. E., & Rugs, D. (1985). Development of conversational responsiveness: Preschoolers' use of responsive listener cues and relevant comments. *Developmental Psychology, 21,* 473–480.

Miller, M. C. (2001). *The Bush dyslexicon.* New York: Norton.

Milliken, B., Joordens, S., Merikle, P. M., & Seiffert, A. E. (1998). Selective attention: A reevaluation of the implications of negative priming. *Psychological Review, 105,* 203–229.

Millis, K. K., & Cohen, R. (1994). Spatial representations and updating situation models. *Reading Research Quarterly, 29,* 369–380.

Millis, K. K., & Graesser, A. C. (1994). The time-course of constructing knowledge-based inferences for scientific texts. *Journal of Memory and Language, 33,* 583–599.

Milner, B. (1966). Amnesia following operation on the temporal lobes. In C. W. M. Whitty & O. L. Zangwill (Eds.), *Amnesia following operation on the temporal lobes* (pp. 109–133). London: Butterworth.

Miozzo, M., & Caramazza, A. (1997). Retrieval of lexical-syntactic features in tip-of-the-tongue states. *Journal of Experimental Psychology: Learning, Memory, and Cognition, 23,* 1410–1423.

Mitchell, K. J., & Johnson, M. K. (2000). Source monitoring: Attributing mental experiences. In E. Tulving & F. I. M. Craik (Eds.), *The Oxford handbook of memory* (pp. 179–195). New York: Oxford University Press.

Miyake, A. (2001a). Individual differences in working memory: Introduction to the special section. *Journal of Experimental Psychology: General, 130,* 163–168.

Miyake, A. (Ed.). (2001b). Individual differences in working memory [Special issue]. *Journal of Experimental Psychology: General, 130,* 163–168.

Miyake, A., Just, M. A., & Carpenter, P. A. (1994). Working memory constraints on the resolution of lexical ambiguity: Maintaining multiple interpretations in neutral contexts. *Journal of Memory and Language, 33,* 175–202.

Miyake, A., & Shah, P. (Eds.). (1999a). *Models of working memory: Mechanisms of active maintenance and executive control* (pp. 442–481). New York: Cambridge University Press.

Miyake, A., & Shah, P. (1999b). Toward unified theories of working memory. In A. Miyake & P. Shah (Eds.), *Models of working memory: Mechanisms of active maintenance and executive control* (pp. 442–481). New York: Cambridge University Press.

Miyashita, Y. (1995). How the brain creates imagery: Projection to primary visual cortex. *Science, 268,* 1719–1720.

Moar, I., & Bower, G. H. (1983). Inconsistency in spatial knowledge. *Memory & Cognition, 11,* 107–113.

Moely, B. E., Olson, F. A., Halwes, T. G., & Flavell, J. H. (1969). Production deficiency in young children's clustered recall. *Developmental Psychology, 1,* 26–34.

Moldoveanu, M., & Langer, E. (2002). When "stupid" is smarter than we are. In R. J. Sternberg (Ed.), *Why smart people can be so stupid* (pp. 212–231). New Haven, CT: Yale University Press.

Moore, J. D., & Wiemer-Hastings, P. (2003). Discourse in computational linguistics and artificial Intelligence. In A. C. Graesser, M. A. Gernsbacher, & S. R. Goldman (Eds.), *Handbook of discourse processes* (pp. 439–485). Mahwah, NJ: Erlbaum.

Moran, A. P. (1996). *The psychology of concentration in sport performers: A cognitive analysis.* East Sussex, England: Psychology Press.

Moravcsik, J. E., & Kintsch, W. (1993). Writing quality, reading skills, and domain knowledge as factors in text comprehension. *Canadian Journal of Experimental Psychology, 47,* 360–374.

Moray, N. (1959). Attention in dichotic listening: Affective cues and the influence of instructions. *Quarterly Journal of Experimental Psychology, 11,* 56–60.

Morris, P. E. (1992). Prospective memory: Remembering to do things. In M. Gruneberg & P. Morris (Eds.), *Aspects of memory* (2nd ed., Vol. 1, pp. 196–222). New York: Routledge.

Morris, R. K., & Binder, K. S. (2001). What happens to the unselected meaning of an ambiguous word in skilled reading? In D. S. Gorfein (Ed.), *On the consequences of meaning selection: Perspectives on resolving lexical ambiguity* (pp. 139–153). Washington, DC: American Psychological Association.

Moscovitch, M., & Craik, F. I. M. (1976). Depth of processing, retrieval cues, and uniqueness of encoding as factors in recall. *Journal of Verbal Learning and Verbal Behavior, 15,* 447–458.

Moses, L., & Baird, J. A. (1999). Metacognition. In R. A. Wilson & F. C. Keil (Eds.), *The MIT encyclopedia of the cognitive sciences* (pp. 533–534). Cambridge, MA: MIT Press.

Moses, Y., Ullman, S., & Edelman, S. (1996). Generalization to novel images in upright and inverted faces. *Perception, 25,* 443–461.

Most, S. B., et al. (2001). How not to be seen: The contribution of similarity and selective ignoring to sustained inattentional blindness. *Psychological Science, 12,* 9–17.

Mountcastle, V. B. (1979). An organizing principle for cerebral function: The unit module and the distributed system. In F. O. Schmitt (Ed.), *The neurosciences: Fourth study program.* Cambridge, MA: The MIT Press.

Moynahan, E. D. (1978). Assessment and selection of paired associate strategies: A developmental study. *Journal of Experimental Child Psychology, 26,* 257–266.

Murdock, B. (2001). Analysis of the serial position curve. In H. L. Roediger, III, J. S. Nairne, I. Neath, & A. M. Surprenant (Eds.), *The nature of remembering* (pp. 151–188). Washington, DC: American Psychological Association.

Murphy, G. L. (2002). *The big book of concepts.* Cambridge, MA: MIT Press.

Murphy, G. L., & Shapiro, A. M. (1994). Forgetting of verbatim information in discourse. *Memory & Cognition, 22,* 85–94.

Murray, B. (1998, August). The latest techno tool: Essay-grading computers. *APA Monitor,* p. 43.

Murray, L. A., Whitehouse, W. G., & Alloy, L. B. (1999). Mood congruence and depressive deficits in memory: A forced-recall analysis. *Memory, 7,* 175–196.

Mussweiler, T., Englich, B., & Strack, F. (2004). Anchoring effects. In R. Pohl (Ed.), *Cognitive illusions: Handbook on fallacies and biases in thinking, judgment, and memory.* Hove, England: Psychology Press.

Myers, D. G. (2002). *Intuition: Its powers and perils.* New Haven, CT: Yale University Press.

Myers, N. A., & Perlmutter, M. (1978). Memory in the years from two to five. In P. A. Ornstein (Ed.), *Memory development in children* (pp. 191–218). Hillsdale, NJ: Erlbaum.

Näätänen, R. (1985). Selective attention and stimulus processing: Reflections in event-related potentials, magnetoencephalogram, and regional cerebral blood flow. In M. I. Posner & O. S. Marin (Eds.), *Attention and performance XI* (pp. 355–373). Hillsdale, NJ: Erlbaum.

Näätänen, R., Alho, K., & Schröger, E. (2002). Electrophysiology of attention. In H. Pashler & J. Wixted (Eds.), *Stevens' handbook of experimental psychology* (3rd ed., Vol. 4, pp. 601–653). New York: Wiley.

Nairne, J. S. (2002). Remembering over the short-term: The case against the standard model. *Annual Review of Psychology, 53,* 53–81.

Nakatani, C. H., & Hirschberg, J. (1994). A corpus-based study of repair cues in spontaneous speech. *Journal of the Acoustical Society of America, 95,* 1603–1616.

National Television Violence Study. (1997). *National television violence study* (Vol. 2). Studio City, CA: Mediascope.

Naveh-Benjamin, M., & Ayres, T. J. (1986). Digit span, reading rate, and linguistic relativity. *Quarterly Journal of Experimental Psychology, 38,* 739–751.

Naveh-Benjamin, M., Craik, F. I. M., Guez, J., & Dori, H. (1998). Effects of divided attention on encoding and retrieval processes in human memory: Further support for an asymmetry. *Journal of Experimental Psychology: Learning, Memory, & Cognition, 24,* 1091–1104.

Neath, I. (1998). *Human memory: An introduction to research, data, and theory.* Pacific Grove, CA: Brooks/Cole.

Needham, D. R., & Begg, I. M. (1991). Problem-oriented training promotes spontaneous analogical transfer: Memory-oriented training promotes memory for training. *Memory & Cognition, 19,* 543–557.

Neisser, U. (1967). *Cognitive psychology.* New York: Appleton.

Neisser, U. (1994). Multiple systems: A new approach to cognitive theory. *European Journal of Cognitive Psychology, 6,* 225–241.

Neisser, U., & Harsch, N. (1992). Phantom flashbulbs: False recollections of hearing the news about *Challenger.* In E. Winograd & U. Neisser (Eds.), *Affect and accuracy in recall: Studies of "flashbulb" memories* (pp. 9–31). New York: Cambridge University Press.

Neisser, U., & Libby, L. K. (2000). Remembering life experiences. In E. Tulving & F. I. M. Craik (Eds.),

The Oxford handbook of memory (pp. 315–332). New York: Oxford University Press.

Neisser, U., et al. (1996). Remembering the earthquake: Direct experience vs. hearing the news. *Memory, 4,* 337–357.

Nelson, K., Aksu-Koç, A., & Johnson, C. (Eds.). (2001). *Children's language: Interactional contributions to language development* (Vol. 11). Mahwah, NJ: Erlbaum.

Nelson, T. O. (1996). Consciousness and metacognition. *American Psychologist, 51,* 102–116.

Nelson, T. O. (1999). Cognition versus metacognition. In R. J. Sternberg (Ed.), *The nature of cognition* (pp. 625–641). Cambridge, MA: MIT Press.

Nelson, T. O., Dunlosky, J., Graf, A., & Narens, L. (1994). Utilization of metacognitive judgments in the allocation of study during multitrial learning. *Psychological Science, 5,* 207–213.

Nelson, T. O., & Leonesio, R. J. (1988). Allocation of self-paced study time and the "labor-in-vain effect." *Journal of Experimental Psychology: Learning, Memory, and Cognition, 14,* 676–686.

Nettle, D. (2001). *Strong imagination: Madness, creativity, and human nature.* New York: Oxford University Press.

Neuschatz, J. S., et al. (2002). The effect of memory schemata on memory and the phenomenological experience of naturalistic situations. *Applied Cognitive Psychology, 16,* 687–708.

Newcombe, N. S. (2002). Spatial cognition. In D. Medin (Ed.), *Stevens' handbook of experimental psychology* (3rd. ed., Vol. 2, pp. 113–163). New York: Wiley.

Newcombe, N. S., & Huttenlocher, J. (2000). *Making space: The development of spatial representation and reasoning.* Cambridge, MA: MIT Press.

Newcombe, N. S., et al. (2000). Remembering early childhood: How much, how, and why (or why not). *Current Directions in Psychological Science, 9,* 55–58.

Newell, A., & Simon, H. A. (1972). *Human problem solving.* Englewood Cliffs, NJ: Prentice-Hall.

Newman, S. D., Just, M. A., & Carpenter, P. A. (2002). The synchronization of the human cortical working memory network. *NeuroImage, 15,* 810–822.

Newmeyer, F. J. (1998). *Language form and language function.* Cambridge, MA: MIT Press.

Ng, W.-K., & Lindsay, R. C. L. (1994). Cross-race facial recognition: Failure of the contact hypothesis. *Journal of Cross-Cultural Psychology, 25,* 217–232.

Nickerson, R. S. (1999). Enhancing creativity. In R. J. Sternberg (Ed.), *Handbook of creativity* (pp. 392–430). New York: Cambridge University Press.

Nickerson, R. S. (2001). The projective way of knowing: A useful heuristic that sometimes misleads. *Current Directions in Psychological Science, 10,* 168–176.

Nickerson, R. S., Perkins, D. N., & Smith, E. E. (1985). *The teaching of thinking.* Hillsdale, NJ: Erlbaum.

Nisbett, R. E., & Wilson, T. D. (1977). Telling more than we can know: Verbal reports on mental processes. *Psychological Review, 84,* 231–259.

Noice, H. (1992). Elaborative memory strategies of professional actors. *Applied Cognitive Psychology, 6,* 417–427.

Noice, T., & Noice, H. (1997a). Effort and active experiencing as factors in verbatim recall. *Discourse Processes, 23,* 149–167.

Noice, T., & Noice, H. (1997b). *The nature of expertise in professional acting: A cognitive view.* Mahwah, NJ: Erlbaum.

Noice, T., & Noice, H. (2002). Very long-term recall and recognition of well-learned material. *Applied Cognitive Psychology, 16,* 259–272.

Noordman, L. G. M., Vonk, W., & Kempff, H. J. (1992). Causal inferences during the reading of expository texts. *Journal of Memory and Language, 31,* 573–590.

Northcraft, G. B., & Neale, M. A. (1987). Experts, amateurs, and real estate: An anchoring-and-adjustment perspective on property pricing decisions. *Organizational Behavior and Human Decision Processes, 39,* 84–97.

Nosek, B. A., Banaji, M. R., & Greenwald, A. G. (2002). Math = male, me = female, therefore math ≠ me. *Journal of Personality and Social Psychology, 83,* 44–59.

Nosofsky, R. M., & Palmeri, T. J. (1998). A rule-plus-exception model for classifying objects in continuous-dimension spaces. *Psychonomic Bulletin & Review, 5,* 345–369.

Noveck, I. A., & Politzer, G. (1998). Leveling the playing field: Investigating competing claims concerning relative inference difficulty. In M. D. S. Braine & D.P. O'Brien (Eds.), *Mental logic* (pp. 367–384). Mahwah, NJ: Erlbaum.

Novick, L. R. (1988). Analogical transfer, problem similarity, and expertise. *Journal of Experimental Psychology: Learning, Memory, and Cognition, 14,* 510–520.

Novick, L. R. (2003). At the forefront of thought: The effect of media exposure on airplane typicality. *Psychonomic Bulletin & Review, 10*, 971–974.

Novick, L. R., & Coté, N. (1992). The nature of expertise in anagram solution. *Proceedings of the Fourteenth Annual Conference of the Cognitive Science Society* (pp. 450–455). Hillsdale, NJ: Erlbaum.

Novick, L. R., Hurley, S. M., & Francis, M. (1999). Evidence for abstract, schematic knowledge of three spatial diagram representations. *Memory & Cognition, 27*, 288–308.

Novick, L. R., & Morse, D. L. (2000). Folding a fish, making a mushroom: The role of diagrams in executing assembly procedures. *Memory & Cognition, 28*, 1242–1256.

Nussbaum, J. F., Pecchioni, L. L., Robinson, J. D., & Thompson, T. L. (2000). *Communication and aging* (2nd ed.). Mahwah, NJ: Erlbaum.

Nyberg, L., & McIntosh, A. R. (2001). Functional neuroimaging: Network analysis. In R. Cabeza & A. Kingstone (Eds.), *Handbook of functional neuroimaging of cognition* (pp. 49–72). Cambridge, MA: MIT Press.

Oaksford, M., & Chater, N. (1994). A rational analysis of the selection task as optimal data selection. *Psychological Review, 101*, 608–631.

Oaksford, M., & Chater, N. (1998). *Rationality in an uncertain world.* East Sussex, England: Psychology Press.

Oberauer, K., Wendland, M., & Kliegl, R. (2003). Age differences in working memory—The roles of storage and selective access. *Memory & Cognition, 31*, 563–569.

Obler, L. K., Fein, D., Nicholas, N., & Albert, M. L. (1991). Auditory comprehension and aging: Decline in syntactic processing. *Applied Psycholinguistics, 12*, 433–452.

O'Brien, E. J., & Myers, J. L. (1999). Text comprehension: A view from the bottom up. In S. Goldman, et al. (Eds.), *Narrative comprehension, causality, and coherence: Essays in honor of Tom Trabasso* (pp. 35–53). Mahwah, NJ: Erlbaum.

O'Brien, E. J., Rizzella, M. L., Albrecht, J. E., & Halleran, J. G. (1998). Updating a situation model: A memory-based text processing view. *Journal of Experimental Psychology: Learning, Memory, and Cognition, 24*, 1200–1210.

O'Brien, L. T., & Crandall, C. S. (2003). Stereotype threat and arousal: Effects on women's math performance. *Personality and Social Psychology Bulletin, 29*, 782–789.

Ohta, A. S. (2001). *Second language acquisition processes in the classroom: Learning Japanese.* Mahwah, NJ: Erlbaum.

Olson, G. M., & Olson, J. S. (2003). Human-computer interaction: Psychological aspects of the human use of computing. *Annual Review of Psychology, 54*, 491–516.

O'Reilly, R. C., & Munakata, Y. (2000). *Computational explorations in cognitive neuroscience: Understanding the mind by simulating the brain.* Cambridge, MA: MIT Press.

Ornstein, P. A., Baker-Ward, L., Gordon, B. N., & Merritt, K. A. (1997). Children's memory for medical experiences: Implications for testimony. *Applied Cognitive Psychology, 11*, S87–S104.

Ornstein, P. A., & Haden, C. A. (2001). Memory development or the development of memory? *Current Directions in Psychological Science, 10*, 202–205.

Ornstein, P. A., Shapiro, L. R., et al. (1997). The influence of prior knowledge on children's memory for salient medical experiences. In N. L. Stein, P.A. Ornstein, B. Tversky, & C. Brainerd (Eds.), *Memory for everyday and emotional events* (pp. 83–111). Mahwah, NJ: Erlbaum.

Ornstein, P. A., et al. (1998). Children's knowledge, expectation, and long-term retention. *Applied Cognitive Psychology, 12*, 387–405.

O'Seaghdha, P., & Marin, J. W. (1997). Mediated semantic-phonological priming: Calling distant relatives. *Journal of Memory and Language, 36*, 226–252.

Osherson, D. N. (1995). Probability judgment. In E. E. Smith & D. N. Osherson (Eds.), *Thinking* (2nd ed., pp. 35–75). Cambridge, MA: MIT Press.

Osterhout, L., Bersick, M., & McLaughlin, J. (1997). Brain potentials reflect violations of gender stereotypes. *Memory & Cognition, 25*, 273–285.

Oswald, M. E., & Grosjean, S. (2004). Confirmation bias. In R. Pohl (Ed.), *Cognitive illusions: Handbook on fallacies and biases in thinking, judgment, and memory.* Hove, England: Psychology Press.

O'Toole, A. J., Deffenbacher, K. A., Valentin, D., & Abdi, H. (1994). Structural aspects of face recognition and the other-race effects. *Memory & Cognition, 22*, 208–224.

Owens, R. E., Jr. (2001). *Language development: An introduction.* Boston: Allyn & Bacon.

Page, M. P. A., & Norris, D. (1998). The primacy model: A new model of immediate serial recall. *Psychological Review, 105,* 761–781.

Paivio, A. (1971). *Imagery and verbal processes.* New York: Holt, Rinehart & Winston.

Paivio, A. (1978). Comparison of mental clocks. *Journal of Experimental Psychology: Human Perception and Performance, 4,* 61–71.

Paivio, A. (1995). Imagery and memory. In M. S. Gazzaniga (Ed.), *The cognitive neurosciences* (pp. 977–986). Cambridge, MA: MIT Press.

Pajares, F. (2003). Self-efficacy beliefs, motivation, and achievement in writing: A review of the literature. *Reading & Writing Quarterly, 19,* 139–158.

Palmer, S. E. (1999). *Vision science: Photons to phenomenology.* Cambridge, MA: MIT Press.

Palmer, S. E. (2002). Perceptual organization in vision. In S. Yantis (Ed.), *Stevens' handbook of experimental psychology* (3rd. ed., Vol. 1, pp. 177–234). New York: Wiley.

Palmer, S. E., & Nelson, R. (2000). Late influences on perceptual grouping: Illusory figures. *Perception & Psychophysics, 62,* 1321–1331.

Pan, B. A., Perlmann, R. Y., & Snow, C. E. (2000). Food for thought: Dinner table as a context for observing parent-child discourse. In L. Menn & N. B. Ratner (Eds.), *Methods for studying language production* (pp. 205–224). Mahwah, NJ: Erlbaum.

Pan, B. A., & Snow, C. E. (1999). The development of conversational and discourse skills. In M. Barrett (Ed.), *The development of language* (pp. 229–249). Hove, England: Psychology Press.

Parasuraman, R. (Ed.). (1998). *The attentive brain.* Cambridge, MA: MIT Press.

Park, D. C., & Hedden, T. (2001). Working memory and aging. In M. Naveh-Benjamin, M. Moscovitch, & H. L. Roediger, III (Eds.), *Perspectives on human memory and cognitive aging: Essays in honour of Fergus Craik* (pp. 148–169). New York: Psychology Press.

Park, D. C., Morrell, R. W., & Shifren, K. (Eds.). (1999). *Processing of medical information in aging patients.* Mahwah, NJ: Erlbaum.

Park, D. C., & Schwarz, N. (2000). *Cognitive aging.* Philadelphia: Psychology Press.

Park, D. C., et al. (1999). Medication adherence in rheumatoid arthritis patients: Older is wiser. *Journal of the American Geriatric Society, 47,* 172–183.

Park, D. C., et al. (2002). Models of visuospatial and verbal memory across the adult life span. *Psychology and Aging, 17,* 299–320.

Parrott, W. G., & Spackman, M. P. (2000). Emotion and memory. In M. Lewis & J. M. Haviland-Jones (Eds.), *Handbook of emotions* (2nd ed., pp. 476–490). New York: Guilford.

Pashler, H. (Ed.). (2002). *Stevens' handbook of experimental psychology.* (3rd ed.) New York: Wiley.

Pashler, H., & Johnston, J. C. (1998). Attention limitations in dual-task performance. In H. Pashler (Ed.), *Attention* (pp. 155–189). East Sussex, England: Psychology Press.

Pashler, H., & Wixted, J. (Eds.). (2002). *Stevens' handbook of experimental psychology* (3rd ed., Vol. 4, pp. 223–269). New York: Wiley.

Pastore, R. E., Li, X.-F., & Layer, J. K. (1990). Categorical perception of nonspeech chirps and bleats. *Perception & Psychophysics, 48,* 151–156.

Pasupathi, M. (2001). The social construction of the personal past and its implications for adult development. *Psychological Bulletin, 127,* 651–672.

Patel, A. D., et al. (1998). Processing syntactic relations in language and music: An event-related potential study. *Journal of Cognitive Neuroscience, 10,* 717–733.

Patterson, J. L. (2002). Relationships of expressive vocabulary to frequency of reading and television experience among bilingual toddlers. *Applied Psycholinguistics, 23,* 493–508.

Payne, D. G., & Wenger, M. J. (1992). Improving memory through practice. In D. J. Herrmann, H. Weingartner, A. Searleman, & C. McEvoy (Eds.), *Memory improvement: Implications for memory theory* (pp. 187–209). New York: Springer-Verlag.

Payne, D. G., et al. (1999). Memory applied. In T. Durso et al. (Eds.) *Handbook of applied psychology* (pp. 83–113). New York: Wiley.

Peal, E., & Lambert, W. E. (1962). The relation of bilingualism to intelligence. *Psychological Monographs, 546.*

Pear, J. J. (2001). *The science of learning.* Philadelphia: Psychology Press.

Pennebaker, J. W., & Graybeal, A. (2001). Patterns of natural language use: Disclosure, personality, and social integration. *Current Directions in Psychological Science, 10,* 90–93.

Pennebaker, J. W., Mehl, M. R., & Niederhoffer, K. G. (2003). Psychological aspects of natural language use: Our words, ourselves. *Annual Review of Psychology, 54,* 547–577.

Penrod, S. D., & Cutler, B. (1999). Preventing mistaken convictions in eyewitness identification trials: The case against traditional safeguards. In R. Roesch, S. D. Hart, & J. R. P. Ogloff (Eds.), *Psychology and law: The state of the discipline.* New York: Kluwer Academic/Plenum Publishers.

Peplau, L. A., & Garnets, L. D. (Eds.). (2000). Women's sexualities: New perspectives on sexual orientation and gender [Special issue]. *Journal of Social Issues, 56* (2).

Perfect, T. (1997). Memory aging as frontal lobe dysfunction. In M. A. Conway (Ed.), *Cognitive models of memory* (pp. 315–339). Cambridge, MA: MIT Press.

Perfect, T. J., & Schwartz, B. L. (Eds.). (2002). *Applied metacognition.* Cambridge, England: Cambridge University Press.

Perfetti, C. A. (1996). *Reading: Universals and particulars across writing systems.* Paper presented at the convention of the Eastern Psychological Association, Philadelphia.

Perfetti, C. A. (1999). Comprehending written language: A blueprint of the reader. In P. Hagoort & C. Brown (Eds.), *Neurocognition of language processing* (pp. 167–208). New York: Oxford University Press.

Perkins, D. (2001). *The Eureka Effect: The art and logic of breakthrough thinking.* New York: Norton.

Perry, S. K. (1999). *Writing in flow: Keys to enhanced creativity.* Cincinnati, OH: Writer's Digest Books.

Peterson, L. R., & Peterson, M. (1959). Short-term retention of individual verbal items. *Journal of Experimental Psychology, 58,* 193–198.

Pezdek, K., Finger, K., & Hodge, D. (1997). Planting false childhood memories: The role of event plausibility. *Psychological Science, 8,* 437–441.

Pezdek, K., & Taylor, J. (2002). Memory for traumatic events in children and adults. In M. L. Eisen, J. A. Quas, & G. S. Goodman (Eds.), *Memory and suggestibility in the forensic interview* (pp. 165–183). Mahwah, NJ: Erlbaum.

Phelps, E. A. (1999). Brain versus behavioral studies of cognition. In R. J. Sternberg (Ed.), *The nature of cognition* (pp. 295–322). Cambridge, MA: MIT Press.

Phillips, W. D. (1995). *Personal communication.*

Phillipson, R. (Ed.). (2000). *Rights to language: Equity, power, and education.* Mahwah, NJ: Erlbaum.

Pickering, M. J., & Branigan, H. P. (1998). The representation of verbs: Evidence from syntactic priming in language production. *Journal of Memory and Language, 39,* 633–651.

Pillemer, D. B. (1998). *Momentous events, vivid memories.* Cambridge, MA: Harvard University Press.

Pinker, S. (1985). Visual cognition: An introduction. In S. Pinker (Ed.), *Visual cognition* (pp. 1–63). Cambridge, MA: MIT Press.

Pinker, S. (1993). The central problem for the psycholinguist. In G. Harman (Ed.), *Conceptions of the human mind* (pp. 59–84). Hillsdale, NJ: Erlbaum.

Pinker, S. (1995). Introduction. In M. S. Gazzaniga (Ed.), *The cognitive neurosciences.* Cambridge, MA: MIT Press.

Pinker, S. (1997). *How the mind works.* New York: Norton.

Pinker, S. (1999). *Words and rules: The ingredients of language.* New York: Basic Books.

Pinker, S., & Prince, A. (1999). The nature of human concepts: Evidence from an unusual source. In R. Jackendoff, P. Bloom, & K. Winn (Eds.), *Language, logic, and concepts* (pp. 221–261). Cambridge, MA: MIT Press.

Pitt, W. R. (2003, November 24). *Donkeys of mass destruction.* Retrieved November 30, 2003, from http://www.truthout.org/docs

Platt, R. D., & Griggs, R. A. (1993). Darwinian algorithms and the Wason selection task: A factorial analysis of social contract selection task problems. *Cognition, 48,* 163–192.

Platt, R. D., & Griggs, R. A. (1995). Facilitation and matching bias in the abstract selection task. *Thinking and Reasoning, 1,* 55–70.

Plucker, J. A., & Renzulli, J. S. (1999). Psychometric approaches to the study of human creativity. In R. J. Sternberg (Ed.), *Handbook of creativity* (pp. 35–61). New York: Cambridge University Press.

Plumert, J. M. (1994). Flexibility in children's use of spatial and categorical organizational strategies in recall. *Developmental Psychology, 30,* 738–747.

Plunkett, K., & Schafer, G. (1999). Early speech perception and word learning. In M. Barrett (Ed.), *The development of language* (pp. 51–71). Hove, England: Psychology Press.

Pohl, R. F. (Ed.) (2004a). *Cognitive illusions: Handbook on fallacies and biases in thinking, judgment, and memory.* Hove, England: Psychology Press.

Pohl, R. F. (2004b). Overconfidence. In R. Pohl (Ed.), *Cognitive illusions: Handbook on fallacies and biases in thinking, judgment, and memory*. Hove, England: Psychology Press.

Pohl, R. F., Bender, M., & Lachmann, G. (2002). Hindsight bias around the world. *Experimental Psychology, 49,* 270–282.

Pohl, R. F., Schwarz, S., Sczesny, S., & Stahlberg, D. (2003). Hindsight bias in gustatory judgments. *Experimental Psychology, 50,* 107–115.

Polk, T. A., et al. (2002). Neural specialization for letter recognition. *Journal of Cognitive Neuroscience, 14,* 145–159.

Posner, M. I., & DiGirolamo, G. J. (2000a). Attention in cognitive neuroscience: An overview. In M. S. Gazzaniga (Ed.), *The new cognitive neurosciences* (2nd ed., pp. 623–621). Cambridge, MA: MIT Press.

Posner, M. I., & DiGirolamo, G. J. (2000b). Cognitive neuroscience: Origins and promise. *Psychological Bulletin, 126,* 873–889.

Posner, M. I., & Fernandez-Duque, D. (1999). Attention in the human brain. In R. A. Wilson & F. C. Keil (Eds.), *The MIT encyclopedia of the cognitive sciences* (pp. 43–46). Cambridge, MA: MIT Press.

Posner, M. I., & McCandliss, B. D. (1999). Brain circuitry during reading. In R. M. Klein & P. A. McMullen (Eds.), *Converging methods for understanding reading and dyslexia* (pp. 305–337). Cambridge, MA: MIT Press.

Posner, M. I., & Raichle, M. E. (1994). *Images of mind*. New York: Freeman.

Potter, M. C. (1999). Understanding sentences and scenes: The role of conceptual short-term memory. In V. Coltheart (Ed.), *Fleeting memories: Cognition of brief visual stimuli* (pp. 13–46). Cambridge, MA: MIT Press.

Potter, M. C., Moryadas, A., Abrahams, I., & Noel, A. (1993). Word perception and misperception in context. *Journal of Experimental Psychology: Learning, Memory, and Cognition, 19,* 3–22.

Poulton, E. C. (1994). *Behavioral decision theory: A new approach*. Cambridge, England: Cambridge University Press.

Powell, M. B., Thomson, D. M., & Ceci, S. J. (2003). Children's memory of recurring events: Is the first event always the best remembered? *Applied Cognitive Psychology, 17,* 127–146.

Powers, S., & López, R. L. (1985). Perceptual, motor and verbal skills of monolingual and bilingual His-panic children: A discriminant analysis. *Perceptual and Motor Skills, 60,* 999–1002.

Press, B. (2004, February 9). It's official: No weapons of mass destruction. *Liberal Opinion*, p. 4.

Pressley, M. (1996). Personal reflections on the study of practical memory in the mid-1990s: The complete cognitive researcher. In D. J. Herrmann, et al. (Eds.), *Basic and applied memory research: Practical applications* (Vol. 2, pp. 19–33). Mahwah, NJ: Erlbaum.

Pressley, M., & Afflerbach, P. (1995). *Verbal protocols of reading: The nature of constructively responsive reading*. Hillsdale, NJ: Erlbaum.

Pressley, M., & Ghatala, E. S. (1988). Delusions about performance on multiple-choice comprehension tests. *Reading Research Quarterly, 23,* 454–464.

Pressley, M., & Grossman, L. R. (Eds.). (1994). Recovery of memories of childhood sexual abuse [Special issue]. *Applied Cognitive Psychology, 8* (4).

Pressley, M., Levin, J. R., & Ghatala, E. S. (1984). Memory strategy monitoring in adults and children. *Journal of Verbal Learning and Verbal Behavior, 23,* 270–288.

Pressley, M., Levin, J. R., & Ghatala, E. S. (1988). Strategy-comparison opportunities promote long-term strategy use. *Contemporary Educational Psychology, 13,* 157–168.

Pressley, M., et al. (1996). Elementary reading instruction. In G. D. Phye (Ed.), *Handbook of academic learning: Construction of knowledge* (pp. 151–198). San Diego: Academic Press.

Protopapas, A. (1999). Connectionist modeling of speech perception. *Psychological Bulletin, 125,* 410–436.

Pulford, B. D., & Colman, A. M. (1997). Overconfidence: Feedback and item difficulty effects. *Personality and Individual Differences, 23,* 125–133.

Pylyshyn, Z. W. (1984). *Computation and cognition*. Cambridge, MA: MIT Press.

Pylyshyn, Z. W. (1989). The role of location indexes in spatial perception: A sketch of the FINST spatial-index model. *Cognition, 32,* 65–97.

Pylyshyn, Z. W. (2003). Return of the mental image: Are there pictures in the brain? *Trends in Cognitive Sciences, 7,* 113–118.

Quilici, J. L., & Mayer, R. E. (2002). Teaching students to recognize structural similarities between statistics word problems. *Applied Cognitive Psychology, 16,* 325–342.

Quinn, D. M., & Spencer, S. J. (2001). The interference of stereotype threat with women's generation of mathematical problem-solving strategies. *Journal of Social Issues, 57,* 55–71.

Quinn, P. C., et al. (2002). Development of form similarity as a Gestalt grouping principle in infancy. *Psychological Science, 13,* 320–328.

Quinn, S., & Markovits, H. (1998). Conditional reasoning, causality, and the structure of semantic memory: Strength of association as a predictive factor for content effects. *Cognition, 68,* B93–B101.

Raaijmakers, J. G. W., & Shiffrin, R. M. (2002). Models of memory. In D. Medin (Ed.), *Stevens' handbook of experimental psychology* (3rd ed., pp. 43–76). New York: Wiley.

Rabbitt, P. (2002). Aging and cognition. In H. Pashler (Ed.), *Stevens' handbook of experimental psychology* (Vol. 4, pp. 793–860). New York: Wiley.

Rachlin, H. (2002). A framework for scientific psychology [Review of the book *The new behaviorism: Mind, mechanism, and society*]. *Contemporary Psychology, 47,* 360–361.

Raichle, M. E. (1999). Positron emission tomography. In R. A. Wilson & F. C. Keil (Eds.), *The MIT encyclopedia of the cognitive sciences* (pp. 656–658). Cambridge, MA: MIT Press.

Raichle, M. E. (2000). Functional imaging in cognitive neuroscience. In M. J. Farah & T. E. Feinberg (Eds.), *Patient-based approaches to cognitive neuroscience* (pp. 35–52). Cambridge, MA: MIT Press.

Raichle, M. E. (2001). Functional neuroimaging: A historical and physiological perspective. In R. Cabeza & A. Kingstone (Eds.), *Handbook of functional neuroimaging of cognition* (pp. 3–26). Cambridge, MA: MIT Press.

Ramsey, W. (1999). Connectionism, philosophical issues. In R. A. Wilson & F. C. Keil (Eds.), *The MIT encyclopedia of the cognitive sciences* (pp. 186–187). Cambridge, MA: MIT Press.

Ransdell, S., & Levy, C. M. (1999). Writing, reading, and speaking memory spans and the importance of resource flexibility. In M. Torrance & G. C. Jeffery (Eds.), *The cognitive demands of writing: Processing capacity and working memory in text production* (pp. 99–113). Amsterdam: Amsterdam University Press.

Rapp, B. (Ed.). (2001). *The handbook of cognitive neuropsychology.* Philadelphia: Psychology Press.

Rapp, B., Folk, J. R., & Tainturier, M. (2001). Word reading. In B. Rapp (Ed.), *Handbook of cognitive neuropsychology* (pp. 233–262). New York: Psychology Press.

Rapp, B., & Goldrick, M. (2000). Discreteness and interactivity in spoken word production. *Psychological Review, 107,* 460–499.

Ratcliff, R. (1990). Connectionist models of recognition memory: Constraints imposed by learning and forgetting functions. *Psychological Review, 97,* 285–308.

Ratner, H. H., Foley, M. A., & Gimpert, N. (2000). In K. Roberts & M. Blades (Eds.), *Children's source monitoring.* Mahwah, NJ: Erlbaum.

Ratner, H. H., Foley, M. A., & Gimpert, N. (2002). The role of collaborative planning in children's source-monitoring errors and learning. *Journal of Experimental Child Psychology, 81,* 44–73.

Ratner, H. H., Foley, M. A., & McCaskill, P. (2001). Understanding children's activity memory: The role of outcomes. *Journal of Experimental Child Psychology, 79,* 162–191.

Ratner, N. B., & Gleason, J. B. (1993). An introduction to psycholinguistics: What do language users know? In J. B. Gleason & N. B. Ratner (Eds.), *Psycholinguistics.* Fort Worth, TX: Harcourt Brace Jovanovich.

Rau, P. S., & Sebrechts, M. M. (1996). How initial plans mediate the expansion and resolution of options in writing. *Quarterly Journal of Experimental Psychology, 49A,* 616–638.

Rayner, K. (1998). Eye movements in reading and information processing: 20 years of research. *Psychological Bulletin, 124,* 372–422.

Rayner, K., & Clifton, C., Jr. (2002). Language processing. In D. Medin (Ed.), *Stevens' handbook of experimental psychology* (3rd ed., Vol. 2, pp. 261–316). New York: Wiley.

Rayner, K., Pollatsek, A., & Binder, K. S. (1998). Phonological codes and eye movements in reading. *Journal of Experimental Psychology: Learning, Memory, and Cognition, 24,* 476–497.

Rayner, K., Pollatsek, A., & Starr, M. S. (2003). Reading. In A. F. Healy & R. W. Proctor (Eds.), *Handbook of psychology* (Vol. 4, pp. 549–574). Hoboken, NJ: Wiley.

Rayner, K., et al. (2001). How psychological science informs the teaching of reading. *Psychological Science in the Public Interest, 2,* 31–74.

Read, J. D., & Lindsay, D. S. (Eds.). (1997). *Recollections of trauma: Scientific evidence and clinical practice.* New York: Plenum.

Read, S. J., & Urada, D. I. (2003). A neural network simulation of the outgroup homogeneity effect. *Personality and Social Psychology Review, 7,* 146–169.

Reason, J. (1984). Absent-mindedness and cognitive control. In J. E. Harris & P. E. Morris (Eds.), *Everyday memory, actions and absent-mindedness* (pp. 113–132). London: Academic Press.

Reason, J., & Mycielska, K. (1982). *Absent-minded? The psychology of mental lapses and everyday errors.* Englewood Cliffs, NJ: Prentice Hall.

Reber, R. (2004). Availability. In R. Pohl (Ed.), *Cognitive illusions: Handbook on fallacies and biases in thinking, judgment, and memory.* Hove, England: Psychology Press.

Recarte, M., & Nunes, L. M. (2000). Effects of verbal and spatial-imagery tasks on eye fixations while driving. *Journal of Experimental Psychology: Applied, 6,* 31–43.

Reddy, V. (1999). Prelinguistic communication. In M. Barrett (Ed.), *The development of language* (pp. 25–50). Hove, England: Psychology Press.

Reed, E. (1997). The cognitive revolution from an ecological point of view. In D. M. Johnson & C. E. Erneling (Eds.), *The future of the cognitive revolution* (pp. 261–273). New York: Oxford University Press.

Reed, S. K. (1974). Structural descriptions and the limitations of visual images. *Memory & Cognition, 2,* 329–336.

Reed, S. K. (1977). Facilitation of problem solving. In N. J. Castellan, Jr., D. B. Pisoni, & G. R. Potts (Eds.), *Cognitive theory* (Vol. 2, pp. 3–20). Hillsdale, NJ: Erlbaum.

Reed, S. K. (1999). *Word problems: Research and curriculum reform.* Mahwah, NJ: Erlbaum.

Reeve, D. K., & Aggleton, J. P. (1998). On the specificity of expert knowledge about a soap opera: An everyday story of farming folk. *Applied Cognitive Psychology, 12,* 35–42.

Reeves, L. M., & Weisberg, R. W. (1993). On the concrete nature of human thinking: Content and context in analogical transfer. *Educational Psychology, 13,* 245–258.

Reeves, L. M., Weisberg, R. W. (1994). The role of content and abstract information in analogical transfer. *Psychological Bulletin, 115,* 381–400.

Reicher, G. M. (1969). Perceptual recognition as a function of meaningfulness of stimuli material. *Journal of Experimental Psychology, 81,* 275–280.

Reichle, E. D., Pollatsek, A., Fisher, D. L., & Rayner, K. (1998). Toward a model of eye movement control in reading. *Psychological Review, 105,* 125–157.

Reisberg, D. (1998). Constraints on image-based discovery: A comment on Rouw et al. (1997). *Cognition, 66,* 95–102.

Reisberg, D., Pearson, D. G., & Kosslyn, S. M. (2003). Intuitions and introspections about imagery: The role of imagery experience in shaping an investigator's theoretical views. *Applied Cognitive Psychology, 17,* 147–160.

Remnick, D. (2003, July 28). Faith-based intelligence. *New Yorker,* pp. 27–29.

Renner, C. H., & Renner, M. J. (2001). But I thought I knew that: Using confidence estimation as a debiasing technique to improve classroom performance. *Applied Cognitive Psychology, 15,* 23–32.

Rensink, R. A. (2002). Change detection. *Annual Review of Psychology, 53,* 245–277.

Rensink, R. A., O'Regan, J. K., & Clark, J. J. (1997). To see or not to see: The need for attention to perceive changes in scenes. *Psychological Science, 8,* 368–373.

Ricciardelli, L. A. (1992). Creativity and bilingualism. *Journal of Creative Behavior, 26,* 242–259.

Riccio, D. C., Millin, P. M., & Gisquet-Verrier, P. (2003). Retrograde amnesia: Forgetting back. *Current Directions in Psychological Science, 12,* 41–44.

Richardson, J. T. E. (1996a). Evolving concepts of working memory. In J. T. E. Richardson et al. (Eds.), *Working memory and human cognition* (pp. 3–30). New York: Oxford University Press.

Richardson, J. T. E. (1996b). Evolving issues in working memory. In J. T. E. Richardson et al. (Eds.), *Working memory and human cognition* (pp. 120–148). New York: Oxford University Press.

Richardson, J. T. E. (1999). *Imagery.* East Sussex, England: Psychology Press.

Richardson, R. C. (1998). Heuristics and satisficing. In W. Bechtel & G. Graham (Eds.), *A companion to cognitive science* (pp. 566–575). Malden, MA: Blackwell.

Richardson-Klavehn, A., & Gardiner, J. M. (1998). Depth-of-processing effects on priming in stem completion: Tests of the voluntary-contamination, conceptual-processing, and lexical-processing hypotheses. *Journal of Experimental Psychology: Learning, Memory, and Cognition, 24,* 593–609.

Riddoch, M. J., & Humphreys, G. W. (2001). Object recognition. In B. Rapp (Ed.), *The handbook of cognitive neuropsychology* (pp. 45–74). Philadelphia: Psychology Press.

Ridley, C. R. (1995). *Overcoming unintentional racism in counseling and therapy.* Thousand Oaks, CA: Sage.

Rips, L. J. (1994). *The psychology of proof: Deductive reasoning in human thinking.* Cambridge, MA: MIT Press.

Rips, L. J. (1995). Deduction and cognition. In E. E. Smith & D. N. Osherson (Eds.), *Thinking* (pp. 297–343). Cambridge, MA: MIT Press.

Rips, L. J. (2002). Reasoning. In D. Medin (Ed.), *Stevens' handbook of experimental psychology* (3rd. ed., Vol. 2, pp. 363–411). New York: Wiley.

Robertson, S. I. (2001). *Problem solving.* East Sussex, England: Psychology Press.

Robins, R. W., Gosling, S. D., & Craik, K. H. (1999). An empirical analysis of trends in psychology. *American Psychologist, 54,* 117–128.

Robinson, J. A. (1996). Perspective, meaning, and remembering. In D. C. Rubin (Ed.), *Remembering our past: Studies in autobiographical memory* (pp. 199–217). New York: Cambridge University Press.

Rodd, J., Gaskell, G., & Marslen-Wilson, W. (2002). Making sense of semantic ambiguity: Semantic competition in lexical access. *Journal of Memory and Language, 46,* 245–266.

Roebers, C. M., & Schneider, W. (2000). The impact of misleading questions on eyewitness memory in children and adults. *Applied Cognitive Psychology, 14,* 509–526.

Roediger, H. L., III. (1996). Prospective memory and episodic memory. In M. Brandimonte, G. O. Einstein, & M. A. McDaniel (Eds.), *Prospective memory: Theory and applications* (pp. 149–155). Mahwah, NJ: Erlbaum.

Roediger, H. L., III. (1997). Remembering [Review of the book *Remembering: A study in experimental and social psychology*]. *Contemporary Psychology, 42,* 488–492.

Roediger, H. L., III. (2000). Why retrieval is the key process in understanding human memory. In E. Tulving (Ed.), *Memory, consciousness, and the brain* (pp. 52–75). Philadelphia: Psychology Press.

Roediger, H. L., III, Balota, D. A., & Watson, J. M. (2001). Spreading activation and arousal of false memories. In H. L. Roediger, III, J. S. Nairne, I. Neath, & A. M. Suprenant (Eds.), *The nature of remembering* (pp. 95–115). Washington, DC: American Psychological Association.

Roediger, H. L., III, & Gallo, D. A. (2001). Levels of processing: Some unanswered questions. In M. Naveh-Benjamin, M. Moscovitch, & H. L. Roediger, III (Eds.), *Perspectives on human memory and cognitive aging: Essays in honour of Fergus Craik* (pp. 28–47). New York: Psychology Press.

Roediger, H. L., III, & Gallo, D. A. (2002). Processes affecting accuracy and distortion in memory: An overview. In M. L. Eisen, J. A. Quas, & G. S. Goodman (Eds.), *Memory and suggestibility in the forensic interview* (pp. 3–28). Mahwah, NJ: Erlbaum.

Roediger, H. L., III, Gallo, D. A., & Geraci, L. (2002). Processing approaches to cognition: The impetus from the levels-of-processing framework. *Memory, 10,* 319–332.

Roediger, H. L., III, & Guynn, M. J. (1996). Retrieval processes. In E. L. Bjork & R. A. Bjork (Eds.), *Memory* (pp. 197–236). San Diego: Academic Press.

Roediger, H. L., III, Guynn, M. J., & Jones, T. C. (1994). Implicit memory: A tutorial review. In G. d'Ydewalle, P. Eelen, & P. Bertelson (Eds.), *International perspectives on psychological science* (Vol. 2, pp. 67–94). Hove, England: Erlbaum.

Roediger, H. L., III, Marsh, E. J., & Lee, S. C. (2002). Kinds of memory. In D. Medin (Ed.), *Stevens' handbook of experimental psychology* (3rd ed., pp. 1–41). New York: Wiley.

Roediger, H. L., III, & McDermott, K. B. (1995). Creating false memories: Remembering words not presented in lists. *Journal of Experimental Psychology: Learning, Memory, and Cognition, 21,* 803–814.

Roediger, H. L., III, & McDermott, K. B. (2000). Distortions of memory. In E. Tulving & F. I. M. Craik (Eds.), *The Oxford handbook of memory* (pp. 149–162). New York: Oxford University Press.

Roediger, H. L., III, Watson, J. M., McDermott, K. B., & Gallo, D. A. (2001). Factors that determine false recall: A multiple regression analysis. *Psychonomic Bulletin & Review, 8,* 385–407.

Roelofs, A., & Baayen, H. (2002). Morphology by itself in planning the production of spoken words. *Psychonomic Bulletin & Review, 9,* 132–138.

Roelofs, A., & Meyer, A. S. (1998). Metrical structure in planning the production of spoken words. *Journal of Experimental Psychology: Learning, Memory, and Cognition, 24*, 922–939.

Rogers, D. (1985). Language development. In A. Branthwaite & D. Rogers (Eds.), *Children growing up* (pp. 82–93). Milton Keynes, England: Open University Press.

Rogers, T. B., Kuiper, N. A., & Kirker, W. S. (1977). Self-reference and the encoding of personal information. *Journal of Personality and Social Psychology, 35*, 677–688.

Rogoff, B. (1990). *Apprenticeship in thinking: Cognitive development in social context.* New York: Oxford University Press.

Rohrbaugh, C. C., & Shanteau, J. (1999). Context, process, and experience: Research on applied judgment and decision making. In F. T. Durso et al. (Eds.), *Handbook of applied cognition* (pp. 115–139). New York: Wiley.

Rojahn, K., & Pettigrew, T. F. (1992). Memory for schema-relevant information: A meta-analytic resolution. *British Journal of Social Psychology, 31*, 81–109.

Rollins, P. R. (2003). Caregivers' contingent comments to 9-month-old infants: Relationships with later language. *Applied Psycholinguistics, 24*, 221–234.

Rolls, E. T., & Tovee, M. J. (1995). Sparseness of the neuronal representation of stimuli in the primate temporal visual cortex. *Journal of Neurophysiology, 73*, 713–726.

Rosch, E. H. (1973). Natural categories. *Cognitive Psychology, 4*, 328–350.

Rosch, E. H. (1975). The nature of mental codes for color categories. *Journal of Experimental Psychology: Human Perception and Performance, 1*, 303–322.

Rosch, E. H., & Mervis, C. B. (1975). Family resemblances: Studies in the internal structure of categories. *Cognitive Psychology, 7*, 573–605.

Rosch, E. H., et al. (1976). Basic objects in natural categories. *Cognitive Psychology, 8*, 382–439.

Rosen, V. M., & Engle, R. W. (1997). The role of working memory capacity in retrieval. *Journal of Experimental Psychology: General, 126*, 211–227.

Rosenthal, J. W. (Ed.). (2000). *Handbook of undergraduate second language education.* Mahwah, NJ: Erlbaum.

Roskos-Ewoldsen, B., McNamara, T. P., Shelton, A. L., & Carr, W. (1998). Mental representations of large and small spatial layouts are orientation de-pendent. *Journal of Experimental Psychology: Learning, Memory, and Cognition, 24*, 215–226.

Ross, B. H., & Makin, V. S. (1999). Prototype versus exemplar models in cognition. In R. J. Sternberg (Ed.), *The nature of cognition* (pp. 205–241). Cambridge, MA: MIT Press.

Ross, M., & Buehler, R. (1994). Creative remembering. In U. Neisser & R. Fivush (Eds.), *The remembering self: Construction and accuracy in the self-narrative* (pp. 205–235). New York: Cambridge University Press.

Rothblum, E. D., & Factor, R. (2001). Lesbians and their sisters as a control group. *Psychological Science, 12*, 63–69.

Rothman, A. J., & Salovey, P. (1997). Shaping perceptions to motivate healthy behavior: The role of message framing. *Psychological Bulletin, 121*, 3–19.

Rouw, R., Kosslyn, S. M., & Hamel, R. (1997). Detecting high-level and low-level properties in visual images and visual precepts. *Cognition, 63*, 209–226.

Rovee-Collier, C. K. (1995). Time windows in cognitive development. *Developmental Psychology, 31*, 147–169.

Rovee-Collier, C. K. (1999). The development of infant memory. *Current Directions in Psychological Science, 8*, 80–85.

Rovee-Collier, C. K., & Barr, R. (2002). Infant cognition. In H. Pashler (Ed.), *Stevens' handbook of experimental psychology* (Vol. 4, pp. 693–791). New York: Wiley.

Rovee-Collier, C. K., & Boller, K. (1995). Current theory and research on infant learning and memory: Application to early intervention. *Infants and Young Children, 7*, 1–12.

Rovee-Collier, C. K., Borza, M. A., Adler, S. A., & Boller, K. (1993). Infants' eyewitness testimony: Effects of postevent information on a prior memory representation. *Memory & Cognition, 21*, 267–279.

Rovee-Collier, C. K., Griesler, P. C., & Earley, L. A. (1985). Contextual determinants of retrieval in three-month-old infants. *Learning and Motivation, 16*, 139–157.

Rovee-Collier, C., & Hayne, H. (2000). Memory in infancy and early childhood. In E. Tulving & F. I. M. Craik (Eds.), *The Oxford handbook of memory* (pp. 267–282). New York: Oxford University Press.

Rovee-Collier, C., Hayne, H., & Colombo, M. (2001). *The development of implicit and explicit memory.* Philadelphia: John Benjamins Publishing Company.

Roy, A. (1997). *The god of small things*. New York: Random House.

Royden, C. S., Wolfe, J. M., & Klempen, N. (2001). Visual search asymmetries in motion and optic flow fields. *Perception & Psychophysics, 63*, 436–444.

Ruben, B. D. (2001, July 13). We need excellence beyond the classroom. *Chronicle of Higher Education*, pp. B15–B16.

Rubin, D. C. (1996). Introduction. In D. C. Rubin (Ed.), *Remembering our past: Studies in autobiographical memory* (pp. 1–15). New York: Cambridge University Press.

Rubin, D. C. (2000). The distribution of early childhood memories. *Memory, 8*, 265–269.

Rubin, E. (1915/1958). Synoplevede Figurer [Figure and ground]. In D. C. Beardslee & M. Wertheimer (Eds.), *Readings in perception* (pp. 194–203). Princeton, NJ: Van Nostrand.

Rueckl, J. G. (1995). Ambiguity and connectionist networks: Still settling into a solution—comment on Joordens and Besner (1994). *Journal of Experimental Psychology: Learning, Memory, and Cognition, 21*, 501–508.

Rueckl, J. G., & Oden, G. C. (1986). The integration of contextual and featural information during word identification. *Journal of Memory and Language, 25*, 445–460.

Rumelhart, D. E., & McClelland, J. L. (1982). An interactive activation model of context effects in letter perception: Part 2. The contextual enhancement effect and some tests and extensions of the model. *Psychological Review, 89*, 60–94.

Rumelhart, D. E., & McClelland, J. L. (1986). On learning the past tenses of English verbs. In J. L. McClelland & D. E. Rumelhart (Eds.), *Parallel distributed processing: Explorations in the microstructure of cognition* (Vol. 2, pp. 216–271). Cambridge, MA: MIT Press.

Rumelhart, D. E., & McClelland, J. L. (1987). Learning the past tenses of English verbs: Implicit rules or parallel distributed processing? In B. MacWhinney (Ed.), *Mechanisms of language acquisition* (pp. 195–248). Hillsdale, NJ: Erlbaum.

Rumelhart, D. E., McClelland, J. L., & the PDP Research Group (Eds.). (1986). *Parallel distributed processing* (Vol. 1). Cambridge, MA: MIT Press.

Runco, M. A., & Pritzker, S. R. (Eds.). (1999). *Encyclopedia of creativity*. San Diego: Academic Press.

Rundus, D. (1971). Analysis of rehearsal processes in free recall. *Journal of Experimental Psychology, 89*, 63–77.

Ruscio, A. M., & Amabile, T. M. (1999). Effects of instructional style on problem-solving creativity. *Creativity Research Journal, 12*, 251–266.

Ruscio, J., Whitney, D. M., & Amabile, T. M. (1998). Looking inside the fishbowl of creativity: Verbal and behavioral predictors of creative performance. *Creativity Research Journal, 11*, 243–263.

Russ, S. W. (2001). Writing creatively: How to do it. [Review of the book *Writing in flow: Keys to enhanced creativity*]. *Contemporary Psychology, 46*, 181–182.

Russo, R., Parkin, A. J., Taylor, S. R., & Wilks, J. (1998). Revising current two-process accounts of spacing effects in memory. *Journal of Experimental Psychology: Learning, Memory, and Cognition, 24*, 161–172.

Ryan, L., & Eich, E. (2000). Mood dependence and implicit memory. In E. Tulving (Ed.), *Memory, consciousness, and the brain* (pp. 91–105). Philadelphia: Psychology Press.

Rychlak, J. F. (1994). *Logical learning theory: A human teleology and its empirical support*. Lincoln: University of Nebraska Press.

Sachs, J. (1967). Recognition memory for syntactic and semantic aspects of a connected discourse. *Perception & Psychophysics, 2*, 437–442.

Saffran, J. R. (2001). Words in a sea of sounds: The output of infant statistical learning. *Cognition, 81*, 149–169.

Saito, A. (Ed.). (2000). *Bartlett, culture and cognition*. East Sussex, England: Psychology Press.

Salthouse, T. A. (1991). *Theoretical perspectives on cognitive aging*. Hillsdale, NJ: Erlbaum.

Salthouse, T. A. (2000). Psychological assumptions in cognitive aging research. In F. I. M. Craik & T. A. Salthouse (Eds.), *The handbook of aging and cognition* (2nd ed.). Mahwah, NJ: Erlbaum.

Salthouse, T. A. (2002). Age-related effects on memory in the context of age-related effects on cognition. In P. Graf & N. Ohta (Eds.), *Lifespan development of human memory* (pp. 139–158). Cambridge, MA: MIT Press.

Sams, H., Paavilainen, P., Alho, K., & Näätänen, N. (1985). Auditory frequency discrimination and event-related potentials. *Electroencephalography and Clinical Neurophysiology, 62*, 437–448.

Samuel, A. G. (1987). Lexical uniqueness effects on phonemic restoration. *Journal of Memory and Language, 26*, 36–56.

Samuel, A. G., & Ressler, W. H. (1986). Attention within auditory word perception: Insights from the phonemic restoration illusion. *Journal of Experimental Psychology: Human Perception and Performance, 12,* 70–79.

Sanbonmatsu, D. M., Posavac, S. S., Kardes, F. R., & Mantel, S. P. (1998). Selective hypothesis testing. *Psychonomic Bulletin & Review, 5,* 197–220.

Sancier, M. L., & Fowler, C. A. (1997). Gestural drift in a bilingual speaker of Brazilian Portuguese and English. *Journal of Phonetics, 25,* 421–436.

Santelmann, L. M., & Jusczyk, P. W. (1998). Sensitivity to discontinuous dependencies in language learners: Evidence for limitations in processing space. *Cognition, 69,* 105–134.

Schacter, D. L. (1996). *Searching for memory: The brain, the mind, and the past.* New York: Basic Books.

Schacter, D. L. (1998). Memory and awareness. *Science, 280,* 59–60.

Schacter, D. L. (1999a). Implicit vs. explicit memory. In R. A. Wilson & F. C. Keil (Eds.), *The MIT encyclopedia of the cognitive sciences* (pp. 394–395). Cambridge, MA: MIT Press.

Schacter, D. L. (1999b). The seven sins of memory: Insights from psychology and cognitive neuroscience. *American Psychologist, 54,* 182–203.

Schacter, D. L. (2000). Introduction. In M. Gazzaniga (Ed.), *The new cognitive neurosciences* (pp. 1273–1276). Cambridge, MA: MIT Press.

Schacter, D. L. (2001). *The seven sins of memory.* Boston: Houghton Mifflin.

Schacter, D. L., & Badgaiyan, R. D. (2001). Neuroimaging of priming: New perspectives on implicit and explicit memory. *Current Directions in Psychological Science, 10,* 1–4.

Schacter, D. L., & Buckner, R. L. (1998). On the relations among priming, conscious recollection, and intentional retrieval: Evidence from neuroimaging research. *Neurobiology of Learning and Memory, 70,* 284–303.

Schacter, D. L., Church, B., & Treadwell, J. (1994). Implicit memory in amnesic patients: Evidence for spared auditory priming. *Psychological Science, 5,* 20–25.

Schacter, D. L., Koutstaal, W., & Norman, K. A. (1999). Can cognitive neuroscience illuminate the nature of traumatic childhood memories? In L. M. Williams & V. L. Banyard (Eds.), *Trauma & memory* (pp. 257–269). Thousand Oaks, CA: Sage.

Schacter, D. L., Norman, K. A., & Koustaal, W. (1998). The cognitive neuroscience of constructive memory. *Annual Review of Psychology, 49,* 289–318.

Schaefer, E. G., & Laing, M. L. (2000). 'Please, remind me . . .': The role of others in prospective remembering. *Applied Cognitive Psychology, 14,* S99–S114.

Schaeken, W., DeVooght, G., Vandierendonck, A., & d'Ydewalle, G. (Eds.). (2000a). *Deductive reasoning and strategies.* Mahwah, NJ: Erlbaum.

Schaeken, W., DeVooght, G., Vandierendonck, A., & d'Ydewalle, G. (2000b). Strategies and tactics in deductive reasoning. In W. Schaeken, G. DeVooght, A. Vandierendonck, & G. d'Ydewalle (Eds.), *Deductive reasoning and strategies* (pp. 301–309). Mahwah, NJ: Erlbaum.

Schank, R. C., & Abelson, R. P. (1977). *Scripts, plans, goals, and understanding.* Hillsdale, NJ: Erlbaum.

Schank, R. C., & Abelson, R. P. (1995). Knowledge and memory: The real story. In R. S. Wyer, Jr. (Ed.), *Knowledge and memory: The real story* (pp. 1–85). Hillsdale, NJ: Erlbaum.

Schawlow, A. (1982, Fall). Going for the gaps. *Stanford Magazine,* p. 42.

Schiffrin, D. (1994). Making a list. *Discourse Processes, 17,* 377–406.

Schmolck, H., Buffalo, E. A., & Squire, L. R. (2000). Memory distortions develop over time: Recollections of the O.J. Simpson trial verdict after 15 and 32 months. *Psychological Science, 11,* 39–45.

Schneider, W. (1998). The development of procedural metamemory in childhood and adolescence. In G. Mazzoni & T. O. Nelson (Eds.), *Metacognition and cognitive neuropsychology* (pp. 1–21). Mahwah, NJ: Erlbaum.

Schneider, W. (1999). The development of metamemory in children. In D. Gopher & A. Koriat (Eds.), *Attention and performance XVII* (pp. 487–514). Cambridge, MA: MIT Press.

Schneider, W. (2002). Memory development in childhood. In U. Goswami (Ed.), *Blackwell handbook of childhood cognitive development* (pp. 236–256). Malden, MA: Blackwell.

Schneider, W., & Bjorklund, D. F. (1998). Memory. In D. Kuhn & R. S. Siegler (Eds.), *Handbook of child psychology* (5th ed., Vol. 2, pp. 467–521). New York: Wiley.

Schneider, W., & Pressley, M. (1997). *Memory development: Between two and twenty* (2nd ed.). Mahwah, NJ: Erlbaum.

Schneider, W., & Shiffrin, R. M. (1977). Controlled and automatic information processing: I. Detection, search, and attention. *Psychological Review, 84,* 1–66.

Schober, M. F., & Brennan, S. E. (2003). Processes of interactive spoken discourse: The role of the partner. In A. C. Graesser, M. A. Gernsbacher, & S. R. Goldman (Eds.), *Handbook of discourse processes* (pp. 123–164). Mahwah, NJ: Erlbaum.

Schoenfeld, A. H. (1982). Some thoughts on problem-solving research and mathematics education. In F. K. Lester & J. Garofalo (Eds.), *Mathematical problem solving: Issues in research* (pp. 27–37). Philadelphia: The Franklin Institute.

Schooler, C., Neumann, E., Caplan, L. J., & Roberts, B. R. (1997). A time course analysis of Stroop interference and facilitation: Comparing normal individuals and individuals with schizophrenia. *Journal of Experimental Psychology: General, 126,* 19–36.

Schooler, J. W. (1994). Seeking the core: The issues and evidence surrounding recovered accounts of sexual trauma. *Consciousness and Cognition, 3,* 452–469.

Schooler, J. W. (2001). Discovering memories of abuse in the light of meta-awareness. In J. J. Freyd & A. P. DePrince (Eds.), *Trauma and cognitive science* (p. 105–136). New York: Haworth.

Schooler, J. W., Bendiksen, M., & Ambadar, Z. (1997). Taking the middle line: Can we accommodate both fabricated and recovered memories of sexual abuse? In M. A. Conway (Ed.), *Recovered memories and false memories* (pp. 251–293). New York: Oxford University Press.

Schooler, J. W., & Eich, E. (2000). Memory for emotional events. In E. Tulving & F. I. M. Craik (Eds.), *The Oxford handbook of memory* (pp. 379–392). New York: Oxford University Press.

Schooler, J. W., Fallshore, M., & Fiore, S. M. (1995). Epilogue: Putting insight into perspective. In R. J. Sternlogue & J. E. Davidson (Eds.), *The nature of insight* (pp. 559–587). Cambridge, MA: MIT Press.

Schooler, J. W., & Melcher, J. (1994). The ineffability of insight. In S. M. Smith, T. B. Ward, & R. A. Finke (Eds.), *The creative cognition approach* (pp. 97–133). Cambridge, MA: MIT Press.

Schooler, J. W., Ohlsson, S., & Brooks, K. (1993). Thoughts beyond words: When language overshad-ows insight. *Journal of Experimental Psychology: General, 122,* 166–183.

Schraagen, J. M. (1993). How experts solve a novel problem in experimental design. *Cognitive Science, 17,* 285–309.

Schrauf, R. W., & Rubin, D. C. (2001). Effects of voluntary immigration on the distribution of autobiographical memory over the lifespan. *Applied Cognitive Psychology, 15,* S75–S88.

Schraw, G. (1994). The effect of metacognitive knowledge on local and global monitoring. *Contemporary Educational Psychology, 19,* 143–154.

Schützwohl, A. (1998). Surprise and schema strength. *Journal of Experimental Psychology: Learning, Memory, and Cognition, 24,* 1182–1199.

Schwartz, B. L. (1999). Sparkling at the end of the tongue: The etiology of tip-of-the-tongue phenomenology. *Psychonomic Bulletin & Review, 6,* 379–393.

Schwartz, B. L. (2001). The relation of tip-of-the-tongue states and retrieval time. *Memory & Cognition, 29,* 117–126.

Schwartz, B. L. (2002). *Tip-of-the-tongue states: Phenomenology, mechanism, and lexical retrieval.* Mahwah, NJ: Erlbaum.

Schwartz, B. L., Benjamin, A. S., & Bjork, R. A. (1997). The inferential and experiential bases of metamemory. *Current Directions in Psychological Science, 6,* 132–137.

Schwartz, B. L., & Perfect, T. J. (2002). Introduction: Toward an applied metacognition. In T. J. Perfect & B. L. Schwartz (Eds.), *Applied metacognition* (pp. 1–11). Cambridge, England: Cambridge University Press.

Schwartz, B. L., & Smith, S. M. (1997). The retrieval of related information influences tip-of-the-tongue states. *Journal of Memory and Language, 36,* 68–86.

Schwartz, B. L., Travis, D. M., Castro, A. M., & Smith, S. M. (2000). The phenomenology of real and illusory tip-of-the-tongue states. *Memory & Cognition, 28,* 18–27.

Schwartz, S. H. (1971). Modes of representation and problem solving: Well evolved is half solved. *Journal of Experimental Psychology, 91,* 347–350.

Schwartz, S. H., & Fattaleh, D. (1972). Representation in deductive problem solving: The matrix. *Journal of Experimental Psychology, 95,* 343–348.

Schwartz, S. H., & Polish, J. (1974). The effect of problem size on representation in deductive problem solving. *Memory & Cognition, 2*, 683–686.

Schwarz, N. (1995). Social cognition: Information accessibility and use in social judgment. In E. E. Smith & D. N. Osherson (Eds.), *Thinking* (2nd ed., pp. 345–376). Cambridge, MA: MIT Press.

Schwarz, N. (2001). Feelings as information: Implications for affective influences on information processing. In L. L. Martin & G. L. Clore (Eds.), *Theories of mood and cognition* (pp. 159–176). Mahwah, NJ: Erlbaum.

Schweickert, R., & Boruff, B. (1986). Short-term memory capacity: Magic number or magic spell? *Journal of Experimental Psychology: Learning, Memory, and Cognition, 12*, 419–425.

Scott, S. (1973). *The relation of divergent thinking to bilingualism: Cause or effect?* Unpublished manuscript, McGill University, Department of Psychology.

Searleman, A., & Herrmann, D. (1994). *Memory from a broader perspective*. New York: McGraw-Hill.

Sebel, P. S., Bonke, B., & Winograd, E. (Eds.). (1993). *Memory and awareness in anesthesia*. Englewood Cliffs, NJ: Prentice Hall.

Sedlmeier, P. (1999). *Improving statistical reasoning: Theoretical models and practical implications*. Mahwah, NJ: Erlbaum.

Sedlmeier, P., Hertwig, R., & Gigerenzer, G. (1998). Are judgments of the positional frequencies of letters systematically biased due to availability? *Journal of Experimental Psychology: Learning, Memory, and Cognition, 24*, 754–770.

Segal, S. J., & Fusella, V. (1970). Influence of imaged pictures and sounds on detection of visual and auditory signals. *Journal of Experimental Psychology, 83*, 458–464.

Seidenberg, M. S. (1995). Visual word recognition: An overview. In J. L. Miller & P. D. Eimas (Eds.), *Speech, language, and communication* (pp. 137–179). San Diego: Academic Press.

Seifert, C. M. (1999). Situated cognition and learning. In R. A. Wilson & F. C. Keil (Eds.), *The MIT encyclopedia of the cognitive sciences* (pp. 767–769). Cambridge, MA: MIT Press.

Sellen, A. J. (1994). Detection of everyday errors. *Applied Psychology: An International Review, 43*, 475–498.

Sereno, S. C., Brewer, C. C., & O'Donnell, P. J. (2003). Context effects in word recognition: Evidence for early interactive processing. *Psychological Science, 14*, 328–333.

Shafir, E. B., & LeBoeuf, R. A. (2002). Rationality. *Annual Review of Psychology, 53*, 491–517.

Shafir, E. B., & Tversky, A. (1995). Decision making. In E. E. Smith & D. N. Osherson (Eds.), *Thinking* (pp. 77–100). Cambridge, MA: MIT Press.

Shammi, P., & Stuss, D. T. (1999). Humour appreciation: A role of the right frontal lobe. *Brain, 122*, 657–666.

Shanks, D. R. (1997). Representation of categories and concept in memory. In M. A. Conway (Ed.), *Cognitive models of memory* (pp. 111–146). Cambridge, MA: MIT Press.

Sharps, M. J. (1998, Winter). Age-related change in visual information processing: Toward a unified theory of aging and visual memory. *Current Psychology, 16*, 284–307.

Sharps, M. J., & Wertheimer, M. (2000). Gestalt perspectives on cognitive science and on exprimental psychology. *Review of General Psychology, 4*, 315–336.

Shatz, M., & Gelman, R. (1973). The development of communication skills: Modifications in the speech of young children as a function of listener. *Monographs of the Society for Research in Child Development, 38*(2, Serial No. 152).

Shavinina, L. V. (Ed.). (2003). *The international handbook on innovation*. Oxford, England: Elsevier Science.

Shepard, R. N. (1978). Externalization of mental images and the act of creation. In B. S. Randhawa & W. E. Coffman (Eds.), *Visual learning, thinking, and communication* (pp. 133–190). New York: Academic Press.

Shepard, R. N., & Chipman, S. (1970). Second-order isomorphism of internal representation: Shapes of states. *Cognitive Psychology, 1*, 1–17.

Shepard, R. N., & Metzler, J. (1971). Mental rotation of three-dimensional objects. *Science, 171*, 701–703.

Sherman, J. W., & Bessenoff, G. R. (1999). Stereotypes as source-monitoring cues: On the interaction between episodic and semantic memory. *Psychological Science, 10*, 106–110.

Sherman, M. A. (1976). Adjectival negation and the comprehension of multiple negated sentences. *Journal of Verbal Learning and Verbal Behavior, 15*, 143–157.

Shi, R., & Werker, J. F. (2001). Six-month-old infants' preference for lexical words. *Psychological Science, 12*, 70–75.

Shiffrin, R. M. (1999). 30 years of memory. In C. Izawa (Ed.), *On human memory* (pp. 127–149). Mahwah, NJ: Erlbaum.

Shiffrin, R. M., & Schneider, W. (1977). Controlled and automatic human information processing: II. Perceptual learning, automatic attending, and a general theory. *Psychological Review, 84,* 127–190.

Shih, M., Pittinsky, T. L., & Ambady, N. (1999). Stereotype susceptibility: Identity salience and shifts in quantitative performance. *Psychological Science, 10,* 80–83.

Shih, S., & Sperling, G. (2002). Measuring and modeling the trajectory of visual spatial attention. *Psychological Review, 109,* 260–305.

Shiloh, S. (1994). Heuristics and biases in health decision making: Their expression in genetic counseling. In L. Heath et al. (Eds.), *Applications of heuristics and biases to social issues* (pp. 13–30). New York: Plenum.

Shimamura, A. P. (1996). The role of the prefrontal cortex in controlling and monitoring memory processes. In L. M. Reder (Ed.), *Implicit memory and metacognition* (pp. 259–274). Mahwah, NJ: Erlbaum.

Shin, H. B., & Bruno, R. (2003, October). *Language use and English-speaking ability: 2000.* Washington, DC: U.S. Census Bureau.

Shoham, V., & Rohrbaugh, M. (1997). Interrupting ironic processes. *Psychological Science, 8,* 151–153.

Shum, M. S. (1998). The role of temporal landmarks in autobiographical memory processes. *Psychological Bulletin, 124,* 423–442.

Siegal, M. (1996). Conversation and cognition. In R. Gelman & T. K. Au (Eds.), *Perceptual and cognitive development* (pp. 243–282). San Diego: Academic Press.

Siegler, R. S. (1998). *Children's thinking* (3rd ed.). Upper Saddle River, NJ: Prentice Hall.

Siegler, R. S., DeLoache, J., & Eisenberg, N. (2003). *How children develop.* New York: Worth.

Silva, T., & Matsuda, P. K. (Eds.). (2001). *Landmark essays on ESL writing.* Mahwah, NJ: Erlbaum.

Simon, D., Pham, L. B., Le, Q. A., & Holyoak, K. J. (2001). The emergence of coherence over the course of decision making. *Journal of Experimental Psychology: Learning, Memory, and Cognition, 27,* 1250–1260.

Simon, H. A. (1995). Technology is not the problem. In P. Baumgartner & S. Payr (Eds.), *Speaking minds: Interviews with twenty eminent cognitive scientists* (pp. 231–248). Princeton, NJ: Princeton University Press.

Simon, H. A. (1996). *The sciences of the artificial* (3rd ed.). Cambridge, MA: MIT Press.

Simon, H. A. (1999). Problem solving. In R. A. Wilson & F. C. Keil (Eds.), *The MIT encyclopedia of the cognitive sciences* (pp. 674–676). Cambridge, MA: MIT Press.

Simon, H. A. (2001). Learning to research about learning. In S. M. Carver & D. Klahr (Eds.), *Cognition and instruction: Twenty-five years of progress* (pp. 205–226). Mahwah, NJ: Erlbaum.

Simon, H. A., & Gobet, F. (2000). Expertise effects in memory recall: Comment on Vicente and Wang (1998). *Psychological Review, 107,* 593–600.

Simons, D. J., & Chabris, C. F. (1999). Gorillas in our midst: Sustained inattentional blindness for dynamic events. *Perception, 28,* 1059–1074.

Simons, D. J., Chabris, C. F., Schnur, T., & Levin, D. T. (2002). Evidence for preserved representations in change blindness. *Consciousness and Cognition, 11,* 78–97.

Simons, D. J., & Levin, D. T. (1997a). Change blindness. *Trends in Cognitive Sciences, 1,* 261–267.

Simons, D. J., & Levin, D. T. (1997b). Failure to detect changes to unattended objects. *Investigative Ophthalmology and Visual Science, 38,* S707.

Simons, D. J., & Levin, D. T. (1998). Failure to detect changes to people during a real-world interaction. *Psychonomic Bulletin & Review, 5,* 644–649.

Simonson, I., et al. (2001). Consumer research: In search of identity. *Annual Review of Psychology, 52,* 249–275.

Simonton, D. K. (1997). Creative productivity: A predictive and explanatory model of career trajectories and landmarks. *Psychological Review, 104,* 66–89.

Simonton, D. K. (1999). Creativity from a historiometric perspective. In R. J. Sternberg (Ed.), *Handbook of creativity* (pp. 116–133). New York: Cambridge University Press.

Simpson, G. B. (1994). Context and the processing of ambiguous words. In M. A. Gernsbacher (Ed.), *Handbook of psycholinguistics* (pp. 359–374). San Diego: Academic Press.

Sims, V. K., & Mayer, R. E. (2002). Domain specificity of spatial expertise: The case of video game players. *Applied Cognitive Psychology, 16,* 97–115.

Slater, A., & Butterworth, G. (1997). Perception of social stimuli: Face perception and imitation. In G. Brenner, A. Slater, & G. Butterworth (Eds.),

Infant development: Recent advances (pp. 223–245). Hove, England: Psychology Press.

Slobin, D. I. (1966). Grammatical transformations and sentence comprehension in childhood and adulthood. *Journal of Verbal Learning and Verbal Behavior, 5,* 219–227.

Slobin, D. I. (1979). *Psycholinguistics* (2nd ed.). Glenview, IL: Scott, Foresman.

Sloman, S. A. (1999). Rational versus arational models of thought. In R. J. Sternberg (Ed.), *The nature of cognition* (pp. 557–585). Cambridge, MA: MIT Press.

Sloman, S. A., Love, B. C., & Ahn, W. (1998). Feature centrality and conceptual coherence. *Cognitive Science, 22,* 189–228.

Slovic, P., Kunreuther, H., & White, G. F. (1974). Decision processes, rationality and adjustment to natural hazards. In G. F. White (Ed.), *Natural hazards, local, national and global.* New York: Oxford University Press.

Small, S. L. (2002). Biological approaches to the treatment of aphasia. In A. E. Hillis (Ed.), *The handbook of adult language disorders* (pp. 397–411). New York: Psychology Press.

Smeets, M. A. M., & Kosslyn, S. M. (2001). Hemispheric differences in body image in anorexia nervosa. *International Journal of Eating Disorders, 29,* 409–416.

Smith, E. E. (1995). Concepts and categorization. In E. E. Smith & D. N. Osherson (Eds.), *Thinking* (2nd ed., pp. 3–33). Cambridge, MA: MIT Press.

Smith, E. E. (2000). Neural bases of human working memory. *Current Directions in Psychological Science, 9,* 45–49.

Smith, E. E., & Jonides, J. (1997). Working memory: A view from neuroimaging. *Cognitive Psychology, 33,* 5–42.

Smith, E. E., & Jonides, J. (1998). Neuroimaging analyses of human working memory. *Proceedings of the National Academy of Science, 95,* 12061–12068.

Smith, E. E., & Jonides, J. (1999). Storage and executive processes in the frontal lobes. *Science, 283,* 1657–1660.

Smith, E. E., Patalano, A. L., & Jonides, J. (1998). Alternative strategies of categorization. *Cognition, 65,* 167–196.

Smith, E. E., Shoben, E. J., & Rips, L. J. (1974). Structure and process in semantic memory: A featural model for semantic decisions. *Psychological Review, 81,* 214–241.

Smith, J., & Baltes, P. B. (1999). Life-span perspectives on development. In M. H. Bornstein & M. E. Lamb (Eds.), *Developmental psychology: An advanced textbook* (4th ed., pp. 47–720). Mahwah, NJ: Erlbaum.

Smith, J. D. (2002). Exemplar theory's predicted typicality gradient can be tested and disconfirmed. *Psychological Science, 13,* 437–442.

Smith, M. (2000). Conceptual structures in language production. In L. Wheeldon (Ed.), *Aspects of language production* (pp. 331–374). Philadelphia: Psychology Press.

Smith, N. (2000). Foreword. In N. Chomsky (Ed.), *On nature and language* (pp. 1–44). Cambridge, Great Britain: Cambridge University Press.

Smith, S. M. (1995a). Fixation, incubation, and insight in memory and creative thinking. In S. M. Smith, T. B. Ward, & R. A. Finke (Eds.), *The creative cognition approach* (pp. 135–156). Cambridge, MA: MIT Press.

Smith, S. M. (1995b). Getting into and out of mental ruts: A theory of fixation, incubation, and insight. In R. J. Sternberg & J. E. Davidson (Eds.), *The nature of insight* (pp. 229–251). Cambridge, MA: MIT Press.

Smith, S. M., Glenberg, A., & Bjork, R. A. (1978). Environmental context and human memory. *Memory & Cognition, 6,* 342–353.

Smith, S. M., Ward, T. B., & Schumacher, J. S. (1993). Constraining effects of examples in a creative generation task. *Memory & Cognition, 21,* 837–845.

Smith, S. M., et al. (2003). Eliciting and comparing false and recovered memories: An experimental approach. *Applied Cognitive Psychology, 17,* 251–279.

Smyth, M. M., Collins, A. F., Morris, P. E., & Levy, P. (1994). *Cognition in action* (2nd ed.). Hove, England: Erlbaum.

Smyth, M. M., Morris, P. E., Levy, P., & Ellis, A. W. (1987). *Cognition in action.* Hillsdale, NJ: Erlbaum.

Snow, C. E. (1998). Bilingualism and second language acquisition. In J. Berko-Gleason & N. Bernstein Ratner (Eds.), *Psycholinguistics* (2nd ed., pp. 453–481). Fort Worth, TX: Harcourt Brace.

Snow, C. E. (1999). Social perspectives on the emergence of language. In B. MacWhinney (Ed.), *The emergence of language* (pp. 257–276). Mahwah, NJ: Erlbaum.

Snow, C. E., & Hoefnagel-Hohle, M. (1978). The critical period for language acquisition. *Child Development, 4,* 1114–1128.

Sobel, C. P. (2001). *The cognitive sciences: An interdisciplinary approach.* Mountain View, CA: Mayfield.

Soderquist, D. R. (2002). *Sensory processes.* Thousand Oaks, CA: Sage Publications.

Son, L. K., & Metcalfe, J. (2000). Metacognitive and control strategies in study-time allocation. *Journal of Experimental Psychology: Learning, Memory, and Cognition, 26,* 204–221.

Son, L. K., & Schwartz, B. L. (2002). The relation between metacognitive monitoring and control. In T. J. Perfect & B. L. Schwartz (Eds.), *Applied metacognition* (pp. 15–38). Cambridge, England: Cambridge University Press.

Sparing, R., et al. (2002). Visual cortex excitability increases during visual mental imagery—a TMS study in healthy human subjects. *Brain Research, 938,* 92–97.

Spelke, E., Hirst, W., & Neisser, U. (1976). Skills of divided attention. *Cognition, 4,* 215–230.

Spencer, S. J., Steele, C. M., & Quinn, D. M. (1999). Stereotype threat and women's math performance. *Journal of Experimental Social Psychology, 35,* 4–28.

Sperling, G. (1960). The information available in brief visual presentations. *Psychological Monographs, 74,* 1–29.

Sporer, S. L. (1991). Deep—deeper—deepest? Encoding strategies and the recognition of human faces. *Journal of Experimental Psychology: Learning, Memory, and Cognition, 17,* 323–333.

Springer, S. P., & Deutsch, G. (1998). *Left brain, right brain: Perspectives from cognitive neuroscience* (5th ed.). New York: Freeman.

Squire, L. R., Knowlton, B., & Musen, G. (1993). The structure and organization of memory. *Annual Review of Psychology, 44,* 453–495.

Staddon, J. (2001). *The new behaviorism: Mind, mechanism, and society.* Philadelphia: Psychology Press.

Stanny, C. J., & Johnson, T. C. (2000). Effects of stress induced by a simulated shooting on recall by police and citizen witnesses. *American Journal of Psychology, 113,* 359–386.

Stanovich, K. E. (1999). *Who is rational? Studies of individual differences in reasoning.* Mahwah, NJ: Erlbaum.

Stanovich, K. E., & West, R. F. (1981). The effect of sentence processing on ongoing word recognition: Tests of a two-process theory. *Journal of Experimental Psychology: Human Perception and Performance, 7,* 658–672.

Stanovich, K. E., & West, R. F. (1983). On priming by a sentence context. *Journal of Experimental Psychology: General, 112,* 1–36.

Stanovich, K. E., & West, R. F. (1997). Reasoning independently of prior belief and individual differences in actively open-minded thinking. *Journal of Educational Psychology, 89,* 342–357.

Stanovich, K. E., & West, R. F. (1998). Individual differences in rational thought. *Journal of Experimental Psychology: General, 127,* 161–188.

Stanovich, K. E., & West, R. F. (2000). Individual differences in reasoning: Implications for the rationality debate? *Behavioral and Brain Sciences, 23,* 645–726.

Statistics Canada. (2003a). *Canadian statistics.* Retrieved December 5, 2003, from http://www.statcan.ca/english/

Statistics Canada. (2003b). *Population by mother tongue, provinces and territories.* Retrieved October 10, 2003, from http:www.statcan.ca/english/Pgdb/demo18a.htm

Statistics Canada (2003c). *Selected dwelling characteristics and household equipment.* Retrieved June 13, 2003, from http://www.statcan.ca/english/Pgdb/famil09b.htm

Steele, C. M. (1997). A threat in the air: How stereotypes shape intellectual identity and performance. *American Psychologist, 52,* 613–629.

Steele, C. M., & Aronson, J. (1995). Stereotype threat and the intellectual test performance of African Americans. *Journal of Personality and Social Psychology, 69,* 797–811.

Stein, N. I., Ornstein, P. A., Tversky, B., & Brainerd, C. (Eds.). (1997). *Memory for everyday and emotional events.* Mahwah, NJ: Erlbaum.

Sternberg, R. J. (1998). A balance theory of wisdom. *Review of General Psychology, 2,* 347–365.

Sternberg, R. J. (1999a). A dialectical basis for understanding the study of cognition. In R. J. Sternberg (Ed.), *The nature of cognition* (pp. 51–78). Cambridge, MA: MIT Press.

Sternberg, R. J. (Ed.). (1999b). *Handbook of creativity.* New York: Cambridge University Press.

Sternberg, R. J. (Ed.). (1999c). *The nature of cognition.* Cambridge, MA: MIT Press.

Sternberg, R. J. (2001). What is the common thread of creativity? *American Psychologist, 56,* 360–362.

Sternberg, R. J. (2002). Smart people are not stupid, but they sure can be foolish. In R. J. Sternberg

(Ed.), *Why smart people can be so stupid* (pp. 232–242). New Haven, CT: Yale University Press.

Sternberg, R. J., & Ben-Zeev, T. (2001). *Complex cognition: The psychology of human thought.* New York: Oxford University Press.

Sternberg, R. J., & Lubart, T. I. (1995). *Defying the crowd: Cultivating creativity in a culture of conformity.* New York: Free Press.

Sternberg, R. J., & Lubart, T. I. (1996). Investing in creativity. *American Psychologist, 51,* 677–688.

Sternberg, R. J., & O'Hara, L. A. (1999). Creativity and intelligence. In R. J. Sternberg (Ed.), *Handbook of creativity* (pp. 251–272). New York: Cambridge University Press.

Sternberg, R. J., & Powell, J. S. (1983). Comprehending verbal comprehension. *American Psychologist, 38,* 878–893.

Stevens, A., & Coupe, P. (1978). Distortions in judged spatial relations. *Cognitive Psychology, 10,* 422–437.

Stillings, N. A., et al. (1995). *Cognitive science: An introduction* (2nd ed.). Cambridge, MA: MIT Press.

Stine, E. L., Wingfield, A., & Poon, L. W. (1989). Speech comprehension and memory through adulthood: The roles of time and strategy. In L. W. Poon, D. C. Rubin, & B. A. Wilson (Eds.), *Everyday cognition in adulthood and later life* (pp. 195–221). New York: Cambridge University Press.

Stine-Morrow, E. A. L., & Miller, L. M. S. (1999). Basic cognitive processes. In J. C. Cavanaugh & S. K. Whitbourne (Eds.), *Gerontology: An interdisciplinary perspective* (pp. 186–212). New York: Oxford University Press.

Stothard, S. E., & Hulme, C. (1996). A comparison of reading comprehension and decoding difficulties in children. In C. Cornoldi & J. Oakhill (Eds.), *Reading comprehension difficulties: Processes and intervention* (pp. 93–112). Mahwah, NJ: Erlbaum.

Strayer, D. L., Drews, F. A., & Johnston, W. A. (2003). Cell phone-induced failures of visual attention during simulated driving. *Journal of Experimental Psychology: Applied, 9,* 23–32.

Stroessner, S. J., & Plaks, J. E. (2001). Illusory correlation and stereotype formation: Tracing the arc of research over a quarter century. In G. B. Moskowitz (Ed.), *Cognitive social psychology* (pp. 247–259). Mahwah, NJ: Erlbaum.

Stromswold, K. (1999). Cognitive and neural aspects of language acquisition. In E. Lepore & Z. Pylyshyn

(Eds.), *What is cognitive science?* (pp. 356–400). Malden, MA: Blackwell.

Stroop, J. R. (1935). Studies of interference in serial verbal reactions. *Journal of Experimental Psychology, 18,* 643–662.

Stuss, D. T., Binns, M. A., Murphy, K. J., & Alexander, M. P. (2002). Dissociations within the anterior attentional system: Effects of task complexity and irrelevant information on reaction time speed and accuracy. *Neuropsychology, 16,* 500–513.

Suh, S., & Trabasso, T. (1993). Inferences during reading: Converging evidence from discourse analysis, talk-aloud protocols, and recognition priming. *Journal of Memory and Language, 32,* 279–300.

Sutherland, R., & Hayne, H. (2001). The effect of postevent information on adults' eyewitness reports. *Applied Cognitive Psychology, 15,* 249–263.

Suzuki-Slakter, N. S. (1988). Elaboration and metamemory during adolescence. *Contemporary Educational Psychology, 13,* 206–220.

Swanson, H. L. (1999). What develops in working memory? A life span perspective. *Developmental Psychology, 35,* 986–1000.

Swinkels, A. (2003). An effective exercise for teaching cognitive heuristics. *Teaching of Psychology, 30,* 120–122.

Swoyer, C. (2002). Judgment and decision making: Extrapolations and applications. In R. Gowda & J. C. Fox (Eds.), *Judgments, decisions, and public policy* (pp. 9–45). New York: Cambridge University Press.

Symons, C. S., & Johnson, B. T. (1997). The self-reference effect in memory: A meta-analysis. *Psychological Bulletin, 121,* 371–394.

Talarico, J. M., & Rubin, D. C. (2003). Confidence, not consistency, characterizes flashbulb memories. *Psychological Science, 14,* 455–461.

Tanaka, J. W., & Curran, T. (2001). A neural basis for expert object recognition. *Psychological Science, 12,* 43–47.

Tanaka, J. W., & Farah, M. J. (1993). Parts and wholes in face recognition. *Quarterly Journal of Experimental Psychology, 46A,* 225–245.

Tanaka, J. W., & Taylor, M. (1991). Object categories and expertise: Is the basic level in the eye of the beholder? *Cognitive Psychology, 23,* 457–482.

Tarr, M. J. (1995). Rotating objects to recognize them: A case study on the role of viewpoint dependency in the recognition of three-dimensional objects. *Psychonomic Bulletin & Review, 2,* 55–82.

Tarr, M. J. (1999). Visual object recognition: Can a single mechanism suffice? In M. A. Peterson & G. Rhodes (Eds.), *Analytic and holistic processes in the perception of faces, objects, and scenes.* New York: JAI: Ablex.

Tarr, M. J., & Bülthoff, H. H. (1998). Image-based object recognition in man, monkey and machine. *Cognition, 67,* 1–20.

Tarr, M. J., Bülthoff, H. H., Zabinski, M., & Blanz, V. (1997). To what extent do unique parts influence recognition across changes in viewpoint? *Psychological Science, 8,* 282–289.

Tarr, M. J., & Vuong, Q. C. (2002). Visual object recognition. In S. Yantis (Ed.), *Stevens' handbook of experimental psychology* (3rd. ed., Vol. 1, pp. 287–314). New York: Wiley.

Tavris, C. (2002, July/August). The high cost of skepticism. *Skeptical Inquirer,* pp. 41–44.

Taylor, H. A., Naylor, S. J., & Chechile, N. A. (1999). Goal-specific influences on the representation of spatial perspective. *Memory & Cognition, 27,* 309–319.

Taylor, I. A., & Taylor, M. M. (1990). *Psycholinguistics: Learning and using language.* Englewood Cliffs, NJ: Prentice Hall.

Taylor, S. E., Phan, L. B., Rivkin, I. D., & Armor, D. A. (1998). Harnessing the imagination: Mental simulation, self-regulation, and coping. *American Psychologist, 53,* 429–439.

Teasdale, J. D., et al. (1995). Stimulus-independent thought depends on central executive resources. *Memory & Cognition, 23,* 551–559.

Teigen, K. H. (2004). Judgment by representativeness. In R. Pohl (Ed.), *Cognitive illusions: Handbook on fallacies and biases in thinking, judgment, and memory.* Hove, England: Psychology Press.

Tetlock, P. E., & Mellers, B. A. (2002). The great rationality debate. *Psychological Science, 13,* 94–99.

Thiede, K. W., Anderson, M. C. M., & Therriault, D. (2003). Accuracy of metacognitive monitoring affects learning of texts. *Journal of Educational Psychology, 95,* 66–73.

Thomas, J. C. (1974). An analysis of behavior in the Hobbits-Orcs program. *Cognitive Psychology, 6,* 257–269.

Thomas, J. C. (1989). Problem solving by human-machine interaction. In K. J. Gilhooly (Ed.), *Human and machine problem solving* (pp. 317–362). New York: Plenum.

Thomas, M. H., & Wang, A. Y. (1996). Learning by the keyword mnemonic: Looking for long-term benefits. *Journal of Experimental Psychology: Applied, 2,* 330–342.

Thomas, R. D. (1998). Learning correlations in categorization tasks using large, ill-defined categories. *Journal of Experimental Psychology: Learning, Memory, and Cognition, 24,* 119–143.

Thompson, C. P., Skowronski, J. J., Larsen, S. F., & Betz, A. (1996). *Autobiographical memory: Remembering what and remembering when.* Mahwah, NJ: Erlbaum.

Thompson, W. L., & Kosslyn, S. M. (2000). Neural systems activated during visual mental imagery: A review and meta-analyses. In A. W. Toga & J. C. Mazziotta (Eds.), *Brain mapping: The systems* (pp. 535–560). San Diego: Academic Press.

Thorndyke, P. W. (1981). Distance estimation from cognitive maps. *Cognitive Psychology, 13,* 526–550.

Thrun, S., et al. (1998). Map learning and high-speed navigation in RHINO. In D. Kortenkamp, R. P. Bonasso, & R. Murphy (Eds.), *Artificial intelligence and mobile robots* (pp. 21–52). Cambridge, MA: MIT Press.

Tiitinen, H., Sinkkonen, J., Reinikainen, K., Alho, K., Lavikainen, J., & Näätänen, R. (1993). Selective attention enhances the auditory 40-Hz transient response in humans. *Nature, 364,* 59–60.

Tincoff, R., & Jusczyk, P. W. (1999). Some beginnings of word comprehension in 6-month-olds. *Psychological Science, 10,* 172–175.

Tippett, L. J., McAuliffe, S., & Farah, M. J. (1995). Preservation of categorical knowledge in Alzheimer's disease: A computational account. In R. A. McCarthy (Ed.), *Semantic knowledge and semantic representations* (pp. 519–533). East Sussex, England: Erlbaum.

Todd, P. M., & Gigerenzer, G. (2000). Précis of *Simple heuristics that make us smart. Behavioral and Brain Sciences, 23,* 727–780.

Toglia, M. P., Neuschatz, J. S., & Goodwin, K. A. (1999). Recall accuracy and illusory memories: When more is less. *Memory, 7,* 233–256.

Tokuhama-Espinosa, T. (2001). *Raising multilingual children: Foreign language acquisition and children.* Westport, CT: Bergin & Garvey.

Tomasello, M. (1998a). Cognitive linguistics. In W. Bechtel & G. Graham (Eds.), *A companion to cognitive science* (pp. 477–487). Malden, MA: Blackwell.

Tomasello, M. (1998b). Introduction: A cognitive-functional perspective on language structure. In M. Tomasello (Ed.), *The new psychology of language: Cognitive and functional approaches to language structure* (pp. vii–xxiii). Mahwah, NJ: Erlbaum.

Tomasello, M., Conti-Ramsden, G., & Ewert, B. (1990). Young children's conversations with their mothers and fathers: Differences in breakdown and repair. *Journal of Child Language, 17,* 115–130.

Toms, M., Morris, N., & Foley, P. (1994). Characteristics of visual interference with visuospatial working memory. *British Journal of Psychology, 85,* 131–144.

Toplak, M. E., & Stanovich, K. E. (2002). The domain specificity and generality of disjunctive reasoning: Searching for generalizable critical thinking skills. *Journal of Educational Psychology, 94,* 197–209.

Torrance, E. P. (Ed.). (2000). *On the edge and keeping on the edge.* Westport, CT: Ablex.

Torrance, M., & Jeffery, G. (1999). Writing processes and cognitive demands. In M. Torrance & G. C. Jeffery (Eds.), *The cognitive demands of writing: Processing capacity and working memory in text production* (pp. 1–11). Amsterdam: Amsterdam University Press.

Torrance, M., Thomas, G. V., & Robinson, E. J. (1996). Finding something to write about: Strategic and automatic processes in idea generation. In C. M. Levy & S. Ransdell (Eds.), *The science of writing: Theories, methods, individual differences, and applications* (pp. 189–205). Mahwah, NJ: Erlbaum.

Torrance, M., Thomas, G. V., & Robinson, E. J. (1999). Individual differences in the writing behaviour of undergraduate students. *British Journal of Educational Psychology, 69,* 189–199.

Toth, J. P. (2000). Nonconscious forms of human memory. In E. Tulving & F. I. M. Craik (Eds.), *The Oxford handbook of memory* (pp. 245–261). New York: Oxford University Press.

Trabasso, T., & Suh, S. (1993). Understanding text: Achieving explanatory coherence through on-line inferences and mental operations in working memory. *Discourse Processes, 16,* 3–34.

Trabasso, T., Suh, S., Payton, P., & Jain, R. (1995). Explanatory inferences and other strategies during comprehension and their effect on recall. In R. F. Lorch & E. J. O'Brien (Eds.), *Sources of coherence in reading* (pp. 219–239). Hillsdale, NJ: Erlbaum.

Trafimow, D., & Wyer, R. S., Jr. (1993). Cognitive representation of mundane social events. *Journal of Personality and Social Psychology, 64,* 365–376.

Trainor, L. J., Austin, C. M., & Desjardins, R. N. (2000). Is infant-directed speech prosody a result of the vocal expression of emotion? *Psychological Science, 11,* 188–195.

Treiman, R., Clifton, C., Jr., Meyer, A. S., & Wurm, L. H. (2003). Language comprehension and production. In A. F. Healy & R. W. Proctor (Eds.), *Handbook of psychology* (Vol. 4, pp. 527–547). Hoboken, NJ: Wiley.

Treisman, A. (1964). Monitoring and storage of irrelevant messages and selective attention. *Journal of Verbal Learning and Verbal Behavior, 3,* 449–459.

Treisman, A. (1986, November). Features and objects in visual processing. *Scientific American, 255*(5), 114B–125.

Treisman, A. (1990). Visual coding of features and objects: Some evidence from behavioral studies. In National Research Council (Ed.), *Advances in the modularity of vision: Selections from a symposium on frontiers of visual science* (pp. 39–61). Washington, DC: National Academy Press.

Treisman, A. (1993). The perception of features and objects. In A. Baddeley & L. Weiskrantz (Eds.), *Attention: Selection, awareness, and control* (pp. 5–35). Oxford, England: Clarendon.

Treisman, A. (2003, Fall/Winter). Eminent women in psychology. *The General Psychologist, 38* (3), 44–45.

Treisman, A., & Gelade, G. (1980). A feature-integration theory of attention. *Cognitive Psychology, 12,* 97–136.

Treisman, A., & Schmidt, H. (1982). Illusory conjunction in the perception of objects. *Cognitive Psychology, 14,* 107–141.

Treisman, A., & Souther, J. (1985). Search asymmetry: A diagnostic for preattentive processing of separable features. *Journal of Experimental Psychology: General, 114,* 285–310.

Treisman, A., & Souther, J. (1986). Illusory words: The roles of attention and of top-down constraints in conjoining letters to form words. *Journal of Experimental Psychology: Human Perception and Performance, 12,* 3–17.

Treisman, A., Viera, A., & Hayes, A. (1992). Automaticity and preattentive processing. *American Journal of Psychology, 105,* 341–362.

Tremblay, S., & Jones, D. M. (1998). Role of habituation in the irrelevant sound effect: Evidence from the effects of token set size and rate of transition. *Journal of Experimental Psychology: Learning, Memory, and Cognition, 24*, 659–671.

Trout, J. D. (2001). The biological basis of speech: What to infer from talking to the animals. *Psychological Review, 108*, 523–549.

Trout, J. D. (2002). Scientific explanation and the sense of understanding. *Philosophy of Science, 69*, 212–233.

Truthout. (2003). *White House credibility defense shifting.* Retrieved September 1, 2003, from http://truthout.org/docs

Tulving, E. (1983). *Elements of episodic memory.* New York: Oxford University Press.

Tulving, E. (1991). Memory research is not a zero-sum game. *American Psychologist, 46*, 41–42.

Tulving, E. (1999a). On the uniqueness of episodic memory. In L. Nilsson & H. J. Markowitsch (Eds.), *Cognitive neuroscience of memory* (pp. 11–42). Kirkland, WA: Hogrefe & Huber.

Tulving, E. (1999b). Study of memory: Processes and systems. In J. K. Foster & M. Jelicic (Eds.), *Memory: Systems, process, or function?* (pp. 11–30). New York: Oxford University Press.

Tulving, E. (2002). Episodic memory: From mind to brain. *Annual Review of Psychology, 53*, 1–25.

Tulving, E., & Craik, F. I. M. (Eds.). (2000). *The Oxford handbook of memory.* New York: Oxford University Press.

Tulving, E., & Lepage, M. (2000). Where in the brain is the awareness of one's past? In D. L. Schacter & E. Scarry (Eds.), *Memory, brain, and belief* (pp. 208–228). Cambridge, MA: MIT Press.

Tunmer, W. E., & Chapman, J. W. (1998). Language prediction skill, phonological recoding ability, and beginning reading. In C. Hulme & R. M. Joshi (Eds.), *Reading and spelling: Development and disorders* (pp. 33–67). Mahwah, NJ: Erlbaum.

Tversky, A., & Fox, C. R. (1995). Weighing risk and uncertainty. *Psychological Review, 102*, 269–283.

Tversky, A., & Kahneman, D. (1971). Belief in the law of small numbers. *Psychological Bulletin, 76*, 105–110.

Tversky, A., & Kahneman, D. (1973). Availability: A heuristic for judging frequency and probability. *Cognitive Psychology, 5*, 207–232.

Tversky, A., & Kahneman, D. (1974). Judgments under uncertainty: Heuristics and biases. *Science, 185*, 1124–1131.

Tversky, A., & Kahneman, D. (1981). The framing of decisions and the psychology of choice. *Science, 211*, 453–458.

Tversky, A., & Kahneman, D. (1982). Judgment under uncertainty: Heuristics and biases. In D. Kahneman, P. Slovic, & A. Tversky (Eds.), *Judgment under uncertainty: Heuristics and biases* (pp. 3–20). New York: Cambridge University Press.

Tversky, A., & Kahneman, D. (1983). Extensional versus intuitive reasoning: The conjunction fallacy in probability judgment. *Psychological Review, 90*, 293–315.

Tversky, B. (1981). Distortions in memory for maps. *Cognitive Psychology, 13*, 407–433.

Tversky, B. (1991). Spatial mental models. *The Psychology of Learning and Motivation, 27*, 109–145.

Tversky, B. (1997). Spatial constructions. In N. L. Stein, P. A. Ornstein, B. Tversky, & C. Brainerd (Eds.), *Memory for everyday and emotional events* (pp. 181–208). Mahwah, NJ: Erlbaum.

Tversky, B. (1998). Three dimensions of spatial cognition. In M. A. Conway, S. E. Gathercole, & C. Cornoldi (Eds.), *Theories of memory* (Vol. 2, pp. 259–275). East Sussex, England: Psychology Press.

Tversky, B. (1999). Talking about space [Review of the book *Representation and processing of spatial expressions*]. *Contemporary Psychology, 44*, 39–40.

Tversky, B. (2000a). Levels and structure of spatial knowledge. In S. M. Freundschuh & R. Kitchin (Eds.), *Cognitive mapping: Past, present, and future* (pp. 24–43). New York: Routledge.

Tversky, B. (2000b), Remembering spaces. In E. Tulving & F. I. M. Craik (Eds.), *The Oxford handbook of memory* (pp. 363–378). New York: Oxford University Press.

Tversky, B., & Lee, P. U. (1998). How space structures language. In C. Freksa, C. Habel, & K. F. Wender (Eds.), *Spatial cognition* (pp. 157–175). New York: Springer.

Tversky, B., Morrison, J. B., Franklin, N., & Bryant, D. J. (1999). Three spaces of spatial cognition. *Professional Geographer, 51*, 516–524.

Tversky, B., & Schiano, D. J. (1989). Perceptual and conceptual factors in distortions in memory for graphs and maps. *Journal of Experimental Psychology: General, 118*, 387–398.

Tweney, R. D. (1998). Toward a cognitive psychology of science: Recent research and its implications. *Current Directions in Psychological Science, 7,* 150–154.

Ucros, C. G. (1989). Mood state-dependent memory: A meta-analysis. *Cognition and Emotion, 3,* 139–167.

Umilta, C. (2001). Mechanisms of attention. In B. Rapp (Ed.), *The handbook of cognitive neuropsychology* (pp. 135–158). Philadelphia: Psychology Press.

Underwood, G. (Ed.). (1998). *Eye guidance in reading and scene perception.* Amsterdam: Elsevier.

Underwood, G., & Batt, V. (1996). *Reading and understanding: An introduction to the psychology of reading.* Cambridge, MA: Blackwell.

van den Broek, P. (1994). Comprehension and memory of narrative texts. In M. A. Gernsbacher (Ed.), *Handbook of psycholinguistics* (pp. 539–588). San Diego: Academic Press.

van den Broek, P., Young, M., Tzeng, Y., & Linderholm, T. (1999). The landscape model of reading: Inferences and the online construction of a memory representation. In H. van Oostendorp & S. R. Goldman (Eds.), *The construction of mental representations during reading.* Mahwah, NJ: Erlbaum.

VanderStoep, S. W., & Seifert, C. M. (1994). Problem solving, transfer, and thinking. In P. R. Pintrich, D. R. Brown, & C. E. Weinstein (Eds.), *Student motivation, cognition, and learning: Essays in honor of Wilbert J. McKeachie* (pp. 27–49). Hillsdale, NJ: Erlbaum.

van Hell, J. G., & Dijkstra, T. (2002). Foreign language knowledge can influence native language performance in exclusively native contexts. *Psychonomic Bulletin & Review, 9,* 780–789.

van Oostendorp, H., & Bonebakker, C. (1999). Difficulties in updating mental representations during reading news reports. In H. van Oostendorp & S. R. Goldman (Eds.), *The construction of mental representations during reading* (pp. 319–339). Mahwah, NJ: Erlbaum.

van Turennout, M., Hagoort, P., & Brown, C. M. (1998). Brain activity during speaking: From syntax to phonology in 40 milliseconds. *Science, 280,* 572–574.

Van Wallendael, L. R., & Kuhn, J. C. (1997). Distinctiveness is in the eye of the beholder: Cross-racial differences in perceptions of faces. *Psychological Reports, 80,* 35–39.

Vecera, S. P. (1998). Visual object representation: An introduction. *Psychobiology, 26,* 281–308.

Vecera, S. P., & O'Reilly, R. C. (1998). Figure-ground organization and object recognition processes: An interactive account. *Journal of Experimental Psychology: Human Perception and Performance, 24,* 441–462.

Vertzberger, Y. Y. I. (1998). *Risk taking and decision making: Foreign military intervention decisions.* Stanford, CA: Stanford University Press.

Vicente, K. J., & Wang, J. H. (1998). An ecological theory of expertise effects in memory recall. *Psychological Review, 105,* 33–57.

Vigliocco, G., & Hartsuiker, R. J. (2002). The interplay of meaning, sound, and syntax in sentence production. *Psychological Bulletin, 128,* 442–472.

Viney, W., & King, D. B. (2003). *A history of psychology: Ideas and context* (3rd ed.). Boston: Allyn and Bacon.

Vingerhoets, G., Berckmoes, C., & Stroobant, N. (2003). Cerebral hemodynamics during discrimination of prosodic and semantic emotion in speech studied by transcranial Doppler ultrasonography. *Neuropsychology, 17,* 93–99.

Visser, T. A. W., Bischof, W. F., & Di Lollo, V. (1999). Attentional switching in spatial and nonspatial domains: Evidence from the attentional blink. *Psychological Bulletin, 125,* 458–469.

Vroomen, J., & de Gelder, B. (1997). Activation of embedded words in spoken word recognition. *Journal of Experimental Psychology: Human Perception and Performance, 23,* 710–720.

Wagman, M. (1999). *The human mind according to artificial intelligence: Theory, research, and implications.* Westport, CT: Praeger.

Wagner, A. D., et al. (1998). Building memories: Remembering and forgetting of verbal experiences as predicted by brain activity. *Science, 281,* 1188–1191.

Wagner, R. K., & Stanovich, K. E. (1996). Expertise in reading. In K. A. Ericsson (Ed.), *The road to excellence: The acquisition of expert performance in the arts and sciences, sports, and games* (pp. 189–225). Mahwah, NJ: Erlbaum.

Walker, I., & Hulme, C. (1999). Concrete words are easier to recall than abstract: Evidence for a semantic contribution to short-term serial recall. *Journal of Experimental Psychology: Learning, Memory, & Cognition, 25,* 1256–1271.

Walker, W. R., Skowronski, J. J., & Thompson, C. P. (2003). Life is pleasant—and memory helps to keep it that way! *Review of General Psychology, 7*, 203–210.

Walker, W. R., Vogl, R. J., & Thompson, C. P. (1997). Autobiographical memory: Unpleasantness fades faster than pleasantness over time. *Applied Cognitive Psychology, 11*, 399–413.

Walker, W. R., et al. (2003). On the emotions that accompany autobiographical memories: Dysphoria disrupts the fading affect bias. *Cognition and Emotion, 7*, 703–724.

Walker-Andrews, A. S. (1986). Intermodal perception of expressive behaviors: Relation of eye and voice? *Developmental Psychology, 22*, 373–377.

Walker-Andrews, A. S. (1997). Infants' perception of expressive behaviors: Differentiation of multimodal information. *Psychological Bulletin, 121*, 437–456.

Wallenstein, G. V., & Hasselmo, M. E. (1998). Are there common neural mechanisms for learning, epilepsy, and Alzheimer's disease? In D. J. Stein & J. Ludik (Eds.), *Neural networks and psychopathology* (pp. 316–345). Cambridge, England: Cambridge University Press.

Walton, G. E., Bower, N. J., & Bower, T. G. R. (1992). Recognition of familiar faces by newborns. *Infant Behavior and Development, 15*, 265–269.

Waltz, J. A., Lau, A., Grewal, S. K., & Holyoak, K. J. (2000). The role of working memory in analogical mapping. *Memory & Cognition, 28*, 1205–1212.

Waltz, J. A., et al. (1999). A system for relational reasoning in human prefrontal cortex. *Psychological Science, 10*, 119–125.

Wang, A. Y., & Thomas, M. H. (1999). In defence of keyword experiments: A reply to Gruneberg's commentary. *Applied Cognitive Psychology, 13*, 283–287.

Wang, G., Tanaka, K., & Tanifuji, M. (1996). Optical imaging of functional organization in the monkey inferotemporal cortex. *Science, 272*, 1665–1668.

Ward, G., & Allport, A. (1997). Planning and problem-solving using the five-disc tower of London task. *Quarterly Journal of Experimental Psychology, 50A*, 49–78.

Ward, T. B. (2001). Creative cognition, conceptual combination, and the creative writing of Stephen R. Donaldson. *American Psychologist, 56*, 350–354.

Ward, T. B., Smith, S. M., & Vaid, J. (Eds.). (1997). *Creative thought: An investigation of conceptual structures and processes.* Washington, DC: American Psychological Association.

Warren, D. H. (1995). From maps to cityscapes: Reactions to modes of spatial representation. In W. Pape & F. Burwick (Eds.), *Reflecting senses: Perception and appearance in literature, culture, and the arts* (pp. 33–52). Berlin: Walter de Gruyter.

Warren, R. M., & Warren, R. P. (1970, December). Auditory illusions and confusions. *Scientific American, 223*(6), 30–36.

Warrington, E. K., & Weiskrantz, L. (1970). Amnesic syndrome: Consolidation or retrieval? *Nature, 228*, 629–630.

Wason, P. C. (1968). Reasoning about a rule. *Quarterly Journal of Experimental Psychology, 20*, 273–281.

Wason, P. C., & Johnson-Laird, P. N. (1972). *Psychology of reasoning: Structure and content.* Cambridge, MA: Harvard University Press.

Watson, J. B. (1913). Psychology as the behaviorist views it. *Psychological Review, 20*, 158–177.

Waxman, S. R. (2002). Early word-learning and conceptual development: Everything had a name and each name gave birth to a new thought. In U. Goswami (Ed.), *Blackwell handbook of childhood cognitive development* (pp. 102–126). Malden, MA: Blackwell.

Weber, E. U., Böckenholt, U., Hilton, D. J., & Wallace, B. (1993). Determinants of diagnostic hypothesis generation: Effects of information, base rates, and experience. *Journal of Experimental Psychology: Learning, Memory, and Cognition, 19*, 1131–1164.

Webster, M. J., & Ungerleider, L. G. (1998). Neuroanatomy of visual attention. In R. Parasuraman (Ed.), *The attentive brain* (pp. 19–34). Cambridge, MA: MIT Press.

Wegner, D. M. (1992). You can't always think what you want: Problems in the suppression of unwanted thoughts. *Advances in Experimental Social Psychology, 25*, 193–225.

Wegner, D. M. (1994). Ironic processes of mental control. *Psychological Review, 101*, 34–52.

Wegner, D. M. (1996). Personal communication.

Wegner, D. M. (1997a). When the antidote is the poison: Ironic mental control processes. *Psychological Science, 8*, 148–153.

Wegner, D. M. (1997b). Why the mind wanders. In J. D. Cohen & J. W. Schooler (Eds.), *Scientific approaches to consciousness* (pp. 295–315). Mahwah, NJ: Erlbaum.

Wegner, D. M. (2002). *The illusion of conscious will.* Cambridge, MA: MIT Press.

Wegner, D. M., Schneider, D. J., Carter, S. R., III, & White, T. L. (1987). Paradoxical effects of thought suppression. *Journal of Personality and Social Psychology, 53,* 5–13.

Weingardt, K. R., Loftus, E. F., & Lindsay, D. S. (1995). Misinformation revisited: New evidence on the suggestibility of memory. *Memory & Cognition, 23,* 72–82.

Weisberg, R. W. (1999). Creativity and knowledge: A challenge to theories. In R. J. Sternberg (Ed.), *Handbook of creativity* (pp. 226–250). New York: Cambridge University Press.

Weiskrantz, L. (1997). *Consciousness lost and found: A neuropsychological explanation.* New York: Oxford University Press.

Weiskrantz, L. (2000). To have but not to hold. In J. J. Bolhuis (Ed.), *Brain, perception, memory* (pp. 310–325). New York: Oxford University Press.

Weist, R. M. (1985). Cross-linguistic perspective on cognitive development. In T. M. Schlechter & M. P. Toglia (Eds.), *New directions in cognitive science* (pp. 191–216). Norwood, NJ: Ablex.

Wellman, H. M. (2000). Early childhood: Cognitive and mental development. In A. E. Kazdin (Ed.), *The encyclopedia of psychology.* New York: Oxford University Press.

Wellman, H. M., & Gelman, S. A. (1992). Cognitive development: Foundational theories of core domains. *Annual Review of Psychology, 43,* 337–375.

Wells, G. L., & Bradfield, A. L. (1998). "Good, you identified the suspect": Feedback to eyewitnesses distorts their reports of the witnessing experience. *Journal of Applied Psychology, 83,* 360–376.

Wells, G. L., & Bradfield, A. L. (1999). Distortions in eyewitnesses' recollections: Can the postidentification-feedback effect be moderated? *Psychological Science, 10,* 138–144.

Wells, G. L., & Olson, E. A. (2003). Eyewitness testimony. *Annual Review of Psychology, 54,* 277–295.

Wells, G. L., et al. (2000). From the lab to the police station: A successful application of eyewitness research. *American Psychologist, 55,* 581–598.

Werker, J. F., & Tees, R. C. (1984). Cross-language speech perception: Evidence for perceptual reorganization during the first year of life. *Infant Behavior and Development, 7,* 49–63.

Werker, J. F., & Tees, R. C. (1999). Influences on infant speech processing: Toward a new synthesis. *Annual Review of Psychology, 50,* 509–535.

West, R., Herndon, R. W., & Ross-Munroe, K. (2000). Event-related neural activity associated with prospective remembering. *Applied Cognitive Psychology 14,* S115–S126.

West, R. L. (1995). Compensatory strategies for age-associated memory impairment. In A. D. Baddeley, B. A. Wilson, & F. N. Watts (Eds.), *Handbook of memory disorders* (pp. 481–500). Chichester, England: Wiley.

Wexler, M., Kosslyn, S. M., & Berthoz, A. (1998). Motor processes in mental rotation. *Cognition, 68,* 77–94.

Wheatley, G. H. (1997). Reasoning with images in mathematical activity. In L. D. English (Ed.), *Mathematical reasoning: Analogies, metaphors, and images* (pp. 281–297). Mahwah, NJ: Erlbaum.

Wheeldon, L. (Ed.). (2000a). *Aspects of language production.* Philadelphia: Psychology Press.

Wheeldon, L. (2000b). Generating prosodic structure. In L. Wheeldon (Ed.), *Aspects of language production* (pp. 249–274). Philadelphia: Psychology Press.

Wheeldon, L. (2000c). Introduction. In L. Wheeldon (Ed.), *Aspects of language production* (pp. 1–47). Philadelphia: Psychology Press.

Wheeler, D. L. (1998, September 11). Neuroscientists take stock of brain-imaging studies. *Chronicle of Higher Education,* pp. A20–A22.

Wheeler, M. A. (2000). Episodic memory and autonoetic awareness. In E. Tulving & F. I. M. Craik (Eds.), *The Oxford handbook of memory* (pp. 597–608). New York: Oxford University Press.

Whitbourne, S. K. (2005). *Adult development and aging: Biopsychosocial perspectives* (2nd ed.). Hoboken, NJ: Wiley.

White, J. A. (2003). *Personal communication.*

Whittlesea, B. W. A. (1997). The representation of general and particular knowledge. In K. Lamberts & D. Shanks (Eds.), *Knowledge, concepts, and categories* (pp. 335–370). Cambridge, MA: MIT Press.

Wickelgren, W. A. (1965). Acoustic similarity and intrusion errors in short-term memory. *Journal of Experimental Psychology, 70,* 102–108.

Wickens, D. D., Dalezman, R. E., & Eggemeier, F. T. (1976). Multiple encoding of word attributes in memory. *Memory & Cognition, 4,* 307–310.

Wikman, A., Nieminen, T., & Summala, H. (1998). Driving experience and time-sharing during in-car tasks on roads of different width. *Ergonomics, 41,* 358–372.

Wilding, J., & Valentine, E. (1997). *Superior memory.* Hove, England: Psychology Press.

Williams, J. D. (1999). *The teacher's grammar book.* Mahwah, NJ: Erlbaum.

Williams, J. M. G., Mathews, A., & MacLeod, C. (1996). The emotional Stroop task and psychopathology. *Psychological Bulletin, 120,* 3–24.

Williams, L. M., & Banyard, V. L. (Eds.). (1999). *Trauma & memory.* Thousand Oaks, CA: Sage.

Wilson, B. A. (1995). Management and remediation of memory problems in brain-injured adults. In A. D. Baddeley, B. A. Wilson, & F. N. Watts (Eds.), *Handbook of memory disorders* (pp. 451–479). Chichester, England: Wiley.

Wilson, M. (2002). Six views of embodied cognition. *Psychonomic Bulletin & Review, 9,* 625–636.

Wilson, R. A., & Keil, F. C. (Eds.). (1999). *The MIT encyclopedia of the cognitive sciences.* Cambridge, MA: MIT Press.

Wilson, T. D. (1997). The psychology of meta-psychology. In J. D. Cohen & J. W. Schooler (Eds.), *Scientific approaches to consciousness* (pp. 317–332). Mahwah, NJ: Erlbaum.

Wingfield, A. (1993). Sentence processing. In J. B. Gleason & N. Bernstein Ratner (Eds.), *Psycholinguistics* (pp. 199–235). Fort Worth, TX: Harcourt Brace.

Wingfield, A., & Kahana, M. J. (2002). The dynamics of memory retrieval in older adulthood. *Canadian Journal of Experimental Psychology, 56,* 187–199.

Wingfield, A., & Stine-Morrow, E. A. L. (2000). Language and speech. In F. I. M. Craik & T. A. Salthouse (Eds.), *The handbook of aging and cognition* (pp. 359–416). Mahwah, NJ: Erlbaum.

Winman, A., & Juslin, P. (1999). "I was well-calibrated all along": Assessing accuracy in retrospect. In P. Juslin & H. Montgomery (Eds.), *Judgments and decision making* (pp. 97–120). Mahwah, NJ: Erlbaum.

Winman, A., Juslin, P., & Björkman, M. (1998). The confidence-hindsight mirror effect in judgment: An accuracy-assessment model for the knew-it-all-along phenomenon. *Journal of Experimental Psychology: Learning, Memory, and Cognition, 24,* 415–431.

Winne, P. H., & Hadwin, A. F. (1998). Studying as self-regulated learning. In D. J. Hacker, J. Dunlosky, & A. C. Graesser (Eds.), *Metacognition in educational theory and practice* (pp. 277–304). Mahwah, NJ: Erlbaum.

Winocur, G., & Hasher, L. (2002). Circadian rhythms and memory in aged humans and animals. In L. Squire & D. Schacter (Eds.), *Neuropsychology of memory* (3rd ed., pp. 273–285). New York: Guilford.

Winograd, E. (1993). Memory in the laboratory and everyday memory: The case for both. In J. M. Puckett & H. W. Reese (Eds.), *Mechanisms of everyday cognition* (pp. 55–70). Hillsdale, NJ: Erlbaum.

Wisniewski, E. J. (2002). Concepts and categorization. In D. Medin (Ed.), *Stevens' handbook of experimental psychology* (3rd ed., Vol. 2, pp. 467–531). New York: Wiley.

Wittgenstein, L. (1953). *Philosophical investigations.* New York: Macmillan.

Wixted, J. T., & Stretch, V. (2000). The case against a criterion-shift account of false memory. *Psychological Review, 107,* 368–376.

Wohlschläger, A. (2001). Mental object rotation and the planning of hand movements. *Perception & Psychophysics, 63,* 709–718.

Wolfe, J. M. (1998). What can 1 million trials tell us about visual search? *Psychological Science, 9,* 33–39.

Wolfe, J. M. (2000). Visual attention. In K. K. De Valois (Ed.), *Seeing* (2nd ed., pp. 335–386). San Diego: Academic Press.

Wolfe, J. M. (2001). Asymmetries in visual search: An introduction. *Perception & Psychophysics, 63,* 381–389.

Wolfe, J. M., & Cave, K. R. (1999). The psychophysical evidence for a binding problem in human vision. *Neuron, 24,* 11–17.

Woll, S. (2002). *Everyday thinking: Memory, reasoning, and judgment in the real world.* Mahwah, NJ: Erlbaum.

Wood, N., & Cowan, N. (1995). The cocktail party phenomenon revisited: How frequent are attention shifts to one's name in an irrelevant auditory channel? *Journal of Experimental Psychology: Learning, Memory, and Cognition, 21,* 255–260.

Woodward, A. L., & Markman, E. M. (1998). Early word learning. In W. Damon (Ed.), *Handbook of child psychology: Cognition, perception, and language* (5th ed., Vol. 2, pp. 371–420). New York: Wiley.

World almanac and book of facts. (2003). New York: World Almanac Books.

Wright, D. B., Boyd, C. E., & Tredoux, C. G. (2003). Inter-racial contact and the own-race bias for face recognition in South Africa and England. *Applied Cognitive Psychology, 17,* 365–373.

Wyer, R. S., Jr. (Ed.). (1998). *Stereotype activation and inhibition.* Mahwah, NJ: Erlbaum.

Wynn, V. E., & Logie, R. H. (1998). The veracity of long-term memories—Did Bartlett get it right? *Applied Cognitive Psychology, 12,* 1–20.

Yantis, S. (Ed.). (2002). *Stevens' handbook of experimental psychology* (3rd ed., vol. 4). New York: Wiley.

Yeni-Komshian, G. H. (1998). Speech perception. In J. Berko-Gleason & N. Bernstein Ratner (Eds.), *Psycholinguistics* (2nd ed., pp. 107–156). Fort Worth, TX: Harcourt Brace.

Yoon, C., May, C. P., & Hasher, L. (2000). Aging, circadian arousal patterns, and cognition. In D. C. Park & N. Schwarz (Eds.), *Cognitive aging* (pp. 151–171). Philadelphia: Psychology Press.

Young, J. E., Klosko, J. S., & Weishaar, M. E. (2003). *Schema therapy: A practitioner's guide.* New York: Guilford.

Yuille, J. C., & Catchpole, M. J. (1977). Imagery and children's associative learning. In A. M. Lesgold, J. W. Pellegrino, S. D. Fokkema, & R. Glaser (Eds.), *Cognitive psychology and instruction.* New York: Plenum.

Yussen, S. R., & Levy, V. M. (1975). Developmental changes in predicting one's own span of short-term memory. *Journal of Experimental Child Psychology, 19,* 502–508.

Zabrucky, K., & Ratner, H. H. (1986). Children's comprehension monitoring and recall of inconsistent stories. *Child Development, 57,* 1401–1418.

Zacks, J. M., Ollinger, J. M., Sheridan, M. A., & Tversky, B. (2002). A parametric study of mental spatial transformations of bodies. *NeuroImage, 126,* 857–872.

Zacks, J. M., Tversky, B., & Iyer, G. (2001). Perceiving, remembering, and communicating structure in events. *Journal of Experimental Psychology: General, 130,* 29–58.

Zaragoza, M. S., Lane, S. M., Ackil, J. K., & Chambers, K. L. (1997). Confusing real and suggested memories: Source monitoring and eyewitness suggestibility. In N. L. Stein, P. A. Ornstein, B. Tversky, & C. Brainerd (Eds.), *Memory for everyday and emotional events* (pp. 401–425). Mahwah, NJ: Erlbaum.

Zatorre, R. J., et al. (1996). Hearing in the mind's ear: A PET investigation of musical imagery and perception. *Journal of Cognitive Neuroscience, 8,* 29–46.

Zelinski, E. M., & Gilewski, M. J. (1988). Memory for prose and aging: A meta-analysis. In M. L. Howe & C. J. Brainerd (Eds.), *Cognitive development in adulthood: Progress in cognitive development research* (pp. 133–158). New York: Springer-Verlag.

Zimmer, H. D., & Engelkamp, J. (1999). Levels-of-processing effects in subject-performed tasks. *Memory & Cognition, 27,* 907–914.

Zwaan, R. A. (1999). Situation models: The mental leap into imagined worlds. *Current Directions in Psychological Science, 8,* 15–18.

Zwaan, R. A., & Singer, M. (2003). Text comprehension. In A. C. Graesser, M. A. Gernsbacher, & S. R. Goldman (Eds.), *Handbook of discourse processes* (pp. 83–121). Mahwah, NJ: Erlbaum.

꧁ Literary Credits

Color Figure 4: Posner, M. I., & Raichle, M. E. (1994). *Images of mind.* New York: W. H. Freeman.

Figure 2.8: Burton, A. M., Wilson, S., Cowan, M., & Bruce, V. (1999). Face recognition in poor-quality video. *Psychological Science, 10,* 243–248, page 245 of the article.

Figure 4.5: Baddeley, A. (2000). The episodic buffer: A new component of working memory? *Trends in Cognitive Sciences, 4,* 417–423.

Figure 4.6: The left and center panels are adapted from Brandimonte, M. A., Hitch, G. J., & Bishop, D. V. M. (1992). Influence of short-term memory codes on visual image processing: Evidence from image transformation tasks. Journal of Experimental Psychology: Learning, Memory, and Cognition, 18, 157–165. Copyright © 1992 by the American Psychological Association. Adapted with permission.

Figure 4.7: Rosen, V. M., & Engle, R. W. (1997). The role of working memory capacity in retrieval. *Journal of Experimental Psychology: General, 126,* 211–227.

Figure 5.2: Talarico, J. M., & Rubin, D. C. (2003). Confidence, not consistency, characterizes flashbulb memories. *Psychological Science, 14,* 455–461.

Figure 6.5: Dunning, D., et al. (2003). Why people fail to recognize their own incompetence. *Current Directions in Psychological Science, 12,* 83–87. This figure is Figure 2 and it appears on page 84.

Table 8.3: Murphy, G. L., & Shapiro, A. M. (1994). Forgetting of verbatim information in discourse. *Memory & Cognition, 22,* 85–94.

Table 10.1: Shin, Hyon B., & Bruno, Rosalind (2003, October). *Language use and English-speaking ability* (2002). Washington, DC: U.S. Census Bureau.

Table 10.2: Statistics Canada, 2001. *Canadian Statistics* "Population by mother tongue, provinces and territories."

Figure 11.2: Quinn, D. M., & Spencer, S. J. (2001). The interference of stereotype threat with women's generation of mathematical problem-solving strategies. *Journal of Social Issues, 57,* 55–71.

Figure 13.3: Rubin, D. C. (2000). The distribution of early childhood memories. *Memory, 8,* 265–269.

Name Index

◉ Subject Index

Note: New terms appear in boldface print.

Color Figure 3 (for Demonstration 3.2)

Part A

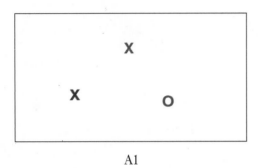

A1

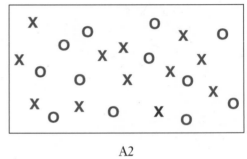

A2

Part B

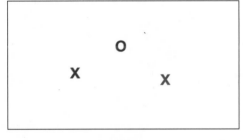

B1

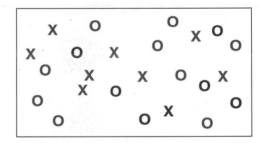

B2